ZONDERVAN BOOKS BY WAYNE GRUDEM

Bible Doctrine

Systematic Theology

Counterpoints/Are
Miraculous Gifts for
Today? (Editor)

BIBLE
doctrine

BIBLE
doctrine

Essential Teachings

of the

Christian Faith

WAYNE GRUDEM

Edited by Jeff Purswell

ZONDERVAN™

GRAND RAPIDS, MICHIGAN 49530

ZONDERVAN™

Bible Doctrine
Copyright © 1999 by Wayne Grudem

Requests for information should be addressed to:

Zondervan, *Grand Rapids, Michigan 49530*

Library of Congress Cataloging-in-Publication Data
  Grudem, Wayne A.
      Bible doctrine : essential teachings of the Christian faith / Wayne Grudem.
    p. cm.
      "Condensed version of . . . Systematic theology"—Pref.
      Includes bibliographical references and index.
      ISBN 0–310–22233–8
      1. Theology, Doctrinal. 2. Bible—Theology. I. Grudem, Wayne A. Systematic theology.
    II. Title.
    BT75.2.G 1999   98-35127
    230'.04624—dc21   CIP

This edition printed on acid-free paper.

All Scripture quotations, unless otherwise noted, are taken from the *Revised Standard Version of the Bible,* copyright © 1946, 1952, 1971, by the Division of Christian Education of the National Council of Churches of Christ in the USA, and are used by permission. However, the author has, with permission, modernized archaic personal pronouns and has changed the verbs accordingly. Scripture quotations marked NASB are from the *New American Standard Bible,* copyright © 1960, 1962, 1963, 1968, 1971, 1972 by the Lockman Foundation, La Habra, California. Used by permission. Those marked NIV are from the *Holy Bible: New International Version®,* copyright © 1973, 1978, 1984 by the International Bible Society. Used by permission of Hodder and Stoughton Ltd. and Zondervan. Use of italics in Scripture quotations indicates Wayne Grudem's emphasis.

Interior design by Sherri L. Hoffman

Printed in the United States of America

04 05 /❖DC / 21 20 19 18 17 16 15 14

To
Dave and Peggy Ekstrom,
Tom and Kaye Forester,
and
Michael and Susie Kelley
whose friendships are special gifts from God

CONTENTS

ABBREVIATIONS

BAGD   *A Greek-English Lexicon of the New Testament and Other Early Christian Literature.* Edited by Walter Bauer. Revised and translated by Wm. Arndt, F. Gingrich, F. Danker. Chicago: Chicago University Press, 1979.

BDB   *A Hebrew and English Lexicon of the Old Testament.* F. Brown, S. R. Driver and C. Briggs. Oxford: Clarendon Press, 1907; reprinted, with corrections, 1968.

cf.   compare

EDT   *Evangelical Dictionary of Theology.* Edited by Walter Elwell. Grand Rapids: Baker Book House, 1984.

JETS   *Journal of the Evangelical Theological Society*

KJV   King James Version (Authorized Version)

LSJ   *A Greek-English Lexicon,* ninth edition. Henry Liddell, Robert Scott, H. S. Jones, R. McKenzie. Oxford: Clarendon Press, 1940.

LXX   Septuagint

NASB   *New American Standard Bible*

NIV   *New International Version*

NKJV   *New King James Version*

RSV   *Revised Standard Version*

TDNT   *Theological Dictionary of the New Testament.* 10 vols. Edited by G. Kittel and G. Friedrich. Translated by G. W. Bromiley. Grand Rapids: Wm. B. Eerdmans Publishing Co., 1964–76.

WTJ   *Westminster Theological Journal*

PREFACE

This book is a condensed version of my 1,264-page *Systematic Theology*.[1] It is intended for students in one-semester classes in Christian doctrine, but I hope it will also prove useful for adult Sunday school classes and home Bible studies in which Christians want to work through a readable and biblically based survey of Christian doctrine.

Jeff Purswell, a recent honors graduate of Trinity Evangelical Divinity School (where he was my teaching assistant and also a Teaching Fellow in New Testament Greek), did the hard work of cutting 740 pages from my *Systematic Theology*. He consulted regularly with me, and we agreed to eliminate whole sections that were more relevant for seminary students (chapters on church government and church discipline, for example, and most of the detailed footnotes that dealt with fine points of interpretation of Scripture verses). In the sections that remained, he left much of the main argument intact, but he found that on subsidiary points he could often summarize longer discussions into one or two clear sentences. To keep the book within manageable size, he also eliminated the bibliographies and (with regret) the hymn at the end of each chapter. Then he added a glossary of special terms and review questions for each chapter. When I read through the resulting manuscript and added some final touches, I found that he had done a wonderful job of preserving both the essential character and the overall tone of the larger book. The result is a more compact book that covers the entire range of essential Christian doctrines.

In the five years since *Systematic Theology* was published, the two most frequent comments I have heard are, "Thank you for writing a theology book that I can understand," and "This book is helping my Christian life." I thank God that he has allowed it to be useful to people in these ways. We have attempted to preserve these two characteristics—clarity and application to life—in this shorter book.

As far as my general approach to writing about theology, much of what I said in the preface to the large book can be said of this book as well, and is contained in what follows.

I have not written this book for other teachers of theology (though I hope many of them will read it). I have written it for students—and not only for students, but also for every Christian who has a hunger to know the central doctrines of the Bible in greater depth.

I have tried to make *Bible Doctrine* understandable even for Christians who have never studied theology before. I have avoided using technical terms without first explaining them. And most of the chapters can be read on their own so that someone can begin at any chapter and grasp it without having read the earlier material.

Introductory studies do not have to be shallow or simplistic. I am convinced that most Christians are able to understand the doctrinal teachings of the Bible in considerable depth, provided that they are presented clearly and without the use of

---

[1] *Systematic Theology: An Introduction to Biblical Doctrine* (Leicester: Inter-Varsity Press and Grand Rapids: Zondervan, 1994).

highly technical language. Therefore, I have not hesitated to treat theological disputes in some detail where it seemed necessary.

The following six distinctive features of this book grow out of my convictions about what systematic theology is and how it should be taught.

1. A clear biblical basis for doctrines. Because I believe that theology should be explicitly based on the teachings of Scripture, in each chapter I have attempted to show where the Bible gives support for the doctrines under consideration. In fact, because I believe that the words of Scripture themselves have power and authority greater than any human words, I have not just given Bible references; I have frequently *quoted* Bible passages at length so that readers can easily examine for themselves the scriptural evidence and in that way be like the noble Bereans, who were "examining the scriptures daily to see if these things were so" (Acts 17:11). This conviction about the unique nature of the Bible as God's words has also led to the inclusion of a Scripture memory passage at the end of each chapter.

2. Clarity in the explanation of doctrines. I do not believe that God intended the study of theology to result in confusion and frustration. A student who comes out of a course in theology filled only with doctrinal uncertainty and a thousand unanswered questions is hardly "able to give instruction in sound doctrine and also to confute those who contradict it" (Titus 1:9). Therefore, I have tried to state the doctrinal positions of this book clearly and to show where in Scripture I find convincing evidence for those positions. I do not expect that everyone reading this book will agree with me at every point of doctrine; I do think that every reader will understand the positions I am arguing for and where Scripture can be found to support those positions.

I think it is only fair to readers of this book to say at the beginning what my own convictions are regarding certain points that are disputed within evangelical Christianity. I hold to a conservative view of biblical inerrancy, very much in agreement with the Chicago Statement of the International Council on Biblical Inerrancy (appendix 1, pp. 473–78). I hold to a traditional Reformed position with regard to questions of God's sovereignty and man's responsibility (ch. 8) and the question of predestination (ch. 18). Consistent with the Reformed view, I hold that those who are truly born again will never lose their salvation (ch. 24). With regard to male-female relationships, I argue for a view that is neither traditional nor feminist, but "complementarian," namely, that God created man and woman equal in value and personhood and equal in bearing his image, but that both creation and redemption indicate some distinct roles for men and women (ch. 12). I argue for a baptistic view of baptism, namely, that those who give a believable profession of personal faith should be baptized (ch. 27). I hold that all the gifts of the Holy Spirit mentioned in the New Testament are still valid for today, but that Christians need to be cautious to follow the Bible's wise directions and avoid abuses in this controversial area (chs. 29, 30). I believe that Christ's second coming could occur any day, that it will be premillennial—that is, it will mark the beginning of his thousand-year reign of perfect peace on the earth—but that it will be posttribulational—that is, that many Christians will go through the great tribulation (chs. 31, 32).

This does not mean that I ignore other views. Where there are doctrinal differences within evangelical Christianity, I have tried to represent other positions fairly and to explain why I disagree with them. I must also say that I do not think that all of the doctrines mentioned above are doctrines that should divide Christians. In fact, when discussing some of them, I say that they do not seem to me to be doctrines of primary importance. Therefore, it would be healthy for us as Christians to recognize that we have limited understanding and limited certainty in many disputed areas and to express tolerance and a willingness to minister with those who hold differing viewpoints.

3. *Application to life*. I do not believe that God intended the study of theology to be dry and boring. Theology is the study of God and all his works! Theology is meant to be *lived* and *prayed* and *sung!* All of the great doctrinal writings of the Bible (such as Paul's epistle to the Romans) are full of praise to God and personal application to life. For this reason, I have incorporated notes on application from time to time in the text and have added "Questions for Personal Application" at the end of each chapter. True theology is "teaching which accords with godliness" (1 Tim. 6:3), and theology when studied rightly will lead to growth in our Christian lives, and to worship.

4. *Focus on the evangelical world*. I do not think that a true system of theology can be constructed from within what we may call the "liberal" theological tradition—that is, by people who deny the absolute truthfulness of the Bible, or who do not think the words of the Bible to be God's very words (see ch. 2 on the authority of Scripture). For this reason, the other writers with whom I interact in this book are mostly within what is today called the larger "conservative evangelical" tradition—from the great Reformers John Calvin and Martin Luther, down to the writings of evangelical scholars today. I write as an evangelical and for evangelicals. This does not mean that those in the liberal tradition have nothing valuable to say; it simply means that differences with them almost always boil down to differences over the nature of the Bible and its authority. The amount of doctrinal agreement that can be reached by people with widely divergent bases of authority is quite limited.

Of course, instructors can always assign supplemental readings from liberal theologians of current interest if they wish to do so, and I am thankful for my evangelical friends who write extensive critiques of liberal theology. But I do not think that everyone is called to do that, or that an extensive analysis of liberal views is the most helpful way to build a positive system of theology based on the total truthfulness of the whole Bible. In fact, somewhat like the boy in Hans Christian Andersen's tale who shouted, "The Emperor has no clothes!" I think someone needs to say that it is doubtful that liberal theologians have given us any significant insights into the doctrinal teachings of Scripture that are not already to be found in evangelical writers. (Incidentally, no one has given me a counterexample to that claim in the five years since it was first published in *Systematic Theology!*) There is some value in academic interaction with liberal scholars and in criticism of their works, but the long-term benefits to the church are limited. Simply out of a consideration of stewardship of time and academic gifts, I personally think that evangelical scholars could wisely pay less attention to liberal theologians and more attention to the positive, constructive task of seeking answers from Scripture for the pressing doctrinal and ethical questions that the church faces today.

It is not always appreciated that the world of conservative evangelical scholarship is so rich and diverse that it affords ample opportunity for exploration of different viewpoints and insights into Scripture. I think that ultimately we will attain much more depth of understanding of Scripture when we are able to study it in the company of a great number of scholars who all begin with the conviction that the Bible is completely true and absolutely authoritative.

5. Hope for progress in doctrinal unity in the church. I believe there is still much hope for the church to attain deeper and purer doctrinal understanding and to overcome old barriers, even those that have persisted for centuries. Jesus is at work perfecting his church "that he might present the church to himself in splendor, without spot or wrinkle or any such thing, that she might be holy and without blemish" (Eph. 5:27), and he has given gifts to equip the church "until we all attain to the unity of the faith and of the knowledge of the Son of God" (Eph. 4:13). Though some persistent areas of disagreement may discourage us, these Scriptures remain true, and I believe the history of the church is largely a history of gradual development of deeper and more precise understanding of Scripture among the main, central bodies of God's people who have continued to believe the whole Bible to be the inerrant Word of God and who have not turned aside into major doctrinal error.

Therefore, we should not abandon hope of greater agreement even at the present time. In fact, in this century we have already seen much greater understanding and some greater doctrinal agreement between Covenant and Dispensational theologians, and between charismatics and noncharismatics; moreover, I think the church's understanding of biblical inerrancy and of spiritual gifts has also increased significantly in the last few decades. I believe that the current debate over appropriate roles for men and women in marriage and the church will eventually result in much greater understanding of the teaching of Scripture as well, painful though the controversy may be at the present time. And one of the most interesting theological surprises in a long time is the October 1997 statement indicating some possibility of wider agreement between evangelicals and Roman Catholics on the nature of salvation and especially on the doctrine of justification by faith alone (see p. 319).

Because the Lord is still in the process of bringing greater doctrinal understanding to his church, in this book I have not hesitated to raise again some of the old differences (over baptism, the Lord's Supper, the millennium and the tribulation, and predestination, for example) in the hope that, in some cases at least, a fresh look at Scripture may provoke a new examination of these doctrines and may perhaps prompt some movement not just toward greater understanding and tolerance of other viewpoints, but even toward greater doctrinal consensus.

6. A sense of the urgent need for greater doctrinal understanding in the whole church. I am convinced that there is an urgent need in the church today for much greater understanding of Christian doctrine, or systematic theology. Not only pastors and teachers need to understand theology in greater depth—the *whole church* does as well. One day by God's grace we may have churches full of Christians who can discuss, apply, and *live* the doctrinal teaching of the Bible as readily as they can discuss the details of their own jobs or hobbies—or the fortunes of their favorite sports team or television program. It is not that Christians lack the *ability* to understand doctrine; it is just that they must have access to it in an understandable form. Once that happens, I think that many Christians will find that understanding (and living) the doctrines of Scripture is one of their greatest joys.

I want to express appreciation to my students at Trinity Evangelical Divinity School (1981–present). Their thoughtful, insightful comments on various sections of *Systematic Theology* resulted in numerous small improvements in the way things are expressed in this book (and their comments even led me to change my position about one aspect of the final judgment—see page 455!).

I do not think I would have undertaken the preparation of this condensed theology book had it not been for the persistent encouragement of Jack Kragt, academic sales manager for Zondervan, who kept telling me that there was a need for a such a book. In the editing process and overall concept of the book, it has once again been a pleasure to work with Jim Ruark and Stan Gundry at Zondervan. In addition, Laura Weller did outstanding work, catching numerous tiny errors in her role as copy editor.

My wife, Margaret, has been a constant encouragement and source of great joy to me as I have worked on this revision, just as she has been for twenty-nine years of marriage. Here in the fiftieth year of my life, I thank the Lord greatly for her. "She is far more precious than jewels. The heart of her husband trusts in her" (Prov. 31:10–11).

"O give thanks to the LORD, for he is good; for his steadfast love endures for ever!" (Ps. 118:29).

"Not to us, O LORD, not to us, but to your name give glory" (Ps. 115:1).

WAYNE GRUDEM
TRINITY EVANGELICAL DIVINITY SCHOOL
2065 HALF DAY ROAD
DEERFIELD, ILLINOIS 60015
USA

CHAPTER ONE

Introduction to
Systematic Theology

+ *What is systematic theology?*
+ *Why should Christians study it?*
+ *How should we study it?*

I. EXPLANATION AND SCRIPTURAL BASIS

A. Definition of Systematic Theology

What is systematic theology? Many definitions have been given, but for the purposes of this book the following definition will be used: *Systematic theology is any study that answers the question, "What does the whole Bible teach us today?" about any given topic.*[1] This definition indicates that systematic theology involves collecting and understanding all the relevant passages in the Bible on various topics and then summarizing their teachings clearly so that we know what to believe about each topic.

1. Relationship to other disciplines. The emphasis of this book will not be on *historical theology* (a historical study of how Christians in different time periods have understood various theological topics) or *philosophical theology* (studying theological topics largely without use of the Bible, but using the tools and methods of philosophical reasoning and what can be known about God from observing the universe) or *apologetics* (providing a defense of the truthfulness of the Christian faith for the purpose of convincing unbelievers). These three subjects, which are worthwhile subjects for Christians to pursue, are sometimes also included in a broader definition of the term *systematic theology*. In fact, some consideration of historical, philosophical, and apologetic matters will be found at points throughout this book. This is because historical study informs us of the insights gained and the mistakes made by others in the past in understanding Scripture; philosophical study helps us understand right and wrong thought forms common in our culture and others; and apologetic study helps us bring the teachings of Scripture to bear on the objections raised by unbelievers. But these areas of study are not the focus of this volume, which rather interacts directly with the biblical text in order to understand what the Bible itself says to us about various theological subjects. While these other areas of study help us to understand theological questions, only Scripture has the final authority to define

---

[1]This definition of systematic theology is taken from Professor John Frame, now of Westminster Seminary in Escondido, California, under whom I was privileged to study in 1971–73 (at Westminster Seminary, Philadelphia).

what we are to believe, and it is therefore appropriate to spend some time focusing on the teaching of Scripture itself.

This book will also not emphasize *Christian ethics*. Although there is inevitably some overlap between the study of theology and the study of ethics, I have tried to maintain a distinction in emphasis. The emphasis of systematic theology is on what God wants us to *believe* and to *know*, while the emphasis in Christian ethics is on what God wants us to *do* and what *attitudes* he wants us to have. Such a distinction is reflected in the following definition: *Christian ethics is any study that answers the question, "What does God require us to do and what attitudes does he require us to have today?" with regard to any given situation.* Thus, theology focuses on ideas while ethics focuses on life situations. Theology tells us how we should think while ethics tells us how we should live. A textbook on ethics, for example, would discuss topics such as marriage and divorce, capital punishment, war, birth control, abortion, euthanasia, homosexuality, lying, racial discrimination, alcohol use, the role of civil government, use of money and private property, care for the poor, and so forth. Such topics belong to the study of ethics and are not covered in this book. However, this book will not hesitate to suggest application of theology to life where such application comes readily.

Systematic theology, as defined above, also differs from *Old Testament theology, New Testament theology,* and *biblical theology*. These three disciplines organize their topics historically and in the order the topics are presented in the Bible. Therefore, in Old Testament theology, one might ask, "What does Deuteronomy teach about prayer?" or "What do the Psalms teach about prayer?" or "What does Isaiah teach about prayer?" or even "What does the whole Old Testament teach about prayer, and how is that teaching developed over the history of the Old Testament?" In New Testament theology, one might ask, "What does John's gospel teach about prayer?" or "What does Paul teach about prayer?" or even "What does the New Testament teach about prayer, and what is the historical development of that teaching as it progresses through the New Testament?"

Biblical theology has a technical meaning in theological studies. It is the larger category that contains both Old Testament theology and New Testament theology. Biblical theology gives special attention to the teachings of *individual authors and sections* of Scripture and to the place of each teaching in the *historical development* of Scripture. So one might ask, "What is the historical development of the teaching about prayer as it is seen throughout the history of the Old Testament and then of the New Testament?" Of course, this question comes very close to the question, "What does the whole Bible teach us today about prayer?" (which would be *systematic theology* by the above definition). It then becomes evident that the boundary lines between these various disciplines often overlap, and parts of one study blend into the next. Yet there is still a difference, for biblical theology traces the historical development of a doctrine and the way in which one's place at some point in that historical development affects one's understanding and application of that particular doctrine. Biblical theology also focuses on the understanding of each doctrine that the biblical authors and their original hearers or readers possessed.

Systematic theology, on the other hand, concentrates on the collection and then the summary of the teaching of *all* the biblical passages on a particular subject. It therefore makes use of the results of biblical theology and often builds upon them. Thus, systematic theology asks, for example, "What does the whole Bible teach us today about prayer?" It attempts to summarize the teaching of Scripture in a brief, understandable, and very carefully formulated statement.

2. *Application to life.* Furthermore, systematic theology focuses on summarizing each doctrine as it should be understood by present-day Christians. This sometimes involves the use of terms and even concepts that were not themselves used by any individual biblical author but are the proper result of combining the teachings of two or more biblical authors on a particular subject. The terms *Trinity, incarnation,* and *deity of Christ,* for example, are not found in the Bible, but they usefully summarize biblical concepts.

Defining systematic theology to include "what the whole Bible *teaches us* today" implies that application to life is a necessary part of the proper pursuit of systematic theology. Thus, all doctrines should be seen in terms of their practical value for living the Christian life. Nowhere in Scripture do we find doctrine studied for its own sake or in isolation from life. The biblical writers consistently apply their teaching to life. Therefore, any Christian reading this book should find his or her Christian life enriched and deepened during this study; indeed, if personal spiritual growth does not occur, then the book has not been written properly by the author or the material has not been rightly studied by the reader.

3. *Systematic theology and disorganized theology.* If we use this definition of systematic theology, it will be seen that most Christians actually do systematic theology (or at least make systematic-theological statements) many times a week. For example: "The Bible says that everyone who believes in Jesus Christ will be saved." "The Bible says that Jesus Christ is the only way to God." "The Bible says that Jesus is coming again."

These are all summaries of what Scripture says and, as such, they are systematic-theological statements. In fact, every time a Christian says something about what the whole Bible says, he or she is in a sense doing "systematic theology"   according ing to the above definition—by thinking about various topics and answering the question, "What does the whole Bible teach us today?"

How then does this book differ from this kind of "systematic theology" that most Christians do? It does so in at least four ways. First, this book treats biblical topics in a *carefully organized way* to guarantee that all important topics will receive thorough consideration. This organization also helps to prevent inaccurate analysis of individual topics, for it means that all doctrines that are treated can be compared with each topic for consistency in methodology and absence of contradictions in the relationships between the doctrines. This also helps to ensure balanced consideration of complementary doctrines: Christ's deity and humanity are studied together, for example, as are God's sovereignty and man's responsibility, so that wrong conclusions will not be drawn from an imbalanced emphasis on only one aspect of the full biblical presentation.

In fact, the adjective *systematic* in systematic theology should be understood to mean something like "carefully organized by topics," with the understanding that the topics studied will be seen to fit together in a consistent way, and will include all the major doctrinal topics of the Bible. Thus "systematic" should be thought of as the opposite of "randomly arranged" or "disorganized." In systematic theology, topics are treated in an orderly or "systematic" way.

A second difference between this book and the way most Christians do systematic theology is that it treats topics in *much more detail* than most Christians do. For example, an ordinary Christian as a result of regular reading of the Bible may make the theological statement, "The Bible says that everyone who believes in Jesus Christ will be saved." That is a perfectly true summary of a major biblical teaching. However, in this book we devote several pages to elaborating more precisely what it means to "believe in Jesus Christ,"[2] and nine chapters (chs. 20–28) will be devoted to explaining what it means to "be saved" in all of the many implications of that term.

Third, a formal study of systematic theology will make it possible to formulate summaries of biblical teachings with *much more accuracy* than Christians would normally arrive at without such a study. In systematic theology, summaries of biblical teachings must be worded precisely to guard against misunderstandings and to exclude false teachings. In fact, one of the marks of maturity in understanding systematic theology is precision in the use of words to summarize the teachings of the Bible.

Fourth, a good theological analysis must find and treat fairly *all the relevant Bible passages* for each particular topic, not just some or a few of the relevant passages. This often means that it must depend on the results of careful exegesis, or interpretation, of Scripture generally agreed upon by evangelical interpreters or, where there are significant differences of interpretation, systematic theology will include detailed interpretation of Bible verses at certain points.

Because of the large number of topics covered in a study of systematic theology and because of the great detail with which these topics are analyzed, it is inevitable that someone studying systematic theology for the first time will have many of his or her own personal beliefs challenged or modified, refined or enriched. It is of utmost importance, therefore, that each person beginning such a course firmly resolve to abandon as false any idea found to be clearly contradicted by the teaching of Scripture. But it is also very important for each person to resolve not to believe any individual doctrine simply because this textbook or some other textbook or teacher says that it is true, unless this book or the instructor in a course can convince the student from the text of Scripture itself. It is Scripture alone, not any human authority, that must function as the normative authority for the definition of what we should believe.

4. What are doctrines? In this book, the word *doctrine* will be understood in the following way: *A doctrine is what the whole Bible teaches us today about some particular topic.* This definition is directly related to our earlier definition of systematic theology, since it shows that a doctrine is simply the result of the process of doing systematic theology with regard to one particular topic. Understood in this way, doctrines can be very broad or very narrow. We can speak of "the doctrine of God" as a major doctrinal category, including a summary of all that the Bible teaches us today about God. Such a doctrine would be exceptionally large. On the other hand, we may also speak more narrowly of the doctrine of God's eternity, the doctrine of the Trinity, or the doctrine of God's justice.

The book is divided into seven major sections according to seven major doctrines or areas of study:

Part 1:   The Doctrine of the Word of God
Part 2:   The Doctrine of God
Part 3:   The Doctrine of Man
Part 4:   The Doctrine of Christ
Part 5:   The Doctrine of the Application of Redemption

---

[2]See ch. 21, pp. 307–9, on saving faith, and chs. 14–16, pp. 229–69, on the person and work of Christ.

Part 6:   The Doctrine of the Church
Part 7:   The Doctrine of the Future

Within each of these major doctrinal categories many more specific teachings have been included. Generally these meet at least one of the following three criteria: (1) they are doctrines that are most emphasized in Scripture; (2) they are doctrines that have been most significant throughout the history of the church and have been important for all Christians at all times; (3) they are doctrines that have become important for Christians in the present situation in the history of the church. Some examples of doctrines in the third category would be the doctrine of the inerrancy of Scripture, the doctrine of baptism in the Holy Spirit, the doctrine of Satan and demons with particular reference to spiritual warfare, the doctrine of spiritual gifts in the New Testament age, and the doctrine of the creation of man as male and female in relation to the understanding of roles appropriate to men and women today. Because of their relevance to the contemporary situation, doctrines such as these have received more emphasis in the present volume than in most traditional textbooks of systematic theology.

5. *Major and minor doctrines.* People sometimes ask what the difference is between a "major doctrine" and a "minor doctrine." Christians often say they want to seek agreement in the church on major doctrines but also allow for differences on minor doctrines. I have found the following guideline useful:

> A major doctrine is one that has a significant impact on our thinking about other doctrines or that has a significant impact on how we live the Christian life. A minor doctrine is one that has very little impact on how we think about other doctrines and very little impact on how we live the Christian life.

By this standard, doctrines such as the authority of the Bible (ch. 2), the Trinity (ch. 6), the deity of Christ (ch. 14), justification by faith (ch. 22), and many others would rightly be considered major doctrines. People who disagree with the historic evangelical understanding of any of these doctrines will have wide areas of difference with Christians who affirm these doctrines. By contrast, it seems to me that differences over forms of church government, or some details about the Lord's Supper (ch. 28), or the timing of the great tribulation (ch. 32), concern minor doctrines. Christians who differ over these things can agree on perhaps every other area of doctrine, and can live Christian lives that differ in no important way, and can have genuine fellowship with one another.

Of course, we may find doctrines that fall somewhere between "major" and "minor" according to this standard. That is only natural, because many doctrines have *some* influence on other doctrines or on life, but we may differ over whether we think it to be a "significant" influence. In such cases, Christians will need to ask God to give them mature wisdom and sound judgment as they try to determine to what extent a doctrine should be considered major in their particular circumstances.

B. Initial Assumptions of This Book

We begin with two assumptions or presuppositions: (1) that the Bible is true and that it is, in fact, our only absolute standard of truth; (2) that the God who is spoken of in the Bible exists, and that he is who the Bible says he is: the Creator of heaven and earth and all things in them. These two assumptions, of course, are always open to later reconsideration or deeper confirmation, but at this point, these assumptions form the point at which we begin.

C. Why Should Christians Study Theology?

Why should Christians study systematic theology? That is, why should we engage in the process of collecting and summarizing the teachings of many individual Bible passages on particular topics? Why is it not sufficient simply to continue regularly reading the Bible every day of our lives?

1. The basic reason. The most important reason for studying systematic theology is that it enables us to obey the command of Jesus to *teach* believers to observe all that he commanded: "Go therefore and make disciples of all nations, baptizing them in the name of the Father and of the Son and of the Holy Spirit, *teaching them* to observe all that I have commanded you; and lo, I am with you always, to the close of the age" (Matt. 28:19–20).

To teach all that Jesus commanded means more than merely teaching the words he spoke while he walked on the earth. Luke implies that the book of Acts contains the story of what Jesus *continued* to do and teach through the apostles after his resurrection (note that Acts 1:1 speaks of Luke's gospel as recording "all that Jesus *began* to do and teach"). "All that Jesus commanded" can also include the Epistles, since they were written under the supervision of the Holy Spirit and were also considered to be a "command of the Lord" (1 Cor. 14:37; see also John 14:26; 16:13; 1 Thess. 4:15; 2 Peter 3:2; Rev. 1:1–3). Thus, in a larger sense, "all that Jesus commanded" includes all of the New Testament.

Furthermore, when we consider that the New Testament writings exhibit the absolute confidence Jesus and the New Testament writers had in the authority and reliability of the Old Testament Scriptures as God's words (see ch. 2), it becomes evident that we cannot teach "all that Jesus commanded" without including all of the Old Testament (rightly understood in the various ways in which it applies to the new covenant age in the history of redemption) as well.

The task of fulfilling the Great Commission includes, therefore, not only evangelism, but also *teaching.* And the task of teaching all that Jesus commanded us is, in a broad sense, the task of teaching what the whole Bible says to us today. This is where systematic theology becomes necessary: To effectively teach ourselves and others what the whole Bible says, it is necessary to *collect* and *summarize* all the Scripture passages on a particular subject.

Because no one will have the time to study what the entire Bible says about every doctrinal question that may arise, it is very helpful to have the benefit of the work of others who have searched Scripture and found answers to various topics. This work enables us to teach others more effectively by directing them to the most relevant passages and suggesting an appropriate summary of the teachings of those passages. Then the person who questions us can inspect those passages quickly for himself or herself and learn much more rapidly what the teaching of the Bible is on a particular subject. Thus, the necessity of systematic theology for teaching what the Bible says comes about primarily because we are finite in our memory and in the amount of time at our disposal.

The basic reason for studying systematic theology, then, is that it enables us to teach ourselves and others what the whole Bible says, thus fulfilling the second part of the Great Commission.

2. The benefits to our lives. Although the basic reason for studying systematic theology is that it is a means of obedience to our Lord's command, there are some additional specific benefits that come from such study.

First, studying theology helps us *overcome our wrong ideas*. Because there is sin in our hearts, and because we have incomplete knowledge of the Bible, all of us from time to time resist or refuse to accept certain teachings of Scripture. For example, we may have only a vague understanding about a doctrine, which makes it easier to resist, or perhaps we know only one verse about a topic and we then try to explain away that verse. It is helpful for us to be confronted with the total weight of the teaching of Scripture on that subject so that we will be persuaded more readily even against our initial wrongful inclinations.

Second, studying systematic theology helps us to be *able to make better decisions later* on new questions of doctrine that may arise. We cannot know what new doctrinal controversies will arise in the future. These new controversies will sometimes include questions that no one has faced very carefully before. To properly answer these questions, Christians will be asking, "What does the whole Bible say about this subject?"

Whatever the new doctrinal controversies are in future years, those who have learned systematic theology well will be much better able to answer the new questions that arise. This is because of the Bible's great consistency; everything that the Bible says is somehow related to everything else the Bible says. Thus, the new question will be related to much that has already been learned from Scripture. The more thoroughly that earlier material has been learned, the better able we will be to deal with those new questions.

This benefit extends even more broadly. We face problems of applying Scripture to life in many more contexts than formal doctrinal discussions. What does the Bible teach about husband-wife relationships? About raising children? About witnessing to a friend at work? What principles does Scripture give us for studying psychology, economics, or the natural sciences? How does it guide us in spending money, in saving, or in tithing? The Bible gives us principles that apply to every area of our lives, and those who have learned well the theological teachings of the Bible will be much better able to make decisions that are pleasing to God in these practical ethical areas as well.

Third, studying systematic theology will *help us grow as Christians*. The more we know about God, about his Word, about his relationships to the world and mankind, the better we will trust him, the more fully we will praise him, and the more readily we will obey him. Studying systematic theology rightly will make us more mature Christians. If it does not do this, we are not studying it in the way God intends.

In fact, the Bible often connects sound doctrine with maturity in Christian living: Paul speaks of *"the teaching which accords with godliness"* (1 Tim. 6:3), and says that his work as an apostle is "to further the faith of God's elect and their knowledge of *the truth which accords with godliness"* (Titus 1:1). By contrast, he indicates that all kinds of disobedience and immorality are "contrary to sound doctrine" (1 Tim. 1:10).

D. How Should Christians Study Systematic Theology?

How then should we study systematic theology? The Bible provides some guidelines for answering this question.

1. We should study systematic theology with prayer. If studying systematic theology is simply a certain way of studying the Bible, the passages in Scripture that talk about the way in which we should study God's Word give guidance to us in this task. Just as the psalmist prays in Psalm 119:18, "Open my eyes that I may behold wondrous things out of your law," so we should pray and seek God's help in understanding his Word. Paul tells us in 1 Corinthians 2:14 that "the unspiritual man does not receive the gifts of the Spirit of God, for they are folly to him, and he is not able to understand them because they are spiritually discerned." Studying theology is therefore a spiritual activity in which we need the help of the Holy Spirit.

No matter how intelligent, if the student does not continue to pray for God to give him or her an understanding mind and a believing and humble heart, and the student does not maintain a personal walk with the Lord, the teachings of Scripture will be misunderstood and disbelieved, doctrinal error will result, and the mind and heart of the student will not be changed for the better but for the worse. Students of systematic theology should resolve at the beginning to keep their lives free from any disobedience to God or any known sin which would disrupt their relationship with him. They should resolve to maintain with great regularity their own personal devotional lives. They should continually pray for wisdom and understanding of Scripture.

Since it is the Holy Spirit who gives us the ability to understand Scripture, we need to realize that the proper thing to do, particularly when we are unable to understand some passage or some doctrine of Scripture, is to pray for God's help. Often what we need is not more data but more insight into the data we already have available. This insight is given only by the Holy Spirit (cf. 1 Cor. 2:14; Eph. 1:17–19).

2. We should study systematic theology with humility. Peter tells us, "Clothe yourselves, all of you, with humility toward one another, for 'God opposes the proud, but gives grace to the humble'" (1 Peter 5:5). Those who study systematic theology will learn many things about the teachings of Scripture that are perhaps not known or not known well by other Christians in their churches or by relatives who are older in the Lord than they are. They may also find that they understand things about Scripture that some of their church officers do not understand, and that even their pastor has perhaps forgotten or never learned well.

In all of these situations, it would be very easy to adopt an attitude of pride or superiority toward others who have not made such a study. But how ugly it would be if anyone were to use this knowledge of God's Word simply to win arguments or to put down a fellow Christian in conversation, or to make another believer feel insignificant in the Lord's work. James' counsel is good for us at this point: "Let every man be quick to hear, slow to speak, slow to anger, for the anger of man does not work the righteousness of God" (James 1:19–20). He tells us that one's understanding of Scripture is to be imparted in humility and love. "Who is wise and understanding among you? By his good life let him show his works in the meekness of wisdom. . . . But the wisdom from above is first pure, then peaceable, gentle, open to reason, full of mercy and good fruits, without uncertainty or insincerity. And the harvest of righteousness is sown in peace by those who make peace" (James 3:13, 17–18). Systematic theology rightly studied will not lead to the knowledge that "puffs up" (1 Cor. 8:1), but to humility and love for others.

3. We should study systematic theology with reason. We find in the New Testament that Jesus and the New Testament authors will often quote a verse of Scripture and then draw logical conclusions from it. They *reason* from Scripture. It is therefore not wrong to use human understanding, human logic, and human reason to draw conclusions from the statements of Scripture. Nevertheless, when we reason and draw what we think to be correct logical deductions from Scripture, we sometimes make mistakes. The deductions we draw from the statements of Scripture are not equal to the statements of Scripture themselves in certainty or authority, for our ability to reason and draw conclusions is not the ultimate standard of truth—only Scripture is.

What then are the limits on our use of our reasoning abilities to draw deductions from the statements of Scripture? The fact that reasoning to conclusions that go beyond the mere statements of Scripture is appropriate for studying Scripture, and the fact that Scripture itself is the ultimate standard of truth, combine to indicate to us that *we are free to use our reasoning abilities to draw deductions from any passage of Scripture so long as these deductions do not contradict the clear teaching of some other passage of Scripture.*[3]

This principle puts a safeguard on our use of what we think to be logical deductions from Scripture. Our supposedly logical deductions may be erroneous, but Scripture itself cannot be erroneous. Thus, for example, we may read Scripture and find that God the Father is called God (1 Cor. 1:3), that God the Son is called God (John 20:28; Titus 2:13), and that God the Holy Spirit is called God (Acts 5:3–4). We might deduce from this that there are three Gods. But then we find the Bible explicitly teaching us that God is one (Deut. 6:4; James 2:19). Thus, we conclude that what we *thought* to be a valid logical deduction about three Gods was wrong and that Scripture teaches both (a) that there are three separate persons (the Father, the Son, and the Holy Spirit), each of whom is fully God, and (b) that there is one God.

We cannot understand exactly how these two statements can both be true, so together they constitute a *paradox* ("a seemingly contradictory statement that may nonetheless be true").[4] We can tolerate a paradox (such as "God is three persons and one God") because we have confidence that ultimately God knows fully the truth about himself and about the nature of reality, and that in his understanding the different elements of a paradox are fully reconciled, even though at this point God's thoughts are higher than our thoughts (Isa. 55:8–9). But a true contradiction (such as, "God is three persons and God is not three persons") would imply ultimate contradiction in God's own understanding of himself or of reality, and this cannot be.

When the psalmist says, "*The sum of your word is truth;* and every one of your righteous ordinances endures for ever" (Ps. 119:160), he implies that God's words are not only true individually but also viewed together as a whole. Viewed collectively, their "sum" is also "truth." Ultimately, there is no internal contradiction either in Scripture or in God's own thoughts.

4. We should study systematic theology with help from others. We need to be thankful that God has put teachers in the church ("And God has appointed in the church first apostles, second prophets, third *teachers . . .*" [1 Cor. 12:28]). We should allow those with gifts of teaching to help us understand Scripture. This means that we should make use of systematic theologies and other books that have been written by

---

[3]This guideline is also adopted from Professor John Frame at Westminster Seminary (see p. 17).

[4]The *American Heritage Dictionary of the English Language,* ed. William Morris (Boston: Houghton-Mifflin, 1980), 950 (first definition).

some of the great teachers that God has given to the church over the course of its history. It also means that our study of theology should include *talking with other Christians* about the things we study. Among those with whom we talk will often be some with gifts of teaching who can explain biblical teachings clearly and help us to understand more easily. In fact, some of the most effective learning in systematic theology courses in colleges and seminaries often occurs outside the classroom in informal conversations among students who are attempting to understand Bible doctrines for themselves.

5. *We should study systematic theology by collecting and understanding all the relevant passages of Scripture on any topic.* This point was mentioned in our definition of systematic theology at the beginning of the chapter, but the actual process needs to be mentioned here. How does one go about making a doctrinal summary of what all the passages of Scripture teach on a certain topic? For topics covered in this book, many people will think that studying the chapters in this book and reading the Bible verses noted in the chapters is enough. But some people will want to do further study of Scripture on a particular topic or study some new topic not covered here. How could a student go about using the Bible to research its teachings on some new subject, perhaps one not discussed explicitly in any of his or her systematic theology textbooks?

The process would look like this: (1) Find all the relevant verses. The best help in this step is a good concordance, which enables one to look up key words and find the verses in which the subject is treated. For example, in studying what it means that man is created in the image and likeness of God, one needs to find all the verses in which *image, likeness,* and *create* occur. (The words *man* and *God* occur too often to be useful for a concordance search.) In studying the doctrine of prayer, many words could be looked up (*pray, prayer, intercede, petition, supplication, confess, confession, praise, thanks, thanksgiving,* et al.)—and perhaps the list of verses would grow too long to be manageable, so that the student would have to skim the concordance entries without looking up the verses, or the search would probably have to be divided into sections or limited in some other way. Verses can also be found by thinking through the overall history of the Bible and then turning to sections where there would be information on the topic at hand—for example, a student studying prayer would want to read the passages like the one about Hannah's prayer for a son (in 1 Sam. 1), Solomon's prayer at the dedication of the temple (in 1 Kings 8), Jesus' prayer in the Garden of Gethsemane (in Matt. 26 and parallels), and so forth. Then in addition to concordance work and reading other passages that one can find on the subject, checking the relevant sections in some systematic theology books will often bring to light other verses that had been missed, sometimes because none of the key words used for the concordance were in those verses.[5]

(2) The second step is to read, make notes on, and try to summarize the points made in the relevant verses. Sometimes a theme will be repeated often and the summary of the various verses will be relatively easy. At other times there will be verses difficult to understand, and the student will need to take some time to study a verse

---

[5]I have read a number of student papers telling me that John's gospel says nothing about how Christians should pray, for example, because they looked at a concordance and found that the word *prayer* was not in John, and the word *pray* occurs only four times in reference to Jesus praying in John 14, 16, and 17. They overlooked the fact that John contains several important verses where the word *ask* rather than the word *pray* is used (John 14:13–14; 15:7, 16 et al.).

in depth (just by reading the verse in context over and over, or by using specialized tools such as commentaries and dictionaries) until a satisfactory understanding is reached.

(3) Finally, the teachings of the various verses should be summarized into one or more points that the Bible affirms about that subject. The summary does not have to take the exact form of anyone else's conclusions on the subject, because we each may see things in Scripture that others have missed, or we may organize the subject differently or emphasize different things.

On the other hand, at this point it is also helpful to read related sections, if any can be found, in several systematic theology books. This provides a useful check against error and oversight, and often makes one aware of other perspectives and arguments that may cause us to modify or strengthen our position. If a student finds that others have argued for strongly differing conclusions, then these other views need to be stated fairly and then answered. Sometimes other theology books will alert us to historical or philosophical considerations that have been raised previously in the history of the church, and these will provide additional insight or warnings against error.

The process outlined above is possible for any Christian who can read his or her Bible and can look up words in a concordance. Of course people will become faster and more accurate in this process with time and experience and Christian maturity, but it would be a tremendous help to the church if Christians generally would give much more time to searching out topics in Scripture for themselves and drawing conclusions in the way outlined above. The joy of discovery of biblical themes would be richly rewarding. Especially pastors and those who lead Bible studies would find added freshness in their understanding of Scripture and in their teaching.

6. We should study systematic theology with rejoicing and praise. The study of theology is not merely an intellectual or mental exercise. It is a study of the living God and of the wonders of all his works in creation and redemption. We cannot study this subject as if our hearts and lives are uninvolved! We must love all that God is, all that he says, and all that he does. "You shall love the LORD your God with all your heart" (Deut. 6:5). Our response to the study of the theology of Scripture should be that of the psalmist who said, "How precious to me are your thoughts, O God!" (Ps. 139:17). In the study of the teachings of God's Word, it should not surprise us if we often find our hearts spontaneously breaking forth in expressions of praise and delight like those of the psalmist:

> The precepts of the LORD are right,
> rejoicing the heart. (Ps. 19:8)

> In the way of your testimonies I delight
> as much as in all riches. (Ps. 119:14)

> How sweet are your words to my taste,
> sweeter than honey to my mouth! (Ps. 119:103)

> Your testimonies are my heritage for ever;
> yea, they are the joy of my heart. (Ps. 119:111)

> I rejoice at your word
> like one who finds great spoil. (Ps. 119:162)

Often in the study of theology the response of the Christian should be similar to that of Paul in reflecting on the long theological argument he has just completed at the end of Romans 11:32. He breaks forth into joyful praise at the richness of the doctrine God has enabled him to express:

> O the depth of the riches and wisdom and knowledge of God! How unsearchable are his judgments and how inscrutable his ways!
>
> > "For who has known the mind of the Lord,
> > or who has been his counselor?"
> > "Or who has given a gift to him
> > that he might be repaid?"
>
> For from him and through him and to him are all things. To him be glory for ever. Amen. (Rom. 11:33–36)

II. REVIEW QUESTIONS

1. Define *systematic theology* and discuss its relationship with other theological disciplines (historical theology, philosophical theology, apologetics, Old Testament theology, New Testament theology, and biblical theology).

2. What is a "doctrine," and how does this relate to the study of systematic theology?

3. Give four reasons why Christians should study systematic theology.

4. Name six attitudes or activities that should characterize or accompany the study of systematic theology.

III. QUESTIONS FOR PERSONAL APPLICATION

Because I believe doctrine is to be felt at the emotional level as well as understood at the intellectual level, in many chapters I have included some questions about how a reader *feels* regarding a point of doctrine. I think these questions will prove quite valuable to those who take the time to reflect on them.

1. In what ways (if any) has this chapter changed your understanding of what systematic theology is? What was your attitude toward the study of systematic theology before reading this chapter? What is your attitude now?

2. What is likely to happen to a church or denomination that gives up learning systematic theology for a generation or longer? Has that been true of your church?

3. Are there any doctrines listed in the contents for which a fuller understanding would help to solve a personal difficulty in your life at the present time? What are the spiritual and emotional dangers that you personally need to be aware of in studying systematic theology?

4. Pray for God to make this study of basic Christian doctrines a time of spiritual growth and deeper fellowship with him, and a time in which you understand and apply the teachings of Scripture rightly.

IV. SPECIAL TERMS

apologetics

biblical theology

Christian ethics

contradiction

doctrine

historical theology

major doctrine

minor doctrine

New Testament theology

Old Testament theology

paradox

philosophical theology

presupposition

systematic theology

V. SCRIPTURE MEMORY PASSAGE

Students have repeatedly mentioned that one of the most valuable parts of any of their courses in college or seminary has been the Scripture passages they were required to memorize. "I have hidden your word in my heart that I might not sin against you" (Ps. 119:11 NIV). In each chapter, therefore, I have included an appropriate memory passage so that instructors may incorporate Scripture memory into the course requirements wherever possible. (Scripture memory passages at the end of each chapter are taken from the RSV, the version used in this book, but some may prefer other versions.)

MATTHEW 28:18–20

Jesus came and said to them, "All authority in heaven and on earth has been given to me. Go therefore and make disciples of all nations, baptizing them in the name of the Father and of the Son and of the Holy Spirit, teaching them to observe all that I have commanded you; and lo, I am with you always, to the close of the age."

PART I

The Doctrine
of the Word of God

CHAPTER TWO

The Authority and Inerrancy of the Bible

+ *How do we know that the Bible is God's Word?*
+ *Are there any errors in the Bible?*

Since we affirmed in chapter 1 that systematic theology attempts to summarize the teaching of the whole Bible on various subjects, we next turn to questions concerning the nature of the Bible from which we draw our data for the discipline of systematic theology. What does the whole Bible teach us about itself?

The major teachings of the Bible about itself can be classified into four characteristics: (1) the authority of Scripture, (2) the clarity of Scripture, (3) the necessity of Scripture, and (4) the sufficiency of Scripture.

With regard to the first characteristic, most Christians would agree that the Bible is our authority in some sense. But in exactly what sense does the Bible claim to be our authority? And how do we become persuaded that the claims of Scripture to be God's Word are true? These are the questions addressed in this chapter.

I. EXPLANATION AND SCRIPTURAL BASIS

The authority of Scripture means that all the words in Scripture are God's words in such a way that to disbelieve or disobey any word of Scripture is to disbelieve or disobey God. This definition may now be examined in its various parts.

A. All the Words in Scripture Are God's Words

1. This is what the Bible claims for itself. There are frequent claims in the Bible that all the words of Scripture are God's words (as well as words that were written down by men). In the Old Testament, this is often seen in the introductory phrase, "Thus says the LORD," which appears hundreds of times. In the world of the Old Testament, this phrase would have been recognized as identical in form to the phrase, "Thus says King . . . ," which was used to preface the edict of a king to his subjects, an edict that could not be challenged or questioned, but that simply had to be obeyed.[1] Therefore, when the prophets say, "Thus says the LORD," they are claiming to be messengers from the sovereign King of Israel, namely, God himself, and

---

[1] See Wayne Grudem, *The Gift of Prophecy in 1 Corinthians* (Lanham, Md.: University Press of America, 1982), pp. 12–13; also Wayne Grudem, "Scripture's Self-Attestation," in *Scripture and Truth,* ed. D. A. Carson and J. Woodbridge (Grand Rapids, Zondervan, 1983), pp. 21–22.

they are claiming that their words are the absolutely authoritative words of God. When a prophet spoke in God's name in this way, every word he spoke had to come from God, or he would be a false prophet (cf. Num. 22:38; Deut. 18:18–20; Jer. 1:9; 14:14; 23:16–22; 29:31–32; Ezek. 2:7; 13:1–16).

Furthermore, God is often said to speak "through" the prophet (1 Kings 14:18; 16:12, 34; 2 Kings 9:36; 14:25; Jer. 37:2; Zech. 7:7, 12). Thus, what the prophet says in God's name, God says (1 Kings 13:26 with v. 21; 1 Kings 21:19 with 2 Kings 9:25–26; Hag. 1:12; cf. 1 Sam. 15:3, 18). In these and other instances in the Old Testament, words which the prophets spoke can also be referred to as words God himself spoke. Therefore, to disbelieve or disobey anything a prophet says is to disbelieve or disobey God himself (Deut. 18:19; 1 Sam. 10:8; 13:13–14; 15:3, 19, 23; 1 Kings 20:35, 36).

These verses by themselves do not claim that *all* the words in the Old Testament are God's words, for these verses themselves are referring only to specific sections of spoken or written words in the Old Testament. But the cumulative force of these passages, including the hundreds of passages that begin "Thus says the LORD," is to demonstrate that within the Old Testament we have written records of words that are said to be God's own words. These words constitute large sections of the Old Testament. When we realize that all of the words that were part of the "law of God" or the "book of the covenant" were considered God's words, we see that the whole Old Testament claims that kind of authority (see Ex. 24:7; Deut. 29:21; 31:24–26; Josh. 24:26; 1 Sam. 10:25; 2 Kings 23:2–3).

In the New Testament, a number of passages indicate that all of the Old Testament writings are thought of as God's words. Second Timothy 3:16 says, "All Scripture is God-breathed and is useful for teaching, rebuking, correcting and training in righteousness" (NIV). Here "scripture" (Gk. *graphē*) must refer to the Old Testament written Scripture, for that is what the word *graphē* refers to in every one of its fifty-one occurrences in the New Testament. Furthermore, the "sacred writings" of the Old Testament are what Paul has just referred to in verse 15.

Paul here affirms that all of the Old Testament writings are *theopneustos,* "breathed out by God." Since it is *writings* that are said to be "breathed out," this breathing must be understood as a metaphor for speaking the words of Scripture. This verse thus states in brief form what was evident in many Old Testament passages: The Old Testament writings are regarded as God's Word in written form. For every word of the Old Testament, God is the one who spoke (and still speaks) it, although God used human agents to write down these words.[2]

A similar indication of the character of all Old Testament writings as God's words is found in 2 Peter 1:21. Speaking of the prophecies of Scripture (v. 20), which means at least the Old Testament Scriptures to which Peter encourages his readers to give careful attention (v. 19), Peter says that none of these prophecies ever came "by the impulse of man," but that "men moved along by the Holy Spirit spoke from God." It is not Peter's intention to deny completely the role of human volition or personality in the writing of Scripture (he says that the men "spoke"), but rather to say that the ultimate source of every prophecy was never a man's decision about

---

[2]Older systematic theologies used the words *inspired* and *inspiration* to speak of the fact that the words of Scripture are spoken by God. I have preferred the NIV rendering of 2 Tim. 3:16, "God-breathed," and have used other expressions to say that the words of Scripture are God's very words. This is because the word *inspired* has a weakened sense in ordinary usage today (e.g., a poet was "inspired" to write, or a basketball player gave an "inspired" performance).

what he wanted to write, but rather the Holy Spirit's action in the prophet's life, carried out in ways unspecified here (or, in fact, elsewhere in Scripture). This indicates a belief that all of the Old Testament prophecies (and, in light of vv. 19–20, this probably includes all of the written Scripture of the Old Testament) are spoken "from God": that is, they are God's own words.

Many other passages could be cited (see Matt. 19:5; Luke 1:70; 24:25; John 5:45–47; Acts 3:18, 21; 4:25; 13:47; 28:25; Rom. 1:2; 3:2; 9:17; 1 Cor. 9:8–10; Heb. 1:1–2, 6–7), but the pattern of attributing to God the words of Old Testament Scripture should be very clear. Moreover, in several places it is all of the words of the prophets or the words of the Old Testament Scriptures that are said to compel belief or to be from God (see Luke 24:25, 27, 44, Acts 3:18; 24:14; Rom. 15:4).

But if Paul meant only the Old Testament writings when he spoke of all "scripture" as God-breathed in 2 Timothy 3:16, how can this verse apply to the New Testament writings as well? Does it say anything about the character of the New Testament writings? To answer that question, we must realize that the Greek word *graphē* ("scripture") was a technical term for the New Testament writers and had a very specialized meaning. Even though it is used fifty-one times in the New Testament, in every one of those instances it refers to the Old Testament writings, not to any other words or writings outside the canon of Scripture. Thus, everything that belonged in the category "scripture" had the character of being "God-breathed": its words were God's very words.

But at two places in the New Testament we see New Testament writings also being called "scripture" along with the Old Testament writings. In 2 Peter 3:15–16, Peter says, "Our beloved brother Paul wrote to you according to the wisdom given him, speaking of this as he does in *all his letters.* There are some things in them hard to understand, which the ignorant and unstable twist to their own destruction, as they do *the other scriptures.*"

Here Peter shows not only an awareness of the existence of written epistles from Paul, but also a clear willingness to classify "all of his [Paul's] letters" with "the other scriptures." This is an indication that very early in the history of the church all of Paul's epistles were considered to be God's written words in the same sense as the Old Testament texts were. Similarly, in 1 Timothy 5:18, Paul writes, "For the scripture says, 'You shall not muzzle an ox when it is treading out the grain,' and, 'The laborer deserves his wages.'" The first quotation is from Deuteronomy 25:4, but the second occurs nowhere in the Old Testament. It is rather a quotation from Luke 10:7. Paul here quotes Jesus' words as found in Luke's gospel and calls them "scripture."

These two passages taken together indicate that during the time of the writing of the New Testament documents there was an awareness that *additions* were being made to this special category of writings called "scripture," writings that had the character of being God's very words. Thus, once we establish that a New Testament writing belongs to the special category "scripture," we are correct in applying 2 Timothy 3:16 to that writing as well, and saying that that writing also has the characteristic Paul attributes to "all scripture": It is "God-breathed," and all its words are the very words of God.

Is there further evidence that the New Testament writers thought of their own writings (not just the Old Testament) as the words of God? In some cases, there is. In 1 Corinthians 14:37, Paul says, "If any one thinks that he is a prophet, or spiritual, he should acknowledge that *what I am writing to you is a command of the Lord.*"

Paul has here instituted a number of rules for church worship at Corinth and has claimed for them the status of "commands of the Lord."

One might think that Paul felt his own commands were inferior to those of Jesus and therefore did not need to be obeyed as carefully. For example, in 1 Corinthians 7:12 he distinguishes his own words from those of Jesus: "To the rest I say, not the Lord. . . ." This, however, simply means that he had possession of *no earthly word that Jesus had spoken on this subject.* We can see that this is the case, because in verses 10–11 he simply repeated Jesus' earthly teaching "that the wife should not separate from her husband" and "that the husband should not divorce his wife." In verses 12–15, however, he gives his own instructions on a subject Jesus apparently did not address. What gave him the right to do this? Paul says that he spoke as one "who by the Lord's mercy is trustworthy" (1 Cor. 7:25). He seems to imply here that his own judgments were to be considered as authoritative as the commands of Jesus!

Indications of a similar view of the New Testament writings are found in John 14:26 and 16:13, where Jesus promised that the Holy Spirit would bring all that he had said to the disciples' remembrance, and would guide them into all the truth. This points to the Holy Spirit's work of enabling the disciples to remember and record without error all that Jesus had said. Similar indications are also found in 2 Peter 3:2; 1 Corinthians 2:13; 1 Thessalonians 4:15; and Revelation 22:18–19.

2. We are convinced of the Bible's claims to be God's words as we read the Bible. It is one thing to affirm that the Bible claims to be the words of God. It is another thing to be convinced that those claims are true. Our ultimate conviction that the words of the Bible are God's words comes only when the Holy Spirit speaks *in* and *through* the words of the Bible to our hearts and gives us an inner assurance that these are the words of our Creator speaking to us. Apart from the work of the Spirit of God, a person will not receive or accept the truth that the words of Scripture are in fact the words of God.

But for those in whom God's Spirit is working there is a recognition that the words of the Bible are the words of God. This process is closely analogous to that by which people who believed in Jesus knew that his words were true. He said, "My sheep hear my voice, and I know them, and they follow me" (John 10:27). Those who are Christ's sheep hear the words of their great Shepherd as they read the words of Scripture, and they are convinced that these words are in fact the words of their Lord.

It is important to remember that this conviction that the words of Scripture are the words of God does not come *apart from* the words of Scripture or *in addition* to the words of Scripture. It is not as if the Holy Spirit one day whispers in our ear, "Do you see that Bible sitting on your desk? I want you to know that the words of that Bible are God's words." It is rather as people read Scripture that they hear their Creator's voice speaking to them in the words of Scripture and realize that the book they are reading is unlike any other book, that it is indeed a book of God's own words speaking to their hearts.

One influential theological movement in the twentieth century was called *neoorthodoxy.* The most prominent representative of this movement was Swiss theologian Karl Barth (pronounced *bart*) (1886–1968).[3] Although much of his writing provided a welcome reaffirmation of the teachings of the Bible in distinction from the unbelief of liberal German theology, Barth still did not affirm that all the

---

[3] For an introduction to Barth's thought, see David L. Mueller, *Karl Barth* (Waco, Tex.: Word, 1972).

words of the Bible are the words of God in the sense that we have argued here. Rather, he said that the words of Scripture *become the words of God to us* as we encounter them. This was the primary reason why evangelicals could not whole-heartedly support the neoorthodoxy of Barth, though they did appreciate many of the individual things he taught.

3. *Other evidence is useful but not finally convincing.* The previous section is not meant to deny the validity of other kinds of arguments that may be used to support the claim that the Bible is God's words. It is helpful for us to learn that the Bible is his-torically accurate, that it is internally consistent, that it contains prophecies that have been fulfilled hundreds of years later, that it has influenced the course of human his-tory more than any other book, that it has continued changing the lives of millions of individuals throughout its history, that through it people come to find salvation, that it has a majestic beauty and a profound depth of teaching unmatched by any other book, and that it claims hundreds of times over to be God's very words. All of these arguments are useful to us and remove obstacles that might otherwise come in the way of our believing Scripture. But all of these arguments taken individually or together cannot finally be convincing. As the Westminster Confession of Faith said in 1643–46,

> We may be moved and induced by the testimony of the Church to an high and reverent esteem of the Holy Scripture. And the heavenliness of the matter, the efficacy of the doctrine, the majesty of the style, the consent of all the parts, the scope of the whole (which is, to give all glory to God), the full discovery it makes of the only way of man's salvation, the many other incomparable excel-lencies, and the entire perfection thereof, are arguments whereby it doth abun-dantly evidence itself to be the Word of God: yet notwithstanding, our full persuasion and assurance of the infallible truth and divine authority thereof, is from the inward work of the Holy Spirit bearing witness by and with the Word in our hearts. (chap. 1, para. 5)

4. *The words of Scripture are self-attesting.* Since the words of Scripture are "self-attesting," they cannot be "proved" to be God's words by appeal to any higher authority. If we make our ultimate appeal, for example, to human logic or to scien-tific truth to prove that the Bible is God's Word, then we assume the thing to which we appeal to be a higher authority than God's words and one that is more true or more reliable. Therefore, the ultimate authority by which Scripture is shown to be God's words must be Scripture itself.

5. *Objection: This is a circular argument.* Someone may object that to say Scripture proves itself to be God's words is to use a circular argument: We believe that Scripture is God's Word because it claims to be that. And we believe its claims because Scripture is God's Word. And we believe that it is God's Word because it claims to be that, and so forth.

It should be admitted that this is a kind of circular argument. However, that does not make its use invalid, for all arguments for an absolute authority must ultimately appeal to that authority for proof; otherwise the authority would not be an absolute or highest authority. This problem is not unique to the Christian who is arguing for the authority of the Bible. Everyone either implicitly or explicitly uses some kind of circular argument when defending his or her ultimate authority for belief.

A few simple examples will illustrate the types of circular arguments people use to support the basis for their beliefs:

"My reason is my ultimate authority because it seems reasonable to me to make it so."

"Logical consistency is my ultimate authority because it is logical to make it so."

"The findings of human sensory experiences are the ultimate authority for discovering what is real and what is not, because our human senses have never discovered anything else: Thus, human sense experience tells me that my principle is true."

Each of these arguments utilizes circular reasoning to establish its ultimate standard for truth.

How then does a Christian, or anyone else, choose among the various claims for absolute authorities? Ultimately, the truthfulness of the Bible will commend itself as being far more persuasive than other religious books (such as the *Book of Mormon* or the *Qur'an*) or than any other intellectual constructions of the human mind (such as logic, human reason, sense experience, scientific methodology, etc.). It will be more persuasive because, in the actual experience of life, all of these other candidates for ultimate authority are seen to be inconsistent or to have shortcomings that disqualify them, while the Bible will be seen to be fully in accord with all that we know about the world around us, about ourselves, and about God.

The Bible will commend itself as being persuasive in this way, that is, if we are thinking rightly about the nature of reality, our perception of it and of ourselves, and our perception of God. The trouble is that because of sin our perception and analysis of God and creation are faulty. Therefore, it requires the work of the Holy Spirit, overcoming the effects of sin, to enable us to be persuaded that the Bible is indeed the Word of God and that the claims it makes for itself are true.

In another sense, then, the argument for the Bible as God's Word and our ultimate authority is not a typical circular argument. The process of persuasion is perhaps better likened to a spiral in which increasing knowledge of Scripture and increasingly correct understanding of God and creation tend to supplement one another in a harmonious way, each tending to confirm the accuracy of the other. This is not to say that our knowledge of the world around us serves as a higher authority than Scripture, but rather that such knowledge, if it is correct knowledge, continues to give greater and greater assurance and deeper conviction that the Bible is the only truly ultimate authority and that other competing claims for ultimate authority are false.

6. This does not imply dictation from God as the sole means of communication. At this point a word of caution is necessary. The fact that all the words of Scripture are God's words should not lead us to think that God dictated every word of Scripture to the human authors.

When we say that all the words of the Bible are God's words, we are talking about the *result* of the process of bringing Scripture into existence. The question of dictation addresses the process that led to that result, or the manner by which God acted in order to ensure the result that he intended. It must be emphasized that the Bible does not speak of only one type of process or one manner by which God communicated to the biblical authors what he wanted to be said. In fact, there is indication of *a wide variety of processes* God used to bring about the desired result.

A few scattered instances of dictation are explicitly mentioned in Scripture. When the apostle John saw the risen Lord in a vision on the island of Patmos, Jesus spoke to him as follows: "To the angel of the church in Ephesus *write* ..." (Rev. 2:1); "And to the angel of the church in Smyrna *write ...*" (Rev. 2:8); "And to the angel of the church in Pergamum *write ...*" (Rev. 2:12). These are examples of dictation pure and simple. The risen Lord tells John what to write, and John writes the words he hears from Jesus.

But in many other sections of Scripture, such direct dictation from God is certainly not the manner by which the words of Scripture were caused to come into being. The author of Hebrews says that God spoke to our fathers by the prophets "in many and various ways" (Heb. 1:1). On the other end of the spectrum from dictation we have, for instance, Luke's ordinary historical research for writing his gospel. He says, "Inasmuch as many have undertaken to compile a narrative of the things which have been accomplished among us, just as they were delivered to us by those who from the beginning were eyewitnesses and ministers of the word, it seemed good to me also, having followed all things closely for some time past, to write an orderly account for you, most excellent Theophilus ..." (Luke 1:1–3).

This is clearly not a process of dictation. Luke used ordinary processes of speaking to eyewitnesses and gathering historical data so that he might write an accurate account of the life and teachings of Jesus. He did his historical research thoroughly, listening to the reports of many eyewitnesses and evaluating his evidence carefully. The gospel he wrote emphasizes what he thought important to emphasize and reflects his own characteristic style of writing.

In between these two extremes of dictation on the one hand and ordinary historical research on the other hand, we have many indications of various ways by which God communicated with the human authors of Scripture. In some cases, Scripture speaks of dreams, visions, or of hearing the Lord's voice. In other cases, it speaks of men who were with Jesus and observed his life and listened to his teaching, men whose memory of these words and deeds was made completely accurate by the working of the Holy Spirit as he brought things to their remembrance (John 14:26). Apparently many different methods were used, but it is not important that we discover precisely what these were in each case.

In instances where the human personality and writing style of the author were prominently involved, as seems the case with the major part of Scripture, all that we are able to say is that God's providential oversight and direction of the life of each author was such that their personalities and skills were just what God wanted them to be for the task of writing Scripture. Their backgrounds and training (such as Paul's rabbinic training or Moses' training in Pharaoh's household or David's work as a shepherd), their abilities to evaluate events in the world around them, their access to historical data, their judgment with regard to the accuracy of information, and their individual circumstances when they wrote were all exactly what God wanted them to be, so that when they actually came to the point of putting pen to paper, the words were fully their own words but also fully the words God wanted them to write, words God would also claim as his own.

B. Therefore, to Disbelieve or Disobey Any Word of Scripture Is to Disbelieve or Disobey God

The preceding section has argued that all the words in Scripture are God's words. Consequently, to disbelieve or disobey any word of Scripture is to disbelieve or disobey God himself. Thus, Jesus can rebuke his disciples for not believing the Old Testament Scriptures (Luke 24:25: "O foolish men, and slow of heart *to believe all that the prophets have spoken!*"). Believers are to keep or obey the disciples' words (John 15:20: "If they kept my word, they will keep yours also"). Christians are encouraged to remember "the commandment of the Lord and Savior through your apostles" (2 Peter 3:2). To disobey Paul's writings was to make oneself liable to church discipline, such as excommunication (2 Thess. 3:14) and spiritual punishment (2 Cor. 13:2–3), including punishment from God (this is the apparent sense of the passive verb "he is not recognized" in 1 Cor. 14:38). By contrast, God delights in everyone who "trembles" at his word (Isa. 66:2).

Throughout the history of the church the greatest preachers have been those who have recognized that they have no authority in themselves, and have seen their task as being to explain the words of Scripture and apply them clearly to the lives of their hearers. Their preaching has drawn its power not from the proclamation of their own Christian experiences or the experiences of others, nor from their own opinions, creative ideas, or rhetorical skills, but from God's powerful words. Essentially, they stood in the pulpit, pointed to the biblical text, and said in effect to the congregation, "This is what this verse means. Do you see that meaning here as well? Then you must believe it and obey it with all your heart, for God himself, your Creator and your Lord, is saying this to you today!" Only the written words of Scripture can give this kind of authority to preaching.

C. The Truthfulness of Scripture

1. God cannot lie or speak falsely. The essence of the authority of Scripture is its ability to compel us to believe and to obey it and to make such belief and obedience equivalent to believing and obeying God himself. Because this is so, it is needful to consider the truthfulness of Scripture, because if we do not think some parts of Scripture are true, we of course will not be able to believe them.

Since the biblical writers repeatedly affirm that the words of the Bible, though human, are God's own words, it is appropriate to look at biblical texts that talk about *the character of God's words* and to apply these to the character of the words of Scripture. Specifically, there are a number of biblical passages that talk about the truthfulness of God's speech. Titus 1:2 speaks of "God, who never lies," or (more literally translated), "the unlying God." Because God is a God who cannot speak a "lie," his words can always be trusted. Since all of Scripture is spoken by God, all of Scripture must be "unlying," just as God himself is. There can be no untruthfulness in Scripture.

Hebrews 6:18 mentions two unchangeable things (God's oath and his promise) "in which it is impossible for God to lie" (author's translation). Here the author says not merely that God does not lie, but that it is not possible for him to lie. Although the immediate reference is only to oaths and promises, if it is impossible for God to lie in these utterances, then certainly it is impossible for him ever to lie.

2. Therefore, all the words in Scripture are completely true and without error in any part. Since the words of the Bible are God's words, and since God cannot lie or speak falsely, it is correct to conclude that there is no untruthfulness or error in any part of the words of Scripture. We find this affirmed several places in the Bible. "The words of the LORD *are words that are pure,* silver refined in a furnace on the ground, purified seven times" (Ps. 12:6, author's translation). Here the psalmist uses vivid imagery to speak of the undiluted purity of God's words; there is no imperfection in them. Also in Proverbs 30:5 we read, "*Every word of God proves true;* he is a shield to those who take refuge in him." It is not just some of the words of Scripture that are true, but every word. In fact, God's Word is fixed in heaven for all eternity: "For ever, O LORD, *your word is firmly fixed in the heavens*" (Ps. 119:89). Jesus can speak of the eternal nature of his own words: "Heaven and earth will pass away, but my words will not pass away" (Matt. 24:35). These verses affirm explicitly what was implicit in the requirement that we believe all the words of Scripture, namely, that there is no untruthfulness or falsehood affirmed in any of the statements of the Bible.

3. God's words are the ultimate standard of truth. In John 17, Jesus prays to the Father, "Sanctify them in the truth; your word is truth" (John 17:17). This verse is interesting because Jesus does not use an adjective, *alēthinos* or *alēthēs* ("true"), which we might have expected, to say, "Your word is true." Rather, he uses a noun, *alētheia* ("truth"), to say that God's Word is not simply "true," but it is truth itself.

The difference is significant, for this statement encourages us to think of the Bible not simply as being "true" in the sense that it conforms to some higher standard of truth, but rather to think of the Bible as itself the final standard of truth. The Bible is God's Word, and God's Word is the ultimate definition of what is true and what is not true: God's Word is itself *truth*. Thus, we are to think of the Bible as the ultimate standard of truth, the reference point by which every other claim to truthfulness is to be measured. Those assertions that conform with Scripture are "true" while those that do not conform with Scripture are not true.

What then is truth? Truth is what God says, and we have what God says (accurately but not exhaustively) in the Bible.

This doctrine of the absolute truthfulness of Scripture stands in clear contrast to a common viewpoint in modern society that is often called *pluralism*. Pluralism is the view that every person has a perspective on truth that is just as valid as everyone else's perspective—therefore, we should not say that anyone else's religion or ethical standard is wrong. According to pluralism, we cannot know any absolute truth; we can only have our own views and perspectives. Of course, if pluralism is true, the Bible cannot be what it claims to be: the words the only true God, the creator and judge of all the world, has spoken to us.[4]

Pluralism is one aspect of an entire contemporary view of the world called *postmodernism*. Postmodernism would not simply hold that we can never find absolute truth; it would say that there is no such thing as absolute truth. All attempts to claim truth for one idea or another are just the result of our own background, culture, biases, and personal agendas (especially our desire for power). Such a view of the world is of course directly opposed to a biblical view, which sees the Bible as truth that has been given to us from God.

4. Might some new fact ever contradict the Bible? Will any new scientific or historical fact ever be discovered that will contradict the Bible? Here we can say with confidence that this will never happen—it is in fact impossible. If any supposed "fact" is ever discovered that is said to contradict Scripture, then (if we have understood Scripture rightly) that "fact" must be false, because God, the author of Scripture, knows all true facts (past, present, and future). No fact will ever turn up that God did not know about ages ago and take into account when he caused Scripture to be written. Every true fact is something that God has known already from all eternity and is something that therefore cannot contradict God's speech in Scripture.

---

[4]For a detailed survey of modern forms of pluralism and a Christian response, see D. A. Carson, *The Gagging of God: Christianity Confronts Pluralism* (Grand Rapids: Zondervan, 1996).

Nevertheless, it must be remembered that scientific or historical study (as well as other kinds of study of creation) can cause us to reexamine Scripture to see if it really teaches what we thought it taught. For example, the Bible does not teach that the sun goes around the earth, for it only uses descriptions of phenomena as we see them from our vantage point and does not purport to be describing the workings of the universe from some arbitrary "fixed" point somewhere out in space. Yet until the study of astronomy advanced enough to demonstrate the rotation of the earth on its axis, people assumed that the Bible taught that the sun goes around the earth. Then the study of scientific data prompted a reexamination of the appropriate biblical texts. Thus, whenever confronted with some "fact" that is said to contradict Scripture, we must not only examine the data adduced to demonstrate the fact in question; we must also reexamine the appropriate biblical texts to see if the Bible really teaches what we thought it to teach. We can do so with confidence, for no true fact will ever contradict the words of the God who knows all facts and who never lies.

D. The Inerrancy of Scripture

1. The meaning of inerrancy. The previous section addressed the truthfulness of Scripture. A key component of this topic is Scripture's inerrancy. This issue is of great concern in the evangelical world today, because on many fronts the truthfulness of Scripture has been brought into question or even abandoned.

With the evidence given above concerning the truthfulness of Scripture, we are now in a position to define biblical inerrancy: *The inerrancy of Scripture means that Scripture in the original manuscripts does not affirm anything which is contrary to fact.*

This definition focuses on the question of truthfulness and falsehood in the language of Scripture. The definition in simple terms just means that the Bible always tells the truth and that it always tells the truth concerning everything it talks about. This definition does not mean that the Bible tells us every fact there is to know about any one subject, but it affirms that what it does say about any subject is true.

It is important to realize at the outset of this discussion that the focus of this controversy is on the question of truthfulness in speech. It must be recognized that absolute truthfulness in speech is consistent with some other types of statements, such as the following:

a. *The Bible can be inerrant and still speak in the ordinary language of everyday speech.* This is especially true in "scientific" or "historical" descriptions of facts or events. The Bible can speak of the sun rising and the rain falling because from the perspective of the speaker this is exactly what happens. From the standpoint of the speaker, the sun does rise and the rain does fall, and these are perfectly true descriptions of the natural phenomena the speaker observes.

A similar consideration applies to numbers when used in counting or in measuring. A reporter can say that 8,000 men were killed in a certain battle without thereby implying that he has counted everyone and that there are not 7,999 or 8,001 dead soldiers. This is also true for measurements. Whether I say, "I don't live far from the library," or "I live a little over a mile from the library," or "I live 1¼ miles from the library," or "I live 1.287 miles from the library," all four statements are still approximations to some degree of accuracy. In both of these examples, and in many others that could be drawn from daily life, the limits of truthfulness would depend on the degree of precision implied by the speaker and expected by his or her original hearers. It should not trouble us, then, to affirm both that the Bible is absolutely truthful in everything it says and that it uses ordinary language to describe natural phenomena or to give approximations or round numbers when those are appropriate in the context.

b. *The Bible can be inerrant and still include loose or free quotations.* The method by which one person quotes the words of another person is a procedure that in large part varies from culture to culture. While in contemporary American and British culture we are used to quoting a person's exact words when we enclose the statement in quotation marks, written Greek at the time of the New Testament had no quotation marks or equivalent kinds of punctuation, and an accurate citation of another person needed to include only a correct representation of the content of what the person said (rather like our use of indirect quotations); it was not expected to cite each word exactly. Thus, inerrancy is consistent with loose or free quotations of the Old Testament or of the words of Jesus, for example, so long as the content is not false to what was originally stated. The original writer did not ordinarily imply that he was using the exact words of the speaker and only those, nor did the original hearers expect verbatim quotation in such reporting.

c. *It is consistent with inerrancy to have unusual or uncommon grammatical constructions in the Bible.* Some of the language of Scripture is elegant and stylistically excellent. Other scriptural writings contain the rough-hewn language of ordinary people. At times this includes a failure to follow the commonly accepted "rules" of grammatical expression (such as the use of a plural verb where grammatical rules would require a singular verb). These stylistically incorrect grammatical statements (several of which are found in the book of Revelation) should not trouble us, for they do not affect the truthfulness of the statements under consideration; a statement can be ungrammatical but still entirely true. For example, an uneducated backwoodsman in some rural area may be the most trusted man in the county even though his grammar is poor, because he has earned a reputation for never telling a lie. Similarly, there are some statements in Scripture (in the original languages) that are ungrammatical (according to current standards of proper grammar at that time) but still inerrant because they are completely true. God used ordinary people who used their own ordinary language. The issue is not elegance in style but truthfulness in speech.

2. Some current challenges to inerrancy. In this section we examine some of the major objections that are commonly made against the concept of inerrancy.

a. *The Bible is only authoritative for "faith and practice."* One of the most frequent objections to inerrancy is raised by those who say that the purpose of Scripture is to teach us in areas that concern "faith and practice" only; that is, in areas that directly relate to our religious faith or to our ethical conduct. This position would allow for the possibility of false statements in Scripture, for example, in other areas such as in minor historical details or scientific facts—these areas, it is said, do not concern the purpose of the Bible, which is to instruct us in what we should believe and how we are to live. Advocates of this position often prefer to say that the Bible is *infallible,* but they hesitate to use the word *inerrant.*[5]

---

[5]Until about 1960 or 1965, the word *infallible* was used interchangeably with the word *inerrant.* But in more recent years, at least in the United States, the word *infallible* has been used in a weaker sense to mean that the Bible will not lead us astray in matters of faith and practice.

The response to this objection can be stated as follows: The Bible repeatedly affirms that *all* of Scripture is profitable for us and that *all* of it is "God-breathed" (2 Tim. 3:16). Thus, it is completely pure (Ps. 12:6), perfect (Ps. 119:96), and true (Prov. 30:5). The Bible itself does not make any restriction on the kinds of subjects to which it speaks truthfully.

The New Testament contains further affirmations of the reliability of all parts of Scripture. In Acts 24:14, Paul says that he worships God, "*believing everything* laid down by the law or written in the prophets." In Luke 24:25, Jesus says that the disciples are "foolish men" because they are "slow of heart to believe *all* that the prophets have spoken." In Romans 15:4, Paul says that "*whatever* was written" in the Old Testament was "written for our instruction." These texts give no indication that there is any part of Scripture that is not to be trusted or relied on completely.

A quick perusal of the historical details of the Old Testament that are cited in the New Testament indicates that the New Testament writers were willing to rely on the truthfulness of any part of the historical narratives of the Old Testament. No detail is too insignificant to be used for the instruction of New Testament Christians (see, for example, Matt. 12:3–4, 41; Luke 4:25–26; John 4:5; 1 Cor. 10:11; Heb. 11; Heb. 12:16–17; James 2:25; 2 Peter 2:16; et al.). There is no indication that they thought of a certain category of scriptural statements as unreliable and untrustworthy (such as "historical and scientific" statements as opposed to doctrinal and moral passages). It seems clear that the Bible itself does not support any restriction on the kinds of subjects to which it speaks with absolute authority and truth; indeed, many passages in Scripture actually exclude the validity of this kind of restriction.

A second response to those who limit the necessary truthfulness of Scripture to matters of "faith and practice" is to note that this position mistakes the *major* purpose of Scripture for the *total* purpose of Scripture. To say that the major purpose of Scripture is to teach us in matters of "faith and practice" is to make a useful and correct summary of God's purpose in giving us the Bible. But as a *summary* it includes only the most prominent purpose of God in giving us Scripture. It is not, however, legitimate to use this summary to deny that it is *part* of the purpose of Scripture to tell us about minor historical details, or about some aspects of astronomy or geography, and so forth. A summary cannot properly be used to deny one of the things it is summarizing! It is better to say that the *whole purpose* of Scripture is to say everything it does say, on whatever subject. Every one of God's words in Scripture was deemed by him to be important for us. Thus, God issues severe warnings to anyone who would take away even one word from what he has said to us (Deut. 4:2; 12:32; Rev. 22:18–19). We cannot add to God's words or take from them, for all are part of his larger purpose in speaking to us. Everything stated in Scripture is there because God intended it to be there. God does not say anything unintentionally!

b. *The term* inerrancy *is a poor term.* People who make this second objection say that the term *inerrancy* is too precise and that in ordinary usage it denotes a kind of absolute scientific precision that we do not want to claim for Scripture. Furthermore, those who make this objection note that the term *inerrancy* is not used in the Bible itself. Therefore, they say, it is probably an inappropriate term for us to insist upon.

The response to this objection may be stated as follows: First, the word has been used by scholars for more than a hundred years, and they have always allowed for the "limitations" that attach to speech in ordinary language. Furthermore, it must be noted that we often use nonbiblical terms to summarize a biblical teaching. The word *Trinity* does not occur in Scripture, nor does the word *incarnation*. Yet both of these terms are very helpful because they allow us to summarize in one word a true biblical concept, and they are therefore helpful in enabling us to discuss a biblical teaching more easily. Finally, in the church today we seem to be unable to carry on the discussion around this topic without the use of the term. People may object to this term if they wish, but, like it or not, this is the term about which the discussion has focused and almost certainly will continue to focus in the next several decades. It therefore seems appropriate to maintain its usage in the discussion over Scripture's complete truthfulness.

c. *We have no inerrant manuscripts; therefore, talk about an inerrant Bible is misleading.* Those who make this objection point to the fact that inerrancy has always been claimed for the first or original copies of the biblical documents. Yet none of these survive; we have only copies of copies of what Moses or Paul or Peter wrote. What is the use, then, of placing so great importance on a doctrine that applies only to manuscripts that no one has?

In reply to this objection, we can first think of an analogy from American history. The original copy of the United States Constitution is housed in a building called the National Archives in Washington, D.C. If through some terrible event that building were destroyed and the original copy of the Constitution lost, could we ever find out what the Constitution said? Of course—we would compare hundreds of copies, and where they all agreed, we would have reason for confidence that we had the exact words of the original document.

A similar process has occurred in determining the original words of the Bible. For over 99 percent of the words of the Bible, we *know* what the original manuscript said. Even for many of the verses where there are textual variants (that is, different words in different ancient copies of the same verse), the correct decision is often quite clear (there may be an obvious copying error, for example), and there are really very few places where the textual variant is both difficult to evaluate and significant in determining the meaning. In the small percentage of cases where there is significant uncertainty about what the original text said, the general sense of the sentence is usually quite clear from the context.

This is not to say that the study of textual variants is unimportant, but it is to say that the study of textual variants has not left us in confusion about what the original manuscripts said.[6] It has rather brought us extremely close to the content of those original manuscripts. For most practical purposes, then, *the current published scholarly texts* of the Hebrew Old Testament and Greek New Testament *are the same as the original manuscripts*. Therefore, the doctrine of inerrancy affects how we think not only about the original manuscripts but also about our present manuscripts as well.

d. *The biblical writers "accommodated" their messages in minor details to the false ideas current in their day and affirmed or taught those ideas in an incidental way.* Those who hold this position argue that it would have been very difficult for the biblical writers to communicate with the people of their time if they had tried to

---

[6]An excellent survey of the work of studying textual variants in the extant manuscripts of the New Testament is Bruce M. Metzger, *The Text of the New Testament: Its Transmission, Corruption, and Restoration,* 2d ed. (Oxford: Clarendon Press, 1968).

correct all the false historical and scientific information believed by their contemporaries (such as a three-storied universe or a flat earth, and so on). Therefore, they say, when the authors of Scripture were attempting to make a larger point, they sometimes *incidentally affirmed some falsehood* believed by the people of their time.

To this objection to inerrancy we can reply that God is Lord of human language who can use human language to communicate perfectly without having to affirm any false ideas that may have been held by people during the time of the writing of Scripture. Furthermore, such "accommodation" by God to our misunderstandings would imply that God had acted contrary to his character as an "unlying God" (Num. 23:19; Titus 1:2; Heb. 6:18). Although God does condescend to speak the language of human beings, no passage of Scripture teaches that he "condescends" so as to act contrary to his moral character. This objection thus at root misunderstands the purity and unity of God as they affect all of his words and deeds.

e. *There are some clear errors in the Bible.* For many who deny inerrancy, the conviction that there are some actual errors in Scripture is a major factor in persuading them to challenge the doctrine of inerrancy. In every case, however, the first answer that should be made to this objection is to ask where such errors are. In which specific verse or verses do these "errors" occur? It is surprising how frequently one finds that this objection is made by people who have little or no idea where the specific errors are, but who believe there are errors because others have told them so.

In other cases, however, people will mention one or more specific passages where, they claim, there is a false statement in Scripture.[7] In many instances, a close examination of the biblical text itself will bring to light one or more possible solutions to the difficulty. In a few passages, no solution to the difficulty may be immediately apparent from reading the English text. At that point it is helpful to consult some commentaries on the text. There are a few texts where a knowledge of Hebrew or Greek may be necessary in order to find a solution, and those who do not have firsthand access to these languages may have to find answers either from a more technical commentary or by asking someone who does have this training.

Of course, our understanding of Scripture is never perfect, and this means that there may be cases where we will be unable to find a solution to a difficult passage at the present time. This may be because the linguistic, historical, or contextual evidence that we need to understand the passage correctly is presently unknown to us. This should not trouble us in a small number of passages so long as the overall pattern of our investigation of these passages has shown that there is, in fact, no error where one has been alleged.

Finally, a historical perspective on this question is helpful. There are no really "new" problems in Scripture. The Bible in its entirety is over nineteen hundred years old, and the alleged "problem texts" have been there all along. Yet throughout the history of the church there has been a firm belief in the inerrancy of Scripture in the sense in which it is defined in this chapter. Moreover, for these hundreds of years, highly competent biblical scholars have read and studied those problem texts and still have found no difficulty in holding to inerrancy. This should give us confidence

---

[7]Some commonly mentioned "problem texts" are texts such as Matt. 1:1–17 with Luke 3:23–38; Matt. 4:1–11 with Luke 4:1–13; Matt. 20:29–30 with Mark 10:46; and Matt. 21:18–21 with Mark 11:12–14, 20–24; Matt. 27:5 with Acts 1:16–25. There are reasonable solutions for all of these in commentaries, but students may find it profitable first to examine the texts for themselves to see if they can discover reasonable ways to reconcile them.

that the solutions to these problems are available and that belief in inerrancy is entirely consistent with a lifetime of detailed attention to the text of Scripture.

3. Problems with denying inerrancy. The problems that come with a denial of biblical inerrancy are not insignificant, and when we understand the magnitude of these problems, it gives us further encouragement not only to affirm inerrancy but also to affirm its importance for the church. Some of the more serious problems are listed here.

a. *If we deny inerrancy a serious moral problem confronts us: May we imitate God and intentionally lie in small matters also?* Ephesians 5:1 tells us to be imitators of God. But a denial of inerrancy that still claims that the words of Scripture are God-breathed words necessarily implies that God intentionally spoke falsely to us in some of the less central affirmations of Scripture. But if this is right for God to do, how can it be wrong for us? Such a line of reasoning would, if we believed it, exert strong pressure on us to begin to speak untruthfully in situations where that might seem to help us communicate better, and so forth. This position would be a slippery slope with ever-increasing negative results in our own lives.

b. *Second, if inerrancy is denied, we begin to wonder if we can really trust God in anything he says.* Once we become convinced that God has spoken falsely to us in some minor matters in Scripture, then we realize that God is capable of speaking falsely to us. This will have a serious detrimental effect on our ability to take God at his word and trust him completely or obey him fully in the rest of Scripture. We may begin to disobey initially those sections of Scripture that we least wish to obey, and to distrust initially those sections that we are least inclined to trust. But such a procedure will eventually increase, to the great detriment of our spiritual lives.

c. *Third, if we deny inerrancy we essentially make our own human minds a higher standard of truth than God's Word itself.* We use our minds to pass judgment on some sections of God's Word and pronounce them to be in error. But this is in effect to say that we know truth more certainly and more accurately than God's Word does (or than God does), at least in these areas. Such a procedure, making our own minds to be a higher standard of truth than God's Word, is the root of all intellectual sin.

d. *Fourth, if we deny inerrancy, we must also say that the Bible is wrong not only in minor details but in some of its doctrines as well.* A denial of inerrancy means that we say that the Bible's teaching about the *nature of Scripture* and about the *truthfulness and reliability of God's words* is also false. These are not minor details but are major doctrinal concerns in Scripture.[8]

E. Written Scripture Is Our Final Authority

It is important to realize that the final form in which Scripture is authoritative is its *written* form. It was the words of God *written* on the tablets of stone that Moses deposited in the ark of the covenant. Later, God commanded Moses and subsequent prophets to *write* their words in a book. And it was *written* Scripture (Gk. *graphē*)

---

[8]Although the undesirable positions listed above are logically related to a denial of inerrancy, a word of caution is in order: Not all who deny inerrancy will also adopt the undesirable conclusions just listed. Some people (probably inconsistently) will deny inerrancy but not take these next logical steps. In debates over inerrancy, as in other theological discussions, it is important that we criticize people on the basis of views they actually hold and that we distinguish those views clearly from positions we think they would hold if they were consistent with their stated views.

that Paul said was "God-breathed" (2 Tim. 3:16). This is important because people sometimes (intentionally or unintentionally) attempt to substitute some other final standard than the written words of Scripture. For example, people will sometimes refer to "what Jesus really said" and claim that when we translate the Greek words of the Gospels back into the Aramaic language Jesus spoke, we can gain a better understanding of Jesus' words than was given by the writers of the Gospels. In other cases, people claim to know "what Paul really thought" even when that is different from the meaning of the words he wrote. Or they speak of "what Paul would have said if he had been consistent with the rest of his theology." Similarly, others speak of "the church situation to which Matthew was writing" and attempt to give normative force either to that situation or to the solution they think Matthew was attempting to bring about in that situation.

In all of these instances, we must admit that asking about the words or situations that lie behind the text of Scripture may at times be helpful to us in understanding what the text means. Nevertheless, our hypothetical reconstructions of these words or situations can never replace or compete with Scripture itself as the final authority, nor should we ever allow them to contradict or call into question the accuracy of any of the words of Scripture. We must continually remember that we have in the Bible God's very words, and we must not try to "improve" on them in some way, for this cannot be done. Rather, we should seek to understand them and then trust them and obey them with our whole heart.

II. REVIEW QUESTIONS

1. Defend the following statement: "All the words in Scripture are God's words."

2. What is meant by the idea that the words of Scripture are "self-attesting"?

3. How can we know that God's words are truthful?

4. Define the term *inerrancy* and discuss how this idea can be consistent with the Bible's use of the language of ordinary, everyday speech.

5. List and respond to three objections to the concept of the inerrancy of Scripture.

6. Name four possible problems that may result from a denial of biblical inerrancy.

III. QUESTIONS FOR PERSONAL APPLICATION

1. Who would try to make people want to disbelieve something in Scripture? To disobey something in Scripture? Is there anything in the Bible that you do not want to believe? To obey? If your answers to either of the preceding two questions were positive, what is the best way to approach and to deal with the desires that you have in this area?

2. Do you know of any proven fact in all of history that has shown something in the Bible to be false? Can the same be said about other religious writings such as the *Book of Mormon* or the *Qur'an*? If you have read in other books such as these, can you describe the spiritual effect they had on you? Compare that with the spiritual effect that reading the Bible has on you.

3. Do you ever find yourself believing something, not because you have external evidence for it, but simply because it is written in Scripture? Is that proper faith according to Hebrews 11:1? Do you think that trusting and obeying everything that Scripture affirms will ever lead you into sin or away from God's blessing in your life?

4. If you thought there were some small errors affirmed by Scripture, how do you think that would affect the way you read Scripture? Would it affect your concern for truthfulness in everyday conversation?

IV. SPECIAL TERMS

absolute authority

authority of Scripture

circular argument

dictation

faith and practice

God-breathed

inerrant

infallible

inspiration

neoorthodoxy

Scripture

self-attesting

textual variant

V. SCRIPTURE MEMORY PASSAGE

2 TIMOTHY 3:16

All scripture is inspired by God and profitable for teaching, for reproof, for correction, and for training in righteousness.

CHAPTER THREE

The Clarity, Necessity, and Sufficiency of the Bible

+ *Can only Bible scholars understand the Bible rightly?*
+ *For what purposes is the Bible necessary?*
+ *Is the Bible enough for knowing what God wants us to think or do?*

Having discussed in chapter 2 the Bible's claim to authority, we now turn to the other three characteristics of Scripture to complete our discussion concerning what the Bible teaches about itself.

I. EXPLANATION AND SCRIPTURAL BASIS

Anyone who has begun to read the Bible seriously will realize that some parts can be understood very easily while other parts seem puzzling. While we must admit that not all parts of Scripture are easily understood, it would be a mistake to think that most of Scripture or Scripture in general is difficult to understand. In fact, the Old Testament and New Testament frequently affirm that Scripture is written in such a way that its teachings are understandable by ordinary believers. We will therefore examine first the doctrine of the clarity of Scripture.

Beyond the issue of our ability to understand Scripture is the question of its necessity: Do we need to know what the Bible says to know that God exists? Or that we are sinners in need of salvation? These are the kinds of questions an investigation of the necessity of Scripture is intended to answer.

Finally, we will look at Scripture's sufficiency. Are we to look for other words from God in addition to those we have in Scripture? Is the Bible enough for knowing what God requires us to believe or to do? The doctrine of the sufficiency of Scripture addresses these questions.

A. The Clarity of Scripture

1. The Bible frequently affirms its own clarity. The Bible often speaks of its own clarity and of the responsibility of believers to read and understand it. In a very familiar passage, Moses tells the people of Israel: "These words which I command you this day shall be upon your heart; and *you shall teach them diligently to your chil-*

dron, and shall *talk of them* when you sit in your house, and when you walk by the way, and when you lie down, and when you rise" (Deut. 6:6–7). All the people of Israel were expected to be able to understand the words of Scripture well enough to be able to "teach them diligently" to their children. This teaching would not have consisted merely of rote memorization devoid of understanding, for the people of Israel were to *discuss* the words of Scripture during their activities of sitting in the house or walking or going to bed or getting up in the morning. God expected that *all* of his people would know and be able to talk about his Word with proper application to ordinary life situations.

The character of Scripture is said to be such that even the "simple" can understand it rightly and be made wise by it. "The testimony of the LORD is sure, *making wise the simple*" (Ps. 19:7). Again we read, "The unfolding of your words gives light; *it imparts understanding to the simple*" (Ps. 119:130). Here the "simple" person is not merely one who lacks intellectual ability, but one who lacks sound judgment, who is prone to making mistakes, and who is easily led astray. God's Word is so understandable, so clear, that even this kind of person is made wise by it. This should be a great encouragement to all believers; no believer should think himself or herself too foolish to read Scripture and understand it sufficiently to be made wise by it.

There is a similar emphasis in the New Testament. Jesus himself, in his teachings, his conversations, and his disputes, never responds to any questions with a hint of blaming the Old Testament Scriptures for being unclear. Instead, whether he is speaking to scholars or untrained common people, his responses always assume that the blame for misunderstanding any teaching of Scripture is not to be placed on the Scriptures themselves, but on those who misunderstand or fail to accept what is written. Again and again he answers questions with statements like, "Have you not read . . . ?" (Matt. 12:3, 5; 19:14; 22:31), "Have you never read in the Scriptures . . . ?" (Matt. 21:42), or even, "You are wrong because you know neither the Scriptures nor the power of God" (Matt. 22:29; see also Matt. 9:13; 12:7; 15:3; 21:13; John 3:10; et al.).

Lest we think that understanding the Bible was somehow easier for first-century Christians than for us, it is important to realize that in many instances the New Testament epistles were written to churches that had large proportions of Gentile Christians. They were relatively new Christians who had no previous background in any kind of Christian society, and who had little or no prior understanding of the history and culture of Israel. The events of Abraham's life (around 2000 B.C.) were as far in the past for them as the events of the New Testament are for us! Nevertheless, the New Testament authors show no hesitancy in expecting even these Gentile Christians to be able to read a translation of the Old Testament in their own language and to understand it rightly (see Rom. 4:1–25; 15:4; 1 Cor. 10:1–11; 2 Tim. 3:16–17; et al.).

2. The moral and spiritual qualities needed for right understanding. The New Testament writers frequently state that the ability to understand Scripture rightly is more a moral and spiritual than intellectual ability: "The unspiritual man does not receive the gifts (literally 'things') of the Spirit of God, for they are folly to him, and he is not able to understand them because they are spiritually discerned" (1 Cor. 2:14; cf. 1:18–3:4; 2 Cor. 3:14–16; 4:3–4, 6; Heb. 5:14; James 1:5–6; 2 Peter 3:5; cf. Mark 4:11–12; John 7:17; 8:43). Thus, although the New Testament authors affirm that the Bible *in itself* is written clearly, they also affirm that it will not be understood rightly by those who are unwilling to receive its teachings. Scripture is able to be understood by all unbelievers who will read it sincerely seeking salvation, and by believers who will read it while seeking God's help in understanding it. This is because in both cases the Holy Spirit is at work overcoming the effects of sin, which otherwise will make the truth appear to be foolish (1 Cor. 1:18–25; 2:14; James 1:5–6, 22–25).

3. Definition of the clarity of Scripture. In order to summarize this biblical material, we can affirm that the Bible is written in such a way that all things necessary for our salvation and for our Christian life and growth are very clearly set forth in Scripture. Although theologians have sometimes defined the clarity of Scripture more narrowly (by saying, for example, only that Scripture is clear in teaching the way of salvation), the texts cited above apply to many different aspects of biblical teaching and do not seem to support any such limitation on the areas to which Scripture can be said to speak clearly. It seems more faithful to those biblical texts to define the clarity of Scripture as follows: *The clarity of Scripture means that the Bible is written in such a way that its teachings are able to be understood by all who will read it seeking God's help and being willing to follow it.* Once we have stated this, however, we must also recognize that many people, even God's people, do in fact misunderstand Scripture.

4. Why do people misunderstand Scripture? During Jesus' lifetime, his own disciples at times failed to understand the Old Testament and Jesus' own teachings (see Matt. 15:16; Mark 4:10–13; 6:52; 8:14–21; 9:32; Luke 18:34; John 8:27; 10:6). Although sometimes this was due to the fact that they simply needed to wait for further events in the history of redemption, and especially in the life of Christ himself (see John 12:16; 13:7; cf. John 2:22), there were also times when this was due to their own lack of faith or hardness of heart (Luke 24:25). Furthermore, there were times in the early church when Christians did not understand or agree on the teachings of the Old Testament or about the letters written by the apostles: note the process of growth in understanding concerning the implications of Gentile inclusion in the church (culminating in "much debate" [Acts 15:7] in the Jerusalem Council of Acts 15), and note Peter's misunderstanding of this issue in Galatians 2:11–15. In fact, throughout the history of the church, doctrinal disagreements have been many, and progress in resolving doctrinal differences has often been slow.

To help people avoid making mistakes in interpreting Scripture, many Bible teachers have developed "principles of interpretation," or guidelines to encourage growth in the skill of proper interpretation. The word *hermeneutics* (from the Greek word *hermēneuō*, "to interpret") is the more technical term for this field of study: *Hermeneutics is the study of correct methods of interpretation* (especially interpretation of Scripture).

Another technical term often used in discussions of biblical interpretation is *exegesis,* a term that refers more to the actual practice of interpreting Scripture, not to theories and principles about how it should be done: *Exegesis is the process of interpreting a text of Scripture.* Consequently, when one studies principles of interpretation, that is called "hermeneutics," but when one applies those principles and begins actually explaining a biblical text, he or she is doing "exegesis."

The existence of many disagreements about the meaning of Scripture throughout history reminds us that the doctrine of the clarity of Scripture does not imply or suggest that all believers will agree on all the teachings of Scripture. Nevertheless, it does tell us something very important—that the problem always lies not with Scripture but with ourselves. We affirm that all the teachings of Scripture are clear and able to be understood, but we also recognize that people often (through their own short-comings) misunderstand what is clearly written in Scripture.

Therefore, as people grow in the Christian life, gaining more knowledge of Scripture as they spend time studying it, they will understand Scripture better. The doctrine of the clarity of Scripture says that Scripture is *able to be understood,* not that all understand it equally well.

5. *Practical encouragement from this doctrine.* The doctrine of the clarity of Scripture has a very important, and ultimately very encouraging, practical implication. It tells us that where there are areas of doctrinal or ethical disagreement (for example, over baptism or predestination or church government), there are only two possible causes for these disagreements: (1) On the one hand, it may be that we are *seeking to make affirmations where Scripture itself is silent.* In such cases, we should be more ready to admit that God has not given us the answer to our quest, and to allow for differences of viewpoint within the church. (This will often be the case with very practical questions, such as methods of evangelism or styles of Bible teaching or appropriate church size.) (2) On the other hand, it is possible that we have made *mistakes in our interpretation* of Scripture. This could have happened because the data we used to decide a question of interpretation were inaccurate or incomplete. Or it could be because there is some personal inadequacy on our part, whether it be, for example, personal pride, greed, lack of faith, selfishness, or even failure to devote enough time to prayerfully reading and studying Scripture.

But in no case are we free to say that the teaching of the Bible on any subject is confusing or incapable of being understood correctly. In no case should we think that persistent disagreements on some subject through the history of the church mean that we will be unable to come to a correct conclusion on that subject ourselves. Rather, if a genuine concern about some such subject arises in our lives, we should sincerely ask God's help and then go to Scripture, searching it with all our ability, believing that God will enable us to understand rightly.

6. *The role of scholars.* Is there any role then for Bible scholars or for those with specialized knowledge of Hebrew (for the Old Testament) and Greek (for the New Testament)? Certainly there is a role for them in at least four areas.

For one thing, they can *teach* Scripture clearly, communicating its content to others, and thus fulfilling the office of "teacher," which is mentioned in the New Testament (1 Cor. 12:28; Eph. 4:11).

Second, they can *explore* new areas of understanding the teachings of Scripture. This exploration will seldom (if ever) involve denial of the main teachings the church has held throughout its centuries, but it will often involve the application of Scripture to new areas of life, the answering of difficult questions that have been raised by both believers and unbelievers at each new period in history, and the continual activity of refining and making more precise the church's understanding of detailed points of interpretation of individual verses or matters of doctrine or ethics.

Third, they can *defend* the teachings of the Bible against attacks by other scholars or those with specialized technical training. The role of teaching God's Word also at times involves correcting false teachings. One must be able not only "to give instruction in sound doctrine," but also "to confute those who contradict it" (Titus 1:9; cf. 2 Tim. 2:25, "correcting his opponents with gentleness"; and Titus 2:7–8). Sometimes those who attack biblical teachings have specialized training and technical knowledge in historical, linguistic, or philosophical study, and they use that training to mount rather sophisticated attacks against the teaching of Scripture. In such cases, believers with similar specialized skills can use their training to understand and respond to such attacks.

Finally, they can *supplement* the study of Scripture for the benefit of the church. Bible scholars often have training that will enable them to relate the teachings of Scripture to the rich history of the church, and to make the interpretation of Scripture more precise and its meaning more vivid with a greater knowledge of the languages and cultures in which the Bible was written.

These four functions benefit the church as a whole, and all believers should be thankful for those who perform them. However, these functions do not include the right to decide for the church as a whole what is true and false doctrine or what is proper conduct in a difficult situation. If such a right were the preserve of formally trained Bible scholars, then they would become a governing elite in the church, and the ordinary functioning of the government of the church as described in the New Testament would cease. The process of decision making for the church must be left to the officers of the church, whether they are scholars or not (and, in churches where there is a congregational form of church government, not only to the officers, but also to the people of the church as a whole).

B. The Necessity of Scripture

The necessity of Scripture may be defined as follows: *The necessity of Scripture means that the Bible is necessary for knowledge of the gospel, for maintaining spiritual life, and for certain knowledge of God's will, but is not necessary for knowing that God exists or for knowing something about God's character and moral laws.*

This definition may now be explained in its various parts.

1. The Bible is necessary for knowledge of the gospel. In Romans 10:13–17, Paul says: "For, 'everyone who calls upon the name of the Lord will be saved.' But how are men to call upon him in whom they have not believed? And *how are they to believe in him of whom they have never heard*? And how are they to hear without a preacher? . . . So *faith comes from what is heard,* and what is heard comes by the preaching of Christ."

This statement indicates the following line of reasoning: (1) It first assumes that one must call upon the name of the Lord in order to be saved. (In Pauline usage generally as well as in this specific context [see v. 9], "the Lord" refers to the Lord Jesus Christ.) (2) People can only call upon the name of Christ if they believe in him (that is, that he is a Savior worthy of calling upon, and one who will answer those who call). (3) People cannot believe in Christ unless they have heard of him. (4) They cannot hear of Christ unless there is someone to tell them about Christ (a "preacher"). (5) The conclusion is that saving faith comes by hearing—that is, by hearing the gospel message—and this hearing of the gospel message comes about through the preaching of Christ. The implication seems to be that without hearing the preaching of the gospel of Christ, no one can be saved.

This passage is one of several that shows that eternal salvation comes only through belief in Jesus Christ, and no other way. Speaking of Christ, John 3:18 says,

"He who believes in him is not condemned; *he who does not believe is condemned already,* because he has not believed in the name of the only Son of God." Similarly, in John 14:6, Jesus says, "I am the way, and the truth, and the life; *no one comes to the Father, but by me.*"[1]

But if people can only be saved through faith in Christ, someone might ask how believers under the old covenant could have been saved. The answer must be that those who were saved under the old covenant were also saved through trusting in Christ, even though their faith was a forward-looking faith based on God's word of promise that a Messiah or a Redeemer would come. Speaking of Old Testament believers such as Abel, Enoch, Noah, Abraham, and Sarah, the author of Hebrews says, "*These all died in faith,* not having received what was promised, but *having seen it and greeted it from afar*" (Heb. 11:13). And Jesus can say of Abraham, "Your father Abraham rejoiced that he was to see my day; *he saw it* and was glad" (John 8:56). This again apparently refers to Abraham's joy in looking forward to the day of the promised Messiah. Thus, even Old Testament believers had saving faith in Christ, to whom they looked forward, not with exact knowledge of the historical details of Christ's life, but with great faith in the absolute reliability of God's word of promise.

The Bible is necessary for salvation, then, in this sense: One must either read the gospel message in the Bible for oneself or hear it from another person. Even those believers who came to salvation in the old covenant did so by trusting in the words of God that promised a Savior to come.

There are other views that differ with this biblical teaching. *Inclusivism* is the view that people can be saved by Christ's work without knowing about him or trusting in him, but simply by sincerely following the religion that they know. Inclusivists often talk about "many different ways to God" even if they emphasize that they personally believe in Christ. *Universalism* is the view that all people will ultimately be saved.[2] The view maintained in this chapter, that people cannot be saved without knowing about Christ and trusting in him, is sometimes called *exclusivism* (though the word itself is unfortunate because it suggests a desire to exclude others, and it thereby fails to convey the outward-reaching missionary theme that is so strong in the New Testament).

2. The Bible is necessary for maintaining spiritual life. Jesus says in Matthew 4:4 (quoting Deut. 8:3), "Man shall not live on bread alone, but on every word that proceeds out of the mouth of God" (NASB). Here Jesus indicates that our spiritual life is maintained by daily nourishment with the Word of God, just as our physical lives are maintained by daily nourishment with physical food. To neglect regular reading of God's Word is as detrimental to the health of our souls as the neglect of physical food is detrimental to the health of our bodies.

3. The Bible is necessary for certain knowledge of God's will. It will be argued below that all people ever born have *some* knowledge of God's will through their consciences. But this knowledge is often indistinct and cannot give certainty. In fact, if there were no written Word of God, we could not gain certainty about God's will through other means such as advice from others, an internal witness of the Holy Spirit, changed circumstances, and the use of sanctified reasoning and common

---

[1]On the question of whether it is fair of God to condemn people who have never heard of Christ, see the discussion in ch. 10, pp. 170–71, and ch. 18, pp. 289–90.

[2]See ch. 10, pp. 170–71, and ch. 18, pp. 291–92, on the fact that not all people will be saved.

sense. These all might give an approximation of God's will in more or less reliable ways, but from these means alone no certainty about God's will could ever be attained, at least in a fallen world where sin distorts our perception of right and wrong, brings faulty reasoning into our thinking processes, and causes us to suppress from time to time the testimony of our consciences (cf. Jer. 17:9; Rom. 2:14–15; 1 Cor. 8:10; Heb. 5:14; 10:22; also 1 Tim. 4:2; Titus 1:15).

In the Bible, however, we have clear and definite statements about God's will. God has not revealed all things to us, but he has revealed enough for us to know his will: "The secret things belong to the LORD our God; but *the things that are revealed belong to us and to our children for ever,* that we may do all the words of this law" (Deut. 29:29). As it was in the time of Moses, so it is now with us: God has revealed his words to us in order that we might obey his laws and thereby do his will. To be "blameless" in God's sight is to "walk in the law of the LORD" (Ps. 119:1). The "blessed" man is one who does not follow the will of wicked people (Ps. 1:1), but delights *"in the law of the LORD,"* and meditates on God's law "day and night" (Ps. 1:2). To love God (and thereby to act in a way that is pleasing to him) is to "keep his commandments" (1 John 5:3). If we are to have a certain knowledge of God's will, then, we must attain it through the study of Scripture.

In fact, in one sense it can be argued that the Bible is necessary for certain knowledge about anything. A philosopher might argue as follows: The fact that we do not know everything requires us to be uncertain about everything we do claim to know. This is because some fact unknown to us may yet turn out to prove that what we thought to be true was actually false. However, God knows all facts that ever have been or ever will be. And this God, who never lies, has spoken to us in Scripture, in which he has told us many true things about himself, about ourselves, and about the universe he has made. No fact can ever turn up to contradict the truth spoken by this One who is omniscient.

Thus, it is appropriate for us to be *more certain* about the truths we read in Scripture than about any other knowledge we have. If we are to talk about degrees of certainty of knowledge we have, then the knowledge we attain from Scripture would have the highest degree of certainty. If the word *certain* can be applied to any kind of human knowledge, it can be applied to this knowledge. Christians who take the Bible as God's Word escape philosophical skepticism about the possibility of attaining certain knowledge with our finite minds. In this sense, then, it is correct to say that for people who are not omniscient, the Bible is necessary for certain knowledge about anything.

4. But the Bible is not necessary for knowing that God exists or for knowing something about God's character and moral laws. What about people who do not read the Bible? Can they obtain any knowledge of God? Can they know anything about his laws? Yes, without the Bible some knowledge of God is possible, even if it is not absolutely certain knowledge.

a. *General revelation and special revelation.* People can obtain a knowledge *that God exists* and a knowledge of *some of his attributes* simply from observation of themselves and the world around them. David says, *"The heavens are telling the glory of God; and the firmament proclaims his handiwork"* (Ps. 19:1). To look at the sky is to see evidence of the infinite power, wisdom, and even beauty of God; it is to observe a majestic witness to the glory of God.

Even those who by their wickedness suppress the truth cannot avoid the evidences of God's existence and nature in the created order:

> For *what can be known about God is plain to them,* because God has shown it to them. Ever since the creation of the world *his invisible nature,* namely, his eternal power and deity, *has been clearly perceived in the things that have been made.* So they are without excuse; for although *they knew God* they did not honor him as God or give thanks to him, but they became futile in their thinking and their senseless minds were darkened. (Rom. 1:19–21)

Here Paul says not only that creation gives evidence of God's existence and character, but also that even wicked men recognize that evidence. What can be known about God is "plain to them" and in fact "they knew God" (apparently, they knew who he was), but "they did not honor him as God or give thanks to him." This passage allows us to say that all persons, even the most wicked, have some internal knowledge or perception that God exists and that he is a powerful Creator. This knowledge is seen "in the things that have been made," a phrase that refers to all creation, including mankind.

Paul goes on in Romans 1 to show that even unbelievers who have no written record of God's laws still have in their consciences some understanding of God's moral demands. Speaking of a long list of sins ("envy, murder, strife, deceit . . ."), Paul says of wicked people who practice them, "Though *they know God's decree that those who do such things deserve to die,* they not only do them but approve those who practice them" (Rom. 1:32). Wicked people know that their sin is wrong, at least in large measure.

Paul then talks about the activity of conscience in Gentiles who do not have the written law: "When Gentiles who have not the law do by nature what the law requires, they are a law to themselves, even though they do not have the law. They show that *what the law requires is written on their hearts,* while their conscience also bears witness and their conflicting thoughts accuse or perhaps excuse them" (Rom. 2:14–15).

The consciences of unbelievers bear witness to God's moral standards, but at times this evidence of God's law on the hearts of unbelievers is distorted or suppressed. Sometimes their thoughts "accuse" them and sometimes their thoughts "excuse" them, Paul says. The knowledge of God's laws derived from such sources is never perfect, but it is enough to give an awareness of God's moral demands to all mankind. (And it is on this basis that Paul argues that all humanity is held guilty before God for sin, even those who do not have the written laws of God in Scripture.)

The knowledge of God's existence, character, and moral law, which comes through creation to all humanity, is often called "general revelation" (because it comes to all people generally). General revelation comes through observing nature, through seeing God's directing influence in history, and through an inner sense of God's existence and his laws that he has placed inside every person. General revelation is distinct from *special revelation,* which refers to God's words addressed to specific people, such as the words of the Bible, the words of the Old Testament prophets and New Testament apostles, and the words of God spoken in personal address, such as at Mount Sinai or at Jesus' baptism.

The fact that all people know something of God's moral laws is a great blessing for society, for unless they did there would be no societal restraint on the evil that people would do and no restraint coming from their consciences. Because there is some common knowledge of right and wrong, Christians can often find much consensus with non-Christians in matters of civil law, community standards, basic ethics for business and professional activity, and acceptable patterns of conduct in ordinary life. The knowledge of God's existence and character also provides a basis of information that enables the gospel to make sense to a non-Christian's heart and mind; unbelievers know that God exists and that they have broken his standards, so the news that Christ died to pay for their sins should truly come as *good news* to them.

b. *Special revelation necessary for salvation.* However, it must be emphasized that Scripture nowhere indicates that people can know the gospel, or the way of salvation, through such general revelation. They may know that God exists, that he is their Creator, that they owe him obedience, and that they have sinned against him. But how the *holiness and justice* of God can ever be reconciled with his *willingness to forgive sins* is a mystery that has never been solved by any religion apart from the Bible. Nor does the Bible give us any hope that it ever can be discovered apart from specific revelation from God. It is the great wonder of our redemption that God himself has provided the way of salvation by sending his own Son, who is both God and man, to be our representative and bear the penalty for our sins, thus combining the justice and love of God in one infinitely wise and amazingly gracious act. This fact, which seems commonplace to the Christian ear, should not lose its wonder for us: It never could have been conceived by man alone apart from God's special, verbal revelation.

C. The Sufficiency of Scripture

We can define the sufficiency of Scripture as follows: *The sufficiency of Scripture means that Scripture contained all the words of God he intended his people to have at each stage of redemptive history, and that it now contains everything we need God to tell us for salvation, for trusting him perfectly, and for obeying him perfectly.*

This definition emphasizes the fact that it is in Scripture alone that we are to search for God's words to us. It also reminds us that God considers what he has told us in the Bible to be enough for us, and that we should rejoice in the great revelation that he has given us and be content with it.

Significant scriptural support and explanation of this doctrine is found in Paul's words to Timothy, "From childhood you have been acquainted with the sacred writings which are *able to instruct you for salvation* through faith in Christ Jesus" (2 Tim. 3:15). The context shows that "sacred writings" here means the written words of Scripture (2 Tim. 3:16). This is an indication that the words of God which we have in Scripture are all the words of God we need in order to be saved; these words are able to make us wise "for salvation."

Other passages indicate that the Bible is sufficient to equip us for living the Christian life. Psalm 119:1 says, "Blessed are those whose way is *blameless* who *walk in the law of the LORD!*" This verse shows an equivalence between being "blameless" and "walking in the law of the LORD"; those who are blameless are those who walk in the law of the Lord. Here we have an indication that all that God requires of us is recorded in his written Word. Simply to do all that the Bible commands us is to be blameless in God's sight. Later we read that a young man can "keep his way pure" by "guarding it according to your word" (Ps. 119:9). Paul says that God gave Scripture in order that we may be "complete, equipped for every good work" (2 Tim. 3:17).

1. We can find all that God has said on particular topics, and we can find answers to our questions. Of course, we realize that we will never perfectly obey all of Scripture in this life (see James 3:2; 1 John 1:8–10; and ch. 13 of this volume). Thus, it may not at first seem very significant to say that all we have to do is what God commands us in the Bible, since we will never be able to obey it all in this life anyway. But the truth of the sufficiency of Scripture is of great significance for our Christian lives, for it enables us to *focus* our search for God's words to us on the Bible alone and saves us from the endless task of searching through all the writings of Christians throughout history, or through all the teachings of the church, or through all the subjective feelings and impressions that come to our minds from day to day, in order to find what God requires of us. In a very practical sense, it means that we are able to come to clear conclusions on many teachings of Scripture.

This doctrine means, moreover, that it is possible to collect all the passages that directly relate to doctrinal issues such as the atonement, or the person of Christ, or the work of the Holy Spirit in the believer's life today. In these and hundreds of other moral and doctrinal questions, the biblical teaching about the sufficiency of Scripture gives us confidence that we *will be able to find* what God requires us to think or to do in these areas. In many of these areas we can attain confidence that we, together with the vast majority of the church throughout history, have found and correctly formulated what God wants us to think or to do. Simply stated, the doctrine of the sufficiency of Scripture tells us that it is possible to study systematic theology and ethics and find answers to our questions.

2. The amount of Scripture given was sufficient at each stage of redemptive history. The doctrine of the sufficiency of Scripture does not imply that God cannot add any more words to those he has already spoken to his people. It rather implies that humans cannot add on their own initiative any words to those that God has already spoken. Furthermore, it implies that in fact *God has not spoken* to mankind any more words he requires us to believe or obey other than those we have now in the Bible.

This point is important, for it helps us to understand how God could tell his people that his words to them were sufficient at many different points in the history of redemption and how he could nevertheless add to those words later. For example, in Deuteronomy 29:29 Moses says, "The secret things belong to the LORD our God; but the things that are revealed belong to us and to our children for ever, that we may do all the words of this law."

This verse reminds us that God has always taken the initiative in revealing things to us. He has decided what to reveal and what not to reveal. At each stage in redemptive history, the things that God had revealed were for his people for that time, and they were to study, believe, and obey those things. With further progress in the history of redemption, more of God's words were added, recording and interpreting that history.

3. Practical applications of the sufficiency of Scripture. The doctrine of the sufficiency of Scripture has several practical applications to our Christian lives. The following list is intended to be helpful but not exhaustive.

a. *An encouragement to search the Bible for answers.* The sufficiency of Scripture should encourage us as we try to discover what God would have us to *think* (about a particular doctrinal issue) or to *do* (in a particular situation). We should be encouraged that *everything* God wants to tell us about that question is to be found in Scripture. This does not mean that the Bible answers all the questions that we might think up, for "the secret things belong to the LORD our God" (Deut. 29:29). But it does mean that when we are facing a problem of genuine importance to our Christian life, we can approach Scripture with the confidence that from it God will provide us with guidance for that problem.

There will of course be some times when the answer we find is that Scripture does not speak directly to our question. (This would be the case, for example, if we tried to find from Scripture what order of worship to follow on Sunday mornings, or whether it is better to kneel or perhaps to stand when we pray, or at what time we should eat our meals during the day, and so on.) In those cases, we may conclude that God has not required us to think or to act in any certain way with regard to that question (except, perhaps, in terms of more general principles regarding our attitudes and goals). But in many other cases, we will find direct and clear guidance from the Lord to equip us for "every good work" (2 Tim. 3:17).

b. *A warning not to add to Scripture.* The sufficiency of Scripture reminds us that *we are to add nothing to Scripture,* and that *we are to consider no other writings of equal value to Scripture.* This principle is violated by almost all cults and sects. Mormons, for example, claim to believe the Bible, but they also claim divine authority for the *Book of Mormon.* Christian Scientists similarly claim to believe the Bible, but in practice they hold the book *Science and Health with a Key to the Scriptures* by Mary Baker Eddy on a par with Scripture or above it in authority. Since these claims violate God's commands not to add to his words, we should not think that any additional words from God to us would be found in these writings. Even in Christian churches a similar error is sometimes made when people go beyond what Scripture says and assert with great confidence new ideas about God or heaven, basing their teachings not on Scripture but on their own speculation or even on claimed experiences of dying and coming back to life.

c. *A warning not to count any other guidance from God equal to Scripture.* The sufficiency of Scripture shows us that *no modern revelations from God are to be placed on a level equal to Scripture in authority.* At various times throughout the history of the church, and particularly in the modern charismatic movement, people have claimed that God has given revelations through them for the benefit of the church. Even people in noncharismatic churches often say that God "led" or "guided" them in a certain way. However we may evaluate such claims,[3] we must be careful never to allow (in theory or in practice) the placing of such revelations on a level equal to Scripture. We must insist that God does not require us to believe anything about himself or his work in the world that is contained in these revelations but not in Scripture. And we must insist that God does not require us to obey any moral directives that come to us through such means but are not confirmed by Scripture. The Bible contains all the words of God we need for trusting and obeying him perfectly.[4]

---

[3]See ch. 29, pp. 402–6, on the possibility of some kinds of revelation from God continuing today when the canon is closed, and especially ch. 30, pp. 408–15, on the gift of prophecy.

[4]I do not wish to imply at this point that I am adopting a "cessationist" view of spiritual gifts (that is, a view that holds that certain gifts, such as prophecy and speaking in tongues, ceased when the apostles died). I only wish at this point to state that there is a danger in explicitly or even implicitly giving these gifts a status that in practice challenges the authority or the sufficiency of Scripture in Christians' lives.

d. *A warning not to add more sins or requirements to those named in Scripture.* With regard to living the Christian life, the sufficiency of Scripture reminds us that *nothing is sin that is not forbidden by Scripture either explicitly or by implication.* To walk in the law of the Lord is to be "blameless" (Ps. 119:1). Therefore, we are not to add prohibitions to those already stated in Scripture. From time to time there may be situations in which it would be wrong, for example, for an individual Christian to drink coffee or Coca-Cola, or to attend movie theaters, or to eat meat offered to idols (see 1 Cor. 8–10), but unless some specific teaching or some general principle of Scripture can be shown to prohibit these (or any other activities) for all believers for all time, we must insist that these activities are not in themselves sinful and they are not in all situations prohibited by God for his people.

The discovery of this great truth could bring tremendous joy and peace to the lives of thousands of Christians who, spending countless hours seeking God's will outside of Scripture are often uncertain about whether they have found it. Instead, Christians who are convinced of the sufficiency of Scripture should begin eagerly to seek and find God's will in Scripture. They should be enthusiastically and regularly growing in obedience to God, knowing great freedom and peace in the Christian life. Then they will be able to say with the psalmist:

> I will keep your law continually,
> for ever and ever;
> and *I shall walk at liberty,*
> *for I have sought your precepts....*
> *Great peace have those who love your law;*
> nothing can make them stumble. (Ps. 119:44–45, 165)

e. *An encouragement to be content with Scripture.* The sufficiency of Scripture reminds us that in our doctrinal and ethical teaching we should *emphasize what Scripture emphasizes and be content with what God has told us in Scripture.* There are some subjects about which God has told us little or nothing in the Bible. We must remember that "the secret things belong to the LORD our God" (Deut. 29:29) and that God has revealed to us in Scripture exactly what he deemed right for us. We must accept this and not think that Scripture is something less than it should be, or begin to wish that God had given us much more information about subjects on which there are very few scriptural references.

The doctrinal matters that have divided evangelical Protestant denominations from one another have almost uniformly been matters on which the Bible places relatively little emphasis and matters in which our conclusions must be drawn from skillful inference much more than from direct biblical statements. For example, abiding denominational differences have occurred or have been maintained over the "proper" form of church government, the exact nature of Christ's presence in the Lord's Supper, and the exact sequence of the events surrounding Christ's return.

We should not say that these issues are all unimportant, nor should we say that Scripture gives no solution to any of them (indeed, with respect to many of them, a specific solution will be defended in subsequent chapters of this book). However, since all of these topics receive *relatively little direct emphasis in Scripture,* it is ironic and tragic that denominational leaders will so often give much of their lives to defending precisely the minor doctrinal points that make their denominations different from others. Is such effort really motivated by a desire to bring unity of understanding to the church, or might it stem in some measure from human pride, a desire to retain power over others, and an attempt at self-justification, which is displeasing to God and ultimately unedifying to the church?

II. REVIEW QUESTIONS

1. Define "clarity of Scripture." Why can we say that Scripture is clear?
2. Given the above definition, why do people sometimes misunderstand Scripture?
3. Name and describe at least three things for which the Bible is necessary.
4. Can people know anything about God apart from the Bible? If so, what can they know about him?
5. Since God added to the words of Scripture over a long period of time, did the doctrine of the sufficiency of Scripture apply to people in the Old Testament who had only portions of what we now call the Bible? Why or why not?
6. Is there anything required of us by God or forbidden to us by God that is not commanded or forbidden in Scripture? Explain.

III. QUESTIONS FOR PERSONAL APPLICATION

1. If the doctrine of the clarity of Scripture is true, why does there seem to be so much disagreement among Christians about the teaching of the Bible? Observing the diversity of interpretations of Scripture, some conclude, "People can make the Bible say anything they want." How do you think Jesus would respond to this statement?
2. Do you think that there are right and wrong interpretations of most or all passages of Scripture? If you thought the Bible was generally unclear, how would your answer change? Will a conviction about the clarity of Scripture affect the care you use when studying a text of Scripture? Will it affect the way you approach Scripture when trying to gain a biblical answer to some difficult doctrinal or moral problem?
3. When you are witnessing to an unbeliever, what is the one thing above all others that you should want him or her to read? Do you know of anyone who ever became a Christian without either reading the Bible or hearing someone tell him what the Bible said? What, then, is the primary task of an evangelistic missionary?
4. When we are actively seeking to know God's will, where should we spend most of our time and effort? In practice, where do you? Do God's principles in Scripture and the apparent guidance we receive from feelings, conscience, advice, circumstances, human reasoning, or society ever seem to conflict? How should we seek to resolve the conflict?
5. Have you ever wished that the Bible would say more than it does about a certain subject? Or less? What do you think motivated that wish? After reading this chapter, how would you approach someone who expressed such a wish today?

IV. SPECIAL TERMS

blameless

clarity of Scripture

exegesis

general revelation

hermeneutics

natural revelation

necessity of Scripture

special revelation

sufficiency of Scripture

V. SCRIPTURE MEMORY PASSAGE

DEUTERONOMY 6:6–7

These words which I command you this day shall be upon your heart; and you shall teach them diligently to your children, and shall talk of them when you sit in your house, and when you walk by the way, and when you lie down, and when you rise.

PART II

The Doctrine of God

CHAPTER FOUR

The Character of God: "Incommunicable" Attributes

+ *How do we know that God exists?*
+ *Can we really know God?*
+ *How is God different from us?*

I. EXPLANATION AND SCRIPTURAL BASIS

This chapter will introduce the doctrine of God, or what is sometimes referred to as "theology proper," since the word theology literally means "the study of God."[1] In this chapter and the next we will examine various aspects of God's character, traditionally referred to as his "attributes."

Before addressing the character of God, it is necessary to begin with the basic question, how do we know that God exists? This question is not a major focus of this text and is treated more fully in courses on apologetics. However, an introduction to some of the evidence for God's existence will provide a helpful foundation for the study of God's character. Beyond this, we can also ask whether, if God does exist, is it possible for us to really know him?

A. The Existence of God

The answer to the first question above can be given in two parts: First, all people have an inner sense of God. Second, we believe the evidence that is found in Scripture and in nature.

1. Humanity's inner sense of God. All persons everywhere have a deep, inner sense that God exists, that they are his creatures, and he is their Creator. Paul says that even Gentile unbelievers "knew God" but did not honor him as God or give thanks to him (Rom. 1:21). He says that wicked unbelievers have "exchanged the truth about God for a lie" (Rom. 1:25), implying that they actively or willfully rejected some truth about God's existence and character that they knew. Paul says that "what can be known about God is plain to them" and adds that this is "because God has shown it to them" (Rom. 1:19).

Yet Scripture also recognizes that some people deny this inner sense of God and even deny that God exists. It is "the *fool*" who says in his heart, "There is no God" (Pss. 14:1; 53:1). It is the wicked person who first "curses and renounces the LORD"

---

[1]The word *theology* is taken from the Greek words *theos* ("God") and *logos* ("word, speech").

and then in pride repeatedly thinks, "There is no God" (Ps. 10:3–4). These passages indicate both that sin leads people to think irrationally and to deny God's existence, and that it is someone who is thinking irrationally or who has been deceived who will say, "There is no God."

In the life of a Christian, this inner awareness of God becomes stronger and more distinct. We begin to know God as our loving Father in heaven (Rom. 8:15); the Holy Spirit bears witness with our spirits that we are children of God (Rom. 8:16); and we come to know Jesus Christ living within our hearts (Phil. 3:8, 10; Eph. 3:17; Col. 1:27; John 14:23). The intensity of this awareness for a Christian is such that though we have not seen our Lord Jesus Christ, we indeed love him (1 Pet. 1:8).

2. Believing the evidence in Scripture and nature. In addition to people's inner awareness of God that bears clear witness to the fact that God exists, clear evidence of his existence is to be seen in Scripture and in nature.

The evidence that God exists is of course found throughout the Bible. In fact, the Bible everywhere assumes that God exists. The first verse of Genesis does not present evidence for the existence of God but begins immediately to tell us what he has done: "In the beginning God created the heavens and the earth." If we are convinced that the Bible is true, then we know from the Bible not only that God exists but also very much about his nature and his acts.

The world also gives abundant evidence of God's existence. Paul says that God's eternal nature and deity have been "clearly perceived in the things that have been made" (Rom. 1:20). This broad reference to "the things that have been made" suggests that in some sense every created thing gives evidence of God's character. Nevertheless, it is man himself, created in the image of God, who most abundantly bears witness to the existence of God: whenever we meet another human being, we should (if our minds are thinking correctly) realize that such an incredibly intricate, skillful, communicative living creature could only have been created by an infinite, all-wise Creator.

In addition to the evidence seen in the existence of living human beings, there is further excellent evidence in nature. The "rains and fruitful seasons" as well as the "food and gladness" that all people benefit from are also said by Barnabas and Paul to be witnesses to God (Acts 14:17). David tells us of the witness of the heavens: "*The heavens are telling the glory of God;* and the firmament proclaims his handiwork. Day to day pours forth speech, and night to night declares knowledge" (Ps. 19:1– 2). To look upward into the sky by day or by night is to see sun, moon, and stars, sky and clouds, all continually declaring by their existence and beauty and greatness that a powerful and wise Creator has made them and sustains them in their order.

Thus, for those who are correctly evaluating the evidence, *everything* in Scripture and *everything* in nature proves clearly that God exists and that he is the powerful and wise Creator that Scripture describes him to be. Therefore, when we believe that God exists, we are basing our belief *not* on some blind hope apart from any evidence, but on *an overwhelming amount of reliable evidence from God's words and God's works.* It is a characteristic of true faith that it is a confidence based on reliable evidence, and faith in the existence of God shares this characteristic.

Furthermore, these evidences can all be seen as valid proofs for the existence of God, even though some people reject them. Their rejection of the evidence does not mean that the evidence is invalid in itself, only that those who reject the evidence are evaluating it wrongly.

B. The Knowability of God

Even if we believe that God does exist, this does not tell us whether it is possible to actually know God, nor does it tell us how much of God we can know. In many cultures it is quite acceptable to profess belief in God's existence, but opinions on whether one can know God are much more diverse. We now move on to address these issues.

1. We can never fully understand God. Because God is infinite and we are finite or limited, we can never fully understand God. In this sense God is said to be *incomprehensible,* where the term "incomprehensible" is used with an older sense, "unable to be fully understood." This sense must be clearly distinguished from the more common meaning, "unable to be understood." It is not true to say that God is unable to be understood, but it is true to say that he cannot be understood fully or exhaustively.

Psalm 145:3 says, "Great is the LORD, and greatly to be praised, and *his greatness is unsearchable.*" God's greatness is beyond searching out or discovering: it is too great ever to be fully known. Regarding God's understanding, Psalm 147:5 says, "Great is our LORD, and abundant in power; *his understanding is beyond measure.*" We will never be able to measure or fully know the understanding of God: it is far too great for us to equal or to understand. Similarly, when thinking of God's knowledge of all his ways, David says, "*Such knowledge is too wonderful for me;* it is high, I cannot attain it" (Ps. 139:6; cf. v. 17).

Paul implies this incomprehensibility of God when he says that "the Spirit searches everything, even the depths of God," and then goes on to say that "no one comprehends the things of God except the Spirit of God" (1 Cor. 2:10–12). At the end of a long discussion on the history of God's great plan of redemption, Paul breaks forth into praise: "O the depth of the riches and wisdom and knowledge of God! How unsearchable are his judgments and how inscrutable his ways!" (Rom. 11:33).

These verses allow us to take our understanding of the incomprehensibility of God one step further. It is not only true that we can never fully understand God; it is also true that *we can never fully understand any single thing about God.* His greatness (Ps. 145:3), his understanding (Ps. 147:5), his knowledge (Ps. 139:6), his riches, wisdom, judgments, and ways (Rom. 11:33) are *all* beyond our ability to understand fully. Thus, we may know *something* about God's love, power, wisdom, and so forth. But we can never know, for example, how God's love relates to every other attribute of God, and to every individual thing in the universe, for all eternity! We can never know any of God's attributes completely or *exhaustively.*

This doctrine of God's incomprehensibility has much positive application for our own lives. It means that we will never be able to know "too much" about God, for we will never run out of things to learn about him, and we will thus never tire in delighting in the discovery of more and more of his excellence and of the greatness of his works.

2. Yet we can know God truly. Even though we cannot know God exhaustively, we can know *true* things about God. In fact, *all that Scripture tells us* about God is true. It is true to say that God is love (1 John 4:8), that God is light (1 John 1:5), that God is spirit (John 4:24), that God is righteous (Rom. 3:26), and so forth. To say this does not imply or require that we know everything about God or about his love or his righteousness or any other attribute. When I say that I have three sons, that statement is entirely true, even though I do not know everything about my sons, nor even about myself. So it is in our knowledge of God: we have true knowledge of God from Scripture, even though we do not have exhaustive knowledge. We can know some of God's thoughts—even many of them—from Scripture, and when we know them we, like David, find them to be "precious" (Ps. 139:17).

Even more significantly, it is *God himself* that we know, not simply facts about him or actions that he does. We make a distinction between knowing *facts* and knowing *persons* in our ordinary use of English. It would be true for me to say that I know many facts about the President of the United States, but it would not be true for me to say that I know *him*. To say that I know him would imply that I had met him and talked with him and that I had developed at least to some degree a personal relationship with him.

Some people say that we cannot know God himself, but only know facts about him or know what he does. Others have said that we cannot know God as he is in himself, but only as he relates to us (and there is an implication that these two are somehow different). But Scripture does not speak that way. Several passages speak of our *knowing God himself*. We read God's words in Jeremiah:

> Let not the wise man glory in his wisdom, let not the mighty man glory in his might, let not the rich man glory in his riches; but let him who glories glory in this, that he understands and *knows me,* that I am the LORD who practice steadfast love, justice, and righteousness in the earth; for in these things I delight, says the LORD. (Jer. 9:23–24)

Here God says that the source of our joy and sense of importance ought to come not from our own abilities or possessions, but from the fact that we know him. Similarly, in praying to his Father, Jesus can say, "And this is eternal life, that *they know you* the only true God, and Jesus Christ whom you have sent" (John 17:3). The promise of the new covenant is that all shall know God, "from the least of them to the greatest" (Heb. 8:11), and John's first epistle tells us that the Son of God has come and given us understanding "*to know him* who is true" (1 John 5:20; see also Gal. 4:9; Phil. 3:10; 1 John 2:3; 4:8). John can say, "I write to you, children, because *you know the Father*" (1 John 2:13).

The fact that we do know God himself is further demonstrated by the realization that the richness of the Christian life includes a personal relationship with God. As these passages imply, we have a far greater privilege than mere knowledge of facts about God. We speak to God in prayer, and he speaks to us through his Word. We commune with him in his presence, we sing his praise, and we are aware that he personally dwells among us and within us to bless us (John 14:23). Indeed, this personal relationship with God the Father, with God the Son, and with God the Holy Spirit may be said to be the greatest of all the blessings of the Christian life.

C. Introduction to the Study of God's Character: God's Attributes

When we come to talk about the character of God, we realize that we cannot say everything the Bible teaches us about God's character at once. We need some way to decide which aspect of God's character to discuss first, which aspect to discuss second, and so forth. In other words, we need some way to categorize the attributes of God. This question is not as unimportant as it may seem. There is the possibility that we would adopt a misleading order of attributes or that we would emphasize some attributes so much that others would not be presented properly.

Several different methods of classifying God's attributes have been used. In this chapter we will adopt probably the most commonly used classification: the *incommunicable attributes* of God (that is, those attributes that God does not share or "communicate" to others), and the *communicable attributes* of God (those that God shares or "communicates" with us).

Examples of the incommunicable attributes are God's eternity (God has existed for all eternity but we have not), unchangeableness (God does not change but we do), or omnipresence (God is everywhere present but we are present in only one place at one time). Examples of the communicable attributes are love (God is love and we are able to love as well), knowledge (God has knowledge and we are able to have knowledge as well), mercy (God is merciful and we are able to be merciful, too), or justice (God is just and we, too, are able to be just). This classification of God's attributes into two major categories is helpful, and most people have an initial sense of which specific attributes should be called incommunicable and which should be called communicable. Thus it makes sense to say that God's love is communicable but his omnipresence is not.

However, upon further reflection we realize that this distinction, although helpful, is not perfect. That is because there is no attribute of God that is *completely* communicable, and there is no attribute of God that is *completely* incommunicable! This will be evident if we think for a moment about some things we already know about God.

For example, God's *wisdom* would usually be called a communicable attribute, because we also can be wise. But we will never be infinitely wise as God is. His wisdom is *to some extent* shared with us, but it is never *fully* shared with us. So it is with all the attributes that are normally called "communicable attributes": God does indeed share them with us *to some degree*, but it must be said that none of these attributes is completely communicable. It is better to say that those attributes that we call "communicable" are those that are *more shared* with us.

On the other hand, those attributes we call "incommunicable" are better defined by saying that they are attributes of God that are *less shared* by us. Not one of the incommunicable attributes of God is completely without at least some likeness in the character of human beings. For example, God is unchangeable, while we change. But we do not change completely, for there are some aspects of our characters that remain largely unchanged: our individual identities, many of our personality traits, and some of our long-term purposes remain substantially unchanged over many years (and will remain largely unchanged once we are set free from sin and begin to live in God's presence forever).

We will use the two categories "incommunicable" and "communicable" attributes, then, while realizing that they are not entirely precise classifications, and that there is in reality much overlap between the categories.

D. The Incommunicable Attributes of God

1. Independence. God's independence is defined as follows: *God does not need us or the rest of creation for anything, yet we and the rest of creation glorify him and bring him joy.* This attribute of God is sometimes called his self-existence or his *aseity* (from the Latin words *a se,* which mean "from himself").

Scripture in several places teaches that God does not need any part of creation in order to exist or for any other reason. God is absolutely independent and self-sufficient. Paul proclaims to the men of Athens, "The God who made the world and everything in it, being Lord of heaven and earth, does not live in shrines made by man, *nor is he served by human hands, as though he needed anything,* since he himself gives to all men life and breath and everything" (Acts 17:24–25). The implication is that God does not need anything from mankind. (See also Job 41:11; Psalm 50:10–12.)

People have sometimes thought that God created human beings because he was lonely and needed fellowship with other persons. If this were true, it would certainly mean that God is not completely independent of creation. It would mean that God would *need* to create persons in order to be completely happy or completely fulfilled in his personal existence.

Yet there are some specific indications in Jesus' words which show this idea to be inaccurate. In John 17:5, Jesus prays, "Father, glorify me in your own presence with *the glory which I had with you before the world was made.*" Here is an indication that there was a sharing of glory between the Father and the Son before creation. Then in John 17:24, Jesus speaks to the Father of "my glory which you have given me *in your love for me before the foundation of the world.*" There was love and communication between the Father and the Son before creation, and in this fellowship there was no lack or shortcoming which required the creation of mankind.

With regard to God's existence, this doctrine also reminds us that only God exists by virtue of his very nature, and that he was never created and never came into being. He always was. This is seen from the fact that all things that exist were made by him ("For you created *all things,* and by your will they existed and were created" [Rev. 4:11]; this is also affirmed in John 1:3; Rom. 11:35–36; 1 Cor. 8:6). Moses tells us that God existed before there was any creation: "*Before* the mountains were brought forth, or ever you had formed the earth and the world, from everlasting to everlasting *you are God*" (Ps. 90:2). God's being has always been and will always be exactly what it is. God is not dependent upon any part of creation for his existence or his nature.

God's being is also something totally unique. It is not just that God *does not* need the creation for anything; God *could not* need the creation for anything. The difference between the creature and the Creator is an immensely vast difference, for God exists in a fundamentally different order of being. It is not just that we exist and God has always existed; it is also that God *necessarily* exists in an infinitely better, stronger, more excellent way. The difference between God's being and ours is more than the difference between the sun and a candle, more than the difference between the ocean and a raindrop, more than the difference between the arctic ice cap and a snowflake, more than the difference between the universe and the room we are sitting in: God's being is *qualitatively different.* No limitation or imperfection in creation should be projected on to our thought of God. He is the Creator; all else is creaturely. All else can pass away in an instant; he necessarily exists forever.

The balancing consideration with respect to this doctrine is the fact that *we and the rest of creation do in fact glorify God and we do bring him joy.* This must be stated in order to guard against any idea that God's independence makes us meaningless. Someone might wonder, if God does not need us for anything, then are we important at all? Is there any significance to our existence or to the existence of the rest of creation? In response it must be said that we are in fact very meaningful because God has created us and he has determined that we would be *meaningful to him.* That is the final definition of genuine significance.

God speaks of his sons and daughters from the ends of the earth as "every one who is called by my name, whom I created *for my glory,* whom I formed and made" (Isa. 43:7). Although God did not have to create us, he chose to do so in a totally free choice. He decided that he would create us to glorify him (cf. Eph. 1:11–12; Rev. 4:11).

It is also true that we are able to bring real joy and delight to God. It is one of the most amazing facts in Scripture that God actually delights in his people and rejoices over them. Zephaniah prophesies that the Lord "will rejoice over you with gladness, he will renew you in his love; *he will exult over you with loud singing* as on a day of festival" (Zeph. 3:17–18; cf. Is. 62:3–5). God does not need us for anything, yet it is the amazing fact of our existence that he chooses to delight in us and to allow us to bring joy to his heart. This is the basis for personal significance in the lives of all God's people: to be significant to God is to be significant in the most ultimate sense. No greater personal significance can be imagined.

2. *Unchangeableness.* We can define the unchangeableness of God as follows: *God is unchanging in his being, perfections, purposes, and promises, yet God does act and feel emotions, and he acts and feels differently in response to different situations.*[2] This attribute of God is also called God's *immutability.*

a. *Evidence in Scripture.* In Psalm 102 we find a contrast between things which we may think to be permanent such as the earth or the heavens, on the one hand, and God, on the other hand. The psalmist says:

Of old you laid the foundation of the earth,
and the heavens are the work of your hands.
They will perish, but you endure;
they will all wear out like a garment.
You change them like raiment, and they pass away;
but *you are the same,* and your years have no end. (Ps. 102:25–27).[3]

God existed before the heavens and earth were made, and he will exist long after they have been destroyed. God causes the universe to change, but in contrast to this change he is "the same."

Referring to his own qualities of patience, long-suffering, and mercy, God says, "For *I the LORD do not change;* therefore you, O sons of Jacob, are not consumed" (Mal. 3:6). Here God uses a general statement of his unchangeableness to refer to some specific ways in which he does not change.

The definition given above specifies that God is unchanging—not in every way that we might imagine, but only in ways that Scripture itself affirms. The Scripture passages already cited refer either to God's own being or to some attribute of his character. From these we can conclude that God is unchanging at least with respect to his "*being,*" and with respect to his "*perfections*" (that is, his attributes or the various aspects of his character).

The definition given above also affirms God's unchangeableness or immutability with respect to his *purposes.* "The counsel of the LORD stands for ever, the

---

[2]These four words (*being, perfections, purposes, promises*) used to summarize the ways in which God is unchanging are taken from Louis Berkhof, *Systematic Theology* (Grand Rapids: Eerdmans, 1939, 1941), p. 58.

[3]It is significant that this passage is quoted in Heb. 1:11–12 and applied to Jesus Christ. Heb. 13:8 also applies the attribute of unchangeableness to Christ: "Jesus Christ is the same yesterday and today and for ever." Thus, God the Son shares fully in this divine attribute.

thoughts of his heart to all generations" (Ps. 33:11). This general statement about God's counsel is supported by several specific verses which talk about individual plans or purposes of God which he has had for all eternity (Matt. 13:35; 25:34; Eph. 1:4, 11; 3:9, 11; 2 Tim. 2:19; 1 Pet. 1:20; Rev. 13:8). Once God has determined that he will assuredly bring something about, his purpose is unchanging and it will be achieved.

Furthermore, God is unchanging in his *promises*. Once he has promised something, he will not be unfaithful to that promise: "God is not a man, that he should lie, or a son of man, that he should repent. Has he said, and will he not do it? Or has he spoken, and will he not fulfil it?" (Num. 23:19; cf. 1 Sam. 15:29).

b. *Does God sometimes change his mind?* Yet when we talk about God being unchanging in his purposes we may wonder about places in Scripture where God said he would judge his people and then because of prayer or the people's repentance (or both) God relented and did not bring judgment as he had said he would. Examples of such withdrawing from threatened judgment include the successful intervention of Moses in prayer to prevent the destruction of the people of Israel (Exod. 32:9–14), the adding of another fifteen years to the life of Hezekiah (Isa. 38:1–6), or the failure to bring promised judgment upon Nineveh when the people repented (Jon. 3:4, 10). Are these not cases where God's purposes in fact did change?

These instances should all be understood as true expressions of God's *present* attitude or intention *with respect to the situation as it exists at that moment*. If the situation changes, then of course God's attitude or expression of intention will also change. This is just saying that *God responds differently to different situations*. The example of Jonah preaching to Nineveh is helpful here. God sees the wickedness of Nineveh and sends Jonah to proclaim, "Yet forty days, and Nineveh shall be overthrown!" (Jon. 3:4). The possibility that God would withhold judgment if the people repented is not explicitly mentioned in Jonah's proclamation as recorded in Scripture, but it is of course *implicit* in that warning: the *purpose* for proclaiming a warning is to bring about repentance. Once the people repented, the situation was different, and God responded differently to that changed situation: "*When God saw what they did*, how they turned from their evil way, *God repented of the evil which he had said he would do to them; and he did not do it*" (Jon. 3:10). As in many other places in Scripture, God responded to the new situation differently, but nevertheless remained unchanging in his being and his purposes. (In fact, if God did *not* respond differently when people acted differently, then people's actions would make no difference to God, and he would not be the kind of just and merciful God portrayed in the Bible—unchanging in his attributes of justice and mercy.)

c. *The question of God's impassibility.* Sometimes in a discussion of God's attributes theologians have spoken of another attribute, namely, the impassibility of God. This attribute, if true, would mean that God does not have passions or emotions, but is "impassible," not subject to passions. Of course, God does not have *sinful* passions or emotions. But the idea that God has no passions or emotions *at all* clearly conflicts with much of the rest of Scripture, and for that reason I have not affirmed God's impassibility in this book. Instead, quite the opposite is true, for God, who is the origin of our emotions and who created our emotions, certainly does feel emotions: God rejoices (Isa. 62:5). He is grieved (Ps. 78:40; Eph. 4:30). His wrath burns hot against his enemies (Exod. 32:10). He pities his children (Ps.

103:13). He loves with everlasting love (Isa. 54.8; Ps. 103:17). He is a God whose passions we are to imitate for all eternity as we—like our Creator—hate sin and delight in righteousness.

d. *God is both infinite and personal.* Unlike other systems of theology, the Bible teaches that God is both *infinite* and *personal:* he is infinite in that he is not subject to any of the limitations of humanity, or of creation in general. He is far greater than everything he has made, far greater than anything else that exists. But he is also personal: he interacts with us as a person, and we can relate to him as persons. We can pray to him, worship him, obey him, and love him, and he can speak to us, rejoice in us, and love us.

Apart from the true religion found in the Bible, no system of religion has a God who is both infinite and personal. For example, the gods of ancient Greek and Roman mythology were *personal* (they interacted frequently with people), but they were not infinite: they had weaknesses and frequent moral failures, even petty rivalries. On the other hand, deism portrays a God who is *infinite* but far too removed from the world to be personally involved in it. Similarly, pantheism holds that God is infinite (since the whole universe is thought to be God), but such a God can certainly not be personal nor relate to us as persons.

Many of the objections raised against Biblical Christianity try to deny one or the other of these truths. People say that if God is infinite, he cannot be personal, or they say that if God is personal, he cannot be infinite. The Bible teaches that God is both infinite and personal. We must affirm both that God is infinite (or unlimited) with respect to change that occurs in the universe (nothing will change God's being, perfections, purposes, or promises), and that God is also personal, and that he relates to us personally and counts us valuable.

e. *The importance of God's unchangeableness.* If we stop for a moment to imagine what it would be like if God *could* change, the importance of this doctrine becomes more clear. For example, if God *could* change (in his being, perfections, purposes, or promises), then any change would be either for the better or for the worse. But if God changed for the better, then he was not the best possible being when we first trusted him. And how could we be sure that he is the best possible being now? But if God could change for the worse (in his very being), then what kind of God might he become? Might he become, for instance, a little bit evil rather than wholly good? And if he could become a little bit evil, then how do we know he could not change to become largely evil—or *wholly* evil? It is hard to imagine any thought more terrifying. How could we ever trust such a God who could change? How could we ever commit our lives to him?

Moreover, if God could change with regard to his purposes, then how can we trust God's promise, for example, that Jesus will come back to rule over a new heaven and new earth? If God can change his purposes, maybe he has abandoned that plan now, and thus our hope in Jesus' return is in vain. Or, if God could change in regard to his promises, then how could we trust him completely for eternal life? Or for anything else the Bible says?

A little reflection like this shows how absolutely important the doctrine of God's unchangeableness is. If God is not unchanging, then the whole basis of our faith begins to fall apart, and our understanding of the universe begins to unravel. This is because our faith and hope and knowledge all ultimately depend on a *person* who is *infinitely worthy of trust*—because he is *absolutely* and *eternally* unchanging in his being, perfections, purposes, and promises.

3. Eternity. God's eternity may be defined as follows: *God has no beginning, end, or succession of moments in his own being, and he sees all time equally vividly, yet God sees events in time and acts in time.*

Sometimes this doctrine is called the doctrine of God's infinity with respect to time. To be "infinite" is to be unlimited, and this doctrine teaches that time does not limit God or change him in any way.

a. *God is timeless in his own being.* The fact that God has no beginning or end is seen in Psalm 90:2: "Before the mountains were brought forth, or ever you had formed the earth and the world, *from everlasting to everlasting you are God.*" Similarly, in Job 36:26, Elihu says of God, "The number of his years is unsearchable."

God's eternity is also suggested by passages that talk about the fact that God always is or always exists. "'*I am the Alpha and the Omega,*' says the Lord God, who is and who was and who is to come, the Almighty" (Rev. 1:8; cf. 4:8).

The fact that God never began to exist can also be concluded from the fact that God created all things and that he himself is an immaterial spirit. Before God made the universe, there was no matter, but then he created all things (Gen. 1:1; John 1:3; 1 Cor. 8:6; Col. 1:16; Heb. 1:2). The study of physics tells us that matter and time and space must all occur together: if there is no matter, there can be no space or time either. Thus, before God created the universe, there was no "time," at least not in the sense of a succession of moments one after another. Therefore, when God created the universe, he also created time. But before there was a universe, and before there was time, God always existed, without beginning, and without being influenced by time.

In some places the Bible speaks of God existing or acting "before" there was any creation or any time. Psalm 90:2 speaks of God "*before* the mountains were brought forth" and "[before] . . . you had formed the earth and the world." Ephesians 1:4 says that God chose us in Christ "*before* the foundation of the world." More remarkably, Jude 25 says this:

> . . . to the only God, our Savior through Jesus Christ our Lord, be glory, majesty, dominion, and authority, *before all time* and now and for ever. Amen.

Here Jude ascribes glory, majesty, dominion, and authority to God "*before all time* (this is a good translation of the Greek *pro pantos tou aiwnos*) and now and forever." It is significant that Jude's three time descriptors indicate a sequence of past-present-future ("before all time"—"now"—"for ever"), thereby indicating that the phrase is correctly translated, "before all time."

The foregoing Scripture passages, and the fact that God always existed, even before there was any time, combine to indicate to us that God's own being does not have a succession of moments or any progress from one state of existence to another. To God himself, all of his existence is always somehow "present," though admittedly that idea is extremely difficult for us to understand, for it is a kind of existence different from that which we experience.

b. *God sees all time equally vividly.* We read in Psalm 90:4, "For a *thousand years* in your sight are but as *yesterday* when it is past, or as a *watch* in the night." In the New Testament, Peter tells us, "with the Lord *one day is as a thousand years,* and a thousand years as one day" (2 Pet. 3:8). These verses taken together help us to imagine the way in which God sees time. On the one hand, God views a thousand years "as yesterday." He can remember all the detailed events of a thousand years at least as clearly as we can remember the events of "yesterday." When we realize that "a thousand years" does not imply that God forgets things after 1,100 or 1,200 years, but rather is here a figurative expression for an extremely long period of time—for as long a time as one might imagine—it becomes evident that *all of past history* is viewed by God with great clarity and vividness: all of time since the creation is to God as if it just happened.

On the other hand, to God "one day is as a thousand years"; that is, any one day from God's perspective seems to last for "a thousand years." It is as if that day never ends, but is always being experienced. Again, since "a thousand years" is a figurative expression for "as long a time as we can imagine," or "all history," we can say from this verse that any one day seems to God to be present to his consciousness forever. These two statements together show an amazing way of viewing time: The whole span of history is as vivid as if it were a brief event that had just happened, but any brief event is as if it is going on forever! No event ever fades from God's consciousness. We can conclude, therefore, that God sees and knows all events—past, present, and future—with equal vividness.

We can picture God's relationship to time as in figure 4.1. This diagram is meant to show that God created time and is Lord over time. Therefore he can see all events in time equally vividly, yet he also can see events in time and act in time.

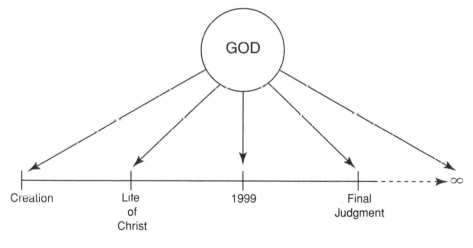

The Relationship of God to Time
figure 4.1

The diagram also anticipates the following discussion, since it indicates that God knows events in the future, even the infinitely long eternal future. With regard to the future, God frequently claims through the Old Testament prophets that *he alone is the one who knows and can declare future events*. We read in Isaiah:

> For I am God, and there is no other;
> I am God, and *there is none like me,*
> *declaring the end from the beginning*

and from ancient times things not yet done,
saying, "My counsel shall stand,
and I will accomplish all my purpose." (Isa. 46:9–10)[4]

Thus God somehow stands above time and is able to see it all as present in his consciousness.

c. *God sees events in time and acts in time.* Yet we must guard against misunderstanding by completing the definition of God's eternity: "*yet God sees events in time and acts in time.*" Paul writes, "*When the time had fully come, God sent forth his Son,* born of woman, born under the law, to redeem those who were under the law" (Gal. 4:4–5). God observed clearly and knew exactly what was happening with events in his creation as they occurred over time. We might say that God watched the progress of time as various events occurred within his creation. Then at the right time, "when the time had fully come," God sent forth his Son into the world. We should never think that God sees all events as happening at the same time, or that he does not know the difference between events happening in 2000 B.C. (Abraham's life), 1000 B.C. (David's life), A.D. 30 (the death of Christ), and 1998 A.D. (the year in which I am writing this page of this book), or between this morning and this afternoon.

It is evident throughout Scripture that God acts within time and acts differently at different points in time. Indeed, the repeated emphasis on God's ability to predict the future in the Old Testament prophets requires us to realize that God predicts his actions at one point in time and then carries out his actions at a later point in time. And on a larger scale, the entire Bible from Genesis to Revelation is God's own record of the way he has acted over time in order to bring redemption for his people.

We must therefore affirm both that God has no succession of moments in his own being and sees all history equally vividly, and that in his creation he sees the progress of events over time and acts differently at different points in time. In short, he is the Lord who created time and who rules over it and uses it for his own purposes. God can act in time *because* he is Lord of time.

4. Omnipresence. Just as God is unlimited or infinite with respect to time, so God is unlimited with respect to space. This characteristic of God's nature is called God's omnipresence (the Latin prefix *omni-* means "all"). *God's omnipresence may be defined as follows: God does not have size or spatial dimensions, and is present at every point of space with his whole being, yet God acts differently in different places.*

The fact that God is Lord of space and cannot be limited by space is evident first from the fact that he created it, for the creation of the material world (Gen. 1:1) implies the creation of space as well. Moses reminded the people of God's lordship over space: "Behold, to the LORD your God belong heaven and the heaven of heavens, the earth with all that is in it" (Deut. 10:14).

a. *God is present everywhere.* Yet there are also specific passages which speak of God's presence in every part of space. We read in Jeremiah, "Am I a God at hand, says the LORD, and not a God afar off? Can a man hide himself in secret places so that I cannot see him? says the LORD. *Do I not fill heaven and earth?* says the LORD" (Jer. 23:23–24). God is here rebuking the prophets who think their words or thoughts are hidden from God. He is everywhere and fills heaven and earth.

---

[4]A list of the Bible passages where God knew what was going to happen in he future would run to several hundred verses. By this he often demonstrates that he is the only true God.

God's omnipresence is beautifully expressed by David:

Whither shall I go from your Spirit?
Or whither shall I flee from your presence?
If I ascend to heaven, you are there!
If I make my bed in Sheol, you are there!
If I take the wings of the morning
and dwell in the uttermost parts of the sea,
even there your hand shall lead me,
and your right hand shall hold me. (Ps. 139:7–10)

There is nowhere in the entire universe, on land or sea, in heaven or in hell, where one can flee from God's presence.

We should note also that there is no indication that simply a *part* of God is in one place and a part of him in another. It is *God himself* who is present wherever David might go. We cannot say that some of God or just part of God is present, for that would be to think of his being in spatial terms, as if he were limited somehow by space. It seems more appropriate to say that God is present *with his whole being* in every part of space. This is difficult for us to imagine, because God's being is of a qualitatively different sort than anything in creation.

b. *God does not have spatial dimensions.* While it seems necessary for us to say that God's whole being is present in every part of space, or at every point in space, it is also necessary to say that *God cannot be contained by any space*, no matter how large. Solomon says in his prayer to God, "But will God indeed dwell on the earth? Behold, *heaven and the highest heaven cannot contain you;* how much less this house which I have built!" (1 Kings 8:27). Heaven and the highest heaven cannot contain God; indeed, he cannot be contained by the largest space imaginable (cf. Isa. 66:1–2; Acts 7:48).

We should guard against thinking that God extends infinitely far in all directions so that he himself exists in a sort of infinite, unending space. Nor should we think that God is somehow a "bigger space" or bigger area surrounding the space of the universe as we know it. All of these ideas continue to think of God's being in spatial terms, as if he were simply an extremely large being. Instead, we should try to avoid thinking of God in terms of size or spatial dimensions. God is a being who exists *without* size or dimensions in space.

We must also be careful not to think that God himself is equivalent to any part of creation, or to all of it. A pantheist believes that everything is God, or that God is everything that exists. The biblical perspective is rather that God is *present* everywhere in his creation, but that he is also *distinct* from his creation. How can this be? The analogy of a sponge filled with water is not perfect, but it is helpful. Water is present everywhere in the sponge, but the water is still completely distinct from the sponge. Now this analogy breaks down at very small points within the sponge, where we could say that there is sponge at one point and not water, or water and not sponge. Yet this is because the analogy is dealing with two materials that have spatial characteristics and dimensions, while God does not.

c. *God can be present to punish, to sustain, or to bless.* The idea of God's omnipresence has sometimes troubled people who wonder how God can be present, for example, in hell. In fact, isn't hell the opposite of God's presence or the absence of God?

This difficulty can be resolved by realizing that *God is present in different ways in different places.* Another way of understanding this is to say that God acts differently in different places in his creation. Sometimes God is *present to punish,* and it seems that this is how God is present in hell. A terrifying passage in Amos vividly portrays this presence of God in judgment:

> Not one of them shall flee away,
> not one of them shall escape.
> Though they dig into Sheol,
> from there shall my hand take them;
> though they climb up to heaven,
> from there I will bring them down.
> Though they hide themselves on the top of Carmel,
> from there I will search out and take them;
> and though they hide from my sight at the bottom of the sea,
> there I will command the serpent, and it shall bite them.
> And though they go into captivity before their enemies,
> there I will command the sword, and it shall slay them;
> and I will set my eyes upon them for evil and not for good. (Amos 9:1–4)

At other times God is present neither to punish nor to bless, but merely *present to sustain,* or to keep the universe existing and functioning in the way he intended it to function. In this sense the divine nature of Christ is everywhere present: "He is before all things, and in him all things hold together" (Col. 1:17). The author of Hebrews says of God the Son that he is (continually) "upholding the universe by his word of power" (Heb. 1:3).

Yet at other times or in other places God is *present to bless.* David says, "in your presence there is fulness of joy, in your right hand are pleasures for evermore" (Ps. 16:11). Here David is speaking not of God's presence to punish or merely to sustain, but of God's presence to bless.

Here we must recognize that we can use the same words in different ways. Sometimes when we speak of God being "present" we simply mean that his being is omnipresent in the universe. But at other times when we speak of God being "present" we mean he is present to give blessing, or to give people a positive awareness of his presence. In fact, most of the time that the Bible talks about God's presence, it is referring to God's presence to bring blessing. For example, it is in this way that we should understand God's presence above the ark of the covenant in the Old Testament. We read of "the ark of the covenant of the LORD of hosts, who is *enthroned on the cherubim*" (1 Sam. 4:4; cf. Exod. 25:22), a reference to the fact that God made his presence known and acted in a special way to bring blessing and protection to his people at the location which he had designated as his throne, namely, the place above the two golden figures of heavenly beings ("cherubim") which were over the top of the ark of the covenant. It is not that God was not present elsewhere, but rather that here he especially made his presence known and here he especially manifested his character and brought blessing to his people. It is in this sense that the biblical authors usually referred to God's "presence."

In a parallel kind of expression, when the Bible talks about God being "far away" it usually means he is "not present to bless." For example, Isaiah 59:2 says, "Your iniquities have made a separation between you and your God," and Proverbs 15:29

declares: "The LORD is far from the wicked, but he hears the prayer of the righteous." These verses do not mean that God's being is not there at all, but that he is not there to bring blessing to the people and give evidence of his presence.

In summary, God is present in every part of space with his whole being, yet God acts differently in different places. Furthermore, when the Bible speaks of God's presence, it usually does not mean his omnipresence in every point, or his presence to punish or to sustain. Instead, it usually means his presence to bless, and it is only normal for our own speech to conform to this biblical usage.

Herman Bavinck, in *The Doctrine of God*, quotes a beautiful paragraph illustrating the practical application of the doctrine of God's omnipresence:

> When you wish to do something evil, you retire from the public into your house where no enemy may see you; from those places of your house which are open and visible to the eyes of men you remove yourself into your room; even in your room you fear some witness from another quarter; you retire into your heart, there you meditate: he is more inward than your heart. Wherever, therefore, you shall have fled, there he is. From yourself, whither will you flee? Will you not follow yourself wherever you shall flee? But since there is One more inward even than yourself, there is no place where you may flee from God angry but to God reconciled. There is no place at all whither you may flee. Will you flee from him? Flee unto him.[5]

5. Unity. The unity of God is defined as follows: *God is not divided into parts, yet we see different attributes of God emphasized at different times.*

When Scripture speaks about God's attributes it never singles out one attribute of God as more important than all the rest. There is an assumption that every attribute is completely true of God and is true of all of God's character. For example, John can say that "God is light" (1 Jn. 1:5) and then a little later say also that "God is love" (1 Jn. 4:8). There is no suggestion that part of God is light and part of God is love, or that God is partly light and partly love. Nor should we think that God is more light than love, or more love than light. Rather it is *God himself* who is light, and it is *God himself* who is also love. God's *whole being* includes all of his attributes: he is *entirely* loving, *entirely* merciful, *entirely* just, and so forth. Every attribute of God that we find in Scripture is true of *all* of God's being, and we therefore can say that *every attribute of God also qualifies every other attribute.*

Why then does Scripture speak of these different attributes of God? It is probably because we are unable to grasp all of God's character at one time, and we need to learn of it from different perspectives over a period of time. Yet these perspectives should never be set in opposition to one another, for they are just different ways of looking at the totality of God's character.

In terms of practical application, this means that we should never think, for example, that God is a loving God at one point in history and a just or wrathful God at another point in history. He is the same God always, and everything he says or does is fully consistent with all his attributes. It is not accurate to say, as some have said, that God is a God of justice in the Old Testament and a God of love in the New Testament. God is and always has been infinitely just and infinitely loving as well, and everything he does in the Old Testament as well as the New Testament is completely consistent with both of those attributes.

---

[5]Herman Bavinck, *The Doctrine of God*, trans. by William Hendriksen (Edinburgh: Banner of Truth, 1977, reprint of 1951 ed.), p. 164. The citation is reproduced in the book with no indication of its source.

Now it is true that some actions of God show certain of his attributes more prominently. Creation demonstrates his power and wisdom, the judgment on Sodom and Gomorrah demonstrates his holiness and justice and wrath, the atonement demonstrates his love and justice, and the radiance of heaven demonstrates his glory and beauty. But all of these events in some way or other *also* demonstrate his knowledge and holiness and mercy and truthfulness and patience and sovereignty, and so forth. It would be difficult indeed to find some attribute of God that is not reflected at least to some degree in any one of his acts of redemption. This is due to the fact mentioned above: God is a unity and everything he does is an act of the whole person of God.

Moreover, the doctrine of the unity of God should caution us against attempting to single out any one attribute of God as more important than all the others. At various times people have attempted to see God's holiness, or his love, or his self-existence, or his righteousness, or some other attribute as the most important attribute of his being. But all such attempts seem to misconceive of God as a combination of various parts, with some parts being somehow larger or more influential than others. Furthermore, it is hard to understand exactly what "most important" might mean. Does it mean that there are some actions of God which are not fully consistent with some of his other attributes? That there are some attributes which God somehow sets aside at times in order to act in ways slightly contrary to those attributes? Certainly we cannot maintain either of these views, for that would mean that God is inconsistent with his own character or that he changes and becomes something different from what he was previously. Rather, when we see all the attributes as merely various aspects of the total character of God, then such a question becomes quite unnecessary and we discover that there is no attribute which can be singled out as more important. It is *God himself in his whole being* who is supremely important, and it is God himself in his whole being whom we are to seek to know and to love.

II. REVIEW QUESTIONS

1. In addition to the Bible, what evidence do we have that God exists?

2. How would you reconcile the incomprehensibility of God and the fact that we can know God truly?

3. Differentiate between incommunicable attributes of God and communicable attributes of God.

4. Define God's "independence." How can the two parts of this definition be reconciled?

5. In light of God's unchangeableness, what does Scripture mean when it speaks of God changing his mind?

6. Does time have any effect on God? Explain.

7. If God is present everywhere, how can he be present in hell if it is a place of terrible suffering?

6. Is there any attribute of God that is *more* true about him than other attributes? Explain.

III. QUESTIONS FOR PERSONAL APPLICATION

1. Do most people today believe in the existence of God? Has this been true throughout history? If they believe that God exists, why have they not worshiped him rightly? Why do some people deny the existence of God? Does Romans 1:18 suggest there is often a moral factor influencing their intellectual denial of God's existence (compare Ps. 14:1–3)?

2. Why do you think God decided to reveal himself to us? Do you learn more about God from his revelation in nature, or his revelation in Scripture? Why do you think it is that God's thoughts are "precious" to us (Ps. 139:17)? Would you call your present relationship to God a personal relationship? How is it similar to your relationships with other people, and how is it different? What would make your relationship with God better?

3. As you think of God's independence, unchangeableness, eternity, omnipresence, and unity, can you see some faint reflections of these five incommunicable attributes in yourself as God created you to be? What would it mean to strive to become more like God in these areas? At what point would it be wrong to even want to be like God in each of these areas because it would be attempting to usurp his unique role as Creator and Lord?

4. Explain how the doctrine of God's immutability or unchangeableness helps to answer the following questions: Will we be able to do a good job of bringing up children in such an evil world as we have today? Is it possible to have the same close fellowship with God that people had during biblical times? What can we think or do in order to make Bible stories seem more real and less removed from our present life? Do you think that God is less willing to answer prayer today than he was in Bible times?

5. If you sin against God today, when would it start bringing sorrow to God's heart? When would it *stop* bringing sorrow to God's heart? Does this reflection help you understand why God's character requires that he punish sin? Why did God have to send his Son to bear the punishment for sin, instead of simply forgetting about sin and welcoming sinners into heaven without having given the punishment for sin to anyone? Does God now think of your sins as forgiven or as unforgiven sins?

IV. SPECIAL TERMS

aseity

communicable attributes

eternity

inner sense of God

immutability

incommunicable attributes

incomprehensible

independence

infinite

infinity with respect to space

infinity with respect to time

knowable

omnipresence

self-existence

unchangeableness

unity

IV. SCRIPTURE MEMORY PASSAGE

PSALM 102:25–27:

> *Of old you laid the foundation of the earth,*
> *and the heavens are the work of your hands.*
> *They will perish, but you endure;*
> *they will all wear out like a garment.*
> *You change them like raiment, and they pass away;*
> *but you are the same, and your years have no end.*

CHAPTER FIVE

The "Communicable" Attributes of God

+ *How is God like us?*

I. EXPLANATION AND SCRIPTURAL BASIS

In this chapter we consider the attributes of God that are "communicable," or more shared with us than those mentioned in the previous chapter. It must be remembered that this division into "incommunicable" and "communicable" is not an absolute division and there is some room for difference of opinion concerning which attributes should fit into which categories. The list of attributes here put in the category "communicable" is a common one, but understanding the definition of each attribute is more important than being able to categorize the attributes in exactly the way presented in this book.[1]

This chapter divides God's "communicable" attributes into five major categories, with individual attributes listed under each category as follows:

A. Attributes Describing God's Being
1. Spirituality
2. Invisibility
B. Mental Attributes
3. Knowledge (or Omniscience)
4. Wisdom
5. Truthfulness (including Faithfulness)
C. Moral Attributes
6. Goodness (including Mercy, Grace)
7. Love
8. Holiness
9. Righteousness (or Justice)
10. Jealousy
11. Wrath
D. Attributes of Purpose
12. Will (including Freedom)
13. Omnipotence (or Power, including Sovereignty)

---

[1]This list is fairly complete but does not cover everything said about God's character in the Bible. Because God's excellence is so rich and full, other attributes than these could be listed, and some of these could be subdivided into other specific attributes.

E. "Summary" Attributes
   14. Perfection
   15. Blessedness
   16. Beauty

Because God's communicable attributes are to be imitated in our lives (Eph. 5:1 tells us to "be imitators of God, as beloved children"), some of these sections will include a short explanation of the way in which the attribute in question is to be imitated by us.

A. Attributes Describing God's Being

1. Spirituality. People have often wondered, what is God made of? Is he made of flesh and blood like ourselves? Certainly not. What then is the material that forms his being? Is God made of matter at all? Or is God pure energy? Or is he in some sense pure thought?

The answer of Scripture is that God is none of these. Rather, we read that "God is *spirit*" (John 4:24). This statement is spoken by Jesus in the context of a discussion with the woman at the well in Samaria. The discussion is about the *location* where people should worship God, and Jesus is telling her that true worship of God does not require that one be *present* either in Jerusalem or in Samaria (John 4:21), for true worship has to do not with physical location but with one's inner spiritual condition. This is because "God is spirit" and this apparently signifies that God is in no way limited to a spatial location. We should therefore not think of God as having *size* or *dimensions,* even infinite ones (see the discussion on God's omnipresence in the previous chapter).

We also find that God forbids his people to think of *his very being* as similar to *anything* else in the physical creation. The second commandment (Ex. 20:4) forbids us to worship or serve "any graven image" or "any likeness of anything" in heaven or earth. This is a reminder that God's being is different from everything that he has created. To think of his being in terms of anything else in the created universe is to misrepresent him, to limit him, to think of him as less than he really is. Indeed, while we must say that God has made all creation so that each part of it reflects something of his own character, we must also affirm that to picture God as existing in a form or mode of being that is like anything else in creation is to think of God in a horribly misleading and dishonoring way.

Thus, God does not have a physical body, nor is he made of any kind of matter like much of the rest of creation. Furthermore, God is not merely energy or thought or some other element of creation. Instead of all these ideas of God, we must say that God is *spirit.* Whatever this means, it is a kind of existence that is unlike anything else in creation. It is a kind of existence that is far superior to all our material existence. At this point we can define God's spirituality: *God's spirituality means that God exists as a being that is not made of any matter, has no parts or dimensions, is unable to be perceived by our bodily senses, and is more excellent than any other kind of existence.*

It might appear that God's spirituality would be better classified as an "incommunicable" attribute since God's being is so different from ours. Nevertheless, the fact remains that God has given us spirits in which we worship him (John 4:24; 1 Cor. 14:14; Phil. 3:3), in which we are united with the Lord's spirit (1 Cor. 6:17), with which the Holy Spirit joins to bear witness to our adoption in God's family (Rom. 8:16), and in which we pass into the Lord's presence when we die (Eccl.

12:7; Luke 23:46; Heb. 12:23, cf. Phil. 1:23–24). Therefore, there is clearly some communication from God to us of a spiritual nature that is something like his own nature, though certainly not in all respects. For this reason, it also seems appropriate to think of God's spirituality as a communicable attribute.

2. Invisibility. Related to God's spirituality is the fact that God is invisible. Yet we also must speak of the visible ways in which God manifests himself. God's invisibility can be defined as follows: *God's invisibility means that God's total essence, all of his spiritual being, will never be able to be seen by us, yet God still shows himself to us through visible, created things.*

Many passages speak of the fact that God is not able to be seen. "No one has ever seen God" (John 1:18). Jesus says, "Not that any one has seen the Father except him who is from God; he has seen the Father" (John 6:46). Paul speaks of God as one "who alone has immortality and dwells in unapproachable light, *whom no man has ever seen or can see*" (1 Tim. 6:16).

We must remember that these passages were all written after many events in Scripture in which people saw some outward manifestation of God. For example, very early in Scripture we read, "Thus the LORD used to speak to Moses face to face, as a man speaks to his friend" (Ex. 33:11). Yet God told Moses, "You cannot see my face; for man shall not see me and live" (Ex. 33:20). The Old Testament also records a number of theophanies. A *theophany* is "an appearance of God." In these theophanies God took on various visible forms to show himself to people. God appeared to Abraham (Gen. 18:1–33), Jacob (Gen. 32:28–30), the people of Israel (as a pillar of cloud by day and fire by night: Ex. 13:21–22), the elders of Israel (Ex. 24:9–11), Manoah and his wife (Judg. 13:21–22), Isaiah (Isa. 6:1), and others.

A much greater visible manifestation of God than these Old Testament theophanies was found in the person of Jesus Christ himself. He could say, "He who has seen me has seen the Father" (John 14:9). And John contrasts the fact that no one has ever seen God with the fact that God's only Son has made him known to us: "No one has ever seen God, but God the One and Only, who is at the Father's side, has made him known" (John 1:18 NIV). Thus, in the person of Jesus we have a unique visible manifestation of God in the New Testament that was not available to believers who saw theophanies in the Old Testament.

It is right, therefore, to say that although God's *total essence* will never be able to be seen by us, nevertheless, God still shows something of himself to us through visible, created things, and especially in the person of Christ.

But how will we see God in heaven? We will never be able to see or know all of God, for "his greatness is unsearchable" (Ps. 145:3; cf. John 6:46; 1 Tim. 1:17; 6:16; 1 John 4:12). And we will not be able to see—at least with our physical eyes—the entire spiritual being of God. Nevertheless, Scripture says that we will see God himself. Jesus says, "Blessed are the pure in heart, for *they shall see God*" (Matt. 5:8). Perhaps the nature of this "seeing" will not be known to us until we reach heaven.

Although what we see will not be an exhaustive vision of God, it will be a completely true, clear, and real vision of God. We shall see "face to face" (1 Cor. 13:12) and "we shall see him as he is" (1 John 3:2). In the heavenly city "his servants shall worship him; they shall see his face" (Rev. 22:3–4).

When we realize that God is the perfection of all that we long for or desire, that he is the summation of everything beautiful or desirable, then we realize that the greatest joy of the life to come will be that we "shall see his face." To look at God will change us and make us like him: "We shall be like him, *for we shall see him as he is*" (1 John 3:2; cf. 2 Cor. 3:18). This vision of God will give us full delight and joy for all eternity.

B. Mental Attributes

3. Knowledge (Omniscience). God's knowledge may be defined as follows: *God fully knows himself and all things actual and possible in one simple and eternal act.*

Elihu says that God is the one "who is *perfect in knowledge*" (Job 37:16), and John says that God *"knows everything"* (1 John 3:20). The quality of knowing everything is called omniscience, and because God knows everything, he is said to be omniscient (that is, "all-knowing").

The definition given above explains omniscience in more detail. It says first that God fully knows himself. This is an amazing fact since God's own being is infinite or unlimited. Of course, only he who is infinite can fully know himself in every detail. This fact is implied by Paul when he says, "For the Spirit searches everything, even the depths of God. For what person knows a man's thoughts except the spirit of the man which is in him? So also no one comprehends the thoughts of God except the Spirit of God" (1 Cor. 2:10–11).

The definition also says that God knows "all things *actual and possible.*" This means all things that exist, all things that happen, and all things that might happen. God's knowledge of all things *actual* applies to the entire creation, for God is the one before whom "no creature is hidden, but all are open and laid bare to the eyes of him with whom we have to do" (Heb. 4:13; cf. 2 Chron. 16:9; Job 28:24; Matt. 10:29–30). God also knows all things *possible,* including events that might happen but do not actually come to pass. For example, Jesus could state that Tyre and Sidon *would have* repented if Jesus' own miracles had been done there in former days (Matt. 11:21; cf. 1 Sam. 23:11–13; 2 Kings 13:19, where Elisha tells what would have happened if King Joash had struck the ground five or six times with the arrows).

Our definition of God's knowledge speaks of God knowing everything in one "simple act." Here the word *simple* is used in the sense "not divided into parts." This means that God is always fully aware of everything. If he should wish to tell us the number of grains of sand on the seashore or the number of stars in the sky, he would not have to count them all quickly like some kind of giant computer, nor would he have to call the number to mind because it was something he had not thought about for a time. Rather, he always knows all things at once. He does not have to reason to conclusions or ponder carefully before he answers, for he knows the end from the beginning, and he never learns and never forgets anything (cf. Ps. 90:4). Every bit of God's knowledge is always fully present in his consciousness; it never grows dim or fades into his nonconscious memory.

Finally, the definition talks about God's knowledge as not only a simple act, but also an "eternal act." This simply means that God's knowledge never changes or grows. If he were ever to learn something new, he would not have been omniscient beforehand. Thus, from all eternity, God has known all things that would happen and all things that he would do.

4. Wisdom. God's wisdom means that God always chooses the best goals and the best means to those goals. This definition goes beyond the idea of God knowing all things and specifies that God's decisions about what he will do are always wise decisions—

that is, they always will bring about the best results (from God's ultimate perspective), and they will bring about those results through the best possible means.

Scripture affirms God's wisdom in general in several places. He is called "the only wise God" (Rom. 16:27). Job says that God "is wise in heart" (Job 9:4), and "with him are wisdom and might; he has counsel and understanding" (Job 12:13). God's wisdom is seen specifically in creation. The psalmist exclaims, "O LORD, how manifold are your works! In wisdom you have made them all; the earth is full of your creatures" (Ps. 104:24). As God created the universe, it was perfectly suited to bring him glory, both in its day-by-day processes and in the goals for which he created it. Even now, while we still see the effects of sin and the curse on the natural world, we should be amazed at how harmonious and intricate God's creation is.

God's wisdom is also shown in our individual lives. "We know that in everything God works for good with those who love him, who are called according to his purpose" (Rom. 8:28, author's translation). Here Paul affirms that God does work wisely in all the things that come into our lives, and that through all these things he advances us toward the goal of conformity to the image of Christ (Rom. 8:29). Every day of our lives, we may quiet our discouragement with the comfort that comes from the knowledge of God's infinite wisdom. If we are his children, we can know that he is working wisely in our lives to bring us into greater conformity to the image of Christ.

God's wisdom is, of course, in part communicable to us. We can ask God confidently for wisdom when we need it, for he promises in his Word, "If any of you lacks wisdom, let him ask God, who gives to all men generously and without reproaching, and it will be given him" (James 1:5). This wisdom, or skill in living a life pleasing to God, comes primarily from reading and obeying his Word: "The testimony of the LORD is sure, making wise the simple" (Ps. 19:7; cf. Deut. 4:6–8). As far as the motivation for gaining true wisdom, "The fear of the LORD is the beginning of wisdom" (Ps. 111:10; Prov. 9:10; cf. Prov. 1:7), because if we fear dishonoring God or displeasing him, and if we fear his fatherly discipline, then we will have the motivation that makes us want to follow his ways and live according to his wise commands.

Yet we must also remember that God's wisdom is not entirely communicable; we can never fully share God's wisdom (Rom. 11:33). In practical terms, this means that there will frequently be times in this life when we will not be able to understand why God allowed something to happen. Then we have simply to trust him and go on obeying his wise commands for our lives: "Therefore let those who suffer according to God's will do right and entrust their souls to a faithful Creator" (1 Peter 4:19; cf. Deut. 29:29; Prov. 3:5–6). God is infinitely wise and we are not, and it pleases him when we have faith to trust his wisdom even when we do not understand what he is doing.

5. Truthfulness (including Faithfulness). God's truthfulness means that he is the true God, and that all his knowledge and words are both true and the final standard of truth. The first part of this definition indicates that the God revealed in Scripture is the true or real God and that all other so-called gods are idols. "The LORD is the true God; he is the living God and the everlasting King. ... The gods who did not make the heavens and the earth shall perish from the earth and from under the heavens" (Jer. 10:10–11). Jesus says to his Father, "This is eternal life, that they know you *the only true God,* and Jesus Christ whom you have sent" (John 17:3; cf. 1 John 5:20).

The above definition also affirms that all of God's *knowledge* is true and is the final standard of truth. Job tells us that God is "perfect in knowledge" (Job 37:16; see also the verses cited above under the discussion of God's omniscience). To say that God knows all things and that his knowledge is perfect is to say that he is never mistaken in his perception or understanding of the world. All that he knows and thinks is true and is a correct understanding of the nature of reality. In fact, since God knows all things infinitely well, we can say that the standard of true knowledge is conformity to God's knowledge. If we think the same thing God thinks about anything in the universe, we are thinking truthfully about it.

Our definition also affirms that God's words are both *true* and the *final standard of truth*. This means that God is reliable and faithful in his words. With respect to his promises, God always does what he promises to do, and we can depend on him never to be unfaithful to his promises. Thus, he is "a God of faithfulness" (Deut. 32:4). In fact, this specific aspect of God's truthfulness is sometimes viewed as a distinct attribute: *God's faithfulness means that God will always do what he has said and fulfill what he has promised* (Num. 23:19; cf. 2 Sam. 7:28; Ps. 141:6; et al.). He can be relied upon, and he will never prove unfaithful to those who trust what he has said. Indeed, the essence of true faith is taking God at his word and relying on him to do as he has promised.

The truthfulness of God is also communicable in that we can in part imitate it by striving to have true knowledge about God and about his world. In fact, as we begin to think true thoughts about God and creation, thoughts that we learn from Scripture and from allowing Scripture to guide us in our observation and interpretation of the natural world, we begin to think God's own thoughts after him! Growth in knowledge is part of the process of becoming more like God. Paul tells us that we have put on the "new nature," which, he says, "is being renewed in knowledge after the image of its creator" (Col. 3:10).

In a society that is exceedingly careless with the truthfulness of spoken words, we as God's children are to imitate our Creator and take great care to be sure that our words are always truthful. "*Do not lie to one another,* seeing that you have put off the old nature with its practices and have put on the new nature" (Col. 3:9–10). Furthermore, we should imitate God's truthfulness in our own emotional reaction to truth and falsehood. Like God, we should *love* truth and *hate* falsehood. The commandment not to bear false witness against our neighbor (Ex. 20:16), like the other commandments, requires not merely outward conformity but also conformity in heart attitude. One who is pleasing to God "speaks truth from his heart" (Ps. 15:2), and strives to be like the righteous man who "hates falsehood" (Prov. 13:5).

C. Moral Attributes

6. Goodness. *The goodness of God means that God is the final standard of good, and that all that God is and does is worthy of approval.* In this definition, "good" can be understood to mean "worthy of approval," but this raises the question, approval by whom? Because we are mere creatures, we are not free to decide by ourselves what is worthy of approval and what is not. Ultimately, therefore, God's being and actions are perfectly worthy of his own approval. He is therefore the final standard of good. Jesus implies this when he says, "No one is good but God alone" (Luke 18:19). The Psalms frequently affirm that "the LORD is good" (Ps. 100:5) or exclaim, "O give thanks to the LORD, for he is good" (Pss. 106:1; 107:1; et al.). We can therefore understand the meaning of "good" as being that which God approves, because there is no higher standard of goodness than God's own character and his approval of whatever is consistent with that character.

Our definition also states that all that God *does* is worthy of approval. We see evidence of this in the creation narrative: "God saw everything that he had made, and behold, it was very good" (Gen. 1:31). Scripture also tells us that God is the source of all good in the world. "Every good endowment and every perfect gift is from above, coming down from the Father of lights with whom there is no variation or shadow due to change" (James 1:17; cf. Ps. 145:9; Acts 14:17). Moreover, God does only good things for his children. We read, "No good thing does the LORD withhold from those who walk uprightly" (Ps. 84:11). Jesus teaches that, much more than an earthly father, our heavenly Father will "give good things to those who ask him" (Matt. 7:11), and the writer of Hebrews notes that even his fatherly discipline is a manifestation of his love and is for our good (Heb. 12:10).

In imitation of this communicable attribute, we should ourselves do good (that is, we should do what God approves) and thereby imitate the goodness of our heavenly Father. Paul writes, "So then, as we have opportunity, let us do good to all men, and especially to those who are of the household of faith" (Gal. 6:10; cf. Luke 6:27, 33–35; 2 Tim. 3:17). Moreover, when we realize that God is the definition and source of all good, we will recognize that God himself is the ultimate good that we seek. We will say with the psalmist:

> Whom have I in heaven but you?
> And there is nothing upon earth that I desire besides you.
> My flesh and my heart may fail,
> but God is the strength of my heart and my portion for ever.
> (Ps. 73:25–26; cf. 16:11; 42:1–2)

God's goodness is closely related to several other characteristics of his nature. For example, God's *mercy* and *grace* may be seen as two separate attributes, or as specific aspects of God's goodness. God's *mercy* means God's goodness toward those in misery and distress. God's *grace* means God's goodness toward those who deserve only punishment.

These two characteristics of God's nature are often mentioned together, especially in the Old Testament. When God proclaimed his name to Moses, he proclaimed, "The LORD, the LORD, a God merciful and gracious, slow to anger, and abounding in steadfast love and faithfulness" (Ex. 34:6). David says in Psalm 103:8, "The LORD is merciful and gracious, slow to anger and abounding in steadfast love."

Grace as God's goodness especially shown to those who do not deserve it is seen frequently in Paul's writings. He emphasizes that salvation by grace is the opposite of salvation by human effort, for grace is a freely given gift. "Since all have sinned and fall short of the glory of God, they are justified by his *grace* as a gift, through the redemption which is in Christ Jesus" (Rom. 3:23–24).

7. Love. God's love means that God eternally gives of himself to others.

This definition understands love as self-giving for the benefit of others. This attribute of God shows that it is part of his nature to give of himself in order to bring about blessing or good for others.

John tells us that "God is love" (1 John 4:8). We see evidence that this attribute of God was active even before creation among the members of the Trinity. Jesus speaks to his Father of "my glory which you have given me in your *love* for me *before the foundation of the world* " (John 17:24), thus indicating that there was love and a giving of honor from the Father to the Son from all eternity. This love is also recip- rocal, for Jesus says, "I do as the Father has commanded me, so that the world may know that I love the Father" (John 14:31). The love between the Father and the Son also presumably characterizes their relationship with the Holy Spirit, even though it is not explicitly mentioned. This eternal love between the Father, the Son, and the Holy Spirit makes heaven a world of love and joy because each person of the Trin- ity seeks to bring joy and happiness to the other two.

The self-giving that characterizes the Trinity finds clear expression in God's rela- tionship to mankind, and especially to sinful people. "In this is love, not that we loved God, but that He loved us and sent His Son *to be* the propitiation for our sins" (1 John 4:10 NASB). Paul writes, "God shows his love for us in that while we were yet sinners Christ died for us" (Rom. 5:8). John also writes, "For God so loved the world that he gave his only Son, that whoever believes in him should not perish but have eter- nal life" (John 3:16). It should cause us great joy to know that it is the purpose of God the Father, Son, and Holy Spirit to give of themselves in order to bring us true joy and happiness. It is God's nature to act that way toward those upon whom he has set his love, and he will continue to act that way toward us for all eternity.

We imitate this communicable attribute of God, first by loving God in return, and second by loving others in imitation of the way God loves them. All our obliga- tions to God can be summarized in this: "You shall love the Lord your God with all your heart, and with all your soul, and with all your mind. . . . You shall love your neighbor as yourself" (Matt. 22:37–38). If we love God, we will obey his command- ments (1 John 5:3) and thus do what is pleasing to him. We will love God, not the world (1 John 2:15), and we will do all this because he first loved us (1 John 4:19).

8. Holiness. *God's holiness means that he is separated from sin and devoted to seek- ing his own honor.* This definition contains both a relational quality (separation from) and a moral quality (the separation is from sin or evil, and the devotion is to the good of God's own honor or glory). The idea of holiness as including both separa- tion from evil and devotion to God's own glory is found in a number of Old Testa- ment passages. The word *holy* is used to describe both parts of the tabernacle, for example. The tabernacle itself was a place separate from the evil and sin of the world, and the first room in it was called the "Holy Place." It was dedicated to God's ser- vice. But then God commanded that there be a veil, "and the veil shall separate for you the holy place from the most holy" (Ex. 26:33). The Most Holy Place, where the ark of the covenant was kept, was the place most separated from evil and sin and most fully devoted to God's service.

God himself is the Most Holy One. He is called the "Holy One of Israel" (Pss. 71:22; 78:41; 89:18; Isa. 1:4; 5:19, 24; et al.). The seraphim around God's throne cry, "Holy, holy, holy is the LORD of hosts; the whole earth is full of his glory" (Isa. 6:3). "The LORD our God is holy!" exclaims the psalmist (Ps. 99:9; cf. 99:3, 5; 22:3).

God's holiness provides the pattern for his people to imitate. He commands them, "*You shall be holy;* for I the LORD your God am holy" (Lev. 19:2; cf. 11:44– 45; 20:26; 1 Peter 1:16). When God called his people out of Egypt and brought them to himself and commanded them to obey his voice, then he said, "You shall be to me a kingdom of priests and a *holy nation*" (Ex. 19:4–6). In this case, the idea of separation from evil and sin (which here included in a very striking way separation from life in Egypt) and the idea of devotion to God (in serving him and in obeying his statutes) are both seen in the example of a "holy nation." New covenant believers are also to "strive. . .for the holiness without which no one will see the Lord" (Heb. 12:14) and to know that God's discipline is given to us "that we may share his holiness" (Heb. 12:10). Not only individuals, but also the church itself, must grow in holiness (Eph. 5:26–27), until that day when everything on earth will be separated from evil, purified from sin, and devoted to the service of God in true moral purity (Zech. 14:20–21).

9. Righteousness (or Justice). In English the terms *righteousness* and *justice* are different words, but in both the Hebrew Old Testament and the Greek New Testament there is only one word group behind these two English terms. Therefore, these two terms will be considered together as speaking of one attribute of God. *God's righteousness means that God always acts in accordance with what is right and is himself the final standard of what is right.*

Speaking of God, Moses says, "All his ways are *justice.* A God of faithfulness and without iniquity, *just* and *right* is he" (Deut. 32:4). Abraham successfully appeals to God's own character of righteousness when he says, "Shall not the Judge of all the earth do right?" (Gen. 18:25). And God says of himself, "I the LORD speak the truth, I declare what is *right*" (Isa. 45:19). As a result of God's righteousness, it is necessary that he treat people according to what they deserve. Thus, it is necessary that God punish sin, for it does not deserve reward; it is wrong and deserves punishment.

When God does not punish sin, it seems to indicate that he is unrighteous, unless some other means of punishing sin can be seen. This is why Paul says that when God sent Christ as a sacrifice to bear the punishment for sin, it "was *to show God's righteousness,* because in his divine forbearance he had passed over former sins; it was to prove at the present time that he himself is righteous and that he justifies him who has faith in Jesus" (Rom. 3:25–26). When Christ died to pay the penalty for our sins, it showed that God was truly righteous, because he did give appropriate punishment to sin, even though he did forgive his people their sins.

With respect to the definition of righteousness given above, we may ask, What is "right"? In other words, what *ought* to happen and what *ought* to be? Here we must respond that *whatever conforms to God's moral character is right.* But why is whatever conforms to God's moral character right? It is right because it conforms to his moral character! If indeed God is the final standard of righteousness, then there can be no standard outside of God by which we measure righteousness or justice. He himself is the final standard.

In answer to Job's questioning about whether God has been righteous in his dealings with him, God answers Job, "Shall a faultfinder contend with the Almighty? . . . Will you even put me in the wrong? Will you condemn me that you may be justified?" (Job 40:2, 8). Then God answers not in terms of an explanation that would allow Job to understand why God's actions were right, but rather in terms of a statement of God's own majesty and power! God does not need to explain the rightness of his actions to Job, for God is the Creator and Job is the creature (cf. Job 40:9ff.).

Nevertheless, it should be a cause for thanksgiving and gratitude when we realize that righteousness and omnipotence are both possessed by God. If he were a

God of perfect righteousness without power to carry out that righteousness, he would not be worthy of worship and we would have no guarantee that justice will ultimately prevail in the universe. But if he were a God of unlimited power, yet without righteousness in his character, how unthinkably horrible the universe would be! There would be unrighteousness at the center of all existence and there would be nothing anyone could do to change it. We ought therefore continually to thank and praise God for who he is, "for *all his ways are justice*. A God of faithfulness and without iniquity, just and right is he" (Deut. 32:4).

10. Jealousy. Although the word *jealous* is frequently used in a negative sense in English, it also takes a positive sense at times. For example, Paul says to the Corinthians, "I feel a divine jealousy for you" (2 Cor. 11:2). Here the sense is "earnestly protective or watchful." It has the meaning of being deeply committed to seeking the honor or welfare of someone, whether oneself or someone else.

Scripture represents God as being jealous in this way. He continually and earnestly seeks to protect his own honor. He commands his people not to bow down to idols or serve them, saying, "for I the LORD your God am a *jealous* God" (Ex. 20:5). He desires that worship be given to himself and not to false gods (Ex. 34:14; cf. Deut. 4:24; 5:9). Thus, God's jealousy may be defined as follows: *God's jealousy means that God continually seeks to protect his own honor.*

People sometimes have trouble thinking that jealousy is a desirable attribute in God. This is because jealousy for our own honor as human beings is almost always wrong. We are not to be proud, but humble. Yet we must realize that the reason pride is wrong is a theological reason: It is that we do not deserve the honor that belongs to God alone (cf. 1 Cor. 4:7; Rev. 4:11).

It is not wrong for God to seek his own honor, however, for he deserves it fully. God freely admits that his actions in creation and redemption are done for his own honor. Speaking of his decision to withhold judgment from his people, God says, "For my own sake, for my own sake, I do it. . . . *My glory I will not give to another*" (Isa. 48:11). It is healthy for us spiritually when we settle in our hearts the fact that God deserves all honor and glory from his creation, and that it is right for him to seek this honor. He alone is infinitely worthy of being praised. To realize this fact and to delight in it is to find the secret of true worship.

11. Wrath. It may surprise us to find how frequently the Bible talks about the wrath of God. Yet if God loves all that is right and good and all that conforms to his moral character, it should not be surprising that he would hate everything that is opposed to his moral character. God's wrath directed against sin is therefore closely related to God's holiness and justice. God's wrath may be defined as follows: *God's wrath means that he intensely hates all sin.*

Descriptions of God's wrath are found frequently when God's people sin greatly against him. God sees the idolatry of the people of Israel and says to Moses, "I have seen this people . . .; now therefore let me alone, that my *wrath* may burn hot against them and I may consume them" (Ex. 32:9–10). Later Moses tells the people, "Remember and do not forget how you provoked the LORD your God to *wrath* in the wilderness. . . . Even at Horeb you provoked the LORD to *wrath,* and the LORD was so angry with you that he was ready to destroy you" (Deut. 9:7–8; cf. 29:23; 2 Kings 22:13).

The doctrine of the wrath of God in Scripture is not limited to the Old Testament, however, as some have falsely imagined. We read in John 3:36, "He who believes in the Son has eternal life; he who does not obey the Son shall not see life, but *the wrath of God rests upon him*." Paul says, "For the wrath of God is revealed from heaven against all ungodliness and wickedness of men" (Rom. 1:18; cf. 2:5, 8; 5:9; 9:22, Col. 3:6; 1 Thess. 1:10; 2:16; 5:9; Heb. 3:11; Rev. 6:16–17; 19:15).

This also is an attribute for which we should thank and praise God. It may not immediately appear to us how this can be done, since wrath seems to be such a negative concept. Yet it is helpful for us to ask what God would be like if he were a God who did not hate sin. He would then be a God who either delighted in sin or at least was not troubled by it. Such a God would not be worthy of our worship, for sin is hateful and it is *worthy* of being hated. Sin ought not to be. It is in fact a virtue to hate evil and sin (cf. Zech. 8:17; Heb. 1:9; et al.), and we rightly imitate this attribute of God when we feel hatred against great evil, injustice, and sin.[2]

Furthermore, we should feel no fear of God's wrath as Christians, for although "we were by nature children of wrath, like the rest of mankind" (Eph. 2:3), we now have trusted in Jesus, "who delivers us from the wrath to come" (1 Thess. 1:10; cf. Rom. 5:10). When we meditate on the wrath of God, we will be amazed to think that our Lord Jesus Christ bore the wrath of God that was due to our sin, in order that we might be saved (Rom. 3:25–26).

Moreover, in thinking about God's wrath, we must also bear in mind his patience. Patience and wrath are mentioned together in Psalm 103: "The LORD is . . . *slow to anger* and abounding in steadfast love. He will not always chide, nor will he keep his anger for ever" (Ps. 103:8–9). In fact, the delay of the execution of God's wrath upon evil is for the purpose of leading people to repentance (see Rom. 2:4).

Thus, when we think of God's wrath to come, we should simultaneously be thankful for his patience in waiting to execute that wrath in order that yet more people may be saved: "The Lord is not slow about his promise as some count slowness, but is forbearing toward you, not wishing that any should perish, but that all should reach repentance. But the day of the Lord will come like a thief, and then the heavens will pass away with a loud noise" (2 Peter 3:9–10). God's wrath should motivate us to evangelism and should also cause us to be thankful that God finally will punish all wrongdoing and will reign over a new heavens and a new earth in which there will be no unrighteousness.

D. Attributes of Purpose

In this category of attributes, we will discuss first God's will in general, then the omnipotence (or infinite power) of God's will.

12. Will. *God's will is that attribute of God whereby he approves and determines to bring about every action necessary for the existence and activity of himself and all creation.* This definition indicates that God's will has to do with deciding and approving the things that God is and does. It concerns God's choices of what to do and what not to do.

a. *God's will in general.* Scripture frequently indicates God's will as the final or most ultimate reason for everything that happens. Paul refers to God as the one "who accomplishes all things according to the counsel of his will" (Eph. 1:11). The phrase here translated "all things" *(ta panta)* is used frequently by Paul to refer to

---

[2]It is appropriate for us in this regard to "hate the sin but love the sinner," as a popular slogan puts it.

everything that exists or everything in creation (see, for example, Eph. 1:10, 23; 3:9; 4:10; Col. 1:16 [twice], 17; Rom. 11:36; 1 Cor. 8:6 [twice]; 15:27–28 [twice]). The word translated "accomplishes" (*energeō*, "works, works out, brings about, produces") is a present participle and suggests continual activity. The phrase might more explicitly be translated "who continually brings about everything in the universe according to the counsel of his will."

More specifically, all things were created by God's will: "You created all things, and *by your will they existed and were created*" (Rev. 4:11). Both Old and New Testaments speak of human government as coming about according to God's will (Dan. 4:32; Rom. 13:1). Even the events connected with the death of Christ were according to God's will. The church at Jerusalem believed this, for in their prayer they said, "Truly in this city there were gathered together against your holy servant Jesus, whom you anointed, both Herod and Pontius Pilate, with all the Gentiles and the peoples of Israel, to do *whatever your hand and your plan had predestined to take place*" (Acts 4:27–28). This implies that not simply the fact of Jesus' death, but all the detailed events connected with it, were predestined by God's will to occur.

James encourages us to see all the events of our lives as subject to God's will. To those who say, "Today or tomorrow we will go into such and such a town and spend a year there and trade and get gain," James says, "You do not know about tomorrow. . . . Instead you ought to say, *'if the Lord wills,* we shall live and we shall do this or that'" (James 4:13–15). Sometimes it is God's will that Christians suffer, as is seen in 1 Peter 3:17, for example: "For it is better to suffer for doing right, *if that should be God's will,* than for doing wrong." To attribute so many events, even evil events, to the will of God, however, often causes misunderstanding and difficulty for Christians. Some of the difficulties connected with this subject will be treated here and others will be dealt with in chapter 9 on God's providence.

b. *Distinctions in aspects of God's will. Secret will and revealed will:* Distinctions are sometimes made between aspects of God's will. Just as we can will or choose something eagerly or reluctantly, happily or with regret, secretly or publicly, so also God in the infinite greatness of his personality is able to will different things in different ways.

One helpful distinction applied to different aspects of God's will is the distinction between God's *secret will* and his *revealed will.* Even in our own experience we know that we are able to will some things secretly and then only later make this will known to others. Sometimes we tell others before the thing that we have willed comes about, and at other times we do not reveal our secret will until the event we willed has happened.

Surely, a distinction between aspects of God's will is evident in many passages of Scripture. According to Moses, "The *secret things* belong to the LORD our God; but the *things that are revealed* belong to us and to our children for ever, that we may do all the words of this law" (Deut. 29:29). Those things that God *has* revealed are given to us for the purpose of obeying God's will: "that we may *do* all the words of this law." There were many other aspects of his plan, however, that he had not revealed to them: many details about future events, specific details of hardship or of blessing in their lives, and so forth. With regard to these matters, they were simply to trust him.

Because God's revealed will usually contains his commands or "precepts" for our moral conduct, God's revealed will is sometimes also called God's *will of precept* or *will of command*. This revealed will of God is God's declared will concerning *what we should do* or what God *commands* us to do.

On the other hand, God's secret will usually includes his hidden decrees by which he governs the universe and determines everything that will happen. He does not ordinarily reveal these decrees to us (except in prophecies of the future), so these purposes or plans really are God's "secret" will. We do not find out what God has secretly purposed until events actually happen. Because this secret will of God has to do with his decreeing of events in the world, this aspect of God's will is sometimes also called God's *will of decree*.

There are several instances where Scripture mentions God's revealed will. In the Lord's Prayer the petition, "*Your will be done*, on earth as it is in heaven" (Matt. 6:10) is a prayer that people would obey God's *revealed* will, his commands, on earth just as they do in heaven (that is, fully and completely). This could not be a prayer that God's secret will (that is, his decrees for events that he has planned) would in fact be fulfilled, for what God has decreed in his secret will shall certainly come to pass. To ask God to bring about what he has already decreed to happen would simply be to pray, "May what is going to happen, happen." That would be a hollow prayer indeed, for it would not be asking for anything at all. Furthermore, since we do not know God's secret will regarding the future, the person praying a prayer for God's secret will to be done would never know for what he or she was praying! It would be a prayer without understandable content and without effect. Rather, the prayer "*Your will* be done" must be understood as an appeal for the *revealed* will of God to be followed on earth.

On the other hand, many passages speak of God's secret will. When James tells us to say, "*If the Lord wills,* we shall live and we shall do this or that" (James 4:15), he cannot be talking about God's revealed will or will of precept, for with regard to many of our actions we *know* that it is according to God's command that we do one or another activity that we have planned. Rather, to trust in the secret will of God overcomes pride and expresses humble dependence on God's sovereign control over the events of our lives.

Another instance is found in Genesis 50:20. Joseph says to his brothers, "As for you, you meant evil against me; but *God meant it for good,* to bring it about that many people should be kept alive, as they are today." Here God's *revealed* will to Joseph's brothers was that they should love him and not steal from him or sell him into slavery or make plans to murder him. But God's *secret* will was that in the disobedience of Joseph's brothers a greater good would be done when Joseph, having been sold into slavery into Egypt, gained authority over the land and was able to save his family.

Both the revealing of the good news of the gospel to some and its hiding from others are said to be according to God's will. Jesus says, "I thank you, Father, Lord of heaven and earth, that you have hidden these things from the wise and understanding and revealed them to babes; yea, Father, *for such was your gracious will*" (Matt. 11:25–26). This again must refer to God's secret will, for his revealed will is that all come to salvation. Indeed, only two verses later, Jesus commands everyone, "Come to me, *all* who labor and are heavy laden, and I will give you rest" (Matt. 11:28). And both Paul and Peter tell us that God wills all men to be saved (see 1 Tim. 2:4 and 2 Peter 3:9). Thus, the fact that some are not saved and some have the gospel hidden from them must be understood as happening according to God's secret will, unknown to us and inappropriate for us to seek to pry into.

There is danger in speaking about evil events as happening according to the will of God, even though we sometimes see Scripture speaking of them in this way. One danger is that we might begin to think that God takes pleasure in evil, which he does not do (see Ezek. 33:11: "I have no pleasure in the death of the wicked, but that the wicked turn from his way and live"), though he can use evil for his good purposes (as he did in Joseph's life and or in the death of Christ).[3] Another danger is that we might begin to blame God for sin, rather than ourselves, or to think that we are not responsible for our evil actions. Scripture, however, does not hesitate to couple statements of God's sovereign will with statements of man's responsibility for evil. Peter could say in the same sentence that Jesus was "delivered up according to the definite plan and foreknowledge of God," and also that "this Jesus . . . *you crucified and killed* by the hands of lawless men" (Acts 2:23). Both God's hidden will of decree and the culpable wickedness of "lawless men" in carrying it out are affirmed in the same statement. However we may understand the secret workings of God's hidden will, we must never understand it to imply that we are freed from responsibility for evil, or that God is ever to be blamed for sin. Scripture never speaks that way, and we may not either, even though how this can be so may remain a mystery for us in this age.

We will also consider God's freedom as part of God's will, but it may be considered a separate attribute. *God's freedom is that attribute of God whereby he does whatever he pleases.* This definition implies that nothing in all creation can hinder God from doing his will. God is not constrained by anything external to himself, and he is free to do whatever he wishes to do. No person or force can ever dictate to God what he should do. He is under no authority or external restraint.

God's freedom is mentioned in Psalm 115, where his great power is contrasted with the weakness of idols: "Our God is in the heavens; *he does whatever he pleases*" (Ps. 115:3). Human rulers are not able to stand against God and effectively oppose his will, for "the king's heart is a stream of water in the hand of the LORD; he turns it wherever he will" (Prov. 21:1). Similarly, Nebuchadnezzar learns in his repentance that it is true to say of God, "*He does according to his will* in the host of heaven and among the inhabitants of the earth; and none can stay his hand or say to him, 'What are you doing?'" (Dan. 4:35). We imitate God's freedom when we exercise our will and make choices, an ability essential to human nature but often misused because of sin.

Since God is free, we should not try to seek any more ultimate answer for God's actions in creation than the fact that he willed to do something and that his will has perfect freedom (so long as the actions he takes are consistent with his own moral character). Sometimes people try to discover the reason why God had to do one or another action (such as create the world or save us). It is better simply to say that it was God's totally free will (working in a way consistent with his character) that was the final reason why he chose to create the world and to save sinners and thereby bring glory to himself.

13. Omnipotence (or Power, including Sovereignty). *God's omnipotence means that God is able to do all his holy will.* The word *omnipotence* is derived from two Latin words, *omni,* "all," and *potens,* "powerful," and means "all-powerful." There are no limits on God's power to do what he decides to do.

---

[3]See ch. 8 for further discussion.

This power is frequently mentioned in Scripture. The rhetorical question, "Is anything too hard for the LORD?" (Gen. 18:14; Jer. 32:27) certainly implies (in the contexts in which it occurs) that nothing is too hard for the Lord. In fact, Jeremiah says to God, "*Nothing* is too hard for you" (Jer. 32:17). In the New Testament, Jesus says, "With God *all things are possible*" (Matt. 19:26); and Paul says that God is "able to do far more abundantly than all that we ask or think" (Eph. 3:20; cf. Luke 1:37; 2 Cor. 6:18; Rev. 1:8). Indeed, the consistent testimony of Scripture is that God's power is infinite.

There are, however, some things that God cannot do. God cannot will or do anything that would deny his own character. This is why the definition of omnipotence is stated in terms of God's ability to do "all his holy will." It is not absolutely everything that God is able to do, but everything that is consistent with his character. For example, God cannot lie (Titus 1:2), he cannot be tempted with evil (James 1:13), and he cannot deny himself (2 Tim. 2:13). Although God's power is infinite, his use of that power is qualified by his other attributes (just as all God's attributes qualify all his actions). This is therefore another instance where misunderstanding would result if one attribute were isolated from the rest of God's character and emphasized in a disproportionate way.

As we conclude our treatment of God's attributes of purpose, it is appropriate to realize that he has made us in such a way that we show in our lives some faint reflection of each of them. God has made us as creatures with a will, and so we exercise choice and make real decisions regarding the events of our lives. We do not of course have infinite power or omnipotence, but God has given us power to bring about results, both physical power and other kinds of power: mental power, spiritual power, persuasive power, and power in various kinds of authority structures (family, church, civil government, and so forth). In all of these areas, the use of power in ways pleasing to God and consistent with his will is again something that brings him glory as it reflects his own character.

E. "Summary" Attributes

14. Perfection. *God's perfection means that God completely possesses all excellent qualities and lacks no part of any qualities that would be desirable for him.* It is possible to include this attribute in the description of the other attributes. However, there are passages that tell us that God is "perfect" or "complete." For instance, Jesus tells us, "You, therefore, must be perfect, as your heavenly Father is perfect" (Matt. 5:48; cf. Deut. 32:4; Ps. 18:30). Thus, it seems proper to state explicitly that God fully possess all excellent attributes and lacks nothing in his excellence.

15. Blessedness. To be "blessed" is to be happy in a very full and rich sense. Scripture often talks about the blessedness of those people who walk in God's ways. Yet in 1 Timothy, Paul calls God "the *blessed* and only Sovereign" (6:15) and speaks of "the glorious gospel of the *blessed* God" (1:11). In both instances the word is not *eulogetos* (often translated "blessed"), but *makarios* ("happy").

Thus, God's blessedness may be defined as follows: *God's blessedness means that God delights fully in himself and in all that reflects his character.* In this definition the idea of God's happiness or blessedness is connected directly to his own person as the focus of all that is worthy of joy or delight. This definition indicates that God is perfectly happy, that he has fullness of joy in himself.

The definition also reflects the fact that God takes pleasure in everything in creation that mirrors his own excellence. When he finished his work of creation, he looked at everything that he had made and saw that it was "very good" (Gen. 1:31). This indicates God's delight in and approval of his creation. Then in Isaiah we read a promise of God's future rejoicing over his people: "As the bridegroom rejoices over the bride, so shall your God rejoice over you" (62:5; cf. Prov. 8:30–31; Zeph. 3:17).

We imitate God's blessedness when we find delight and happiness in all that is pleasing to God, both those aspects of our own lives that are pleasing to God and the deeds of others. In fact, when we are thankful for and delight in the specific way God has created us as individuals, then we also imitate his attribute of blessedness. Furthermore, we imitate God's blessedness by rejoicing in the creation as it reflects various aspects of his excellent character. And we find our greatest blessedness, our greatest happiness, in delighting in the source of all good qualities, God himself.

16. Beauty. *God's beauty is that attribute of God whereby he is the sum of all desirable qualities.* This attribute of God is especially related to God's perfection: "Perfection" means that God doesn't lack anything desirable; "beauty" means that God has everything desirable. They are two different ways of affirming the same truth.

Nevertheless, there is value in affirming God's positive possession of everything that is desirable. It reminds us that all of our good and righteous desires, all of the desires that really ought to be in us or in any other creature, find their ultimate fulfillment in God and in no one else.

David speaks of the beauty of the Lord in Psalm 27:4:

> One thing have I asked of the LORD,
>   that will I seek after;
> that I may dwell in the house of the LORD
>   all the days of my life,
> to behold *the beauty of the LORD,*
>   and to inquire in his temple.

A similar idea is expressed in another psalm: "Whom have I in heaven but you? And there is nothing upon earth that I desire besides you" (Ps. 73:25). In both cases, the psalmist recognizes that his desire for God, who is the sum of everything desirable, far surpasses all other desires.

II. REVIEW QUESTIONS

1. Name and differentiate between the two attributes that describe God's being.
2. What does it mean that God knows all things "actual and possible"?
3. Differentiate between God's attributes of mercy, grace, and patience.
4. Why is it appropriate for God to be jealous for his own honor?
5. Is God's wrath inconsistent with his love? Explain.
6. What is the difference between God's secret will and his revealed will?
7. Are there any limitations to God's power? Explain, using the definition of his attribute of omnipotence.

III. QUESTIONS FOR PERSONAL APPLICATION

1. (Spirituality) Why is God so strongly displeased at carved idols, even those that are intended to represent him? How then shall we picture God or think of God in our minds when we pray to him?

2. (Knowledge) With regard to the circumstances of your life, will God ever make a mistake, or fail to plan ahead, or fail to take into account all the eventualities that occur? How is the answer to this question a blessing in your life?

3. (Wisdom) Do you really believe that God is working wisely in your life today? In the world? If you find this difficult to believe at times, what might you do to change your attitude?

4. (Truthfulness) Why are people in our society, sometimes even Christians, quite careless with regard to truthfulness in speech? Do you need to ask God's help to more fully reflect his truthfulness in speech in any of the following areas: promising to pray for someone; saying that you will be some place at a certain time; exaggerating events in order to make a more exciting story; taking care to remember and then be faithful to what you have said in business commitments; reporting what other people have said or what you think someone else is thinking; fairly representing your opponent's viewpoint in an argument?

5. (Love) Is it possible to decide to love someone and then to act on that decision, or does love between human beings simply depend on spontaneous emotional feelings? In what ways could you imitate God's love specifically today?

6. (Mercy) If you were to reflect God's mercy more fully, for whom among those you know would you show special care during the next week?

7. (Holiness) Are there activities or relationships in your present pattern of life that are hindering your growth in holiness because they make it difficult for you to be separated from sin and devoted to seeking God's honor?

8. (Righteousness) Do you ever find yourself wishing that some of God's laws were different than they are? If so, does such a wish reflect a dislike for some aspect of God's moral character? What passages of Scripture might you read to convince yourself more fully that God's character and his laws are right in these areas?

9. (Jealousy) Do you reflect God's jealousy for his own honor instinctively when you hear him dishonored in conversation or on television or in other contexts? What can we do to deepen our jealousy for God's honor?

10. (Wrath) Should we love the fact that God is a God of wrath who hates sin? In what ways is it right for us to imitate this wrath, and in what ways is it wrong for us to do so?

11. (Will) As children grow toward adulthood, what are proper and improper ways for them to show in their own lives greater and greater exercise of individual will and freedom from parental control? Are these to be expected as evidence of our creation in the image of God?

12. (Power) If God's power is his ability to do what he wills to do, then is power for us the ability to obey God's will and bring about results in the world that are pleasing to him? Name several ways in which we can increase in such power in our lives.

13. (Perfection) How does God's attribute of perfection remind us that we can never be satisfied with the reflection of only some of God's character in our own lives? Can you describe some aspects of what it would mean to "be perfect" as our heavenly Father is perfect, with respect to your own life?

14. (Blessedness) Are you happy with the way God created you—with the physical, emotional, mental, and relational traits he gave you? In what ways is it right to be happy or pleased with our own personalities, physical characteristics, abilities, positions, etc.? In what ways is it wrong to be pleased or happy about these things? Will we ever be fully "blessed" or happy? When will that be and why?

15. (Beauty) If we refuse to accept our society's definition of beauty, or even the definitions we ourselves may have worked with previously, and decide that that which is truly beautiful is the character of God himself, then how will our understanding of beauty be different from the one we previously held? Will we still be able to rightly apply our new idea of beauty to some of the things we previously thought to be beautiful? Why or why not?

IV. SPECIAL TERMS

attributes of being

attributes of purpose

beauty

blessedness

communicable attributes

faithfulness

freedom

goodness

grace

holiness

invisibility

jealousy

justice

knowledge

love

mental attributes

mercy

moral attributes

omnipotence

omniscience

perfection

power

revealed will

righteousness

secret will

sovereignty

spirituality

"summary attributes"

theophany

truthfulness

will

wisdom

wrath

V. SCRIPTURE MEMORY PASSAGE

Exodus 34:6–7

The LORD passed before him, and proclaimed, "The LORD, the LORD, a God merciful and gracious, slow to anger, and abounding in steadfast love and faithfulness, keeping steadfast love for thousands, forgiving iniquity and transgression and sin, but who will by no means clear the guilty, visiting the iniquity of the fathers upon the children and the children's children, to the third and the fourth generation."

CHAPTER SIX

The Trinity

+ *How can God be three persons, yet one God?*

The preceding chapters have discussed many attributes of God. But if we understood only those attributes, we would not rightly understand God at all, for we would not understand that God, in his very being, has always existed as more than one person. In fact, God exists as three persons, yet he is one God.

The doctrine of the Trinity is one of the most important doctrines of the Christian faith. To study the Bible's teachings on the Trinity gives us great insight into the question that is at the center of all of our seeking after God: What is God like in himself? Here we learn that in himself, in his very being, God exists in the persons of Father, Son, and Holy Spirit, yet he is one God.

I. EXPLANATION AND SCRIPTURAL BASIS

We may define the doctrine of the Trinity as follows: *God eternally exists as three persons, Father, Son, and Holy Spirit, and each person is fully God, and there is one God.*

A. The Doctrine of the Trinity Is Progressively Revealed in Scripture

1. Partial revelation in the Old Testament. The word *trinity* is never found in the Bible, though the idea represented by the word is taught in many places. The word *trinity* means "triunity" or "three-in-oneness." It is used to summarize the teaching of Scripture that God is three persons yet one God.

Sometimes people think the doctrine of the Trinity is only found in the New Testament, not in the Old. But if God has eternally existed as three persons, it would be surprising to find no indications of that in the Old Testament. Although the doctrine of the Trinity is not explicitly found in the Old Testament, several passages suggest or even imply that God exists as more than one person.

For instance, according to Genesis 1:26, God said, "Let *us* make man in *our* image, after *our* likeness." What do the plural verb ("let us") and the plural pronoun ("our") mean? Some have suggested they are plurals of majesty, a form of speech a king would use in saying, for example, "We are pleased to grant your request." However, in Old Testament Hebrew there are no other examples of a monarch using plural verbs or plural pronouns of himself in such a "plural of majesty," so this suggestion has no evidence to support it. Another suggestion is that God is here speaking to angels. But angels did not participate in the creation of man, nor was man created in the image and likeness of angels, so this suggestion is not convincing. The best explanation, and the one held almost unanimously by the church fathers and earlier theologians, is that already in the first chapter of Genesis we have an indication of a plurality of persons in God himself. We are not told how many persons, and we have nothing approaching a complete doctrine of the Trinity, but it is implied that more than one person is involved. The same can be said of Genesis 3:22 ("Behold, the man has become like one of *us*, knowing good and evil"), Genesis 11:7 ("Come, let *us* go down, and there confuse their language"), and Isaiah 6:8 ("Whom shall I send, and who will go for *us?*"). (Note the combination of singular and plural in the same sentence in the last passage.)

Moreover, there are passages where one person is called "God" or "the Lord" and is distinguished from another person who is also said to be God. In Psalm 45:6–7 (NIV), the psalmist says, "Your throne, O God, will last for ever and ever. . . . You love righteousness and hate wickedness; therefore God, your God, has set you above your companions by anointing you with the oil of joy." Here the psalm passes beyond describing anything that could be true of an earthly king and calls the king "God" (v. 6), whose throne will last "for ever and ever." But then, still speaking to the person called "God," the author says that "God, your God, has set you above your companions" (v. 7). So two separate persons are called "God" (Heb. *'Elōhîm*). In the New Testament, the author of Hebrews quotes this passage and applies it to Christ: "Your throne, O God, is for ever and ever" (Heb. 1:8).

Similarly, in Psalm 110:1, David says, "The LORD says to my lord: 'Sit at my right hand until I make your enemies a footstool for your feet'" (NIV). Jesus rightly understands that David is referring to two separate persons as "Lord" (Matt. 22:41–46), but who is David's "Lord" if not God himself? And who could be saying to God, "Sit at my right hand" except someone else who is also fully God? From a New Testament perspective, we can paraphrase this verse: "God the Father said to God the Son, 'Sit at my right hand.'" But even without the New Testament teaching on the Trinity, it seems clear that David was aware of a plurality of persons in one God.

Isaiah 63:10 says that God's people "rebelled and grieved his Holy Spirit" (NIV), apparently suggesting both that the Holy Spirit is distinct from God himself (it is "his Holy Spirit"), and that this Holy Spirit can be "grieved," thus suggesting emotional capabilities characteristic of a distinct person.

Furthermore, several Old Testament passages about "the angel of the LORD" suggest a plurality of persons in God. The word translated "angel" (Heb. *mal'ak*) means simply "messenger." If this angel of the Lord is a "messenger" of the Lord, he is then distinct from the Lord himself. Yet at some points the angel of the Lord is called "God" or "the LORD" (see Gen. 16:13; Ex. 3:2–6; 23:20–22; Num. 22:35 with 38; Judg. 2:1–2; 6:11 with 14). At other points in the Old Testament "the angel of the LORD" simply refers to a created angel, but at least at these texts the special angel (or "messenger") of the Lord seems to be a distinct person who is fully divine.

2. More complete revelation of the Trinity in the New Testament. When the New Testament opens, we enter into the history of the coming of the Son of God to earth. It is to be expected that this great event would be accompanied by more explicit teaching about the trinitarian nature of God, and that is in fact what we find. Before looking at this in detail, we can simply list several passages where all three persons of the Trinity are named together.

When Jesus was baptized, "the heavens were opened and he saw the Spirit of God descending like a dove, and alighting on him; and lo, a voice from heaven, saying, 'This is my beloved Son, with whom I am well pleased'" (Matt. 3:16–17). Here at one moment we have three members of the Trinity performing three distinct activities. God the Father is speaking from heaven; God the Son is being baptized, and is then spoken to from heaven by God the Father; and God the Holy Spirit is descending from heaven to rest upon and empower Jesus for his ministry.

At the end of Jesus' earthly ministry, he tells the disciples that they should go "and make disciples of all nations, baptizing them in the name of the Father and of the Son and of the Holy Spirit" (Matt. 28:19). The very names "Father" and "Son," drawn as they are from the family, the most familiar of human institutions, indicate very strongly the distinct personhood of both the Father and the Son. When "the Holy Spirit" is put in the same expression and on the same level as the other two persons, it is hard to avoid the conclusion that the Holy Spirit is also viewed as a person and of equal standing with the Father and the Son.

When we realize that the New Testament authors generally use the name "God" (Gk. *theos*) to refer to God the Father and the name "Lord" (Gk. *kyrios*) to refer to God the Son, then it is clear that there is another trinitarian expression in 1 Corinthians 12:4–6: "Now there are varieties of gifts, but the same *Spirit;* and there are varieties of service, but the same *Lord;* and there are varieties of working, but it is the same *God* who inspires them all in every one."

Similarly, the last verse of 2 Corinthians is trinitarian in its expression: "The grace of the *Lord Jesus Christ* and the love of *God* and the fellowship of the *Holy Spirit* be with you all" (2 Cor. 13:14). We see the three persons mentioned separately in Ephesians 4:4–6 as well: "There is one body and one *Spirit,* just as you were called to the one hope that belongs to your call, one *Lord,* one faith, one baptism, one *God and Father* of us all, who is above all and through all and in all."

All three persons of the Trinity are mentioned together in the opening sentence of 1 Peter: "According to the foreknowledge of God the Father, by the sanctifying work of the Spirit, that you may obey Jesus Christ and be sprinkled with his blood" (1 Peter 1:2 NASB). And in Jude 20–21, we read: "But you, beloved, build yourselves up on your most holy faith; pray in the Holy Spirit; keep yourselves in the love of God; wait for the mercy of our Lord Jesus Christ unto eternal life."

B. Three Statements Summarize the Biblical Teaching

In one sense, the doctrine of the Trinity is a mystery that we will never be able to fully understand. However, we can understand something of its truth by summarizing the teaching of Scripture in three statements:

1. God is three persons.
2. Each person is fully God.
3. There is one God.

The following section will develop each of these statements in more detail.

1. God is three persons. The fact that God is three persons means that the Father is not the Son; they are distinct persons. It also means that the Father is not the Holy Spirit, but that they are distinct persons. And it means that the Son is not the Holy Spirit. These distinctions are seen in a number of the passages quoted in the earlier section as well as in many additional New Testament passages.

John 1:1–2 tells us: "In the beginning was the Word, and the Word was with God, and the Word was God. He was in the beginning with God." The fact that the

"Word" (who is seen to be Christ in vv. 9–18) is "with" God shows distinction from God the Father. In John 17:24 (NIV), Jesus speaks to God the Father about "my glory, the glory you have given me because you loved me before the creation of the world," thus showing distinction of persons, sharing of glory, and a relationship of love between the Father and the Son before the world was created.

We are told that Jesus continues as our High Priest and Advocate before God the Father: "If any one does sin, we have an advocate with the Father, Jesus Christ the righteous" (1 John 2:1). Christ is the one who "is able for all time to save those who draw near to God through him, since he always lives to make intercession for them" (Heb. 7:25). Yet in order to intercede for us before God the Father, it is necessary that Christ be a person distinct from the Father.

Moreover, the Father is not the Holy Spirit, and the Son is not the Holy Spirit. They are distinguished in several verses. Jesus says, "The Counselor, the Holy Spirit, whom the Father will send in my name, he will teach you all things, and bring to your remembrance all that I have said to you" (John 14:26). The Holy Spirit also prays or "intercedes" for us (Rom. 8:27), indicating a distinction between the Holy Spirit and God the Father to whom the intercession is made.

Finally, the fact that the Son is not the Holy Spirit is also indicated in the several trinitarian passages mentioned earlier, such as the Great Commission (Matt. 28:19), and in passages that indicate that Christ went back to heaven and then sent the Holy Spirit to the church. Jesus said, "It is to your advantage that I go away, for if I do not go away, the Counselor will not come to you; but if I go, I will send him to you" (John 16:7).

Some have questioned whether the Holy Spirit is indeed a distinct person, rather than just the "power" or "force" of God at work in the world. But the New Testament evidence is quite clear and strong.[1] First are the several verses mentioned earlier where the Holy Spirit is put in a coordinate relationship with the Father and the Son (Matt. 28:19; 1 Cor. 12:4–6; 2 Cor. 13:14; Eph. 4:4–6; 1 Peter 1:2). Since the Father and Son are both persons, the coordinate expression strongly intimates that the Holy Spirit is a person also. Then there are places where the masculine pronoun *he* (Gk. *ekeinos*) is applied to the Holy Spirit (John 14:26; 15:26; 16:13–14), which one would not expect from the rules of Greek grammar, for the word *spirit* (Gk. *pneuma*) is neuter, not masculine, and would ordinarily be referred to with the neuter pronoun *ekeino*. Moreover, the name *counselor* or *comforter* (Gk. *Parakletos*) is a term commonly used to speak of a person who helps or gives comfort or counsel to another person or persons, but is used of the Holy Spirit in John's gospel (14:16, 26; 15:26; 16:7).

Other personal activities are ascribed to the Holy Spirit, such as teaching (John 14:26), bearing witness (John 15:26; Rom. 8:16), interceding or praying on behalf of others (Rom. 8:26–27), searching the depths of God (1 Cor. 2:10), knowing the thoughts of God (1 Cor. 2:11), willing to distribute some gifts to some and other gifts to others (1 Cor. 12:11), forbidding or not allowing certain activities (Acts 16:6–7), speaking (Acts 8:29; 13:2; and many times in both Old and New Testaments), evaluating and approving a wise course of action (Acts 15:28), and being grieved by sin in the lives of Christians (Eph. 4:30).

Finally, if the Holy Spirit is understood simply to be the power of God, rather than a distinct person, then a number of passages would simply not make sense,

---

[1]The following section on the distinct personality of the Holy Spirit follows quite closely the excellent material in Louis Berkhof, *Introduction to Systematic Theology* (Grand Rapids: Eerdmans, 1932; reprint, Grand Rapids: Baker, 1979), p. 96.

because in them the Holy Spirit and his power or the power of God are both mentioned. For example, Luke 4:14, "Jesus returned in the power of the Spirit into Galilee," would have to mean, "Jesus returned in the power of the power of God into Galilee." In Acts 10:38, "God anointed Jesus of Nazareth with the Holy Spirit and with power," would mean, "God anointed Jesus with the power of God and with power" (see also Rom. 15:13; 1 Cor. 2:4). We can conclude that the Holy Spirit is a distinct person.

2. Each person is fully God. In addition to the fact that all three persons are distinct, the abundant testimony of Scripture is that each person is fully God as well.

First, *God the Father is clearly God*. This is evident from the first verse of the Bible, where God created the heavens and the earth. It is evident through the Old and New Testaments, where God the Father is clearly viewed as sovereign Lord over all and where Jesus prays to his Father in heaven.

Next, *the Son is fully God*. Although this point will be developed in greater detail in chapter 15, "The Person of Christ," we can briefly note several explicit passages at this point. John 1:1–4 clearly affirms the full deity of Christ: "In the beginning was the Word, and the Word was with God, and the Word was God. He was in the beginning with God; all things were made through him, and without him was not anything made that was made. In him was life, and the life was the light of men."

Here Christ is referred to as "the Word," and John says both that he was "with God" and that he "was God." The Greek text echoes the opening words of Genesis 1:1 ("In the beginning . . .") and reminds us that John is talking about something that was true before the world was made. God the Son was always fully God.

The translation "the Word was God" has been challenged by the Jehovah's Witnesses, who translate it "the Word was a god," implying that the Word was simply a heavenly being but not fully divine. They justify this translation by pointing to the fact that the definite article (Gk. *ho*, "the") does not occur before the Greek word *theos* ("God"). They say therefore that *theos* should be translated "a god." However, their interpretation has been followed by no recognized Greek scholar anywhere, for it is commonly known that the sentence follows a regular rule of Greek grammar, and the absence of the definite article merely indicates that "God" is the predicate rather than the subject of the sentence.

The inconsistency of the Jehovah's Witnesses' position can further be seen in their translation of the rest of the chapter. For various other grammatical reasons the word *theos* also lacks the definite article at other places in this chapter, such as verse 6 ("There was a man sent from God"), verse 12 ("power to become children of God"), and verse 18 ("No one has ever seen God"). If the Jehovah's Witnesses were consistent with their argument about the absence of the definite article, they would have to translate all of these with the phrase "a god," but they translate "God" in every case.

John 20:28 in its context is also a strong proof for the deity of Christ. Thomas had doubted the reports of the other disciples that they had seen Jesus raised from the dead, and he said he would not believe unless he could see the nail prints in Jesus' hands and place his hand in his wounded side (John 20:25). Then Jesus appeared to the disciples when Thomas was with them. He said to Thomas, "Put your finger here, and see my hands; and put out your hand, and place it in my side; do not be faithless, but believing" (John 20:27). In response to this, we read,

"Thomas answered him, 'My Lord and my God!'" (John 20:28). Here Thomas calls Jesus "my God." The following verses (vv. 29–31) show that both John in writing his gospel and Jesus himself approve of what Thomas has said and encourage everyone who hears about Thomas to believe the same things that Thomas did.

Other passages speaking of Jesus as fully divine include Hebrews 1, where the author says that Christ is the "exact representation" (v. 3, Gk. *Charaktēr,* "exact duplicate") of the nature or being (Gk. *hypostasis*) of God—meaning that God the Son exactly duplicates the being or nature of God the Father in every way; whatever attributes or power God the Father has, God the Son has them as well. The author goes on to refer to the Son as "God" in verse 8 ("But of the Son he says, 'Your throne, O God, is for ever and ever'"), and he attributes the creation of the heavens to Christ when he says of him, "You, Lord, did found the earth in the beginning, and the heavens are the work of your hands" (Heb. 1:10, quoting Ps. 102:25).

Many other passages will be discussed in chapter 15 below, but these should be sufficient to demonstrate that the New Testament clearly refers to Christ as fully God. As Paul says in Colossians 2:9, "In him the whole fulness of deity dwells bodily."

Next, *the Holy Spirit is also fully God.* Once we understand God the Father and God the Son to be fully God, then the trinitarian expressions in verses like Matthew 28:19 ("baptizing them in the name of the Father and of the Son and of the Holy Spirit") assume significance for the doctrine of the Holy Spirit, because they show that the Holy Spirit is classified on an equal level with the Father and the Son. This can be seen if we recognize how unthinkable it would have been for Jesus to say something like, "baptizing them in the name of the Father and of the Son and of the archangel Michael"—this would give to a created being a status entirely inappropriate even to an archangel. Believers throughout all ages can only be baptized into the name (and thus into a taking on of the character) of God himself. (Note also the other trinitarian passages mentioned above: 1 Cor. 12:4–6; 2 Cor. 13:14; Eph. 4:4–6; 1 Peter 1:2; Jude 20–21.)

In Acts 5:3–4, Peter asks Ananias, "Why has Satan filled your heart to lie to the Holy Spirit . . . ? You have not lied to men but *to God.*" According to Peter's words, to lie to the Holy Spirit is to lie to God. Paul says in 1 Corinthians 3:16, "Do you not know that you are God's temple and that God's Spirit dwells in you?" God's temple is the place where God himself dwells, which Paul explains by the fact that "God's Spirit" dwells in it, thus apparently equating God's Spirit with God himself.

David asks in Psalm 139:7–8, "Whither shall I go from your Spirit? Or whither shall I flee from your presence? If I ascend to heaven, you are there!" This passage attributes the divine characteristic of omnipresence to the Holy Spirit, something that is not true of any of God's creatures. It seems that David is equating God's Spirit with God's presence. To go from God's Spirit is to go from his presence, but if there is nowhere that David can flee from God's Spirit, then he knows that wherever he goes he will have to say, "You are there."

Paul attributes the divine characteristic of omniscience to the Holy Spirit in 1 Corinthians 2:10–11: "For the Spirit searches everything, even the depths of God. For what person knows a man's thoughts except the spirit of the man which is in him? So also no one comprehends the thoughts of God [Gk., lit. 'the things of God'] except the Spirit of God."

Moreover, the activity of giving new birth to everyone who is born again is the work of the Holy Spirit. Jesus said, "Unless one is born of water and the Spirit, he cannot enter the kingdom of God. That which is born of the flesh is flesh, and that which is born of the Spirit is spirit. Do not marvel that I said to you, 'You must be born anew'" (John 3:5–7). But the work of giving new spiritual life to people when they become Christians is something that only God can do (cf. 1 John 3:9, "born of God"). This passage therefore gives another indication that the Holy Spirit is fully God.

Up to this point we have two conclusions, both abundantly taught throughout Scripture:

1. God is three persons.
2. Each person is fully God.

If the Bible only taught these two facts, there would be no logical problem at all in fitting them together, for the obvious solution would be that there are three Gods. The Father is fully God, the Son is fully God, and the Holy Spirit is fully God. We would have a system in which there are three equally divine beings. Such a system of belief would be called polytheism—or, more specifically, "tritheism," or belief in three Gods. But that is far from what the Bible teaches.

3. There is one God. Scripture is abundantly clear that there is one and only one God. The three different persons of the Trinity are one not only in purpose and in agreement on what they think, but they are one in essence, one in their essential nature. In other words, God is only *one being*. There are not three Gods. There is only one God.

One of the most familiar passages of the Old Testament is Deuteronomy 6:4– 5 (NIV): "Hear, O Israel: The LORD our God, *the LORD is one*. Love the LORD your God with all your heart and with all your soul and with all your strength."

When God speaks, he repeatedly makes it clear that he is the only true God; the idea that there are three Gods to be worshiped rather than one would be unthinkable in the light of these extremely strong statements. God *alone* is the one true God and there is no one like him. When he speaks, he alone is speaking—he is not speaking as one God among three who are to be worshiped. He says:

"I am the LORD, and there is no other,
     besides me there is no God;
     I gird you, though you do not know me,
that men may know, from the rising of the sun
     and from the west, that there is none besides me;
I am the LORD, and there is no other." (Isa. 45:5–6)

The New Testament also affirms that there is one God. Paul writes, "For there is *one God*, and there is one mediator between God and men, the man Christ Jesus" (1 Tim. 2:5). Paul affirms that "God is one" (Rom. 3:30). Finally, James acknowledges that even demons recognize that there is one God, even though their intellectual assent to that fact is not enough to save them: "You believe that God is one; you do well. Even the demons believe—and shudder" (James 2:19). But clearly James affirms that one "does well" to believe that "God is one."

4. All analogies have shortcomings. If we cannot adopt any of these simple solutions, then how can we put the three truths of Scripture together and maintain the doctrine of the Trinity? Sometimes people have used several analogies drawn from nature or human experience to attempt to explain this doctrine. Although these analogies can be helpful at an elementary level of understanding, they all turn out to be inadequate or misleading on further reflection. To say, for example, that God is like a three-leaf clover, which has three parts yet remains one clover, fails because each leaf is only part of the clover, and any one leaf cannot be said to be the whole clover. But in the Trinity, each of the persons is not just a separate part of God, each person is fully God.

The analogy of the three forms of water (steam, water, and ice) is also inadequate because (a) no quantity of water is ever all three of these at the same time, (b) they have different properties or characteristics, (c) the analogy has nothing that corresponds to the fact that there is only one God (there is no such thing as "one water" or "all the water in the universe"), and (d) the element of intelligent personality is lacking.

Other analogies have been drawn from human experience. It might be said that the Trinity is something like a man who is both a farmer, the mayor of his town, and an elder in his church. He functions in different roles at different times, but he is one man. However, this analogy is very deficient because there is only one person doing these three activities at different times, and the analogy cannot deal with the personal interaction among the members of the Trinity. (In fact, this analogy simply teaches the heresy called modalism, discussed below.)

So what analogy shall we use to teach the Trinity? Although the Bible uses many analogies from nature and life to teach us various aspects of God's character (God is like a rock in his faithfulness, he is like a shepherd in his care, and so on) it is interesting that Scripture nowhere uses any analogies to teach the doctrine of the Trinity. The closest we come to an analogy is found in the titles "Father" and "Son" themselves, titles that clearly speak of distinct persons and of the close relationship that exists between them in a human family. But on the human level, of course, we have two entirely separate human beings, not one being comprised of three distinct persons. It is best to conclude that no analogy adequately teaches about the Trinity, and all are misleading in significant ways.

5. Simplistic solutions must all deny one strand of biblical teaching. We now have three statements, all of which are taught in Scripture:

1. God is three persons.
2. Each person is fully God.
3. There is one God.

Throughout the history of the church there have been attempts to come up with a simple solution to the doctrine of the Trinity by denying one or another of these statements. If someone *denies the first statement,* then we are simply left with the fact that each of the persons named in Scripture (Father, Son, and Holy Spirit) is God, and there is one God. But if we do not have to say that they are distinct persons, then there is an easy solution: These are just different names for one person who acts differently at different times. Sometimes this person calls himself Father, sometimes he calls himself Son, and sometimes he calls himself Spirit. But such a solution would deny the fact that the three persons are distinct individuals, that God the Father sends God the Son into the world, that the Son prays to the Father, and that the Holy Spirit intercedes before the Father for us.

Another simple solution might be found by *denying the second statement*—that is, denying that some of the persons named in Scripture are really fully God. If we simply hold that God is three persons and that there is one God, then we might be tempted to say that some of the "persons" are not fully God, but are only subordinate or created parts of God. This solution would be taken, for example, by those who deny the full deity of the Son (and of the Holy Spirit). But, as we saw above, this solution would have to deny an entire category of biblical teaching.

Finally, as we noted above, a simple solution could come by *denying that there is one God.* But this would result in a belief in three Gods, something clearly contrary to Scripture.

Though the third error has not been common, each of the first two errors has appeared at one time or another in the history of the church, and each persists today in some groups.

C. Errors Have Come by Denying Any of the Three Statements Summarizing the Biblical Teaching

In the previous section we saw how the Bible requires that we affirm the following three statements:

1. God is three persons.
2. Each person is fully God.
3. There is one God.

Before we discuss further the differences between the Father, Son, and Holy Spirit, and the way they relate to one another, it is important that we examine some of the doctrinal errors about the Trinity that have been made in the history of the church. In this historical survey we will see some of the mistakes that we ourselves should avoid in thinking about this doctrine. In fact, the major trinitarian errors that have arisen have come through a denial of one or another of these three primary statements.[2]

1. Modalism claims that there is one person who appears to us in three different forms (or "modes"). At various times people have taught that God is not really three distinct persons, but only one person who appears to people in different "modes" at different times. For example, in the Old Testament, God appeared as "Father." Throughout the Gospels, this same divine person appeared as "the Son" as seen in the human life and ministry of Jesus. After Pentecost, this same person then revealed himself as the "Spirit" active in the church.

Modalism gains its attractiveness from the desire to emphasize clearly the fact that there is only one God. It may claim support not only from the passages talking about one God, but also from passages such as John 10:30 ("I and the Father are one") and John 14:9 ("He who has seen me has seen the Father"). However, the last passage can simply mean that Jesus fully reveals the character of God the Father, and the former passage (John 10:30), in a context in which Jesus affirms that he will accomplish all that the Father has given him to do and save all whom the Father has given to him, seems to mean that Jesus and the Father are one in purpose.

The fatal shortcoming of modalism is the fact that it must deny the personal relationships within the Trinity that appear in so many places in Scripture (or it must affirm that these were simply an illusion and not real). Thus, it must deny three separate persons at the baptism of Jesus, where the Father speaks from heaven and the

---

[2]An excellent discussion of the history and theological implications of the trinitarian heresies discussed in this section is found in Harold O. J. Brown, *Heresies: The Image of Christ in the Mirror of Heresy and Orthodoxy from the Apostles to the Present* (Garden City, N.Y.: Doubleday, 1984; reprint, Peabody, Mass.: Hendrickson, 1998), pp. 95–157.

Spirit descends on Jesus like a dove. And it must say that all those instances where Jesus is praying to the Father are an illusion or a charade. The idea of the Son or the Holy Spirit interceding for us before God the Father is lost. Finally, modalism ultimately loses the heart of the doctrine of the atonement—that is, the idea that God sent his Son as a substitutionary sacrifice, and that the Son bore the wrath of God in our place, and that the Father, representing the interests of the Trinity, saw the suffering of Christ and was satisfied (Isa. 53:11).

2. Arianism denies the full deity of the Son and the Holy Spirit. The term *Arianism* is derived from Arius, a bishop of Alexandria whose views were condemned at the Council of Nicea in A.D. 325, and who died in A.D. 336. Arius taught that God the Son was at one point created by God the Father, and that before that time the Son did not exist, nor did the Holy Spirit, but the Father only. Thus, though the Son is a heavenly being who existed before the rest of creation and who is far greater than all the rest of creation, he is still not equal to the Father in all his attributes— he may even be said to be "like the Father" or "similar to the Father" in his nature, but he cannot be said to be "of the same nature" as the Father.

The Arians depended heavily on texts that called Christ God's "only begotten" Son (John 1:14; 3:16, 18; 1 John 4:9). If Christ were "begotten" by God the Father, they reasoned, it must mean that he was brought into existence by God the Father (for the word *beget* in human experience refers to the father's role in conceiving a child). Further support for the Arian view was found in Colossians 1:15, "He is the image of the invisible God, the first-born of all creation." Does not "first-born" here imply that the Son was at some point brought into existence by the Father? And if this is true of the Son, it must necessarily be true of the Holy Spirit as well.

But these texts do not require us to believe the Arian position. Colossians 1:15, which calls Christ "the first-born of all creation," is better understood to mean that Christ has the rights or privileges of the "first-born"—that is, according to biblical usage and custom, the right of leadership or authority in the family for one's generation. (Note Heb. 12:16 where Esau is said to have sold his "first-born status," or "birthright"—the Greek word *prōtotokia* is cognate to the term *prōtotokos,* "first-born," in Col. 1:15.) So Colossians 1:15 means that Christ has the privileges of authority and rule, the privileges belonging to the "first-born," but with respect to the whole creation. The NIV translates it helpfully, "the firstborn *over all creation.*"

Arian arguments that used texts that refer to Christ as God's "only begotten Son" are based on a misunderstanding of the Greek word *monogenēs* (translated by, for example, the KJV as "only begotten" in John 1:14, 18; 3:16, 18; 1 John 4:9). For many years it was thought that the word derived from two Greek terms, *mono* meaning "only" and *gennaō,* meaning "beget," or "bear." But linguistic study in the twentieth century has shown that the second half of the word is actually related to the word *genos,* meaning "class," or "kind." Thus, the word means rather "one of a kind" or "unique" son (see also Heb. 11:17, where Isaac is Abraham's *monogenēs,* even though he was not an only child). Rather than referring in some way to Christ's descent from the Father, these verses affirm Christ's unique status as God's Son.

In spite of the early church's misunderstanding of this term *monogenēs,* it felt so strongly the force of many other texts showing that Christ was fully and completely God that it concluded that, whatever "only begotten" meant, it did not mean "created." Therefore the Nicene Creed in 325 affirmed that Christ was "begotten, not made":

We believe in one God, the Father Almighty, Maker of all things visible and invisible.

And in one Lord Jesus Christ, the Son of God, begotten of the Father, the only-begotten; that is, of the essence of the Father, God of God, Light of Light, very God of very God, *begotten, not made*, being of one substance *[homoousion]* with the Father. . . .[3]

In further repudiation of the teaching of Arius, the Nicene Creed insisted that Christ was "of the same substance as the Father." The dispute with Arius concerned two words that have become famous in the history of Christian doctrine, *homoousios* ("of the same nature") and *homoiousios* ("of a similar nature"). The difference depends on the different meaning of two Greek prefixes, *homo-*, meaning "same," and *homoi-*, meaning "similar." Arius was happy to say that Christ was a supernatural heavenly being and that he was created by God before the creation of the rest of the universe, and even that he was "similar" to God in his nature. Thus, Arius would agree to the word *homoiousios*. But the Council of Nicea in 325 and the Council of Constantinople in 381 realized that this did not go far enough, for if Christ is not of exactly the same nature as the Father, then he is not fully God. So both councils insisted that orthodox Christians confess Jesus to be *homoousios*, of the *same* nature as God the Father. While the difference between the two words was only one letter, this difference was indeed profound, marking the difference between biblical Christianity and heresy, between a true doctrine of the Trinity and a heresy that did not accept the full deity of Christ and therefore was nontrinitarian and ultimately destructive to the whole Christian faith.

In affirming that the Son was of the same nature as the Father, the early church also excluded a related false doctrine, *subordinationism*. While Arianism held that the Son was created and was not divine, subordinationism held that the Son was eternal (not created) and divine, but still not equal to the Father in being or attributes—the Son was inferior or "subordinate" in being to God the Father.[4] Like Arianism, this idea was clearly rejected at the Council of Nicea.

3. Tritheism denies that there is only one God. A final possible way to attempt an easy reconciliation of the biblical teaching about the Trinity would be to deny that there is only one God. The result is to say that God is three persons and each person is fully God. Therefore, there are three Gods. Technically this view would be called "tritheism."

Few persons have held this view in the history of the church. It has similarities to many ancient pagan religions that held to a multiplicity of gods. This view would result in confusion in the minds of believers. There would be no absolute worship or loyalty or devotion to one true God. We would wonder to which God we should give our ultimate allegiance. And, at a deeper level, this view would destroy any sense of ultimate unity in the universe; even in the very being of God, there would be plurality but no unity.

---

[3]This is the original form of the Nicene Creed, but it was later modified at the Council of Chalcedon in A.D. 381 and there took the form that is commonly called the Nicene Creed by churches today. This text is taken from Philip Schaff, *Creeds of Christendom*, 3 vols. (Grand Rapids: Baker, 1983; reprint of 1931 ed.), 1:28–29.

[4]The heresy of subordinationism, which holds that the Son is inferior in *being* to the Father, should be clearly distinguished from the orthodox doctrine that the Son is eternally subordinate to the Father in *role or function*. Without this truth, we would lose the doctrine of the Trinity, for we would not have any eternal personal distinctions between the Father and the Son, and they would not eternally be Father and Son. (See section D below on the differences between the Father, Son, and Holy Spirit.)

Although no modern groups advocate tritheism, perhaps many evangelicals today unintentionally tend toward tritheistic views of the Trinity, recognizing the distinct personhood of the Father, the Son, and the Holy Spirit, but seldom being aware of the unity of God as one undivided being.

4. The importance of the doctrine of the Trinity. Why was the church so concerned about the doctrine of the Trinity? Is it really essential to hold to the full deity of the Son and the Holy Spirit? Yes it is, for this teaching has implications for the very heart of the Christian faith.

First, the atonement is at stake. If Jesus is merely a created being, and not fully God, then it is hard to see how he, a creature, could bear the full wrath of God against all of our sins. Could any creature, no matter how great, really save us? Second, justification by faith alone is threatened if we deny the full deity of the Son. (This is seen today in the teaching of the Jehovah's Witnesses, who do not believe in justification by faith alone.) If Jesus is not fully God, we would rightly doubt whether we can really trust him to save us completely. Could we really depend on any creature fully for our salvation? Third, if Jesus is not infinite God, should we pray to him or worship him? Who but an infinite, omniscient God could hear and respond to all the prayers of all God's people? And who but God himself is worthy of worship? Indeed, if Jesus is merely a creature, no matter how great, it would be idolatry to worship him—yet the New Testament commands us to do so (Phil. 2:9–11; Rev. 5:12–14). Fourth, if someone teaches that Christ is a created being but nonetheless one who saved us, this teaching wrongly begins to attribute credit for salvation to a creature and not to God himself. This teaching wrongfully exalts the creature rather than the Creator, something Scripture never allows us to do. Fifth, the independence and personal nature of God are at stake: If there is no Trinity, then there were no interpersonal relationships within the being of God before creation, and, without personal relationships, it is difficult to see how God could be genuinely personal or be without the need for a creation to relate to. Sixth, the unity of the universe is at stake: If there is not perfect plurality and perfect unity in God himself, then we have no basis for thinking there can be any ultimate unity among the diverse elements of the universe either. Clearly, in the doctrine of the Trinity, the heart of the Christian faith is at stake.

D. What Are the Distinctions Between the Father, the Son, and the Holy Spirit?

After completing this survey of errors concerning the Trinity, we may now go on to ask if anything more can be said about the distinctions between the Father, Son, and Holy Spirit. If we say that each member of the Trinity is fully God, and that each person fully shares in all the attributes of God, then is there any difference at all among the persons?

1. The persons of the Trinity have different primary functions in relating to the world. When Scripture discusses the way in which God relates to the world, both in creation and in redemption, the persons of the Trinity are said to have different functions or primary activities. Sometimes this has been called the "economy of the Trinity," using *economy* in an old sense meaning "ordering of activities." (In this sense, people used to speak of the "economy of a household" or "home economics," meaning not just the financial affairs of a household, but all of the "ordering of activities" within the household.) The "economy of the Trinity" means the different ways the three persons act as they relate to the world and (as we shall see in the next section) to each other for all eternity.

We see these different functions in the work of creation. God the Father spoke the creative words to bring the universe into being. But it was God the Son, the eternal Word of God, who carried out these creative decrees. "All things were made through him, and without him was not anything made that was made" (John 1:3; see also 1 Cor. 8:6; Col 1:16; Heb. 1:2). The Holy Spirit was active as well in a different way, in "moving" or "hovering" over the face of the waters (Gen. 1:2), apparently sustaining and manifesting God's immediate presence in his creation (cf. Ps. 33:6, where "breath" should perhaps be translated "Spirit"; see also Ps. 139:7).

We can also see distinct functions in the work of redemption. God the Father planned redemption and sent his Son into the world (John 3:16; Gal. 4:4; Eph. 1:9–10). The Son obeyed the Father and accomplished redemption for us (John 6:38; Heb. 10:5–7; et al.). God the Father did not come and die for our sins, nor did God the Holy Spirit. That was the particular work of the Son. Then, after Jesus ascended back into heaven, the Holy Spirit was sent by the Father and the Son to apply redemption to us. Jesus speaks of "the Holy Spirit, whom the Father will send in my name" (John 14:26), but also says that he himself will send the Holy Spirit, for he says, "If I go, I will send him to you" (John 16:7). It is especially the role of the Holy Spirit to give us regeneration, or new spiritual life (John 3:5–8), to sanctify us (Rom. 8:13; 15:16; 1 Peter 1:2), and to empower us for service (Acts 1:8; 1 Cor. 12:7–11). In general, the work of the Holy Spirit seems to be to bring to completion the work that has been planned by God the Father and begun by God the Son.

So we may say that the role of the Father in creation and redemption has been to plan and direct and send the Son and Holy Spirit. This is not surprising, for it shows that the Father and the Son relate to one another as a father and son relate to one another in a human family: The father directs and has authority over the son, and the son obeys and is responsive to the directions of the father. The Holy Spirit is obedient to the directives of both the Father and the Son.

Thus, while the persons of the Trinity are equal in all their attributes, they nonetheless differ in their relationships to the creation. The Son and Holy Spirit are equal in deity to God the Father, but they are subordinate in their roles.

2. The persons of the Trinity eternally existed as Father, Son, and Holy Spirit. But why do the persons of the Trinity take these different roles in relating to creation? Was it accidental or arbitrary? Could God the Father have come instead of God the Son to die for our sins? Could the Holy Spirit have sent God the Father to die for our sins, and then sent God the Son to apply redemption to us?

No, it does not seem that these things could have happened, for the role of commanding, directing, and sending is appropriate to the position of the Father, after whom all human fatherhood is patterned (Eph. 3:14–15). And the role of obeying, going as the Father sends, and revealing God to us is appropriate to the role of the Son, who is also called the Word of God (cf. John 1:1–5, 14, 18; 17:4; Phil. 2:5–11). These roles could not have been reversed or the Father would have ceased to be the Father and the Son would have ceased to be the Son. And by analogy from that relationship, we may conclude that the role of the Holy Spirit is similarly one that was appropriate to the relationship he had with the Father and the Son before the world was created.

Second, before the Son came to earth, and even before the world was created, for all eternity the Father has been the Father, the Son has been the Son, and the

Holy Spirit has been the Holy Spirit. These relationships are eternal, not something that occurred only in time. We may conclude this first from the unchangeableness of God (see ch. 4). If God now exists as Father, Son, and Holy Spirit, then he has always existed as Father, Son, and Holy Spirit.

We may also conclude that the relationships are eternal from other verses in Scripture that speak of the relationships the members of the Trinity had to one another before the creation of the world. For instance, when Scripture speaks of God's work of election (see ch. 18) before the creation of the world, it speaks of the Father choosing us "in" the Son: "Blessed be the God and Father of our Lord Jesus Christ. . . . *he chose us in him* before the foundation of the world, that we should be holy and blameless before him" (Eph. 1:3–4). The initiatory act of choosing is attributed to God the Father, who regarded us as united to Christ or "in Christ" before we ever existed (see also Rom. 8:29: The Father "predestined" us "to be conformed to the image of his Son"). Even the fact that the Father "*gave* his only Son" (John 3:16) and "*sent* the Son into the world" (John 3:17) indicate that there was a Father-Son relationship before Christ came into the world.

When Scripture speaks of creation, once again it speaks of the Father creating *through* the Son, indicating a relationship prior to when creation began (see John 1:3; 1 Cor. 8:6; Heb. 1:2). But nowhere does it say that the Son or Holy Spirit created *through* the Father. These passages again imply that there was a relationship of Father (as originator) and Son (as active agent) before creation, and that this relationship made it appropriate for the different persons of the Trinity to fulfill the roles they actually did fulfill.

Therefore, the different functions that we see the Father, Son, and Holy Spirit performing are simply outworkings of an eternal relationship between the three persons, one that has always existed and will always exist for eternity. God has always existed as three distinct persons: Father, Son, and Holy Spirit. These distinctions are essential to the very nature of God himself, and they could not be otherwise.

Finally, it may be said that there are no differences in deity, attributes, or essential nature between the Father, Son, and Holy Spirit. Each person is fully God and has all the attributes of God. *The only distinctions between the members of the Trinity are in the ways they relate to each other and to the creation.* In those relationships they carry out roles that are appropriate to each person.

This truth about the Trinity has sometimes been summarized in the phrase "ontological equality but economic subordination," where the word *ontological* means "being" and *economic* refers to different activities or roles. Another way of expressing this more simply would be to say "equal in being but subordinate in role." Both parts of this phrase are necessary to a true doctrine of the Trinity: If we do not have ontological equality, not all the persons are fully God. But if we do not have economic subordination,[5] then there is no inherent difference in the way the three persons relate to one another, and consequently we do not have the three distinct persons existing as Father, Son, and Holy Spirit for all eternity.

Some recent evangelical writings have denied an eternal subordination in role among the members of the Trinity, perhaps thinking that a subordinate role necessarily implies lesser importance or lesser personhood. Of course, there is no inferiority

---

[5]Economic subordination should be carefully distinguished from the error of "subordinationism," which holds that the Son and Holy Spirit are inferior *in being* to the Father (see section C.2 above, pp. 113–14.)

of being or status among the members of the Trinity in spite of their different functions, and the idea of eternal subordination in role has clearly been part of the church's doctrine of the Trinity at least since the Council of Nicea (A.D. 325). So Charles Hodge says:

> The Nicene doctrine includes, (1) the principle of the subordination of the Son to the Father, and of the Spirit to the Father and the Son. But this subordination does not imply inferiority. . . . The subordination intended is only that which concerns the mode of subsistence and operation. . . .
>
> The creeds are nothing more than a well-ordered arrangement of the facts of Scripture which concern the doctrine of the Trinity. They assert the distinct personality of the Father, Son, and Spirit . . . and their consequent perfect equality; and the subordination of the Son to the Father, and of the Spirit to the Father and the Son, as to the mode of subsistence and operation. These are scriptural facts, to which the creeds in question add nothing; *and it is in this sense they have been accepted by the Church universal.*[6]

3. What is the relationship between the three persons and the being of God? After the preceding discussion, the question that remains unresolved is, "What is the difference between *person* and *being* in this discussion? How can we say that God is one undivided being, yet that in this one being there are three persons?"

First, it is important to affirm that each person is *completely* and *fully* God; that is, that each person has the whole fullness of God's being in himself. The Son is not partly God or just one-third of God, but the Son is wholly and fully God, and so are the Father and the Holy Spirit. Thus, it would not be right to think of the Trinity according to figure 6.1, with each person representing only one-third of God's being.

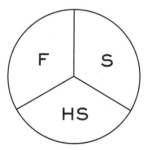

God's Being Is Not Divided Into Three Equal Parts
Belonging to the Three Members of the Trinity

figure 6.1

Rather, we must say that the person of the Father possesses the *whole being* of God in himself. Similarly, the Son possesses the *whole being* of God in himself, and the Holy Spirit possesses the *whole being* of God in himself. When we speak of the Father, Son, and Holy Spirit together, we are not speaking of any greater being than when we speak of the Father alone, or the Son alone, or the Holy Spirit alone. The

---

[6]*Systematic Theology,* 3 vols. (Grand Rapids: Eerdmans, 1970; first published 1871–73), 1:460–62 (italics mine).

Father is *all* of God's being. The Son also is *all* of God's being. And the Holy Spirit is *all* of God's being.

But if each person is *fully God* and has *all* of God's being, then we also should not think that the personal distinctions are any kind of additional attributes added on to the being of God, something after the pattern of figure 6.2.

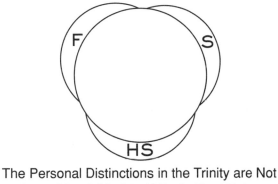

The Personal Distinctions in the Trinity are Not
Something Added onto God's Real Being

figure 6.2

Rather, each person of the Trinity has all of the attributes of God, and no one person has any attributes that are not possessed by the others.

On the other hand, we must say that the persons are *real*, that they are not just different ways of looking at the one being of God. (This would be modalism, as discussed above.) So figure 6.3 would not be appropriate.

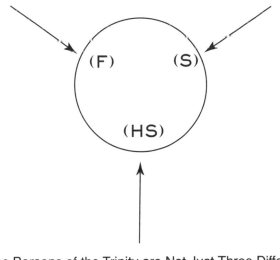

The Persons of the Trinity are Not Just Three Different
Ways of Looking at the One Being of God

figure 6.3

Rather, we need to think of the Trinity in such a way that the reality of the three persons is maintained, and each person is seen as relating to the others as an "I" (a first person) and a "you" (a second person) and a "he" (a third person).

The only way it seems possible to do this is to say that the distinction between the persons is not a difference in "being" but a difference in "relationships." This is something far removed from our human experience, where every different human "person" is a different being as well. Somehow God's being is so much greater than ours that within his one undivided being there can be an unfolding into interpersonal relationships so that there can be three distinct persons.

What then are the differences between Father, Son, and Holy Spirit? There is no difference in attributes at all. The only difference between them is the way they *relate* to each other and to the creation. The unique quality of the Father is the way he *relates as Father* to the Son and Holy Spirit. The unique quality of the Son is the way he *relates as Son.* And the unique quality of the Holy Spirit is the way he *relates as Spirit.*

Figure 6.4 may be helpful in thinking about the existence of three persons in the one undivided being of God.

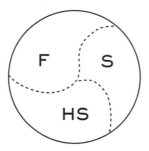

There are Three Distinct Persons, and the Being of
Each Person is Equal to the Whole Being of God

figure 6.4

In figure 6.4, the Father is represented as the section of the circle designated by F and also the rest of the circle moving around clockwise from the letter F; the Son is represented as the section of the circle designated by S and also the rest of the circle moving around clockwise from the letter S; and the Holy Spirit is represented as the section of the circle marked HS and also the rest of the circle moving around clockwise from the HS. Thus, there are three distinct persons, but each person is fully and wholly God. Of course the representation is imperfect, for it cannot represent God's infinity, personality, or indeed any of his attributes. It also requires looking at the circle in more than one way in order to understand it. The dotted lines must be understood to indicate personal relationship, not any division in the one being of God. Thus, the circle itself represents God's being while the dotted lines represent a form of personal existence other than a difference in being. But the diagram may nonetheless help guard against some misunderstanding.

From this discussion it is clear that this tri-personal form of being is far beyond our ability to comprehend. *It is a kind of existence far different from anything we have experienced* and far different from anything else in the universe. Because the existence of three persons in one God is something beyond our understanding, Christian theology has come to use the word *person* to speak of these differences in relationship, not because we fully understand what is meant by the word *person* when referring to the Trinity, but rather so that we might say something instead of saying nothing at all.

4. Can we understand the doctrine of the Trinity? We should be warned by the errors that have been made in the past. They have all come about through attempts to simplify the doctrine of the Trinity and make it completely understandable, removing all mystery from it. This we can never do. However, it is not correct to say that we cannot understand the doctrine of the Trinity at all. Certainly we can understand and know that God is three persons, and that each person is fully God, and that there is one God. We can know these things because the Bible teaches them. Moreover, we can know some things about the way in which the persons relate to each other (see the section above). But what we cannot understand fully is how to fit together those distinct biblical teachings. We wonder how there can be three distinct persons and each person have the whole being of God in himself, and yet God is only one undivided being. This we are unable to understand. In fact, it is spiritually healthy for us to acknowledge openly that God's very being is far greater than we can ever comprehend. This humbles us before God and draws us to worship him without reservation.

But it should also be said that Scripture does not ask us to believe in a contradiction. A contradiction would be "There is one God and there is not one God," or "God is three persons and God is not three persons," or even (which is similar to the previous statement) "God is three persons and God is one person." But to say that "God is three persons and there is one God" is not a contradiction. It is something we do not understand, and it is therefore a mystery or a paradox, but that should not trouble us as long as the different aspects of the mystery are clearly taught by Scripture, for as long as we are finite creatures and not omniscient deity, there will always (for all eternity) be things that we do not fully understand.

E. Application

Because God in himself has both unity and diversity, it is not surprising that unity and diversity are also reflected in the human relationships he has established. We see this first in marriage. When God created man in his own image, he did not create merely isolated individuals, but Scripture tells us, "Male and female he created them" (Gen. 1:27). And in the unity of marriage (see Gen. 2:24) we see, not a tri-unity as with God, but at least a remarkable unity of two persons, persons who remain distinct individuals yet also become one in body, mind, and spirit (cf. 1 Cor. 6:16–20; Eph. 5:31). In fact, in the relationship between man and woman in marriage, we see also a picture of the relationship between the Father and Son in the Trinity. Paul says, "But I want you to understand that the head of every man is Christ, the head of a woman is her husband, and the head of Christ is God" (1 Cor. 11:3). Here, just as the Father has authority over the Son in the Trinity, so the husband has authority over the wife in marriage. The husband's role is parallel to that of God the Father and the wife's role is parallel to that of God the Son. Moreover, just as Father and Son are equal in deity and importance and personhood, so the husband and wife are equal in humanity and importance and personhood. And, although it is not explicitly mentioned in Scripture, the gift of children within marriage, coming from both the father and the mother, and subject to the authority of both father and mother, is analogous to the relationship of the Holy Spirit to the Father and Son in the Trinity.

We also see a reflection of God's diversity and unity in the church, which has "many members" yet "one body" (1 Cor. 12:12). We have many different members in our churches with different gifts and interests, and we depend on and help each other, thereby demonstrating great diversity and great unity at the same time. When we see different people doing many different things in the life of a church, we ought to thank God that this allows us to glorify him by reflecting something of the unity and diversity of the Trinity.

We should also notice that God's purpose in the history of the universe has frequently been to display unity in diversity, and thus to display his glory. We see this not only in the church but also in the unity of Jews and Gentiles, so that all races, diverse as they are, are united in Christ (Eph. 2:16; 3:8–10; see also Rev. 7:9). Paul is amazed that God's plans for the history of redemption have been like a great symphony so that his wisdom is beyond finding out (Rom. 11:33–36). Even in the mysterious unity between Christ and the church, in which we are called the bride of Christ (Eph. 5:31–32), we see unity beyond what we ever would have imagined, unity with the Son of God himself. Yet in all this we never lose our individual identity but remain distinct persons always able to worship and serve God as unique individuals.

Eventually, the entire universe will partake of this unity of purpose with every diverse part contributing to the worship of God the Father, Son, and Holy Spirit, for one day, at the name of Jesus every knee will bow "in heaven and on earth and under the earth, and every tongue confess that Jesus Christ is Lord, to the glory of God the Father" (Phil. 2:10–11).

On a more everyday level, there are many activities that we carry out as human beings (in the labor force, in social organizations, in musical performances, and in athletic teams, for example) in which many distinct individuals contribute to a unity of purpose or activity. As we see in these activities a reflection of the wisdom of God in allowing us both unity and diversity, we can see a faint reflection of the glory of God in his trinitarian existence. Though we will never fully comprehend the mystery of the Trinity, we can worship God for who he is both in our songs of praise, and in our words and actions as they reflect something of his excellent character.

II. REVIEW QUESTIONS

1. Provide scriptural evidence for the doctrine of the Trinity from both the Old and New Testaments.
2. List the three statements given in the chapter that summarize the biblical teaching on the Trinity, and give scriptural support for each one.
3. Which of the above three statements does each of the following heresies deny?
    - Modalism
    - Arianism
    - Subordinationism
    - Tritheism
4. What are the distinctions between the persons of the Trinity? How do these distinctions apply to the work of creation? Of redemption?

III. QUESTIONS FOR PERSONAL APPLICATION

1. Why is God pleased when people exhibit faithfulness, love, and harmony within a family? What are some ways in which members of your family reflect the diversity found in the members of the Trinity? What are some ways in which your family relationships could reflect the unity of the Trinity more fully? How might the diversity of persons in the Trinity encourage parents to allow their children to develop different interests from each other, and from their parents, without thinking that the unity of the family will be damaged?

2. Have you ever thought that if your church allows new or different kinds of ministries to develop, it might hinder the unity of the church? How might the fact of unity and diversity in the Trinity help you to approach those questions?

3. Do you think that the trinitarian nature of God is more fully reflected in a church in which all the members have the same racial background, or one in which the members come from many different races (see Eph. 3:1–10)?

4. In addition to our relationships within our families, we all exist in other relationships to human authority—as in government, employment, voluntary societies, educational institutions, and athletics. Whether in the family or one of these other areas, give one example of a way in which your use of authority or your response to authority might become more like the pattern of relationships in the Trinity.

5. In the being of God we have infinite unity combined with the preservation of distinct personalities belonging to the members of the Trinity. How can this fact reassure us if we ever begin to fear that becoming more united to Christ, and to one another in the church, might tend to obliterate our individual personalities? In heaven, do you think you will be exactly like everyone else, or will you have a personality that is distinctly your own? How do Eastern religions (such as Buddhism) differ from Christianity in this regard?

IV. SPECIAL TERMS

Arianism

economic subordination

homoiousios

homoousios

modalism

only-begotten

ontological equality

subordinationism

Trinity

tritheism

V. SCRIPTURE MEMORY PASSAGE

MATTHEW 3:16–17

And when Jesus was baptized, he went up immediately from the water, and behold, the heavens were opened and he saw the Spirit of God descending like a dove, and alighting on him; and lo, a voice from heaven, saying, "This is my beloved Son, with whom I am well pleased."

Chapter Seven

Creation

+ *Why, how, and when did God create the universe?*

I. EXPLANATION AND SCRIPTURAL BASIS

How did God create the world? Did he create every different kind of plant and animal directly, or did he use some kind of evolutionary process, guiding the development of living things from the simplest to the most complex? And how quickly did God bring about creation? Was it all completed within six twenty-four-hour days, or did he use thousands or perhaps millions of years? How old is the earth, and how old is the human race?

These questions face us when we deal with the doctrine of creation. Unlike most of the earlier material in this book, this chapter treats several questions on which evangelical Christians have differing viewpoints, sometimes very strongly held ones.

This chapter is organized to move from those aspects of creation that are most clearly taught in Scripture, and on which almost all evangelicals would agree (creation out of nothing, special creation of Adam and Eve, and the goodness of the universe), to other aspects of creation about which evangelicals have had disagreements (whether God used a process of evolution to bring about much of creation, and how old the earth and the human race are).

We may define the doctrine of creation as follows: *God created the entire universe out of nothing; it was originally very good; and he created it to glorify himself.*

A. God Created the Universe Out of Nothing

1. Biblical evidence for creation out of nothing. The Bible clearly requires us to believe that God created the universe out of nothing. (Sometimes the Latin phrase *ex nihilo,* "out of nothing," is used; it is then said that the Bible teaches creation *ex nihilo.*) This means that before God began to create the universe, nothing else existed except God himself.

This is the implication of Genesis 1:1, which says, "In the beginning God created the heavens and the earth." The phrase "the heavens and the earth" includes the entire universe. Psalm 33 also tells us, "By the word of the LORD the heavens were made, and all their host by the breath of his mouth. . . . For he spoke, and it came to be; he commanded, and it stood forth" (Ps. 33:6, 9). In the New Testament we find a universal statement at the beginning of John's gospel: "*All things were made through him, and without him was not anything made that was made*" (John 1:3). The phrase "all things" is best taken to refer to the entire universe (cf. Acts 17:24; Heb. 11:3). Paul is quite explicit in Colossians 1 when he specifies all the parts of the universe, both visible and invisible things: "In him *all things* were created, in heaven and on earth, *visible and invisible,* whether thrones or dominions or principalities or authorities—all things were created through him and for him" (Col. 1:16).

Hebrews 11:3 says, "By faith we understand that the worlds were prepared by the word of God, so that what is seen was not made out of things which are visible" (NASB). This translation (as well as the NIV) most accurately reflects the Greek text. Though the text does not quite teach the doctrine of creation out of nothing, it comes close to doing so, since it says that God did not create the universe out of anything that is visible. The somewhat strange idea that the universe might have been created out of something that was invisible is probably not in the author's mind. He is contradicting the idea of creation out of previously existing matter, and for that purpose the verse is quite clear.

Because God created the entire universe out of nothing, no matter in the universe is eternal. All that we see—the mountains, the oceans, the stars, the earth itself—all came into existence when God created them. This reminds us that God rules over all the universe and that nothing in creation is to be worshiped instead of God or in addition to him. However, were we to deny creation out of nothing, we would have to say that some matter has always existed and that it is eternal like God. This idea would challenge God's independence, his sovereignty, and the fact that worship is due to him alone. If matter existed apart from God, then what inherent right would God have to rule over it and use it for his glory? And what confidence could we have that every aspect of the universe will ultimately fulfill God's purposes if some parts of it were not created by him?

The positive side of the fact that God created the universe out of nothing is that it has meaning and a purpose. God, in his wisdom, created it *for something.* We should try to understand that purpose and use creation in ways that fit that purpose, namely, to bring glory to God himself.[1] Moreover, whenever the creation brings us joy (cf. 1 Tim. 6:17), we should give thanks to the God who made it all.

2. *The direct creation of Adam and Eve.* The Bible also teaches that God created Adam and Eve in a special, personal way. "The LORD God formed man of dust from the ground, and breathed into his nostrils the breath of life; and man became a living being" (Gen. 2:7). After that, God created Eve from Adam's body: "So the LORD God caused a deep sleep to fall upon the man, and while he slept took one of his ribs and closed up its place with flesh; and the rib which the LORD God had taken from the man he made into a woman and brought her to the man" (Gen. 2:21–22). God apparently let Adam know something of what had happened, for Adam says,

> "This at last is bone of my bones
> and flesh of my flesh;
> she shall be called Woman,
> because she was taken out of Man." (Gen. 2:23)

As we shall see below, Christians differ on the extent to which evolutionary developments may have occurred after creation, perhaps (according to some) leading to the development of more and more complex organisms. While there are sincerely

---

[1]See section C below (pp. 130–31) on God's purpose for creation.

held differences on that question among Christians with respect to the plant and animal kingdoms, these texts are so explicit that it would be very difficult for someone to hold to the complete truthfulness of Scripture and still hold that human beings are the result of a long evolutionary process. This is because when Scripture says that the Lord "formed man of dust from the ground" (Gen. 2:7), it does not seem possible to understand that to mean that he did it over a process that took millions of years and employed the random development of thousands of increasingly complex organisms. Even more impossible to reconcile with an evolutionary view is the fact that this narrative clearly portrays Eve as having no female parent; she was created directly from Adam's rib while Adam slept (Gen. 2:21). But on a purely evolutionary view, this would not be possible, for even the very first female "human being" would have been descended from some nearly human creature that was still an animal. The New Testament reaffirms the historicity of this special creation of Eve from Adam when Paul says, "For man was not made from woman, but woman from man. Neither was man created for woman, but woman for man" (1 Cor. 11:8–9).

The special creation of Adam and Eve shows that, though we may be like animals in many respects in our physical bodies, nonetheless we are very different from animals. We are created "in God's image," the pinnacle of God's creation, more like God than any other creature, appointed to rule over the rest of creation. Even the brevity of the Genesis account of creation (compared with the story of human beings in the rest of the Bible) places a wonderful emphasis on the importance of man in distinction from the rest of the universe. It thus resists modern tendencies to see man as meaningless against the immensity of the universe.

3. The work of the Son and of the Holy Spirit in creation. God the Father was the primary agent in initiating the act of creation. But the Son and the Holy Spirit were also active. The Son is often described as the one "through" whom creation came about. "All things were made *through* him, and without him was not anything made that was made" (John 1:3). Paul says there is "one Lord, Jesus Christ, *through* whom are all things and *through* whom we exist" (1 Cor. 8:6), and, "all things were created *through* him and for him" (Col. 1:16). These passages give a consistent picture of the Son as the active agent carrying out the plans and directions of the Father.

The Holy Spirit was also at work in creation. He is generally pictured as completing, filling, and giving life to God's creation. In Genesis 1:2, "the Spirit of God was moving over the face of the waters," indicating a preserving, sustaining, governing function. Job says, "The spirit of God has made me, and the breath of the Almighty gives me life" (Job 33:4). In a number of Old Testament passages, it is important to realize that the same Hebrew word *(rûach)* can mean, in different contexts, "spirit," "breath," or "wind." But in many cases there is not much difference in meaning, for even if one decided to translate some phrases as the "breath of God" or even the "wind of God," it would still seem to be a figurative way of referring to the activity of the Holy Spirit in creation. So the psalmist, in speaking of the great variety of creatures on the earth and in the sea, says, "When you send forth your Spirit, they are created" (Ps. 104:30; note also, on the Holy Spirit's work, Job 26:13; Isa. 40:13; 1 Cor. 2:10).

B. Creation Is Distinct from God Yet Always Dependent on God

The teaching of Scripture about the relationship between God and creation is unique among the religions of the world. The Bible teaches that God is distinct from his creation. He is not part of it, for he has made it and rules over it. The term often used to say that God is much greater than creation is the word *transcendent*. Very simply, this means that God is far "above" the creation in the sense that he is greater than the creation and he is independent of it.

God is also very much involved in creation, for it is continually dependent on him for its existence and its functioning. The technical term used to speak of God's involvement in creation is the word *immanent*, meaning "remaining in" creation. The God of the Bible is no abstract deity removed from and uninterested in his creation. The Bible is the story of God's involvement with his creation and particularly with the people in it. Job affirms that even the animals and plants depend on God: "In his hand is the life of every living thing and the breath of all mankind" (Job 12:10). In the New Testament, Paul affirms that God "gives to all men life and breath and everything" and that "in him we live and move and have our being" (Acts 17:25, 28). Indeed, in Christ "all things hold together" (Col. 1:17), and he is continually "upholding the universe by his word of power" (Heb. 1:3). God's transcendence and immanence are both affirmed in a single verse when Paul speaks of "one God and Father of us all, who is above all and through all and in all" (Eph. 4:6).

The fact that creation is distinct from God yet always dependent on God, that God is far above creation yet always involved in it (in brief, that God is both *transcendent* and *immanent*), may be represented as in figure 7.1.

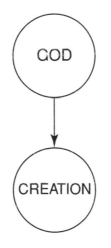

Creation Is Distinct From God Yet Always Dependent on God
(God Is Both Transcendent and Immanent)

figure 7.1

This is clearly distinct from *materialism*, which is the most common philosophy of unbelievers today and which denies the existence of God altogether. Materialism would say that the material universe is all there is. It may be represented as in figure 7.2.

Materialism

figure 7.2

Christians today who focus almost the entire effort of their lives on earning more money and acquiring more possessions become "practical" materialists in their activity, since their lives would be not much different if they did not believe in God at all.

The scriptural account of God's relation to his creation is also distinct from *pantheism*. The Greek word *pan* means "all" or "every," and *pantheism* is the idea that everything, the whole universe, is God, or is part of God. This can be pictured as in figure 7.3.

Pantheism

figure 7.3

Pantheism denies several essential aspects of God's character. If the whole universe is God, then God has no distinct personality. God is no longer unchanging, because as the universe changes, God also changes. Moreover, God is no longer holy, because the evil in the universe is also part of God. Another difficulty is that ultimately most pantheistic systems (such as Buddhism and many other Eastern religions) end up denying the importance of individual human personalities: Since everything is God, the goal of an individual should be to blend in with the universe and become more and more united with it, thus losing his or her individual distinctiveness. If God himself (or itself) has no distinct personal identity separate from the universe, then we should certainly not strive to have one either. Thus, pantheism destroys not only the personal identity of God, but also, ultimately, of human beings as well.

The biblical account also rules out *dualism*. This is the idea that both God and the material universe have eternally existed side by side. Thus, there are two ultimate forces in the universe, God and matter. This may be represented as in figure 7.4.

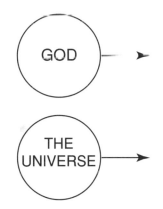

Dualism

figure 7.4

The problem with dualism is that it indicates an eternal conflict between God and the evil aspects of the material universe. Will God ultimately triumph over evil in the universe? We cannot be sure, because both God and evil have apparently always existed side by side. This philosophy would deny both God's ultimate lordship over creation, and also that creation came about because of God's will, that it is to be used solely for his purposes, and that it is to glorify him. This viewpoint would also deny that all of the universe was created inherently good (Gen. 1:31) and would encourage people to view material reality as somewhat evil in itself, in contrast with a genuine biblical account of a creation that God made to be good and that he rules over for his purposes.

One example of dualism in modern culture is the *Star Wars* trilogy, which postulates the existence of a universal "Force" that has both a good and an evil side. There is no concept of one holy and transcendent God who rules over all and will certainly triumph over all. When non-Christians today begin to be aware of a spiritual aspect to the universe, they often become dualists, merely acknowledging that there are good and evil aspects to the supernatural or spiritual world. Most New Age religion is dualistic. Of course, Satan is delighted to have people think that there is an evil force in the universe that is perhaps equal to God himself.

The Christian view of creation is also distinct from the viewpoint of *deism*. Deism is the view that God is not now directly involved in the creation. It may be represented as in figure 7.5 on the following page.

Deism generally holds that God created the universe and is far greater than the universe (God is "transcendent"). Some deists also agree that God has moral standards and will ultimately hold people accountable on a day of judgment. But they deny God's present involvement in the world, thus leaving no place for his immanence in the created order. Rather, God is viewed as a divine clock maker who wound up the "clock" of creation at the beginning but then left it to run on its own.

While deism does affirm God's transcendence in some ways, it denies almost the entire history of the Bible, which is the history of God's active involvement in the world. Many "lukewarm" or nominal Christians today are, in effect, practical

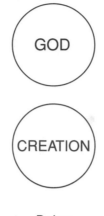

Deism

figure 7.5

deists, since they live lives almost totally devoid of genuine prayer, worship, fear of God, or moment-by-moment trust in God to care for needs that arise.

C. God Created the Universe to Show His Glory

It is clear that God created his people for his own glory, for he speaks of his sons and daughters as those "whom I created *for my glory,* whom I formed and made" (Isa. 43:7). But it is not only human beings that God created for this purpose. The entire creation is intended to show God's glory. Even the inanimate creation, the stars and sun and moon and sky, testify to God's greatness: "The heavens are telling the glory of God; and the firmament proclaims his handiwork. Day to day pours forth speech, and night to night declares knowledge" (Ps. 19:1–2). The song of heavenly worship in Revelation 4 connects God's creation of all things with the fact that he is worthy to receive glory from them:

> "*You are worthy,* our Lord and God,
> *to receive glory* and honor and power,
> for you have created all things,
> and by your will they existed and were created." (Rev. 4:11)

What does creation show about God? Primarily it shows his great power and wisdom, far above anything that could be imagined by any creature.[2] "It is he who made the earth by his power, who established the world by his wisdom, and by his understanding stretched out the heavens" (Jer. 10:12). One glance at the sun or the stars convinces us of God's infinite power. And even a brief inspection of any leaf on a tree, or of the wonder of the human hand, or of any one living cell, convinces us of God's great wisdom. Who could make all of this? Who could make it out of nothing? Who could sustain it day after day for endless years? Such infinite power, such intricate skill, is completely beyond our comprehension. When we meditate on it, we give glory to God.

---

[2]See ch. 3, pp. 54–58, for a discussion of the necessity of Scripture if we are to interpret creation rightly.

When we affirm that God created the universe to show his glory, it is important that we realize that he did not need to create it. We should not think that God needed more glory than he had within the Trinity for all eternity or that he was somehow incomplete without the glory that he would receive from the created universe. This would be to deny God's independence and imply that God needed the universe in order to be fully God.[3] Rather, we must affirm that the creation of the universe was a *totally free act of God*. It was not a necessary act but something that God chose to do. "You created all things, and *by your will* they existed and were created" (Rev. 4:11). God desired to create the universe to demonstrate his excellence. The creation shows his great wisdom and power, and ultimately it shows all of his other attributes as well.[4] It seems that God created the universe, then, to take delight in his creation, for as creation shows forth various aspects of God's character, to that extent he does take delight in it.

This explains why we take spontaneous delight in all sorts of creative activities ourselves. People with artistic, musical, or literary skills enjoy creating things and seeing, hearing, or pondering their creative work. God has so made us that we enjoy imitating, in a creaturely way, his creative activity. And one of the amazing aspects of humanity—in distinction from the rest of creation—is our ability to create new things. This also explains why we take delight in other kinds of "creative" activity: Many people enjoy cooking, decorating their home, gardening, working with wood or other materials, producing scientific inventions, or devising new solutions to problems in industrial production. Even children enjoy coloring pictures or building houses out of blocks. In all of these activities, we reflect in small measure the creative activity of God, and we should delight in it and thank him for it.

D. The Universe God Created Was "Very Good"

This point follows from the previous point. If God created the universe to show his glory, then we would expect that the universe would fulfill the purpose for which he created it. In fact, when God finished his work of creation, he did take delight in it. At the end of each stage of creation, God saw that what he had done was "good" (Gen. 1:4, 10, 12, 18, 21, 25). Then at the end of the six days of creation, "God saw everything that he had made, and behold, *it was very good*" (Gen. 1:31). God delighted in the creation that he had made just as he had purposed to do.

Even though there is now sin in the world, the material creation is still good in God's sight and should be seen as "good" by us as well. This knowledge will free us from a false asceticism that sees the use and enjoyment of the material creation as wrong. Paul says that "everything created by God *is good*, and nothing is to be rejected if it is received with thanksgiving; for then it is consecrated by the word of God and prayer" (1 Tim. 4:4–5).

Though the created order can be used in sinful or selfish ways, and can turn our affections away from God, nonetheless we must not let the danger of the abuse of God's creation keep us from a positive, thankful, joyful use of it for our own enjoyment and for the good of his kingdom. Shortly after Paul has warned against the desire to be rich and the "love of money" (1 Tim. 6:9–10), he affirms that it is God himself "who richly furnishes us with everything to enjoy" (1 Tim. 6:17). This fact

---

[3]See the discussion of God's independence in ch. 4, pp. 71–73, and his freedom in ch. 5, pp. 95–99.

[4]See the discussion in ch. 4, p. 68, on the ways in which all of creation reveals various aspects of God's character.

gives warrant for Christians to encourage proper industrial and technological development (together with care for the environment), and joyful and thankful use of all the products of the abundant earth that God has created—amazing varieties of food, clothing, and housing, as well as thousands of modern products like automobiles, airplanes, cameras, telephones, and computers. All these things can be overvalued and misused, but in themselves they are not evil; they are developments from God's good creation and should be seen as good gifts from God.

E. The Relationship Between Scripture and the Findings of Modern Science

At various times in history, Christians have found themselves dissenting from the accepted findings of contemporary science. In the vast majority of cases, sincere Christian faith and strong trust in the Bible have led scientists to the discovery of new facts about God's universe, and these discoveries have changed scientific opinion for all of subsequent history. The lives of Isaac Newton, Galileo Galilei, Johannes Kepler, Blaise Pascal, Robert Boyle, Michael Faraday, James Clerk Maxwell, and many others are examples of this.

On the other hand, there have been times when accepted scientific opinion has been in conflict with people's understanding of what the Bible said. For example, when the Italian astronomer Galileo (1564–1642) began to teach that the earth was not the center of the universe but that the earth and other planets revolved around the sun (thus following the theories of the Polish astronomer Copernicus [1472–1543]), he was criticized, and eventually his writings were condemned by the Roman Catholic Church. This was because many people thought that the Bible taught that the sun revolved about the earth. In fact, the Bible does not teach that at all, but it was Copernican astronomy that made people look again at Scripture to see if it really taught what they thought it taught. Descriptions in the Bible of the sun rising and setting (Eccl. 1:5; et al.) merely portray events as they appear from the perspective of the human observer, and from that perspective, they give an accurate description. The lesson of Galileo, who was forced to recant his teachings and who had to live under house arrest for the last few years of his life, should remind us that careful observation of the natural world can cause us to go back to Scripture and reexamine whether Scripture actually teaches what we think it teaches. Sometimes, on closer examination of the text, we may find that our previous interpretations were incorrect.

In the following section, we have listed some principles by which the relationship between creation and the findings of modern science can be approached.

1. When all the facts are rightly understood, there will be "no final conflict" between Scripture and natural science. The phrase "no final conflict" is taken from a very helpful book by Francis Schaeffer, *No Final Conflict*.[5] Regarding questions about the creation of the universe, Schaeffer lists several areas where, in his judgment, there is room for disagreement among Christians who believe in the total truthfulness of Scripture. Among these areas he includes the possibility that God created a "grown-up" universe, the possibility of a break between Genesis 1:1 and 1:2 or between 1:2 and 1:3, the possibility of a long day in Genesis 1, and the possibility that the flood affected the geological data. Schaeffer makes clear that he is not saying that any of these positions is his own; only that they are theoretically possi-

---

[5]Downers Grove, Ill.: InterVarsity Press, 1975.

ble. Schaeffer's major point is that in both our understanding of the natural world and in our understanding of Scripture, our knowledge is not perfect. But we can approach both scientific and biblical study with the confidence that when all the facts are correctly understood, and when we have understood Scripture rightly, our findings will never be in conflict with each other; there will be "no final conflict." This is because God, who speaks in Scripture, knows all facts, and he has not spoken in a way that would contradict any true fact in the universe.

2. Some theories about creation seem clearly inconsistent with the teachings of Scripture. In this section we will examine three types of explanation of the origin of the universe that seem clearly inconsistent with Scripture.

a. *Secular theories.* For the sake of completeness, we mention here only briefly that any purely secular theories of the origin of the universe would be unacceptable for those who believe in Scripture. A "secular" theory is any theory of the origin of the universe that does not see an infinite-personal God as responsible for creating the universe by intelligent design. Thus, the "big bang" theory (in a secular form in which God is excluded), or any theories that hold that matter has always existed, would be inconsistent with the teaching of Scripture that God created the universe out of nothing, and that he did so for his own glory. (When Darwinian evolution is thought of in a totally materialistic sense, as it most often is, it would belong in this category also.)[6]

b. *Theistic evolution.* Ever since the publication of Charles Darwin's *Origin of Species by Means of Natural Selection* (1859), some Christians have proposed that living organisms came about by the process of evolution Darwin propounded but that God guided that process so that the result was just what he wanted it to be. This view is called *theistic evolution* because it advocates belief in God (it is "theistic") and in evolution too. Many who hold to theistic evolution would propose that God intervened in the process at some crucial points, usually (1) the creation of matter at the beginning, (2) the creation of the simplest life form, and (3) the creation of man. But with the possible exception of those points of intervention, theistic evolutionists hold that evolution proceeded in the ways now discovered by natural scientists and that it was the process God decided to use in allowing all of the other forms of life on earth to develop. They believe that the random mutation of living things led to the evolution of higher life forms through the fact that those that had an "adaptive advantage" (a mutation that allowed them to be better fitted to survive in their environment) lived when others did not.

An examination of the scriptural data reveals that theistic evolution is at odds with the biblical account of creation. The clear teaching of Scripture that there is purposefulness in God's work of creation seems incompatible with the randomness demanded by evolutionary theory. When Scripture reports that God said, "Let the earth bring forth living creatures according to their kinds: cattle and creeping things and beasts of the earth according to their kinds" (Gen. 1:24), it pictures God as doing things intentionally and with a purpose for each thing he does. But this is the opposite of allowing mutations to proceed entirely randomly, with no purpose for the millions of mutations that would have to come about, under evolutionary theory, before a new species could emerge.

---

[6]See pp. 135–38 below, for a discussion of Darwinian evolution.

The fundamental difference between a biblical view of creation and theistic evolution lies here: The driving force that brings about change and the development of new species in all evolutionary schemes is *randomness*. Without the random mutation of organisms, you do not have evolution in the modern scientific sense at all. Random mutation is the underlying force that brings about eventual development from the simplest to the most complex life forms. But the driving force in the development of new organisms according to Scripture is God's intelligent design. "God made the wild animals according to their kinds, the livestock according to their kinds, and all the creatures that move along the ground according to their kinds. And God saw that it was good" (Gen. 1:25 NIV). These statements seem inconsistent with the idea of God creating or directing or observing millions of random mutations, none of which were "very good" in the way he intended, none of which really were the kinds of plants or animals he wanted to have on the earth. The theistic evolution view has to understand events to have occurred something like this: "And God said, 'Let the earth bring forth living creatures according to their kinds.' And after three hundred eighty-seven million, four hundred ninety-two thousand, eight hundred seventy-one attempts, God finally made a mouse that worked."

That may seem a strange explanation, but it is precisely what the theistic evolutionist must postulate for each of the hundreds of thousands of different kinds of plants and animals on the earth: They all developed through a process of random mutation over millions of years, gradually increasing in complexity as the vast majority of mutations were harmful but occasional mutations turned out to be advantageous to the creature.

A theistic evolutionist may object that God intervened in the process and guided it at many points in the direction he wanted it to go. But once this is allowed, there is purpose and intelligent design in the process—we no longer have evolution at all, because there is no longer random mutation (at the points of divine interaction, the points that really bring about the results).

Theistic evolution also seems incompatible with Scripture's picture of God's creative word as bringing immediate response. When the Bible talks about God's creative word, it emphasizes the power of his word and its ability to accomplish his purpose.

> By the word of the LORD the heavens were made,
>   and all their host by the breath of his mouth.
> . . . For he spoke, and it came to be;
>   he commanded, and it stood forth. (Ps. 33:6, 9)

This kind of statement seems at odds with the idea that God spoke, and after millions of years and millions of random mutations in living things, his power brought about the result that he had called for. Rather, as soon as God says, "Let the earth put forth vegetation," the very next sentence tells us, "And it was so" (Gen. 1:11).

God's present active role in creating or forming every living thing that now comes into being is also hard to reconcile with the distant "hands off" kind of oversight of evolution that is proposed by theistic evolution. David is able to confess, "You formed my inward parts, you knit me together in my mother's womb" (Ps. 139:13). And God said to Moses, "Who has made man's mouth? Who makes him dumb, or deaf, or seeing, or blind? Is it not I, the LORD?" (Ex. 4:11). God makes the grass grow (Ps. 104:14; Matt. 6:30) and feeds the birds (Matt. 6:26) and the other creatures of the forest (Ps. 104:21, 27–30). If God is so involved in causing the growth and development of every step of every living thing even now, does it seem consistent with Scripture to say that these life forms were originally brought about by an evolutionary process directed by random mutation rather than by God's direct, purposeful creation?

Finally, the special creation of Adam, and Eve from him, is a strong reason to break with theistic evolution. Those theistic evolutionists who argue for a special creation of Adam and Eve because of the statements in Genesis 1–2, have really broken with evolutionary theory at the point that is of most concern to human beings anyway. But if, on the basis of Scripture, we insist upon God's special intervention at the point of the creation of Adam and Eve, then what is to prevent our allowing that God intervened, in a similar way, in the creation of living organisms?

We must realize that the special creation of Adam and Eve as recorded in Scripture shows them to be far different from creatures that evolutionists would say were the first humans, primitive and minimally skilled creatures who descended from highly developed nonhuman creatures and were just barely superior to them. Scripture pictures the first man and woman, Adam and Eve, as possessing highly developed linguistic, moral, and spiritual abilities from the moment they were created. They can talk with each other. They can even talk with God. They are very different from the nearly animal first humans, descended from nonhuman apelike creatures, of evolutionary theory.

It seems most appropriate to conclude in the words of geologist Davis A. Young, "The position of theistic evolutionism as expressed by some of its proponents is not a consistently Christian position. It is not a truly biblical position, for it is based in part on principles that are imported into Christianity."[7] According to Louis Berkhof, "theistic evolution is really a child of embarrassment, which calls God in at periodic intervals to help nature over the chasms that yawn at her feet. It is neither the biblical doctrine of creation, nor a consistent theory of evolution."[8]

c. *Notes on the Darwinian theory of evolution.*

(1) *Current challenges to evolution.* The word *evolution* can be used in different ways. Sometimes it is used to refer to "micro-evolution"—small developments within one species, so that we see flies or mosquitoes becoming immune to insecticides, or human beings growing taller, or different colors and varieties of roses being developed. Innumerable examples of such micro-evolution are evident today, and no one denies that they exist. But that is not the sense in which the word *evolution* is usually used when discussing theories of creation and evolution.

The term *evolution* is more commonly used to refer to macro-evolution—that is, the "general theory of evolution," or the view that "nonliving substance gave rise to the first living material, which subsequently reproduced and diversified to produce all extinct and extant organisms."[9] In this chapter, when we use the word *evolution*, it is used to refer to macro-evolution or the general theory of evolution. In modern Darwinian evolutionary theory, the history of the development of life began when a

---

[7]Davis A. Young, *Creation and the Flood: An Alternative to Flood Geology and Theistic Evolution* (Grand Rapids: Baker, 1977), p. 38. Young includes a discussion of the views of Richard H. Bube, a leading proponent of theistic evolution (pp. 33–35).

[8]Louis Berkhof, *Introduction to Systematic Theology* (Grand Rapids: Eerdmans, 1932; reprint, Grand Rapids: Baker, 1979), pp. 139–40.

mix of chemicals present on the earth spontaneously produced a very simple, probably one-celled life form. This living cell reproduced itself, and eventually there were some mutations or differences in the new cells produced. These mutations led to the development of more complex life forms. A hostile environment meant that many of them would perish, but those that were better suited to their environment would survive and multiply. Thus, nature exercised a process of "natural selection" in which the differing organisms most fitted to the environment survived. More and more mutations eventually developed into more and more varieties of living things, so that from the very simplest organism all the complex life forms on earth eventually developed through this process of mutation and natural selection.

Since Charles Darwin first published his *Origin of Species by Means of Natural Selection* in 1859, there have been challenges to his theory by Christians and non-Christians alike. Modern critics are producing increasingly devastating critiques of evolutionary theory, demonstrating points such as the following:[10]

(a) After more than one hundred years of experimental breeding of various kinds of animals and plants, the amount of variation that can be produced (even with *intentional,* not random, breeding) is extremely limited, due to the limited range of genetic variation in each type of living thing.[11] Dogs that are selectively bred for generations are still dogs; fruit flies are still fruit flies, and so forth.

(b) The vast and complex mutations required to produce complex organs such as an eye or a bird's wing (or hundreds of other organs) could not have occurred in tiny mutations accumulating over thousands of generations, because the individual parts of the organ are useless (and give no "advantage") unless the entire organ is functioning. (The hundreds of parts needed for an eye or a bird's wing to work have to all be there, or the other parts are useless and confer no adaptive advantage.) But the mathematical probability of hundreds of such *random* mutations happening together in one generation is effectively zero.

(c) The subsequent 130 years of intensive archaeological activity since Darwin's time has still failed to produce even one convincing example of a needed "intermediate (or transitional) type," a fossil that would show some characteristics of one animal and a few characteristics of the next developmental type, which would be necessary to fill in the gaps in the fossil record between distinct kinds of animals.[12]

(d) Advances in molecular biology increasingly reveal the incredible complexity of even the simplest of organisms, and no satisfactory explanation for the origin of those differences has been given.[13]

(e) Probably the greatest difficulty of all for evolutionary theory is explaining how any life could have begun in the first place. The spontaneous generation of even

[9]Wayne Frair and Percival Davis, *A Case for Creation,* 3d ed. (Norcross, Ga.: CRS Books, 1983), p. 25.

[10]These points are drawn from Phillip E. Johnson, *Darwin on Trial* (Downers Grove, Ill.: InterVarsity Press, 1991). See also his *Reason in the Balance: The Case Against Naturalism in Science, Law, and Education* (Downers Grove, Ill.: InterVarsity Press, 1995), and *Defeating Darwinism by Opening Minds* (Downers Grove, Ill.: InterVarsity Press, 1997).

[11]Johnson, *Darwin on Trial,* pp. 15–20.

[12]Ibid., pp. 73–85, discusses the two examples sometimes claimed out of perhaps 100 million fossils that have been discovered, *Archaeopteryx* (a bird with some characteristics that resemble those of reptiles), and some apelike examples thought to be prehuman hominids. *Archaeopteryx* is still very much a bird, not a near-reptile. Study of the characteristics of the supposedly prehuman fossils includes large amounts of subjective speculation, resulting in strong differences among experts who have examined them.

[13]Ibid., pp. 86–99. An especially strong argument of irreducible complexity in living cells that can only be explained by intelligent design is found in Michael Behe, *Darwin's Black Box: The Biochemical Challenge to Evolution* (New York: Free Press, 1996).

the simplest living organism capable of independent life (the prokaryote bacterial cell) from inorganic materials on the earth could not happen by random mixing of chemicals; it requires intelligent design and craftsmanship so complex that no advanced scientific laboratory in the world has been able to do it.

It is important to notice that the preceding five arguments are not based on "the Bible versus science" (which the secular scientific community regularly dismisses as mere superstition or irrationalism), but are based on "science versus science"— that is, the arguments are simply examining the evidence found in the natural world and asking where the evidence leads. If the evidence leads one direction (for example, if it gives strong evidence of intelligent design) and a scientist's philosophical commitment to a materialistic, naturalistic explanation of the origin of life leads another direction, then what will the scientist do? Will he continue to insist that life must have a naturalistic explanation, not because scientific facts prove it, but because he has a prior commitment to explaining everything in a naturalistic way? Then we must ask, is his commitment to naturalism as a methodology founded on some evidence he has seen in investigating the world, or is it based on some philosophical ideas that he has adopted for other reasons?

Phillip Johnson quotes Richard Lewontin, an eminent Harvard biologist, who states clearly that he will always choose a naturalistic explanation in such a situation:

> We take the side of science *in spite of* the patent absurdity of some of its constructs, *in spite of* its failure to fulfill many of its extravagant promises of health and life, *in spite of* the tolerance of the scientific community for unsubstantiated, just-so stories, because we have a prior commitment, a commitment to materialism. It is not that the methods and institutions of science somehow compel us to accept a material explanation of the phenomenal world, but, on the contrary, that we are forced by our a priori adherence to material causes to create an apparatus of investigation and a set of concepts that produce material explanations, no matter how counterintuitive, no matter how mystifying to the uninitiated. Moreover, that materialism is absolute, for we cannot allow a Divine Foot in the door.[14]

Numerous challenges to the theory of evolution continue to be published. Yet it is tragic that the common opinion, perpetuated in many science textbooks today, that evolution is an established "fact," has continued to persuade many people that they should not consider the total truthfulness of the Bible to be an intellectually acceptable viewpoint for responsible, thinking individuals to hold today. One only hopes it will not be too long before the scientific community publicly acknowledges the implausibility of evolutionary theory, and textbooks written for high school and college students openly acknowledge that evolution simply is not a satisfactory explanation for the origin of life on the earth.

(2) *The destructive influences of evolutionary theory in modern thought.* It is important to understand the incredibly destructive influences that evolutionary theory has had on modern thinking. If in fact life was not created by God, and if human beings in particular are not created by God or responsible to him, but are simply the result of random occurrences in the universe, then of what significance is human life? We are merely the product of matter plus time plus chance, and so to think that

---

[14]Phillip E. Johnson, "The Unraveling of Scientific Materialism," in *First Things* 77 (November 1997), p. 22.

we have any eternal importance, or really any importance at all in the face of an immense universe, is simply to delude ourselves. Honest reflection on this notion should lead people to a profound sense of despair.

Moreover, if all of life can be explained by evolutionary theory apart from God, and if there is no God who created us (or at least if we cannot know anything about him with certainty), then there is no supreme Judge to hold us morally accountable. Therefore, there are no moral absolutes in human life, and people's moral ideas are only subjective preferences, good for them perhaps but not to be imposed on others. In fact, in such a case, the only thing forbidden is to say that one knows that certain things are right and certain things are wrong.

There is another ominous consequence of evolutionary theory: If the inevitable processes of natural selection continue to bring about improvement in life forms on earth through the survival of the fittest, then why should we hinder this process by caring for those who are weak or less able to defend themselves? Should we not rather allow them to die without reproducing, so that we might move toward a new, higher form of humanity, even a "master race"? In fact, Marx, Nietzsche, and Hitler all justified war on these grounds.

In addition, if human beings are continually evolving for the better, the wisdom of earlier generations (and particularly of earlier religious beliefs) is not likely to be as valuable as modern thought. In addition, the effect of Darwinian evolution on people's opinions of the trustworthiness of Scripture has been a very negative one.

Contemporary sociological and psychological theories that see human beings as simply higher forms of animals are another outcome of evolutionary thought. And the extremes of the modern "animal rights" movement that oppose all killing of animals (for food, leather coats, or medical research, for example) also flow naturally out of evolutionary thought.

3. The age of the earth. Up to this point, the discussions in this chapter have advocated conclusions that we hope will find broad assent among evangelical Christians. The question of the age of the earth, however, is a perplexing question about which Bible-believing Christians have differed for many years, sometimes very sharply. The two primary options to choose from for a date of the earth are the "old earth" position, which agrees with the consensus of modern science that the earth is 4.5 billion years old, and the "young earth" position, which says that the earth is 10,000 to 20,000 years old, and that secular scientific dating schemes are incorrect.

Those who advocate old earth theories of creation propose that the six "days" of creation in Genesis 1 refer not to periods of twenty-four hours, but rather to long periods of time, millions of years, during which God carried out the creative activities described in Genesis 1.[15] They point out that the Hebrew word translated "day" is sometimes used to refer not to a literal twenty-four-hour day but to a longer period of time (the same Hebrew word is used, for example, in Gen. 2:4, Ex. 20:12; Job 20:28; Prov. 24:10; 25:13; Eccl. 7:14; et al.). Other factors supporting the old earth view include the fact that the genealogies of the Bible contain gaps and are not intended to be used to calculate the age of the earth, and the evidences of antiquity in the universe (such as evidence from continental drift, the protracted formation of coral reefs, astronomical measurements, and various kinds of radiometric dating).

---

[15]An alternative view among some "old earth" advocates is that the six days of Genesis 1 are not intended to indicate a chronological sequence of events, but are rather a literary "framework," which the author uses to teach us about God's creative activity.

Those who hold to "young earth" theories of creation argue that the "days" in Genesis 1 represent literal twenty-four-hour periods of time, pointing to the fact that each of the days of Genesis 1 ends with an expression such as, "And there was evening, and there was morning—the first day" (Gen. 1:5 NIV). Some advocates of the young earth position suggest that the original creation must have had an "appearance of age" even from the first day. Those who hold this position often combine it with certain objections to current scientific dating processes, questioning the reliability of radiometric dating and assumptions concerning the rates of decay of certain elements. Other young earth advocates claim that the tremendous natural forces unleashed by the flood at the time of Noah (Gen. 6–9) significantly altered the face of the earth, exerting extremely high pressures on the earth and depositing fossils in layers of incredibly thick sediment all over the earth's surface.

While the various arguments for the two basic views of the age of the earth are complex and our conclusions are tentative, at this point in our understanding, Scripture seems to be more easily understood to *suggest* (but not to require) a young earth view, while the observable facts of creation seem increasingly to favor an old earth view. Perhaps this situation will change in the next few years as Christians examine both the Bible and the evidence in nature more thoroughly. It is theoretically possible that the young earth advocates will be able to advance more detailed arguments from Scripture showing not just that the verses are easily read in a young earth way, but that the words of Scripture actually *require* us to hold to a young earth view (those are two very different claims, for in a number of other passages—such as those on the sun rising and falling—our casual first reading of Scripture is not the correct one). On the other hand, it is possible that more investigation of the facts of the universe will provide an increasing avalanche of data on one side or the other— either surprising reversals in modern scientific claims about the antiquity of the earth, or overwhelming additional evidence that the earth is indeed extremely old. It is likely that scientific research in the next ten or twenty years will tip the weight of evidence decisively toward either a young earth or an old earth view, and the weight of Christian scholarly opinion (from both biblical scholars and scientists) will begin to shift decisively in one direction or the other. This should not cause alarm to advocates of either position, because the truthfulness of Scripture is not threatened (our interpretations of Genesis 1 have enough uncertainty that either position is possible).

However, it should be said at this point that, with the information we now have, it is not at all easy to decide this question with certainty. The possibility must be left open that God has chosen not to give us enough information to come to a clear decision on this question, and the real test of faithfulness to him may be the degree to which we can act charitably toward those who in good conscience and full belief in God's Word hold to a different position on this matter. Both views are possible, but neither one seems to me now to be certain. Given this situation, it would seem best (1) to admit that God may not allow us to find a clear solution to this question before Christ returns, and (2) to encourage evangelical scientists and theologians who fall in both the young earth and old earth camps to begin to work together with much less arrogance, much more humility, and a much greater sense of cooperation in a larger common purpose.

F. Application

The doctrine of creation has many applications for Christians today. It makes us realize that the material universe is good in itself, for God created it good and wants us to use it in ways pleasing to him. Therefore, we should seek to be like the early Christians, who "partook of food with glad and generous hearts" (Acts 2:46), always with thanksgiving to God and trust in his provisions. A healthy appreciation of creation will keep us from false asceticism that denies the goodness of creation and the blessings that come to us through it. It will also encourage some Christians to do scientific and technological research to discover more of the goodness of God's abundant creation, or to support such research. The doctrine of creation will also enable us to recognize more clearly that scientific and technological study in itself glorifies God, for it enables us to discover how incredibly wise, powerful, and skillful God was in his work of creation. "Great are the works of the LORD, studied by all who have pleasure in them" (Ps. 111:2).

The doctrine of creation also reminds us that God is sovereign over the universe he created. He made it all, and he is Lord of all of it. We owe all that we are and have to him, and we may have complete confidence that he will ultimately defeat all his enemies and be manifested as sovereign King to be worshiped forever. In addition, the incredible size of the universe and the amazing complexity of every created thing will, if our hearts are right, draw us continually to worship and praise him for his greatness.

Finally, as we indicated above, we can wholeheartedly enjoy creative activities (artistic, musical, athletic, domestic, literary, etc.) with an attitude of thanksgiving that our Creator God enables us to imitate him in our creativity.

II. REVIEW QUESTIONS

1. Define the doctrine of creation.
2. How does the Bible's description of creation give special significance to the creation of man?
3. Distinguish between the Bible's teaching about God's relationship to creation and each of the following philosophies:
   - Materialism
   - Pantheism
   - Dualism
   - Deism
4. Why did God create the universe? Was it necessary that he do so?
5. Why is the theory of theistic evolution inconsistent with Scripture's teaching on creation?
6. List four scientific arguments against the theory of evolution.

III. QUESTIONS FOR PERSONAL APPLICATION

1. Are there ways in which you could be more thankful to God for the excellence of his creation? Look around you and give some examples of the goodness of the creation that God has allowed you to enjoy. Are there ways in which you could be a better steward of the parts of God's creation that he has entrusted to your care?

2. Might the goodness of all that God created encourage you to try to enjoy different kinds of foods than those you normally prefer? Can children be taught to thank God for variety in the things God has given us to eat?

3. To understand something of the despair felt by contemporary non-Christians, try to imagine for a moment that you believe that there is no God and that you are just a product of matter plus time plus chance, the spontaneous result of random variation in organisms over millions of years. How would you feel differently about yourself? About other people? About the future? About right and wrong?

4. Why do we feel joy when we are able to "subdue" even a part of the earth and make it useful for serving us—whether it be in growing vegetables, developing a better kind of plastic or metal, or using wool to knit a piece of clothing? Should we feel joy at such times? What other attitudes of heart should we feel as we do them?

5. When you think about the immensity of the stars, and that God put them in place to show us his power and glory, how does it make you feel about your place in the universe? Is this different from the way a non-Christian would feel?

IV. SPECIAL TERMS

asceticism	micro-evolution
creation	natural selection
creation *ex nihilo*	old earth theory
deism	pantheism
dualism	random mutation
immanent	theistic evolution
intelligent design	transcendent
macro-evolution	transitional types
materialism	young earth theory

V. SCRIPTURE MEMORY PASSAGE

NEHEMIAH 9:6

And Ezra said: "You are the Lord, you alone; you have made heaven, the heaven of heavens, with all their host, the earth and all that is on it, the seas and all that is in them; and you preserve all of them; and the host of heaven worships you."

Chapter Eight

God's Providence

+ *What is the extent of God's control over creation?*
+ *If God controls all things, how can our actions have real meaning?*

I. EXPLANATION AND SCRIPTURAL BASIS

Once we understand that God is the all-powerful Creator (see ch. 7), it seems reasonable to conclude that he also preserves and governs everything in the universe as well. Though the term *providence* is not found in Scripture, it has been used to summarize God's ongoing relationship to his creation.

We may define God's providence as follows: *God is continually involved with all created things in such a way that he (1) keeps them existing and maintaining the properties with which he created them; (2) cooperates with created things in every action, directing their distinctive properties to cause them to act as they do; and (3) directs them to fulfill his purposes.*

Under the general category of providence we have three subtopics according to the three elements in the definition above: (1) preservation, (2) concurrence, and (3) government. We shall examine each of these separately then consider differing views and objections to the doctrine of providence. It should be noted that this is a doctrine on which there has been substantial disagreement among Christians since the early history of the church, particularly with respect to God's relationship to the willing choices of moral creatures. We will first present a summary of the position favored in this textbook (what is commonly called the "Reformed" or "Calvinist" position),[1] then consider arguments that have been made from another position (what is commonly called the "Arminian" position).

---

[1]Though philosophers may use the term *determinism* (or *soft determinism*) to categorize the position I advocate in this chapter, I do not use that term because it is too easily misunderstood in everyday English: (1) It suggests a system in which human choices are not real and make no difference in the outcome of events; and (2) it suggests a system in which the ultimate cause of events is a mechanistic universe rather than a wise and personal God. Moreover, (3) it too easily allows critics to group the biblical view with non-Christian deterministic systems and blur the distinctions between them.

The view advocated in this chapter is also sometimes called "compatibilism" because it holds that absolute divine sovereignty is compatible with human significance and real human choices. I have no objection to the nuances of this term, but I have decided not to use it because (1) I want to avoid the proliferation of technical terms in studying theology, and (2) it seems preferable simply to call my position a traditional Reformed view of God's providence and thereby to place myself within a widely understood theological tradition.

An excellent recent defense of the type of Reformed theology that I present in this chapter (and elsewhere in this book) is found in Thomas Schreiner and Bruce Ware, eds., *The Grace of God, the Bondage of the Will: Biblical and Practical Perspectives on Calvinism*, 2 vols. (Grand Rapids: Baker, 1995).

A. Preservation

God keeps all created things existing and maintaining the properties with which he created them.

Hebrews 1:3 tells us that Christ is "upholding the universe by his word of power." The Greek word translated "upholding" is *pherō*, "carry, bear." This is commonly used in the New Testament for carrying something from one place to another, such as bringing a paralyzed man on a bed to Jesus (Luke 5:18), bringing wine to the steward of the feast (John 2:8), or bringing a cloak and books to Paul (2 Tim. 4:13). It does not mean simply "sustain," but has the sense of active, purposeful control over the thing being carried from one place to another. In Hebrews 1:3, the use of the present participle indicates that Jesus is "*continually* carrying along all things" in the universe by his word of power.

Similarly, in Colossians 1:17, Paul says of Christ that "in him all things hold together." The phrase "all things" refers to every created thing in the universe (see v. 16), and the verse affirms that Christ keeps all things existing—in him they continue to exist or "endure" (NASB mg.). Both verses indicate that if Christ were to cease his ongoing activity of sustaining all things in the universe, then everything except the triune God would instantly cease to exist. Such teaching is also affirmed by Paul when he says, "In him we live and move and *have our being*" (Acts 17:28), and by Ezra: "You are the LORD, you alone; you have made heaven, the heaven of heavens, with all their host, the earth and all that is on it, the seas and all that is in them; *and you preserve all of them;* and the host of heaven worships you" (Neh. 9:6).

God, in preserving all things he has made, also causes them to maintain the properties with which he created them. God preserves water in such a way that it continues to act like water. He causes grass to continue to act like grass, with all its distinctive characteristics. He causes the paper on which this sentence is written to continue to act like paper—so that it does not spontaneously dissolve into water and float away or change into a living thing and begin to grow! Until it is acted on by some other part of creation and thereby its properties are changed (for instance, until it is burned with fire and it becomes ash), this paper will continue to act like paper so long as God preserves the earth and the creation that he has made.

God's providence provides a basis for science: God has made and continues to sustain a universe that acts in predictable ways. If a scientific experiment gives a certain result today, then we can have confidence that (if all the factors are the same) it will give the same result tomorrow and a hundred years from tomorrow. The doctrine of providence also provides a foundation for technology: I can be confident that gasoline will make my car run today just as it did yesterday, not simply because "it has always worked that way," but because God's providence sustains a universe in which created things maintain the properties with which he created them.

B. Concurrence

God cooperates with created things in every action, directing their distinctive properties to cause them to act as they do.

This second aspect of providence, *concurrence,* is an expansion of the idea contained in the first aspect, *preservation.* In fact, some theologians (such as John Calvin) treat the fact of concurrence under the category of preservation, but it is helpful to treat it as a distinct category.

In Ephesians 1:11, Paul says that God "accomplishes all things according to the counsel of his will." The word translated "accomplishes" (Gk. *Energeō*) indicates that God "works" or "brings about" *all things* according to his own will. No event in creation falls outside of his providence. Of course, this fact is hidden from our eyes unless we read it in Scripture. Like preservation, God's work of concurrence is not clearly evident from observation of the natural world around us.

In giving scriptural proof for concurrence, we will begin with the inanimate creation, then move to animals, and finally to different kinds of events in the life of human beings.

1. Inanimate creation. These are many things in creation that we think of as merely "natural" occurrences. Yet Scripture says that God causes them to happen. We read of "fire and hail, snow and frost, stormy wind fulfilling his command!" (Ps. 148:8). Similarly,

> To the *snow* he says, "Fall on the earth";
>   and to the shower and the *rain*, "Be strong." . . .
> By the breath of God *ice* is given
>   and the broad waters are frozen fast.
> He loads the thick cloud with moisture;
>   the clouds scatter his *lightning*.
> They turn round and round by his guidance,
>   to accomplish all that he commands them
>   on the face of the habitable world.
> Whether for correction, or for his land,
>   or for love, he causes it to happen.
>   (Job 37:6–13; cf. similar statements in 38:22–30)

God also causes the grass to grow: "*You cause the grass to grow* for the cattle, and plants for man to cultivate, that he may bring forth food from the earth" (Ps. 104:14). God directs the stars in the heavens, asking Job, "Can you bring forth the constellations in their seasons or lead out the Bear with its cubs?" (Job 38:32 NIV; "the Bear" or Ursa Major is commonly called the Big Dipper; v. 31 refers to the constellations Pleiades and Orion). Moreover, God continually directs the coming of the morning (Job 38:12), a fact Jesus affirmed when he said that God "*makes his sun rise* on the evil and on the good, and *sends rain* on the just and on the unjust" (Matt. 5:45).

2. Animals. Scripture affirms that God feeds the wild animals of the field, for,

> These all look to you,
>   to give them their food in due season.
> When you give to them, they gather it up;
>   when you open your hand, they are filled with good things.
> When you hide your face, they are dismayed.
>   (Ps. 104:27–29; cf. Job 38:39–41)

Jesus also affirmed this when he said, "Look at the *birds* of the air. . . . your heavenly Father *feeds them*" (Matt. 6:26). And he said that not one sparrow "will fall to the ground without your Father's will" (Matt. 10:29).

3. Seemingly "random" or "chance" events. From a human perspective, the casting of lots (or its modern equivalent, the rolling of dice) is the most typical of random events that occur in the universe. But Scripture affirms that the outcome of such an event is from God: "The lot is cast into the lap, but the decision is wholly from the LORD" (Prov. 16:33).

4. Events fully caused by God and fully caused by the creature as well. For any of these foregoing events (rain and snow, grass growing, sun and stars, the feeding of animals, or casting of lots), we could (at least in theory) give a completely satisfactory "natural" explanation. A botanist can detail the factors that cause grass to grow, and a meteorologist can give a complete explanation of factors that cause rain (humidity, temperature, atmospheric pressure, and so on). Yet Scripture says that *God* causes grass to grow and that *God* causes the rain.

This shows us that it is incorrect for us to reason that if we know the "natural" cause of something in this world, then God did not cause it. Nor is it correct to think that events are partly caused by God and partly by factors in the created world. If that were the case, then we would always be looking for some small feature of an event that we could not explain, and attribute that (say 1 percent of the cause) to God. Rather, these passages affirm that such events are entirely caused by God. Yet we know that (in another sense) they are entirely caused by factors in the creation as well.

The doctrine of concurrence affirms that God *directs* and *works through* the distinctive properties of each created thing, so that these things themselves bring about the results that we see. In this way it is possible to affirm that in one sense events are fully (100 percent) caused by God and fully (100 percent) caused by the creature as well. However, divine and creaturely causes work in different ways. The divine cause of each event works as an invisible, behind-the-scenes directing cause and therefore could be called the "primary cause" that plans and initiates everything that happens. But the created thing brings about actions in ways consistent with the creature's own properties, ways that can often be discerned through observation. These creaturely factors and properties can therefore be called the "secondary" causes of everything that happens, even though they are the causes that are most evident to us.

5. The affairs of nations. Scripture also speaks of God's providential control of human affairs. We read that God "makes nations great, and he destroys them: he enlarges nations, and leads them away" (Job 12:23). "Dominion belongs to the LORD, and he rules over the nations" (Ps. 22:28). He has determined the time of existence and the place of every nation on the earth, for Paul says, "he made from one every nation of men to live on all the face of the earth, having determined allotted periods and the boundaries of their habitation" (Acts 17:26; cf. Acts 14:16).

6. All aspects of our lives. It is amazing to see the extent to which Scripture affirms that God brings about various events in our lives. For example, our dependence on God to give us food each day is affirmed every time we pray, "Give us this day our daily bread" (Matt. 6:11), even though we work for our food and (as far as mere human observation can discern) obtain it through entirely "natural" causes. Similarly, Paul, looking at events with the eye of faith, affirms that "my God will supply every need" of his children (Phil. 4:19), even though God may use "ordinary" means (such as other people) to do so.

God plans our days before we are born, for David affirms, "In your book were written, every one of them, the days that were formed for me, when as yet there was none of them" (Ps. 139:16). And Job says that man's "days are determined, and the number of his months is with you, and you have appointed his bounds that he cannot pass" (Job 14:5). This can be seen in the life of Paul, who says that God "had set me apart before I was born" (Gal. 1:15), and Jeremiah, to whom God said, "Before I formed you in the womb I knew you, and before you were born I consecrated you; I appointed you a prophet to the nations" (Jer. 1:5).

All our actions are under God's providential care, for "in him we live and *move*" (Acts 17:28). The individual steps we take each day are directed by the Lord. Jeremiah confesses, "I know, O LORD, that the way of man is not in himself, that it is not in man who walks to direct his steps" (Jer. 10:23). We read that "a man's steps are ordered by the LORD" (Prov. 20:24), and that "A man's mind plans his way, but the LORD directs his steps" (Prov. 16:9). Success and failure come from God, for we read, "Not from the east or from the west and not from the wilderness comes lifting up; but it is God who executes judgment, putting down one and lifting up another" (Ps. 75:6–7). Even all of our talents and abilities are from the Lord, for Paul can ask the Corinthians, "What have you that you did not receive? If then you received it, why do you boast as if it were not a gift?" (1 Cor. 4:7).

God influences the desires and decisions of people, for he looks down "on all the inhabitants of the earth" and "fashions the hearts of them all" (Ps. 33:14–15). When we realize that the heart in Scripture is the location of our inmost thoughts and desires, this is a significant passage. Yes, we know that we make willing choices, but who formed our will to make those choices? God "fashions the hearts" of "all the inhabitants of the earth." God especially guides the desires and inclination of believers, working in us "both *to will* and to work for his good pleasure" (Phil. 2:13).

All of these passages, reporting both general statements about God's work in the lives of all people and specific examples of God's work in the lives of individuals, lead us to conclude that God's providential work of concurrence extends to all aspects of our lives. Our words, our steps, our movements, our hearts, and our abilities are all from the Lord.

But we must guard against misunderstanding. Here also, as with the lower creation, God's providential direction as an unseen, behind-the-scenes, "primary cause" should not lead us to deny the reality of our choices and actions. Again and again Scripture affirms that we really do *cause* events to happen. We are significant and we are responsible. We do have choices, and these are real choices that bring about real results. Just as God has created things in nature with certain properties (e.g., rocks are hard, water is wet), God has made us in such a wonderful way that he has endowed us with the property of willing choice.

One approach to these passages about God's concurrence is to say that if our choices are real, they cannot be caused by God (see below for further discussion of this viewpoint). But the number of passages that affirm this providential control of God is so considerable, and the difficulties involved in giving them some other interpretation are so formidable, that it does not seem to me that this can be the right approach to them. It seems better simply to affirm that God causes all things that happen, but that he does so in such a way that he somehow upholds our ability to make *willing, responsible choices,* choices that have *real and eternal results,* and for which we are *held accountable.* Exactly how God combines his providential control with our willing and significant choices, Scripture simply does not explain to us. But rather than deny one aspect or the other (simply because we cannot explain how both can be true), we should accept both in an attempt to be faithful to the teaching of all of Scripture.

7. **What about evil?** If God does indeed cause, through his providential activity, everything that comes about in the world, then the question arises, "What is the relationship between God and evil in the world?" Does God actually cause the evil actions that people do? If he does, then is God not responsible for sin?

In approaching this question, it is best first to read the passages of Scripture that most directly address it. We can begin by looking at several passages that affirm that God did, indeed, cause evil events to come about and evil deeds to be done. But we must remember that in all these passages it is very clear that Scripture nowhere shows God as *directly doing anything evil,* but rather as bringing about evil deeds through the willing actions of moral creatures. Moreover, Scripture never blames God for evil or shows God as taking pleasure in evil, and Scripture never excuses human beings for the wrong they do. However we understand God's relationship to evil, we must never come to the point where we think that we are not responsible for the evil we do or that God takes pleasure in evil or is to be blamed for it. Such a conclusion is clearly contrary to Scripture.

A very clear example is found in the story of Joseph. Scripture clearly says that Joseph's brothers were wrongly jealous of him (Gen. 37:11), hated him (Gen. 37:4, 5, 8), wanted to kill him (Gen. 37:20), and did wrong when they cast him into a pit (Gen. 37:24) and then sold him into slavery in Egypt (Gen. 37:28). Yet later Joseph could say to his brothers, "*God sent me before you* to preserve life" (Gen. 45:5), and again "You meant evil against me; but *God meant it for good,* to bring it about that many people should be kept alive, as they are today" (Gen. 50:20). Here we have a combination of evil deeds brought about by sinful men who are rightly held accountable for their sin and the overriding providential control of God whereby God's own purposes were accomplished. Both are clearly affirmed.

The story of the exodus from Egypt repeatedly affirms that God hardened the heart of Pharaoh: God says, "I will harden his heart" (Ex. 4:21), "I will harden Pharaoh's heart" (Ex. 7:3, repeated in 14:4), "The LORD hardened the heart of Pharaoh" (Ex. 9:12, repeated in 14:8), and "The LORD hardened Pharaoh's heart" (Ex. 10:20, repeated in 10:27 and again in 11:10). It is sometimes objected that Scripture also says that Pharaoh hardened his own heart (Ex. 8:15, 32; 9:34) and that God's act of hardening Pharaoh's heart was only in response to the initial rebellion and hardness of heart Pharaoh himself exhibited of his own free will. But it should be noted that God's promises that he would harden Pharaoh's heart (Ex. 4:21; 7:3) are made long before Scripture tells us that Pharaoh hardened his own heart (we read of this for the first time in Ex. 8:15). Moreover, our analysis of concurrence given above, in which both divine and human agents can cause the same event, should show us that both factors can be true at the same time. Even when Pharaoh hardens his own heart, that is not inconsistent with saying that God is causing Pharaoh to do this and thereby God is hardening Pharaoh's heart. Finally, if someone would object that God is just intensifying the evil desires and choices that were already in Pharaoh's heart, this kind of action could still—in theory at least—cover all the evil in the world today, since all people have evil desires still in their hearts and all people do in fact make evil choices.

What was God's purpose in this? Paul reflects on Exodus 9:16 and says, "The scripture says to Pharaoh, 'I have raised you up for the very purpose of showing my power in you, so that my name may be proclaimed in all the earth'" (Rom. 9:17). Then Paul infers a general truth from this specific example: "So then he has mercy upon whomever he wills, and he hardens the heart of whomever he wills" (Rom. 9:18). In fact, God also hardened the hearts of the Egyptian people so that they pursued Israel into the Red Sea: "I will harden the hearts of the Egyptians so that they shall go in after them, and I will get glory over Pharaoh and all his host, his chariots, and his horsemen" (Ex. 14:17). This theme is repeated in Psalm 105:25: "He turned their hearts to hate his people."

In the story of Job, though the Lord gave Satan permission to bring harm to Job's possessions and children, and though this harm came through the evil actions of the Sabeans and the Chaldeans, as well as a windstorm (Job 1:12, 15, 17, 19), yet Job looks beyond those secondary causes and, with the eyes of faith, sees it all as from the hand of the Lord: "The LORD gave, and the LORD has taken away; *blessed be the name of the LORD*" (Job 1:21). The Old Testament author follows Job's statement immediately with the sentence, "In all this Job did not sin or charge God with wrong" (Job 1:22). Job had just been told that evil marauding bands had destroyed his flocks and herds, yet with great faith and patience in adversity, he says, "*The LORD has taken away.*" Yet Job does not blame God for the evil or say that God had done wrong; he says, "Blessed be the name of the LORD." To *blame* God for evil that he had brought about through secondary agents would have been to sin. Job does not do this, Scripture never does this, and neither should we.

Examples similar to these could be multiplied. In many such passages, God brings evil and destruction on people in judgment for their sins. They have been disobedient or have strayed into idolatry, and the Lord uses evil human beings or demonic forces or "natural" disasters to bring judgment on them. (This is not always said to be the case—Joseph and Job, for example, suffered but not because of their own sin—but it is often so.) Perhaps this idea of judgment on sin can help us to understand, at least in part, how God can righteously bring about evil events. All human beings are sinful, for Scripture tells us that "all have sinned and fall short of the glory of God" (Rom. 3:23). None of us deserves God's favor or his mercy, but only eternal condemnation. Therefore, when God brings evil on human beings, whether to discipline his children, or to lead unbelievers to repentance, or to bring a judgment of condemnation and destruction upon hardened sinners, none of us can charge God with doing wrong. Ultimately, all will work in God's good purposes to bring glory to him and good to his people. Yet we must realize that in punishing evil in those who are not redeemed (such as Pharaoh, the Canaanites, and the Babylonians), God is also glorified through the demonstration of his justice, holiness, and power (see Ex. 9:16; Rom. 9:14–24).

The most evil deed of all history, the crucifixion of Christ, was ordained by God—not just the fact that it would occur, but also all the individual actions connected with it. The church at Jerusalem recognized this, for they prayed: "For truly in this city there were gathered together against your holy servant Jesus, whom you anointed, both Herod and Pontius Pilate, with the Gentiles and the peoples of Israel, *to do whatever your hand and your plan had predestined to take place*" (Acts 4:27). All the actions of all the participants in the crucifixion of Jesus had been "predestined" by God. Yet the apostles clearly attach no moral blame to God, for the actions resulted from the willing choices of sinful men. Peter makes this clear in his sermon at Pentecost: "This Jesus, delivered up according to the definite plan and foreknowledge of God, *you crucified and killed by the hands of lawless men*" (Acts 2:23). In one sentence, he links God's plan and foreknowledge with the moral blame that attaches to the actions of "lawless men." They were not forced by God to act against their wills; rather, God brought about his plan *through their willing choices,* for which they were nevertheless responsible.

8. Analysis of verses relating to God and evil. After looking at so many verses that speak of God's providential use of the evil actions of men and demons, what can we say by way of analysis?

a. *God uses all things to fulfill his purposes and even uses evil for his glory and for our good.* Thus, when evil comes into our lives to trouble us, we can have from the doctrine of providence a deeper assurance that "God causes all things to work together for good to those who love God, to those who are called according to his purpose" (Rom. 8:28 NASB). This kind of conviction enabled Joseph to say to his brothers, "You meant evil against me; but *God meant it for good*" (Gen. 50:20).

We can also realize, with trembling, that God is glorified even in the punishment of evil. Scripture tells us that "the LORD has made everything for its purpose, even the wicked for the day of trouble" (Prov. 16:4). Similarly, the psalmist affirms, "Surely the wrath of men shall praise you" (Ps. 76:10). And the case of Pharaoh (Rom. 9:14–24) is a clear example of the way God uses evil for his own glory and for the good of his people.

b. *Nevertheless, God never does evil and is never to be blamed for evil.* In a statement similar to those cited above from Acts 2:23 and 4:27–28, Jesus also combines God's predestination of the crucifixion with moral blame on those who carry it out: "For the Son of man goes *as it has been determined;* but woe to that man by whom he is betrayed!" (Luke 22:22; cf. Matt. 26:24; Mark 14:21). And in a more general statement about evil in the world, Jesus says, "Woe to the world for temptations to sin! For it is necessary that temptations come, but woe to the man by whom the temptation comes!" (Matt. 18:7).

James speaks similarly in warning us not to blame God for the evil we do when he says, "Let no one say when he is tempted, 'I am tempted by God'; for God cannot be tempted with evil and he himself tempts no one; but each person is tempted when he is lured and enticed by his own desire" (James 1:13–14). The verse does not say that God never causes evil; it affirms that we should never think of him as the personal agent who is tempting us or who is to be held accountable for the temptation. We can never blame God for temptation or think that he will approve of us if we give in to it. We are to resist evil and always blame ourselves or others who tempt us, but we must never blame God.

These verses all make it clear that "secondary causes" (human beings, angels, and demons) are real and that human beings do cause evil and are responsible for it. Though God ordained that it would come about, both in general terms and in specific details, yet *God is removed from actually doing evil,* and his bringing it about through "secondary causes" does not impugn his holiness or render him blameworthy.

We should notice that the alternatives to saying that God uses evil for his purposes, but that he never does evil and is not to be blamed for it, are not desirable ones. If we were to say that God himself does evil, we would have to conclude that he is not a good and righteous God, and therefore that he is not really God at all. On the other hand, if we maintain that God does not use evil to fulfill his purposes, then we would have to admit that there is evil in the universe that God did not intend, is not under his control, and might not fulfill his purposes. This would make it very difficult for us to affirm that "all things" work together for good for those who love God and are called according to his purpose (Rom. 8:28). If evil came into the world in spite of the fact that God did not intend it and did not want it to be there, then what guarantee do we have that there will not be more and more evil that he does not intend and that he does not want? And what guarantee do we have that he will be able to use it for his purposes, or even that he can triumph over it? Surely this is an undesirable alternative position.

c. *God rightfully blames and judges moral creatures for the evil they do.* Many passages in Scripture affirm this. One is found in Isaiah:

These have *chosen* their own ways,
    and their soul *delights in* their abominations;
I also will choose affliction for them,
    and bring their fears upon them;
because, when I called, no one answered,
    when I spoke they did not listen;
but they did what was evil in my eyes,
    and *chose* that in which I did not delight. (Isa. 66:3–4)

Similarly, we read, "God made man upright, but they have sought out many devices" (Eccl. 7:29). *The blame for evil is always on the responsible creature,* whether man or demon, who does it, and *the creature who does evil is always worthy of punishment.* Scripture consistently affirms that God is righteous and just to punish us for our sins. And if we object that he should not find fault with us because we cannot resist his will, then we must ponder the apostle Paul's own response to that question: "You will say to me then, 'Why does he still find fault? For who can resist his will?' But who are you, a man, to answer back to God? Will what is molded say to its molder, 'Why have you made me thus?'" (Rom. 9:19–20). In every case where we do evil, we know that we *willingly* choose to do it, and we realize that we are rightly to be blamed for it.

d. *Evil is real, not an illusion, and we should never do evil, for it will always harm us and others.* Scripture consistently teaches that we never have a right to do evil and that we should persistently oppose it in ourselves and in the world. We are to pray, "Deliver us from evil" (Matt. 6:13), and if we see anyone wandering from the truth and doing wrong, we should attempt to bring him back. Scripture says, "If any one among you wanders from the truth and someone brings him back, let him know that whoever brings back a sinner from the error of his way will save his soul from death and will cover a multitude of sins" (James 5:19–20). We should never even *will* evil to be done, for entertaining sinful desires in our minds is to allow them to "wage war" against our souls (1 Peter 2:11) and thereby to do us spiritual harm.

In thinking about God using evil to fulfill his purposes, we should remember that there are some things that are right for God to do but wrong for us to do. For example, he requires others to worship him, and he accepts worship from them. He seeks glory for himself. He will execute final judgment on wrongdoers. And he also uses evil to bring about good purposes, but he does not allow us to do so. Calvin quotes a statement of Augustine with approval: "There is a great difference between what is fitting for man to will and what is fitting for God. . . . For through the bad wills of evil men God fulfills what he righteously wills."[2] And Herman Bavinck uses the analogy of a parent who will himself use a very sharp knife but will not allow his child to use it, to show that God himself uses evil to bring about good purposes but never allows his children to do so. Though we are to imitate God's moral character in many ways (cf. Eph. 5:1), this is one of the ways in which we are not to imitate him.

e. *In spite of all of the foregoing statements, we have to come to the point where we confess that we do not understand how it is that God can ordain that we carry out evil deeds and yet hold us accountable for them and not be blamed himself.* We can affirm that all of these things are true, because Scripture teaches them. But Scripture does not tell us exactly *how* God brings this situation about or how it can be that God holds us accountable for what he ordains will come to pass. Here Scripture is silent, and we have to agree with Berkhof that ultimately "the problem of God's relation to sin remains a mystery."[3]

9. Are we "free"? Do we have "free will"? If God exercises providential control over all events, are we in any sense free? The answer depends on what is meant by the word *free*. Sometimes people will argue endlessly over this question because they never define clearly what they or their opponent in argument means by "free," and the word is then used in various ways that confuse the discussion.

The kind of freedom that is often assumed by those who deny God's providential control of all things is a freedom to act outside of God's sustaining and controlling activity, a freedom that includes being able to make decisions that are not caused by anything external to ourselves. Scripture nowhere says we are free in those senses. That kind of freedom would be impossible if Jesus Christ is indeed "continually carrying along things by his word of power" (Heb. 1:3, author's translation) and if God "accomplishes all things according to the counsel of his will" (Eph. 1:11). If this is true, to be outside of that providential control would simply be not to exist! An absolute "freedom," totally free of God's control, is simply not possible in a world providentially sustained and directed by God himself. If that is what someone means by "free will," it is inconsistent with Scripture to say that we have free will.

On the other hand, we are free in the greatest sense that any creature of God could be free—we make *willing* choices, choices that have *real effects*. We are aware of no restraints on our will from God when we make decisions, and we act in accord with our own desires. In this sense, it is certainly consistent with Scripture to say that we have "free will." Clearly we must insist that we have the power of willing choice and that our choices have real results in the universe; otherwise we will fall into the error of fatalism or determinism and thus conclude that our choices do not matter or that we cannot really make willing choices.

C. Government

We have discussed the first two aspects of providence, (1) preservation and (2) concurrence. This third aspect of God's providence indicates that *God has a purpose in all he does in the world and that he providentially governs or directs all things in order that they accomplish his purposes.* We read in the Psalms, "His kingdom rules

---

[2] John Calvin, *Institutes of the Christian Religion,* Library of Christian Classics, ed. John T. McNeill, trans. F. L. Battles, 2 vols. (Philadelphia: Westminster, 1960), 1:234 (1.18.3).

[3] Louis Berkhof, *Introduction to Systematic Theology* (Grand Rapids: Eerdmans, 1932; reprint, Grand Rapids: Baker, 1979), p. 175.

over all" (103:19). Moreover, "he does according to his will in the host of heaven and among the inhabitants of the earth; and none can stay his hand or say to him, 'What are you doing?'" (Dan. 4:35). Paul affirms that "from him and through him and to him are all things" (Rom. 11:36). It is because Paul knows that God is sovereign over all and works his purposes in every event that happens that he can declare that "God causes all things to work together for good to those who love God, to those who are called according to his purpose" (Rom. 8:28 NASB).

D. The Importance of Our Human Actions

We may sometimes forget that God works *through human actions* in his providential management of the world. If we do, then we begin to think that our actions and our choices do not make much difference or do not have much effect on the course of events. To guard against any misunderstanding of God's providence, we make the following points of emphasis.

1. We are still responsible for our actions. God has made us *responsible* for our actions, which have *real and eternally significant results.* In all his providential acts, God will preserve these characteristics of responsibility and significance. If we do right and obey God, he will reward us, and things will go well with us both in this age and in eternity. If we do wrong and disobey God, he will discipline and perhaps punish us, and things will go ill with us. The realization of these facts will help us have wisdom in talking to others and in encouraging them to avoid laziness and disobedience.

2. Our actions have real results and do change the course of events. In the ordinary working of the world, if I neglect to take care of my health and have poor eating habits, or if I abuse my body through alcohol or tobacco, I am likely to die sooner. God has ordained that our *actions* do have effects. God has ordained that *events* will come about *by our causing them.* Of course, we do not know what God has planned—even for the rest of this day, to say nothing of next week or next year. But we do know that *if we trust God and obey him,* we will discover that he has planned *good things* to come about through that obedience!

This should encourage us not only to obey God, but also to exercise wisdom and ordinary caution in our lives, realizing that these are often the means God uses to bring about certain results in our lives. By contrast, if we anticipate that some dangers or evil events may come in the future, and if we do not use reasonable means to avoid them, then we may in fact discover that our lack of action was the means God used to allow them to come about!

3. Prayer is one specific kind of action that has definite results and that does change the course of events. God has also ordained that prayer is a very significant means of bringing about results in the world.[4] When we earnestly intercede for a specific person or situation, we will often find that God had ordained that our prayer would be a *means* he would use to bring about the changes in the world. Scripture reminds us of this when it tells us, "You do not have, because you do not ask" (James 4:2). Jesus says, "Hitherto you have asked nothing in my name; ask, and you will receive, that your joy may be full" (John 16:24).

4. In conclusion, we must act! The doctrine of providence in no way encourages us to sit back in idleness to await the outcome of certain events. Of course, God

---

[4]See chapter 9 for a more extensive discussion of prayer.

may impress on us the need to wait on him before we act and to trust in him rather than in our own abilities—that is certainly not wrong. But simply to say that we are trusting in God *instead of* acting responsibly is sheer laziness and is a distortion of the doctrine of providence.

In practical terms, if one of my sons has school work that must be done the next day, I am right to make him complete that work before he can go out to play. I realize that his grade is in God's hands and that God has long ago determined what it would be, but I do not know what it will be and neither does he. What I do know is that if he studies and does his school work faithfully, he will receive a good grade. If he doesn't, he will not. The doctrine of providence, then, should encourage us to combine complete trust in God's sovereign control with a realization that the use of ordinary means is necessary for things to come out the way God has planned them to come out. A hearty belief in God's providence is not a discouragement, but a spur to action.

5. What if we cannot understand this doctrine fully? Every believer who meditates on God's providence will sooner or later come to a point where he or she will have to say, "I cannot understand this doctrine fully." In some ways that must be said about every doctrine, since our understanding is finite and God is infinite (see ch. 1, pp. 24–25). But particularly is this so with the doctrine of providence. Because Scripture teaches it, we should believe it, even when we do not understand fully how it fits in with other teachings of Scripture.

E. Another Evangelical View: The Arminian Position

There is a major alternative position held by many evangelicals, which for convenience we shall call the "Arminian" view.[5] Those who hold an Arminian position maintain that to preserve the *real human freedom* and *real human choices* that are necessary for genuine human personhood, God cannot cause or plan our voluntary choices. Therefore, they conclude that God's providential involvement in or control of history must not include every specific detail of every event that happens, but that God instead simply responds to human choices and actions as they come about and does so in such a way that his purposes are ultimately accomplished in the world. Arminian proponents also argue that God's purposes in the world are more general and could be accomplished through many different kinds of specific events.

The Arminian position can be summarized in the following four major points:

1. The verses cited as examples of God's providential control are exceptions and do not describe the way God ordinarily works in human activity.
2. The Calvinist view wrongly makes God responsible for sin.
3. Choices caused by God cannot be real choices.
4. The Arminian view encourages responsible Christian living, while the Calvinistic view encourages a dangerous fatalism.

These objections illustrate the primary concerns common to proponents of the Arminian position, which focus especially on the preservation of human freedom and human choice.

---

[5]This position is named after Jacob Arminius (1560–1609), a Dutch theologian who differed with the predominant Calvinism of his day, especially with respect to God's providence in general (the subject of this chapter) and specifically with respect to predestination or election (the subject of ch. 18).

F. Response to the Arminian Position

Many within the evangelical world will find these four Arminian points convincing. They will feel that these arguments represent what they intuitively know about themselves, their own actions, and the way the world functions, and that these arguments best account for the repeated emphasis in Scripture on our responsibility and the real consequences of our choices. However, there are some answers that can be given to the Arminian position.

1. Are these Scripture passages unusual examples, or do they describe the way God ordinarily works? In response to the objection that the examples of God's providential control only refer to limited or specific events, it may be said first that the examples are so numerous (see above, pp. 143–49) that they seem to be designed to describe to us the ways in which God works all the time. Moreover, many of the verses that speak of God's providence are very general: Christ "continually carries along *all things* by his word of power" (Heb. 1:3, author's translation), and God "accomplishes *all things* according to the counsel of his will" (Eph. 1:11). Such Scripture passages have in view more than exceptional examples of an unusual intervention by God in the affairs of human beings; they describe the way God always works in the world.

2. Does the Calvinistic doctrine of God's providence make God responsible for sin? The Arminian contention that says that God is not responsible for sin and evil *because he did not ordain them or cause them in any way* simply seems unable to account for the many texts that clearly say that God ordains that some people sin or do evil (see section B.7 above, pp. 147–49). While on a human level it may be difficult to reconcile God's ordaining of events with the voluntary actions of personal moral agents, Scripture repeatedly affirms that both are true. The Arminian position seems to have failed to show why God cannot work in this way in the world, preserving both his holiness and our individual human responsibility for sin.

3. Can choices ordained by God be real choices? In response to the claim that choices ordained by God cannot be real choices, it must be said that this is simply an assumption based once again on human experience and intuition, not on specific Scripture texts. Scripture repeatedly indicates that God works through our will, our power to choose, and our personal volition, and it consistently affirms that our choices are genuine choices, that they have *real* results, and that those results last for eternity. The contention that such choices are not real seems to place a limitation on God based merely on finite human experience. After all, God alone determines what is significant, what is real, and what is genuine personal responsibility in the universe.

4. Does a Calvinistic view of providence encourage a dangerous fatalism? The objection that a Calvinistic view of providence encourages dangerous fatalism fails to understand the Reformed doctrine of providence, which emphasizes both God's sovereign control and the need for responsible obedience. When this doctrine is held consistently, the fruit will be a more comprehensive trust in God in all circumstances, gratitude for all of God's blessings, and patience in all kinds of adversity. Such are the benefits of knowing that nothing falls outside the bounds of God's wise and loving plans.

5. Additional objections to the Arminian position. In addition to responding to the four specific Arminian claims mentioned above, some remaining objections to it need to be considered.

a. *On an Arminian view, how can God know the future?* To this objection some Arminians respond that God is not able to know details of future human choices, while others say that God knows the future because he is able to see into the future, not because he has planned or caused what will happen. The first response radically revises the idea of divine omniscience and seems to be clearly denied by dozens of texts in Scripture. The second response fails to render our choices free in the way the Arminian wishes them to be free. If our future choices are known, then they are fixed and therefore predetermined by something (whether fate or the inevitable cause-and-effect mechanism of the universe). And if they are fixed, then they are not "free" (undetermined or uncaused) in the Arminian sense.

b. *On an Arminian view, how can evil exist if God did not want it?* If evil happens in spite of the fact that God does not want it to happen, this seems to deny God's omnipotence: He wanted to prevent evil, but he was unable to do so. The common Arminian response is to say that God was *able* to prevent evil but he chose to *allow for the possibility* of evil in order to guarantee that angels and humans would have the freedom necessary for meaningful choices. But this is not a satisfactory response, for if choices must include the possibility of sinful choices in order to be real, this implies that God will have to allow for the possibility of sinful choices in heaven eternally (assuming that we will have genuine choices in heaven). More troubling than this, however, is the issue of *God's* choices. Either God's choices are not real, since he cannot do evil, or God's choices are real, and the possibility exists that he might someday choose to do evil. Both implications are incorrect, and they therefore provide good reason for rejecting the Arminian position that real choices must allow the possibility of choosing evil. But this puts us back to the earlier question for which there does not seem to be a satisfactory answer from the Arminian position: How can evil exist if God did not want it to exist?

c. *On an Arminian view, how can we know that God will triumph over evil?* If all the evil now in the world came into the world even though God did not want it, how can we be sure that God will triumph over it in the end? Of course, God says in Scripture that he will triumph over evil. But if he was unable to keep it out of his universe in the first place and it came in against his will, and if he is unable to predict the outcome of any future events that involve free choices, how then can we be sure that God's declaration that he will triumph over all evil is in itself true?

Both of these last two objections regarding evil make us realize that, while we may have difficulties in thinking about the Reformed view of evil as ordained by God and completely under the control of God, there are far more serious difficulties with the Arminian view of evil as not ordained or even willed by God and therefore not assuredly under the control of God.

d. *The difference in the unanswered questions.* Since we are finite in our understanding, we inevitably will have some unanswered questions about every biblical doctrine. Yet on this issue the questions that Calvinists and Arminians must leave unanswered are quite different. On the one hand, Calvinists must say that they do not know the answer to the following questions: (1) exactly how God can ordain that we do evil willingly, and yet God not be blamed for evil, and (2) exactly how God can cause us to choose something willingly.

To both, Calvinists would say that the answer is somehow to be found in an awareness of God's infinite greatness, in the knowledge of the fact that he can do far more than we could ever think possible. So the effect of these unanswered questions is to increase our appreciation of the greatness of God.

On the other hand, Arminians must leave unanswered questions regarding God's knowledge of the future, why he would allow evil when it is against his will, and whether he will certainly triumph over evil. Their failure to resolve these questions tends to diminish the greatness of God—his omniscience, his omnipotence, and the absolute reliability of his promises for the future. And these unanswered questions tend to exalt the greatness of man (his freedom to do what God does not want) and the power of evil (it comes and remains in the universe even though God does not want it). Moreover, by denying that God can make creatures who have real choices that are nevertheless caused by him, the Arminian position seems to diminish the wisdom and skill of God the Creator.

II. REVIEW QUESTIONS

1. Define and give scriptural support for the doctrine of preservation. How does this teaching provide a basis for scientific activity?

2. How can an event be fully caused by God and fully caused by a creature as well?

3. How would you describe the relationship of God to evil in the world?

4. From the perspective of the author, in what way can we say that people have "free will"?

5. If God is in control of all things, are human actions significant? Why?

6. What is the primary difference between the doctrine of providence as described in this chapter and the viewpoint of Arminianism?

III. QUESTIONS FOR PERSONAL APPLICATION

1. Has thinking about the doctrine of providence increased your trust in God? How has it changed the way you think about the future? Cite an example of a specific difficulty that you are now facing, and explain how the doctrine of providence will help you in the way you think about it.

2. Can you name five good things that have happened to you so far today? Were you thankful to God for any of them?

3. Do you sometimes think of luck or chance as causing events that happen in your life? Does that thought increase or decrease your anxiety about the future? Think about some events that you might have attributed to luck in the past and, instead, begin to think about those events as under the control of your wise and loving heavenly Father. How does that make you feel differently about them and about the future generally?

4. Do you ever fall into a pattern of little "superstitious" actions or rituals that you think will bring good luck or prevent bad luck (such as not walking under a ladder or being afraid when a black cat walks across your path)? Do you think those actions tend to increase or decrease your trust in God during the day and your obedience to him?

5. Explain how a proper understanding of the doctrine of providence should lead a Christian to a more active prayer life.

IV. SPECIAL TERMS

Arminian

Calvinist

concurrence

free choices

free will

government

preservation

primary cause

providence

Reformed

secondary cause

voluntary choices

willing choices

V. SCRIPTURE MEMORY PASSAGE

Romans 8:28

We know that in everything God works for good with those who love him, who are called according to his purpose.

CHAPTER NINE

Prayer

+ *Why does God want us to pray?*
+ *How can we pray effectively?*

I. EXPLANATION AND SCRIPTURAL BASIS

The character of God and his relationship to the world, as discussed in the previous chapters, lead naturally to a consideration of the doctrine of prayer. Prayer may be defined as follows: *Prayer is personal communication from us to God.*

This definition is very broad. What we call "prayer" includes prayers of request for ourselves or for others (sometimes called prayers of petition or intercession), confession of sin, adoration, praise, and thanksgiving.

A. Why Does God Want Us to Pray?

Prayer is not made so that God can find out what we need, because Jesus tells us, "Your Father knows what you need before you ask him" (Matt. 6:8). God wants us to pray because prayer expresses our trust in God and is a means whereby our trust in him can increase. In fact, perhaps the primary emphasis of the Bible's teaching on prayer is that we are to pray with faith, which means trust or dependence on God. God as our Creator delights in being trusted by us as his creatures, for an attitude of dependence is most appropriate to the Creator-creature relationship.

The first words of the Lord's Prayer, "Our Father who art in heaven" (Matt. 6:9), acknowledge our dependence on God as a loving and wise Father and also recognize that he rules over all from his heavenly throne. Scripture many times emphasizes our need to trust God as we pray. For example, Jesus compares our praying to a son asking his father for a fish or an egg (Luke 11:9–12) and then concludes, "If you then, who are evil, know how to give good gifts to your children, how much more will the heavenly Father give the Holy Spirit to those who ask him!" (Luke 11:13). As children look to their fathers to provide for them, so God expects us to look to him in prayer. Since God is our Father, we should ask in faith. Jesus says, "Whatever you ask in prayer, you will receive, if you have faith" (Matt. 21:22; cf. Mark 11:24; James 1:6–8; 5:14–15).

But God does not only want us to trust him. He also wants us to love him and have fellowship with him. This, then, is a second reason why God wants us to pray: Prayer brings us into deeper fellowship with God, and he loves us and delights in our fellowship with him. When we truly pray, we as persons, in the wholeness of our character, are relating to God as a person, in the wholeness of his character. Thus, all that we think or feel about God comes to expression in our prayer. It is only natural that God would delight in such activity and place much emphasis on it in his relationship with us.

A third reason God wants us to pray is that in prayer God allows us as creatures to be involved in activities that are eternally important. When we pray, the work of the kingdom is advanced. In this way, prayer gives us opportunity to be involved in a significant way in the work of the kingdom and thus gives expression to our amazing significance as creatures made in God's image.

A fourth reason God wants us to pray is that in praying we give glory to God. Praying in humble dependence on God indicates that we are genuinely convinced of his wisdom, love, goodness, and power.

B. The Effectiveness of Prayer

How exactly does prayer work? Does prayer not only do us good but also affect God and the world?

1. Prayer often changes the way God acts. James tells us, "You do not have, because you do not ask" (James 4:2). He implies that failure to ask deprives us of what God would otherwise have given to us. We pray, and God responds. Jesus also says, "Ask, and it will be given you; seek, and you will find; knock, and it will be opened to you. For every one who asks receives, and he who seeks finds, and to him who knocks it will be opened" (Luke 11:9–10). He makes a clear connection between seeking things from God and receiving them. When we ask, God responds.

We see this happening many times in the Old Testament. The Lord declared to Moses that he would destroy the people of Israel for their sin (Ex. 32:9–10), "But Moses besought the LORD his God, and said, 'O Lord, . . . Turn from your fierce wrath, and repent of this evil against your people'" (Ex. 32:11–12). Then we read, "And the LORD repented of the evil which he thought to do to his people" (Ex. 32:14). Moses prayed, and God responded. When God threatens to punish his people for their sins, he declares, "If my people who are called by my name humble themselves, *and pray and seek my face*, and turn from their wicked ways, *then I will hear* from heaven, and will forgive their sin and heal their land" (2 Chron. 7:14). If and when God's people pray (with humility and repentance), *then* he will hear and forgive them. The prayers of his people clearly affect how God acts. Similarly, "If we confess our sins, he is faithful and just, and will forgive our sins and cleanse us from all unrighteousness" (1 John 1:9). We confess, and then he forgives.

If we were really convinced that prayer often changes the way God acts, and that God does bring about remarkable changes in the world in response to prayer (as Scripture repeatedly teaches that he does), then we would pray much more than we do. If we pray little, it is probably because we do not really believe that prayer accomplishes much at all.

2. Effective prayer is made possible by our mediator, Jesus Christ. Because we are sinful and God is holy, we have no right on our own to enter into his presence. We need a mediator to come between us and God and to bring us into God's presence. Scripture clearly teaches, "There is one God, and there is one mediator between God and men, the man Christ Jesus" (1 Tim. 2:5).

But if Jesus is the only mediator between God and man, will God hear the prayers of unbelievers, those who do not trust in Jesus? The answer depends on what we mean by "hear." Since God is omniscient, he always "hears" in the sense that he is aware of the prayers made by unbelievers who do not come to him through Christ. God may even, from time to time, answer their prayers out of his mercy and in a desire to bring them to salvation through Christ. However, God has nowhere promised to respond to the prayers of unbelievers. The only prayers that he has promised to "hear" in the sense of listening with a sympathetic ear and undertaking to answer when they are made according to his will, are the prayers of Christians offered through the one mediator, Jesus Christ (cf. John 14:6).

Then what about believers in the Old Testament? How could they come to God through Jesus the mediator? The answer is that the work of Jesus as our mediator was foreshadowed by the sacrificial system and the offerings made by the priests in the temple (Heb. 7:23–28; 8:1–6; 9:1–14; et al.). There was no saving merit in that system of sacrifices (Heb. 10:1–4), however. Through the sacrificial system, believers were accepted by God only on the basis of the future work of Christ foreshadowed by that system (Rom. 3:23–26).

Jesus' activity as a mediator is especially seen in his work as a priest: He is our "great high priest who has passed through the heavens," one who "in every respect has been tempted as we are, yet without sin" (Heb. 4:14–15).

As recipients of the new covenant, we do not need to stay "outside the temple," as all believers except the priests were required to do under the old covenant. Nor do we need to stay outside of the "Holy of Holies" (Heb. 9:3), the inner room of the temple where God himself was enthroned above the ark of the covenant and where only the high priest could go, and he but once a year. But now, since Christ has died as our mediational High Priest (Heb. 7:26–27), he has gained for us boldness and access to the very presence of God. Therefore, "we have confidence to enter *into the holy places* by the blood of Jesus" (Heb. 10:19, author's literal translation), that is, into the Holy Place and into the Holy of Holies, the very presence of God himself! Christ's mediational work gives us confidence to approach God in prayer.

3. What is praying "in Jesus' name"? Jesus says, "Whatever you ask *in my name,* I will do it, that the Father may be glorified in the Son; if you ask anything *in my name,* I will do it" (John 14:13–14). He also says that he chose his disciples "so that whatever you ask the Father *in my name,* he may give it to you" (John 15:16). Similarly, he says, "Truly, truly, I say to you, if you ask anything of the Father, he will give it to you *in my name.* Hitherto you have asked nothing *in my name;* ask, and you will receive, that your joy may be full" (John 16:23–24; cf. Eph. 5:20). But what does this mean?

Clearly it does not simply mean adding the phrase "in Jesus' name" after every prayer, because Jesus did not say, "If you ask anything and add the words 'in Jesus' name' after your prayer, I will do it." Jesus is not merely speaking about adding certain words as if these were a kind of magical formula that would give power to our prayers. In fact, none of the prayers recorded in Scripture have the phrase "in Jesus' name" at the end of them (see Matt. 6:9–13; Acts 1:24–25; 4:24–30; 7:59; 9:13–14; 10:14; Rev. 6:10; 22:20).

To come in the name of someone means that another person has authorized us to come on his authority, not on our own. When Peter commands the lame man, "in the name of Jesus Christ of Nazareth, walk" (Acts 3:6), he is speaking on the authority of Jesus, not on his own authority. When the Sanhedrin asks the disciples, "By what power or *by what name* did you do this?" (Acts 4:7), they are asking, "By whose authority did you do this?" When Paul rebukes an unclean spirit "in the name of

Jesus Christ" (Acts 16:18), he makes it clear that he is doing so on Jesus' authority, not his own. When Paul pronounces judgment "in the name of the Lord Jesus" (1 Cor. 5:4) on a church member who is guilty of immorality, he is acting with the authority of the Lord Jesus. *Praying in Jesus' name is therefore prayer made on his authorization on the basis of his mediatorial work for us.*

In a broader sense, the "name" of a person in the ancient world represented the person himself and therefore all of his character. To have a "good name" (Prov. 22:1; Eccl. 7:1) was to have a good reputation. Thus, the name of Jesus represents all that he is, his entire character. This means that praying "in Jesus' name" is not only praying in his authority, but also praying in a way that is consistent with his character, that truly represents him and reflects his manner of life and his own holy will. *Praying in Jesus' name also means praying according to his character.* In this sense, to pray in Jesus' name comes close to the idea of praying "according to his will" (1 John 5:14–15).

Does this mean it is wrong to add "in Jesus' name" to the end of our prayers? It is certainly not wrong, as long as we understand what is meant by it and that it is not necessary to do so. There may be some danger, however, if we add this phrase to every public or private prayer we make, for very soon it will become to people simply a formula to which they attach very little meaning and say without thinking about it. It may even begin to be viewed, at least by younger believers, as a sort of magic formula that makes prayer more effective. To prevent such misunderstanding, it would probably be wise to decide not to use the formula frequently and to express the same thought in other words or simply in the overall attitude and approach we take toward prayer. For example, prayers could begin, "Father, we come to you in the authority of our Lord Jesus, your Son . . ." or, "Father, we do not come on our own merits but on the merits of Jesus Christ, who has invited us to come before you . . ." or, "Father, we thank you for forgiving our sins and giving us access to your throne by the work of Jesus your Son. . . ." At other times even these formal acknowledgments should not be thought necessary, so long as our hearts continually realize that it is our Savior who enables us to pray to the Father at all. Genuine prayer is conversation with a person whom we know well and who knows us. Such genuine conversation between persons who know each other never depends on the use of certain formulas or required words, but is a matter of sincerity in our speech and in our heart, a matter of right attitudes, and a matter of the condition of our spirit.

4. Should we pray to Jesus and to the Holy Spirit? A survey of the prayers of the New Testament indicates that they are usually addressed neither to God the Son nor to the Holy Spirit, but to God the Father. Yet a mere count of such prayers may be misleading, for the majority of the prayers we have recorded in the New Testament are those of Jesus himself, who constantly prayed to God the Father but of course did not pray to himself as God the Son. Moreover, in the Old Testament, the trinitarian nature of God was not so clearly revealed, and it is not surprising that we do not find much evidence of prayer addressed directly to God the Son or God the Holy Spirit before the time of Christ.

Though there is a clear pattern of prayer directly to God the Father through the Son (Matt. 6:9; John 16:23; Eph. 5:20), there are other indications that prayer spoken directly to Jesus is also appropriate. The fact that it was Jesus himself who appointed all of the other apostles suggests that the prayer in Acts 1:24 is addressed to him: "*Lord*, who knows the hearts of all men, show which one of these two you have chosen. . . ." The dying Stephen prays, "Lord Jesus, receive my spirit" (Acts

7:59). The conversation between Ananias and "the Lord" in Acts 9:10–16 is with Jesus, because in verse 17 Ananias tells Saul, "The Lord Jesus . . . has sent me that you may regain your sight." The prayer, "Our Lord, come!" (1 Cor. 16:22) is addressed to Jesus, as is the prayer in Revelation 22:20, "Come, Lord Jesus!" And Paul also prayed to "the Lord" in 2 Corinthians 12:8 concerning his thorn in the flesh.[1]

Moreover, the fact that Jesus is "a merciful and faithful high priest" (Heb. 2:17) who is able to "sympathize with our weaknesses" (Heb. 4:15) is an encouragement to us to come boldly before the "throne of grace" in prayer "that we may receive mercy and find grace to help in time of need" (Heb. 4:16). These verses must give us encouragement to come directly to Jesus in prayer, expecting that he will sympathize with our weaknesses as we pray.

There is therefore clear enough scriptural warrant to encourage us to pray not only to God the Father (which seems to be the primary pattern, and certainly follows the example that Jesus taught us in the Lord's Prayer), but also to pray directly to God the Son, our Lord Jesus Christ. Both are correct, and we may pray either to the Father or to the Son.

But should we pray to the Holy Spirit? Though no prayers directly addressed to the Holy Spirit are recorded in the New Testament, there is nothing that would forbid such prayer, for the Holy Spirit, like the Father and the Son, is fully God, is worthy of prayer, and is powerful to answer our prayers. He also relates to us in a personal way since he is a "Comforter" or "Counselor" (John 14:16, 26). Believers "know him" (John 14:17), and he teaches them (cf. John 14:26), bears witness to us that we are children of God (Rom. 8:16), and can be grieved by our sin (Eph. 4:30). Moreover, the Holy Spirit exercises personal volition in the distribution of spiritual gifts, for he "continually distributes to each one individually *as he wills*" (1 Cor. 12:11, author's translation). Therefore, it does not seem wrong to pray directly to the Holy Spirit at times, particularly when we are asking him to do something that relates to his special areas of ministry or responsibility.[2] But this is not the New Testament pattern, and it should not become the dominant emphasis in our prayer life.

C. Some Important Considerations in Effective Prayer

Scripture indicates a number of considerations that need to be taken into account if we would offer the kind of prayer that God desires from us.

1. Praying according to God's will. John tells us, "This is the confidence which we have in him, that if we ask anything *according to his will* he hears us. And if we know that he hears us in whatever we ask, we know that we have obtained the requests made of him" (1 John 5:14–15). Jesus teaches us to pray, "Your will be

---

[1]The name "Lord" (Greek *kyrios*) is used in Acts and the epistles primarily to refer to the Lord Jesus Christ.

[2]Regarding worship of the Holy Spirit, the entire church, Catholic, Orthodox, and Protestant, has unanimously agreed that this is proper, as stated in the Nicene Creed in A.D. 381: ". . . And in the Holy Spirit, the Lord and Giver of Life; who proceedeth from the Father and the Son; who with the Father and the Son together *is worshiped and glorified*." Similarly, the Westminster Confession of Faith says, "Religious worship is to be given to God, the Father, Son, and Holy Ghost; and to him alone; not to angels, saints, or any other creature . . ." (21.2). Many hymns in use for centuries give praise to the Holy Spirit, such as the Gloria Patri ("Glory be to the Father, and to the Son, and to the Holy Ghost . . .") or the Doxology ("Praise God from whom all blessings flow . . . Praise Father, Son, and Holy Ghost"). This practice is based on the conviction that God is worthy of worship, and since the Holy Spirit is fully God, he is worthy of worship. Such words of praise are one kind of prayer to the Holy Spirit, and if they are appropriate, there seems no reason to think that other kinds of prayer to the Holy Spirit are inappropriate.

done" (Matt. 6:10), and he himself gives us an example, by praying in the Garden of Gethsemane, "nevertheless, not as I will, but as you will" (Matt. 26:39).

But how do we know what God's will is when we pray? If the matter we are praying about is covered in a passage of Scripture in which God gives us a *command* or a direct *declaration of his will,* then the answer to this question is easy: His will is that his Word be obeyed and that his commands be kept. We are to seek for perfect obedience to God's moral will on earth so that God's will may be done "on earth as it is in heaven" (Matt. 6:10). For this reason, knowledge of Scripture is a tremendous help in prayer, enabling us to follow the pattern of the first Christians who quoted Scripture when they prayed (see Acts 4:25–26). The regular reading and memorization of Scripture, cultivated over many years of a Christian's life, will increase the depth, power, and wisdom of his or her prayers. Jesus encourages us to have his words within us as we pray, for he says, "If you abide in me, *and my words abide in you,* ask whatever you will, and it shall be done for you" (John 15:7).

We should have great confidence that God will answer our prayer when we ask him for something that accords with a specific promise or command of Scripture like this. In such cases, we know what God's will is, because he has told us, and we simply need to pray believing that he will answer.

However, there are many other situations in life where we do not know what God's will is. We may not be sure, because no promise or command of Scripture applies, whether it is God's will that we get the job we have applied for, or win an athletic contest in which we are participating (a common prayer among children, especially), or be chosen to hold office in the church, and so on. In all of these cases, we should bring to bear as much of Scripture as we understand, perhaps to give us some general principles within which our prayer can be made. But beyond this, we often must admit that we simply do not know what God's will is. In such cases, we should ask him for deeper understanding and then pray for what seems best to us, giving reasons to the Lord why, in our present understanding of the situation, what we are praying for seems to be best. But it is always right to add, either explicitly or at least in the attitude of our heart, "Nevertheless, if I am wrong in asking this, and if this is not pleasing to you, then do as seems best in your sight," or, more simply, "If it is your will." Sometimes God will grant what we have asked. Sometimes he will give us deeper understanding or change our hearts so that we are led to ask something differently. Sometimes he will not grant our request at all but will simply indicate to us that we must submit to his will (see 2 Cor. 12:9–10).

Some Christians object that to add the phrase "if it is your will" to our prayers "destroys our faith." What it actually does is express uncertainty about whether what we pray for is God's will or not. It is appropriate when we do not really know what God's will is, but at other times it is inappropriate. For example, to ask God to give us wisdom to make a decision and then say, "If it is your will to give me wisdom here" would be inappropriate, for it would be saying that we do not believe God meant what he said when he told us to ask in faith and he would grant this request ("If any of you lacks wisdom, let him ask God, who gives to all men generously and without reproaching, and it will be given him," James 1:5).

2. Praying with faith. Jesus says, "Therefore I tell you, whatever you ask in prayer, *believe that you have received it,* and it will be yours" (Mark 11:24). Some translations vary, but the Greek text actually says, "believe that you *have received it.*" Jesus is apparently saying that when we ask for something, the kind of faith that will bring results is a settled assurance that at the time we prayed for something (or perhaps after we had been praying over a period of time), God agreed to grant our specific request. In the personal communion with God that occurs in genuine prayer, this kind of faith on our part could only come *as God gives us a sense of assurance that he has agreed to grant our request.* Of course, we cannot "work up" this kind of genuine faith by any sort of frenzied prayer or great emotional effort to try to make ourselves believe, nor can we force it upon ourselves by saying words we don't think to be true. This is something that only God can give us and that he may or may not give us each time we pray. This assured faith will often come when we ask God for something and then quietly wait before him for an answer.

In fact, Hebrews 11:1 tells us that "faith is the *assurance* of things hoped for, the *conviction* of things not seen." Biblical faith is never a kind of wishful thinking or a vague hope that doesn't have any secure foundation on which to rest. It is rather *trust* in a person, God himself, based on the fact that we take him at his word and believe what he has said. This trust or dependence on God, when it also has an element of assurance or confidence, is genuine biblical faith.

3. Obedience. Since prayer occurs within our relationship with God as a person, anything in our lives that displeases him will be a hindrance to prayer. The psalmist says, "If I had cherished iniquity in my heart, the LORD would not have listened" (Ps. 66:18). Though "the sacrifice of the wicked is an abomination to the LORD," by contrast, "the prayer of the upright is his delight" (Prov. 15:8). Again we read that "The LORD . . . hears the prayer of the righteous" (Prov. 15:29). But God is not favorably disposed to those who reject his laws: "If one turns away his ear from hearing the law, even his prayer is an abomination" (Prov. 28:9).

The apostle Peter quotes Psalm 34 to affirm that "the eyes of the Lord are upon the righteous, and his ears are open to their prayer" (1 Peter 3:12). Since the previous verses encourage good conduct in everyday life, in speaking and turning away from evil and doing right, Peter is saying that God readily hears the prayers of those who live lives of obedience to him. Similarly, Peter warns husbands to "live considerately" with their wives, "in order that your prayers may not be hindered" (1 Peter 3:7). Likewise, John reminds us of the need for a clear conscience before God when we pray, for he says, "If our hearts do not condemn us, we have confidence before God; and we receive from him whatever we ask, because we keep his commandments and do what pleases him" (1 John 3:21–22).

Now this teaching must not be misunderstood. We do not need to be freed from sin completely before God can be expected to answer our prayers. If God only answered the prayers of sinless people, then no one in the whole Bible except Jesus would have had a prayer answered. When we come before God through his grace, we come cleansed by the blood of Christ (Rom. 3:25; 5:9; Eph. 2:13; Heb. 9:14; 1 Peter 1:2). Yet we must not neglect the biblical emphasis on personal holiness of life. Prayer and holy living go together. There is much grace in the Christian life, but growth in personal holiness is also a route to much greater blessing, and that is true with respect to prayer as well. The passages quoted teach that, all other things being equal, more exact obedience will lead to increased effectiveness in prayer (cf. Heb. 12:14; James 4:3–4).

4. Confession of sins. Because our obedience to God is never perfect in this life, we continually depend on his forgiveness of our sins. Confession of sins is necessary in order for God to "forgive us" in the sense of restoring his day-by-day relationship with us (see Matt. 6:12; 1 John 1:9). When we pray, it is good to confess all known sin to the Lord and to ask for his forgiveness. Sometimes when we wait on him, he will bring other sins to mind that we need to confess. With respect to those sins that we do not remember or of which we are unaware, it is appropriate to pray the general prayer of David, "Clear me from hidden faults" (Ps. 19:12).

Sometimes confessing our sins to other trusted Christians will bring an assurance of forgiveness and encouragement to overcome sin as well. James relates mutual confession to prayer, for in a passage discussing powerful prayer, James encourages us, "Therefore *confess your sins to one another,* and pray for one another, that you may be healed" (James 5:16).

5. *Forgiving others.* Jesus says, "If you forgive men their trespasses, your heavenly Father also will forgive you; but if you do not forgive men their trespasses, neither will your Father forgive your trespasses" (Matt. 6:14–15). Similarly, Jesus says, "Whenever you stand praying, forgive, if you have anything against any one; so that your Father also who is in heaven may forgive you your trespasses" (Mark 11:25). Our Lord does not have in mind the initial experience of forgiveness we know when we are justified by faith, for that would not belong in a prayer that we pray every day (see Matt. 6:12, 14–15). He refers rather to the day-by-day relationship with God that we need to have restored when we have sinned and displeased him.

Since prayer presumes a relationship with God as a *person,* this is not surprising. If we have sinned against him and grieved the Holy Spirit (cf. Eph. 4:30), and the sin has not been forgiven, it interrupts our relationship with God (cf. Isa. 59:1–2). Until sin is forgiven and the relationship is restored, prayer will, of course, be difficult. Moreover, if we have unforgiveness in our hearts against someone else, then we are not acting in a way that is pleasing to God or helpful to us. So God declares (Matt. 6:12, 14–15) that he will distance himself from us until we forgive others.

6. *Humility.* James tells us that "God opposes the proud, but gives grace to the humble" (James 4:6; also 1 Peter 5:5). Therefore, he says, "Humble yourselves before the Lord and he will exalt you" (James 4:10). Humility is thus the right attitude to have in praying to God, whereas pride is altogether inappropriate.

Jesus' parable about the Pharisee and the tax collector illustrates this. When the Pharisee stood to pray, he was boastful: "God, I thank you that I am not like other men, extortioners, unjust, adulterers, or even like this tax collector. I fast twice a week, I give tithes of all that I get" (Luke 18:11–12). By contrast, the humble tax collector "would not even lift up his eyes to heaven, but beat his breast, saying, 'God, be merciful to me a sinner!'" (Luke 18:13). Jesus said that he "went down to his house justified," rather than the Pharisee, "for every one who exalts himself will be humbled, but he who humbles himself will be exalted" (Luke 18:14). This is why Jesus condemned those who "for a pretense make long prayers" (Luke 20:47), and those hypocrites who "love to stand and pray in the synagogues and at the street corners, that they may be seen by men" (Matt. 6:5).

God is rightly jealous for his own honor.[3] Therefore, he is not pleased to answer the prayers of the proud who take honor to themselves rather than giving it to him. True humility before God, which will also be reflected in genuine humility before others, is necessary for effective prayer.

---

[3]See discussion of God's attribute of jealousy, p. 94, above.

7. What about unanswered prayer? We must begin by recognizing that as long as God is God and we are his creatures, there must be some unanswered prayers. This is because God keeps hidden his own wise plans for the future, and even though people pray, many events will not come about until the time that God has decreed. The Jews prayed for centuries for the Messiah to come, and rightly so, but it was not until "the time had fully come" that "God sent forth his Son" (Gal. 4:4). The souls of martyrs in heaven, free from sin, cry out for God to judge the earth (Rev. 6:10), but God does not immediately answer; rather, he tells them "to rest a little longer" (Rev. 6:11). It is clear that there can be long periods of delay during which prayers go unanswered because the people praying do not know God's wise timing.

Prayer will also be unanswered because we do not always know how to pray as we ought (Rom. 8:26), we do not always pray according to God's will (James 4:3), and we do not always ask in faith (James 1:6–8). And sometimes we think that one solution is best, but God has a better plan, even to fulfill his purpose through suffering and hardship. Joseph no doubt prayed earnestly to be rescued from the pit and from being carried off into slavery in Egypt (Gen. 37:23–36), but many years later he found how in all of these events "God meant it for good" (Gen. 50:20).

When we face unanswered prayer, we join the company of Jesus, who prayed, "Father, if you are willing, remove this cup from me; nevertheless not my will, but yours, be done" (Luke 22:42). We join also the company of Paul, who asked the Lord "three times" that his thorn in the flesh be removed, but it was not; rather the Lord told him, "My grace is sufficient for you, for my power is made perfect in weakness" (2 Cor. 12:8–9). When prayer remains unanswered, we must continue to trust God, who "causes all things to work together for good" (Rom. 8:28 NASB) and to cast our cares on him, knowing that he continually cares for us (1 Peter 5:7). We must keep remembering that he will give strength sufficient for each day (Deut. 33:25) and that he has promised, "I will never fail you nor forsake you" (Heb. 13:5; cf. Rom. 8:35–39).

We also must continue to pray. Sometimes an answer, long awaited, will suddenly be given, as it was when Hannah after many years bore a child (1 Sam. 1:19–20), or when Simeon saw with his own eyes the long-expected Messiah come to the temple (Luke 2:25–35).

But sometimes prayers will remain unanswered in this life. At times, God will answer those prayers after the believer dies. At other times he will not, but even then, the faith expressed in those prayers, and their heartfelt expressions of love for God and for the people he has made, will still ascend as a pleasing incense before God's throne (Rev. 5:8; 8:3–4), and will result in "praise and glory and honor at the revelation of Jesus Christ" (1 Peter 1:7).

D. Praise and Thanksgiving

Praise and thanksgiving to God are an essential element of prayer. The model prayer that Jesus left us begins with a word of praise: "Hallowed be your name" (Matt. 6:9). And Paul tells the Philippians, "In everything by prayer and supplication *with thanksgiving* let your requests be made known to God" (Phil. 4:6), and the Colossians, "Continue steadfastly in prayer, being watchful in it *with thanksgiving*" (Col. 4:2). Thanksgiving, like every other aspect of prayer, should not be a mechanical mouthing of a "thank you" to God, but the expression of words that reflect the thankfulness of our hearts. Moreover, we should never think that thanking God for the answer to something we ask for can somehow force God to give it to us, for that changes the prayer from a genuine, sincere request to a demand that assumes we can make God do what we want him to do. Such a spirit in our prayers really denies the essential nature of prayer as dependence on God.

By contrast, the kind of thanksgiving that appropriately accompanies prayer must express thankfulness to God for all circumstances, for every event of life that he allows to come to us. When we join our prayers with humble, childlike thanksgiving to God "in all circumstances" (1 Thess. 5:18), this is praying that is acceptable to God.

II. REVIEW QUESTIONS

1. Give three reasons why God wants us to pray.
2. In what way does Jesus make our prayers effective?
3. What does it mean to pray "according to God's will"?
4. What role does our obedience play in answers to our prayers?
5. Give three reasons why our prayers may go unanswered.

III. QUESTIONS FOR PERSONAL APPLICATION

1. Do you often have difficulty with prayer? What things in this chapter have been helpful to you in this regard?
2. When have you known the most effective times of prayer in your own life? What factors contributed to making those times more effective?
3. How does it help and encourage you (if it does) when you pray together with other Christians?
4. Have you ever tried waiting quietly before the Lord after making an earnest prayer request? If so, what has been the result?
5. Do you have a regular time each day for private Bible reading and prayer? Are you sometimes easily distracted and turned aside to other activities? If so, how can distractions be overcome?

IV. SPECIAL TERMS

faith

"in Jesus' name"

mediator

prayer

V. SCRIPTURE MEMORY PASSAGE

HEBREWS 4:14–16

Since then we have a great high priest who has passed through the heavens, Jesus, the Son of God, let us hold fast our confession. For we have not a high priest who is unable to sympathize with our weaknesses, but one who in every respect has been tempted as we are, yet without sin. Let us then with confidence draw near to the throne of grace, that we may receive mercy and find grace to help in time of need.

CHAPTER TEN

Angels, Satan, and Demons

+ *What are angels?*
+ *Why did God create them?*
+ *How should Christians think of Satan and demons today?*

I. EXPLANATION AND SCRIPTURAL BASIS

A. What Are Angels?

We may define angels as follows: *Angels are created spiritual beings with moral judgment and high intelligence but without physical bodies.*

1. Created spiritual beings. Angels have not always existed; they are part of the universe that God created. In a passage that refers to angels as the "host" of heaven (or "armies of heaven"), Ezra says, "You are the LORD, you alone; you have made heaven, the heaven of heavens, *with all their host* ... and the host of heaven worships you" (Neh. 9:6; cf. Ps. 148:2, 5). Paul tells us that God created all things "visible and invisible" through Christ and for him, and then specifically includes the angelic world with the phrase "whether thrones or dominions or principalities or authorities" (Col. 1:16).

That angels exercise moral judgment is seen in the fact that some of them sinned and fell from their positions (2 Peter 2:4; Jude 6; see pp. 174-75). Their high intelligence is seen throughout Scripture as they speak to people (Matt. 28:5; Acts 12:6–11; et al.) and sing praise to God (Rev. 4:11; 5:11).

Since angels are "spirits" (Heb. 1:14), or spiritual creatures, they do not ordinarily have physical bodies (Luke 24:39: Jesus says, "A spirit has not flesh and bones as you see that I have"). Therefore, they cannot usually be seen by us unless God gives us a special ability to see them (Num. 22:31; 2 Kings 6:17; Luke 2:13). In their ordinary activities of guarding and protecting us (Ps. 34:7; 91:11; Heb. 1:14), and joining with us in worship to God (Heb. 12:22), they are invisible. However, from time to time angels took on a bodily form to appear to various people in Scripture (Matt. 28:5; Heb. 13:2).

2. Other names for angels. Scripture sometimes uses other terms for angels, such as "sons of God" (Job 1:6; 2:1), "holy ones" (Ps. 89:5, 7), "spirits" (Heb. 1:14), "watchers" (Dan. 4:13, 17, 23), "thrones," "dominions," "principalities," "authorities" (Col. 1:16), and "powers" (Eph. 1:21).

3. Other kinds of heavenly beings. There are three other specific types of heavenly beings named in Scripture. Whether we think of these as special types of "angels" (in a broad sense of the term), or whether we think of them as heavenly beings distinct from angels, they are nonetheless created spiritual beings who serve and worship God.

a. *The "cherubim."*[1] The cherubim were given the task of guarding the entrance to the Garden of Eden (Gen. 3:24), and God himself is said to be enthroned on the cherubim or to travel with the cherubim as his chariot (Ps. 18:10; Ezek. 10:1–22). Over the ark of the covenant in the Old Testament were two golden figures of cherubim with their wings stretched out above the ark, and it was there that God promised to come to dwell among his people: "There I will meet with you, and from above the mercy seat, from between the two cherubim that are upon the ark of testimony, I will speak with you of all that I will give you in commandment for the people of Israel" (Ex. 25:22; cf. vv. 18–21).

b. *The "seraphim."*[2] Another group of heavenly beings, the seraphim, are mentioned only in Isaiah 6:2–7, where they continually worship the Lord and call to one another, "Holy, holy, holy is the LORD of hosts; the whole earth is full of his glory" (Isa. 6:3).

c. *The living creatures.* Both Ezekiel and Revelation tell us of yet other kinds of heavenly beings known as "living creatures" around God's throne (Ezek. 1:5–14; Rev. 4:6–8). With their appearances like a lion, an ox, a man, and an eagle, they are the mightiest representatives of various parts of God's entire creation (wild beasts, domesticated animals, human beings, and birds), and they worship God continually: "Day and night they never cease to sing, 'Holy, holy, holy, is the Lord God Almighty, who was and is and is to come!'" (Rev. 4:8).

4. Rank and order among the angels. Scripture indicates that there is rank and order among the angels. One angel, Michael, is called an "archangel" in Jude 9, a title that indicates rule or authority over other angels. He is called "one of the chief princes" in Daniel 10:13. Michael also appears to be a leader in the angelic army: "Now war arose in heaven, Michael and his angels fighting against the dragon; and the dragon and his angels fought, but they were defeated" (Rev. 12:7–8). And Paul tells us that the Lord will return from heaven "with the archangel's call" (1 Thess. 4:16). Whether this refers to Michael as the only archangel, or whether there are other archangels, Scripture does not tell us.

5. Do people have individual guardian angels? Scripture clearly tells us that God sends angels for our protection: "He will give his angels charge of you to guard you in all your ways. On their hands they will bear you up, lest you dash your foot against a stone" (Ps. 91:11–12). But some people have gone beyond this idea of general protection and wondered if God gives a specific "guardian angel" for each individual in the world, or at least for each Christian. Support for this idea has been found in Jesus' words about little children, "in heaven *their angels* always behold the face of my Father who is in heaven" (Matt. 18:10). However, our Lord may simply be saying that angels who are assigned the task of protecting little children have

---

[1]The Hebrew word *cherub* is singular, while *cherubim* is the plural form.
[2]The Hebrew word *seraph* is singular, while *seraphim* is the plural form.

ready access to God's presence. (To use an athletic analogy, the angels may be play-ing "zone" rather than "man-on-man" defense.) When the disciples in Acts 12:15 say that Peter's "angel" must be knocking at the door, this does not necessarily imply belief in an individual guardian angel. It could be that an angel was guarding or car-ing for Peter at that time. There seems to be, therefore, no convincing support for the idea of individual "guardian angels" in the text of Scripture. But we do find that angels in general have the task of protecting God's people.

6. The power of angels. Angels apparently have very great power. They are called "you mighty ones who do his word" (Ps. 103:20) and "powers" (cf. Eph. 1:21) and "dominions" and "authorities" (Col. 1:16). Angels are seemingly "greater in might and power" than rebellious human beings (2 Peter 2:11; cf. Matt. 28:2). At least for the time of their earthly existence, human beings are made "lower than the angels" (Heb. 2:7). Though the power of angels is great, it is certainly not infinite, but it is used to battle against the evil demonic powers under the control of Satan (Dan. 10:13; Rev. 12:7–8; 20:1–3). Nonetheless, when the Lord returns, we will be raised to a position higher than that of angels (1 Cor. 6:3; see section B.1 below).

B. The Place of Angels in God's Purpose

1. Angels show the greatness of God's love and plan for us. Human beings and angels are the only moral, highly intelligent creatures that God has made. There-fore, we can understand much about God's plan and love for us when we compare ourselves with angels.

The first distinction to be noted is that angels are never said to be made "in the image of God," while human beings are several times said to be in God's image (Gen. 1:26–27; 9:6). Since being in the image of God means to be like God,[3] it seems fair to conclude that we are more like God even than the angels are.

This is supported by the fact that God will someday give us authority over angels, to judge them: "Do you not know that *we are to judge angels?*" (1 Cor. 6:3). Though we are "for a little while lower than the angels" (Heb. 2:7), when our salvation is complete, we will be exalted above angels and rule over them. In fact, even now, angels already serve us: "Are they not all ministering spirits sent forth *to serve,* for the sake of those who are to obtain salvation?" (Heb. 1:14).

The ability of human beings to bear children like themselves (Adam "became the father of a son in his own likeness, after his image," Gen. 5:3) is another element of our superiority to angels, who apparently cannot bear children (cf. Matt. 22:30; Luke 20:34–36).

Angels also demonstrate the greatness of God's love for us in that, though many angels sinned, none were saved. Peter tells us that "*God did not spare the angels when they sinned,* but cast them into hell and committed them to pits of nether gloom to be kept until the judgment" (2 Peter 2:4). Jude says that "the angels that did not keep their own position but left their proper dwelling have been kept by him in eter-nal chains in the nether gloom until the judgment of the great day" (Jude 6). And we read in Hebrews, "For surely it is not with angels that he is concerned but with the descendants of Abraham" (Heb. 2:16).

We see, therefore, that God created two groups of intelligent moral creatures. Among the angels, many sinned, but God decided to redeem none of them. This was

---

[3]See ch. 11, pp. 189–93.

perfectly just for God to do, and no angel can ever complain that he has been treated unfairly by God. However, even though all human beings have sinned and turned away from him, God decided to do much more than merely meet the demands of justice; he decided to save some sinful human beings. In fact, he has decided to redeem out of sinful mankind a great multitude, whom no man can number, "from every tribe and tongue and people and nation" (Rev. 5:9). This is incalculable mercy and love, far beyond our comprehension. It is all undeserved favor; it is all of grace. The striking contrast with the fate of angels brings this truth home to us.

2. Angels remind us that the unseen world is real. Just as the Sadducees in Jesus' day said that "there is no resurrection, nor angel, nor spirit" (Acts 23:8), so many in our day deny the reality of anything they cannot see. But the biblical teaching on the existence of angels is a constant reminder to us that there is an unseen world that is very real. It was only when the Lord opened the eyes of Elisha's servant to the reality of this invisible world that the servant saw that "the mountain was full of horses and chariots of fire round about Elisha" (2 Kings 6:17; this was a great angelic army sent to Dothan to protect Elisha from the Syrians). The psalmist, too, shows an awareness of the unseen world when he encourages the angels, "Praise him, all his angels, praise him, all his host!" (Ps. 148:2). The author of Hebrews reminds us that when we worship we come into the heavenly Jerusalem to gather with "innumerable angels in festal gathering" (Heb. 12:22), whom we do not see, but whose presence should fill us with both awe and joy. An unbelieving world may dismiss talk of angels as mere superstition, but Scripture offers these statements as insight into the state of affairs as they really are.

3. Angels are examples for us. In both their obedience and their worship angels provide helpful examples for us to imitate. Jesus teaches us to pray, "Your will be done, on earth as it is in heaven" (Matt. 6:10). In heaven God's will is done by angels, immediately, joyfully, and without question. We are to pray daily that our obedience and the obedience of others would be like that of the angels in heaven. Their delight is to be God's humble servants, each faithfully and joyfully performing their assigned tasks, whether great or small. Our desire and prayer should be that we ourselves and all others on earth would do the same.

Angels also serve as our examples in their worship of God. The seraphim before God's throne see God in his holiness and continue to cry out, "Holy, holy, holy is the LORD of hosts; the whole earth is full of his glory" (Isa. 6:3). And John sees around God's throne a great angelic army, "numbering myriads of myriads and thousands of thousands, saying with a loud voice, 'Worthy is the Lamb who was slain, to receive power and wealth and wisdom and might and honor and glory and blessing!'" (Rev. 5:11–12). As angels find it their highest joy to praise God continuously, should we not also delight each day to sing God's praise, counting this as the highest and most worthy use of our time and our greatest joy?

4. Angels carry out some of God's plans. Scripture sees angels as God's servants who carry out some of his plans in the earth. They bring God's messages to people (Luke 1:11–19; Acts 8:26; 10:3–8, 22; 27:23–24). They carry out some of God's judgments, bringing a plague upon Israel (2 Sam. 24:16–17), smiting the leaders of the Assyrian army (2 Chron. 32:21), striking King Herod dead because he did not give God glory (Acts 12:23), or pouring out bowls of God's wrath on the earth (Rev. 16:1). When Christ returns, angels will come with him as a great army accompanying their King and Lord (Matt. 16:27; Luke 9:26; 2 Thess. 1:7).

Angels also patrol the earth as God's representatives (Zech. 1:10–11), and carry out war against demonic forces (Dan. 10:13; Rev. 12:7–8). John in his vision saw an angel coming down from heaven, and he records that the angel "seized the dragon, that ancient serpent, who is the Devil and Satan, and bound him for a thousand years, and threw him into the pit" (Rev. 20:1–3). When Christ returns, an archangel will proclaim his coming (1 Thess. 4:16; cf. Rev. 18:1–2, 21; 19:17–18; et al.).

5. Angels directly glorify God. Angels also serve another function: They minister directly to God by glorifying him. Thus, in addition to human beings, there are other intelligent moral creatures who glorify God in the universe.

Angels glorify God for who he is in himself, for his excellence.

> Bless the LORD, O you his angels,
> you mighty ones who do his word,
> hearkening to the voice of his word! (Ps. 103:20; cf. 148:2)

The seraphim continually praise God for his holiness (Isa. 6:2–3), as do the four living creatures (Rev. 4:8).

Angels also glorify God for his great plan of salvation as they see it unfold. When Christ was born in Bethlehem, a multitude of angels praised God and said, "Glory to God in the highest, and on earth peace among men with whom he is pleased!" (Luke 2:14; cf. Heb. 1:6). Jesus tells us, "There is joy before the angels of God over one sinner who repents" (Luke 15:10), indicating that angels rejoice every time someone turns from his or her sins and trusts in Christ as Savior.

When Paul proclaims the gospel so that people from diverse racial backgrounds, both Jews and Greeks, are brought into the church, he sees God's wise plan for the church as being displayed before the angels (and demons), for he says that he was called to preach to the Gentiles "that through the church the manifold wisdom of God might now be *made known to the principalities and powers in the heavenly places*" (Eph. 3:10). And Peter tells us that "angels long to look" (1 Peter 1:12) into the glories of the plan of salvation as it works out in the lives of individual believers each day. Moreover, the fact that in church worship women were to wear clothing that appropriately signaled that they were women, "because of the angels" (1 Cor. 11:10), indicates that angels witness the lives of Christians and glorify God for our worship and obedience.

C. Our Relationship to Angels

1. We should be aware of angels in our daily lives. Scripture makes it clear that God wants us to be aware of the existence of angels and of the nature of their activity. We should not therefore assume that its teaching about angels has nothing whatsoever to do with our lives today. Rather, there are several ways in which our Christian lives will be enriched by an awareness of the existence and ministry of angels in the world even today.

When we come before God in worship, we are joining not only with the great company of believers who have died and come into God's presence in heaven, "the spirits of just men made perfect," but also with a great throng of angels, "innumerable angels in festal gathering" (Heb. 12:22–23). Though we do not ordinarily see or hear evidence of this heavenly worship, it certainly enriches our sense of reverence and joy in God's presence if we appreciate the fact that angels join us in the worship of God.

Moreover, we should be aware that angels are watching our obedience or disobedience to God through the day. Even if we think our sins are done in secret and bring grief to no one else (except, of course, God himself), we should be sobered by the thought that perhaps even hundreds of angels witness our disobedience and are grieved. On the other hand, when we are discouraged and think that our faithful obedience to God is witnessed by no one and is an encouragement to no one, we can be comforted by the realization that perhaps hundreds of angels witness our lonely struggle, daily "longing to look" at the way Christ's great salvation finds expression in our lives.

As if to make the reality of angelic observation of our service to God more vivid, the author of Hebrews suggests that angels can sometimes take human form, apparently to make "inspection visits," something like the newspaper's restaurant critic who disguises himself and visits a new restaurant. We read, "Do not neglect to show hospitality to strangers, for thereby some have entertained angels unawares" (Heb. 13:2; cf. Gen. 18:2–5; 19:1–3). This should make us eager to minister to the needs of others whom we do not know, all the while wondering if someday we will reach heaven and meet the angel whom we helped when he appeared temporarily as a human being in distress here on earth.

When we are suddenly delivered from a danger or distress, we might suspect that angels have been sent by God to help us, and we should be thankful. An angel shut the mouths of the lions so they would not hurt Daniel (Dan. 6:22), delivered the apostles from prison (Acts 5:19–20), later delivered Peter from prison (Acts 12:7–11), and ministered to Jesus in the wilderness at a time of great weakness, immediately after his temptations had ended (Matt. 4:11). Does not Scripture promise, "For he will give his angels charge of you to guard you in all your ways. On their hands they will bear you up, lest you dash your foot against a stone" (Ps. 91:11–12)? Should we not therefore thank God for sending angels to protect us at such times? It seems right that we should do so.

2. Cautions regarding our relationship to angels.

a. *Beware of receiving false doctrine from angels.* The Bible warns against receiving false doctrine from supposed angels: "Even if we, or an angel from heaven, should preach to you a gospel contrary to that which we preached to you, let him be accursed" (Gal. 1:8). Paul makes this warning because he knows that there is a possibility of deception. He says, "Even Satan disguises himself as an angel of light" (2 Cor. 11:14). Similarly, the lying prophet who deceived the man of God in 1 Kings 13 claimed, "*An angel spoke to me* by the word of the LORD, saying, 'Bring him back with you into your house that he may eat bread and drink water'" (1 Kings 13:18). Yet the text of Scripture immediately adds in the same verse, "But he lied to him."

These are instances of *false* doctrine or guidance being conveyed by angels or people claiming that angels spoke to them. It is interesting that these examples show the clear possibility of satanic deception tempting us to disobey the clear teachings of Scripture or the clear commands of God (cf. 1 Kings 13:9). These warnings should keep any Christians from being fooled by the claims of Mormons, for example, that an angel (Moroni) spoke to Joseph Smith and revealed to him the basis of the Mormon religion. Such "revelation" is contrary to the teachings of Scripture at many points (with respect to such doctrines as the Trinity, the person of Christ, justification by faith alone, and many others), and Christians should be warned against accepting these claims.

b. *Do not worship angels, pray to them, or seek them.* "Worship of angels" (Col. 2:18) was one of the false doctrines being taught at Colossae. Moreover, an angel speaking to John in the book of Revelation warns John not to worship him: "You must not do that! I am a fellow servant with you and your brethren who hold the testimony of Jesus. Worship God" (Rev. 19:10).

Nor should we pray to angels. We are to pray to God alone, who alone is omnipotent and thus able to answer prayer and who alone is omniscient and therefore able to hear the prayers of all his people at once. Paul warns us against thinking that any other "mediator" can come between us and God: "There is one God, and there is *one mediator* between God and men, the man Christ Jesus" (1 Tim. 2:5). If we were to pray to angels, it would be implicitly attributing to them a status equal to God, which we must not do. There is no example in Scripture of anyone praying to any specific angel or asking angels for help.

Moreover, Scripture gives us no warrant to seek for appearances of angels to us. They manifest themselves unsought. To seek such appearances would seem to indicate an unhealthy curiosity or a desire for some kind of spectacular event rather than a love for God and devotion to him and his work. Though angels did appear to people at various times in Scripture, the people apparently never sought those appearances. Our role is rather to talk to the Lord, who is himself the commander of all angelic forces. However, it would not seem wrong to ask God to fulfill his promise in Psalm 91:11 to send angels to protect us in times of need.

D. Demons and Their Origin

The previous discussion leads naturally to a consideration of Satan and demons, since they are evil angels who once were like the good angels but who sinned and lost their privilege of serving God. Like angels, they are also created spiritual beings with moral judgment and high intelligence but without physical bodies. We may define demons as follows: *Demons are evil angels who sinned against God and who now continually work evil in the world.*

When God created the world, he "saw everything that he had made, and behold, it was very good" (Gen. 1:31). This means that even the angelic world that God had created did not have evil angels or demons in it at that time. But by the time of Genesis 3, we find that Satan, in the form of a serpent, is tempting Eve to sin (Gen. 3:1–5). Therefore, sometime between the events of Genesis 1:31 and Genesis 3:1, there must have been a rebellion in the angelic world with many angels turning against God and becoming evil.

The New Testament speaks of this in two places. Peter tells us, "God did not spare the angels when they sinned, but cast them into hell and committed them to pits of nether gloom to be kept until the judgment" (2 Peter 2:4).[4] Jude also says that "the angels that did not keep their own position but left their proper dwelling have been kept by him in eternal chains in the nether gloom until the judgment of the great day" (Jude 6). Once again the emphasis is on the fact that they are removed from the glory of God's presence and their activity is restricted (metaphorically, they

---

[4]This does not mean that these sinful angels have no current influence on the world, for in v. 9 Peter says that the Lord also knows how "to keep the unrighteous under punishment until the day of judgment," here referring to sinful human beings who were obviously still having influence in the world and even troubling Peter's readers. Verse 4 simply means that the wicked angels have been removed from the presence of God and are kept under some kind of restraining influence until the final judgment, but this does not rule out their continued activity in the world meanwhile.

are in "eternal chains"), but the text does not imply either that the influence of demons has been removed from the world or that some demons are kept in a place of punishment apart from the world while others are able to influence it. Rather, both 2 Peter and Jude tell us that some angels rebelled against God and became hostile opponents to his word. Their sin seems to have been pride, a refusal to accept their assigned place, for they "did not keep their own position but left their proper dwelling" (Jude 6).

It is also possible that there is a reference to the fall of Satan, the prince of demons, in Isaiah 14. As Isaiah is describing the judgment of God on the king of Babylon (an earthly, human king), he then comes to a section where he begins to use language that seems too strong to refer to any merely human king:

> How you are fallen from heaven,
>> O Day Star, son of Dawn!
> How you are cut down to the ground,
>> you who laid the nations low!
> You said in your heart,
>> "*I will ascend to heaven;*
> *above the stars of God*
>> *I will set my throne on high;*
> I will sit on the mount of assembly
>> in the far north;
> I will ascend above the heights of the clouds,
>> *I will make myself like the Most High.*"
> But you are brought down to Sheol,
>> to the depths of the Pit. (Isa. 14:12–15; cf. Ezek. 28:11–19)

This language of ascending to heaven and setting his throne on high and saying, "I will make myself like the Most High" strongly suggests a rebellion by an angelic creature of great power and dignity. It would not be uncommon for Hebrew prophetic speech to pass from descriptions of human events to descriptions of heavenly events that are parallel to them and that the earthly events picture in a limited way.[5] If this is so, then the sin of Satan is described as one of pride and attempting to be equal to God in status and authority.

E. Satan as Head of the Demons

"Satan" is the personal name of the head of the demons. This name is mentioned in Job 1:6, where "the sons of God came to present themselves before the LORD, and *Satan* also came among them" (see also Job 1:7–2:7). Here he appears as the enemy of the Lord who brings severe temptations against Job. Similarly, near the end of David's life, "Satan stood up against Israel, and incited David to number Israel" (1 Chron. 21:1). Moreover, Zechariah saw a vision of "Joshua the high priest standing before the angel of the LORD, and Satan standing at his right hand to accuse him" (Zech. 3:1). The name "Satan" is a Hebrew word *(sātān)* that means "adversary." The New Testament also uses the name "Satan," simply taking it over from the Old Testament. So Jesus, in his temptation in the wilderness, speaks to Satan directly saying, "Begone, Satan!" (Matt. 4:10), or "I saw Satan fall like lightning from heaven" (Luke 10:18).

---

[5]See, for example, Ps. 45, which moves from a description of an earthly king to a description of a divine Messiah.

The Bible uses other names for Satan as well. He is called "the devil" (only in the New Testament: Matt. 4:1; 13:39; 25:41; Rev. 12:9; 20:2; et al.), "the serpent" (Gen. 3:1, 14; 2 Cor. 11:3; Rev. 12:9; 20:2), "Be-elzebul" (Matt. 10:25; 12:24, 27; Luke 11:15), "the ruler of this world" (John 12:31; 14:30; 16:11), "the prince of the power of the air" (Eph. 2:2), or "the evil one" (Matt. 13:19; 1 John 2:13). When Jesus says to Peter, "Get behind me, Satan! You are a hindrance to me; for you are not on the side of God, but of men" (Matt. 16:23), he recognizes that Peter's attempt to keep him from suffering and dying on the cross is really an attempt to keep Jesus from obedience to the Father's plan. Jesus realizes that opposition ultimately comes not from Peter, but from Satan himself.

F. The Activity of Satan and Demons

1. Satan was the originator of sin. Satan sinned before any human beings did so, as is evident from the fact that he (in the form of the serpent) tempted Eve (Gen. 3:1–6; 2 Cor. 11:3). The New Testament also informs us that Satan was a "murderer from the beginning" and is "a liar and the father of lies" (John 8:44). It also says that "the devil has sinned *from the beginning*" (1 John 3:8). In both of these texts, the phrase "from the beginning" does not imply that Satan was evil from the time God began to create the world ("from the beginning of the world") or from the beginning of his existence ("from the beginning of his life"), but rather from the "beginning" parts of the history of the world (Gen. 3 and even before). The devil's characteristic has been to originate sin and tempt others to sin.

2. Demons oppose and try to destroy every work of God. Just as Satan tempted Eve to sin against God (Gen. 3:1–6), so he tried to get Jesus to sin and thus fail in his mission as Messiah (Matt. 4:1–11). The tactics of Satan and his demons are to use lies (John 8:44), deception (Rev. 12:9), murder (Ps. 106:37; John 8:44), and every other kind of destructive activity to attempt to cause people to turn away from God and destroy themselves. Demons will try every tactic to blind people to the gospel (2 Cor. 4:4) and keep them in bondage to things that hinder them from coming to God (Gal. 4:8). They will also try to use temptation, doubt, guilt, fear, confusion, sickness, envy, pride, slander, or any other means possible to hinder a Christian's witness and usefulness.

3. Demons are limited by God's control and have limited power. The story of Job makes it clear that Satan could do only what God gave him permission to do, and nothing more (Job 1:12; 2:6). Demons are kept in "eternal chains" (Jude 6) and can be successfully resisted by Christians through the authority that Christ gives them (James 4:7: "Resist the devil and he will flee from you").

Moreover, the power of demons is limited. After rebelling against God, they do not have the power they had when they were angels, for sin is a weakening and destructive influence. The power of demons, though significant, is therefore probably less than the power of angels.

In the area of knowledge, *we should not think that demons can know the future or that they can read our minds or know our thoughts.* In many places in the Old Testament, the Lord shows himself to be the true God in distinction from the false (demonic) gods of the nations by the fact that *he alone can know the future:* "I am God, and there is none like me, declaring the end from the beginning and from ancient times things not yet done" (Isa. 46:9–10). Even angels do not know the time of Jesus' return (Mark 13:32), and there is no indication in Scripture that they or demons know anything else about the future either.

With respect to knowing our thoughts, the Bible tells us that Jesus knew people's thoughts (Matt. 9:4; 12:25; Mark 2:8; Luke 6:8; 11:17) and that God knows people's thoughts (Gen. 6:5; Ps. 139:2, 4, 23; Isa. 66:18), but there is no indication that angels or demons can know our thoughts. In fact, Daniel told King Nebuchadnezzar that no one speaking by any other power than the God of heaven could tell the king what he had dreamed (see Dan. 2:27–28).

But if demons cannot read people's minds, how shall we understand contemporary reports of witch doctors, fortune-tellers, or other people evidently under demonic influence who are able to tell people details of their lives that they thought no one knew, such as, for example what food they had for breakfast or where they keep some money hidden in their house? Most of these things can be explained by realizing that demons can *observe* what goes on in the world and probably can draw some conclusions from those observations. A demon may know what I ate for breakfast simply because it saw me eat breakfast! It may know what I said in a private telephone conversation because it listened to the conversation. Christians should not be led astray if they encounter members of the occult or of other false religions who seem to demonstrate such unusual knowledge from time to time. These results of observation do not prove that demons can read our thoughts, however, and nothing in the Bible would lead us to think they have that power.

G. Our Relationship to Demons

1. Are demons active in the world today? Some people, influenced by a naturalistic worldview that only admits the reality of what can be seen or touched or heard, deny that demons exist today. They maintain that angels and demons are simply myths that belong to an obsolete worldview taught in the Bible and other ancient culture.

If, however, Scripture gives us a true account of the world as it really is, then we must take seriously its portrayal of intense demonic involvement in human society. Our failure to perceive that involvement with our five senses merely tells us that we have some deficiencies in our ability to understand the world, not that demons do not exist. In fact, there is no reason to think that there is any less demonic activity in the world today than there was at the time of the New Testament. We are in the same time period in God's overall plan for history (the church age or the new covenant age), and the millennium has not yet come when Satan's influence will be removed from the earth. From a biblical perspective, the refusal of modern society to recognize the presence of demonic activity today is simply due to people's blindness to the true nature of reality.

But what kind of activity do demons engage in today? Are there some distinguishing characteristics that will enable us to recognize demonic activity when it occurs?

2. Not all evil and sin is from Satan and demons, but some is. If we think of the overall emphasis of the New Testament epistles, we realize that very little space is given to discussing demonic activity in the lives of believers or methods to resist and oppose such activity. The emphasis is on telling believers not to sin but to live lives of righteousness. For example, in 1 Corinthians, when there is a problem of "dissensions,"

Paul does not tell the church to rebuke a spirit of dissension, but simply urges them to "agree" and "be united in the same mind and the same judgment" (1 Cor. 1:10). When there is a problem of incest, he does not tell the Corinthians to rebuke a spirit of incest, but tells them that they ought to be outraged and that they should exercise church discipline until the offender repents (1 Cor. 5:1–5). These examples could be duplicated many times in the other New Testament epistles.

Therefore, though the New Testament clearly recognizes the influence of demonic activity in the world, and even, as we shall see, upon the lives of believers, its primary focus regarding Christian growth is not on demonic activity, but on the choices and actions taken by Christians themselves (see also Gal. 5:16–26; Eph. 4:1–6:9; Col. 3:1–4:6; et al.). Similarly, this should be the primary focus of our efforts today when we strive to grow in holiness and faith and to overcome the sinful desires and actions that remain in our lives (cf. Rom. 6:1–23) and to overcome the temptations that come against us from an unbelieving world (1 Cor. 10:13). We need to accept our own responsibility to obey the Lord and not to shift blame for our own misdeeds onto some demonic force.

Nevertheless, a number of passages show that the New Testament authors were definitely aware of the presence of demonic influence in the world and in the lives of Christians themselves. Paul warned Timothy that in the latter days some would "depart from the faith by giving heed to deceitful spirits and *doctrines of demons*" (1 Tim. 4:1) and that this would lead to claims for avoiding marriage and avoiding certain foods (v. 3), both of which God had created as "good" (v. 4). Thus, he saw some false doctrine as being demonic in origin. In 2 Timothy, Paul implies that those who oppose sound doctrine have been captured by the devil to do his will: "The Lord's servant must not be quarrelsome but kindly to every one, an apt teacher, forbearing, correcting his opponents with gentleness. God may perhaps grant that they will repent and come to know the truth, and they may *escape from the snare of the devil, after being captured by him to do his will*" (2 Tim. 2:24–26).

Jesus had similarly asserted that the Jews who obstinately opposed him were following their father the devil: "*You are of your father the devil*, and your will is to do your father's desires. He was a murderer from the beginning and has nothing to do with the truth, because there is no truth in him. When he lies, he speaks according to his own nature, for he is a liar and the father of lies" (John 8:44).

Emphasis on the hostile deeds of unbelievers as having demonic influence or sometimes demonic origin is made more explicit in John's first epistle. He makes a general statement that "he who commits sin is of the devil" (1 John 3:8), and goes on to say, "By this it may be seen who are the children of God, and who are the children of the devil: whoever does not do right is not of God, nor he who does not love his brother" (1 John 3:10). Here John characterizes all those who are not born of God as children of the devil and subject to his influence and desires.

When we combine all of these statements, we see that Satan is thought of as the originator of lies, murder, deception, false teaching, and sin generally. Because of this, it seems reasonable to conclude that the New Testament wants us to understand that there is some degree of demonic influence in nearly all wrongdoing and sin that occurs today. Not all sin is caused by Satan or demons, nor is the major influence or cause of sin demonic activity, but demonic activity is probably a factor in almost all sin and almost all destructive activity that opposes the work of God in the world today.

In the lives of Christians, as we noted above, the emphasis of the New Testament is not on the influence of demons, but on the sin that remains in the believer's life. Nevertheless, we should recognize that sinning (even by Christians) does give a foothold for some kind of demonic influence in our lives. Thus, Paul could say, "Be angry but do not sin; do not let the sun go down on your anger, and *give no opportunity to the devil*" (Eph. 4:26). Wrongful anger apparently can give opportunity for the devil (or demons) to exert some kind of negative influence in our lives—perhaps by attacking us through our emotions and perhaps by increasing the wrongful anger that we already feel against others. Similarly, Paul mentions "the breastplate of righteousness" (Eph. 6:14) as part of the armor that we are to use standing against "the wiles of the devil" and in contending "against the principalities, against the powers, against the world rulers of this present darkness, against the spiritual hosts of wickedness in the heavenly places" (Eph. 6:11–12). If we have areas of continuing sin in our lives, there are weaknesses and holes in our "breastplate of righteousness," and these are areas in which we are vulnerable to demonic attack. By contrast, Jesus, who was perfectly free from sin, could say of Satan, "He has no power over me" (John 14:30). We may also note the connection in 1 John 5:18 between not sinning and not being touched by the evil one: "We know that any one born of God does not sin,[6] but He who was born of God keeps him, and the evil one does not touch him."

3. Can a Christian be demon possessed? The term *demon possession* is an unfortunate term that has found its way into some English translations of the Bible but is not really reflected in the Greek text. The Greek New Testament can speak of people who "have a demon" (Matt. 11:18; Luke 7:33; 8:27; John 7:20; 8:48, 49, 52; 10:20), or it can speak of people who are suffering from demonic influence (Gk. *daimonizomai*), but it never uses language that suggests that a demon actually "possesses" someone.

The problem with both the terms *demon possession* and *demonized* is that they give the nuance of such strong demonic influence that they seem to imply that the person who is under demonic attack has no choice but to succumb to it. They suggest that the person is unable any longer to exercise his or her will and is completely under the domination of the evil spirit. While this may have been true in extreme cases such as that of the Gerasene demoniac (see Mark 5:1–20; note that after Jesus cast the demons out of him, he was then "in his right mind," v. 15), it is certainly not true with many cases of demonic attack or conflict with demons in many people's lives.[7]

So what should we say to the question, "Can a Christian be demon possessed?" While my own preference is not to use the phrase *demon possessed* at all, for any kinds of cases, the answer to this question will depend on what is meant by "demon

---

[6]The present tense of the Greek verb here gives the sense "does not continue to sin."

[7]The word *diamonizomai*, which may be translated "under demonic influence" or "to be demonized" occurs thirteen times in the New Testament, all in the Gospels: Matt. 4:24; 8:16, 28, 33; 9:32; 12:22; 15:22 ("badly demonized"); Mark 1:32; 5:15, 16, 18; Luke 8:36; and John 10:21. All of these instances seem to indicate quite severe demonic influence. In light of this, it is perhaps better to reserve the English word *demonized* for more extreme or severe cases. The word *demonized* in English seems to me to suggest very strong demonic influence or control. (Cf. other similar "-ized" words: pasteurized, homogenized, tyrannized, materialized, nationalized, etc. These words all speak of a total transformation of the object being spoken about, not simply of mild or moderate influence.) But it has become common in some Christian literature today to speak of people under any kind of demonic attack as being "demonized." It would be wiser to reserve the term for more severe cases of demonic influence, lest our language imply stronger influence than is actually the case.

possessed." If by "demon possessed" one means that a person's will is completely dominated by a demon, so that a person has no power left to chose to do right and obey God, then the answer to whether a Christian could be demon possessed would certainly be no, for Scripture guarantees that sin shall have no dominion over us since we have been raised with Christ (Rom. 6:14, see also vv. 4, 11).

On the other hand, most Christians would agree that there can be differing degrees of demonic attack or influence in the lives of believers. A believer may come under demonic attack from time to time in a milder or stronger sense. (Note the "daughter of Abraham" whom "Satan bound for eighteen years" so that she "had a spirit of infirmity" and "was bent over and could not fully straighten herself" [Luke 13:16, 11].) Though Christians after Pentecost have a fuller power of the Holy Spirit working within them to enable them to triumph over demonic attacks, they do not always call upon or even know about the power that is rightfully theirs. We would do well to avoid categorizing this influence with the term *demon possession* (as well as with other terms such as *oppressed* or *obsessed*), and simply to recognize that *there can be varying degrees of demonic attack or influence on people, even on Christians*, and to leave it at that. In all cases, the remedy will be the same anyway: Rebuke the demon in the name of Jesus and command it to leave.[8]

4. Jesus gives all believers authority to rebuke demons and command them to leave. When Jesus sent the twelve disciples ahead of him to preach the kingdom of God, he "gave them power and authority *over all demons*" (Luke 9:1). After the seventy had preached the kingdom of God in towns and villages, they returned with joy, saying, "Lord, even the demons are subject to us in your name!" (Luke 10:17), and Jesus told them, "I have given you authority . . . over all the power of the enemy" (Luke 10:19). When Philip the evangelist went down to Samaria to preach the gospel of Christ, "unclean spirits came out of many who had them" (Acts 8:7, author's translation), and Paul used spiritual authority over demons to say to a spirit of divination in a soothsaying girl, "I charge you in the name of Jesus Christ to come out of her" (Acts 16:18).

Paul was aware of the spiritual authority he had, both in face-to-face encounters such as the one in Acts 16, and in his prayer life as well. He said, "For though we live in the world we are not carrying on a worldly war, for *the weapons of our warfare* are not worldly but *have divine power to destroy strongholds*" (2 Cor. 10:3–4). Moreover, he spoke at some length of the struggle Christians have against "the wiles of the devil" in his description of conflict "against the spiritual hosts of wickedness in the heavenly places" (see Eph. 6:10–18). James tells all his readers (in many churches) to "*resist the devil* and he will flee from you" (James 4:7). Similarly, Peter tells his readers in many churches in Asia Minor, "Your adversary the devil prowls around like a roaring lion, seeking some one to devour. *Resist him*, firm in your faith" (1 Peter 5:8–9).

It is important that we recognize that the work of Christ on the cross is the ultimate basis for our authority over demons.[9] Though Christ won a victory over Satan in the wilderness, the New Testament epistles point to the cross as the moment when

---

[8]In addition, if there is some specific sin that has given the demon a basis for influence, the sin should be confessed and forsaken (see above). But not all demonic attack can be linked to a specific sin, since Jesus himself was severely tempted by Satan, as was Eve before the fall.

[9]In this paragraph and the following one on adoption I am indebted to the fine work of Timothy M. Warner, *Spiritual Warfare* (Wheaton, Ill.: Crossway, 1991), pp. 55–63.

Satan was decisively defeated. Jesus took on flesh and blood, "that through death he might render powerless him who had the power of death, that is, the devil" (Heb. 2:14 NASB). At the cross God "disarmed the principalities and powers and made a public example of them, triumphing over them in him" (Col. 2:15). Therefore, Satan hates the cross of Christ, because there he was decisively defeated forever. Because of Christ's death on the cross, our sins are completely forgiven, and Satan has no rightful authority over us.

In addition, our membership as children in God's family is the firm spiritual position from which we engage in spiritual warfare. Paul says to every Christian, "In Christ Jesus you are all sons of God, through faith" (Gal. 3:26). When Satan comes to attack us, he is attacking one of *God's own children,* a member of God's own family. This truth gives us authority to defeat him and successfully to wage war against him.

If we as believers find it appropriate to speak a word of rebuke to a demon, it is important to remember that we need not fear demons. Although Satan and demons have much less power than the power of the Holy Spirit at work within us, one of Satan's tactics is to attempt to cause us to be afraid. Instead of giving in to such fear, Christians should remind themselves of the truths of Scripture, which tell us, "You are of God, and have overcome them; for *he who is in you is greater than he who is in the world*" (1 John 4:4); and "God did not give us a spirit of timidity but a spirit of power and love and self-control" (2 Tim. 1:7). Paul tells the Ephesians that in their spiritual warfare they are to use the "shield of faith" with which they can "quench all the flaming darts of the evil one" (Eph. 6:16). This is very important, since the opposite of fear is faith in God. He also tells them to be bold in their spiritual conflict, so that, having taken the whole armor of God, they "may be able to withstand in the evil day, and having done all, *to stand*" (Eph. 6:13). Paul says that Christians, in their conflict with hostile spiritual forces, should not run away in retreat or cower in fear, but should stand their ground boldly, knowing that their weapons and their armor "have divine power to destroy strongholds" (2 Cor. 10:4; cf. 1 John 5:18).

In actual practice, this authority to rebuke demons may result in briefly speaking a command to an evil spirit to leave when we suspect the presence of demonic influence in our personal lives or the lives of those around us. We are to "resist the devil" (James 4:7), and he will flee from us. Sometimes a very brief command in the name of Jesus will be enough. At other times it will be helpful to quote Scripture in the process of commanding an evil spirit to leave a situation. Paul speaks of "the sword of the Spirit, which is the word of God" (Eph. 6:17). And Jesus, when he was tempted by Satan in the wilderness, repeatedly quoted Scripture in response to Satan's temptations (Matt. 4:1–11). Appropriate Scriptures may include general statements of the triumph of Jesus over Satan (Matt. 12:28–29; Luke 10:17–19; 2 Cor. 10:3–4; Col. 2:15; Heb. 2:14; James 4:7; 1 Peter 5:8–9; 1 John 3:8; 4:4; 5:18), but also verses that speak directly to the particular temptation or difficulty at hand.

It is important to remember that the power to cast out demons comes not from our own strength or the power of our own voice, but from the Holy Spirit (Matt. 12:28; Luke 11:20). Moreover, Jesus issues a clear warning that we should not rejoice too much or become proud in our power over demons, but that we should rejoice rather in our great salvation. We must keep this in mind lest we become proud and the Holy Spirit should then withdraw his power from us. When the seventy returned with joy saying, "Lord, even the demons are subject to us in your name!"

(Luke 10:17), Jesus told them, "Do not rejoice in this, that the spirits are subject to you; but rejoice that your names are written in heaven" (Luke 10:20).

5. We should expect the gospel to come in power to triumph over the works of the devil. When Jesus came preaching the gospel in Galilee, "demons also came out of many" (Luke 4:41). When Philip went to Samaria to preach the gospel, "unclean spirits came out of many . . . crying with a loud voice" (Acts 8:7). Jesus commissioned Paul to preach among the Gentiles "that they may turn from darkness to light and from the power of Satan to God, that they may receive forgiveness of sins and a place among those who are sanctified by faith in me" (Acts 26:18). Paul's proclamation of the gospel, he said, was "not in plausible words of wisdom, but in demonstration of the Spirit and of power, that your faith might not rest in the wisdom of men but in the power of God" (1 Cor. 2:4–5; cf. 2 Cor. 10:3–4). If we really believe the scriptural testimony to the existence and activity of demons, and if we really believe that "the reason the Son of God appeared was *to destroy the works of the devil*" (1 John 3:8), then it would seem appropriate to expect that even today when the gospel is proclaimed to unbelievers, and when prayer is made for believers who have perhaps been unaware of this dimension of spiritual conflict, there will be a genuine and often immediately recognizable triumph over the power of the enemy. We should expect that this would happen, think of it as a normal part of the work of Christ in building up his kingdom, and rejoice in Christ's victory in it.

II. REVIEW QUESTIONS

1. What are angels?
2. Name three purposes for angels.
3. What should be our relationship to angels?
4. How did demons originate?
5. Can Christians be influenced by demons? Explain.
6. In what ways can Christians exert authority over demons?

III. QUESTIONS FOR PERSONAL APPLICATION

1. Do you think there are angels watching you right now? What attitude or attitudes do you think they have as they watch you? What difference would it make in your attitude in worship if you consciously thought about being in the presence of angels when you were singing praises to God?
2. Have you ever had a remarkable rescue from physical or other kinds of danger and wondered if angels were involved in helping you at the time?
3. Before reading this chapter, did you think that most demonic activity was confined to the time of the New Testament or to other cultures than your own? After reading this chapter, are there areas in your own society where you think there might be some demonic influence today? Do you feel some fear at the prospect of encountering demonic activity in your own life or the lives of others around you? What does the Bible say that will specifically address that feeling of fear? Do you think that the Lord wants you to feel that fear, if you do?

4. Are there any areas of sin in your own life now that might give a foothold to some demonic activity? If so, what would the Lord have you do with respect to that sin?

IV. SPECIAL TERMS

angel	living creature
archangel	Michael
cherubim	principalities and powers
demon possession	Satan
demonized	seraphim
demons	watchers

V. SCRIPTURE MEMORY PASSAGES

Two Scripture passages are suggested for this chapter:

REVELATION 5:11—12

Then I looked, and I heard around the throne and the living creatures and the elders the voice of many angels, numbering myriads of myriads and thousands of thousands, saying with a loud voice, "Worthy is the Lamb who was slain, to receive power and wealth and wisdom and might and honor and glory and blessing!"

JAMES 4:7—8

Submit yourselves therefore to God. Resist the devil and he will flee from you. Draw near to God and he will draw near to you. Cleanse your hands, you sinners, and purify your hearts, you men of double mind.

PART III

The Doctrine of Man

CHAPTER ELEVEN

The Creation of Man

+ *Why did God create us?*
+ *How did God make us like himself?*
+ *What does Scripture mean by "soul" and "spirit"?*

I. EXPLANATION AND SCRIPTURAL BASIS

The previous chapters have discussed the nature of God and his creation of the universe, the spiritual beings that he created, and his relationship to the world in terms of answering prayer. In this next section, we focus on the pinnacle of God's creative activity, his creation of human beings, both male and female, to be more like him than anything else he has made. We will consider first God's purpose in creating man and the nature of man as God created him to be (chs. 11–12). Then we will look at the nature of sin and man's disobedience to God (ch. 13).

A. The Use of the Word *Man* to Refer to the Human Race

Before discussing the subject matter of this chapter, it is necessary to consider briefly whether it is appropriate to use the word *man* to refer to the entire human race (as in the title for this chapter). Some people today object to ever using the word *man* to refer to the human race in general (including both men and women), because it is claimed that such usage is insensitive to women. Those who make this objection would prefer that we use only gender neutral terms such as *humanity, humankind, human beings,* or *persons* to refer to the human race.

After considering this suggestion, I decided to continue to use the word *man* (as well as several of these other terms) to refer to the human race in this book because such usage has divine warrant in Genesis 5, and because I think there is a theological issue at stake. In Genesis 5:1–2 we read, "When God created man, he made him in the likeness of God. Male and female he created them, and he blessed them *and named them Man* when they were created" (cf. Gen. 1:27). The Hebrew term translated "Man" is *'ādām,* the same term used for the name of Adam, and the same term that is sometimes used of man in distinction from woman (Gen. 2:22, 25; 3:12; Eccl. 7:28). Therefore, the practice of using the same term to refer (1) to male human beings and (2) to the human race generally is a practice that originated with God himself, and we should not find it objectionable or insensitive.

Someone might object that this is just an accidental feature of the Hebrew language, but this argument is not persuasive, because Genesis 5:2 specifically describes God's activity of choosing a name that would apply to the human race as a whole.

I am not here arguing that we must always duplicate biblical patterns of speech or that it is wrong to sometimes use gender-neutral terms to refer to the human race (as I just did in this sentence), but rather that God's *naming* activity reported in Genesis 5:2 indicates that the use of "man" to refer to the entire race is a good and very appropriate choice, and one that we should not avoid.[1]

The theological issue is whether there is a suggestion of male leadership or headship in the family from the beginning of creation. The fact that God did not choose to call the human race "woman," but "man," probably has some significance for understanding God's original plan for men and women. Of course, this question of the name we use to refer to the race is not the only factor in that discussion, but it is one factor, and our use of language in this regard does have some significance in the discussion of male-female roles today.

B. Why Was Man Created?

1. God did not need to create man, yet he created us for his own glory. In the discussion of God's independence in chapter 5 (see pp. 95–98), we noted several Scripture passages that teach that God does not need us or the rest of creation for anything, yet we and the rest of creation glorify him and bring him joy. Since there was perfect love and fellowship among members of the Trinity for all eternity (John 17:5, 24), God did not create us because he was lonely or because he needed fellowship with other persons—God did not need us for any reason.

Nevertheless, *God created us for his own glory.* In our treatment of God's independence, we noted that he speaks of his sons and daughters from the ends of the earth as those "whom I created for my glory" (Isa. 43:7; cf. Eph. 1:11–12). Therefore, we are to "do all to the glory of God" (1 Cor. 10:31).

This fact guarantees that our lives are significant. When we first realize that God did not need to create us and does not need us for anything, we could conclude that our lives have no importance at all. But Scripture tells us that we were created to glorify God, indicating that we are important to God himself. This is the final definition of genuine importance or significance to our lives: If we are truly important to God for all eternity, then what greater measure of importance or significance could we want?

2. What is our purpose in life? The fact that God created us for his own glory determines the correct answer to the question, "What is our purpose in life?" Our purpose must be to fulfill the reason that God created us: to glorify him. When we are speaking with respect to God himself, that is a good summary of our purpose. But when we think of our own interests, we make the happy discovery that we are to enjoy God and take delight in him and in our relationship to him.[2] Jesus says, "I came that they may have life, and have it abundantly" (John 10:10). David tells God, "In your presence there is fulness of joy, in your right hand are pleasures for evermore" (Ps. 16:11). He longs to dwell in the house of the Lord forever, "to behold the beauty of the LORD" (Ps. 27:4), and Asaph cries out:

---

[1]However, the question of whether to use *man* to refer to a person indefinitely, as in, "If any *man* would come after me, let him deny himself and take up his cross daily and follow me" (Luke 9:23), is a different question, because the naming of the human race is not in view. In these cases, considerateness toward women as well as men, and present-day language patterns, would make it appropriate to use gender-neutral language, such as, "If any *one* would come after me."

[2]For an excellent description of how enjoying God works out in practical ways in everyday life, see John Piper, *Desiring God: Meditations of a Christian Hedonist* (Portland, Ore.: Multnomah, 1986).

> Whom have I in heaven but you?
>   And there is nothing upon earth that I desire besides you.
> My flesh and my heart may fail,
>   but God is the strength of my heart
>   and my portion for ever. (Ps. 73:25–26)

Fullness of joy is found in knowing God and delighting in the excellence of his character. To be in his presence, to enjoy fellowship with him, is a greater blessing than anything that can be imagined. Therefore, the normal heart attitude of a Christian is rejoicing in the Lord and in the lessons of the life he gives us (Rom. 5:2–3; Phil. 4:4; 1 Thess. 5:16–18; James 1:2; 1 Peter 1:6, 8; et al.).[3]

As we glorify God and enjoy him, Scripture tells us that he rejoices in us. We read, "As the bridegroom rejoices over the bride, so shall your God rejoice over you" (Isa. 62:5), and Zephaniah prophesies that the Lord "will rejoice over you with gladness, he will renew you in his love; he will exult over you with loud singing as on a day of festival" (Zeph. 3:17–18).

This understanding of the doctrine of the creation of man has very practical results. When we realize that God created us to glorify him, and when we start to act in ways that fulfill that purpose, then we begin to experience an intensity of joy in the Lord that we have never before known. When we add to that the realization that God himself is rejoicing in our fellowship with him, our joy becomes "inexpressible and filled with heavenly glory" (1 Peter 1:8, author's expanded paraphrase).

C. Man in the Image of God

1. The meaning of "image of God." Out of all the creatures God made, only one creature, man, is said to be made "in the image of God." What does that mean? We may use the following definition: *The fact that man is in the image of God means that man is like God and represents God.*

When God says, "Let us make man in our image, after our likeness" (Gen. 1:26), the meaning is that God plans to make a creature similar to himself. Both the Hebrew word for "image" *(tselem)* and the Hebrew word for "likeness" *(demût)* refer to something that is similar but not identical to the thing it represents or is an "image" of. The word *image* can also be used of something that represents something else.

Theologians have spent much time attempting to specify one characteristic of man, or a very few, in which the image of God is primarily seen. Some have thought that the image of God consists in man's intellectual ability, others in his power to make moral decisions and willing choices. Others have thought that the image of God referred to man's original moral purity, or his creation as male and female (see Gen. 1:27), or his dominion over the earth.

In this discussion it would be best to focus attention primarily on the *meanings* of the words *image* and *likeness*. As we have seen, these terms had quite clear meanings to the original readers. When we realize that the Hebrew words for "image" and "likeness" simply informed the original readers that man was like God, and would in many ways represent God, much of the controversy over the meaning of "image of God" is seen to be a search for too narrow and too specific a meaning. When

---

[3]The first question in the Westminster Larger Catechism is "What is the chief and highest end of man?" The answer is, "Man's chief and highest end is to glorify God, and fully to enjoy Him forever."

Scripture reports that God said, "Let us make man in our image, after our likeness" (Gen. 1:26), it simply would have meant to the original readers, "Let us make man to be *like* us and to *represent* us."

Because "image" and "likeness" had these meanings, Scripture does not need to say something like, "The fact that man is in the image of God means that man is like God in the following ways: intellectual ability, moral purity, spiritual nature, dominion over the earth, creativity, ability to make ethical choices, and immortality" (or some similar statement). Such an explanation is unnecessary, not only because the terms had clear meanings, but also because no such list could do justice to the subject: The text only needs to affirm that man is *like God,* and the rest of Scripture fills in more details to explain this. In fact, as we read the rest of Scripture, we realize that a full understanding of man's likeness to God would require a full understanding of who God is in his being and in his actions and a full understanding of who man is and what he does. The more we know about God and man the more similarities we will recognize and the more fully we will understand what Scripture means when it says that man is in the image of God. The expression refers to every way in which man is like God.

2. The fall: God's image is distorted, but not lost. We might wonder whether man could still be thought to be *like God* after he sinned. This question is answered quite early in Genesis where God gives Noah the authority to establish the death penalty for murder among human beings just after the flood: God says, "Whoever sheds the blood of man, by man shall his blood be shed; *for God made man in his own image*" (Gen. 9:6). Even though people are sinful, there is still enough likeness to God remaining in them that to murder another person (to "shed blood" is an Old Testament expression for taking a human life) is to attack the part of creation that most resembles God, and it betrays an attempt or desire (if one were able) to attack God himself. Man is still in God's image. The New Testament gives confirmation to this when James 3:9 says that men generally, not just believers, "are made in the likeness of God."

However, since man has sinned, he is certainly not as fully like God as he was before. His moral purity has been lost and his sinful character certainly does not reflect God's holiness. His intellect is corrupted by falsehood and misunderstanding; his speech no longer continually glorifies God; his relationships are often governed by selfishness rather than love, and so forth. Though man is still in the image of God, in every aspect of life some parts of that image have been distorted or lost. In short, "God made man upright, but they have sought out many devices" (Eccl. 7:29). After the fall, then, we are still in God's image—we are still like God and we still represent God—but the image of God in us is distorted; we are less fully like God than we were before the entrance of sin.

Therefore it is important that we understand the full meaning of the image of God not simply from observation of human beings as they currently exist, but from the biblical indications of the nature of Adam and Eve when God created them and when all that God had made was "very good" (Gen. 1:31). The full measure of the excellence of our humanity will not be seen again in life on earth until Christ returns and we have obtained all the benefits of the salvation he earned for us.

3. Redemption in Christ: A progressive recovering of more of God's image. Nonetheless, it is encouraging to turn to the New Testament and see that our redemption in Christ means that we can, even in this life, progressively grow into more and more likeness to God. For example, Paul says that as Christians we have a new nature that is "being renewed in knowledge after the image of its creator" (Col. 3:10). As we gain in true understanding of God, his Word, and his world, we begin to think more and more of the thoughts that God himself thinks. In this way, we are "renewed in knowledge" and become more like God in our thinking. This is a description of the ordinary course of the Christian life. So Paul also can say that we "are being changed into his likeness [lit. 'image,' Gk. *Eikōn*] from one degree of glory to another" (2 Cor. 3:18). Throughout this life, as we grow in Christian maturity, we grow in greater likeness to God. More particularly, we grow in likeness to Christ in our lives and in our character. In fact, the goal for which God has redeemed us is that we might be "conformed to the image of his Son" (Rom. 8:29) and thus be exactly like Christ in our moral character.

4. At Christ's return: Complete restoration of God's image. The amazing promise of the New Testament is that just as we have been like Adam (subject to death and sin), we shall also be like Christ (morally pure, never subject to death again): "Just as we have borne the image of the man of dust, we shall also bear the image of the man of heaven" (1 Cor. 15:49). The full measure of our creation in the image of God is not seen in the life of Adam who sinned, nor is it seen in our lives now, for we are imperfect. But the New Testament emphasizes that God's purpose in creating man in his image was completely realized in the person of Jesus Christ. He himself "is the image of God" (2 Cor. 4:4 NASB); "He is the image of the invisible God" (Col. 1:15). In Jesus we see human likeness to God as it was intended to be, and it should cause us to rejoice that God has predestined us "to be conformed to the image of his son" (Rom. 8:29; cf. 1 Cor. 15:49): "When he appears we shall be like him" (1 John 3:2).

5. Specific aspects of our likeness to God. Though we have argued above that it would be difficult to define all the ways in which we are like God, we can nevertheless mention several aspects of our existence that show us to be more like God than all the rest of creation.

a. *Moral aspects.* We are creatures who are morally accountable before God for our actions. Corresponding to that accountability, we have an inner sense of right and wrong that sets us apart from animals (who have little if any innate sense of morality or justice but simply respond from fear of punishment or hope of reward). When we act according to God's moral standards, our likeness to God is reflected in behavior that is holy and righteous before him, but, by contrast, our *un*likeness to God is reflected whenever we sin.

b. *Spiritual aspects.* We have not only physical bodies but also immaterial spirits, and we can therefore act in ways that are significant in the immaterial, spiritual realm of existence. This means that we have a spiritual life that enables us to relate to God as persons, and we also have immortality; we will not cease to exist, but will live forever.

c. *Mental aspects.* We have an ability to reason and think logically and learn that sets us apart from the animal world. Animals sometimes exhibit remarkable behavior in solving mazes or working out problems in the physical world, but they certainly do not engage in abstract reasoning—there is no such thing as the "history of canine philosophy," for example, nor have any animals since creation developed at all in their understanding of ethical problems or use of philosophical concepts and the like. No group of chimpanzees will ever sit around the table arguing about the doctrine of the Trinity or the relative merits of Calvinism or Arminianism! In fact, even in developing physical and technical skills, we are far different from animals. Beavers still build the same kind of dams they have built for a thousand generations, birds still build the same kind of nests, and bees still build the same kinds of hives. But we continue to develop greater skill and complexity in technology, in agriculture, in science, and in nearly every field of endeavor.

Our likeness to God is also illustrated by our use of complex, abstract language; our awareness of the distant future; and the entire spectrum of human creative activity in such areas as art, music, literature, and science. Such aspects of human existence reveal the ways in which we differ from animals absolutely, not merely in degree. Furthermore, the degree and complexity of human emotions indicate just how vast is the difference between humankind and the rest of creation.

d. *Relational aspects.* In addition to our unique ability to relate to God (discussed above), there are other relational aspects of being in God's image. Although animals no doubt have some sense of community with each other, the depth of interpersonal harmony experienced in human marriage, in a human family when it functions according to God's principles, and in a church when a community of believers is walking in fellowship with the Lord and with one another, is much greater than the interpersonal harmony experienced by any animals. Man is like God also in his relationship to the rest of creation. Specifically, man has been given the right to rule over the creation and has even been given the authority when Christ returns to sit in judgment over angels (Gen. 1:26, 28; Ps. 8:6–8; 1 Cor. 6:3).

6. Our great dignity as bearers of God's image. It would be good for us to reflect on our likeness to God more often. It will probably amaze us to realize that when the Creator of the universe wanted to create something "in his image," something *more like himself* than all the rest of creation, he made us! This realization will give us a profound sense of dignity and significance as we reflect on the excellence of all the rest of God's creation: The starry universe, the abundant earth, the world of plants and animals, and the angelic kingdoms are remarkable, even magnificent. But we are more like our Creator than any of these things. We are the culmination of God's infinitely wise and skillful work of creation. Even though sin has greatly marred that likeness, we nonetheless now reflect much of it, and shall even more as we grow in likeness to Christ.

Yet we must remember that even fallen, sinful man has the status of being in God's image (see discussion of Gen. 9:6 above). Every single human being, no matter how much the image of God is marred by sin, or illness, or weakness, or age, or any other disability, still has the status of being in God's image and therefore must be treated with the dignity and respect that is due to God's image-bearer. This has profound implications for our conduct toward others. It means that people of every race deserve equal dignity and rights. It means that elderly people, those seriously ill, the mentally retarded, and unborn children deserve full protection and honor as human beings. If we ever deny our unique status in creation as God's only image-bearers, we will soon begin to depreciate the value of human life, will tend to see humans as merely a higher form of animal, and will begin to treat others as such. We will also lose much of our sense of meaning in life.

D. The Essential Nature of Man

1. Trichotomy, dichotomy, and monism. How many parts are there to man? Everyone agrees that we have physical bodies. Most people (both Christians and non-Christians) sense that they also have an immaterial part—a "soul" that will live on after their bodies die.

But here the agreement ends. Some people believe that in addition to "body" and "soul" we have a third part, a "spirit" that most directly relates to God. The view that man is made of three parts *(body, soul, and spirit)* is called *trichotomy.* Though this has been a common view in popular evangelical Bible teaching, there are few if any scholarly defenses of it today.[4] What does this view teach?

According to many trichotomists, man's *soul* includes his intellect, his emotions, and his will. They maintain that all people have such a soul and that the different elements of the soul can either serve God or be yielded to sin. They argue that man's *spirit* is a higher faculty that comes alive when a person becomes a Christian (see Rom. 8:10: "If Christ is in you, although your bodies are dead because of sin, your spirits are alive because of righteousness"). The spirit of a person then would be the part that most directly worships and prays to God (see John 4:24; Phil. 3:3).

Another view is called *dichotomy.* This view teaches that "spirit" is not a separate part of man, but simply another term for "soul" and that both terms are used interchangeably in Scripture to talk about the immaterial part of man, the part that lives on after our bodies die. Therefore, man is made up of *two parts* (body and soul/spirit). Those who hold this view often agree that Scripture uses the word "spirit" (Heb. *rûach* and Gk. *pneuma*) more frequently when referring to our relationship to God, but such usage, they say, is not uniform, and the word *soul* is also used in all the ways that *spirit* can be used. (However, many people who hold to some kind of dichotomy also affirm that the Bible most often views man as a unity, and that there is much interaction between our material and immaterial parts.)

Outside the realm of evangelical thought, we find yet another view, the idea that man cannot exist at all apart from a physical body, and therefore there can be no separate existence for any "soul" after the body dies (although this view can allow for the resurrection of the whole person at some future time). The view that man is only one element and that his body is the person, is called *monism.* According to monism, the scriptural terms *soul* and *spirit* are just other expressions for the "person" himself, or for the person's "life." This view has not generally been adopted by evangelical theologians because so many scriptural texts seem clearly to affirm that our souls or spirits live on after our bodies die (see Gen. 35:18; Ps. 31:5; Luke 23:43, 46; Acts 7:59; Phil. 1:23–24; 2 Cor. 5:8; Heb. 12:23; Rev. 6:9; 20:4; and ch. 25, on the intermediate state).

2. Biblical data. Before asking whether Scripture views "soul" and "spirit" as distinct parts of man, we must at the outset make it clear that there is a strong emphasis in Scripture on the overall unity of man as created by God. When God made man, he "breathed into his nostrils the breath of life; and man became a living

---

[4]I am not aware of any scholarly defense of trichotomy written in the twentieth century. The work by Franz Delitzsch, *A System of Biblical Psychology*, trans. R. E. Wallis [Edinburgh: T. & T. Clark, 1899], is the most recent.

being" (Gen. 2:7). Here Adam is a unified person with body and soul living and acting together. This original harmonious and unified state of man will occur again
when Christ returns and we are fully redeemed in our bodies as well as our souls to
live with him forever (see 1 Cor. 15:51–54). Moreover, we are to grow in holiness
and love for God in every aspect of our lives, in our bodies as well as in our spirits
or souls (cf. 1 Cor. 7:34). We are to "cleanse ourselves from every defilement *of body
and spirit,* and make holiness perfect in the fear of God" (2 Cor. 7:1).

But once we have emphasized that God created us to have a unity between body
and soul, we can go on to point out that Scripture quite clearly teaches that there is
an immaterial part of man's nature. Furthermore, when we look at the usage of the
biblical words translated "soul" (Heb. *nephesh* and Gk. *psychē*) and "spirit" (Heb.
rûach and Gk. *pneuma*),[5] it appears that they are sometimes used interchangeably.
For example, in John 12:27, Jesus says, "Now is my *soul* troubled," whereas in a
very similar context in the next chapter John says that Jesus was "troubled in *spirit*"
(John 13:21). Similarly, we read Mary's words in Luke 1:46–47: "My *soul* magnifies the Lord, and my *spirit* rejoices in God my Savior." This seems to be an evident
example of Hebrew parallelism, the poetic device in which often the same idea is
repeated using different but synonymous words. This interchangeability of terms
also explains why people who have died and gone to heaven or hell can be called
either "spirits" (Heb. 12:23, "the *spirits* of just men made perfect"; also 1 Peter
3:19, "*spirits* in prison") or "souls" (Rev. 6:9, "the *souls* of those who had been slain
for the word of God and for the witness they had borne"; 20:4, "the *souls* of those
who had been beheaded for their testimony to Jesus").

In addition to this interchange between the words *soul* and *spirit,* we can also
observe that man is said to be either "body and soul" or "body and spirit." Jesus
tells us not to fear those who "kill the body but cannot kill the soul," but that we
should rather "fear him who can destroy both soul and body in hell" (Matt. 10:28).
Here "soul" clearly must refer to the part of a person that exists after death. Moreover, when Jesus talks about "soul and body," he seems quite clearly to be talking
about the entire person even though he does not mention "spirit" as a separate component. "Soul" seems to stand for the entire nonphysical part of man.

On the other hand, man is sometimes said to be "body and spirit." Paul wants
the Corinthian church to deliver an erring brother to Satan "for the destruction of
the flesh, that his spirit may be saved in the day of the Lord Jesus" (1 Cor. 5:5). It
is not that Paul has forgotten the salvation of the man's soul as well; he simply uses
"spirit" to refer to the whole of the person's immaterial existence. Similarly, James
says that "the body apart from the spirit is dead" (James 2:26) but mentions nothing about a separate soul. Moreover, when Paul speaks of growth in personal holiness, he approves the woman who is concerned with "how to be holy in body and
spirit" (1 Cor. 7:34), and he suggests that this covers the whole of the person's life.
Even more explicit is 2 Corinthians 7:1, where he says, "Let us cleanse ourselves
from every defilement of *body and spirit,* and make holiness perfect in the fear of

---

[5]Throughout this chapter it is important to keep in mind that some recent Bible translations (especially the NIV)
do not consistently translate the Hebrew and Greek terms noted above as "soul" and "spirit," but sometimes substitute
other terms, such as "life," "mind," "heart," or "person," where the translators thought those senses were more suitable to the contexts. The terms do have a range of meanings and can take at least some of these other senses in some
contexts. The RSV, which I quote here unless another version is specified, tends to translate these terms more regularly
as "soul" and "spirit" wherever those senses are possible.

God." Cleansing ourselves from defilement of the "soul" or of the "spirit" covers the whole immaterial side of our existence (see also Rom. 8:10; 1 Cor. 5:3; Col. 2:5).

In a similar way, everything that the soul is said to do, the spirit is also said to do, and everything that the spirit is said to do, the soul is also said to do. Those who advocate trichotomy face a difficult problem defining clearly just what the difference is between the soul and the spirit (from their perspective). If Scripture gave clear support to the idea that our spirit is the part of us that directly relates to God in worship and prayer, while our soul includes our intellect (thinking), our emotions (feeling), and our will (deciding), then trichotomists would have a strong case. However, Scripture appears not to allow such a distinction to be made.

On one hand, the activities of thinking, feeling, and deciding things are not said to be done by our souls only. Our spirits can also experience emotions, for example, as when Paul's "spirit was provoked within him" (Acts 17:16), or when Jesus was "troubled in spirit" (John 13:21). It is also possible to have a "downcast spirit," which is the opposite of a "cheerful heart" (Prov. 17:22).

Moreover, the functions of knowing, perceiving, and thinking are also said to be done by our spirits. For instance, Mark speaks of Jesus "perceiving [Gk. *Epiginōskō*, 'knowing'] in his spirit" (Mark 2:8). When the Holy Spirit "bears witness with our spirit that we are children of God" (Rom. 8:16), our spirits receive and understand that witness, which is certainly a function of knowing something. In fact, our spirits seem to know our thoughts quite deeply, for Paul asks, "What person knows a man's thoughts except the spirit of the man which is in him?" (1 Cor. 2:11).

The point of these verses is not to say that it is the spirit rather than the soul that feels and thinks things, but rather that *soul* and *spirit* are both terms used of the immaterial side of people generally, and it is difficult to see any real distinction between the use of the terms.

On the other hand, the trichotomist claim that our spirit is that element of us that relates most directly to God in worship and in prayer does not seem to be borne out by Scripture. We often read about our soul worshiping God and relating to him in other kinds of spiritual activity. "To you, O LORD, I lift up my *soul*" (Ps. 25:1). "For God alone my *soul* waits in silence" (Ps. 62:1). "Bless the LORD, O my *soul;* and all that is within me, bless his holy name!" (Ps. 103:1). "Praise the LORD, O my *soul!*" (Ps. 146:1). "My *soul* magnifies the Lord" (Luke 1:46).

These passages indicate that our souls can worship God, praise him, and give thanks to him. Our souls can pray to God, as Hannah implies when she says, "I have been pouring out my soul before the LORD" (1 Sam. 1:15). In fact, the great commandment is to "love the LORD your God with all your heart, and with all your *soul,* and with all your might" (Deut. 6:5; cf. Mark 12:30). There seems to be no area of life or relationship to God in which Scripture says our spirits are active rather than our souls. Both terms are used to speak of all of the aspects of our relationship to God.

The trichotomist view generally thinks of the spirit as purer than the soul, and, when renewed, as free from sin and responsive to the prompting of the Holy Spirit. This understanding (which sometimes finds its way into popular Christian preaching and writing) is not really supported by the biblical text, however. When Paul encourages the Corinthians to cleanse themselves "from every defilement of body and spirit" (2 Cor. 7:1), he clearly implies that there can be defilement (or sin) in our spirits. Similarly, he speaks of the unmarried woman who is concerned with how to be holy "in body and spirit" (1 Cor. 7:34). Other verses speak in similar ways. For example, the Lord hardened the "spirit" of Sihon the king of Heshbon (Deut. 2:30). Psalm 78 speaks of the rebellious people of Israel "whose *spirit* was not faithful to God" (v. 8). A "haughty spirit" goes before a fall (Prov. 16:18), and it is possible for sinful people to be "proud in spirit" (Eccl. 7:8). Isaiah speaks of those "who err in spirit" (Isa. 29:24). Nebuchadnezzar's "spirit was hardened so that he dealt proudly" (Dan. 5:20). The fact that "all the ways of a man are pure in his own eyes, but the LORD weighs the spirit" (Prov. 16:2) implies that it is possible for our spirits to be wrong in God's sight. Other verses imply a possibility of sin in our spirits (see Pss. 32:2; 51:10). Finally, the fact that Scripture approves of one "who rules his spirit" (Prov. 16:32) implies that our spirits are not simply the spiritually pure parts of our lives that are to be followed in all cases, but that they can have sinful desires or directions as well.

What then does Paul mean when he says, "May the God of peace himself sanctify you wholly; and may your *spirit* and *soul* and *body* be kept sound and blameless at the coming of our Lord Jesus Christ" (1 Thess. 5:23)? Does not this verse clearly speak of three parts to man? The phrase "your spirit and soul and body" is by itself inconclusive. Paul is probably here piling up synonyms for emphasis, as is sometimes done elsewhere in Scripture. For example, Jesus says, "You shall love the Lord your God with all your *heart,* and with all your *soul,* and with all your *mind*" (Matt. 22:37). Does this mean that the soul is different from the mind or from the heart?[6] The problem is even greater in Mark 12:30: "You shall love the Lord your God with all your *heart,* and with all your *soul,* and with all your *mind,* and with all your *strength.*" If we go on the principle that such lists of terms tell us about more parts to man, then if we also add *spirit* to this list (and perhaps *body* as well), we would have five or six parts to man! But that is certainly a false conclusion. It is far better to understand Jesus as piling up roughly synonymous terms for emphasis to demonstrate that we must love God with all of our being. Likewise, in 1 Thessalonians 5:23, Paul is not saying that soul and spirit are distinct entities, but simply that, whatever we may call our immaterial part, he wants God to continue to sanctify us wholly to the day of Christ.

3. The benefits of holding to dichotomy with overall unity. The benefits of adhering to a view of dichotomy that upholds the overall unity of man are significant. This view makes it much easier to avoid the error of depreciating the value of our intellects, emotions, or physical bodies (according to trichotomy, these would be parts of the "soul" and therefore less spiritual). We will not think of our bodies as inherently evil or unimportant. Such a view of dichotomy within unity will also help us to remember that, in this life, there is a continual interaction between our body and our spirit, and that they affect each other: "A cheerful heart is good medicine, but a downcast spirit dries up the bones" (Prov. 17:22).

Moreover, a healthy emphasis on dichotomy within an overall unity reminds us that Christian growth must include all aspects of our lives. We are continually to "cleanse ourselves from every defilement of *body* and *spirit,* and make holiness perfect in the fear of God" (2 Cor. 7:1). We are to be "increasing in the knowledge of God" (Col. 1:10), and our emotions and desires are to conform increasingly to the "desires of the Spirit" (Gal. 5:17), including an increase in godly emotions such as peace, joy, love, and so forth (Gal. 5:22).

---

[6]The "heart" in Scripture is an expression for the deepest inmost thoughts and feelings of a person (see Gen. 6:5, 6; Lev. 19:17; Pss. 14:1; 15:2; 37:4; 119:10; Prov. 3:5; Acts 2:37; Rom. 2:5; 10:9; 1 Cor. 4:5; 14:25; Heb. 4:12; 1 Peter 3:4; Rev. 2:23; et al.).

II. REVIEW QUESTIONS

1. What was the purpose for which God created man? On that basis, what is to be the primary purpose of our lives?

2. What does it mean to be made "in the image of God"? In what ways is our existence like God's?

3. What effect did the fall of mankind have on our being made in the image of God? What is God's remedy for this?

4. Differentiate between the trichotomist and the dichotomist views of man.

5. Does there appear to be any difference between Scripture's use of the word *spirit* and its use of the word *soul*? Explain.

6. List two of the Scripture passages that are used to support the trichotomist position and give the dichotomist response to them.

III. QUESTIONS FOR PERSONAL APPLICATION

1. According to Scripture, what should be the major purpose of your life? If you consider the major commitments or goals of your life at the present time (with respect to friendships, marriage, education, job, use of money, church relationships, etc.), are you acting as though your goal were the one that Scripture specifies? Or do you have some other goals that you have acted upon (perhaps without consciously deciding to do so)?

2. How does it make you feel to think that you, as a human being, are more like God than any other creature in the universe? How does that knowledge make you want to act? Do you think that God has made us so that we become happier or less happy when we grow to become more like him? In which areas would you now like to make more progress in likeness to God?

3. Do you think an understanding of the image of God might change the way you think and act toward people who are racially different, or elderly, or weak, or unattractive to the world? How would this affect your relationship with non-Christians?

4. In your own Christian experience, are you aware that you have a nonphysical part that might be called a soul or spirit? Can you describe what it is like to have in your spirit a consciousness of God's presence (John 4:23; Rom. 8:16; Phil. 3:3), or to be troubled in your spirit (John 12:27; 13:21; Acts 17:16), or to have your spirit worship God (Ps. 103:1; Luke 1:47)?

IV. SPECIAL TERMS

dichotomy	soul
image of God	spirit
likeness	trichotomy
monism	

V. SCRIPTURE MEMORY PASSAGE

GENESIS 1:26–27

Then God said, "Let us make man in our image, after our likeness; and let them have dominion over the fish of the sea, and over the birds of the air, and over the cattle, and over all the earth, and over every creeping thing that creeps upon the earth." So God created man in his own image, in the image of God he created him; male and female he created them.

Chapter Twelve

Man as Male and Female

+ *Why did God create two sexes?*
| *Can men and women be equal and yet have different roles?*

I. EXPLANATION AND SCRIPTURAL BASIS

We noted in the preceding chapter that one aspect of our creation in the image of God is our creation as male and female: "So God created man *in his own image,* in the image of God he created him; *male and female he created them*" (Gen. 1:27). The same connection between creation in the image of God and creation as male and female is made in Genesis 5:1–2: "When God created man, he made him in the likeness of God. *Male and female* he created them, and he blessed them and named them Man when they were created." Although the creation of man as male and female is not the only way in which we are in the image of God, it is a significant enough aspect of our creation in the image of God that Scripture mentions it in the very same verse in which it describes God's initial creation of man. We may summarize the ways in which our creation as male and female represents something of our creation in God's image as follows:

The creation of man as male and female shows God's image in (1) harmonious interpersonal relationships, (2) equality in personhood and importance, and (3) difference in role and authority.[1]

A. Personal Relationships

God did not create human beings to be isolated persons, but, in making us in his image, he made us in such a way that we can attain interpersonal unity of various sorts in all forms of human society. Interpersonal unity can be especially deep in the human family and also in our spiritual family, the church. Between men and women, interpersonal unity comes to its fullest expression (in this present age) in marriage, where husband and wife become, in a sense, two persons in one: "Therefore a man leaves his father and his mother and cleaves to his wife, and they become

---

[1]For a more extensive discussion of the theological implications of male-female differentiation in Genesis 1–3, see Raymond C. Ortlund, Jr., "Male-Female Equality and Male Headship: Genesis 1–3," in *Recovering Biblical Manhood and Womanhood: A Response to Evangelical Feminism*, ed. John Piper and Wayne Grudem (Wheaton, Ill.: Crossway, 1991), p. 98. I have depended on Dr. Ortlund's analysis at several points in this chapter, but more detailed responses to objections to these points may be found in his essay. Other material on biblical manhood and womanhood may be obtained from the Council on Biblical Manhood and Womanhood, P.O. Box 7337, Libertyville, IL 60048 (www.cbmw.org).

one flesh" (Gen. 2:24). This unity is not only a physical unity; it is also a spiritual and emotional unity of profound dimensions. A husband and wife joined together in marriage are people whom "God has joined together" (Matt. 19:6). Sexual union with someone other than one's own wife or husband is a specially offensive kind of sin against one's own body (1 Cor. 6:16, 18–20), and, within marriage, husbands and wives no longer have exclusive rule over their own bodies, but share them with their spouses (1 Cor. 7:3–5). Husbands "should love their wives as their own bodies" (Eph. 5:28). The union between husband and wife is not temporary but lifelong (Matt. 19:6; Mal. 2:14–16; Rom. 7:2), and it is not trivial but is a profound relationship created by God to picture the relationship between Christ and his church (Eph. 5:23–32).

The fact that God created two distinct persons who were male and female, rather than just one man, is part of our being in the image of God because it can be seen to reflect to some degree the plurality of persons within the Trinity. In the verse prior to the one that tells of our creation as male and female, we see the first explicit indication of a plurality of persons within God: "Then God said, 'Let *us* make man in *our* image, after *our* likeness; and let them have dominion'" (Gen. 1:26). There is some similarity here: just as there was fellowship and communication and sharing of glory among the members of the Trinity before the world was made (see John 17:5, 24, and ch. 6 above on the Trinity), so God made Adam and Eve in such a way that they would share love and communication and mutual giving of honor to one another in their interpersonal relationship. Of course, such reflection of the Trinity would come to expression in various ways within human society, but it would certainly exist from the beginning in the close interpersonal unity of marriage.

B. Equality in Personhood and Importance

Just as the members of the Trinity are equal in their importance and in their full existence as distinct persons (see ch. 6), so men and women have been created by God to be equal in their importance and personhood. When God created the human race, he created both "male and female" in his image (Gen. 1:27; 5:1–2). Men and women are made equally in God's image, and both men and women reflect God's character in their lives. This means that we should see aspects of God's character reflected in each other's lives. If we lived in a society consisting of only Christian men or a society consisting of only Christian women, we would not gain as full a picture of the character of God as when we see both godly men and godly women in their complementary differences together reflecting the beauty of God's character.

But if we are equally in God's image, then certainly men and women are equally important to God and equally valuable to him. We have equal worth before him for all eternity. The fact that both men and women are said by Scripture to be "in the image of God" should exclude all feelings of pride or inferiority and any idea that one sex is "better" or "worse" than the other. In particular, in contrast to many non-Christian cultures and religions, no one should feel proud or superior because he is a man, and no one should feel disappointed or inferior because she is a woman. If God thinks us to be equal in value, then that settles the question, for God's evaluation is the true standard of personal value for all eternity.

Our equality as persons before God, reflecting the equality of persons in the Trinity, should lead naturally to men and women giving honor to one another. Proverbs 31 is a beautiful picture of the honor given to a godly woman:

A good wife who can find?
> She is far more precious than jewels. . . .
Her children rise up and call her blessed;
> her husband also, and he praises her:
"Many women have done excellently,
> but you surpass them all."
Charm is deceitful, and beauty is vain,
> but a woman who fears the LORD is to be praised.
> (Prov. 31:10, 28–30)

Similarly, Peter tells husbands that they are to "bestow honor" on their wives (1 Peter 3:7), and Paul emphasizes, "In the Lord woman is not independent of man nor man of woman; for as woman was made from man, so man is now born of woman" (1 Cor. 11:11–12). Both men and women are equally important; both depend on each other; both are worthy of honor.

The equality in personhood with which men and women were created is emphasized in a new way in the new covenant church. At Pentecost we see the fulfillment of Joel's prophecy in which God promises:

"I will pour out my Spirit upon all flesh,
and your *sons* and your *daughters* shall prophesy
. . . and on my *menservants* and my *maidservants* in those days
I will pour out my Spirit; and they shall prophesy." (Acts 2:17–18;
> quoting Joel 2:28–29)

The Holy Spirit is poured out in new power on the church, and men and women both are given gifts to minister in remarkable ways. Spiritual gifts are distributed to all men and women, beginning at Pentecost and continuing throughout the history of the church. Paul regards every Christian as a valuable member of the body of Christ, for "To *each* is given the manifestation of the Spirit for the common good" (1 Cor. 12:7). Peter also, in writing to many churches throughout Asia Minor, says, "As *each* has received a gift, employ it for one another, as good stewards of God's varied grace" (1 Peter 4:10). These texts do not teach that all believers have the same gifts, but they do mean that both men and women will have valuable gifts for the ministry of the church, and that we should expect that these gifts will be widely and freely distributed to both men and women.

Equality before God is further emphasized in the new covenant church in the ceremony of baptism. At Pentecost, both men and women who believed were baptized: "Those who received his word were baptized, and there were added that day about three thousand souls" (Acts 2:41). This is significant because in the old covenant, the sign of membership of God's people was circumcision, which was given only to men. But the new sign of membership of God's people, the sign of baptism, given to both men and women, is further evidence that both should be seen as fully and equally members of the people of God.

Equality in status among God's people is also emphasized by Paul in Galatians: "For as many of you as were baptized into Christ have put on Christ. There is neither Jew nor Greek, there is neither slave nor free, *there is neither male nor female;* for you are all one in Christ Jesus" (Gal. 3:27–28). Paul is here underlining the fact that no class of people, such as the Jewish people who had come from Abraham by physical descent, or the freedmen who had greater economic and legal power, could claim special status or privilege in the church. Slaves should not think themselves inferior to free men or women, nor should the free think themselves superior to slaves. Jews should not think themselves superior to Greeks, nor should Greeks think themselves inferior to Jews. Similarly, Paul wants to ensure that men will not adopt some of the attitudes of the surrounding culture, or even some of the attitudes of first-century Judaism, and think that they have greater importance than women or are of superior value before God. Nor should women think themselves inferior or less important in the church. Both men and women, Jews and Greeks, slaves and free, are equal in importance and value to God and equal in membership in Christ's body, the church, for all eternity.

In practical terms, we must never think that there are any second-class citizens in the church. Whether someone is a man or woman, employer or employee, Jew or Gentile, black or white, rich or poor, healthy or ill, strong or weak, attractive or unattractive, extremely intelligent or slow to learn, all are equally valuable to God and should be equally valuable to one another as well. This equality is an amazing and wonderful element of the Christian faith and sets Christianity apart from almost all religions and societies and cultures. The true dignity of godly manhood and womanhood can be fully realized only in obedience to God's redeeming wisdom as found in Scripture.

C. Differences in Roles

1. The relationship between the Trinity and male headship in marriage. Between the members of the Trinity there has been equality in importance, personhood, and deity throughout all eternity. But there have also been differences in roles between the members of the Trinity.[2] God the Father has always been the Father and has always related to the Son as a Father relates to his Son. Though all three members of the Trinity are equal in power and in all other attributes, the Father has a greater authority. He has a leadership role among all the members of the Trinity that the Son and Holy Spirit do not have. In creation, the Father speaks and initiates, but the work of creation is carried out through the Son and sustained by the continuing presence of the Holy Spirit (Gen. 1:1–2; John 1:1–3; 1 Cor. 8:6; Heb. 1:2). In redemption, the Father sends the Son into the world, and the Son comes and is obedient to the Father and dies to pay for our sins (Luke 22:42; Phil. 2:6–8). After the Son has ascended into heaven, the Holy Spirit comes to equip and empower the church (John 16:7; Acts 1:8; 2:1–36). The Father did not come to die for our sins, nor did the Holy Spirit. The Father was not poured out on the church at Pentecost in new covenant power, nor was the Son. Each member of the Trinity has distinct roles or functions. Differences in roles and authority between the members of the Trinity are thus completely consistent with equal importance, personhood, and deity.

If human beings are to reflect the character of God, then we would expect some similar differences in roles among human beings, even with respect to the most basic of all differences among human beings, the difference between male and female. And this is certainly what we find in the biblical text.

Paul makes this parallel explicit when he says, "I want you to understand that the head of every man is Christ, the head of a woman is her husband, and the head of Christ is God" (1 Cor. 11:3). Here is a distinction in authority that may be represented as in figure 12.1.

---

[2]See ch. 6, pp. 115–18, on differences in role among the members of the Trinity.

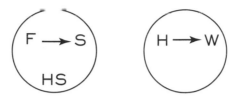

Equality and Differences in the Trinity Are Reflected in Equality and Differences in Marriage

figure 12.1

Just as God the Father has authority over the Son, though the two are equal in deity, so in a marriage, the husband has authority over the wife, though they are equal in personhood. In this case, the man's role is like that of God the Father and the woman's role is parallel to that of God the Son. They are equal in importance, but they have different roles. In the context of 1 Corinthians 11:2–16, Paul sees this as a basis for telling the Corinthians to wear the different kinds of clothing appropriate for the men and women of that day, so that the distinctions between men and women might be outwardly evident in the Christian assembly.

2. Indications of distinct roles before the fall. But were these distinctions between male and female roles part of God's original creation, or were they introduced as part of the punishment of the fall? When God told Eve, "Your desire shall be for your husband, and he shall rule over you" (Gen. 3:16), was that the time when Eve began to be subject to Adam's authority?

The idea that differences in authority were introduced only after there was sin in the world has been advocated by several writers such as Aida B. Spencer[3] and Gilbert Bilezikian.[4] Bilezikian says, "Because it resulted from the Fall, the rule of Adam over Eve is viewed as satanic in origin, no less than is death itself."

However, if we examine the text of the creation narrative in Genesis, we see several indications of differences in role between Adam and Eve even before there was sin in the world.

a. *Adam was created first, then Eve.* The fact that God first created Adam then after a period of time created Eve (Gen. 2:7, 18–23), suggests that God saw Adam as having a leadership role in his family. No such two-stage procedure is mentioned for any of the animals God made, but here it seems to have a special purpose. The creation of Adam first is consistent with the Old Testament pattern of "primogeniture," the idea that the firstborn in any generation in a human family has leadership in the family for that generation. The right of primogeniture is assumed throughout the Old Testament text, even when at times because of God's special purposes the birthright is sold or otherwise transferred to a younger person (see Gen. 25:27–34; 35:23; 38:27–30; 49:3–4; Deut. 21:15–17; 1 Chron. 5:1–2). The "birthright" belongs to the firstborn son and is his unless special circumstances intervene to change that fact. The fact that we are correct in seeing a purpose of God in creating

---

[3] *Beyond the Curse*, 2d ed. (Nashville: Thomas Nelson, 1985), pp. 20–42.
[4] *Beyond Sex Roles* (Grand Rapids: Baker, 1985), p. 58. See also pp. 21–58.

Adam first, and that this purpose reflects an abiding distinction in the roles God has given to men and women, is supported by 1 Timothy 2:13, where Paul uses the fact that "Adam was formed first, then Eve" as a reason for restricting some distinct governing and teaching roles in the church to men. (The fact that animals were created before Adam does not contradict this, for the idea of primogeniture only applied to members of a human family.)

b. *Eve was created as a helper for Adam.* Scripture specifies that God made Eve for Adam, not Adam for Eve. God said, "It is not good that the man should be alone; *I will make him a helper fit for him*" (Gen. 2:18). Paul sees this as significant enough to base a requirement for differences between men and women in worship on it. He says, "Neither was man created for woman, but *woman for man*" (1 Cor. 11:9). This should not be taken to imply lesser importance, but it does indicate that there was a difference in role from the beginning.

c. *Adam named Eve.* The fact that Adam gave names to all the animals (Gen. 2:19–20) indicated Adam's authority over the animal kingdom, because in Old Testament thought the right to name someone implied authority over that person (this is seen both when God gives names to people such as Abraham and Sarah, and when parents give names to their children). Since a Hebrew name designated the character or function of someone, Adam was specifying the characteristics or functions of the animals he named. Therefore, when Adam named Eve by saying, "She shall be called Woman, because she was taken out of Man" (Gen. 2:23), it indicated a leadership role on his part as well. This is true before the fall, where Adam names his wife "Woman," and it is true after the fall as well, when "the man called his wife's name Eve, because she was the mother of all living" (Gen. 3:20). Some have objected that Adam doesn't really name Eve before the fall.[5] But certainly calling his wife "Woman" (Gen. 2:23), just as he called all the living creatures by their names (Gen. 2:19–20), is giving her a name (the same verb *qārā'*, "to call," is used in both places). The fact that mothers sometimes give their children names in the Old Testament does not contradict the idea of name-giving as representing authority, since both mothers and fathers have parental authority over their children.

d. *God named the human race "man," not "woman."* The fact that God named the human race "man," rather than "woman" or some gender-neutral term was explained in chapter 11.[6] Genesis 5:2 specifies that "in the day when they were created" (NASB) God *"named them Man."* The naming of the human race with a term that also referred to Adam in particular, or man in distinction from woman, suggests a leadership role belonging to the man. This is similar to the custom of a woman taking the last name of the man when she marries; it signifies his headship in the family.

e. *God spoke to Adam first after the fall.* Just as God spoke to Adam on his own even before Eve was created (Gen. 2:15–17), so, after the fall, even though Eve had sinned first, God came first to Adam and called him to account for his actions: "But the LORD *God called to the man,* and said to *him,* 'Where are you?'" (Gen. 3:9). God thought of Adam as the leader of his family, the one to be called to account first for what had happened in the family. It is significant that though this is after sin has

---

[5]See Gilbert Bilezikian, *Beyond Sex Roles*, pp. 260–61.
[6]See pp. 187–88.

occurred, it is before the statement to Eve, "He shall rule over you" in Genesis 3:16, where some writers today claim male headship in the family began.

f. *Adam, not Eve, represented the human race.* Even though Eve sinned first (Gen. 3:6), we are counted sinful because of Adam's sin, not because of Eve's sin. The New Testament tells us, "*In Adam* all die" (1 Cor. 15:22; cf. v. 49), and, "Many died through *one man's* trespass" (Rom. 5:15; cf. vv. 12–21). This indicates that God had given Adam headship or leadership with respect to the human race, a role that was not given to Eve.

g. *The curse brought a distortion of previous roles, not the introduction of new roles.* In the punishments God gave to Adam and Eve, he did not introduce new roles or functions, but simply introduced pain and distortion into the functions they previously had. Thus, Adam would still have primary responsibility for tilling the ground and raising crops, but the ground would bring forth "thorns and thistles," and in the sweat of his face he would eat bread (Gen. 3:18–19). Similarly, Eve would still have the responsibility of bearing children, but to do so would become painful: "In pain you shall bring forth children" (Gen. 3:16). Then God also introduced conflict and pain into the previously harmonious relationship between Adam and Eve. God said to Eve, "Your *desire* shall be *for your husband,* and he shall rule over you" (Gen. 3:16). Susan Foh has effectively argued that the word translated "desire" (Heb. *teshúqāh*) means "desire to rule," and that it indicates that Eve would have a wrongful desire to usurp authority over her husband.[7] If this understanding of the word translated "desire" is correct, as it seems to be, then it would indicate that God is introducing *a conflict into the relationship* between Adam and Eve and a desire on Eve's part to rebel against Adam's authority.

Concerning Adam, God told Eve, "He shall *rule* over you" (Gen. 3:16). Here the word "rule" (Heb. *Meāshal*) is a strong term usually used of monarchical governments, not generally of authority within a family.[8] The word certainly does not imply any "participatory" government by those who are ruled, but rather has nuances of rule by greater power or strength. It suggests leadership with harshness rather than with kindness and love. The sense here is that Adam will use his greater strength and power to rule over his wife, again introducing pain and conflict into a relationship that was previously harmonious. It is not that Adam had no authority before the fall; it is simply that he will misuse it after the fall.

So in both cases, the curse brought a *distortion* of Adam's humble, considerate leadership and Eve's intelligent, willing submission to that leadership that existed before the fall.

h. *Redemption in Christ reaffirms the creation order.* If the previous argument about the distortion of roles introduced at the fall is correct, then what we would expect to find in the New Testament is an undoing of the painful aspects of the relationship that resulted from sin and the curse. We would expect that in Christ, redemption would encourage wives not to rebel against their husbands' authority, and would encourage husbands not to use their authority harshly. In fact, that is indeed what we do find: "Wives, *be subject to your husbands,* as is fitting in the Lord.

---

[7] See Susan. T. Foh, "What Is the Woman's Desire?" in *WTJ* 37 (1975): 376–83.

[8] See Deut. 15:6, "You shall rule over many nations, but they shall not rule over you"; Prov. 22:7, "The rich rules over the poor"; Judg. 14:4; 15:11 (of the Philistines ruling over Israel); also Gen. 37:8; Prov. 12:24; et al.

Husbands, *love your wives,* and *do not be harsh with them*" (Col. 3:18–19; cf. Eph. 5:22–33; Titus 2:5; 1 Peter 3:1–7). If it were a sinful pattern for wives to be subject to their husbands' authority, Peter and Paul would not have commanded it to be maintained in Christian marriages! They do not say, for example, "Encourage thorns to grow in your garden," or "Make childbirth as painful as possible," or "Stay alienated from God, cut off from fellowship with him!" The redemption of Christ is aimed at *removing* the results of sin and of the fall in every way: "The reason the Son of God appeared was to *destroy* the works of the devil" (1 John 3:8). *New Testament commands concerning marriage do not perpetuate any elements of the curse or any sinful behavior patterns;* they rather reaffirm the order and distinction of roles that were there from the beginning of God's good creation.

In terms of practical application, as we grow in maturity in Christ, we will grow to delight in and rejoice in the God-ordained and wisely created differences in roles within the human family. When we understand this biblical teaching, both men and women should be able to say in their hearts, "This is what God has planned, and it is beautiful and right, and I rejoice in the way he has made me and the distinct role he has given me." There is eternal beauty and dignity and rightness in this differentiation in roles both within the Trinity and within the human family. With no sense of "better" or "worse," and with no sense of "more important" or "less important," both men and women should be able to rejoice fully in the way they have been made by God.

i. *The question of application to the church.* The question of how the New Testament teachings on manhood and womanhood apply to the church today is a highly disputed one, and space does not allow extensive treatment of that topic here. The major difference among evangelicals on this matter can be reduced to one key question: *Should some governing and teaching roles in the church be reserved for men?* Christians who answer no to that question are called *egalitarians* (because they emphasize "equality" between men and women). They hold that no governing or teaching roles in the church are reserved for men—that all positions are open to men and women alike. They would emphasize Galatians 3:28 as well as Judges 4–5; Acts 2:17–18; 18:26; 21:9; Romans 16:7; and 1 Timothy 3:11. Further information on an egalitarian position is available from an organization devoted to promoting that position, Christians for Biblical Equality (CBE).[9] Their statement of principles is called "Men, Women and Biblical Equality."[10]

Christians who answer yes to the same question are called *complementarians* (because they emphasize that men and women, while equal in value, have "complementary" differences). They hold that "some" governing and teaching roles in the church are reserved for men, although exactly which roles would vary according to how individual denominations and congregations applied 1 Timothy 2:11–15 to their governing structures. They would emphasize 1 Timothy 2:11–15·as well as Matthew 10:2–4 (Jesus chose twelve men to be apostles); 1 Corinthians 14:33–35;

---

[9]Christians for Biblical Equality may be contacted at 122 West Franklin Ave., Suite 218, Minneapolis, MN 55404-2451. Their web site is www.goldengate.net/mall/cbe. Books representing the egalitarian position include Richard and Catherine Kroeger, *I Suffer Not a Woman: Rethinking 1 Timothy 2:11–15 in Light of Ancient Evidence* (Grand Rapids: Baker, 1992) (Kroeger is the founding president of CBE); Gilbert Bilezikian, *Beyond Sex Roles* (Grand Rapids: Baker, 1985); Craig Keener, *Paul, Women and Wives* (Peabody, Mass.: Hendrickson, 1992); and Rebecca Merrill Groothuis, *Good News for Women* (Grand Rapids: Baker, 1997).

[10]First published in *Christianity Today,* April 9, 1990, pp. 36–37, and available on the CBE web site.

1 Timothy 3:2; Titus 1:6; and the connection between leadership in the home and the church (1 Tim. 3:5). Further information on a complementarian position is available from an organization devoted to promoting that position, the Council on Biblical Manhood and Womanhood (CBMW).[11] Their statement of principles is called "The Danvers Statement."[12]

My own position is complementarian, and I have written extensively on that position elsewhere. In a brief summary, my conviction would be that none of the passages emphasized by egalitarians are really addressed to the question of whether women can have governing or teaching authority over the whole church: It is true that women can prophesy in the New Testament churches (Acts 21:9; 1 Cor. 11:5), but the gift of prophecy is always distinguished from teaching, and elders are not required to have the gift of prophecy but to be "apt teachers" (see 1 Tim. 3:2). Private prophesying like that of Deborah (Judges 4) and private teaching like that of Aquila and Priscilla (Acts 18:26) are certainly appropriate for women today, but these activities differ significantly from the authority over the whole church that is prohibited to women in 1 Timothy 2:11-15. Regarding Romans 16:7, there is simply not enough evidence to know with any amount of confidence (even after massive amounts of research) whether the person named is a man (Junias) or a woman (Junia).[13] It is true that we are "all one in Christ Jesus" (Gal. 3:28), but that simply affirms our unity; it does not mean that we are all the same or have the same functions, any more than the fact that all the members of the body are "one body" (1 Cor. 12:12) means that all the parts of our bodies have the same functions.

By contrast, the passages emphasized by complementarians directly address the central question of whether women should have governing or teaching authority over the whole church. Passages like 1 Timothy 3:2, Titus 1:6, and Matthew 10:2–4 are talking about apostles or elders, who did have such authority over a whole church (or, with respect to the apostles, over all the churches). Other passages talk about not an office but about a teaching or governing role over the entire assembled church (1 Tim. 2:11–15; 1 Cor. 14:33–35). The claims that these statements depend on some cultural circumstances such as women teaching false doctrine or women having inadequate education do not seem to me to be supported with reliable evidence, and they are not the reason Paul gives. (He refers rather to Adam and Eve before they sinned). Therefore, I see no reason to take these statements as applying to anything less than the entire "church age" (the period from Pentecost until Christ returns).

---

[11]The Council on Biblical Manhood and Womanhood may be contacted at P.O. Box 7337, Libertyville, IL 60048. Their web site is www.cbmw.org. Books representing the complementarian position include John Piper and Wayne Grudem, eds., *Recovering Biblical Manhood and Womanhood: A Response to Evangelical Feminism* (Wheaton, Ill.: Crossway, 1991); Mary Kassian, *Women, Creation, and the Fall* (Westchester, Ill.: Crossway, 1990), Stephen B. Clark, *Man and Woman in Christ* (Ann Arbor, Mich.: Servant, 1980), and Andreas Köstenberger, Thomas Schreiner, and Scott Baldwin, eds., *Women in the Church: A Fresh Analysis of 1 Timothy 2:9–15* (Grand Rapids: Baker, 1995).

[12]First published in *Christianity Today*, January 13, 1989, pp. 40–41, and available on the CBMW web site.

[13]It is interesting that the source of the only additional historical information we have about this person from outside the New Testament calls him "Junias" (and refers to him with a masculine pronoun) and says he ""became bishop of Apameia in Syria" (see Epiphanius [A.D. 315–403], *Index disciplulorum*, 125.19–20). Another author, Chrysostom (A.D. 347–407), assumes that this was a woman, Junia, but seems to know nothing about this person except what is in the biblical text (*Homily on Romans*, on 16:7).

In addition to the ambiguity of the name, the word *apostle* here is ambiguous; the Greek term *apostolos* sometimes just means "messenger" (as in John 13:16; 2 Cor. 8:23; Phil. 2:25) and in other places refers to the office "apostle of Jesus Christ." Because the context gives so little information in Romans 16:7, it is impossible to be sure of its meaning here.

However, many churches have been far too restrictive in their views of types of ministry open to women, and this has often been aggravated by an excessively clergy-dominated view of ministry. Wise pastors and elders will listen often to the insight and counsel of women in their churches and will open many more doors for hundreds of other kinds of valuable ministries for women while still seeking to be faithful to Scripture, as they best understand it, and therefore restricting "some governing and teaching roles in the church" to men.

II. REVIEW QUESTIONS

1. Explain how the creation of mankind as male and female reflects the image of God in interpersonal relationships.
2. If man and woman are created equally in God's image, what does this say about their relative importance before God?
3. What can the differences in roles among the members of the Trinity teach us about the roles of men and women in marriage?
4. Name five indications that distinct roles for men and women existed before the Fall.
5. What effect did the Fall have on the roles and functions of Adam and Eve?
6. What effect does our redemption in Christ have on these roles?

III. QUESTIONS FOR PERSONAL APPLICATION

1. If you are being honest about your feelings, do you think it is better to be a man or a woman? Are you happy with the gender God gave you, or would you rather be a member of the opposite sex? How do you think God wants you to feel about that question?
2. Can you honestly say that you think members of the opposite sex are *equally valuable* in God's sight?
3. Before reading this chapter, had you thought of relationships in the family as reflecting something of the relationships between members of the Trinity? Do you think that is a helpful way of looking at the family? Are there ways in which you might reflect God's character more fully in your own family?
4. How does the teaching of this chapter on differences in roles between men and women compare with some of the attitudes expressed in society today? If there are differences between what much of society is teaching and what Scripture teaches, do you think there will be times when it will be difficult to follow Scripture? What could your church do to help you in those situations?

IV. SPECIAL TERMS

complementarian	egalitarian
difference in role	equality in personhood
distortion of roles	primogeniture

V. SCRIPTURE MEMORY PASSAGE

COLOSSIANS 3:18—19

Wives, be subject to your husbands, as is fitting in the Lord. Husbands, love your wives, and do not be harsh with them.

Chapter Thirteen

Sin

+ *What is sin?*

+ *Where did it come from?*

+ *Do we inherit a sinful nature from Adam?*

I. EXPLANATION AND SCRIPTURAL BASIS

A. The Definition of Sin

The history of the human race as presented in Scripture is primarily a history of man in a state of sin and rebellion against God, and of God's plan of redemption to bring many people back to himself. Therefore, it is appropriate now to consider the nature of the sin that separates people from God.

We may define sin as follows: *Sin is any failure to conform to the moral law of God in act, attitude, or nature.* Sin is here defined in relation to God and his moral law. Sin consists not only of individual *acts*, such as stealing or lying or committing murder, but also in *attitudes* that are contrary to the attitudes God requires of us. We see this in the Ten Commandments, which not only prohibit sinful actions, but also wrong attitudes: "*You shall not covet* your neighbor's house. *You shall not covet* your neighbor's wife, or his manservant or maidservant, his ox or donkey, or anything that belongs to your neighbor" (Ex. 20:17 NIV). Here God specifies that a *desire* to steal or to commit adultery is also sin in his sight. The Sermon on the Mount also prohibits sinful attitudes such as anger (Matt. 5:22) or lust (Matt. 5:28). Paul also lists attitudes such as jealousy, anger, and selfishness (Gal. 5:20) as things that are works of the flesh opposed to the desires of the Spirit (Gal. 5:20). Therefore, a life that is pleasing to God is one that has moral purity not only in its actions, but also in its desires of heart. In fact, the greatest commandment of all requires that our heart be filled with an attitude of love for God: "You shall love the Lord your God with all your heart, and with all your soul, and with all your mind, and with all your strength" (Mark 12:30).

The definition of sin given above specifies that sin is a failure to conform to God's moral law not only in *action* and in *attitude*, but also in our *moral nature*. Our very nature, the internal character that is the essence of who we are as persons, can also be sinful. Before we were redeemed by Christ, not only did we do sinful acts and have sinful attitudes, we were also sinners by nature. So Paul can say that "while *we were yet sinners* Christ died for us" (Rom. 5:8), or that previously "we were *by nature* children of wrath, like the rest of mankind" (Eph. 2:3). Even while asleep, an unbeliever, though not committing sinful actions or actively nurturing sinful attitudes, is still a "sinner" in God's sight; he or she still has a sinful nature that does not conform to God's moral law.

It is far better to define sin in the way Scripture does, in relationship to God's law and his moral character, than in other, more arbitrary ways. John tells us that "sin is lawlessness" (1 John 3:4, with reference to the law of God). When Paul seeks to demonstrate the universal sinfulness of mankind, he appeals to the law of God, whether the written law given to the Jew (Rom. 2:17–29) or the unwritten law which operates in the consciences of Gentiles who, by their behavior, "show that what the law requires is written on their hearts" (Rom. 2:15). In each case their sinfulness is demonstrated by their lack of conformity to the moral law of God.

Finally, we should note that this definition emphasizes the seriousness of sin. We realize from experience that sin is harmful to our lives, that it brings pain and destructive consequences to us and to others affected by it. But when we define sin as failure to conform to the moral law *of God,* we emphasize that sin is more than simply painful and destructive—it is also wrong in the deepest sense of the word. In a universe created by God, sin ought not to be approved. Sin is directly opposite to all that is good in God's character, and just as God necessarily and eternally delights in himself and in all that he is, so God necessarily and eternally hates sin. It is, in essence, the contradiction of the excellence of his moral character. Because sin contradicts God's holiness, he must hate it.

B. The Origin of Sin

Where did sin come from? How did it come into the universe? First, we must clearly affirm that God himself did not sin, and God is not to be blamed for sin. It was man who sinned, and it was angels who sinned, and in both cases they did so by willful, voluntary choice. To blame God for sin would be blasphemy against the character of God. "His work is perfect; for all his ways are justice. A God of faithfulness and *without iniquity,* just and right is he" (Deut. 32:4). Elihu rightly says, "Far be it from God that he should do wickedness, and from the Almighty that he should do wrong" (Job 34:10). In fact, it is impossible for God even to desire to do wrong: "God cannot be tempted with evil and he himself tempts no one" (James 1:13).

Yet, on the other hand, we must guard against an opposite error: It would be wrong for us to say there is an eternally existing evil power in the universe similar to or equal to God himself in power. To say this would be to affirm what is called an ultimate "dualism" in the universe, the existence of two equally ultimate powers, one good and the other evil.[1] We must also never think that sin surprised God or challenged or overcame his omnipotence or his providential control over the universe. Therefore, even though we must never say that God himself sinned or he is to be blamed for sin, yet we must also affirm that the God who "accomplishes all things according to the counsel of his will" (Eph. 1:11), did ordain that sin would come into the world, even though he does not delight in it and even though he ordained that it would come about through the voluntary choices of moral creatures.[2]

Even before the disobedience of Adam and Eve, sin was present in the angelic world with the fall of Satan and demons. But with respect to the human race, the first sin was that of Adam and Eve in the Garden of Eden (Gen. 3:1–19). Their eating of the fruit of the tree of the knowledge of good and evil is in many ways typical of sin generally. First, their sin struck at the basis for knowledge, for it gave a different

---

[1]See discussion of dualism in ch. 7, pp. 128–29.
[2]See ch. 8, pp. 147–51, for further discussion of God's providence in relationship to evil.

answer to the question, "What is true?" Whereas God had said that Adam and Eve would die if they ate from the tree (Gen. 2:17), the serpent said, "You will not die" (Gen. 3:4). Eve decided to doubt the veracity of God's word and conduct an experiment to see whether God spoke truthfully.

Second, their sin struck at the basis for moral standards, for it gave a different answer to the question, "What is right?" God had said that it was morally right for Adam and Eve not to eat from the fruit of that one tree (Gen. 2:17). But the serpent suggested that it would be right to eat of the fruit, and that in eating it Adam and Eve would become "like God" (Gen. 3:5). Eve trusted her own evaluation of what was right and what would be good for her, rather than allowing God's words to define right and wrong. She "saw that the tree was good for food, and that it was a delight to the eyes, and that the tree was to be desired to make one wise," and therefore she "took of its fruit and ate" (Gen. 3:6).

Third, their sin gave a different answer to the question, "Who am I?" The correct answer was that Adam and Eve were creatures of God, dependent on him and always to be subordinate to him as their Creator and Lord. But Eve, and then Adam, succumbed to the temptation to "be like God" (Gen. 3:5), thus attempting to put themselves in the place of God.

It is important to insist on the historical truthfulness of the narrative of the fall of Adam and Eve. Just as the account of the creation of Adam and Eve is tied in with the rest of the historical narrative in the book of Genesis,[3] so also this account of the fall of man, which follows the history of man's creation, is presented by the author as straightforward, narrative history. Moreover, the New Testament authors look back on this account and affirm that "sin came into the world through one man" (Rom. 5:12) and insist that "the judgment following one trespass brought condemnation" (Rom. 5:16) and that "the serpent deceived Eve by his cunning" (2 Cor. 11:3; cf. 1 Tim. 2:14). The serpent was no doubt, a real, physical serpent, but one that was talking because of the empowerment of Satan speaking through it (cf. Gen. 3:15 with Rom. 16:20; also Num. 22:28–30; Rev. 12:9; 20:2).

Finally, we should note that all sin is ultimately irrational. It really did not make sense for Satan to rebel against God in the expectation of being able to exalt himself above God. Nor did it make sense for Adam and Eve to think that there could be any gain in disobeying the words of their Creator. These were foolish choices. The persistence of Satan in rebelling against God even today is still a foolish choice, as is the decision on the part of any human being to continue in a state of rebellion against God. It is not the wise man but "the fool" who "says in his heart, 'There is no God'" (Ps. 14:1). It is the "fool" in the book of Proverbs who recklessly indulges in all kinds of sins (see Prov. 10:23; 12:15; 14:7, 16; 15:5; 18:2; et al.). Though people sometimes persuade themselves that they have good reasons for sinning, when examined in the cold light of truth on the last day, it will be seen in every case that sin ultimately just does not make sense.

---

[3]Note the phrase "These are the generations of" introducing successive sections in the Genesis narrative at Gen. 2:4 (heavens and the earth); 5:1 (Adam); 6:9 (Noah); 10:1 (the sons of Noah); 11:10 (Shem); 11:27 (Terah, the father of Abraham); 25:12 (Ishmael); 25:19 (Isaac); 36:1 (Esau); and 37:2 (Jacob). The translation of the phrase may differ in various English versions, but the Hebrew expression is the same and literally says, "These are the generations of. . . ." By this literary device, the author has introduced various sections of his historical narrative, tying it all together in a unified whole and indicating that it is to be understood as history writing of the same sort throughout. If the author intends us to understand Abraham, Isaac, and Jacob as historical figures, then he also intends us to understand Adam and Eve as historical figures, part of the same historical narrative.

C. The Doctrine of Inherited Sin[4]

How does the sin of Adam affect us? Scripture teaches that we inherit sin from Adam in two ways.

1. Inherited guilt: We are counted guilty because of Adam's sin. Paul explains the effects of Adam's sin in the following way: "Therefore . . . sin came into the world through one man and death through sin, and so death spread to all men because all men sinned" (Rom. 5:12). The context shows that Paul is not talking about actual sins that people commit every day of their lives, for the entire paragraph (Rom. 5:12–21) is taken up with the comparison between Adam and Christ. And when Paul says, "*so* [Gk. *houtos,* 'thus, in this way'   that is, through Adam's sin] death spread to all men because all men sinned," he is saying that through the sin of Adam "all men sinned."

This idea, that "all men sinned" means that God thought of us all as having sinned when Adam disobeyed, is further indicated by the next two verses, where Paul says: "Sin indeed was in the world before the law was given, but sin is not counted where there is no law. Yet death reigned from Adam to Moses, even over those whose sins were not like the transgression of Adam, who was a type of the one who was to come" (Rom. 5:13 14).

Here Paul points out that from the time of Adam to the time of Moses, people did not have God's written laws. Though their sins were "not counted" (as infractions of the law), they still died. The fact that they died is very good proof that God counted people guilty on the basis of Adam's sin.

The idea that God counted us guilty because of Adam's sin is further affirmed in Romans 5:18–19: "Then as one man's trespass led to condemnation for all men, so one man's act of righteousness leads to acquittal and life for all men. For as *by one man's disobedience many were made sinners,* so by one man's obedience many will be made righteous."

Here Paul says explicitly that through the trespass of one man "many were made [Gk. *katestathēsan,* an aorist indicative indicating completed past action] sinners." When Adam sinned, God thought of all who would descend from Adam as sinners. Though we did not yet exist, God, looking into the future and knowing that we would exist, began thinking of us as those who were guilty like Adam. This is also consistent with Paul's statement that "while we were yet sinners Christ died for us" (Rom. 5:8). Of course, some of us did not even exist when Christ died. But God nevertheless regarded us as sinners in need of salvation.

The conclusion to be drawn from these verses is that all members of the human race were represented by Adam in the time of testing in the Garden of Eden. As our representative, Adam sinned, and God counted us guilty as well as Adam. (A technical term that is sometimes used in this connection is *impute,* meaning "to think of as belonging to someone, and therefore to cause it to belong to that person.") God counted Adam's guilt as belonging to us, and since God is the ultimate Judge of all things in the universe, and since his thoughts are always true, Adam's guilt does in fact belong to us. God rightly *imputed* Adam's guilt to us.

---

[4]I have used the phrase "inherited sin" rather than the more common designation "original sin" because the phrase "original sin" seems so easily to be misunderstood to refer to Adam's first sin rather than to the sin that is ours as a result of Adam's fall (traditionally the technical meaning).

Sometimes the doctrine of inherited sin from Adam is termed the doctrine of "original sin." As explained above,[5] I have not used this expression. If this term is used, it should be remembered that the sin spoken of does not refer to Adam's first sin, but to the guilt and tendency to sin with which we are born. It is "original" in that it comes from Adam, and it is also original in that we have it from the beginning of our existence as persons, but it is still our sin, not Adam's sin, that is meant. Parallel to the phrase "original sin" is the phrase "original guilt." This is that aspect of inherited sin from Adam that we have been discussing above, namely, the idea that we inherit the guilt from Adam. Rather than calling it "original guilt," I have called it "inherited guilt."

When we first confront the idea that we have been counted guilty because of Adam's sin, our tendency is to protest because it seems unfair. *We* did not actually decide to sin, did we? Then how can we be counted guilty? Is it just for God to act this way?

In response, three things may be said. First, everyone who protests that this is unfair has also voluntarily committed many actual sins for which God also holds us guilty. These will constitute the primary basis of our judgment on the last day, for God "will render to every man according to his works" (Rom. 2:6) and "the wrongdoer will be paid back for the wrong he has done" (Col. 3:25).

Second, some have argued, "If any one of us were in Adam's place, we also would have sinned as he did, and our subsequent rebellion against God demonstrates that." I think this is probably true, but it does not seem to be a conclusive argument, for it assumes too much about what would or would not happen. Such uncertainty may not help very much to lessen someone's sense of unfairness.

Third, the most persuasive answer to the objection is to point out that if we think it is unfair for us to be represented by Adam, then we should also think it is unfair for us to be represented by Christ and to have his righteousness imputed to us by God. For the procedure that God used was just the same, and that is exactly Paul's point in Romans 5:12–21: "*As* by one man's disobedience many were made sinners, *so* by one man's obedience many will be made righteous" (Rom. 5:19). Adam, our first representative sinned—and God counted us guilty. But Christ, the representative of all who believe in him, obeyed God perfectly—and God counted us righteous. That is simply the way in which God set up the human race to work. God regards the human race as an organic whole, a unity, represented by Adam as its head. And God also thinks of the new race of Christians, those who are redeemed by Christ, as an organic whole, a unity represented by Christ as head of his people.

Not all evangelical theologians, however, agree that we are counted guilty because of Adam's sin. Some, especially Arminian theologians, think this to be unfair of God and do not believe that it is taught in Romans 5.[6] However, evangelicals of all persuasions do agree that we receive a sinful disposition or a tendency to sin as an inheritance from Adam, a subject we shall now consider.

2. Inherited corruption: *We have a sinful nature because of Adam's sin.* In addition to the legal guilt that God imputes to us because of Adam's sin, we also inherit a sinful nature because of Adam's sin. This inherited sinful nature is some-

---

[5]See n. 4 above.

[6]See, for example, the thorough discussion in H. Orton Wiley, *Christian Theology,* 3 vols. (Kansas City, Mo.: Beacon Hill Press, 1941–49), 3:109–40.

times simply called "original sin" and sometimes more precisely called "original pollution." I have used instead the term "inherited corruption" because it seems to express more clearly the specific idea in view.

David says, "Behold, I was brought forth in iniquity, and in sin did my mother conceive me" (Ps. 51:5). Some have mistakenly thought that the sin of David's mother is in view here, but this is incorrect, for the entire context has nothing to do with David's mother. David is confessing his own personal sin throughout this section. He says:

> Have mercy on *me,* O God
>   . . . blot out *my* transgressions.
> Wash *me* thoroughly from *my* iniquity
>   . . . I know *my* transgressions.
>   . . . Against you . . . have *I* sinned. (Ps. 51:1–4)

David is so overwhelmed with the consciousness of his own sin that as he looks back on his life he realizes that he was sinful from the beginning. As far back as he can think of himself, he realizes that he has had a sinful nature. In fact, when he was born or "brought forth" from his mother's womb, he was "brought forth in iniquity" (Ps. 51:5). Moreover, even before he was born, he had a sinful disposition: He affirms that at the moment of conception he had a sinful nature, for "in sin did my mother *conceive* me" (Ps. 51:5). Here is a strong statement of the inherent tendency to sin that attaches to our lives from the very beginning. A similar idea is affirmed in Psalm 58:3, "The wicked go astray from the womb, they err from their birth, speaking lies."

Therefore, our nature includes a disposition to sin so that Paul can affirm that before we were Christians "we were by nature children of wrath, like the rest of mankind" (Eph. 2:3). Anyone who has raised children can give experiential testimony to the fact that we are all born with a tendency to sin. Children do not have to be taught how to do wrong; they discover that by themselves. What we have to do as parents is to teach them how to do right, to "bring them up in the discipline and instruction of the Lord" (Eph. 6:4).

This inherited tendency to sin does not mean that human beings are all as bad as they could be, nor does it mean that we can do no good in any sense of the word. However, our inherited corruption, our tendency to sin, which we received from Adam, means that as far as God is concerned, we are not able to do anything that pleases him. This may be seen in two ways:

a. *In our natures we totally lack spiritual good before God.* It is not just that some parts of us are sinful and others are pure. Rather, *every part of our being* is affected by sin—our intellects, our emotions and desires, our hearts (the center of our desires and decision-making processes), our goals and motives, and even our physical bodies. Paul says, "I know that nothing good dwells within me, that is, in my flesh" (Rom. 7:18), and, "to the corrupt and unbelieving nothing is pure; their very minds and consciences are corrupted" (Titus 1:15). Moreover, Jeremiah tells us that "the heart is deceitful above all things, and desperately corrupt; who can understand it?" (Jer. 17:9). In these passages Scripture is not denying that unbelievers can do good in human society *in some senses.* But it is denying that they can do any *spiritual* good or be good in *terms of a relationship with God.* Apart from the work of Christ in our lives, we are like all other unbelievers who are "darkened in their understanding, alienated from the life of God because of the ignorance that is in them, due to their hardness of heart" (Eph. 4:18).[7]

b. *In our actions we are totally unable to do spiritual good before God.* This idea is related to the previous one. Not only do we as sinners lack any spiritual good in ourselves, but we also lack the ability to do anything that will in itself please God, and we lack the ability to come to God in our own strength. Paul says that "those who are in the flesh cannot please God" (Rom. 8:8). Moreover, in terms of bearing fruit for God's kingdom and doing what pleases him, Jesus says, "apart from me you can do nothing" (John 15:5). In fact, unbelievers are not pleasing to God, if for no other reason, simply because their actions do not proceed from faith in God or from love to him, and "without faith it is impossible to please him" (Heb. 11:6). Unbelievers are in a state of bondage or enslavement to sin, because "every one who commits sin is a slave to sin" (John 8:34). Though from a human standpoint people might be able to do much good, Isaiah affirms that "all our righteous deeds are like a polluted garment" (Isa. 64:6; cf. Rom. 3:9–20). Nor can we come to God in our own power, for Jesus says, "No one can come to me unless the Father who sent me draws him" (John 6:44).

But if we have a total inability to do any spiritual good in God's sight, then do we still have any freedom of choice? Certainly, those who are outside of Christ do still make voluntary choices—that is, they decide what they want to do, then they do it. In this sense there is still a kind of "freedom" in the choices that people make.[8] Yet because of their inability to do good and to escape from their fundamental rebellion against God and their fundamental preference for sin, unbelievers do not have freedom in the most important sense of freedom—that is, the freedom to do right and to do what is pleasing to God.

The application to our lives is quite evident: If God gives anyone a desire to repent and trust in Christ, he should not delay and should not harden his heart (cf. Heb. 3:7–8; 12:17). This ability to repent and desire to trust in God is not naturally ours but is given by the prompting of the Holy Spirit, and it will not last forever. "Today, when you hear his voice, do not harden your hearts" (Heb. 3:15).

3. Are infants guilty before they commit actual sins? Some maintain that Scripture teaches an "age of accountability" before which young children are not held responsible for sin and are not counted guilty before God.[9] However, the passages noted above about "inherited sin" indicate that *even before birth* children have a guilty standing before God and a sinful nature that not only gives them a tendency to sin but also causes God to view them as "sinners" in his sight. "Behold, I was brought forth in iniquity, and in sin did my mother conceive me" (Ps. 51:5). The passages that speak of final judgment in terms of actual sinful deeds that have been done (e.g., Rom. 2:6–11) do not say anything about the basis of judgment when there have been no individual actions of right or wrong, as with children dying in early infancy. In

---

[7]This total lack of spiritual good before God has traditionally been called "total depravity," but I will not use the phrase here because it is easily subject to misunderstanding. It can give the impression that no good in any sense can be done by unbelievers, a meaning that is certainly not intended by that term or by this doctrine.

[8]See discussion of the question of free will in ch. 8, pp. 151–53.

[9]This is the position of Millard Erickson, for example, in *Christian Theology* (Grand Rapids: Baker, 1985), 639. He uses the term *age of responsibility* rather than *age of accountability.*

such cases, we must accept the Scriptures that talk about ourselves as having a sinful nature from before the time of birth. Furthermore, we must realize that a child's sinful nature manifests itself very early, certainly within the first two years of a child's life, as anyone who has raised children can affirm. (David says, in another place, "The wicked go astray from the womb, they err from their birth," Ps. 58:3.)

4. How can infants who die be saved? But then what do we say about infants who die before they are old enough to understand and believe the gospel? Can they be saved?

Here we must say that if such infants are saved, it cannot be on their own merits, or on the basis of their own righteousness or innocence, but it must be entirely on the basis of Christ's redemptive work and regeneration by the work of the Holy Spirit within them. "There is one God, and there is one mediator between God and men, the man Christ Jesus" (1 Tim. 2:5). "Unless one is born anew, he cannot see the kingdom of God" (John 3:3).

However, it certainly is possible for God to bring regeneration (that is, new spiritual life) to an infant even before he or she is born. This was true of John the Baptist, for the angel Gabriel, before John was born, said, "He will be filled with the Holy Spirit, *even from his mother's womb*" (Luke 1:15). We might say that John the Baptist was "born again" before he was born! There is a similar example in Psalm 22:10: David says, "*Since my mother bore me* you have been my God." It is clear, therefore, that God is able to save infants in an unusual way, apart from their hearing and understanding the gospel, by bringing regeneration to them very early, sometimes even before birth. This regeneration is probably also followed at once by a nascent, intuitive awareness of God and trust in him at an extremely early age, but this is something we simply cannot understand.[10]

We must, however, affirm very clearly that this is not the usual way for God to save people. Salvation usually occurs when someone hears and understands the gospel and then places trust in Christ. But in unusual cases like John the Baptist, God brought salvation before this understanding. And this leads us to conclude that it certainly is possible that God would also do this where he knows the infant will die before hearing the gospel.

How many infants does God save in this way? Scripture does not tell us, so we simply cannot know. Where Scripture is silent, it is unwise for us to make definitive pronouncements. However, we should recognize that it is God's frequent pattern throughout Scripture to save the children of those who believe in him (see Gen. 7:1; also Heb. 11:7; Josh. 2:18; Ps. 103:17; John 4:53; Acts 2:39; 11:14; 16:31; 18:8; 1 Cor. 1:16; 7:14; Titus 1:6). These passages do not show that God automatically saves the children of all believers (for we all know of children of godly parents who have grown up and rejected the Lord), but they do indicate that God's ordinary pattern, the "normal" or expected way in which he acts, is to bring the children of believers to himself. With regard to believers' children who die very young, we have no reason to think that it would be otherwise.

Particularly relevant here is the case of the first child Bathsheba bore to King David. When the infant child had died, David said, "*I shall go to him,* but he will not

---

[10]However, we all know that infants almost from the moment of birth show an instinctive trust in their mothers and awareness of themselves as persons distinct from their mothers. Thus, we should not insist that it is impossible that they would also have an intuitive awareness of God, and if God gives it, an intuitive ability to trust in God as well.

return to me" (2 Sam. 12:23). David, who through his life had such great confidence that he would live forever in the Lord's presence (see Ps. 23:6 and many of David's psalms), also had confidence that he would see his infant son again when he died. This can only imply that he would be with his son in the presence of the Lord forever.[11] This passage, together with the others mentioned above, should be of similar assurance to all believers who have lost children in their infancy, that they will one day see them again in the glory of the heavenly kingdom.

Regarding the children of unbelievers who die at a very early age, Scripture is silent. We simply must leave that matter in the hands of God and trust him to be both just and merciful. If they are saved, it will not be on the basis of any merit of their own or any innocence that we might presume that they have. If they are saved, it will be on the basis of Christ's redeeming work; and their regeneration, like that of John the Baptist before he was born, will be by God's mercy and grace. Salvation is always because of God's mercy, not because of our merits (see Rom. 9:14–18). Scripture does not allow us to say more than that.

D. Actual Sins in Our Lives

1. All people are sinful before God. Scripture in many places testifies to the universal sinfulness of mankind. "They have all gone astray, they are all alike corrupt; there is none that does good, no, not one" (Ps. 14:3). David says, "No man living is righteous before you" (Ps. 143:2). And Solomon says, "There is no man who does not sin" (1 Kings 8:46; cf. Prov. 20:9).

In the New Testament, Paul has an extensive argument in Romans 1:18–3:20, showing that all people, both Jews and Greeks, stand guilty before God. He says, "All men, both Jews and Greeks, are under the power of sin, as it is written: 'None is righteous, no, not one'" (Rom. 3:9–10). He is certain that "all have sinned and fall short of the glory of God" (Rom. 3:23). John, the beloved disciple, who was especially close to Jesus, said: "If we say we have no sin, we deceive ourselves, and the truth is not in us. If we confess our sins, he is faithful and just, and will forgive our sins and cleanse us from all unrighteousness. If we say we have not sinned, we make him a liar, and his word is not in us" (1 John 1:8–10).

2. Does our ability limit our responsibility? Pelagius, a popular Christian teacher active in Rome about A.D. 383–410 and then later (until A.D. 424) in Palestine, taught that God holds man responsible only for those things that man is *able* to do. Since God warns us to do good, therefore, we must have the ability to do the good that God commands. The Pelagian position rejects the doctrine of "inherited sin" (or "original sin") and maintains that sin consists only in separate sinful acts.

However, the idea that we are responsible before God only for what we are able to do is contrary to the testimony of Scripture, which affirms both that we "were *dead* through the trespasses and sins" in which we once walked (Eph. 2:1), and thus unable to do any spiritual good, and also that we are all guilty before God. Moreover, if our responsibility before God were limited by our ability, then extremely hardened sinners, who are in great bondage to sin, could be less guilty before God than mature

---

[11]Someone might object that David is only saying that he would go to the state of death just as his son had. But this interpretation does not fit the language of the verse: David does not say, "I shall go *where he is,*" but rather, "I shall go *to him.*" This is the language of personal reunion, and it indicates David's expectation that he would one day see and be with his son.

Christians who were striving daily to obey him. And Satan himself, who is eternally able to do only evil, would have no guilt at all—surely an incorrect conclusion.

The true measure of our responsibility and guilt is not our own ability to obey God, but rather the absolute perfection of God's moral law and his own holiness (which is reflected in that law). "You, therefore, must be perfect, as your heavenly Father is perfect" (Matt. 5:48).

3. Are there degrees of sin? Are some sins worse than others? The question may be answered either yes or no, depending on the sense in which it is intended.

a. *Legal guilt.* In terms of our legal standing before God, any one sin, even what may seem to be a very small one, makes us legally guilty before God and therefore worthy of eternal punishment. Adam and Eve learned this in the Garden of Eden, where God told them that one act of disobedience would result in the penalty of death (Gen. 2:17). And Paul affirms that "the judgment following one trespass brought condemnation" (Rom. 5:16). This one sin made Adam and Eve sinners before God, no longer able to stand in his holy presence.

This truth remains valid through the history of the human race. Paul (quoting Deut. 27:26) affirms it: "Cursed be every one who does not abide by *all things* written in the book of the law, and do them" (Gal. 3:10). And James declares, "Whoever keeps *the whole law* but fails in one point has become guilty of all of it. For he who said, 'Do not commit adultery,' said also, 'Do not kill.' If you do not commit adultery but do kill, you have become a transgressor of the law" (James 2:10–11). Therefore, in terms of legal guilt, our sins are equally bad because they make us legally guilty before God and constitute us as sinners.

b. *Results in life and in relationship with God.* On the other hand, some sins are worse than others in that they have more harmful consequences in our lives and in the lives of others, and, in terms of our personal relationship to God as Father, they arouse his displeasure more and bring more serious disruption to our fellowship with him.

Scripture sometimes speaks of degrees of seriousness of sin. When Jesus stood before Pontius Pilate, he said, "He who delivered me to you has the *greater sin*" (John 19:11). The reference is apparently to Judas, who had known Jesus intimately for three years and yet willfully betrayed him to death. Though Pilate had authority over Jesus by virtue of his governmental office and was wrong to allow an innocent man to be condemned to death, the sin of Judas was far "greater," probably because of the far greater knowledge and malice connected with it.

In the Sermon of the Mount, when Jesus says, "Whoever then relaxes one of *the least of these commandments* and teaches men so, shall be called least in the kingdom of heaven" (Matt. 5:19), he implies that there are lesser and greater commandments. Similarly, though he agrees that it is appropriate to give a tithe even on the household spices that people use, he pronounces woes on the Pharisees for neglecting "the *weightier matters of the law,* justice and mercy and faith" (Matt. 23:23). In both cases, Jesus distinguishes between lesser and greater commandments, thus implying that some sins are worse than other sins in terms of God's own evaluation of their importance.

In general, we may say that some sins have more harmful consequences than others if they bring more dishonor to God or if they cause more harm to ourselves, to others, or to the church. Moreover, those sins that are done willfully, repeatedly, and knowingly, with a callous heart, are more displeasing to God than those that are done out of ignorance and are not repeated, or are done with a mixture of good and impure motives and are followed by remorse and repentance. Thus, the laws that God gave Moses in Leviticus make provisions for cases where people sin "unwittingly" (Lev. 4:2, 13, 22). Unintentional sin is still sin: "If any one sins, doing any of the things which the LORD has commanded not to be done, *though he does not know it,* yet he is guilty and shall bear his iniquity" (Lev. 5:17). Nonetheless, the penalties required and the degree of God's displeasure that results from the sin are less than in the case of intentional sin.

On the other hand, sins committed with "a high hand," that is, with arrogance and disdain for God's commandments, were viewed very seriously: "But the person who does anything with a high hand, whether he is native or a sojourner, reviles the LORD, and that person shall be cut off from among his people" (Num. 15:30; cf. vv. 27–29).

We can readily see how some sins have more harmful consequences for ourselves and others, and for our relationship with God. If I were to covet my neighbor's car, that would be sin before God. But if my coveting led me to actually steal the car, that would be more serious sin. If in the course of stealing the car I also fought with my neighbor and injured him or recklessly injured someone else as I drove the car, that would be even more serious sin.

Similarly, if a new Christian, who previously had a tendency to lose his temper and get into fights, begins witnessing to his unbelieving friends and, one day, is so provoked he loses his temper and actually strikes someone, that is certainly sin in God's sight. But if a mature pastor or other prominent Christian leader were to lose his temper publicly and strike someone, that would be even more serious in God's sight, both because of the harm that would come to the reputation of the gospel and because those in leadership positions are held to a higher standard of accountability by God: "We who teach shall be judged with greater strictness" (James 3:1; cf. Luke 12:48). Our conclusion, then, is that in terms of results and in terms of the degree of God's displeasure, some sins are certainly worse than others.

The distinction Scripture makes in degrees of sin does have positive value. First, it helps us to know where we should put more effort in our own attempts to grow in personal holiness. Second, it helps us to decide when we should simply overlook a minor fault in a friend or family member and when it would be appropriate to talk with an individual about some evident sin (see James 5:19–20). Third, it may help us decide when church discipline is appropriate, and it provides an answer to the objection that is sometimes raised against exercising church discipline, in which it is said that "we are all guilty of sin, so we have no business meddling in anyone else's life." Though we are all indeed guilty of sin, nonetheless, there are some sins that so evidently harm the church and relationships within the church that they must be dealt with directly. Fourth, this distinction may also help us realize that there is some basis for civil governments to have laws and penalties prohibiting certain kinds of wrongdoing (such as murder or stealing), but not other kinds of wrongdoing (such as anger, jealousy, greed, or selfish use of one's possessions). It is not inconsistent to say that some kinds of wrongdoing require civil punishment but not all kinds of wrongdoing require it.

4. What happens when a Christian sins? Though this subject could be treated later in relation to adoption or sanctification within the Christian life, it is quite appropriate to treat it at this point. What are the results of sin in the life of a Christian?

a. *Our legal standing before God is unchanged.* When a Christian sins, his or her legal standing before God is unchanged. He or she is still forgiven, for "there is therefore now no condemnation for those who are in Christ Jesus" (Rom. 8:1). Salvation is not based on our merits but is a free gift of God (Rom. 6:23), and Christ's death certainly paid for all our sins—past, present, and future. Christ died "for our sins" (1 Cor. 15:3) without distinction. In theological terms, we still keep our "justification."[12]

Moreover, we are still children of God and we still retain our membership in God's family. In the same epistle in which John says, "If we say we have no sin, we deceive ourselves, and the truth in not in us" (1 John 1:8), he also reminds his readers, "Beloved, *we are God's children* now" (1 John 3:2) The fact that we have sin remaining in our lives does not mean that we lose our status as God's children. In theological terms, we keep our "adoption."[13]

b. *Our fellowship with God is disrupted and our Christian life is damaged.* When we sin, even though God does not cease to love us, he is displeased with us. (Even among human beings, it is possible to love someone and be displeased with that person at the same time, as any parent, wife, or husband will attest.) Paul tells us that it is possible for Christians to "grieve the Holy Spirit of God" (Eph. 4:30); when we sin, we cause him sorrow and he is displeased with us. The author of Hebrews reminds us that "the Lord disciplines him whom he loves" (Heb. 12:6, quoting Prov. 3:11–12), and that "the Father of spirits . . . disciplines us for our good, that we may share his holiness" (Heb. 12:9–10). When we disobey, God the Father is grieved, much as an earthly father is grieved with his children's disobedience, and he disciplines us. A similar theme is found in Revelation 3, where the risen Christ speaks from heaven to the church of Laodicea, saying, "Those whom I love, I reprove and chasten; so be zealous and repent" (Rev. 3:19). Here again love and reproof of sin are connected in the same statement. Thus, the New Testament attests to the displeasure of all three members of the Trinity when Christians sin. (See also Isa. 59:1–2; 1 John 3:21.)

The Westminster Confession of Faith wisely says, concerning Christians, "Although they never can fall from the state of justification, yet they may, by their sins, fall under their God's fatherly displeasure, and not have the light of His countenance restored unto them, until they humble themselves, confess their sins, beg pardon, and renew their faith and repentance" (chap. 11, sec. 5).

When we sin as Christians, it is not only our personal relationship with God that is disrupted. Our Christian life and fruitfulness in ministry are also damaged. Jesus warns us, "As the branch cannot bear fruit by itself, unless it abides in the vine, neither can you, *unless you abide in me*" (John 15:4). When we stray from fellowship from Christ because of sin in our lives, we diminish the degree to which we are abiding in Christ.

The New Testament writers frequently speak of the destructive consequences of sin in the lives of believers. In fact, many sections of the Epistles are taken up with rebuking and discouraging Christians from sin that they are committing. Paul says that if Christians yield themselves to sin, they increasingly become "slaves" of sin (Rom. 6:16), whereas God wants Christians to progress upward on a path of ever-increasing righteousness in life. If our goal is to grow in increasing fullness of life

---

[12]See ch. 22, pp. 316–23, on justification.
[13]See ch. 22, pp. 323–24, on adoption.

until the day we die and pass into the presence of God in heaven, to sin is to do an about-face and begin to walk downhill away from the goal of likeness to God; it is to go in a direction that "leads to death" (Rom. 6:16) and eternal separation from God, the direction from which we were rescued when we became Christians.[14]

Moreover, when we sin as Christians, we suffer a loss of heavenly reward. A person who has built on the work of the church not with gold, silver, and precious stones, but with "wood, hay, stubble" (1 Cor. 3:12) will have his work "burned up" on the day of judgment and "he will suffer loss, though he himself will be saved, but only as through fire" (1 Cor. 3:15). Paul realizes that "we must all appear before the judgment seat of Christ, so that each one may receive good or evil, according to what he has done in the body" (2 Cor. 5:10). Paul implies that there are degrees of reward in heaven and that sin has negative consequences in terms of loss of heavenly reward.

c. *The danger of "unconverted evangelicals."* While a genuine Christian who sins does not lose his or her justification or adoption before God (see above), there needs to be a clear warning that mere association with an evangelical church and outward conformity to accepted "Christian" patterns of behavior does not guarantee salvation. Particularly in societies and cultures where it is easy (or even expected) for people to profess to be Christians, there is a real possibility that some will associate with the church who are not genuinely born again. If such people then become more and more disobedient to Christ in their pattern of life, they should not be lulled into complacency by assurances that they still have justification or adoption in God's family. A consistent pattern of disobedience to Christ coupled with a lack of the elements of the fruit of the Holy Spirit such as love, joy, peace, and so forth (see Gal. 5:22–23) is a warning signal that the person is probably not a true Christian inwardly, that there probably has been no genuine heart-faith from the beginning and no regenerating work of the Holy Spirit. Jesus warns that he will say to some who have prophesied, cast out demons, and done many mighty works in his name, "I never knew you; depart from me, you evildoers" (Matt. 7:23). And John tells us that "he who says 'I know him' but disobeys his commandments is a liar, and the truth is not in him" (1 John 2:4, where John speaks of a persistent pattern of life). A long-term pattern of increasing disobedience to Christ should be taken as evidence for decreasing reason to believe that the person in question is really a Christian at all.

5. What is the unpardonable sin? Several passages of Scripture speak about a sin that will not be forgiven. Jesus says: "Therefore I tell you, every sin and blasphemy will be forgiven men, but the blasphemy against the Spirit will not be forgiven. And whoever says a word against the Son of man will be forgiven; but whoever speaks against the Holy Spirit will not be forgiven, either in this age or in the age to come" (Matt. 12:31–32).

A similar statement occurs in Mark 3:29–30, where Jesus says that "whoever blasphemes against the Holy Spirit never has forgiveness" (cf. Luke 12:10). Similarly, Hebrews 6 says: "For it is *impossible to restore again to repentance* those who have once been enlightened, who have tasted the heavenly gift, and have become par-

---

[14]Paul is not saying in Rom. 6:16 that true Christians might actually regress to a point at which they fall under eternal condemnation, but he does seem to be saying that when we yield to sin we are (in a spiritual/moral sense) traveling in that direction.

takers of the Holy Spirit, and have tasted the goodness of the word of God and the powers of the age to come, *if they then commit apostasy,* since they crucify the son of God on their own account and hold him up to contempt" (vv. 4–6; cf. 10:26–27).

Some have held that the sin is that of unbelief that continues until the time of death; therefore, everyone who dies in unbelief (or at least everyone who has heard of Christ and then dies in unbelief) has committed this sin. It is true, of course, that those who persist in unbelief until death will not be forgiven, but the question is whether that fact is what is being discussed in these verses. On close reading of the verses, that explanation does not seem to fit the language of the texts cited, for they do not talk of unbelief in general but specifically of someone who "speaks against the Holy Spirit" (Matt. 12:32), "blasphemes against the Holy Spirit" (Mark 3:29), or commits "apostasy" (Heb. 6:6). They have in view a specific sin—willful rejection of the work of the Holy Spirit and speaking evil about it, or willful rejection of the truth of Christ and holding Christ up to "contempt" (Heb. 6:6). Moreover, the idea that this sin is unbelief that persists until death does not fit well with the context of a rebuke to the Pharisees for what they were saying in both Matthew and Mark (see discussion of context below).

A better possibility is that this sin consists of *unusually malicious, willful rejection and slander against the Holy Spirit's work attesting to Christ, and attributing that work to Satan.* A closer look at the context of Jesus' statement in Matthew and Mark shows that Jesus was speaking in response to the accusation of the Pharisees that "it is only by Be-elzebul, the prince of demons, that this man casts out demons" (Matt. 12:24). The Pharisees had seen Jesus' works repeatedly. He had just healed a blind and dumb demoniac so that he could see and speak (Matt. 12:22). The people were amazed and were following Jesus in large numbers, and the Pharisees themselves had repeatedly seen clear demonstrations of the amazing power of the Holy Spirit working through Jesus to bring life and health to many people. But the Pharisees, *in spite of clear demonstrations of the work of the Holy Spirit in front of their eyes,* willfully rejected Jesus' authority and his teaching and attributed it to the devil. It was irrational and foolish for the Pharisees to attribute Jesus' exorcisms to the power of Satan—it was a classic, willful, malicious lie. Jesus says in this context, "Therefore I tell you, every sin and blasphemy will be forgiven men, but the blasphemy against the Spirit will not be forgiven" (Matt. 12:31). The willful, malicious slander of the work of the Holy Spirit through Jesus, by attributing the Holy Spirit's work to Satan, would not be forgiven.

The context indicates that Jesus is speaking about a sin that is not simply unbelief or rejection of Christ, but one that includes (1) a clear knowledge of who Christ is, (2) knowledge that the Holy Spirit is working through him, (3) a willful rejection of these facts, and then (4) slanderously attributing the work of the Holy Spirit in Christ to the power of Satan.

Why would this sin be unpardonable? In such a case, the hardness of heart would be so great that any ordinary means of bringing a sinner to repentance would already have been rejected. In such a case, persuasion of the truth will not work, for these people have already known the truth and have willfully rejected it. Demonstration of the power of the Holy Spirit to heal and bring life will not work, for they have seen it and rejected it. It is not that the sin itself is so horrible that it could not be covered by Christ's redemptive work, but rather that the sinner's hardened heart puts him or her beyond the reach of God's ordinary means of bringing forgiveness through repentance and trusting Christ for salvation. The sin is unpardonable because it cuts off the sinner from repentance and saving faith through belief in the truth.

The fact that the unpardonable sin involves such extreme hardness of heart and lack of repentance indicates that those who fear they have committed it, yet still have sorrow for sin in their heart and desire to seek after God, certainly do not fall in the category of those who are guilty of it. Berkhof says that "we may be reasonably sure that those who fear that they have committed it and worry about this, and desire the prayers of others for them, have not committed it."[15]

This understanding of the unpardonable sin also fits well with Hebrews 6:4–6. There the persons who "commit apostasy" have had all sorts of knowledge and conviction of the truth: They have "been enlightened" and have "tasted the heavenly gift"; they have participated in some ways in the work of the Holy Spirit and "have tasted the goodness of the word of God and the powers of the age to come," yet they then willfully turn away from Christ and "hold him up to contempt" (Heb. 6:6). They too have put themselves beyond the reach of God's ordinary means of bringing people to repentance and faith. *Knowing* and *being convinced* of the truth, they willfully reject it.

E. The Punishment of Sin

Although God's punishment of sin does serve as a deterrent against further sinning and as a warning to those who observe it, this is not the primary reason why God punishes sin. The primary reason is that God's righteousness demands it, so that he might be glorified in the universe that he has created. He is the Lord who practices "steadfast love, *justice,* and *righteousness* in the earth; for in these things I delight, says the LORD" (Jer. 9:24).

Paul speaks of Christ Jesus "whom God put forward as a propitiation by his blood, through faith" (Rom. 3:25, author's translation). Paul then explains why God put forward Jesus as a "propitiation" (that is, a sacrifice that bears the wrath of God against sin and thereby turns God's wrath into favor): "This was *to show God's righteousness,* because in his divine forbearance he had passed over former sins" (Rom. 3:25). Paul realizes that if Christ had not come to pay the penalty for sins, God could not be shown to be righteous. Because he had passed over sins and not punished them in the past, people could rightly accuse God of unrighteousness, the assumption being that a God who does not punish sins is not a righteous God. Therefore, when God sent Christ to die and pay the penalty for our sins, he showed how he could still be righteous—he had stored up the punishment due to previous sins (those of Old Testament saints) and then, in perfect righteousness, gave that penalty to Jesus on the cross. The propitiation of Calvary thereby clearly demonstrated that God is perfectly righteous: "*It was to prove at the present time that he himself is righteous* and that he justifies him who has faith in Jesus" (Rom. 3:26).

Therefore, in the cross we have a clear demonstration of the reason God punishes sin: If he did not punish sin, he would not be a righteous God, and there would be no ultimate justice in the universe. But when sin is punished, God is showing himself to be a righteous judge over all, and justice is being done in his universe.

---

[15]Louis Berkhof, *Introduction to Systematic Theology* (Grand Rapids: Eerdmans, 1932; reprint, Grand Rapids: Baker, 1979), p. 254.

II. REVIEW QUESTIONS

1. Define sin.
2. Explain the term "inherited guilt." How would you respond to the objection that this teaching is unfair?
3. How did Adam's sin affect our own human natures? Does this mean that all people are as bad as they could be? Explain.
4. What effect does our ability to obey God have on our responsibility before God?
5. When a Christian sins, how does this affect his legal standing before God? What effect does sin have on a Christian?
6. What is the primary reason that God punishes sin?

III. QUESTIONS FOR PERSONAL APPLICATION

1. Has reading this chapter increased your awareness of the sin remaining in your own life? Did the chapter increase in you any sense of the hatefulness of sin? Why do you not feel more often a deeper sense of the hatefulness of sin? What do you think the overall effect of this chapter will be on your personal relationship with God?
2. Would it ultimately be more comforting to you to think that sin came into the world because God ordained that it would come through secondary agents, or because he could not prevent it, even though it was against his will? How would you feel about the universe and your place in it if you thought that evil had always existed and there was an ultimate "dualism" in the universe?
3. Can you name some parallels between the temptation faced by Eve and temptations that you face even now in your Christian life?
4. How can the biblical teaching of degrees of seriousness of sin help your Christian life at this point? Have you known a sense of God's "fatherly displeasure" when you have sinned? What is your response to that sense?

IV. SPECIAL TERMS

dualism	original sin
impute	Pelagius
inherited corruption	propitiation
inherited guilt	sin
inherited sin	the unpardonable sin
original guilt	total depravity
original pollution	total inability

V. SCRIPTURE MEMORY PASSAGE

PSALM 51:1–4

Have mercy on me, O God; according to your steadfast love;
    according to your abundant mercy blot out my transgressions.
Wash me thoroughly from my iniquity,
    and cleanse me from my sin!
For I know my transgressions,
    and my sin is ever before me.
Against you, you only, have I sinned,
    and done that which is evil in your sight,
so that you are justified in your sentence
    and blameless in your judgment.

PART IV

The Doctrine of Christ

CHAPTER FOURTEEN

The Person of Christ

+ *How is Jesus fully God and fully man, yet one person?*

I. EXPLANATION AND SCRIPTURAL BASIS

We may summarize the biblical teaching about the person of Christ as follows: *Jesus Christ was fully God and fully man in one person, and will be so forever.*

The scriptural material supporting this definition is extensive. We will discuss first the humanity of Christ, then his deity, and then attempt to show how Jesus' deity and humanity are united in the one person of Christ.

A. The Humanity of Christ

1. Virgin birth. When we speak of the humanity of Christ, it is appropriate to begin with a consideration of the virgin birth of Christ. Scripture clearly asserts that Jesus was conceived in the womb of his mother, Mary, by a miraculous work of the Holy Spirit and without a human father.

"Now the birth of Jesus Christ took place in this way. When his mother Mary had been betrothed to Joseph, *before they came together* she was found to be with child of the Holy Spirit" (Matt. 1:18) Shortly after that an angel of the Lord said to Joseph, who was engaged to Mary, "Joseph, son of David, do not fear to take Mary your wife, for *that which is conceived in her is of the Holy Spirit*" (Matt. 1:20). Then we read that Joseph "did as the angel of the Lord commanded him; he took his wife, but knew her not until she had borne a son; and he called his name Jesus" (Matt. 1:24–25).

The same fact is affirmed in Luke's gospel, where we read about the appearance of the angel Gabriel to Mary. After the angel had told her that she would bear a son, Mary said, "How shall this be, since I have no husband?" The angel answered,

"The Holy Spirit will come upon you,
    and the power of the Most High will overshadow you;
therefore the child to be born will be called holy,
the Son of God." (Luke 1:34–35; cf. 3:23)

This scriptural affirmation of the virgin birth of Christ alone should give us sufficient warrant to embrace this doctrine. However, there are also critical doctrinal implications of the virgin birth that illustrate its importance. We can see these in at least three areas.

a. *It shows that salvation ultimately must come from the Lord.* The virgin birth of Christ is an unmistakable reminder of the fact that salvation can never come through human effort, but must be the supernatural work of God. That fact was evident at the very beginning of Jesus' life when "God sent forth his Son, born of woman, born under the law, to redeem those who were under the law, so that we might receive adoption as sons" (Gal. 4:4–5).

b. *The virgin birth made possible the uniting of full deity and full humanity in one person.* This was the means God used to send his Son (John 3:16; Gal. 4:4) into the world as a man. If we think for a moment of other possible ways in which Christ might have come to the earth, none of them would so clearly unite humanity and deity in one person. It probably would have been possible for God to create Jesus as a complete human being in heaven and send him to descend from heaven to earth without the benefit of any human parent. But then it would have been very hard for us to see how Jesus could be fully human as we are. On the other hand, it probably would have been possible for God to have Jesus come into the world with two human parents, both a father and a mother, and with his full divine nature miraculously united to his human nature at some point early in his life. But then it would have been hard for us to understand how Jesus was fully God, since his origin was like ours in every way. When we think of these two other possibilities, it helps us to understand how God, in his wisdom, ordained a combination of human and divine influence in the birth of Christ, so that his full humanity would be evident to us from the fact of his ordinary human birth from a human mother, and his full deity would be evident from the fact of his conception in Mary's womb by the powerful work of the Holy Spirit.

c. *The virgin birth also makes possible Christ's true humanity without inherited sin.* As we noted in chapter 14, all human beings have inherited legal guilt and a corrupt moral nature from their first father, Adam. But the fact that Jesus did not have a human father means that the line of descent from Adam is partially interrupted. Jesus did not descend from Adam in exactly the same way in which every other human being has descended from Adam. And this helps us to understand why the legal guilt and moral corruption that belong to all other human beings did not belong to Christ.

But why did Jesus not inherit a sinful nature from Mary? The Roman Catholic Church answers this question by saying that Mary herself was free from sin, but Scripture nowhere teaches this, and it would not really solve the problem anyway (for why then did Mary not inherit sin from her mother?). A better solution is to say that the work of the Holy Spirit in Mary must have prevented not only the transmission of sin from Joseph (for Jesus had no human father) but also, in a miraculous way, the transmission of sin from Mary: "The Holy Spirit will come upon you. . . . *therefore* the child to be born will be called *holy*" (Luke 1:35).[1]

2. Human weakness and limitations.

a. *Jesus had a human body.* The fact that Jesus had a human body just like our human bodies is seen in many passages of Scripture. He was born just as all human

---

[1]This is the translation of the RSV, which seems to me to be more likely than NIV's "so the holy one to be born will be called the Son of God" (similarly, NASB). This is because other examples from ancient literature show the Greek expression *to gennōmenon* to be commonly understood as "the child to be born."

babies are born (Luke 2:7). He grew through childhood to adulthood just as other children grow: "The child grew and became strong, filled with wisdom; and the favor of God was upon him" (Luke 2:40). Moreover, Luke tells us that "Jesus increased in wisdom *and in stature,* and in favor with God and man" (Luke 2:52).

Jesus became tired just as we do, for we read that "Jesus, *wearied* as he was with his journey, sat down beside the well" in Samaria (John 4:6). He became thirsty, for when he was on the cross he said, *"I thirst"* (John 19:28). After he had fasted for forty days in the wilderness, we read that "he was *hungry"* (Matt. 4:2). He was at times physically weak, for during his temptation in the wilderness he fasted for forty days (the point at which a human being's physical strength is almost entirely gone and beyond which irreparable physical harm will occur if the fast continues). At that time "angels came and ministered to him" (Matt. 4:11), apparently to care for him and provide nourishment until he regained enough strength to come out of the wilderness. The culmination of Jesus' limitations in terms of his human body was seen when he died on the cross (Luke 23:46). His human body ceased to have life in it and ceased to function, just as ours does when we die.

Jesus also rose from the dead in a physical, human body, though one that was made perfect and was no longer subject to weakness, disease, or death. He demonstrates repeatedly to his disciples that he does have a real physical body. He says, "See my hands and my feet, that it is I myself; handle me, and see; for *a spirit has not flesh and bones as you see that I have"* (Luke 24:39). He is showing them and teaching them that he has "flesh and bones" and is not merely a "spirit" without a body. Another evidence of this fact is that "they gave him a piece of broiled fish, and he took it and ate before them" (Luke 24:42; cf. v. 30; John 20:17, 20, 27; 21:9, 13).

In this same human body (though a resurrection body that was made perfect), Jesus also ascended into heaven. He said before he left, "I am leaving the world and going to the Father" (John 16:28; cf. 17:11). The way in which Jesus ascended up to heaven was calculated to demonstrate the continuity between his existence in a physical body here on earth and his continuing existence in that body in heaven. Just a few verses after Jesus had told them, "A spirit has not flesh and bones as you see that I have" (Luke 24:39), we read in Luke's gospel that Jesus "led them out as far as Bethany, and lifting up his hands he blessed them. While he blessed them, he parted from them, and was carried up into heaven" (Luke 24:50–51). Similarly, we read in Acts, "As they were looking on, he was lifted up, and a cloud took him out of their sight" (Acts 1:9).

All of these verses taken together show that, as far as Jesus' human body is concerned, it was like ours in every respect before his resurrection, and after his resurrection it was still a human body with "flesh and bones," but made perfect, the kind of body that we will have when Christ returns and we are raised from the dead as well.[2] Jesus continues to exist in that human body in heaven, as the ascension is designed to teach.

b. *Jesus had a human mind.* The fact that Jesus *"increased in wisdom"* (Luke 2:52) says that he went through a learning process just as all other children do—he learned how to eat, how to talk, how to read and write, and how to be obedient to his parents (see Heb. 5:8). This ordinary learning process was part of the genuine humanity of Christ.

---

[2]See ch. 16, pp. 265–66, and ch. 25, pp. 356–58, on the nature of our resurrection body.

We also see that Jesus had a human mind like ours when he speaks of the day on which he will return to earth: "But of that day or that hour no one knows, not even the angels in heaven, nor the Son, but only the Father" (Mark 13:32).[3]

c. *Jesus had a human soul and human emotions.* We see several indications that Jesus had a human soul (or spirit). Just before his crucifixion, Jesus said, "Now is my soul *troubled*" (John 12:27). John writes just a little later, "When Jesus had thus spoken, he was *troubled* in spirit" (John 13:21). In both verses the word *troubled* represents the Greek term *tarassō*, a word often used of people when they are anxious or suddenly very surprised by danger. Moreover, before Jesus' crucifixion, as he realized the suffering he would face, he said, "My soul is very sorrowful, even to death" (Matt. 26:38). So great was the sorrow he felt that it seemed as though, if it were to become any stronger, it would take his very life.

Jesus had a full range of human emotions. He "marveled" at the faith of the centurion (Matt. 8:10). He wept with sorrow at the death of Lazarus (John 11:35). And he prayed with a heart full of emotion, for "in the days of his flesh, Jesus offered up prayers and supplications, *with loud cries and tears,* to him who was able to save him from death, and he was heard for his godly fear" (Heb. 5:7).

The author of Hebrews also tells us, "Although he was a Son, *he learned obedience* through what he suffered; and being made perfect he became the source of eternal salvation to all who obey him" (Heb. 5:8–9). Yet if Jesus never sinned, how could he "learn obedience"? Apparently as Jesus grew toward maturity he, like all other human children, was able to take on more and more responsibility. The older he became the more demands his father and mother could place on him in terms of obedience, and the more difficult the tasks that his heavenly Father could assign to him to carry out in the strength of his human nature. With each increasingly difficult task, even when it involved some suffering (as Heb. 5:8 specifies), Jesus' human moral ability, his ability to obey under more and more difficult circumstances, increased. We might say that his "moral backbone" was strengthened by more and more difficult exercise. Yet in all this he never once sinned.

3. Sinlessness. Though the New Testament clearly affirms that Jesus was fully human just as we are, it also affirms that Jesus was different in one important respect: He was without sin, and he never committed sin during his lifetime. Some have objected that if Jesus did not sin, then he was not truly human, for all humans sin. But that objection simply fails to realize that human beings are now in an abnormal situation. God did not create us sinful, but holy and righteous. Adam and Eve in the Garden of Eden before they sinned were truly human, and we now, though human, do not match the pattern that God intends for us when our full, sinless humanity is restored.

The sinlessness of Jesus is taught frequently in the New Testament. We see that Satan was unable to tempt Jesus successfully, but failed, after forty days, to persuade him to sin: "And when the devil had ended every temptation, he departed from him until an opportune time" (Luke 4:13). We also see in the Synoptic Gospels (Matthew, Mark, and Luke) no evidence of wrongdoing on Jesus' part. To the Jews who opposed him, Jesus asked, "Which of you convicts me of sin?" (John 8:46), and received no answer.

---

[3]See further discussion of this verse below, pp. 245–46.

The statements about Jesus' sinlessness are more explicit in John's gospel. Jesus made the amazing proclamation, "I am the light of the world" (John 8:12). If we understand light to represent both truthfulness and moral purity, then Jesus is here claiming to be the source of truth and the source of moral purity and holiness in the world—an astounding claim, and one that could only be made by someone who was free from sin. Moreover, with regard to obedience to his Father in heaven, he said, "I always do what is pleasing to him" (John 8:29; the present tense gives the sense of continual activity, "I am always doing what is pleasing to him"). At the end of his life, Jesus could say, "I have kept my Father's commandments and abide in his love" (John 15:10). It is significant that when Jesus was put on trial before Pilate, in spite of the accusations of the Jews, Pilate could only conclude, "I find no crime in him" (John 18:38).

When Paul speaks of Jesus coming to live as a man, he is careful not to say that he took on "sinful flesh," but rather says that God sent his own Son "*in the likeness of* sinful flesh and for sin" (Rom. 8:3). And he refers to Jesus as "him . . . who knew no sin" (2 Cor. 5:21). The author of Hebrews affirms that Jesus was tempted but simultaneously insists that he did not sin: Jesus is "one who in every respect has been tempted as we are, *yet without sin*" (Heb. 4:15). He is a high priest who is "holy, blameless, unstained, separated from sinners, exalted above the heavens" (Heb. 7:26). Peter speaks of Jesus as "a lamb without blemish or spot" (1 Peter 1:19), using Old Testament imagery to affirm his freedom from any moral defilement. Peter directly states, "He committed no sin; no guile was found on his lips" (1 Peter 2:22). When Jesus died, it was "the righteous for the unrighteous, that he might bring us to God" (1 Peter 3:18). And John, in his first epistle, calls him "Jesus Christ the righteous" (1 John 2:1) and says, "In him there is no sin" (1 John 3:5). It is hard to deny, then, that the sinlessness of Christ is taught clearly in all the major sections of the New Testament. He was truly man yet without sin.

The fact that Jesus was tempted "in every respect" (Heb. 4:15) has great significance for our lives. As difficult as it may be for us to comprehend, Scripture affirms that in these temptations Jesus gained an ability to understand and help us in our temptations. "Because he himself has suffered and been tempted, he is able to help those who are tempted" (Heb. 2:18). The author goes on to connect Jesus' ability to sympathize with our weaknesses to the fact that he was tempted as we are: "For we have not a high priest who is unable to sympathize with our weaknesses, but one who in every respect has been tempted as we are, yet without sin. Let us then [lit. 'therefore'] with confidence draw near to the throne of grace, that we may receive mercy and find grace to help in time of need" (Heb. 4:15–16).

This has practical application for us: In every situation in which we are struggling with temptation, we should reflect on the life of Christ and ask if there were not similar situations that he faced. Usually, after reflecting for a moment or two, we will be able to think of some instances in the life of Christ where he faced temptations that, though they were not the same in every detail, were very similar to the situations that we face every day.

4. Could Jesus have sinned? The question is sometimes raised, "Was it possible for Christ to have sinned?" Some people argue for the *impeccability* of Christ, in which the word *impeccable* means "not able to sin." (The Latin word *peccare* means "to sin.") Others object that if Jesus were not able to sin, his temptations could not have been real, for how can a temptation be real if the person being tempted is not able to sin anyway?

To answer this question, we must distinguish what Scripture clearly affirms, on the one hand, and, on the other hand, what is more in the nature of speculation on our part. (1) Scripture clearly affirms that Christ never actually sinned (see above). There should be no question in our minds at all on this fact. (2) It also clearly affirms that Jesus was tempted and that these were real temptations (Luke 4:2). If we believe Scripture, then we must insist that Christ *"in every respect has been tempted as we are, yet without sin"* (Heb. 4:15). (3) We also must affirm with Scripture that "God cannot be tempted with evil" (James 1:13). But here the question becomes difficult: If Jesus was fully God as well as fully man (and we shall argue below that Scripture clearly and repeatedly teaches this), then must we not also affirm that (in some sense) Jesus also "could not be tempted with evil"?

These explicit affirmations of Scripture present us with a dilemma similar to a number of other doctrinal dilemmas where Scripture seems to be teaching things that are, if not directly contradictory, at least very difficult to combine together in our understanding. In this instance, we do not have an actual contradiction. Scripture does not tell us that "Jesus was tempted" and that "Jesus was not tempted" (a contradiction if "Jesus" and "tempted" are used exactly in the same sense in both sentences). The Bible tells us that "Jesus was tempted" and "Jesus was fully man" and "Jesus was fully God" and "God cannot be tempted." This combination of teachings from Scripture leaves open the possibility that as we understand the way in which Jesus' human nature and divine nature work together, we might understand more of the way in which he could be tempted in one sense and yet, in another sense, not be tempted. (This possibility will be discussed further below.)

At this point, then, we pass beyond the clear affirmations of Scripture and attempt to suggest a solution to the problem of whether Christ could have sinned. But it is important to recognize that the following solution is more in the nature of a suggested means of combining various biblical teachings and is not directly supported by explicit statements of Scripture. With this in mind, it is appropriate for us to say:[4] (1) If Jesus' human nature had existed by itself, independent of his divine nature, then it would have been a human nature just like that which God gave Adam and Eve. It would have been free from sin but nonetheless *able to sin*. (2) But Jesus' human nature never existed apart from union with his divine nature. From the moment of his conception, he existed as truly God and truly man as well. Both his human nature and his divine nature were united in one person. (3) Although there were some things (such as being hungry or thirsty or weak) that Jesus experienced in his human nature alone, things that were not experienced in his divine nature (see below), nonetheless, an act of sin would have been a moral act that apparently would have involved the whole person of Christ. Therefore, if he had sinned, it would have involved both his human and divine natures. (4) But if Jesus as a person had sinned, involving both his human and divine natures in sin, then God himself would have sinned and he would have ceased to be God. Yet that is clearly impossible because of the infinite holiness of God's nature. (5) Therefore, it seems that if we are asking if it was *actually* possible for Jesus to have sinned, it seems that we must conclude that it was not possible. The union of his human and divine natures in one person prevented it.

---

[4]In this discussion I am largely following the conclusions of Geerhardus Vos, *Biblical Theology* (Grand Rapids: Eerdmans, 1948), pp. 339–42.

But the question remains, "How then could Jesus' temptations be real?" The example of the temptation to change the stones into bread is helpful in this regard. Jesus had the ability, by virtue of his divine nature, to perform this miracle, but if he had done it, he would no longer have been obeying God the Father in the strength of his human nature alone, he would have failed the test that Adam also failed, and he would not have earned our salvation for us. Therefore, Jesus refused to rely on his divine nature to make obedience easier for him. In like manner, it seems appropriate to conclude that Jesus met every temptation to sin, not by his divine power, but on the strength of his human nature alone (though, of course, it was not "alone," because Jesus, in exercising the kind of faith that humans should exercise, was perfectly depending on God the Father and the Holy Spirit at every moment). The moral strength of his divine nature was there as a sort of "backstop" that would have prevented him from sinning in any case (and therefore we can say that it was not possible for him to sin), but he did not rely on the strength of his divine nature to make it easier for him to face temptations, and his refusal to turn the stones into bread at the beginning of his ministry is a clear indication of this.

Were the temptations real then? Many theologians have pointed out that only he who successfully resists a temptation to the end most fully feels the force of that temptation. Just as a champion weightlifter who successfully lifts and holds overhead the heaviest weight in the contest feels the force of it more fully than one who attempts to lift it and drops it, so any Christian who has successfully faced a temptation to the end knows that that is far more difficult than giving in to it at once. So it was with Jesus: Every temptation he faced, he faced to the end, and triumphed over it. The temptations were real, even though he did not give in to them—in fact, they were most real *because* he did not give in to them.

5. *Why was Jesus' full humanity necessary?* When John wrote his first epistle, a heretical teaching was circulating in the church to the effect that Jesus was not a man. This heresy became known as *docetism,* from the Greek verb *dokeō,* "to seem, to appear to be"; this position holds that Jesus was not really a man but only *appeared* to be one. So serious was this denial of truth about Christ, that John could say it was a doctrine of the antichrist: "By this you know the Spirit of God: every spirit which confesses *that Jesus Christ has come in the flesh* is of God, and every spirit which does not confess Jesus is not of God. This is the spirit of antichrist" (1 John 4:2–3). The apostle John understood that to deny Jesus' true humanity was to deny something at the very heart of Christianity, so that no one who denied that Jesus had come in the flesh was sent from God.

As we look through the New Testament, we see several reasons why Jesus had to be fully man if he was going to be the Messiah and earn our salvation. Two of the most vital reasons are listed here.

a. *For representative obedience.* As we noted in the chapter on sin, Adam served as our representative in the Garden of Eden, and through his disobedience God counted us guilty as well.[5] In a similar way, Jesus was our representative and obeyed for us where Adam had disobeyed and failed. We see this in the parallels between Jesus' temptation (Luke 4:1–13) and the time of testing for Adam and Eve in the garden (Gen. 2:15–3:7). It is also clearly reflected in Paul's discussion of the parallels between Adam and Christ: "Then as one man's trespass led to condemnation for

---

[5]See ch. 13, pp. 213–18.

all men, so *one man's act of righteousness* leads to acquittal and life for all men. For as by one man's disobedience many were made sinners, so *by one man's obedience* many will be made righteous" (Rom. 5:18–19).

This is why Paul can call Christ "the last Adam" (1 Cor. 15:45) and can call Adam the "first man" and Christ the "second man" (1 Cor. 15:47). Jesus had to be a man in order to be our representative and obey in our place.

b. *To be a substitute sacrifice.* If Jesus had not been a man, he could not have died in our place and paid the penalty that was due to us. The author of Hebrews tells us that "surely it is not with angels that he is concerned but with the descendants of Abraham. Therefore he *had to* be made like his brethren in every respect, so that he might become a merciful and faithful high priest in the service of God, to make expiation [more accurately, 'propitiation'] for the sins of the people" (Heb. 2:16–17; cf. v. 14). Jesus *had to become a man*, not an angel, because God was concerned with saving men, not with saving angels. But to do this he *"had to"* be made like us in every way, so that he might become "the propitiation" for us, the sacrifice that is an acceptable substitute for us. Unless Christ was fully man, he could not have died to pay the penalty for man's sins. He could not have been a substitute sacrifice for us.

There are also other reasons for the necessity of Jesus' humanity. Jesus had to be fully man as well as fully God to fulfill the role of a mediator between God and man (cf. 1 Tim. 2:5). The fact that Jesus was a man and experienced temptations enabled him to sympathize more fully with us as our "high priest" (Heb. 2:18; cf. 4:15–16). Jesus' humanity also provides an example and pattern for our lives (cf. 1 John 2:6; 1 Peter 2:21). All of these reasons point to the vital importance of affirming that Jesus was not only fully God but also was fully man and thus was able to fully secure our salvation.

B. The Deity of Christ

To complete the biblical teaching about Jesus Christ, we must affirm not only that he was fully human, but also that he was fully divine. Although the word does not explicitly occur in Scripture, the church has used the term *incarnation* to refer to the fact that Jesus was God in human flesh. The *incarnation* was the act of God the Son whereby he took to himself a human nature. The scriptural proof for the deity of Christ is very extensive in the New Testament. We shall examine it under several categories.

1. Direct scriptural claims. In this section we examine direct statements of Scripture that Jesus is God or that he is divine.

a. *The word* God (theos) *used of Christ.* Although the word *theos,* "God," is usually reserved in the New Testament for God the Father, nonetheless, there are several passages where it is also used to refer to Jesus Christ. In all of these passages "God" is used in the strong sense to refer to the one who is the creator of heaven and earth, the ruler over all. These passages include John 1:1; 1:18 (in older and better manuscripts); 20:28; Romans 9:5; Titus 2:13; Hebrews 1:8 (quoting Ps. 45:6); and 2 Peter 1:1. As some of these passages have been discussed in some detail in the chapter on the Trinity,[6] the discussion will not be repeated here. It is enough

---

[6]See ch. 6, pp. 108–9, for discussion of passages that refer to Jesus as "God." See also Murray J. Harris, *Jesus as God* (Grand Rapids: Baker, 1992), for the most extensive exegetical treatment ever published dealing with New Testament passages that refer to Jesus as "God."

to note that there are at least these seven clear passages in the New Testament that explicitly refer to Jesus as God.

One Old Testament example of the name *God* applied to Christ is seen in a familiar messianic passage: "For to us a child is born, to us a son is given, and the government will be upon his shoulder, and his name will be called 'Wonderful Counselor, *Mighty God . . .*'" (Isa. 9:6).

b. *The word* Lord (kyrios) *used of Christ.* Sometimes the word *Lord* (Gk. *kyrios*) is used simply as a polite address to a superior, roughly equivalent to our word *sir* (see Matt. 13:27; 21:30; 27:63; John 4:11). Sometimes it can simply mean "master" of a servant or slave (Matt. 6:24; 21:40). Yet the same word is also used in the Septuagint (the Greek translation of the Old Testament, which was commonly used at the time of Christ) as a translation for the Hebrew *yhwh,* "Yahweh," or (as it is frequently translated) "the LORD," or "Jehovah." The word *kyrios* is used to translate the name of the Lord 6,814 times in the Greek Old Testament. Therefore, any Greek-speaking reader at the time of the New Testament who had any knowledge at all of the Greek Old Testament would have recognized that, in contexts where it was appropriate, the word *Lord* was the name of the one who was the creator and sustainer of heaven and earth, the omnipotent God.

Now there are many instances in the New Testament where "Lord" is used of Christ in what can only be understood as this strong Old Testament sense, "the Lord" who is Yahweh or God himself. This use of "Lord" is quite striking in the word of the angel to the shepherds of Bethlehem: "For to you is born this day in the city of David a Savior, who is Christ *the Lord* " (Luke 2:11). Though these words are familiar to us from frequent reading of the Christmas story, we should realize how surprising it would be to any first-century Jew to hear that someone born as a baby was the "Christ" (or "Messiah"),[7] and, moreover, that this one who was the Messiah was also "the Lord"—that is, the Lord God himself!

We see another example when Matthew says that John the Baptist is the one who cries out in the wilderness, "Prepare the way of *the Lord,* make his paths straight" (Matt. 3:3). John is quoting Isaiah 40:3, which speaks about the Lord God himself coming among his people. But the context applies this passage to John's role of preparing the way for Jesus to come. The implication is that when Jesus comes, *the Lord himself* will come.

Jesus also identifies himself as the sovereign Lord of the Old Testament when he asks the Pharisees about Psalm 110:1, "The Lord said to *my Lord,* Sit at my right hand, till I put your enemies under your feet" (Matt. 22:44). The force of this statement is that "God the Father said to God the Son (David's Lord), 'Sit at my right hand. . . .'" The Pharisees know he is talking about himself and identifying himself as one worthy of the Old Testament title *kyrios,* "Lord."

Such usage is seen frequently in the Epistles, where "the Lord" is a common name to refer to Christ. Paul says, "There is one God, the Father, from whom are all things and for whom we exist, and *one Lord,* Jesus Christ, through whom are all things and through whom we exist" (1 Cor. 8:6; cf. 12:3, and many other passages in both the Pauline and the general epistles).

c. *Other strong claims to deity.* In addition to the uses of the word *God* and *Lord* to refer to Christ, we have other passages that strongly claim deity for Christ. When

---

[7]The word *Christ* is the Greek translation of the Hebrew word *Messiah.*

Jesus told his Jewish opponents that Abraham had seen his (Christ's) day, they challenged him, "You are not yet fifty years old, and have you seen Abraham?" (John 8:57). Here a sufficient response to prove Jesus' eternity would have been, "Before Abraham was, I was." But Jesus did not say this. Instead, he made a much more startling assertion: "Truly, truly, I say to you, before Abraham was, *I am*" (John 8:58). Jesus combined two assertions whose sequence seemed to make no sense: "Before something in the past happened [Abraham was], something in the present happened [I am]." The Jewish leaders recognized at once that he was not speaking in riddles or uttering nonsense. When he said, "I am," he was repeating the very words God used when he identified himself to Moses as "*I AM* WHO I AM" (Ex. 3:14). Jesus was claiming for himself the title "I AM," by which God designates himself as the eternal existing One, the God who is the source of his own existence and who has always been and always will be. When the Jews heard this unusual, emphatic, solemn statement, they knew that he was claiming to be God. "So they took up stones to throw at him; but Jesus hid himself, and went out of the temple" (John 8:59).[8]

Another strong claim to deity is Jesus' statement at the end of Revelation, "I am the Alpha and the Omega, the first and the last, the beginning and the end" (Rev. 22:13). When this is combined with the statement of God the Father in Revelation 1:8, "I am the Alpha and the Omega," it also constitutes a strong claim to equal deity with God the Father. Sovereign over all of history and all of creation, Jesus is the beginning and the end.

Further evidence of claims to deity can be found in the fact that Jesus calls himself "*the* Son of man." This title is used eighty-four times in the four Gospels, but only by Jesus and only to speak of himself (note, e.g., Matt. 16:13 with Luke 9:18). In the rest of the New Testament, the phrase "*the* Son of man" (with the definite article *the*) is used only once, in Acts 7:56, where Stephen refers to Christ as the Son of Man. This unique term has as its background the vision in Daniel 7 where Daniel saw one like a "son of man" who "came to the Ancient of Days" and was given "dominion and glory and kingdom, *that all peoples, nations, and languages should serve him; his dominion is an everlasting dominion,* which shall not pass away" (vv. 13–14). It is striking that this "son of man" came "with the clouds of heaven" (Dan. 7:13). This passage clearly speaks of someone who had heavenly origin and who was given *eternal rule* over the *whole world.* The high priests did not miss the point of this passage when Jesus said, "Hereafter you will see the Son of man *seated at the right hand of Power, and coming on the clouds of heaven*" (Matt. 26:64). The reference to Daniel 7:13–14 was unmistakable, and the high priest and his council knew that Jesus was claiming to be the eternal world ruler of heavenly origin spoken of in Daniel's vision. Immediately they said, "He has uttered blasphemy. . . . He deserves death" (Matt. 26:65–66). Here Jesus finally made explicit the strong claims to eternal world rule that were earlier hinted at in his frequent use of the title "the Son of man" to apply to himself.

Though the title "Son of God" can sometimes be used simply to refer to Israel (Matt. 2:15), or to man as created by God (Luke 2:38), or to redeemed man generally (Rom. 8:14, 19, 23), there are nevertheless instances in which the phrase "Son

---

[8]The other "I am" sayings in John's gospel, where Jesus claims to be the bread of life (6:35), the light of the world (8:12), the door of the sheep (10:7), the good shepherd (10:11), the resurrection and the life (11:25), the way, the truth, and the life (14:6), and the true vine (15:1), also contribute to the overall picture of deity that John paints of Christ: see Donald Guthrie, *New Testament Theology,* pp. 330–32.

of God" refers to Jesus as the heavenly, eternal Son who is equal to God himself (see Matt. 11:25–30; 17:5; 1 Cor. 15:28; Heb. 1:1–3, 5, 8). This is especially true in John's gospel where Jesus is seen as a unique Son from the Father (John 1:14, 18, 34, 49) who fully reveals the Father (John 8:19; 14:9). As Son he is so great that we can trust in him for eternal life (something that could be said of no created being: John 3:16, 36; 20:31). He is also the one who has all authority from the Father to give life, pronounce eternal judgment, and rule over all (John 3:36; 5:20–22, 25; 10:17; 16:15). As Son he has been sent by the Father, and therefore he existed before he came into the world (John 3:37; 5:23; 10:36).

These passages combine to indicate that the title "Son of God" *when applied to Christ* strongly affirms his deity as the eternal Son in the Trinity, one equal to God the Father in all his attributes.

2. Evidence that Jesus possessed attributes of deity. In addition to the specific affirmation of Jesus' deity seen in the many passages quoted above, we see many examples of actions in Jesus' lifetime that point to his divine character.

(a) Jesus demonstrated his *omnipotence* when he stilled the storm at sea with a word (Matt. 8:26–27), multiplied the loaves and fish (Matt. 14:19), and changed water into wine (John 2:1–11).

(b) Jesus asserted his *eternity* when he said, "Before Abraham was, I am" (John 8:58, see discussion above), or "I am the Alpha and the Omega" (Rev. 22:13).

(c) The *omniscience* of Jesus is demonstrated in his knowing people's thoughts (Mark 2:8) and in knowing "from the first who those were that did not believe, and who it was that would betray him" (John 6:64). Jesus' knowledge was much more extensive than the revelation of information that people could receive through the gift of prophecy, for he even knew the belief or unbelief that was in the hearts of all people (see John 2:25; 16:30).

(d) The divine attribute of *omnipresence* is not directly affirmed to be true of Jesus during his earthly ministry. However, while looking forward to the time that the church would be established, Jesus could say, "Where two or three are gathered in my name, *there am I* in the midst of them" (Matt. 18:20). Moreover, before he left the earth, he told his disciples, "I am with you always, to the close of the age" (Matt. 28:20).

(e) That Jesus possessed divine *sovereignty,* a kind of authority possessed by God alone, is seen in the fact that he could forgive sins (Mark 2:5–7). Unlike the Old Testament prophets who declared, "Thus says the LORD," he could preface his statements with the phrase, "But *I say to you*" (Matt. 5:22, 28, 32, 34, 39, 44)—an amazing claim to his own authority. He could speak with the authority of God himself because he was himself fully God.

(f) Another clear attestation to the deity of Christ is the fact that he is counted *worthy to be worshiped,* something that is true of no other creature, including angels (see Rev. 19:10), but only God alone. Yet Scripture says of Christ that "God has highly exalted him and bestowed on him the name which is above every name, that at the name of Jesus every knee should bow, in heaven and on earth and under the earth, and every tongue confess that Jesus Christ is Lord, to the glory of God the Father" (Phil. 2:9–11). Similarly, God commands the angels to worship Christ, for we read, "when he brings the first-born into the world, he says, 'Let all God's angels *worship him*'" (Heb. 1:6).

3. Did Jesus give up some of his divine attributes while on earth (the kenosis theory)? Paul writes to the Philippians, "Have this mind among yourselves, which is yours in Christ Jesus, who, though he was in the form of God, did not count equality with God a thing to be grasped, but *emptied himself,* taking the form of a servant, being born in the likeness of men" (Phil. 2:5–7). Beginning with this text, several theologians in the nineteenth century advocated a novel view of the incarnation called the "kenosis theory," which holds that Christ gave up some of his divine attributes while he was on earth as a man. (The word *kenosis* is taken from the Greek verb *kenoō,* which generally means "to empty," and is translated "emptied himself" in Phil. 2:7.) According to this theory, Christ "emptied himself" of some of his divine attributes, such as omniscience, omnipresence, and omnipotence, while he was on earth as a man. This was viewed as a voluntary self-limitation on Christ's part, which he carried out in order to fulfill his work of redemption.

Upon closer examination, we can see that Philippians 2:7 does not say that Christ "emptied himself of some powers" or "emptied himself of divine attributes" or anything like that. Rather, the text describes what Jesus did in this "emptying": He did not do it by giving up any of his attributes but by "taking the form of a servant," that is, by coming to live as a man, and "being found in human form he humbled himself and became obedient unto death, even death on a cross" (Phil. 2:8). Thus, the context itself interprets this "emptying" as equivalent to "humbling himself" and taking on a lowly status and position. Thus, the NIV, instead of translating the phrase "he emptied himself," translates it "but made himself nothing." The emptying includes role and status, not essential attributes or nature. It means he took a humble role.

The larger context of this passage also makes this interpretation clear. Paul's purpose has been to persuade the Philippians that they should "Do nothing from selfishness or conceit, but in humility count others better than yourselves" (Phil. 2:3), and he continues by telling them, "Let each of you look not only to his own interests, but also to the interests of others" (Phil. 2:4). To persuade them to be humble and to put the interests of others first, he then points to Christ as the supreme example of one who did just that: He put the interests of others first and was willing to give up some of the privilege and status that was his as God. Paul wants the Philippians to imitate Christ. But certainly he is not asking the Philippian Christians to "give up" or "lay aside" any of their essential attributes or abilities! He is not asking them to "give up" their intelligence or strength or skill and become a diminished version of what they were. Rather, he is asking them to put the interests of others first: "Let each of you look not only to his own interests, but also to the interests of others" (Phil. 2:4).

Therefore, the best understanding of this passage is that it talks about Jesus giving up the *status* and *privilege* that were his in heaven: He "did not count equality with God a thing to be grasped" (or "clung to for his own advantage"), but "emptied himself" or "humbled himself" for our sake, and came to live as a man. Jesus speaks elsewhere of the "glory" he had with the Father "before the world was made" (John 17:5), a glory which he had given up and was going to receive again when he returned to heaven. And Paul could speak of Christ who, "though he was rich, yet for your sake he became poor" (2 Cor. 8:9), once again speaking of the privilege and honor that he deserved but temporarily gave up for us.

The "kenosis theory" therefore is not a correct understanding of Philippians 2:5–7. In fact, if the kenosis theory were true (and this is a foundational objection against it), then we could no longer affirm that Jesus was fully God while he was here on earth. The kenosis theory ultimately denies the full deity of Jesus Christ and makes him something less than fully God.

4. Conclusion: Christ is fully divine. The New Testament affirms again and again the full, absolute deity of Jesus Christ. It does this in hundreds of explicit verses that call Jesus "God," "Lord," and "Son of God," as well as in many verses that use other titles of deity to refer to him, and in many passages that attribute actions or words to him that could only be true of God. "In him *all the fulness of God* was pleased to dwell" (Col. 1:19), and "in him the *whole fulness of deity* dwells bodily" (Col. 2:9). In an earlier section we argued that Jesus is truly and fully man. Now we conclude that he is truly and fully God as well. His name is rightly called "Emmanuel," that is, "God with us" (Matt. 1:23).

5. Why was Jesus' deity necessary? In the previous section, we listed several reasons why it was necessary for Jesus to be fully man in order to earn our redemption. Here it is appropriate to recognize that it is crucially important to insist on the full deity of Christ as well, not only because it is clearly taught in Scripture, but also because (1) only someone who is infinite God could bear the full penalty for all the sins of all those who would believe in him—any finite creature would have been incapable of bearing that penalty; (2) salvation is from the Lord (Jonah 2:9 NASB), and the whole message of Scripture is designed to show that no human being, no creature, could ever save man—only God himself; and (3) only someone who was truly and fully God could be the one mediator between God and man (1 Tim. 2:5), both to bring us back to God and also to reveal God most fully to us (John 14:9).

Thus, if Jesus is not fully God, we have no salvation and ultimately no Christianity. It is no accident that throughout history those groups that have given up belief in the full deity of Christ have not remained long within the Christian faith but have soon drifted toward the kind of religion represented by Unitarianism in the United States and elsewhere. "No one who denies the Son has the Father" (1 John 2:23). "Any one who goes ahead and does not abide in the doctrine of Christ does not have God; he who abides in the doctrine has both the Father and the Son" (2 John 9).

C. The Incarnation: Deity and Humanity in the One Person of Christ

The biblical teaching about the full deity and full humanity of Christ is so extensive that both have been believed from the earliest times in the history of the church. But a precise understanding of how full deity and full humanity could be combined together in one person was formulated only gradually in the church and did not reach the final form until the Chalcedonian Definition in A.D. 451. Before that point, several inadequate views of the person of Christ were proposed and then rejected. One view, Arianism, which held that Jesus was not fully divine, was discussed above in the chapter on the doctrine of the Trinity.[9] But three other views that were eventually rejected as heretical should be mentioned at this point.

1. Three inadequate views of the person of Christ.

a. *Apollinarianism.* Apollinaris, who became bishop in Laodicea about A.D. 361, taught that the one person of Christ had a human body but not a human mind or

---

[9]See the discussion of Arianism in ch. 6, pp. 113–14.

spirit, and that the mind and spirit of Christ were from the divine nature of the Son of God. This view may be represented as in figure 14.1.

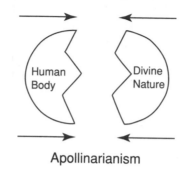

Apollinarianism

figure 14.1

But the views of Apollinaris were rejected by the leaders of the church at that time, who realized that it was not just our human body that needed salvation and needed to be represented by Christ in his redemptive work, but our human minds and spirits (or souls) as well: Christ had to be fully and truly man if he was to save us (Heb. 2:17). Apollinarianism was rejected by several church councils, from the Council of Alexandria in A.D. 362 to the Council of Constantinople in A.D. 381.

b. *Nestorianism.* Nestorianism is the doctrine that there were two separate persons in Christ, a human person and a divine person, a teaching that is distinct from the biblical view that sees Jesus as one person. Nestorianism may be diagrammed as in figure 14.2.

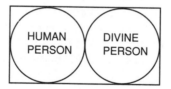

Nestorianism

figure 14.2

Nestorius was a popular preacher at Antioch, and from A.D. 428 was bishop of Constantinople. Although Nestorius himself probably never taught the heretical view that goes by his name (the idea that Christ was two persons in one body, rather than one person), through a combination of several personal conflicts and a good deal of ecclesiastical politics, he was removed from his office of bishop and his teachings were condemned.

It is important to understand why the church could not accept the view that Christ was two distinct persons. Nowhere in Scripture do we have an indication that the human nature of Christ, for example, is an independent person, deciding to do something contrary to the divine nature of Christ. Nowhere do we have an indication of the human and divine natures talking to each other or struggling within Christ, or any such thing. Rather, we have a consistent picture of a single person acting in wholeness and unity. Jesus always speaks as "I," not as "we," though he can refer to himself and the Father together as "we" (John 14:23). The Bible always speaks of Jesus as "he," not as "they." And, though we can sometimes distinguish actions of his divine nature and actions of his human nature in order to help us understand some of the statements and actions recorded in Scripture, the Bible itself does not say "Jesus' human nature did this" or "Jesus' divine nature did that," as though they were separate persons, but always talks about what the *person* of Christ did. Therefore, the church continued to insist that Jesus was one person, although possessing both a human nature and a divine nature.

c. *Monophysitism (Eutychianism)*. A third inadequate view is called *monophysitism*, the view that Christ had one nature only (Gk. *monos*, "one," and *physis*, "nature"). The primary advocate of this view in the early church was Eutyches (c. A.D. 378–454), who was the leader of a monastery at Constantinople. Eutyches taught the opposite error from Nestorianism, for he denied that the human nature and divine nature in Christ remained fully human and fully divine. He held rather that the human nature of Christ was taken up and absorbed into the divine nature, so that both natures were changed somewhat and *a third kind of nature* resulted. An analogy to Eutychianism can be seen if we put a drop of ink in a glass of water: The mixture resulting is neither pure ink nor pure water, but some kind of third substance, a mixture of the two in which both the ink and the water are changed. Similarly, Eutyches taught that Jesus was a mixture of divine and human elements in which both were somewhat modified to form one new nature. This may be represented as in figure 14.3.

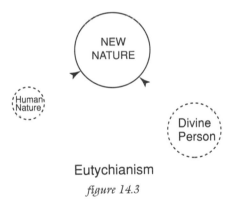

Eutychianism

figure 14.3

Monophysitism also rightly caused great concern in the church, because, by this doctrine, Christ was neither truly God nor truly man. And if that was so, he could not truly represent us as a man nor could he be true God and able to earn our salvation.

2. The solution to the controversy: The Chalcedonian Definition of A.D. 451. In order to attempt to solve the problems raised by the controversies over the person of Christ, a large church council was convened in the city of Chalcedon near Constantinople (or modern Istanbul), from October 8 to November 1, A.D. 451. The resulting statement, called the Chalcedonian Definition, guarded against Apollinarianism, Nestorianism, and Eutychianism. It has been taken as the standard, orthodox definition of the biblical teaching on the person of Christ since that day by Catholic, Protestant, and Orthodox branches of Christianity alike.

The statement is not long, and we may quote it in its entirety:[10]

We, then, following the holy Fathers, all with one consent, teach men to confess one and the same Son, our Lord Jesus Christ, the same perfect in Godhead and also perfect in manhood; truly God and truly man, of a reasonable [rational] soul and body; *consubstantial [coessential] with the Father according to the Godhead, and consubstantial with us according to the Manhood;* in all things like unto us, without sin; begotten before all ages of the Father according to the Godhead, and in these latter days, for us and for our salvation, born of the Virgin Mary, the Mother of God, according to the Manhood; one and the same Christ, Son, Lord, Only-begotten, to be acknowledged in *two natures, inconfusedly, unchangeably, indivisibly, inseparably;* the distinction of natures being by no means taken away by the union, but rather *the property of each nature being preserved,* and concurring in *one Person* and one Subsistence, not parted or divided into two persons, but one and the same Son, and only begotten, God, the Word, the Lord Jesus Christ, as the prophets from the beginning [have declared] concerning him, and the Lord Jesus Christ himself has taught us, and the Creed of the holy Fathers has been handed down to us.

Against the view of Apollinaris that Christ did not have a human mind or soul, we have the statement that he was "*truly man,* of a *reasonable soul* and body . . . *consubstantial with us* according to the Manhood; in all things like unto us."

In opposition to the view of Nestorianism that Christ was two persons united in one body, we have the words "*indivisibly, inseparably* . . . concurring in *one Person* and one Subsistence, not parted or divided into two persons."

Against the view of Eutychianism that Christ had only one nature and that his human nature was lost in the union with the divine nature, we have the words "to be acknowledged in *two natures, inconfusedly, unchangeably* . . . the distinction of natures being by no means taken away by the union, but rather *the property of each nature being preserved.*" The human and the divine natures were not confused or changed when Christ became man, but the human nature remained a truly human nature, and the divine nature remained a truly divine nature.

Figure 14.4 may be helpful in showing this, in contrast to the earlier diagrams. It indicates that the eternal Son of God took to himself a truly human nature, and that Christ's divine and human natures remain distinct and retain their own properties, yet they are eternally and inseparably united together in one person.

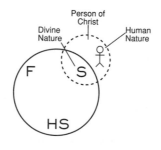

Chalcedonian Christology

figure 14.4

---

[10]English translation taken from Philip Schaff, *Creeds of Christendom,* 2:62–63 (italics added).

3. Combining specific biblical texts on Christ's deity and humanity. When we examine the New Testament, as we did above in the sections on Jesus' humanity and deity, there are several passages that seem difficult to fit together (How could Jesus be omnipotent and yet weak? How could he leave the world and yet be present everywhere? How could he learn things and yet be omniscient?). As the church struggled to understand these teachings, it finally came up with the Chalcedonian Definition, which spoke of two distinct natures in Christ that retain their own properties yet remain together in one person. This distinction, which helps us in our understanding of the biblical passages mentioned earlier, also seems to be demanded by those passages.

a. *One nature does some things that the other nature does not do.* If we are willing to affirm the Chalcedonian statement about "the *property of each nature* being preserved" in the person of Christ, it is necessary to distinguish between things done by Christ's human nature but not his divine nature, or by his divine nature but not his human nature.

For example, when we are talking about Jesus' human nature, we can say that he ascended to heaven and is no longer in the world (John 16:28; 17:11; Acts 1:9–11). But with respect to his divine nature, we can say that Jesus is everywhere present: "Where two or three are gathered in my name, *there am I* in the midst of them" (Matt. 18:20); "*I am with you always,* to the close of the age" (Matt. 28:20); "If a man loves me, he will keep my word, and my Father will love him, and *we* will come to him and make our home with him" (John 14:23). So we can say that both things are true about the *person* of Christ—he has returned to heaven *and* he is also present with us.

Similarly, we can say that Jesus was about thirty years old (Luke 3:23), if we are speaking with respect to his human nature, but we can say that he eternally existed (John 1:1–2; 8:58) if we are speaking of his divine nature.

In his human nature, Jesus was weak and tired (Matt. 4:2; 8:24; Mark 15:21; John 4:6), but in his divine nature he was omnipotent (Matt. 8:26–27; Col. 1:17; Heb. 1:3). Particularly striking is the scene of the Sea of Galilee where Jesus was asleep on the stern of the boat, presumably because he was weary (Matt. 8:24). But he was able to arise from his sleep and calm the wind and sea with a word (Matt. 8:26–27)! Tired yet omnipotent! Here Jesus' weak human nature completely hid his omnipotence until that omnipotence broke forth in a sovereign word from the one who is Lord of heaven and earth.

In a similar way, we can understand that in his human nature, Jesus died (Luke 23:46; 1 Cor. 15:3). But with respect to his divine nature, he did not die, but was able to raise himself from the dead (John 2:19; 10:17–18; Heb. 7:16). Yet here we must give a note of caution: It is true that when Jesus died his physical body died and his human soul (or spirit) was separated from his body and passed into the presence of God the Father in heaven (Luke 23:43, 46). In this way he experienced a death that is like the one we as believers experience if we die before Christ returns. And it is not correct to say that Jesus' divine nature died, or could die, if "die" means a cessation of activity, a cessation of consciousness, or a diminution of power. Nevertheless, by virtue of union with Jesus' human nature, his divine nature somehow tasted something of what it was like to go through death. The *person* of Christ experienced death. Moreover, it seems difficult to understand how Jesus' human nature alone could have borne the wrath of God against the sins of millions of people. It seems that Jesus' divine nature had somehow to participate in the bearing of wrath against sin that was due to us (though Scripture nowhere explicitly affirms this). Therefore, even though

Jesus' divine nature did not actually die, Jesus went through the experience of death as a whole person, and both human and divine natures somehow shared in that experience. Beyond that, Scripture does not enable us to say more.

The distinction between Jesus' human and divine natures also helps us understand Jesus' temptations. With respect to his human nature, he certainly was tempted in every way as we are, yet without sin (Heb. 4:15). With respect to his divine nature, however, he was not tempted, because God cannot be tempted with evil (James 1:13).

b. *Anything either nature does, the person of Christ does.* In the previous section, I mentioned a number of things that were done by one nature but not the other in the person of Christ. Now we must affirm that anything that is true of the human or the divine nature is true of the person of Christ. Thus, Jesus can say, "Before Abraham was, *I am*" (John 8:58). He does not say, "Before Abraham was, my divine nature existed," because he is free to talk about anything done by his divine nature alone or his human nature alone as something that *he* did.

In the human sphere, this is certainly true of our conversation as well. If I type a letter, even though my feet and toes had nothing to do with typing the letter, I do not tell people, "My fingers typed a letter and my toes had nothing to do with it" (though that is true). Rather, I tell people, "*I* typed a letter." That is true because anything that is done by one part of me is done by *me*.

Thus, "*Christ* died for our sins" (1 Cor. 15:3). Even though actually only his human body ceased living and ceased functioning, it was nonetheless *Christ* as a person who died for our sin. This is simply a means of affirming that whatever can be said of one nature or the other can be said of the *person* of Christ.

Therefore, it is correct for Jesus to say, "*I* am leaving the world" (John 16:28), or "*I* am no more in the world" (John 17:11), but at the same time to say, "*I* am with you always" (Matt. 28:20). Anything done by one nature or the other is done by the *person* of Christ.

c. *Conclusion.* At the end of this long discussion, it may be easy for us to lose sight of what is actually taught in Scripture. It is by far the most amazing miracle of the entire Bible—far more amazing than the resurrection and more amazing even than the creation of the universe. The fact that the infinite, omnipotent, eternal Son of God could become man and join himself to a human nature forever, so that infinite God became one person with finite man, will remain for eternity the most profound miracle and the most profound mystery in all the universe.

II. REVIEW QUESTIONS

1. Give three evidences from Scripture for the humanity of Christ.
2. Why was it necessary for Jesus to be fully human? Give two reasons.
3. Name three ways in which the Bible explicitly states that Jesus is God or that he is divine.
4. Why was Jesus' deity necessary?
5. In what ways were the following views erroneous in their view of Christ?
   - Arianism
   - Apollinarianism
   - Nestorianism
   - Monophysitism

6. Describe the Chalcedonian Definition's contribution to a proper understanding of the person of Christ.

III. QUESTIONS FOR PERSONAL APPLICATION

1. After reading this chapter, are there specific ways in which you now think of Jesus as being more like you than you did before? What are these? How can a clearer understanding of Jesus' humanity help you face temptations? How can it help you to pray?

2. What are the most difficult situations in your life right now? Can you think of any similar situations that Jesus might have faced? Does that encourage you to pray confidently to him?

3. Can you picture what it would have been like if you had been present when Jesus said, "Before Abraham was, I am"? What would you have felt? Now try visualizing yourself as present when Jesus made some of the other "I am" statements recorded in John's gospel.[11]

4. After reading this chapter, is there anything that you understand more fully about the deity of Jesus? Do you think Jesus is the one person you would be able to trust with your life for all eternity? Will you be happy to join with thousands of others in worshiping around his throne in heaven? Do you delight in worshiping him now?

IV. SPECIAL TERMS

Apollinarianism	kenosis theory
Arianism	Lord
Chalcedonian Definition	monophysitism
docetism	Nestorianism
Eutychianism	Son of God
God	Son of Man
impeccability	virgin birth
incarnation	

V. SCRIPTURE MEMORY PASSAGE

JOHN 1:14

The Word became flesh and dwelt among us, full of grace and truth; we have beheld his glory, glory as of the only Son from the Father.

---

[11]See the list of "I am" statements at p. 238, n. 8, above.

CHAPTER FIFTEEN

The Atonement

+ *Was it necessary for Christ to die?*
+ *What really happened in the atonement?*
+ *Did Christ descend into hell?*

I. EXPLANATION AND SCRIPTURAL BASIS

We may define the atonement as follows: *The atonement is the work Christ did in his life and death to earn our salvation.* This definition indicates that we are using the word *atonement* in a broader sense than it is sometimes used. Sometimes it is used to refer only to Jesus' dying and paying for our sins on the cross. But, as will be seen below, since saving benefits also come to us from Christ's life, we have included that in our definition as well.

A. The Cause of the Atonement

What was the ultimate cause that led to Christ's coming to earth and dying for our sins? To find this we must trace the question back to something in the character of God himself. And here Scripture points to two things: the *love* and *justice* of God.

The love of God as a cause of the atonement is seen in the most familiar passage in the Bible: "For God *so loved the world* that he gave his only Son, that whoever believes in him should not perish but have eternal life" (John 3:16). But the justice of God also required that God find a way that the penalty due to us for our sins would be paid (for he could not accept us into fellowship with himself unless the penalty was paid). Paul explains that this was why God sent Christ to be a "propitiation" (Rom. 3:25 NASB)—that is, a sacrifice that bears God's wrath so that God becomes "propitious" or favorably disposed toward us: it was "*to show God's righteousness,* because in his divine forbearance he had passed over former sins" (Rom. 3:25). Here Paul says that God had been forgiving sins in the Old Testament but no penalty had been paid—a fact that would make people wonder whether God was indeed just and ask how he could forgive sins without a penalty. No God who was truly just could do that, could he? Yet when God sent Christ to die and pay the penalty for our sins, "it was to prove at the present time *that he himself is righteous* and that he justifies him who has faith in Jesus" (Rom. 3:26).

Therefore, both the love and the justice of God were the ultimate cause of the atonement. It is not helpful for us to ask which is more important, however, because without the love of God, he never would have taken any steps to redeem us, yet without the justice of God, the specific requirement that Christ should earn our salvation by dying for our sins would not have been met. Both the love and justice of God were equally important.

B. The Necessity of the Atonement

Was there any other way for God to save human beings than by sending his Son to die in our place?

Before answering this question, it is important to realize that it was not necessary for God to save any people at all. When we appreciate that "God did not spare the angels when they sinned, but cast them into hell and committed them to pits of nether gloom to be kept until the judgment" (2 Peter 2:4), then we realize that God also could have chosen with perfect justice to have left us in our sins awaiting judgment. He could have chosen to save no one, just as he did with the sinful angels. So in this sense the atonement was not absolutely necessary.

But once God, in his love, decided to save some human beings, then several passages in Scripture indicate that there was no other way for God to do this than through the death of his Son. Therefore, the atonement was not absolutely necessary, but, as a "consequence" of God's decision to save some human beings, the atonement was absolutely necessary. This is sometimes called the "consequent absolute necessity" view of the atonement.

In the Garden of Gethsemane Jesus prays, "*If it be possible,* let this cup pass from me; nevertheless, not as I will, but as you will" (Matt. 26:39). We may be confident that Jesus always prayed according to the will of the Father, and that he always prayed with fullness of faith. Thus it seems that this prayer, which Matthew takes pains to record for us, shows that it was *not possible* for Jesus to avoid the death on the cross that was soon to come to him (the "cup" of suffering he had said would be his). If he was going to accomplish the work that the Father sent him to do, and if people were going to be redeemed for God, it was necessary for him to die on the cross.

Jesus said something similar after his resurrection, when he was talking with two disciples on the road to Emmaus. They were sad that Jesus had died, but his response was, "O foolish men, and slow of heart to believe all that the prophets have spoken! Was it not *necessary* that the Christ should suffer these things and enter into his glory?" (Luke 24:25–26). Jesus understood that God's plan of redemption (which he explained for the disciples from many Old Testament Scriptures, Luke 24:27) made it necessary for the Messiah to die for the sins of his people.

As we saw above, Paul in Romans 3 also shows that if God were to be righteous, and still save people, he had to send Christ to pay the penalty for sins: "It was to prove at the present time that he himself is righteous and that he justifies him who has faith in Jesus" (Rom. 3:26). The epistle to the Hebrews emphasizes that Christ *had* to suffer for our sins: "He *had to* be made like his brethren in every respect, so that he might become a merciful and faithful high priest in the service of God, to make expiation [lit. 'propitiation'] for the sins of the people" (Heb. 2:17). The author of Hebrews also argues that since "it is impossible that the blood of bulls and goats should take away sins" (Heb. 10:4), a better sacrifice is required (Heb. 9:23). Only the blood of Christ, that is, his death, would be able really to take away sins (Heb. 9:25–26). There was no other way for God to save us than for Christ to die in our place.

C. The Nature of the Atonement

In this section, we consider two aspects of Christ's work: (1) Christ's obedience for us, in which he obeyed the requirements of the law in our place and was perfectly obedient to the will of God the Father as our representative, and (2) Christ's sufferings for us, in which he took the penalty due for our sins and as a result died for our sins.

It is important to notice that in both of these categories the primary emphasis and the primary influence of Christ's work of redemption is not on us, but on God the Father. Jesus obeyed the Father in our place and perfectly met the demands of the law. And he suffered in our place, receiving in himself the penalty that God the Father would have visited upon us. In both cases, the atonement is viewed as *objective;* that is, something that has primary influence directly on God himself. Only secondarily does it have application to us, and this is only because there was a definite event in the relationship between God the Father and God the Son that secured our salvation.

1. Christ's obedience for us (sometimes called his "active obedience"). If Christ had only earned forgiveness of sins for us, then we would not merit heaven. Our guilt would have been removed, but we would simply be in the position of Adam and Eve before they had done anything good or bad and before they had passed a time of probation successfully. To be established in righteousness forever and to have their fellowship with God made sure forever, Adam and Eve had to obey God perfectly over a period of time. Then God would have looked on their faithful obedience with pleasure and delight, and they would have lived with him in fellowship forever.

For this reason, Christ had to live a life of perfect obedience to God in order to earn righteousness for us. He had to obey the law for his whole life on our behalf so that the positive merits of his perfect obedience would be counted for us. Sometimes this is called Christ's "active obedience," while his suffering and dying for our sins is called his "passive obedience." Paul says his goal is that he may be found in Christ, "*not having a righteousness of [his] own,* based on law, but *that which is through faith in Christ,* the righteousness from God that depends on faith" (Phil. 3:9). It is not just moral neutrality that Paul knows he needs from Christ (that is, a clean slate with sins forgiven), but a positive moral righteousness. And he knows that that cannot come from himself but must come through faith in Christ. Similarly, Paul says that Christ has been made *"our righteousness"* (1 Cor. 1:30). And he quite explicitly says, "For as by one man's disobedience many were made sinners, so by one man's obedience many will be *made righteous"* (Rom. 5:19).

Some theologians have not taught that Christ needed to achieve a lifelong record of perfect obedience for us. They have simply emphasized that Christ had to die and thereby pay the penalty for our sins. But such a position does not adequately explain why Christ did more than just die for us; he also became our "righteousness" before God. Jesus said to John the Baptist, before he was baptized by him, "It is fitting for us to fulfil all righteousness" (Matt. 3:15).

It might be argued that Christ had to live a life of perfect righteousness for his own sake, not for ours, before he could be a sinless sacrifice for us. But Jesus had no need to live a life of perfect obedience for his own sake—he had shared love and fellowship with the Father for all eternity and was in his own character eternally wor-

thy of the Father's good pleasure and delight. He rather had to "fulfil all righteousness" for our sake—that is, for the sake of the people whom he was representing as their head. Unless he had done this for us, we would have no record of
obedience by which we would merit God's favor and merit eternal life with him.
Moreover, if Jesus had needed only sinlessness and not also a life of perfect obedience, he could have died for us when he was a young child rather than when he was
thirty-three years old.

By way of application, we ought to ask ourselves whose lifelong record of obedience we would rather rely on for our standing before God, Christ's or our own?
As we think about the life of Christ, we ought to ask ourselves, was it good enough
to deserve God's approval? And are we willing to rely on his record of obedience
for our eternal destiny?

2. Christ's sufferings for us (sometimes called his "passive obedience"). In addition to obeying the law perfectly for his whole life on our behalf, Christ also took
on himself the sufferings necessary to pay the penalty for our sins.

a. *Suffering for his whole life.* In a broad sense, the penalty Christ bore in paying
for our sins was suffering in both his body and soul throughout his life. Though
Christ's sufferings culminated in his death on the cross (see below), his whole life in
a fallen world involved suffering. For example, Jesus endured tremendous suffering
during the temptation in the wilderness (Matt. 4:1–11), when he was assaulted for
forty days by the attacks of Satan. He also suffered in growing to maturity, for we
read, "Although he was a Son, he learned obedience through what he *suffered*"
(Heb. 5:8). He knew suffering in the intense opposition he faced from Jewish leaders throughout much of his earthly ministry (see Heb. 12:3–4). We may suppose too
that he experienced suffering and grief at the death of his earthly father[1] and certainly he experienced grief at the death of his close friend Lazarus (John 11:35). In
predicting the coming of the Messiah, Isaiah said he would be "a man of sorrows and
acquainted with grief" (Isa. 53:3).

b. *The pain of the cross.* The sufferings of Jesus intensified as he drew near to the
cross. He told his disciples something of the agony he was going through when he
said, "My soul is very sorrowful, even to death" (Matt. 26:38). It was especially on
the cross that Jesus' sufferings for us reached their climax, for it was there that he
bore the penalty for our sin and died in our place. Scripture teaches us that there
were four different aspects of the pain that Jesus experienced.

(1) *Physical pain and death.* We do not need to hold that Jesus suffered
more physical pain than any human being has ever suffered, for the Bible nowhere
makes such a claim. But we still must not forget that death by crucifixion was one
of the most horrible forms of execution ever devised by man.

Many readers of the Gospels in the ancient world would have witnessed cruci-
fixions and thus would have had a painfully vivid mental picture upon reading the
simple words "And they crucified him" (Mark 15:24). A criminal who was crucified
was essentially forced to inflict upon himself a very slow death by suffocation. When
the criminal's arms were outstretched and fastened by nails to the cross, he had to
support most of the weight of his body with his arms. The chest cavity would be

---

[1]Although Scripture does not explicitly say that Joseph died during Jesus' life, we hear nothing of him after Jesus
is twelve years old.

pulled upward and outward, making it difficult to exhale in order to be able to draw a fresh breath. But when the victim's longing for oxygen became unbearable, he would have to push himself up with his feet, thus giving more natural support to the weight of his body, releasing some of the weight from his arms, and enabling his chest cavity to contract more normally. By pushing himself upward in this way, the criminal could fend off suffocation, but it was extremely painful because it required putting the body's weight on the nails holding the feet, and bending the elbows and pulling upward on the nails driven through the wrists. The criminal's back, which had been torn open repeatedly by a previous flogging, would scrape against the wooden cross with each breath. Thus, Seneca (first century A.D.) spoke of a crucified man "drawing the breath of life amid long-drawn-out agony" (Epistle 101, to Lucilius, sec. 14).

A physician writing in the *Journal of the American Medical Association* in 1986 explained the pain that would have been experienced in death by crucifixion:

> Adequate exhalation required lifting the body by pushing up on the feet and by flexing the elbows. . . . However, this maneuver would place the entire weight of the body on the tarsals and would produce searing pain. Furthermore, flexion of the elbows would cause rotation of the wrists about the iron nails and cause fiery pain along the damaged median nerves. . . . Muscle cramps and paresthesias of the outstretched and uplifted arms would add to the discomfort. As a result, each respiratory effort would become agonizing and tiring and lead eventually to asphyxia.[2]

In some cases, crucified men would survive for several days, nearly suffocating but not quite dying. This was why the executioners would sometimes break the legs of a criminal, so that death would come quickly, as we see in John 19:31–33:

> Since it was the day of Preparation, in order to prevent the bodies from remaining on the cross on the sabbath (for that sabbath was a high day), the Jews asked Pilate that their legs might be broken, and that they might be taken away. So the soldiers came and broke the legs of the first, and of the other who had been crucified with him; but when they came to Jesus and saw that he was already dead, they did not break his legs.

(2) *The pain of bearing sin.* More awful than the pain of physical suffering Jesus endured was the psychological pain of bearing the guilt for our sin. In our own experience as Christians, we know something of the anguish we feel when we know we have sinned. The weight of guilt is heavy on our hearts, and there is a bitter sense of separation from all that is right in the universe, an awareness of something that in a very deep sense ought not to be. In fact, the more we grow in holiness as God's children, the more intensely we feel this instinctive revulsion against evil.

Now Jesus was perfectly holy. He hated sin with his entire being. The thought of evil, of sin, contradicted everything in his character. Far more than we do, Jesus instinctively rebelled against evil. Yet in obedience to the Father, and out of love for us, Jesus took on himself all the sins of those who would someday be saved. Taking on himself all the evil against which his soul rebelled created deep revulsion in the center of his being. All that he hated most deeply was poured out fully upon him.

Scripture frequently says that our sins were put on Christ: "The LORD has laid on him the iniquity of us all" (Isa. 53:6), and "He *bore the sin* of many" (Isa. 53:12).

---

[2]William Edwards, M.D., et al., *Journal of the American Medical Association* 255, no. 11 (March 21, 1986): 1461.

John the Baptist calls Jesus "the Lamb of God, who takes away the sin of the world" (John 1:29). Paul declares that God made Christ *"to be sin"* (2 Cor. 5:21) and that Christ became "a curse for us" (Gal. 3:13). The author of Hebrews says that Christ was "offered once to bear the sins of many" (Heb. 9:28). And Peter says, "He himself *bore our sins* in his body on the tree" (1 Peter 2:24).

The passage from 2 Corinthians quoted above, together with the verses from Isaiah, indicate that it was God the Father who put our sins on Christ. How could that be? In the same way in which Adam's sins were imputed to us,[3] so God imputed our sins to Christ—that is, he *thought of them as belonging to Christ*, and, since God is the ultimate judge and definer of what really is in the universe, when God thought of our sins as belonging to Christ then in fact they *actually did* belong to Christ. This does not mean that God thought that Christ had himself committed the sins, or that Christ himself actually had a sinful nature, but rather that the guilt for our sins (that is, the liability to punishment) was thought of by God as belonging to Christ rather than to us.

Some have objected that it was not fair for God to transfer the guilt of sin from us to an innocent person, Christ. Yet we must remember that Christ voluntarily took on himself the guilt for our sins, so this objection loses much of its force. Moreover, God himself (Father, Son, and Holy Spirit) is the ultimate standard of what is just and fair in the universe, and he decreed that the atonement would take place in this way and that it did in fact satisfy the demands of his own righteousness and justice.

(3) *Abandonment.* The physical pain of crucifixion and the pain of taking on himself the absolute evil of our sins were aggravated by the fact that Jesus faced this pain alone. In the Garden of Gethsemane, when Jesus took with him Peter, James, and John, he confided something of his agony to them: "My soul is very sorrowful, even to death; remain here, and watch" (Mark 14:34). This is the kind of confidence one would disclose to a close friend, and it implies a request for support in his hour of greatest trial. Yet as soon as Jesus was arrested, "all the disciples forsook him and fled" (Matt. 26:56).

Here also there is a very faint analogy in our experience, for we cannot live long without tasting the inward ache of rejection, whether it be rejection by a close friend, by a parent or child, or even by a wife or husband. Yet in all those cases there is at least a sense that we could have done something differently, that at least in small part we may be at fault. It was not so with Jesus and the disciples, for "having loved his own who were in the world, he loved them to the end" (John 13:1). He had done nothing but love them; in return they all abandoned him.

But far worse than desertion by even the closest of human friends was the fact that Jesus was deprived of the closeness to the Father that had been the deepest joy of his heart for all his earthly life. When Jesus cried out "Eli, Eli, lama sabachthani?" that is, "My God, my God, why have you forsaken me?" (Matt. 27:46), he showed that he was finally cut off from the sweet fellowship with his heavenly Father that had been the unfailing source of his inward strength and the element of greatest joy in a life filled with sorrow. As Jesus bore our sins on the cross, he was abandoned by his heavenly Father, who is "of purer eyes than to behold evil" (Hab. 1:13). He faced the weight of the guilt of millions of sins alone.

---

[3]See ch. 13, pp. 213–18, for a discussion of the imputation of Adam's sin to us.

(4) *Bearing the wrath of God.* Yet more difficult than these three previous aspects of Jesus' pain was the pain of bearing the wrath of God upon himself. As Jesus bore the guilt of our sins alone, God the Father, the mighty Creator, the Lord of the universe, poured out on Jesus the fury of his wrath: Jesus became the object of the intense hatred of sin and vengeance against sin that God had patiently stored up since the beginning of the world.

Romans 3:25 tells us that God put forward Christ as a *"propitiation"* (NASB), a word that means "a sacrifice that bears God's wrath to the end and in so doing changes God's wrath toward us into favor." Paul tells us that "this was to show God's righteousness, because in his divine forbearance he had passed over former sins; it was to prove at the present time that he himself is righteous and that he justifies him who has faith in Jesus" (Rom. 3:25–26). God had not simply forgiven sin and forgotten about the punishment in generations past. He had forgiven sins and stored up his righteous anger against those sins. But at the cross the fury of all that stored-up wrath against sin was unleashed against God's own Son.

Many theologians outside the evangelical world have strongly objected to the idea that Jesus bore the wrath of God against sin. Their basic assumption is that since God is a God of love, it would be inconsistent with his character to show wrath against the human beings he has created and for whom he is a loving Father. But evangelical scholars have convincingly argued that the idea of the wrath of God is solidly rooted in both the Old and New Testaments: "The whole of the argument of the opening part of Romans is that all men, Gentiles and Jews alike, are sinners, and that they come under the wrath and the condemnation of God."[4]

Three other crucial passages in the New Testament refer to Jesus' death as a "propitiation": Hebrews 2:17; 1 John 2:2 and 4:10. The Greek terms (the verb *hilaskomai,* "to make propitiation" and the noun *hilasmos,* "a sacrifice of propitiation") used in these passages have the sense of "a sacrifice that turns away the wrath of God—and thereby makes God propitious (or favorable) toward us." This is the consistent meaning of these words outside the Bible where they were well understood in reference to pagan Greek religions. These verses simply mean that Jesus bore the wrath of God against sin.

It is important to insist on this fact, because it is the heart of the doctrine of the atonement. It means that there is an eternal, unchangeable requirement in the holiness and justice of God that sin be paid for. Furthermore, before the atonement ever could have an effect on our subjective consciousness, it first had an effect on God and his relation to the sinners he planned to redeem. Apart from this central truth, the death of Christ really cannot be adequately understood (see discussion of other views of the atonement below).

The view of Christ's death presented here has frequently been called the theory of "penal substitution." Christ's death was "penal" in that he bore a *penalty* when he died. His death was also a "substitution" in that he was a *substitute* for us when he died. This has been the orthodox understanding of the atonement held by evangelical theologians, in contrast to other views that attempt to explain the atonement apart from the idea of the wrath of God or payment of the penalty for sin (see below).

---

[4]Leon Morris, "Propitiation," *EDT*, p. 888 (includes brief bibliography). Morris's own work has represented the best of evangelical scholarship on this question. See his *The Apostolic Preaching of the Cross,* 3d ed. (London: Tyndale Press, 1965), pp. 144–213. See also the discussion of the wrath of God in ch. 5, pp. 94–95.

This view of the atonement is sometimes called the theory of *vicarious atonement*. A "vicar" is someone who stands in the place of another or who represents another. Christ's death was therefore "vicarious" because he stood in our place and represented us. As our representative, he took the penalty that we deserve.

c. *New Testament terms describing different aspects of the atonement.* The atoning work of Christ is a complex event that has several effects on us. It can therefore be viewed from several different aspects. The New Testament uses different words to describe these; we shall examine four of the more important terms.

The four terms show how Christ's death met the four needs that we have as sinners:

1. We deserve to die as the *penalty* for sin.
2. We deserve to bear God's *wrath* against sin.
3. We are *separated* from God by our sins.
4. We are in *bondage* to sin and to the kingdom of Satan.

These four needs are met by Christ's death in the following ways:

(1) *Sacrifice.* To pay the penalty of death that we deserved because of our sins, Christ died as a sacrifice for us. "He has appeared once for all at the end of the age to put away sin by the sacrifice of himself" (Heb. 9:26).

(2) *Propitiation.* To remove from us the wrath of God we deserved, Christ died as a propitiation for our sins. "In this is love, not that we loved God, but that He loved us and sent His Son to be the propitiation for our sins" (1 John 4:10 NASB).

(3) *Reconciliation.* To overcome our separation from God, we needed someone to provide reconciliation and thereby bring us back into fellowship with God. Paul says that God "through Christ reconciled us to himself and gave us the ministry of reconciliation, that is, in Christ God was reconciling the world to himself" (2 Cor. 5:18–19).

(4) *Redemption.* Because we as sinners are in bondage to sin and to Satan, we need someone to provide redemption and thereby "redeem" us out of that bondage. When we speak of redemption, the idea of a "ransom" comes into view. A ransom is the price paid to redeem someone from bondage or captivity. Jesus said of himself, "For the Son of man also came not to be served but to serve, and to give his life as a ransom for many" (Mark 10:45). If we ask to whom the ransom was paid, we realize that the human analogy of a ransom payment does not fit the atonement of Christ in every detail. Though we were in bondage to sin and to Satan, there was no "ransom" paid either to "sin" or to Satan himself, for they did not have power to demand such payment, nor was Satan the one whose holiness was offended by sin and who required a penalty to be paid for sin. As we saw earlier, the penalty for sin was paid by Christ and received and accepted by God the Father. But we hesitate to speak of paying a "ransom" to God the Father, because it was not he who held us in bondage but Satan and our own sins. Therefore, at this point the idea of a ransom payment cannot be pressed in every detail. It is sufficient to note that a price was paid (the death of Christ) and the result was that we were "redeemed" from bondage.

We were redeemed from bondage to Satan because "the whole world is in the power of the evil one" (1 John 5:19), and when Christ came he died in order to "deliver all those who through fear of death were subject to lifelong bondage" (Heb.

2:15). In fact, God the Father "has delivered us from the dominion of darkness and transferred us to the kingdom of his beloved Son" (Col. 1:13).

As for deliverance from bondage to sin, Paul says, "So you also must consider yourselves dead to sin and alive to God in Christ Jesus. . . . For sin will have no dominion over you, since you are not under law but under grace" (Rom. 6:11, 14). We have been delivered from bondage to the guilt of sin and from bondage to its ruling power in our lives.

d. *Other views of the atonement.* In contrast to the penal substitution view of the atonement presented in this chapter, several other views have been advocated in the history of the church.

(1) *The ransom to Satan theory.* This view was held by Origen (c. A.D. 185– c. 254), a theologian from Alexandria and later Caesarea, and after him by some others in the early history of the church. According to this view, the ransom Christ paid to redeem us was paid to Satan, in whose kingdom all people were by virtue of sin.

This theory finds no direct confirmation in Scripture, and has few supporters in the history of the church. It falsely thinks of Satan rather than God as the one who required that a payment be made for sin, and thus completely neglects the demands of God's justice with respect to sin. It views Satan as having much more power than he actually does, namely, power to demand whatever he wants from God, rather than as one who has been cast down from heaven and has no right to demand anything of God. Nowhere does Scripture say that we as sinners owe anything to Satan, but it repeatedly says that God requires of us a payment for our sins. This view also fails to deal with the texts that speak of Christ's death as a propitiation offered to God the Father for our sins, or with the fact that God the Father represented the Trinity in accepting the payment for sins from Christ (see discussion above).

(2) *The moral influence theory.* First advocated by Peter Abelard (1079– 1142), a French theologian, the moral influence theory of the atonement holds that God did not require the payment of a penalty for sin, but that Christ's death was simply a way in which God showed how much he loved human beings by identifying with their sufferings, even to the point of death. Christ's death therefore becomes a great teaching example that shows God's love to us and draws from us a grateful response, so that in loving him we are forgiven.

The great difficulty with this viewpoint is that it is contrary to so many passages of Scripture that speak of Christ dying for sin, bearing our sin, or dying as a propitiation. Moreover, it robs the atonement of its objective character, because it holds that the atonement had no effect on God himself. Finally, it has no way of dealing with our guilt—if Christ did not die to pay for our sins, we have no right to trust in him for forgiveness of sins.

(3) *The example theory.* The example theory of the atonement was taught by the Socinians, the followers of Faustus Socinus (1539–1604), an Italian theologian who settled in Poland in 1578 and attracted a wide following. The example theory, like the moral influence theory, also denies that God's justice requires payment for sin; it says that Christ's death simply provides us with an example of how we should trust and obey God perfectly, even if that trust and obedience leads to a horrible death. Whereas the moral influence theory says that Christ's death teaches us *how much God loves us,* the example theory says that Christ's death teaches us *how we*

should live. Support for this view could be found in 1 Peter 2:21, "For to this you have been called, because Christ also suffered for you, leaving you an example, that you should follow in his steps."

While it is true that Christ is an example for us even in his death, the question is whether this fact is the complete explanation of the atonement. The example theory fails to account for the many Scriptures that focus on Christ's death as a payment for sin, the fact that Christ bore our sins, and the fact that he was the propitiation for our sins. These considerations alone mean that the theory must be rejected. Moreover, this view really ends up arguing that man can save himself by following Christ's example and by trusting and obeying God just as Christ did. Thus, it fails to show how the guilt of our sin can be removed, because it does not hold that Christ actually paid the penalty for our sins or made provision for our guilt when he died.

(4) *The governmental theory.* The governmental theory of the atonement was first taught by a Dutch theologian and jurist, Hugo Grotius (1583–1645). This theory holds that God did not actually have to require payment for sin, but, since he was omnipotent God, he could have set aside that requirement and simply forgiven sins without the payment of a penalty. Then what was the purpose of Christ's death? It was God's demonstration of the fact that his laws had been broken, that he is the moral lawgiver and governor of the universe, and that some kind of penalty would be required whenever his laws were broken. Thus Christ did not exactly pay the penalty for the actual sins of any people, but simply suffered to show that when God's laws are broken there must be some penalty paid.

The problem with this view again is that it fails to account adequately for all the Scriptures that speak of Christ bearing our sins on the cross, of God laying on Christ the iniquity of us all, of Christ dying specifically for our sins, and of Christ being the propitiation for our sins. Moreover, it takes away the objective character of the atonement by making its purpose not the satisfaction of God's justice but simply that of influencing us to realize that God has laws that must be kept. This view also implies that we cannot rightly trust in Christ's completed work for forgiveness of sin, because he has not actually made payment for those sins. Moreover, it makes the actual earning of forgiveness for us something that happened in God's own mind apart from the death of Christ on the cross—he had already decided to forgive us without requiring any penalty from us and then punished Christ only to demonstrate that he was still the moral governor of the universe. But this means that Christ (in this view) did not actually earn forgiveness or salvation for us, and thus the value of his redemptive work is greatly minimized. Finally, this theory fails to take adequate account of the unchangeableness of God and the infinite purity of his justice. To say that God can forgive sins without requiring any penalty (in spite of the fact that throughout Scripture sin always requires the payment of a penalty) is seriously to underestimate the absolute character of the justice of God.

e. *Did Christ descend into hell?* It is sometimes argued that Christ descended into hell after he died. Although the phrase "he descended into hell" does not occur in the Bible, its appearance in the widely used Apostles' Creed has generated much discussion as to its meaning and implications.

The Creed contains the words, "was crucified, dead, and buried, *he descended into hell;* the third day he rose again from the dead." Does this phrase accurately represent the biblical teaching concerning Christ's death? Did Christ endure further suffering after his death on the cross? Here we will briefly examine the history of this phrase and the biblical texts relevant to this idea.[5]

It may first be said that a murky background lies behind the history of the phrase "he descended into hell." Unlike the Nicene Creed and the Chalcedonian Definition, the Apostles' Creed was not written or approved by a single church council at one specific time, but rather developed gradually from about A.D. 200 to 750. A summary of the Creed's development by the great church historian Philip Schaff shows that the phrase in question was not found in any of the early versions of the Creed.[6] Prior to A.D. 650, the phrase "he descended into hell" appeared in only one version of the Creed, by Rufinus in A.D. 390. Moreover, Rufinus understood the phrase simply to mean that Christ was "buried."[7] In other words, he took it to mean that Christ "descended into the grave." (The Greek form has *hadēs*, which can mean just "grave," not *geenna*, "hell, place of punishment.") This means, therefore, that until A.D. 650 no version of the Creed included this phrase with the intention of saying that Christ "descended into hell." Indeed, after the phrase began to be incorporated into different versions of the Creed, all sorts of attempts were made to explain "he descended into hell" in some way that did not contradict the rest of Scripture. Given this history, one wonders if the term *apostolic* can in any sense be applied to this phrase, or if it really has a rightful place in a creed whose title claims for itself descent from the earliest apostles of Christ.

When we turn to the scriptural evidence for this doctrine, we find that there are a number of texts that argue against the possibility of Christ's going to hell after his death. Jesus' words to the thief on the cross, "Today you will be with me in Paradise" (Luke 23:43), imply that after Jesus died his soul (or spirit) went immediately to the presence of the Father in heaven, even though his body remained on earth and was buried.[8] In addition, the cry of Jesus, "It is finished" (John 19:30) strongly suggests that Christ's suffering was finished at that moment and so was his alienation from the Father because of bearing our sin. Finally, the cry, "Father, into your hands I commit my spirit" (Luke 23:46), also suggests that Christ expected (correctly) the immediate end of his suffering and estrangement and the welcoming of his spirit into heaven by God the Father.

These texts indicate, then, that Christ in his death experienced the same things believers in this present age experience when they die: His dead body remained on earth and was buried (as ours will be), but his spirit (or soul) passed immediately into the presence of God in heaven (just as ours will). Then on the first Easter morning, Christ's spirit was reunited with his body and he was raised from the dead—just as Christians who have died will (when Christ returns) be reunited to their bodies and raised in their perfect resurrection bodies to new life. Furthermore, these texts indicate that Christ in his death on the cross completely satisfied the demands of God's righteous judgment of sin and fully bore the wrath of God against that sin; there was no need for Christ to suffer further after his death on the cross.

---

[5]The following points are developed much more extensively in Wayne Grudem, "He Did Not Descend into Hell: A Plea for Following Scripture Instead of the Apostles' Creed," *JETS* 34, no. 1 (March 1991): 103–13.

[6]See the chart in Philip Schaff, *The Creeds of Christendom*, 3 vols. (Grand Rapids: Baker, 1983, reprint of 1931 edition), 2:52–55.

[7]See ibid., 1:21, n. 6; see also 1:46, n. 2.

[8]In both of the other New Testament uses, the word "Paradise" (Gk. *paradeisos*) clearly means "heaven." In 2 Cor. 12:4 it is the place to which Paul was caught up in his revelation of heaven, and in Rev. 2:7 it is the place where we find the tree of life—which is clearly heaven in Rev. 22:2, 14.

II. REVIEW QUESTIONS

1. To which two aspects of God's character can we trace the ultimate cause of the atonement?

2. Was the atonement necessary? Explain.

3. Explain the two aspects of Christ's obedience in the atonement.

4. Why was it necessary for Jesus to bear the wrath of God?

5. What do both the moral influence theory of the atonement and the example theory of the atonement deny that the penal substitution theory affirms?

6. Give the scriptural evidence against the view that Christ descended into hell after he died.

III. QUESTIONS FOR PERSONAL APPLICATION

1. In what ways has this chapter enabled you to appreciate Christ's death more than you did before? Has it given you more or less confidence in the fact that your sins have actually been paid for by Christ?

2. If the ultimate cause of the atonement is found in the love and justice of God, then was there anything in you (as a sinner in rebellion against him) that required God to love you or to take steps to save you? Does your answer to this question help you to appreciate the character of God's love for you as a person who did not at all deserve that love? How does that realization make you feel in your relationship to God?

3. Do you think that Christ's sufferings were enough to pay for your sins? Are you willing to rely on his work to pay for all your sins? Do you think he is a sufficient Savior, worthy of your trust? Will you now and always rely on him with your whole heart for complete salvation?

4. If Christ bore all the guilt for our sins, all the wrath of God against sin, and all the penalty of the death that we deserved, then will God ever turn his wrath against you as a believer (see Rom. 8:31–39)? Can any of the hardships or sufferings that you experience in life be due to the wrath of God against you? If not, then why do we as Christians experience difficulties and sufferings in this life (see Rom. 8:28; Heb. 12:3–11)?

5. If Christ has indeed redeemed you from bondage to sin and to the kingdom of Satan, are there areas of your life in which you could more fully realize this to be true? Could this realization give you more encouragement in your Christian life?

IV. SPECIAL TERMS

active obedience

atonement

consequent absolute necessity

example theory

governmental theory

impute

moral influence theory

passive obedience

penal substitution

propitiation

ransom to Satan theory

reconciliation

redemption

sacrifice

vicarious atonement

V. SCRIPTURE MEMORY PASSAGE

ROMANS 3:23–26

Since all have sinned and fall short of the glory of God, they are justified by his grace as a gift, through the redemption which is in Christ Jesus, whom God put forward as an expiation by his blood, to be received by faith. This was to show God's righteousness, because in his divine forbearance he had passed over former sins; it was to prove at the present time that he himself is righteous and that he justifies him who has faith in Jesus.

CHAPTER SIXTEEN

Resurrection and Ascension

+ *What was Christ's resurrection body like?*
+ *What is its significance for us?*
+ *What happened to Christ when he ascended into heaven?*

I. EXPLANATION AND SCRIPTURAL BASIS

A. Resurrection

1. New Testament evidence. The Gospels contain abundant testimony to the resurrection of Christ (see Matt. 28:1–20; Mark 16:1–8; Luke 24:1–53; John 20:1–21:25). In addition to these detailed narratives in the four gospels, the book of Acts is a story of the apostles' proclamation of the resurrection of Christ, and of continued prayer to Christ and trust in him as the one who is alive and reigning in heaven. The Epistles depend entirely on the assumption that Jesus is a living, reigning Savior who is now the exalted head of the church, who is to be trusted, worshiped, and adored, and who will some day return in power and great glory to reign as King over the earth. The book of Revelation repeatedly shows the risen Christ reigning in heaven and predicts his return to conquer his enemies and reign in glory. Therefore, the entire New Testament bears witness to the fact of the resurrection of Christ.[1]

2. The nature of Christ's resurrection. Christ's resurrection was not simply a coming back from the dead, as had been experienced by others before such as Lazarus (John 11:1–44), for then Jesus would have been subject to weakness and aging, and eventually would have died again just as all other human beings die. Rather, when he rose from the dead, Jesus was the "first fruits"[2] (1 Cor. 15:20, 23)

---

[1]The historical arguments for the resurrection of Christ are substantial and have persuaded many skeptics who started to examine the evidence for the purpose of disproving the resurrection. The best-known account of such a change from skepticism to belief is Frank Morison, *Who Moved the Stone?* (London: Faber and Faber, 1930; reprint, Grand Rapids: Zondervan, 1958). A widely used booklet summarizing the arguments is J. N. D. Anderson, *The Evidence for the Resurrection* (London and Downers Grove, Ill.: InterVarsity Press, 1966). (Both Morison and Anderson were trained as lawyers.) More recent and detailed presentations are found in William Lane Craig, *The Son Rises: The Historical Evidence for the Resurrection of Jesus* (Chicago: Moody, 1981); Gary Habermas and Anthony Flew, *Did Jesus Rise from the Dead? The Resurrection Debate*, ed. Terry L. Miethe (New York: Harper and Row, 1987); Gary Habermas, "Resurrection of Christ," in *EDT*, pp. 938–41. An extensive collection of arguments and quotations from recognized scholars affirming the overwhelming reliability of the evidence for Christ's resurrection is found in Josh McDowell, *Evidence that Demands a Verdict*, rev. ed., vol. 1 (San Bernardino, Calif.: Here's Life Publishers, 1979), pp. 179–263.

[2]See discussion of the term "first fruits" on p. 265 below.

of a new kind of human life, a life in which his body was made perfect, no longer subject to weakness, aging, or death, but able to live eternally.

It is true that two of Jesus' disciples did not recognize him when they walked with him on the road to Emmaus (Luke 24:13–32), but Luke specifically tells us that this was because "their eyes were kept from recognizing him" (Luke 24:16), and later "their eyes were opened and they recognized him" (Luke 24:31). Mary Magdalene failed to recognize Jesus only for a moment (John 20:14–16), but it may have been still quite dark and she was not at first looking at him—she had come the first time "while it was still dark" (John 20:1), and she "turned" to speak to Jesus once she recognized him (John 20:16).

On other occasions the disciples seemed to have recognized Jesus fairly quickly (Matt. 28:9, 17; John 20:19–20, 26–28; 21:7, 12). When Jesus appeared to the eleven disciples in Jerusalem, they were initially startled and frightened (Luke 24:33, 37), yet when they saw Jesus' hands and his feet and watched him eat a piece of fish, they were convinced that he had risen from the dead. These examples indicate that there was a considerable degree of continuity between the physical appearance of Jesus before his death and after his resurrection. Yet Jesus did not look exactly as he had before he died, for in addition to the initial amazement of the disciples at what they apparently thought could not happen, there was probably sufficient difference in his physical appearance for Jesus not to be immediately recognized. Perhaps that difference in appearance was simply the difference between a man who had lived a life of suffering, hardship, and grief, and one whose body was restored to its full youthful appearance of perfect health: though Jesus' body was still a physical body, it was raised as a transformed body, never able again to suffer, be weak or ill, or die; it had "put on immortality" (1 Cor. 15:53). Paul says the resurrection body is raised "imperishable . . . in glory . . . in power . . . a spiritual body" (1 Cor. 15:42–44). (By "spiritual body" Paul does not mean "immaterial," but rather "suited to and responsive to the guidance of the Spirit.")[3]

There are at least ten pieces of evidence in the New Testament showing that Jesus had a physical body after the resurrection: The disciples "took hold of his feet" (Matt. 28:9); he appeared to the disciples on the road to Emmaus to be just another traveler on the road (Luke 24:15–18, 28–29); he took bread and broke it (Luke 24:30); he ate a piece of broiled fish to demonstrate clearly that he had a physical body and was not just a spirit; Mary thought him to be a gardener (John 20:15); "he showed them his hands and his side" (John 20:20); he invited Thomas to put his finger out to touch his hands and put out his hand and touch his side (John 20:27); he prepared breakfast for his disciples (John 21:12–13); and he explicitly told them, "See my hands and my feet, that it is I myself; handle me, and see; for *a spirit has not flesh and bones as you see that I have*" (Luke 24:39). Finally, Peter said that the disciples "ate and drank with him after he rose from the dead" (Acts 10:41).

It is true that Jesus apparently was able to appear and disappear out of sight quite suddenly (Luke 24:31, 36; John 20:19, 26). Yet we should be careful not to draw too many conclusions from this fact, for not all the passages affirm that Jesus could suddenly appear or disappear; some just say that Jesus came and stood among the disciples. When Jesus suddenly vanished from the sight of the disciples in

---

[3]In the Pauline epistles, the word "spiritual" (Gk. *pneumatikos*) never means "nonphysical" but rather "consistent with the character and activity of the Holy Spirit" (see, e.g., Rom. 1:11; 7:14; 1 Cor. 2:13, 15; 3:1; 14:37; Gal. 6:1 ["you who are spiritual"]; Eph. 5:19).

Emmaus, this may have been a special miraculous occurrence, such as happened when "the Spirit of the Lord caught up Philip; and the eunuch saw him no more" (Acts 8:39). Nor should we make too much of the fact that Jesus came and stood among the disciples on two occasions when the doors were "shut"[4] (John 20:19, 26), for no text says that Jesus "passed through walls" or anything like that. Indeed, on another occasion in the New Testament where someone needed to pass through a locked door, the door miraculously opened (see Acts 12:10).

Finally, there is a larger doctrinal consideration. The physical resurrection of Jesus, and his eternal possession of a physical resurrection body, give clear affirmation of the goodness of the material creation that God originally made: "And God saw everything that he had made, and behold, *it was very good*" (Gen. 1:31). We as resurrected men and women will live forever in "new heavens and a new earth in which righteousness dwells" (2 Peter 3:13). We will live in a renewed earth that "will be set free from its bondage to decay" (Rom. 8:21) and the whole earth will become like a new Garden of Eden. There will be a new Jerusalem, and people "shall bring into it the glory and the honor of the nations" (Rev. 21:26), and there will be "the river of the water of life, bright as crystal, flowing from the throne of God and of the Lamb through the middle of the street of the city; also, on either side of the river, the tree of life with its twelve kinds of fruit, yielding its fruit each month" (Rev. 22:1–2).

In this very material, physical, renewed universe, it seems that we will need to live as human beings with physical bodies, suitable for life in God's renewed physical creation. Specifically, Jesus' physical resurrection body affirms the goodness of God's original creation of man not as a mere spirit like the angels, but *as a creature with a physical body that was "very good."* We must not fall into the error of thinking that nonmaterial existence is somehow a better form of existence for creatures: When God made us as the pinnacle of his creation, he gave us physical bodies. In a perfected physical body Jesus rose from the dead, now reigns in heaven, and will return to take us to be with himself forever.

3. Both the Father and the Son participated in the resurrection. Some texts affirm that God the Father specifically raised Christ from the dead (Acts 2:24; Rom. 6:4; 1 Cor. 6:14; Gal. 1:1; Eph. 1:20), but other texts speak of Jesus as participating in his own resurrection: Jesus says, "The reason my Father loves me is that I lay down my life—*only to take it up again.* No one takes it from me, but I lay it down of my own accord. I have authority to lay it down *and authority to take it up again.* This command I received from my Father" (John 10:17–18 NIV; cf. 2:19–21). It is best to conclude that both the Father and the Son were involved in the resurrection. Indeed, Jesus says, "I am the resurrection and the life" (John 11:25; cf. Heb. 7:16).

4. Doctrinal significance of the resurrection.

a. *Christ's resurrection insures our regeneration.* Peter says that "we have been born anew to a living hope *through the resurrection of Jesus Christ from the dead*" (1 Peter 1:3). Here he explicitly connects Jesus' resurrection with our regeneration or new birth. When Jesus rose from the dead he had a new quality of life, a "resurrection life" in a human body and human spirit that were perfectly suited for fellowship and obedience to God forever. In his resurrection, Jesus earned for us a new

---

[4]The Greek perfect participle *kekleismenon* may mean either that the doors were "shut" or that they were "locked."

life just like his. We do not receive all of that new "resurrection life" when we become Christians, for our bodies remain as they were, still subject to weakness, aging, and death. But in our spirits we are made alive with new resurrection power.[5] Thus, it is through his resurrection that Christ earned for us the new kind of life we receive when we are "born again." This is why Paul can say that God "made us alive together with Christ (by grace you have been saved), and *raised us up with him*" (Eph. 2:5–6; cf. Col. 3:1). When God raised Christ from the dead, he thought of us as somehow being raised "with Christ" and therefore deserving of the merits of Christ's resurrection. Paul says his goal in life is "that I may know him *and the power of his resurrection*" (Phil. 3:10). Paul knew that even in this life the resurrection of Christ gave new power for Christian ministry and obedience to God.

There is much positive application in this to our Christian lives, especially because it has implications for our ability to live the Christian life. Paul connects the resurrection of Christ with the spiritual power at work within us when he tells the Ephesians that he is praying that they would know "what is the immeasurable greatness of *his power in us* who believe, according to the working of his great might which he accomplished in Christ *when he raised him from the dead* and made him sit at his right hand in the heavenly places" (Eph. 1:19–20). Here Paul says that the power by which God raised Christ from the dead is the same power at work within us. Paul further sees us as raised in Christ when he says, "We were buried therefore with him by baptism into death, so that as Christ was raised from the dead by the glory of the Father, we too might walk in newness of life. . . . So you also must consider yourselves dead to sin and alive to God in Christ Jesus" (Rom. 6:4, 11).

This new resurrection power in us includes *power to gain more and more victory over remaining sin* in our lives—"sin will have no dominion over you" (Rom. 6:14; cf. 1 Cor. 15:17)—even though we will never be perfect in this life. This resurrection power also includes *power for ministry in the work of the kingdom*. It was after Jesus' resurrection that he promised his disciples, "You shall receive *power* when the Holy Spirit has come upon you; and you shall be my witnesses in Jerusalem and in all Judea and Samaria and to the end of the earth" (Acts 1:8). This new, intensified power for proclaiming the gospel and working miracles and triumphing over the opposition of the enemy was given to the disciples after Christ's resurrection from the dead and was part of the new resurrection power that characterized their Christian lives.

b. *Christ's resurrection insures our justification.* In only one passage does Paul explicitly connect Christ's resurrection with our justification (or our receiving a declaration that we are not guilty but righteous before God).[6] Paul says that Jesus "was put to death for our trespasses and *raised for our justification*" (Rom. 4:25). When Christ was raised from the dead, it was God's declaration of approval of Christ's work of redemption. Because Christ "humbled himself and became obedient unto death, even death on a cross" (Phil. 2:8), "God has highly exalted him" (Phil. 2:9). By raising Christ from the dead, God the Father was in effect saying that he approved of Christ's work of suffering and dying for our sins, that his work was completed, and that Christ no longer had any need to remain dead. There was no penalty left to pay for sin, no more wrath of God to bear, no more guilt or liability to punishment—

---

[5]See ch. 20, pp. 300–305, for a discussion of regeneration.
[6]See ch. 22, pp. 316–23, on justification.

all had been completely paid for and no guilt remained. In the resurrection, God was saying to Christ, "I approve of what you have done and you find favor in my sight."

This explains how Paul can say that Christ was "raised for our justification" (Rom. 4:25). If God "raised us up with him" (Eph. 2:6), then, by virtue of our union with Christ, God's declaration of approval of Christ is also his declaration of approval of us. When the Father in essence said to Christ, "All the penalty for sins has been paid and I find you not guilty but righteous in my sight," he was thereby making the declaration that would also apply to us once we trusted in Christ for salvation. In this way Christ's resurrection also gave final proof that he had earned our justification.

c. *Christ's resurrection insures that we will receive perfect resurrection bodies as well.* The New Testament several times connects Jesus' resurrection with our final bodily resurrection. "God raised the Lord and *will also raise us up* by his power" (1 Cor. 6:14). Similarly, "he who raised the Lord Jesus *will raise us also* with Jesus and bring us with you into his presence" (2 Cor. 4:14). But the most extensive discussion of the connection between Christ's resurrection and our own is found in 1 Corinthians 15:12–58. There Paul says that Christ is the "first fruits of those who have fallen asleep" (1 Cor. 15:20). In calling Christ the "first fruits" (Gk. *Aparchē*), Paul uses a metaphor from agriculture to indicate that we will be like Christ. Just as the "first fruits" or the first taste of the ripening crop show what the rest of the harvest will be like for that crop, so Christ as the "first fruits" shows what our resurrection bodies will be like when, in God's final "harvest," he raises us from the dead and brings us into his presence.[7]

After Jesus' resurrection, he still had the nail prints in his hands and feet and the mark from the spear in his side (John 20:27). People sometimes wonder if that indicates that the scars of serious injuries that we have received in this life will also remain on our resurrection bodies. The answer is that we probably will not have any scars from injuries or wounds received in this life, but our bodies will be made perfect, "incorruptible" and raised "in glory." The scars from Jesus' crucifixion were unique because they are an eternal reminder of his sufferings and death for us. In fact, the evidences of the severe beating and disfigurement that Jesus suffered before his crucifixion were probably all healed, and only the scars in his hands, feet, and side remained as testimony to his death for us. The fact the he retains those scars does not necessarily mean that we shall retain ours. Rather, all will be healed, and all will be made perfect and whole.

5. Ethical significance of the resurrection. Paul also sees that the resurrection has application to our obedience to God in this life. After a long discussion of the resurrection, Paul concludes by encouraging his readers, "*Therefore,* my beloved brethren, be steadfast, immovable, always abounding in the work of the Lord, knowing that in the Lord your labor is not in vain" (1 Cor. 15:58). It is because Christ was raised from the dead, and we too shall be raised from the dead, that we should *continue steadfastly in the Lord's work.* This is because everything that we do to bring people into the kingdom and build them up will indeed have eternal significance, because we shall all be raised on the day when Christ returns, and we shall live with him forever.

---

[7]See ch. 25, pp. 357–58, for a more detailed discussion of the nature of our resurrection bodies.

Second, Paul encourages us, when we think about the resurrection, to *focus on our future heavenly reward* as our goal. He sees the resurrection as a time when all the struggles of this life will be repaid. But if Christ has not been raised and if there is no resurrection, then "your faith is futile and you are still in your sins. Then those also who have fallen asleep in Christ have perished. If for this life only we have hoped in Christ, *we are of all men most to be pitied*" (1 Cor. 15:17–19; cf. v. 32). But because Christ has been raised, and because we have been raised with him, we are to seek for a heavenly reward and set our mind on things of heaven: "*If then you have been raised with Christ, seek the things that are above*, where Christ is, seated at the right hand of God. Set your minds on things that are above, not on things that are on earth. For you have died, and your life is hid with Christ in God. When Christ who is our life appears, then you also will appear with him in glory" (Col. 3:1–4).

A third ethical application of the resurrection is the obligation to *stop yielding to sin in our lives.* When Paul says we are to consider ourselves "dead to sin and alive to God in Christ Jesus" by virtue of the resurrection of Christ and his resurrection power within us (Rom. 6:11), he then goes on immediately to say, "*Let not sin therefore reign* in your mortal bodies. . . . Do not yield your members to sin" (Rom. 6:12–13). The fact that we have this new resurrection power over the domination of sin in our lives is used by Paul as a reason to exhort us not to sin any more.

B. Ascension into Heaven

1. Christ ascended to a place. After Jesus' resurrection, he was on earth for forty days (Acts 1:3), then he led his followers out to Bethany, just outside Jerusalem, and "lifting up his hands, he blessed them. While he blessed them, *he parted from them, and was carried up into heaven*" (Luke 24:50–51).

A similar account is given by Luke in the opening section of Acts: "When he had said this, as they were looking on, *he was lifted up, and a cloud took him out of their sight.* And while they were gazing into heaven as he went, behold, two men stood by them in white robes, and said, 'Men of Galilee, why do you stand looking into heaven? This Jesus, who was taken up from you into heaven, will come in the same way as you saw him go into heaven'" (Acts 1:9–11).

These narratives describe an event that is clearly designed to show the disciples that Jesus went to a place. He did not suddenly disappear from them, never to be seen by them again, but gradually ascended as they were watching, and then a cloud (apparently the cloud of God's glory) took him from their sight. But the angels immediately said that he would come back *in the same way* in which he had gone into heaven. The fact that Jesus had a resurrection body that was subject to spatial limitations (it could be at only one place at one time) means that Jesus went *somewhere* when he ascended into heaven.[8]

2. Christ received glory and honor that had not been his before as the God-man. When Jesus ascended into heaven, he received glory, honor, and authority that had never been his before as one who was both God and man. Before Jesus died, he prayed, "Father, glorify me in your own presence with the glory which I had with you before the world was made" (John 17:5). In his sermon at Pentecost, Peter said that Jesus was "exalted at the right hand of God" (Acts 2:33), and Paul declared

---

[8]See ch. 34, pp. 466–67, for further discussion on heaven as a place.

that "God has highly exalted him" (Phil. 2:9), and that he was "taken up in glory" (1 Tim. 3:16; cf. Heb. 1:4). Christ is now in heaven with the angelic choirs singing praise to him with the words, "Worthy is the Lamb who was slain, to receive power and wealth and wisdom and might and honor and glory and blessing!" (Rev. 5:12).

3. Christ was seated at God's right hand (Christ's session). One specific aspect of Christ's ascension into heaven and receiving of honor was the fact that he *sat down* at the right hand of God. This is sometimes called his *session* at God's right hand.

The Old Testament predicted that the Messiah would sit at the right hand of God: "The LORD says to my lord: '*Sit at my right hand*, till I make your enemies your footstool'" (Ps. 110:1). When Christ ascended back into heaven, he received the fulfillment of that promise: "When he had made purification for sins, he *sat down* at the right hand of the Majesty on high" (Heb. 1:3). This welcoming into the presence of God and sitting at God's right hand is a dramatic indication of the completion of Christ's work of redemption. Just as a human being will sit down at the completion of a large task to enjoy the satisfaction of having accomplished it, so Jesus sat at the right hand of God, visibly demonstrating that his work of redemption was completed.

In addition to showing the completion of Christ's work of redemption, the act of sitting at God's right hand is an indication that he received authority over the universe. Paul says that God "raised him from the dead and made him sit at his right hand in the heavenly places, far above all rule and authority and power and dominion, and above every name that is named" (Eph. 1:20–21). Similarly, Peter says that Jesus "has gone into heaven and is at the right hand of God, with angels, authorities, and powers subject to him" (1 Peter 3:22). Paul also alludes to Psalm 110:1 when he says that Christ "must reign until he has put all his enemies under his feet" (1 Cor. 15:25).

One additional aspect of the authority that Christ received from the Father when he sat at his right hand was the authority to pour out the Holy Spirit on the church. Peter says on the Day of Pentecost, "Being therefore exalted at the right hand of God, and *having received from the Father the promise of the Holy Spirit*, he has poured out this which you see and hear" (Acts 2:33).

The fact that Jesus now sits at the right hand of God in heaven does not mean that he is perpetually "fixed" there or that he is inactive. He is also seen as standing at God's right hand (Acts 7:56) and as walking among the seven golden lampstands in heaven (Rev. 2:1). Just as a human king sits on his royal throne at his accession to the kingship but then engages in many other activities throughout each day, so Christ sat at the right hand of God as a dramatic evidence of the completion of his redemptive work and his reception of authority over the universe, but he is certainly engaged in other activities in heaven as well.

4. Christ's ascension has doctrinal significance for our lives. Just as the resurrection has profound implications for our lives, so Christ's ascension has significant implications for us. First, since we are united with Christ in every aspect of his work of redemption, Christ's going up into heaven foreshadows our future ascension into heaven with him. "We who are alive, who are left, shall be caught up together with them in the clouds to meet the Lord in the air; and so we shall always be with the Lord" (1 Thess. 4:17). The author of Hebrews wants us to run the race of life with the knowledge that we are following in Jesus' steps and will eventually arrive at the blessings of life in heaven that he is now enjoying: "Let us run with perseverance the race that is set before us, looking to Jesus the pioneer and perfecter of our faith, who for the joy that was set before him endured the cross, despising the shame, and is seated at the right hand of the throne of God" (Heb. 12:1–2). And Jesus himself says that he will one day take us to be with himself (John 14:3).

Second, Jesus' ascension gives us assurance that our final home will be in heaven with him. "In my Father's house are many rooms; if it were not so, would I have told you that I go to prepare a place for you? And when I go and prepare a place for you, I will come again and will take you to myself, that where I am you may be also" (John 14:2–3). Jesus was a man like us in every way yet without sin, and he has gone before us so that eventually we might follow him there and live with him forever. The fact that Jesus has already ascended into heaven and achieved the goal set before him gives great assurance to us that we will eventually go there also.

Third, because of our union with Christ in his ascension, we are able to share now (in part) in Christ's authority over the universe, and we will later share in it more fully. This is what Paul points to when he says that God "raised us up with him, and made us *sit with him in the heavenly places* in Christ Jesus" (Eph. 2:6). We are not physically present in heaven, of course, for we remain here on earth at the present time. But if Christ's session at God's right hand refers to his reception of authority, then the fact that God has made us sit with Christ means that *we now share in some measure in the authority that Christ has,* authority to contend against "the spiritual hosts of wickedness in the heavenly places" (Eph. 6:12; cf. vv. 10–18) and to do battle with weapons that "have divine power to destroy strongholds" (2 Cor. 10:4).

This sharing in Christ's authority over the universe will be made more fully our possession in the age to come: "Do you not know that we are to judge angels?" (1 Cor. 6:3). Moreover, we will share with Christ in his authority over the creation that God has made (Heb. 2:5–8). Jesus promises, "He who conquers and who keeps my works until the end, *I will give him power over the nations,* and he shall rule them with a rod of iron, as when earthen pots are broken in pieces, even as I myself have received power from my Father" (Rev. 2:26–27). He also promises, "He who conquers, *I will grant him to sit with me on my throne,* as I myself conquered and sat down with my Father on his throne" (Rev. 3:21). These are amazing promises of our future sharing in Christ's sitting at the right hand of God, promises that we will not fully understand until the age to come.

II. REVIEW QUESTIONS

1. Did Jesus have a physical body after his resurrection? Give scriptural support for your answer.

2. Give three reasons for the significance of Christ's resurrection.

3. What implications does Christ's resurrection have for the state of Christians after they die?

4. Where did Christ go when he ascended? Is this an actual place?

5. What significance does Christ's ascension have for our lives as believers?

III. QUESTIONS FOR PERSONAL APPLICATION

1. As you read this chapter, what aspects of the Bible's teaching about Christ's resurrection body were new to your understanding? As you realize that we will someday have a body like his, can you think of some characteristics of the resurrection body that you especially look forward to? How does the thought of having such a body make you feel?

2. What things would you like to do now but find yourself unable to do because of the weakness or limitations of your own physical body? Do you think these activities would be appropriate to your life in heaven? Will you be able to do them then?

3. When you were born again, you received new spiritual life within. If you think of this new spiritual life as part of the resurrection power of Christ working within you, how does that give you encouragement in living the Christian life and in ministering to people's needs?

4. The Bible says that you are now seated with Christ in the heavenly places (Eph. 2:6). As you meditate on this fact, how will it affect your prayer life and your engaging in spiritual warfare against demonic forces?

5. When you think of Christ now in heaven, does it cause you to focus more attention on things that will have eternal significance? Does it increase your assurance that you will someday be with him in heaven? How do you feel about the prospect of reigning with Christ over the nations and over angels as well?

IV. SPECIAL TERMS

ascension	raised in power
first fruits	resurrection
incorruptible	session
raised in glory	spiritual body

V. SCRIPTURE MEMORY PASSAGE

1 Corinthians 15:20–23

But in fact Christ has been raised from the dead, the first fruits of those who have fallen asleep. For as by a man came death, by a man has come also the resurrection of the dead. For as in Adam all die, so also in Christ shall all be made alive. But each in his own order: Christ the first fruits, then at his coming those who belong to Christ.

PART V

The Doctrine of the Application of Redemption

CHAPTER SEVENTEEN

Common Grace

+ *What are the undeserved blessings that God gives to all people, both believers and unbelievers?*

I. EXPLANATION AND SCRIPTURAL BASIS

A. Introduction and Definition

When Adam and Eve sinned, they became worthy of eternal punishment and separation from God (Gen. 2:17). In the same way, when human beings sin today, they become liable to the wrath of God and to eternal punishment: "The wages of sin is death" (Rom. 6:23). This means that once people sin, God's justice would require only one thing—that they be eternally separated from God, cut off from experiencing *any* good from him, and that they live forever in hell, receiving only his wrath eternally. In fact, this was what happened to angels who sinned, and it could justly have happened to us as well: "*God did not spare the angels when they sinned,* but cast them into hell and committed them to pits of nether gloom to be kept until the judgment" (2 Peter 2:4).

But in fact Adam and Eve did not die at once (though the sentence of death *began* to be worked out in their lives on the day they sinned). The full execution of the sentence of death was delayed for many years. Moreover, millions of their descendants even to this day do not die and go to hell as soon as they sin, but continue to live for many years, enjoying countless blessings in this world. How can this be? *How can God continue to give blessings to sinners who deserve only death*—not only to those who will ultimately be saved, but also to millions who will never be saved, whose sins will never be forgiven?

The answer to these questions is that God bestows *common grace.* We may define common grace as follows: *Common grace is the grace of God by which he gives people innumerable blessings that are not part of salvation.* The word *common* here means something that is common to all people and is not restricted to believers or to the elect only.

In distinction from common grace, the grace of God that brings people to salvation is often called "saving grace." Of course, when we talk about "common grace" and "saving grace," we are not implying that there are two different kinds of grace in God himself, but only that God's grace manifests itself in the world in two different ways. Common grace is different from saving grace in its *results* (it does not bring about salvation), in its *recipients* (it is given to believers and unbelievers alike), and in its *source* (it does not directly flow from Christ's atoning work, since Christ's death did not earn any measure of forgiveness for unbelievers and therefore did not merit the blessings of common grace for them either). However, on this last point, it should be said that common grace does flow *indirectly* from Christ's redemptive work, because the fact that God did not judge the world at once when sin entered it was primarily or perhaps exclusively due to the fact that he planned eventually to save some sinners through the death of his Son.

B. Examples of Common Grace

If we look at the world around us and contrast it with the fires of hell that the world deserves, we can immediately see abundant evidence of God's common grace in thousands of examples in everyday life. We can distinguish several specific categories in which this common grace is seen.

1. The physical realm. Unbelievers continue to live in this world solely because of God's common grace—every breath that people take is of grace, for the wages of sin is death, not life. Moreover, the earth does not produce only thorns and thistles (Gen. 3:18), or remain a parched desert, but by God's common grace it produces food and materials for clothing and shelter, often in great abundance and diversity. Jesus said, "Love your enemies and pray for those who persecute you, so that you may be sons of your Father who is in heaven; for *he makes his sun rise on the evil and on the good, and sends rain on the just and on the unjust*" (Matt. 5:44–45). Here Jesus appeals to God's abundant common grace as an encouragement to his disciples that they too should bestow love and prayer for blessing on unbelievers (cf. Luke 6:35–36). Similarly, Paul told the people of Lystra, "In past generations he allowed all the nations to walk in their own ways; yet he did not leave himself without witness, for he did good and *gave you from heaven rains and fruitful seasons, satisfying your hearts with food and gladness*" (Acts 14:16–17).

The Old Testament also speaks of the common grace of God that comes to unbelievers as well as to believers. One specific example is Potiphar, the Egyptian captain of the guard who purchased Joseph as a slave: "*The LORD blessed the Egyptian's house* for Joseph's sake; the blessing of the LORD was upon all that he had, in house and field" (Gen. 39:5). David speaks in a much more general way about all the creatures God has made:

> The LORD is good to all,
>   and his compassion is over all that he has made. . . .
> The eyes of all look to you,
>   and you give them their food in due season.
> You open your hand,
>   you satisfy the desire of every living thing. (Ps. 145:9, 15–16)

These verses are another reminder that the goodness that is found in the whole creation did not "just happen" automatically—it is due to God's goodness and compassion.

2. The intellectual realm. Satan is "a liar and the father of lies" and "there is no truth in him" (John 8:44), because he is fully given over to evil and to the irrationality and commitment to falsehood that accompanies radical evil. But human beings in the world today, even unbelievers, are not totally given over to lying, irrationality, and ignorance. All people are able to have some grasp of truth; indeed, some have great intelligence and understanding. This also must be seen as a result of God's grace. John speaks of Jesus as "the true light that *enlightens every man*" (John 1:9), for in his role as creator and sustainer of the universe (not particularly in his role as redeemer) the Son of God allows enlightenment and understanding to come to all people in the world.

God's common grace in the intellectual realm is seen in the fact that all people have a knowledge of God: "Although *they knew God* they did not honor him as God or give thanks to him" (Rom. 1:21). This means that there is a sense of God's existence and often a hunger to know God that he allows to remain in people's hearts, even though it often results in many differing man-made religions. Therefore, even when speaking to people who held to false religions, Paul could find a point of contact regarding knowledge of God's existence, as he did when speaking to the Athenian philosophers: "Men of Athens, I perceive that in every way you are very religious. . . . What therefore you worship as unknown, this I proclaim to you" (Acts 17:22–23).

The common grace of God in the intellectual realm also results in an ability to grasp truth and distinguish it from error, and to experience growth in knowledge that can be used in the investigation of the universe and in the task of subduing the earth. This means that *all science and technology carried out by non-Christians is a result of common grace,* allowing them to make incredible discoveries and inventions, to develop the earth's resources into many material goods, to produce and distribute those resources, and to have skill in their productive work. In a practical sense, this means that every time we walk into a grocery store or ride in an automobile or enter a house we should remember that we are experiencing the results of the abundant common grace of God poured out so richly on all mankind.

3. The moral realm. God also by common grace restrains people from being as evil as they could be. Once again the demonic realm, totally devoted to evil and destruction, provides a clear contrast with human society in which evil is clearly restrained. If people persist hard-heartedly and repeatedly in following sin over a course of time, God will eventually "give them up" to greater and greater sin (cf. Ps. 81:12; Rom. 1:24, 26, 28), but in the case of most human beings they do not fall to the depths to which their sin would otherwise take them, because God intervenes and puts restraints on their conduct. One very effective restraint is the force of conscience: Paul says, "When Gentiles who have not the law do by nature what the law requires, they are a law to themselves, even though they do not have the law. They show that *what the law requires is written on their hearts,* while *their conscience also bears witness* and their conflicting thoughts accuse or perhaps excuse them" (Rom. 2:14–15).

This inward sense of right and wrong that God gives to all people means that they will frequently approve of moral standards that reflect many of the moral standards in Scripture. Even those who are given up to the most base sin, Paul says, "*Know God's decree* that those who do such things deserve to die" (Rom. 1:32). And in many other cases, this inward sense of conscience leads people to establish laws and customs in society that are, in terms of the outward behavior they approve or prohibit, quite like the moral laws of Scripture. People often establish laws or have customs that respect the sanctity of marriage and the family, protect human life, and prohibit theft and falsehood in speech. Because of this, people will frequently live in ways that are morally upright and outwardly conform to the moral standards found in Scripture. Though their moral behavior cannot earn merit with God (since Scripture clearly says that "no man is justified before God by the law," Gal. 3:11, and "All have turned aside, together they have gone wrong; no one does good, not even one," Rom. 3:12), nevertheless, in some sense less than earning God's eternal approval or merit, unbelievers do "do good." Jesus implies this when he says, "If you do good to those *who do good to you*, what credit is that to you? For *even sinners do the same*" (Luke 6:33).

4. The creative realm. God has allowed significant measures of skill in artistic and musical areas, as well as in other spheres in which creativity and skill can be expressed, such as athletics, cooking, writing, and so forth. Moreover, God gives to us an ability to appreciate beauty in many areas of life. And in this area as well as in the physical and intellectual realm, the blessings of common grace are sometimes poured out on unbelievers even more abundantly than on believers. Yet in all cases, it is a result of the grace of God.

5. The societal realm. God's grace is also evident in the existence of various organizations and structures in human society. We see this first in the human family, evidenced in the fact that Adam and Eve remained husband and wife after the fall and then had children, both sons and daughters (Gen. 5:4). Adam and Eve's children married and formed families for themselves (Gen. 4:17, 19, 26). The human family persists today, not simply as an institution for believers, but for all people.

Human government is also a result of common grace. It was instituted in principle by God after the flood (see Gen. 9:6) and is clearly stated to be given by God in Romans 13:1: "There is no authority except from God, and those that exist have been instituted by God." It is clear that government is a gift from God for mankind generally, for Paul says the ruler is "God's servant for your good" and that he is "the servant of God to execute his wrath on the wrongdoer" (Rom. 13:4). One of the primary means God uses to restrain evil in the world is human government. Human laws and police forces and judicial systems provide a powerful deterrent to evil actions, and these are necessary, for there is much evil in the world that is irrational and that can only be restrained by force, because it will not be deterred by reason or education. Of course, the sinfulness of people can also affect governments themselves, so that they become corrupt and actually encourage evil rather than encourage good. This is just to say that human government, like all the other blessings of common grace that God gives, can be used either for good or for evil purposes.

Other organizations in human society include educational institutions, businesses and corporations, voluntary associations (such as many charitable and public service groups), and countless examples of ordinary human friendship. All of these function to bring some measure of good to human beings, and all are expressions of the common grace of God.

6. The religious realm. Even in the realm of human religion, God's common grace brings some blessings to unbelieving people. Jesus tells us, "Love your enemies and *pray for those who persecute you*" (Matt. 5:44), and since there is no restriction in the context simply to pray for their salvation, and since the command to pray for our persecutors is coupled with a command to love them, it seems reasonable to conclude that God intends to answer our prayers even for our persecutors with regard to many areas of life. In fact, Paul specifically commands that we pray "for kings and all who are in high positions" (1 Tim. 2:1–2). When we seek good for unbelievers, it is consistent with God's own practice of granting sunshine and rain "on the just and on the unjust" (Matt. 5:45) and also consistent with the practice of Jesus during his earthly ministry when he healed every person who was brought to him (Luke 4:40). There is no indication that he required all of them to believe in him or to agree that he was the Messiah before he granted physical healing to them.

Does God answer the prayers of unbelievers? Although God has not promised to answer the prayers of unbelievers as he has promised to answer the prayers of those who come in Jesus' name, and although he has no obligation to answer the prayers of unbelievers, nonetheless, God may out of his common grace still hear and grant the prayers of unbelievers, thus demonstrating his mercy and goodness in yet another way (cf. Ps. 145:9, 15; Matt. 7:22; Luke 6:35–36). This is apparently the sense of 1 Timothy 4:10, which says that God is "the Savior of all men, especially of those who believe." Here "Savior" cannot be restricted in meaning to "one who forgives sins and gives eternal life," because these things are not given to those who do not believe. "Savior" must have a more general sense here—namely, "one who rescues from distress, one who delivers." In cases of trouble or distress, God often does hear the prayers of unbelievers and graciously delivers them from their trouble. Moreover, even unbelievers often have a sense of gratitude toward God for the goodness of creation, for deliverance from danger, and for the blessings of family, home, friendships, and country.

7. *Common grace does not save people.* In spite of all of this, we must realize that common grace is different from saving grace. Common grace does not change the human heart or bring people to genuine repentance and faith—it cannot and does not save people (though in the intellectual and moral sphere it can give some preparation to make people more disposed toward accepting the gospel). Common grace restrains sin but does not change anyone's foundational disposition to sin, nor does it in any significant measure purify fallen human nature.

We must also recognize that the actions of unbelievers performed by virtue of common grace do not in themselves merit God's approval or favor. These actions do not spring from faith ("Whatever does not proceed from faith is sin," Rom. 14:23), nor are they motivated by a love for God (Matt. 22:37), but rather love of self in some form or another. Therefore, although we may readily say that the works of unbelievers that externally conform to the laws of God are "good" in some sense, they nonetheless are not good in terms of meriting God's approval nor of making God obligated to the sinner in any way.

Finally, we should recognize that unbelievers often receive more common grace than believers—they may be more skillful, harder working, more intelligent, more creative, or have more of the material benefits of this life to enjoy. This in no way indicates that they are more favored by God in an absolute sense or that they will gain any share in eternal salvation, but only that God distributes the blessings of common grace in various ways, often granting very significant blessings to unbelievers. In all of this, they should, of course, acknowledge God's goodness (Acts 14:17) and should recognize that God's revealed will is that "God's kindness" should eventually lead them "to repentance" (Rom. 2:4).

C. Reasons for Common Grace

Why does God bestow common grace on undeserving sinners who will never come to salvation? We can suggest at least four reasons.

1. To redeem those who will be saved. Peter says that the day of judgment and final execution of punishment is being delayed because there are yet more people who will be saved: "The Lord is not slow about his promise as some count slowness, but is forbearing toward you, *not wishing that any should perish, but that all should reach repentance.* But the day of the Lord will come like a thief" (2 Peter 3:9–10). In fact, this reason was true from the beginning of human history, for if God wanted to save any people out of the whole mass of sinful humanity, he could not have destroyed all sinners immediately (for then there would be no human race left). He chose rather to allow sinful humans to live for some time so that they might have an opportunity to repent and also so that they would bear children and enable subsequent generations to live and then hear the gospel and repent.

2. To demonstrate God's goodness and mercy. God's goodness and mercy are not only seen in the salvation of believers, but also in the blessings he gives to undeserving sinners. When God "is kind to the ungrateful and the selfish" (Luke 6:35), his kindness is revealed in the universe, to his glory. David says, "The LORD is *good to all,* and his compassion is over all that he has made" (Ps. 145:9). In the story of Jesus talking with the rich young ruler, we read, "Jesus looking upon him *loved him*" (Mark 10:21), even though the man was an unbeliever and would in a moment turn away from Jesus because of his great possessions. Berkhof says that God "showers untold blessings upon all men and also clearly indicates that these are the expressions of a favorable disposition in God, which falls short however of the positive volition to pardon their sin, to lift their sentence, and to grant them salvation."[1]

It is not unjust for God to delay the execution of punishment upon sin and to give temporary blessings to human beings, because the punishment is not forgotten, but just delayed. In delaying punishment, God shows clearly that he has no pleasure in executing final judgment, but rather delights in the salvation of men and women. "As I live, says the Lord GOD, I have no pleasure in the death of the wicked, but that the wicked turn back from his way and live" (Ezek. 33:11). God "desires all men to be saved and to come to the knowledge of the truth" (1 Tim. 2:4). In all of this the delay of punishment gives clear evidence of God's mercy and goodness and love.

3. To demonstrate God's justice. When God repeatedly invites sinners to come to faith and when they repeatedly refuse his invitations, the justice of God in condemning them is seen much more clearly. Paul warns that those who persist in unbelief are simply storing up more wrath for themselves: "By your hard and impenitent heart you are storing up wrath for yourself on the day of wrath when God's righteous judgment will be revealed" (Rom. 2:5). On the day of judgment, "every mouth" will be "stopped" (Rom. 3:19), and no one will be able to object that God has been unjust.

4. To demonstrate God's glory. Finally, God's glory is shown in many ways by the activities of human beings in all the areas in which common grace is operative. In developing and exercising dominion over the earth, men and women demonstrate and reflect the wisdom of their Creator, demonstrate Godlike qualities of skill and moral virtue and authority over the universe, and so forth. Though all of these activities are tainted by sinful motives, they nonetheless reflect the excellence of our Creator and therefore bring glory to God, not fully or perfectly, but nonetheless significantly.

---

[1]Louis Berkhof, *Introduction to Systematic Theology* (Grand Rapids: Eerdmans, 1932; reprint, Grand Rapids: Baker, 1979), p. 445.

D. Our Response to the Doctrine of Common Grace

In thinking about the varying kinds of goodness seen in the lives of unbelievers because of God's abundant common grace, we should keep three points in mind:

1. Common grace does not mean that those who receive it will be saved. Even exceptionally large amounts of common grace do not imply that those who receive it will be saved. Even the most skilled, most intelligent, most wealthy and powerful people in the world still need the gospel of Jesus Christ or they will be condemned for eternity! Even the most moral and kind of our neighbors still need the gospel of Jesus Christ or they will be condemned for eternity! They may appear outwardly to have no needs, but Scripture still says that unbelievers are "enemies" of God (Rom. 5:10; cf. Col. 1:21; James 4:4) and are "against" Christ (Matt. 12:30). They "live as enemies of the cross of Christ" and have their "minds set on earthly things" (Phil. 3:18–19) and are "by nature children of wrath, like the rest of mankind" (Eph. 2:3).

2. We must be careful not to reject the good things that unbelievers do as totally evil. By common grace, unbelievers do *some* good, and we should see God's hand in it and be thankful for common grace as it operates in every friendship, every act of kindness, every way in which it brings blessing to others. All of this—though the unbeliever does not know it—is ultimately from God, and he deserves the glory for it.

3. The doctrine of common grace should stir our hearts to much greater thankfulness to God. When we walk down a street and see houses and gardens and families dwelling in security, or when we do business in the marketplace and see the abundant results of technological progress, or when we walk through the woods and see the beauty of nature, or when we are protected by government, or when we are educated from the vast storehouse of human knowledge, we should realize not only that God in his sovereignty is ultimately responsible for all of these blessings, but also that God has granted them all to sinners who are *totally undeserving* of any of them! These blessings in the world are not only evidence of God's power and wisdom, they are also continually a manifestation of his abundant *grace*. The realization of this fact should cause our hearts to swell with thanksgiving to God in every activity of life.

II. REVIEW QUESTIONS

1. If the punishment for sin is death (Rom. 6:23), how can God continue to give blessings to mankind?
2. Differentiate between "saving grace" and "common grace."
3. Give an example of common grace in each of the following realms:
    - The physical realm
    - The intellectual realm
    - The moral realm
    - The creative realm
    - The societal realm
    - The religious realm
4. List four reasons for God's bestowal of common grace.

III. QUESTIONS FOR PERSONAL APPLICATION

1. Before you read this chapter, did you have a different viewpoint on whether unbelievers deserved the ordinary benefits of the world around them? How has your perspective changed, if at all?

2. Do you know of examples when God has answered the prayers of unbelievers who were in difficulty, or answered your prayers for the needs of an unbelieving friend? Has it provided an opening for sharing the gospel? Did the unbeliever eventually come to salvation in Christ? Do you think that God often uses the blessings of common grace as a means to prepare people to receive the gospel?

3. In what ways will this doctrine change the way you relate to an unbelieving neighbor or friend? Will it tend to make you thankful for the good that you see in their lives?

4. Has this chapter changed the way you view demonstrations of skill and creativity in areas such as music, art, architecture, or poetry, or (something that is very similar) the creativity expressed in athletic activities?

5. If you are kind to an unbeliever and he or she never comes to accept Christ, has it done any good in God's sight (see Matt. 5:44–45; Luke 6:32–36)? What good has it done? Why do you think that God is good even to those who will never be saved? Do you think we have any obligation to give more effort to showing good to believers than to unbelievers?

IV. SPECIAL TERMS

common grace

saving grace

V. SCRIPTURE MEMORY PASSAGE

LUKE 6:35–36

Love your enemies, and do good, and lend, expecting nothing in return; and your reward will be great, and you will be sons of the Most High; for he is kind to the ungrateful and the selfish. Be merciful, even as your Father is merciful.

CHAPTER EIGHTEEN

Election

+ *When and why did God choose us?*
+ *Are some not chosen?*

In the earlier chapters, we talked about the fact that we all have sinned and deserve eternal punishment from God, and the fact that Christ died and *earned* salvation for us. But now in the remaining chapters of this unit (chs. 18–25) we will look at the way God *applies* that salvation to our lives. We begin in this chapter with God's work of election, that is, his decision to choose us to be saved before the foundation of the world. This act of election is, of course, not (strictly speaking) part of the *application* of salvation to us, since it came before Christ earned our salvation when he died on the cross. But we treat election at this point because it is chronologically the *beginning* of God's dealing with us in a gracious way. Therefore, it is rightly thought of as the first step in the process of God's bringing salvation to us individually.

Other steps in God's work of applying salvation to our lives include our hearing the gospel call, our being regenerated by the Holy Spirit, our responding in faith and repentance, and God forgiving us and giving us membership in his family, as well as granting us growth in the Christian life and keeping us faithful to himself throughout life. At the end of our life, we die and go into his presence, then when Christ returns, we receive resurrection bodies, and the process of acquiring salvation is complete.

Various theologians have given specific terms to a number of these events and have often listed them in a specific order in which they believe that they occur in our lives. Such a list of the events in which God applies salvation to us is called the *order of salvation* and is sometimes referred to by a Latin phrase, *ordo salutis,* which simply means "order of salvation." Before discussing any of these elements in the application of salvation to our lives, we can give a complete list here of the elements that will be treated in the following chapters:

The Order of Salvation

1. Election (God's choice of people to be saved)
2. The gospel call (proclaiming the message of the gospel)
3. Regeneration (being born again)
4. Conversion (faith and repentance)
5. Justification (right legal standing)
6. Adoption (membership in God's family)
7. Sanctification (right conduct of life)

8. Perseverance (remaining a Christian)
9. Death (going to be with the Lord)
10. Glorification (receiving a resurrection body)

We should note here that items 2–6 and part of 7 are all involved in "becoming a Christian." Numbers 7 and 8 work themselves out in this life, number 9 occurs at the end of this life, and number 10 occurs when Christ returns.

We begin our discussion of the order of salvation with the first element, election. In connection with this, we will also discuss at the end of this chapter the question of "reprobation," the decision of God to pass over those who will not be saved, and to punish them for their sins. As will be explained below, election and reprobation are different in several important respects, and it is important to distinguish these so that we do not think wrongly about God or his activity.

The term *predestination* is also frequently used in this discussion. In this textbook, and in Reformed theology generally, *predestination* is a broader term and includes the two aspects of election (for believers) and reprobation (for unbelievers). However, the term *double predestination* is not a helpful term because it gives the impression that both election and reprobation are carried out in the same way by God and have no essential differences between them, which is certainly not true. Therefore, the term *double predestination* is not generally used by Reformed theologians, though it is sometimes used to refer to Reformed teaching by those who criticize it. The term *double predestination* will not be used in this book to refer to election and reprobation since it blurs the distinctions between them and does not give an accurate indication of what is actually being taught.

I. EXPLANATION AND SCRIPTURAL BASIS

We may define election as follows: *Election is an act of God before creation in which he chooses some people to be saved, not on account of any foreseen merit in them, but only because of his sovereign good pleasure.*

There has been much controversy in the church and much misunderstanding over this doctrine. Many of the controversial questions regarding man's will and responsibility and regarding the justice of God with respect to human choices have been discussed at some length in connection with God's providence (ch. 8). We will focus here only on those additional questions that apply specifically to the question of election.

Our approach in this chapter will be first simply to cite a number of passages from the New Testament that discuss election. Then we will attempt to understand the purpose of God that the New Testament authors see in the doctrine of election. Finally, we will attempt to clarify our understanding of this doctrine and answer some objections, and also to consider the doctrine of reprobation.

A. Does the New Testament Teach Predestination?

Several passages in the New Testament seem to affirm quite clearly that God ordained beforehand those who would be saved. For example, when Paul and Barnabas began to preach to the Gentiles in Antioch in Pisidia, Luke writes, "When the Gentiles heard this, they were glad and glorified the word of God; and *as many as were ordained to eternal life believed*" (Acts 13:48). It is significant that Luke mentions the fact of election almost in passing. It is as if this were the normal occurrence when the gospel was preached. How many believed? "As many as were ordained to eternal life believed."

In Romans 8:28–30, we read: "We know that in everything God works for good with those who love him, who are called according to his purpose. *For those whom he foreknew he also predestined to be conformed to the image of his Son,* in order that he might be the first-born among many brethren. *And those whom he predestined he also called; and those whom he called he also justified; and those whom he justified he also glorified.*"

In the following chapter, when talking about God's choosing Jacob and not Esau, Paul says it was not because of anything that Jacob or Esau had done, but simply in order that God's purpose of election might continue: "Though they were not yet born and had done nothing either good or bad, *in order that God's purpose of election might continue,* not because of works but because of his call, she was told, 'The elder will serve the younger.' As it is written, 'Jacob I loved, but Esau I hated'" (Rom. 9:11–13).

Regarding the fact that some of the people of Israel were saved but others were not, Paul says, "Israel failed to obtain what it sought. *The elect* obtained it, but the rest were hardened" (Rom. 11:7). Here again Paul indicates two distinct groups within the people of Israel. Those who were "the elect" obtained the salvation that they sought, while those who were not the elect simply "were hardened."

Paul talks explicitly about God's choice of believers before the foundation of the world in the beginning of Ephesians: "*He chose us in him before the foundation of the world,* that we should be holy and blameless before him. *He destined us in love* to be his sons through Jesus Christ, according to the purpose of his will, to the praise of his glorious grace" (Eph. 1:4–6).

Here Paul is writing to believers, and he specifically says that God "chose us" in Christ, referring to believers generally. In a similar way, several verses later he says, "We who first hoped in Christ have been *destined and appointed* to live for the praise of his glory" (Eph. 1:12).

He writes to the Thessalonians, "For we know, brethren beloved by God, that *he has chosen you;* for our gospel came to you not only in word, but also in power and in the Holy Spirit and with full conviction" (1 Thess. 1:4–5).

Paul says that the fact that the Thessalonians *believed* the gospel when he preached it ("for our gospel came to you . . . in power . . . and with full conviction") *is the reason he knows that God chose them.* As soon as they came to faith, Paul concluded that long ago God had chosen them, and therefore they had believed when he preached. He later writes to the same church, "We are bound to give thanks to God always for you, brethren beloved by the Lord, because *God chose you from the beginning to be saved,* through sanctification by the Spirit and belief in the truth" (2 Thess. 2:13).

When Paul talks about the reason why God saved us and called us to himself, he explicitly denies that it was because of our works but points rather to God's own purpose and his unmerited grace in eternity past. He says God is the one "who saved us and called us with a holy calling, not in virtue of our works but in virtue of *his own purpose* and the *grace which he gave us in Christ Jesus ages ago*" (2 Tim. 1:9).

When Peter writes an epistle to hundreds of Christians in many churches in Asia Minor, he writes, "To *God's elect* . . . scattered throughout Pontus, Galatia, Cappadocia, Asia and Bithynia" (1 Peter 1:1 NIV). He later calls them "a *chosen* race" (1 Peter 2:9).

In John's vision in Revelation, those who do not give in to persecution and begin to worship the beast are persons whose names have been written in the book of life before the foundation of the world: "And authority was given it over every tribe and people and tongue and nation, and all who dwell on earth will worship it, *every one whose name has not been written before the foundation of the world in the book of life* of the Lamb that was slain" (Rev. 13:7–8). In a similar way, we read of the beast from the bottomless pit in Revelation 17: "The dwellers on earth *whose names have not been written in the book of life from the foundation of the world*, will marvel to behold the beast, because it was and is not and is to come" (Rev. 17:8).

B. How Does the New Testament Present the Teaching of Election?

After reading this list of verses on election, it is important to view this doctrine in the way the New Testament itself views it.

1. As a comfort. The New Testament authors often present the doctrine of election as a comfort to believers. When Paul assures the Romans that "in everything God works for good with those who love him, who are called according to his purpose" (Rom. 8:28), he gives God's work of predestination as a reason why we can be assured of this truth. He explains in the next verse, "*For* those whom he foreknew he also predestined to be conformed to the image of his Son. . . . And those whom he predestined he also called . . . justified . . . glorified" (Rom. 8:29–30). Paul's point is to say that God has *always* acted for the good of those whom he called to himself. If Paul looks into the distant past before the creation of the world, he sees that God *foreknew and predestined* his people to be conformed to the image of Christ.[1] If he looks at the recent past, he finds that God *called and justified* his people whom he had predestined. And if he then looks toward the future when Christ returns, he sees that God has determined to give perfect, *glorified bodies* to those who believe in Christ. From eternity to eternity God has acted with the good of his people in mind. But if God has *always* acted for our good and will in the future act for our good, Paul reasons, then *will he not also in our present circumstances* work every circumstance together for our good as well? In this way predestination is seen as a comfort for believers in the everyday events of life.

2. As a reason to praise God. Paul says, "He destined us in love to be his sons through Jesus Christ, according to the purpose of his will, *to the praise of his glorious grace*" (Eph. 1:5–6). Similarly, he says, "We who first hoped in Christ have been destined and appointed to live *for the praise of his glory*" (Eph. 1:12).

Paul tells the Christians at Thessalonica, "*We give thanks to God* always for you all. . . . *For we know,* brethren beloved by God, *that he has chosen you*" (1 Thess. 1:2, 4). The reason Paul can give thanks to God for the Thessalonian Christians is that he knows God is ultimately responsible for their salvation and has in fact chosen them to be saved. This is made even clearer in 2 Thessalonians 2:13: "But *we are bound to give thanks to God* always for you, brethren beloved by the Lord, *because God chose you* from the beginning to be saved." Paul was obligated to give thanks to God for the Christians at Thessalonica because he knew that their salvation was ultimately due to God's choice of them. Therefore, it is appropriate for Paul to thank God for them rather than praising them for their own saving faith.

---

[1]See the discussion below (p. 286) on the meaning of "foreknow" here.

Understood in this way, the doctrine of election does increase praise given to God for our salvation and seriously diminishes any pride that we might feel if we thought that our salvation was due to something good in us or something for which we should receive credit.

3. As an encouragement to evangelism. Paul says, "I endure everything for the sake of the elect, that they also may obtain salvation in Christ Jesus with its eternal glory" (2 Tim. 2:10). He knows that God has chosen some people to be saved, and he sees this as an encouragement to preach the gospel, even if it means enduring great suffering. Election is Paul's guarantee that there will be some success for his evangelism, for he knows that some of the people he speaks to will be the elect, and they will believe the gospel and be saved. It is as if someone invited us to come fishing and said, "I guarantee that you will catch some fish—they are hungry and waiting."

C. Misunderstandings of the Doctrine of Election

1. Election is not fatalistic or mechanistic. Sometimes those who object to the doctrine of election say that it is "fatalism" or that it presents a "mechanistic system" for the universe. By "fatalism" is meant a system in which human choices and human decisions really do not make any difference. In fatalism, no matter what we do, things are going to turn out as they have been previously ordained. As a result, our humanity is destroyed and the motivation for moral accountability is removed. In a mechanistic system, the picture is one of an impersonal universe in which all things that happen have been inflexibly determined by an impersonal force long ago, and the universe functions in a mechanical way so that human beings are more like machines or robots than genuine persons. Here also genuine human personality would be reduced to the level of a machine that simply functions in accordance with predetermined plans and in response to predetermined causes and influences.

By contrast to the mechanistic picture, the New Testament presents the entire outworking of our salvation as something brought about by a personal God in relationship with personal creatures. God "destined us *in love* to be his sons through Jesus Christ" (Eph. 1:5). God's act of election was neither impersonal nor mechanistic, but was permeated with personal love for those whom he chose. Moreover, when talking about our response to the gospel offer, Scripture continually views us not as mechanistic creatures or robots but as *genuine persons,* personal creatures who make willing choices to accept or reject the gospel.[2] Jesus invites everyone, "*Come to me,* all who labor and are heavy laden, and I will give you rest" (Matt. 11:28). And we read the invitation at the end of Revelation: "The Spirit and the Bride say, 'Come.' And let him who hears say, 'Come.' And let him who is thirsty come, let *him who desires* take the water of life without price" (Rev. 22:17). This invitation and many others like it are addressed to genuine persons who are capable of hearing the invitation and responding to it by a decision of their wills.

In contrast to the charge of fatalism, we also see a much different picture in the New Testament. Not only do we make willing choices as real persons, but these choices are also real choices because they do affect the course of events in the world. They affect our own lives and they affect the lives and destinies of others. So, "*he who believes in him is not condemned; he who does not believe is condemned* already, because

---

[2]See ch. 8, pp. 145–46, for a more extensive discussion of how we can be genuine persons and make real choices when God has beforehand ordained what we do.

he has not believed in the name of the only Son of God" (John 3:18). Our personal decisions to believe or not believe in Christ have eternal consequences in our lives, and Scripture is quite willing to talk about our decision to believe or not believe as the factor that decides our eternal destiny.

The implication of this is that we certainly must preach the gospel, and people's eternal destiny hinges on whether we proclaim the gospel or not. Therefore, when the Lord one night told Paul, "Do not be afraid, but speak and do not be silent; for I am with you, and no man shall attack you to harm you; for *I have many people in this city*" (Acts 18:9–10), Paul did not simply conclude that the "many people" who belong to God would be saved whether he stayed there preaching the gospel or not. Rather, "*he stayed a year and six months,* teaching the word of God among them" (Acts 18:11)—this was longer than Paul stayed in any other city except Ephesus during his three missionary journeys. When Paul was told that God had many elect people in Corinth, he stayed a long time and preached so that those elect people might be saved!

2. Election is not based on God's foreknowledge of our faith. Quite commonly people will agree that God predestines some to be saved, but they will say that he does this by looking into the future and seeing who will believe in Christ and who will not. If he sees that a person is going to come to saving faith, then he will predestine that person to be saved, *based on foreknowledge of that person's faith.* If he sees that a person will not come to saving faith, then he does not predestine that person to be saved. In this way, it is thought, the ultimate reason why some are saved and some are not lies *within the people themselves,* not within God. All that God does in his predestining work is to give confirmation to the decision he knows people will make on their own. The verse commonly used to support this view is Romans 8:29: "For those *whom he foreknew* he also predestined to be conformed to the image of his Son."

a. *Foreknowledge of persons, not facts.* Romans 8:29 can hardly be used to demonstrate that God based his predestination on foreknowledge of *the fact that a person would believe.* The passage speaks rather of the fact that God knew *persons* ("*those whom* he foreknew"), not that he knew some *fact about them,* such as the fact that they would believe. It is a personal, relational knowledge that is spoken of here: God, looking into the future, thought of certain people in saving relationship to himself, and in that sense he "knew them" long ago. This is the sense in which Paul can talk about God's "knowing" someone, for example, in 1 Corinthians 8:3: "But if one loves God, one is *known by him.*" Similarly, he says, "but now that you have come to know God, or rather *to be known by God . . .*" (Gal. 4:9). When people *know* God in Scripture, or when God *knows* them, it is personal knowledge that involves a saving relationship. Therefore, in Romans 8:29, "those whom he *foreknew*" is best understood to mean, "those whom he long ago *thought of in a saving relationship to himself*" (cf. also Rom. 11:2). The text actually says nothing about God foreknowing or foreseeing that certain people would believe, nor is that idea mentioned in any other text of Scripture.

b. *Scripture never speaks of our faith as the reason God chose us.* In addition, when we look beyond these specific passages that speak of foreknowledge and look at verses that talk about the *reason* God chose us, we find that Scripture never speaks of our faith or the fact that we would come to believe in Christ as the reason God chose us. In fact, Paul seems explicitly to exclude the consideration of anything people would do in life from his understanding of God's choice of Jacob rather than Esau. He says, "Though they were not yet born and had done nothing either good or bad, *in order that God's purpose of election might continue,* not because of works but because of his call, she was told, 'The elder will serve the younger.' As it is written, 'Jacob I loved, but Esau I hated'" (Rom. 9:11–13). Nothing that Jacob or Esau would do in life influenced God's decision; it was simply in order that his purpose of election might continue.

When discussing the Jewish people who have come to faith in Christ, Paul says, "So too at the present time there is a remnant, *chosen by grace.* But if it is by grace, it is no longer on the basis of works" (Rom. 11:5–6). Here again Paul emphasizes God's grace and the complete absence of human merit in the process of election. Similarly, when Paul talks about election in Ephesians, there is no mention of any foreknowledge of the fact that we would believe, or any idea that there was anything worthy or meritorious in us (such as a tendency to believe) that was the basis for God's choosing us. Rather, Paul says, "He destined us *in love* to be his sons through Jesus Christ, *according to the purpose of his will,* to the praise of his glorious grace *which he freely bestowed on us* in the Beloved" (Eph. 1:5–6). Now if God's grace is to be praised for election, and not human ability to believe or decision to believe, then once again it is consistent for Paul to mention nothing of human faith but only to mention God's predestining activity, his purpose and will, and his freely given grace.

c. *Election based on something good in us (our faith) would be the beginning of salvation by merit.* Yet another kind of objection can be brought against the idea that God chose us because he foreknew that we would come to faith. If the ultimate determining factor in whether we will be saved or not is our own decision to accept Christ, then we shall be more inclined to think that we deserve some credit for the fact that we were saved. In distinction from other people who continue to reject Christ, we were wise enough in our judgment or good enough in our moral tendencies or perceptive enough in our spiritual capacities to decide to believe in Christ. By contrast, if election is solely based on God's own good pleasure and his sovereign decision to love us in spite of our lack of goodness or merit, then certainly we have a profound sense of appreciation to him for a salvation that is totally undeserved, and we will forever be willing to praise his "glorious grace" (Eph. 1:6).

In the final analysis, the difference between two views of election can be seen in the answer to a very simple question. Given the fact that in the final analysis some people will choose to accept Christ and some people will not, the question is, "What makes people differ?" That is, what ultimately makes the difference between those who believe and those who do not? If our answer is that it is ultimately based on something God does—namely, his sovereign election of those who would be saved—then we see that salvation at its most foundational level is based on *grace alone.* On the other hand, if we answer that the ultimate difference between those who are saved and those who are not is because of *something in man*—that is, a tendency or disposition to believe or not believe—then salvation ultimately depends on a combination of grace plus human ability.

d. *Predestination based on foreknowledge still does not give people free choice.* The idea that God's predestination of some to believe is based on foreknowledge of their faith encounters still another problem: Upon reflection, this system turns out to give no real freedom to people either. For if God can look into the future and see that person A will come to faith in Christ, and that person B will not come to faith in Christ, then those facts are already fixed, they are already determined. If we assume that God's knowledge of the future is true—which it must be—then it is absolutely certain that person A will believe and person B will not. There is no way that their lives could turn out any differently than this. Therefore, it is fair to say that their destinies are still determined, for they could not be otherwise. But by what are these destinies determined? If they are determined by God himself, then we no longer have election based ultimately on foreknowledge of faith, but rather on God's sovereign will. But if these destinies are not determined by God, then who or what determines them? Certainly no Christian would say that there is some powerful being other than God controlling people's destinies. Therefore, it seems that the only other possible solution is to say they are determined by some impersonal force, some kind of fate, operative in the universe, making things turn out as they do. But what kind of benefit is this? We have then sacrificed election in love by a personal God for a kind of determinism by an impersonal force, and God is no longer to be given the ultimate credit for our salvation.

e. *Conclusion: Election is unconditional.* It seems best, for the previous four reasons, to reject the idea that election is based on God's foreknowledge of our faith. We conclude instead that the reason for election is simply God's sovereign choice— he "destined us in love to be his sons" (Eph. 1:5). God chose us simply because he decided to bestow his love upon us. It was not because of any foreseen faith or foreseen merit in us.

This understanding of election has traditionally been called "unconditional election."[3] It is "unconditional" because it is not conditioned upon anything that God sees in us that makes us worthy of his choosing us.

D. Objections to the Doctrine of Election

It must be said that the doctrine of election as presented here is by no means universally accepted in the Christian church, either in Catholicism or Protestantism. There is a long history of acceptance of the doctrine as presented here, but many others have objected to it. Among current evangelicalism, those in more Reformed or Calvinistic circles (conservative Presbyterian denominations, for example) will accept this view, as will many Lutherans and Anglicans (Episcopalians) and a large number of Baptists and people in independent churches, but it will be rejected quite decisively by nearly all Methodists, as well as by many others in Baptist, Anglican, and independent churches. While a number of the objections to election are more specific forms of objection to the doctrine of providence presented in chapter 9, and have been answered in more detail there, a few specific objections should be mentioned here.

1. Election means that we do not have a choice in whether we accept Christ or not. According to this objection, the doctrine of election denies all the gospel invitations that appeal to the will of man and ask people to make a choice in whether to

---

[3]Unconditional election is the U in the acronym TULIP, which stands for "the five points of Calvinism." The other letters stand for *T*otal depravity (see ch. 13, p. 216), *L*imited atonement, *I*rresistible grace (see ch. 20, p. 301), and *P*erseverance of the saints (see ch. 24, pp. 336–46). Limited atonement (or "particular redemption") is the idea that Christ's death paid the penalty for all who would believe in him but not for those who would not ultimately be saved. This doctrine is not discussed in this book, but see the discussion in Wayne Grudem, *Systematic Theology*, pp. 594–603.

respond to Christ's invitation or not. In response to this, we must affirm that the doctrine of election is fully able to accommodate the idea that we have a voluntary choice and we make willing decisions in accepting or rejecting Christ. Our choices are voluntary because they are what we want to do and what we decide to do, and in that sense they are "free." This does not mean that our choices are absolutely free, because (as explained in ch. 8, on providence) God can sovereignly work through our desires so that he guarantees that our choices come about as he has ordained; but this can still be understood as a real choice, because God has created us, and he ordains that such a choice is real. In short, we can say that God causes us to choose Christ voluntarily. The mistaken assumption underlying this objection is that a choice must be absolutely free (that is, not in any way caused by God) in order for it to be a genuine human choice. However, if God makes us in a certain way and then tells us that our voluntary choices are real and genuine choices, then we must agree that they are.

2. The doctrine of election means that unbelievers never had a chance to believe. This objection to election says that if God had decreed from eternity that some people would not believe, then there was no genuine chance for them to believe, and the entire system functions unfairly. Two responses can be made to this objection. First, we must note that the Bible does not allow us to say that unbelievers "had no chance" to believe, for such a way of expressing the situation puts the blame on God and makes it appear as if unbelievers are not responsible for their unbelief and did not choose it. When people rejected Jesus, he always put the blame on their willful choice to reject him, not on anything decreed by God the Father. "Why do you not understand what I say? It is because you cannot bear to hear my word. You are of your father the devil, and *your will is to do your father's desires*" (John 8:43–44). He said to the Jews who rejected him, "*You refuse to come to me* that you may have life" (John 5:40). Romans 1 makes it plain that all people are confronted with a revelation from God of such clarity that they are "without excuse" (Rom. 1:20). This is the consistent pattern in Scripture: People who remain in unbelief do so because they are unwilling to come to God, and the blame for such unbelief always lies with the unbelievers themselves, never with God.

But the second response to this objection must simply be Paul's answer to a similar objection: "But who are you, a man, to answer back to God? Will what is molded say to its molder, 'Why have you made me thus?'" (Rom. 9:20; note the similarity of the objection Paul mentions in v. 19). This then is related to the next objection.

3. Election is unfair. Sometimes people regard the doctrine of election as unfair, since it teaches that God chooses some to be saved and passes over others, deciding not to save them. How can this be fair?

Two responses may be given at this point. First, we must remember that *it would be perfectly fair for God not to save anyone,* just as he did with the angels: "God did not spare the angels when they sinned, but cast them into hell and committed them to pits of nether gloom to be kept until the judgment" (2 Peter 2:4). What would be perfectly fair for God would be to do with human beings as he did with angels, that is, to save none of those who sinned and rebelled against him. But if he does save some at all, this is a demonstration of grace that goes far beyond the requirements of fairness and justice.

But at a deeper level, this objection would say that it is not fair for God to create some people who he knew would sin and be eternally condemned and whom he would not redeem. Paul raises this objection in Romans 9. After saying that God "has mercy upon whomever he wills, and he hardens the heart of whomever he wills" (Rom. 9:18), Paul then raises this precise objection: "You will say to me then, 'Why does he still find fault? For who can resist his will?'" (Rom. 9:19). Here is the heart of the "unfairness" objection against the doctrine of election. If each person's ultimate destiny is determined by God, not by the person himself or herself—that is, even when people make willing choices that determine whether they will be saved or not, if God is actually behind those choices somehow causing them to occur—how can this be fair?

Paul's response is not one that appeals to our pride, nor does he attempt to give a philosophical explanation of why this is just. He simply calls on God's rights as an omnipotent Creator:

> But who are you, a man, to answer back to God? Will what is molded say to its molder, "Why have you made me thus?" Has the potter no right over the clay, to make out of the same lump one vessel for beauty and another for menial use? What if God, desiring to show his wrath and to make known his power, has endured with much patience the vessels of wrath made for destruction, in order to make known the riches of his glory for the vessels of mercy, which he has prepared beforehand for glory, even us whom he has called, not from the Jews only but also from the Gentiles? (Rom. 9:20–24)

Paul simply says that there is a point beyond which we cannot answer back to God or question his justice. He has done what he has done according to his sovereign will. He is the Creator; we are the creatures, and we ultimately have no basis from which to accuse him of unfairness or injustice. When we read these words of Paul, we are confronted with a decision whether or not to accept what God says here, and what he does, simply because he is God and we are not. It is a question that reaches deep into our understanding of ourselves as creatures and of our relationship to God as our Creator.

4. The Bible says that God wills to save everyone. Another objection to the doctrine of election is that it contradicts certain passages of Scripture that say that God wills for all to be saved. Paul writes of God our Savior, *"who desires all men to be saved and to come to the knowledge of the truth"* (1 Tim. 2:4). And Peter says, "The Lord is not slow about his promise as some count slowness, but is forbearing toward you, *not wishing that any should perish,* but that all should reach repentance" (2 Peter 3:9). Do not these passages contradict the idea that God has only chosen certain people to be saved?

A common solution to this question (from the Reformed perspective advocated in this book) is to say that these verses speak of God's *revealed will* (telling us what we should do), not his *secret will* (his eternal plans for what will happen).[4] The verses simply tell us that God invites and commands every person to repent and come to Christ for salvation, but they do not tell us anything about God's secret decrees regarding who will be saved.

While Arminian theologians sometimes object to the idea that God has a secret and a revealed will, ultimately they also must say that God wills something more

---

[4]For a discussion of the difference between God's revealed will and his secret will, see ch. 5, pp. 96–98.

strongly than he wills the salvation of all people, for in fact all are not saved. Arminians claim that the reason why all are not saved is that God wills to preserve the free
will of man more than he wills to save everyone. But this seems also to be making a
distinction in two aspects of the will of God. On the one hand, God wills that all be
saved (1 Tim. 2:5–6; 2 Peter 3:9). But on the other hand, he wills to preserve man's
absolutely free choice. In fact, he wills the second thing more than the first.

Here the difference between the Reformed and the Arminian conception of
God's will is clearly seen. Both Calvinists and Arminians agree that God's commands
in Scripture reveal to us what he wants us to do, and both agree that the commands
in Scripture invite us to repent and trust in Christ for salvation. Therefore, in one
sense both agree that God wills that we be saved—it is the will that he reveals to us
explicitly in the gospel invitation.

But both sides must also say that there is something else that God deems more
important than saving everyone. Reformed theologians say that God deems his own
glory more important than saving everyone, and that (according to Rom. 9) God's
glory is also furthered by the fact that some are not saved. Arminian theologians also
say that something else is more important to God than the salvation of all people,
namely, the preservation of man's free will. So in a Reformed system, God's highest
value is his own glory, and in an Arminian system, God's highest value is the free will
of man. These are two distinctly different conceptions of God's nature, and it seems
that the Reformed position has much more explicit biblical support than the Arminian position does on this question.

E. The Doctrine of Reprobation

When we understand election as God's sovereign choice of some persons to be
saved, then there is necessarily another aspect of that choice, namely, God's sovereign decision to pass over others and not to save them. This decision of God in eternity past is called reprobation. *Reprobation is the sovereign decision of God before
creation to pass over some persons, in sorrow deciding not to save them, and to punish
them for their sins, and thereby to manifest his justice.*

In many ways, the doctrine of reprobation is the most difficult of all the teachings of Scripture for us to think about and to accept, because it deals with such horrible and eternal consequences for human beings made in God's image. The love
God gives us for our fellow human beings and the love he commands us to have
toward our neighbor cause us to recoil against this doctrine, and it is right that we
feel such dread in contemplating it. It is something that we would not want to
believe, and would not believe, unless Scripture clearly taught it.

But are there Scripture passages that speak of such a decision by God? Certainly
there are some. Jude speaks of some persons "who *long ago were designated for this
condemnation,* ungodly persons who pervert the grace of our God into licentious-
ness and deny our only Master and Lord, Jesus Christ" (Jude 4).

Moreover, Paul, in the passage referred to above, speaks in the same way of
Pharaoh and others: "For the Scripture says to Pharaoh, 'I have raised you up for the
very purpose of showing my power in you, so that my name may be proclaimed in
all the earth.' So then he has mercy upon whomever he wills, and he hardens the
heart of whomever he wills. . . . What if God, desiring to show his wrath and to make
known his power, has endured with much patience the vessels of wrath made for
destruction?" (Rom. 9:17–22). Regarding the results of the fact that God failed to

choose all for salvation, Paul says, "The elect obtained it, but *the rest were hardened*" (Rom. 11:7). And Peter says of those who reject the gospel, "they stumble because they disobey the word, *as they were destined to do*" (1 Peter 2:8).

In spite of the fact that we recoil against this doctrine, we must be careful of our attitude toward God and toward these passages of Scripture. We must never begin to wish that the Bible was written in another way, or that it did not contain these verses. Moreover, if we are convinced that these verses teach reprobation, then we are obligated both to believe it and accept it as fair and just of God, even though it still causes us to tremble in horror as we think of it.

It may help us to recognize that somehow, in God's wisdom, the fact of reprobation and the eternal condemnation of some will show God's justice and also result in his glory. Paul says, "What if God, *desiring to show his wrath and to make known his power,* has endured with much patience the vessels of wrath made for destruction . . . ?" (Rom. 9:22). Paul also notes that the fact of such punishment on the "vessels of wrath" serves to show the greatness of God's mercy toward us: God does this "in order to make known the riches of his glory for the vessels of mercy" (Rom. 9:23).

We also must remember that *there are important differences between election and reprobation as they are presented in the Bible.* Election to salvation is viewed as a cause for rejoicing and praise to God, who is worthy of praise and receives all the credit for our salvation (see Eph. 1:3–6; 1 Peter 1:1–3). God is viewed as actively choosing us for salvation and doing so in love and with delight. But reprobation is viewed as something that brings God sorrow, not delight (see Ezek. 33:11), and the blame for the condemnation of sinners is always put on the men or angels who rebel, never on God himself (see John 3:18–19; 5:40). So in the presentation of Scripture, the cause of election lies in God, and the cause of reprobation lies in the sinner. Another important difference is that the ground of election is God's grace, whereas the ground of reprobation is God's justice. Therefore, "double predestination" is not a helpful or accurate phrase, because it neglects these differences between election and reprobation.

F. Practical Application of the Doctrine of Election

In terms of our own relationship with God, the doctrine of election does have significant practical application. When we think of the biblical teaching on both election and reprobation, it is appropriate to apply it to our own lives individually. It is right for each Christian to ask of himself or herself, "Why am I a Christian? What is the final reason why God decided to save me?"

The doctrine of election tells us that I am a Christian simply because God in eternity past decided to set his love on me. But why did he decide to set his love on me? Not for anything good in me, but simply because he decided to love me. There is no more ultimate reason than that.

It humbles us before God to think in this way. It makes us realize that we have no claim on God's grace whatsoever. Our salvation is totally due to grace alone. Our only appropriate response is to give God eternal praise.

II. REVIEW QUESTIONS

1. Define election, and give three evidences from the New Testament in support of this doctrine.
2. Give three ways in which the New Testament views the doctrine of election.
3. Is God's election of people based on his foreknowledge of their faith? Explain.
4. What is the relationship between God's election and a person's choice to accept Christ?
5. Since both Reformed and Arminian theologians agree that in some sense God wills everyone to be saved (1 Tim. 2:4; 2 Peter 3:9), and since it is also true that not all *are* saved, how would each side of the debate answer the question, "What does God apparently deem more important than saving everyone?"
6. What are the differences between Scripture's presentation of the doctrine of election and the doctrine of reprobation?

III. QUESTIONS FOR PERSONAL APPLICATION

1. Do you think that God chose you individually to be saved before he created the world? Do you think he did it on the basis of the fact that he knew you would believe in Christ, or was it "unconditional election," not based on anything that he foresaw in you that made you worthy of his love? No matter how you answered the previous question, explain how your answer makes you feel when you think about yourself in relationship to God.
2. Does the doctrine of election give you any comfort or assurance about your future?
3. After reading this chapter, do you honestly feel that you would like to give thanks or praise to God for choosing you to be saved? Do you sense any unfairness in the fact that God did not decide to save everyone?
4. If you agree with the doctrine of election as presented in this chapter, does it diminish your sense of individual personhood or make you feel somewhat like a robot or a puppet in God's hands? Do you think it should make you feel this way?
5. What effect do you think this chapter will have on your motivation for evangelism? Is this a positive or negative effect? Can you think of ways in which the doctrine of election can be used as a positive encouragement to evangelism (see 1 Thess. 1:4–5; 2 Tim. 2:10)?

IV. SPECIAL TERMS

determinism	order of salvation
election	predestination
fatalism	reprobation
foreknowledge	

V. SCRIPTURE MEMORY PASSAGE

EPHESIANS 1:3–6

Blessed be the God and Father of our Lord Jesus Christ, who has blessed us in Christ with every spiritual blessing in the heavenly places, even as he chose us in him before the foundation of the world, that we should be holy and blameless before him. He destined us in love to be his sons through Jesus Christ, according to the purpose of his will, to the praise of his glorious grace which he freely bestowed on us in the Beloved.

CHAPTER NINETEEN

The Gospel Call

+ *What is the gospel message?*
+ *How does it become effective?*

I. EXPLANATION AND SCRIPTURAL BASIS

When Paul talks about the way that God brings salvation into our lives, he says, "Those whom he *predestined* he also *called;* and those whom he called he also *justified;* and those whom he justified he also *glorified*" (Rom. 8:30). Here Paul points to a definite order in which the blessings of salvation come to us. Although long ago, before the world was made, God "predestined" us to be his children and to be conformed to the image of his Son, Paul points to the fact that in the actual outworking of his purpose in our lives God "called" us. Then Paul immediately lists justification and glorification, showing that these come after calling. Paul indicates that there is a definite order in God's saving purpose (though not every aspect of our salvation is mentioned here). So we will begin our discussion of the different parts of our experience of salvation with the topic of calling.

A. Effective Calling

When Paul says, "Those whom he predestined *he* also called; and those whom *he* called he also justified" (Rom. 8:30), he indicates that calling is an act of God. In fact, it is specifically an act of God the Father, for he is the one who predestines people "to be conformed to the image of his Son" (Rom. 8:29). Other verses describe more fully what this calling is. When God calls people in this powerful way, he calls them "out of darkness into his marvelous light" (1 Peter 2:9); he calls them "into the fellowship of his Son" (1 Cor. 1:9; cf. Acts 2:39) and "into his own kingdom and glory" (1 Thess. 2:12; cf. 1 Peter 5:10; 2 Peter 1:3). People who have been called by God "belong to Jesus Christ" (Rom. 1:6). They are called to "be saints" (Rom. 1:7; 1 Cor. 1:2), and have come into a realm of peace (1 Cor. 7:15; Col. 3:15), freedom (Gal. 5:13), hope (Eph. 1:18; 4:4), holiness (1 Thess. 4:7), patient endurance of suffering (1 Peter 2:20–21; 3:9), and eternal life (1 Tim. 6:12).

These verses indicate that no powerless, merely human calling is in view. This calling is rather a kind of "summons" from the King of the universe, and it has such power that it brings about the response that it asks for in people's hearts. It is an act of God that *guarantees* a response, because Paul specifies in Romans 8:30 that all who were "called" were also "justified." This calling has the capacity to draw us out of the kingdom of darkness and bring us into God's kingdom and join in full fellowship with him: "God is faithful, by whom you were *called into the fellowship of his Son,* Jesus Christ our Lord" (1 Cor. 1:9).

This powerful act of God is often referred to as *effective calling*, to distinguish it from the general gospel invitation that goes to all people, and which some people reject. This is not to say that human gospel proclamation is not involved. In fact, God's effective calling comes *through* the human preaching of the gospel, because Paul says, "To this he called you *through our gospel*, so that you may obtain the glory of our Lord Jesus Christ" (2 Thess. 2:14). Of course, there are many who hear the general call of the gospel message and do not respond. But in some cases the gospel call is made so effective by the working of the Holy Spirit in people's hearts that they do respond; we can say that they have received "effective calling."

We may define effective calling as follows: *Effective calling is an act of God the Father, speaking through the human proclamation of the gospel, in which he summons people to himself in such a way that they respond in saving faith.*

It is important that we not give the impression that people will be saved by the power of this call *apart from* their own willing response to the gospel (see ch. 21 on the personal faith and repentance that are necessary for conversion). Although it is true that effective calling awakens and brings forth a response from us, we must always insist that this response still has to be a voluntary, willing response in which the individual puts his or her trust in Christ.

This is why prayer is so important to effective evangelism. Unless God works in peoples' hearts to make the proclamation of the gospel effective, there will be no genuine saving response. Jesus said, "No one can come to me unless the Father who sent me draws him" (John 6:44).

An example of the gospel call working effectively is seen in Paul's first visit to Philippi. When Lydia heard the gospel message, "The Lord *opened her heart* to give heed to what was said by Paul" (Acts 16:14).

In distinction from effective calling, which is entirely an act of God, we may talk about the *gospel call* in general, which comes through human speech. This gospel call is offered to all people, even those who do not accept it. Sometimes this gospel call is referred to as *external calling* or *general calling*. By contrast, the effective calling of God that actually brings about a willing response from the person who hears it is sometimes called *internal calling*. The gospel call is general and external and often rejected, while the effective call is particular, internal, and *always* effective. However, this is not to diminish the importance of the gospel call—it is the means God has appointed through which effective calling will come. Without the gospel call, no one could respond and be saved! "How are they to believe in him of whom they have never heard?" (Rom. 10:14). Therefore, it is important to understand exactly what the gospel call is.

B. The Elements of the Gospel Call

Three important elements must be included in human preaching of the gospel.

1. Explanation of the facts concerning salvation. Anyone who comes to Christ for salvation must have at least a basic understanding of who Christ is and how he meets our needs for salvation. Therefore, an explanation of the facts concerning salvation must include at least the following:

    a. All people have sinned (Rom. 3:23).
    b. The penalty for our sin is death (Rom. 6:23).
    c. Jesus Christ died to pay the penalty for our sins (Rom. 5:8).

But understanding those facts and even agreeing that they are true is not enough for a person to be saved. There must also be an invitation for a personal response on the part of the individual who will repent of his or her sins and trust personally in Christ.

2. Invitation to respond to Christ personally in repentance and faith. When the New Testament talks about people coming to salvation, it speaks in terms of a personal response to an invitation from Christ himself. That invitation is beautifully expressed, for example, in the words of Jesus: "*Come to me,* all you who are weary and burdened, and I will give you rest. Take my yoke upon you and learn from me, for I am gentle and humble in heart, and you will find rest for your souls. For my yoke is easy and my burden is light" (Matt. 11:28–30 NIV).

It is important to make clear that these are not just words spoken a long time ago by a religious leader in the past. Every non-Christian hearing these words should be encouraged to think of them as words that Jesus Christ is *even now,* at *this very moment,* speaking to him or to her individually. Jesus Christ is a Savior who is now alive in heaven, and each non-Christian should think of Jesus as speaking directly to him or to her, saying, "*Come to me* . . . and I will give you rest" (Matt. 11:28). This is a genuine *personal* invitation that seeks a personal response from each one who hears it.

John also talks about the need for personal response when he says, "He came to his own home, and his own people received him not. *But to all who received him,* who believed in his name, he gave power to become children of God" (John 1:11–12). In emphasizing the need to "receive" Christ, John, too, points to the necessity of an individual response. To those inside a lukewarm church who do not realize their spiritual blindness the Lord Jesus again issues an invitation that calls for personal response: "Behold, I stand at the door and knock; if any one hears my voice and opens the door, I will come in to him and eat with him, and he with me" (Rev. 3:20).

But what is involved in coming to Christ? Although this will be explained more fully in chapter 23, it is sufficient to note here that if we come to Christ and trust him to save us from our sin, we cannot any longer cling to sin but must willingly renounce it in genuine repentance. In some cases in Scripture both repentance and faith are mentioned together when referring to someone's initial conversion (Paul said that he spent his time "testifying both to Jews and to Greeks of *repentance* to God and of *faith* in our Lord Jesus Christ," Acts 20:21). At other times only repentance of sins is named and saving faith is assumed as an accompanying factor ("that *repentance* and forgiveness of sins should be preached in his name to all nations," Luke 24:47; cf. Acts 2:37–38; 3:19; 5:31; 17:30; Rom. 2:4; 2 Cor. 7:10; et al.). Therefore, any genuine gospel proclamation must include an invitation to make a conscious decision to forsake one's sins and come to Christ in faith, asking Christ for forgiveness of sins. If either the need to repent of sins or the need to trust in Christ for forgiveness is neglected, there is not a full and true proclamation of the gospel.

But what is promised for those who come to Christ? This is the third element of the gospel call.

3. A promise of forgiveness and eternal life. Although Christ's words of personal invitation do have promises of rest, power to become children of God, and access to the water of life, it is helpful to make explicit just what Christ promises to those who come to him in repentance and faith. The primary thing that is promised in the gospel message is the promise of forgiveness of sins and eternal life with God. "For God so loved the world that he gave his only Son, that whoever believes in him *should not perish but have eternal life*" (John 3:16). And in Peter's preaching of the gospel he says, "Repent therefore, and turn again, *that your sins may be blotted out*" (Acts 3:19; cf. 2:38).

Coupled with the promise of forgiveness and eternal life should be an assurance that Christ will accept all who come to him in sincere repentance and faith seeking salvation: "Him who comes to me I will not cast out" (John 6:37).

C. The Importance of the Gospel Call

The doctrine of the gospel call is important, because if there were no gospel call, we could not be saved. "How are they to believe in him of whom they have never heard?" (Rom. 10:14).

The gospel call is important also because through it God addresses us in the fullness of our humanity. He does not simply save us "automatically" without seeking for a response from us as whole persons. Rather, he addresses the gospel call to our intellects, our emotions, and our wills. He speaks to our intellects by explaining the facts of salvation to us in his Word. He speaks to our emotions by issuing a heartfelt personal invitation to us to respond. He speaks to our wills by asking us to hear his invitation and respond willingly in repentance and faith—to decide to turn from our sins and receive Christ as Savior and rest our hearts in him for salvation.

II. REVIEW QUESTIONS

1. In what order would you place the following three aspects of the blessings of salvation: effective calling, justification, and predestination. Why?

2. What is the difference between "effective calling" and "general calling" (or the "gospel call")?

3. What three elements must be present in the gospel call?

4. In light of the doctrine of election (ch. 18), is the gospel call really necessary? Why?

III. QUESTIONS FOR PERSONAL APPLICATION

1. Can you remember the first time you heard the gospel and responded to it? Can you describe what it felt like in your heart? Do you think the Holy Spirit was working to make that gospel call effective in your life? Did you resist it at the time?

2. In your explanation of the gospel call to other people, have some elements been missing? If so, what difference would it make if you added those elements to your explanation of the gospel? What is the one thing most needed to make your proclamation of the gospel more effective?

3. Before reading this chapter, have you thought of Jesus in heaven speaking the words of the gospel invitation personally to people even today? If non-Christians do begin to think of Jesus speaking to them in this way, how do you think it will affect their response to the gospel?

4. Do you understand the elements of the gospel call clearly enough to present them to others? Could you easily turn in the Bible to find four or five appropriate verses that would explain the gospel call clearly to people? (Memorizing the elements of the gospel call and the verses that explain it should be one of the first disciplines of the Christian life.)

IV. SPECIAL TERMS

effective calling

external calling

internal calling

the gospel call

V. SCRIPTURE MEMORY PASSAGE

Matthew 11:28–30

Come to me, all who labor and are heavy laden, and I will give you rest. Take my yoke upon you, and learn from me; for I am gentle and lowly in heart, and you will find rest for your souls. For my yoke is easy, and my burden is light.

CHAPTER TWENTY

Regeneration

+ *What does it mean to be born again?*

I. EXPLANATION AND SCRIPTURAL BASIS

We may define regeneration as follows: *Regeneration is a secret act of God in which he imparts new spiritual life to us.* This is sometimes called "being born again" (using language from John 3:3–8).

A. Regeneration Is Totally a Work of God

In some of the elements of the application of redemption that we will discuss in subsequent chapters, we play an active part (this is true, for example, of conversion, sanctification, and perseverance). But in the work of regeneration, we play no active role at all. It is instead totally a work of God. We see this, for example, when John talks about those to whom Christ gave power to become children of God—they "were born, not of blood *nor of the will of the flesh nor of the will of man,* but of God" (John 1:13). Here John specifies that children of God are those who are "born . . . of God" and our human will ("the will of man") does not bring about this kind of birth.

The fact that we are passive in regeneration is also evident when Scripture refers to it as being "born" or being "born again" (cf. James 1:18; 1 Peter 1:3; John 3:3–8). We did not choose to be made physically alive and we did not choose to be born—it is something that happened to us; similarly, these analogies in Scripture suggest that we are entirely passive in regeneration.

This sovereign work of God in regeneration was also predicted in the prophecy of Ezekiel. Through him God promised a time in the future when he would give new spiritual life to his people: "A *new heart* I will give you, and *a new spirit I will put within you;* and I will take out of your flesh the heart of stone and give you a heart of flesh. And I will put my spirit within you, and cause you to walk in my statutes and be careful to observe my ordinances" (Ezek. 36:26–27).

Which member of the Trinity is the one who causes regeneration? When Jesus speaks of being "born of the Spirit" (John 3:8), he indicates that it is especially God the Holy Spirit who produces regeneration. But other verses also indicate the involvement of God the Father in regeneration: Paul specifies that it is God who "made us alive together with Christ" (Eph. 2:5; cf. Col. 2:13). And James says that it is the "Father of lights" who gave us new birth: "Of his own will *he brought us forth* by the word of truth that we should be a kind of first fruits of his creatures" (James 1:17–18). Finally, Peter says that God "according to his abundant mercy *has*

which is symbolized by water in Ezekiel's prophecy in Ezek. 36:25–26.) Our inability to come to Christ on our own, without an initial work of God within us, is also emphasized when Jesus says, "No one can come to me unless the Father who sent me draws him" (John 6:44), and "No one can come to me unless it is granted him by the Father" (John 6:65). This inward act of regeneration is described beautifully when Luke says of Lydia, "*The Lord opened her heart* to give heed to what was said by Paul" (Acts 16:14). First the Lord opened her heart, then she was able to give heed to Paul's preaching and to respond in faith.

By contrast, Paul tells us, "The man without the Spirit (lit. 'the natural man') does not accept the things that come from the Spirit of God, for they are foolishness to him, and he cannot understand them, because they are spiritually discerned" (1 Cor. 2:14 NIV). He also says of people apart from Christ, "No one understands, no one seeks for God" (Rom. 3:11).

The solution to this spiritual deadness and inability to respond only comes when God gives us new life within. "But God, who is rich in mercy, out of the great love with which he loved us, even *when we were dead through our trespasses,* made us alive together with Christ" (Eph. 2:4–5). Paul also says, "*When you were dead in your sins* and in the uncircumcision of your sinful nature, *God made you alive with Christ*" (Col. 2:13 NIV).

The idea that regeneration comes before saving faith is not always understood by evangelicals today. Sometimes people will even say something like, "If you believe in Christ as your Savior, then (after you believe) you will be born again." But Scripture itself never says anything like that. This new birth is viewed by Scripture as something that God does within us in order to enable us to believe.

The reason that evangelicals often think that regeneration comes after saving faith is that they *see the results* (such as a love for God and his Word, and turning from sin) *after* people come to faith, and they think that regeneration must therefore have come after saving faith. In fact, some evangelical statements of faith contain wording that suggests that regeneration comes after saving faith. In these statements, the word *regeneration* apparently means the *outward evidence of regeneration* that is seen in a changed life, evidence that certainly does come after saving faith. Thus, "being born again" is thought of not in terms of the initial impartation of new life, but in terms of the *total life change that results* from that impartation. If the term *regeneration* is understood in this way, then it would be true that regeneration comes after saving faith.

Nevertheless, if we are to use language that closely conforms to the actual wording of Scripture, it would be better to restrict the word *regeneration* to the instantaneous, *initial* work of God in which he imparts spiritual life to us. Then we can emphasize that we do not see regeneration itself, but we only see the results of it in our lives, and that faith in Christ for salvation is the first result that we see. In fact, we can never know that we have been regenerated until we come to faith in Christ, for that is the outward evidence of this hidden, inward work of God. Once we do come to saving faith in Christ, we know that we have been born again.

By way of application, we should realize that the explanation of the gospel message in Scripture does not take the form of a command, "Be born again and you will be saved," but rather, "Believe in Jesus Christ and you will be saved." This is the consistent pattern in the preaching of the gospel throughout the book of Acts and also in the descriptions of the gospel given in the Epistles.

D. Genuine Regeneration Must Bring Results in Life

In the previous section, we noted that the ability to respond to God in saving faith is the first result of regeneration. Thus, John says, "Everyone who believes that Jesus is the Christ *is born of God*" (1 John 5:1 NIV). But there are also other results of regeneration, many of which are specified in John's first epistle. For example, John says, "No one who is born of God will continue to sin, because God's seed remains in him; he *cannot go on sinning,* because he has been born of God" (1 John 3:9 NIV). Here John explains that a person who is born again has that spiritual "seed" (that life-generating and growing power) within him and that this keeps the person living a life free of continual sin. This does not of course mean that the person will have a perfect life, but only that the pattern of life will not be one of continuing indulgence in sin. We should notice that John says this is true of everyone who is truly born again: "*No one* who is born of God will continue to sin." Another way of looking at this is to say that "every one who does what is right has been born of him" (1 John 2:29).

A genuine, Christlike *love* will be one specific result in life: "Everyone who loves has been born of God and knows God" (1 John 4:7 NIV). Another effect of the new birth is *overcoming the world:* "His commands are not burdensome, for everyone born of God has overcome the world" (1 John 5:3–4 NIV). Here John explains that regeneration gives the ability to overcome the pressures and temptations of the world that would otherwise keep us from obeying God's commandments and following his paths. John says that we will overcome these pressures and therefore it will not be "burdensome" to obey God's commands but, he implies, it will rather be joyful.

Finally, John notes that another result of regeneration is *protection from Satan* himself: "We know that anyone born of God does not continue to sin; the one who was born of God [that is, Jesus] keeps him safe, *and the evil one cannot harm him*" (1 John 5:18 NIV). Though there may be attacks from Satan, John reassures his readers that "the one who is in you is greater than the one who is in the world" (1 John 4:4 NIV), and this greater power of the Holy Spirit within us keeps us safe from ultimate spiritual harm by the evil one.

We should realize that John emphasizes these as *necessary* results in the lives of those who are born again. If there is genuine regeneration in a person's life, he or she *will* believe that Jesus is the Christ, and *will* refrain from a life pattern of continual sin, and *will* love his or her brother and sister, and *will* overcome the temptations of the world, and *will* be kept safe from ultimate harm by the evil one. These passages show that it is impossible for a person to be regenerated and not become truly converted.

Other results of regeneration are listed by Paul where he speaks of the *"fruit of the Spirit,"* that is, the result in life that is produced by the power of the Holy Spirit working within every believer: "But the fruit of the Spirit is love, joy, peace, patience, kindness, goodness, faithfulness, gentleness, self-control" (Gal. 5:22–23). If there is true regeneration, these elements of the fruit of the Spirit will be more and more evident in that person's life. But by contrast, those who are unbelievers, including those who are pretending to be believers but are not, will clearly lack these character traits in their lives. Jesus told his disciples:

> Beware of false prophets, who come to you in sheep's clothing but inwardly are ravenous wolves. *You will know them by their fruits.* Are grapes gathered from thorns, or figs from thistles? So, every sound tree bears good fruit, but the bad

tree bears evil fruit. A sound tree cannot bear evil fruit, nor can a bad tree bear good fruit. Every tree that does not bear good fruit is cut down and thrown into the fire. Thus you will know them by their fruits. (Matt. 7:15–20)

Neither Jesus nor Paul nor John point to activity in the church or miracles as evidence of regeneration. They rather point to character traits in life. In fact, immediately after the verses quoted above, Jesus warns that on the day of judgment many will say to him, "Lord, Lord, did we not prophesy in your name, and cast out demons in your name, and do many mighty works in your name?" But he will declare to them, "*I never knew you;* depart from me, you evildoers" (Matt. 7:22–23). Prophecy, exorcism, and many miracles and mighty works in Jesus' name (to say nothing of other kinds of intensive church activity in the strength of the flesh over perhaps decades of a person's life) do not provide convincing evidence that a person is truly born again. Apparently all these can be produced in the natural man or woman's own strength, or with the help of the evil one. But genuine love for God and his people, heartfelt obedience to his commands, and the Christlike character traits that Paul calls the fruit of the Spirit, demonstrated consistently over a period of time in a person's life, simply *cannot* be produced by Satan or by the natural man or woman working in his or her own strength. These can only come about by the Spirit of God working within and giving us new life.

II. REVIEW QUESTIONS

1. Does a person play any active role in regeneration? Explain.
2. Compare and contrast effective calling and regeneration.
3. What is the relationship between regeneration and saving faith?
4. Can a person be regenerated and show no evidence in his life? Support your answer from Scripture.

III. QUESTIONS FOR PERSONAL APPLICATION

1. Have you been born again? Is there evidence of the new birth in your life? Do you remember a specific time when regeneration occurred in your life? Can you describe how you knew that something had happened?
2. If you (or a friend who comes to you) are not sure whether you have been born again, what would Scripture encourage you to do in order to gain greater assurance (or to be truly born again for the first time)? (Note: Further discussion of repentance and saving faith are given in the next chapter.)
3. What do you think about the fact that your regeneration was totally a work of God and that you contributed nothing to it? How does it make you feel toward yourself? How does it make you feel toward God?
4. Are there areas where the results of regeneration are not very clearly seen in your own life? Do you think it is possible for a person to be regenerated and then stagnate spiritually so that there is little or no growth? Under what conditions might that happen? To what degree do the kind of church one attends, the teaching one receives, the kind of Christian fellowship one has, and the regularity of one's personal time of Bible reading and prayer affect one's own spiritual life and growth?

IV. SPECIAL TERMS

born again

born of the spirit

born of water

irresistible grace

regeneration

V. SCRIPTURE MEMORY PASSAGE

JOHN 3:5–8

> Jesus answered, "Truly, truly, I say to you, unless one is born of water and the Spirit, he cannot enter the kingdom of God. That which is born of the flesh is flesh, and that which is born of the Spirit is spirit. Do not marvel that I said to you, 'You must be born anew.' The wind blows where it wills, and you hear the sound of it, but you do not know whence it comes or whither it goes; so it is with every one who is born of the Spirit."

CHAPTER TWENTY-ONE

Conversion (Faith and Repentance)

+ *What is true repentance?*
+ *What is saving faith?*
+ *Can people accept Jesus as Savior and not as Lord?*

I. EXPLANATION AND SCRIPTURAL BASIS

The previous two chapters have explained how God himself (through the human preaching of the Word) issues the gospel call to us and, by the work of the Holy Spirit, regenerates us, imparting new spiritual life within. In this chapter we examine our response to the gospel call. We may define conversion as follows: *Conversion is our willing response to the gospel call, in which we sincerely repent of sins and place our trust in Christ for salvation.*

The word *conversion* itself means "turning"—here it represents a spiritual turn, a turning *from* sin *to* Christ. The turning from sin is called *repentance,* and the turning to Christ is called *faith.* We can look at each of these elements of conversion, and in one sense it does not matter which one we discuss first, for neither one can occur without the other, and they must occur together when true conversion takes place. For the purposes of this chapter, we shall examine saving faith first and then repentance.

A. True Saving Faith Includes Knowledge, Approval, and Personal Trust

1. Knowledge alone is not enough. Personal saving faith, in the way Scripture understands it, involves more than mere knowledge. *It is necessary that we have some knowledge of who Christ is and what he has done,* for "how are they to believe in him of whom they have never heard?" (Rom. 10:14). But knowledge about the *facts* of Jesus' life, death, and resurrection for us is not enough, for people can know facts but rebel against them or dislike them. For example, Paul tells us that many people know God's laws but dislike them: "Though they *know* God's decree that those who do such things deserve to die, they not only do them but approve those who practice them" (Rom. 1:32). Even the demons know who God is and know the facts about Jesus' life and saving works, for James says, "You believe that God is one; you do well. Even the demons believe—and shudder" (James 2:19). But that knowledge certainly does not mean that the demons are saved.

2. Knowledge and approval are not enough. Moreover, merely knowing the facts and *approving* of them or *agreeing* that they are true is not enough. Nicodemus knew that Jesus had come from God, for he said, "Rabbi, we know that you are a teacher come from God; for no one can do these signs that you do, unless God is with him" (John 3:2). Nicodemus had evaluated the facts of the situation, including Jesus' teaching and his remarkable miracles, and had drawn a correct conclusion from those facts: Jesus was a teacher come from God. But this alone did not mean that Nicodemus had saving faith, for he still had to put his trust in Christ for salvation; he still had to "believe in him." King Agrippa provides another example of knowledge and approval without saving faith. Paul realized that King Agrippa knew and apparently viewed with approval the Jewish Scriptures (what we now call the Old Testament). When Paul was on trial before Agrippa, he said, "King Agrippa, do you believe the prophets? I know that *you believe*" (Acts 26:27). Yet Agrippa did not have saving faith, for he said to Paul, "In a short time you think to make me a Christian!" (Acts 26:28).

3. I must decide to depend on Jesus to save me personally. In addition to knowledge of the facts of the gospel and approval of those facts, in order to be saved, I must decide to depend on Jesus to save me. In doing this, I move from being an interested observer of the facts of salvation and the teachings of the Bible to being someone who enters into a new relationship with Jesus Christ as a living person. We may therefore define saving faith in the following way: *Saving faith is trust in Jesus Christ as a living person for forgiveness of sins and eternal life with God.*

This definition emphasizes that saving faith is not just a belief in facts but *personal trust in Jesus* to save *me*. As we will explain in the following chapters, much more is involved in salvation than simply forgiveness of sins and eternal life, but someone who initially comes to Christ seldom realizes the extent of the blessings of salvation that will come. The main thing that concerns an unbeliever who comes to Christ is the fact that sin has separated him or her from the fellowship with God for which we were made. The unbeliever comes to Christ seeking to have sin and guilt removed and to enter into a genuine relationship with God that will last forever. We may rightly summarize the two major concerns of a person who trusts in Christ as "forgiveness of sins" and "eternal life with God."

The definition emphasizes *personal trust* in Christ, not just belief in facts about Christ. Because saving faith in Scripture involves this personal trust, *trust* is often a better word to use in contemporary culture than the word *faith* or *belief.* The reason is that we can "believe" something to be true with no personal commitment or dependence involved in it. I can *believe* that Canberra is the capital of Australia or that 7 times 6 is 42 but have no personal commitment or dependence on anyone when I simply believe those facts. The word *faith* on the other hand, is sometimes used today to refer to an almost irrational commitment to something in spite of strong evidence to the contrary, a sort of irrational decision to believe something that we are quite sure is not true! (If your favorite football team continues to lose games, someone might encourage you to "have faith" even though all the facts point the opposite direction.) In these two popular senses, *belief* and *faith* have a meaning contrary to the biblical sense.

The word *trust* is closer to the biblical idea, since we are familiar with trusting persons in everyday life. The more we come to know a person, and the more we see in that person a pattern of life that warrants trust, the more we find ourselves able to place trust in him to do what he promises, or to act in ways on which we can rely.

This fuller sense of personal trust is indicated in several passages of Scripture in which initial saving faith is spoken of in very personal terms, often using analogies drawn from personal relationships. John says, "To all who *received him,* who believed in his name, he gave power to become children of God" (John 1:12). Much as we would receive a guest into our homes, John speaks of receiving Christ.

John 3:16 tells us that "whoever *believes in him* should not perish but have eternal life." Here John uses a surprising phrase when he does not simply say, "whoever *believes him*" (that is, believes that what he says is true and able to be trusted), but rather, "whoever *believes in him.*" The Greek phrase *pisteuō eis auton* could also be translated "believe *into* him" with the sense of trust or confidence that goes *into* and rests *in* Jesus as a person. Leon Morris can say, "Faith, for John, is an activity which takes men right out of themselves and makes them one with Christ." He understands the Greek phrase *pisteuō eis* to be a significant indication that New Testament faith is not just intellectual assent but includes a "moral element of personal trust."[1] Such an expression was rare or perhaps nonexistent in the secular Greek found outside the New Testament, but it was well suited to express the personal trust in Christ that is involved in saving faith.

Jesus speaks of "coming to him" in several places. He says, "All that the Father gives me will *come to me;* and him who comes to me I will not cast out" (John 6:37). He also says, "If any one thirst, let him *come to me* and drink" (John 7:37). In a similar way, he says, "*Come to me,* all who labor and are heavy laden, and I will give you rest. Take my yoke upon you, and learn from me; for I am gentle and lowly in heart, and you will find rest for your souls. For my yoke is easy, and my burden is light" (Matt. 11:28–30). In these passages we have the idea of coming to Christ and asking for acceptance, for living water to drink, and for rest and instruction. All of these give an intensely personal picture of what is involved in saving faith.

With this understanding of true New Testament faith, we may now appreciate that when a person comes to trust in Christ, all three elements must be present. There must be some basic knowledge or understanding of the facts of the gospel. There must also be approval of, or agreement with, these facts. Such agreement includes a conviction that the facts spoken of the gospel are true, especially the fact that I am a sinner in need of salvation and that Christ alone has paid the penalty for my sin and offers salvation to me. It also includes an awareness that I need to trust in Christ for salvation and that he is the only way to God and the only means provided for my salvation. This approval of the facts of the gospel will also involve a desire to be saved through Christ. But all this still does not add up to true saving faith. That comes only when I make a decision of my will to depend on, or put my *trust* in, Christ as *my* Savior. This personal decision to place my trust in Christ is something done with my heart, the central faculty of my entire being, which makes personal commitments for me as a whole person.

B. Faith and Repentance Must Come Together

We may define repentance as follows: *Repentance is a heartfelt sorrow for sin, a renouncing of it, and a sincere commitment to forsake it and walk in obedience to Christ.*

This definition indicates that repentance is something that can occur at a specific point in time and is not equivalent to a demonstration of change in a person's

---

[1]Leon Morris, *The Gospel According to John*, New International Commentary on the New Testament (Grand Rapids: Eerdmans, 1971), p. 336.

pattern of life. Repentance, like faith, is an intellectual *understanding* (that sin is wrong), an emotional *approval* of the teachings of Scripture regarding sin (a sorrow for sin and a hatred of it), and a *personal decision* to turn from it (a renouncing of sin and a decision of the will to forsake it and lead a life of obedience to Christ instead). We cannot say that someone has to actually live that changed life over a period of time before repentance can be genuine, or else repentance would be turned into a kind of obedience we could do to merit salvation for ourselves. Of course, genuine repentance will result in a changed life. In fact, a truly repentant person will begin at once to live a changed life, and we can call that changed life the fruit of repentance. But we should never attempt to require that there be a period of time in which a person actually lives a changed life before we give assurance of forgiveness. Repentance is something that occurs in the heart and involves the whole person in a decision to turn from sin.

It is important to realize that mere sorrow for one's actions, or even deep remorse over one's actions, does not constitute genuine repentance unless it is accompanied by a sincere decision to forsake sin that is being committed against God. Genuine repentance involves a deep sense that the worst thing about one's sin is that it has offended a holy God. Paul preached about "repentance *to God* and of faith in our Lord Jesus Christ" (Acts 20:21). He says that he rejoiced over the Corinthians, "not because you were grieved, but because you were *grieved into repenting*.... *For godly grief produces a repentance that leads to salvation and brings no regret, but worldly grief produces death*" (2 Cor. 7:9–10). A worldly sort of grief may involve great sorrow for one's actions and probably also fear of punishment but no genuine renouncing of sin or commitment to forsake it in one's life. Hebrews 12:17 tells us that Esau wept over the consequences of his actions but did not truly repent. Moreover, as 2 Corinthians 7:9–10 indicates, even true godly grief is just one factor that leads to genuine repentance, but such grief is not itself the sincere decision of the heart in the presence of God that makes genuine repentance.

Scripture puts repentance and faith together as different aspects of the one act of coming to Christ for salvation. It is not that a person first turns from sin and next trusts in Christ, or first trusts in Christ and then turns from sin, but rather that both occur at the same time. When we turn to Christ *for* salvation from our sins, we are simultaneously turning *away* from the sins that we are asking Christ to save us from. If that were not true, our turning to Christ for salvation from sin could hardly be a genuine turning to him or trusting in him.

The fact that repentance and faith are simply two different sides of the same coin, or two different aspects of the one event of conversion, may be seen in figure 21.1. In this diagram, the person who genuinely turns to Christ for salvation must at the same time release the sin to which he or she has been clinging and turn away from that sin in order to turn to Christ. Thus, neither repentance nor faith comes first; they must come together. John Murray speaks of "penitent faith" and "believing repentance."[2]

Therefore, it is clearly contrary to the New Testament evidence to speak about the possibility of having true saving faith without having any repentance for sin. It is also contrary to the New Testament to speak about the possibility of someone accepting Christ "as Savior" but not "as Lord," if that means simply depending on him for salvation but not committing oneself to forsake sin and to be obedient to Christ from that point on.

---

[2]John Murray, *Redemption Accomplished and Applied* (Grand Rapids: Eerdmans, 1955), p. 113.

Conversion is a Single Action of Turning from Sin in
Repentance and Turning to Christ in Faith

figure 21.1

When Jesus invites sinners, "Come to me, all who labor and are heavy laden, and I will give you rest," he immediately adds, "*Take my yoke upon you, and learn from me*" (Matt. 11:28–29). To come to him includes taking his yoke upon us, being subject to his direction and guidance, learning from him and being obedient to him. If we are unwilling to make such a commitment, then we have not truly placed our trust in him.

When Scripture speaks of trusting in God or in Christ, it frequently connects such trust with genuine repentance. For example, Isaiah gives an eloquent testimony that is typical of the message of many of the Old Testament prophets:

> Seek the LORD while he may be found,
>> call upon him while he is near;
> let the wicked *forsake his way*,
>> and the unrighteous man his thoughts;
> let him *return to the LORD*, that he may have mercy on him,
>> and to our God, for he will abundantly pardon. (Isa. 55:6–7)

Here both repentance of sin and coming to God for pardon are mentioned. In the New Testament, Paul summarizes his gospel ministry as one of "testifying both to Jews and to Greeks of *repentance* to God and of *faith* in our Lord Jesus Christ" (Acts 20:21). The author of Hebrews includes as the first two elements in a list of elementary doctrines "*repentance* from dead works" and "*faith* toward God" (Heb. 6:1).

Of course, sometimes faith alone is named as the thing necessary for coming to Christ for salvation (see John 3:16; Acts 16:31; Rom. 10:9; Eph. 2:8–9; et al.). These are familiar passages, and we emphasize them often when explaining the gospel to others. But what we do not often realize is that there are many other passages where *only repentance* is named, for it is simply assumed that true repentance will also involve faith in Christ for forgiveness of sins. The New Testament authors understood so well that genuine repentance and genuine faith had to go together that they often simply mentioned repentance alone with the understanding that faith would also be included, because turning *from* sins in a genuine way is impossible apart from a genuine turning *to* God. Therefore, just before Jesus ascended into heaven, he told his disciples, "Thus it is written, that the Christ should suffer and on the third day rise from the dead, and that *repentance* and forgiveness of sins should be preached in his name to all nations" (Luke 24:46–47). Saving faith is implied in the phrase "forgiveness of sins," but it is not explicitly named.

The preaching recorded in the book of Acts shows the same pattern. After Peter's sermon at Pentecost, the crowd asked, "Brethren, what shall we do?" Peter replied, "*Repent,* and be baptized every one of you in the name of Jesus Christ for the forgiveness of your sins" (Acts 2:37–38).[3] In his second sermon, Peter spoke to his hearers in a similar way saying, "*Repent* therefore, and turn again, that your sins may be blotted out, that times of refreshing may come from the presence of the Lord" (Acts 3:19). Later, when the apostles were on trial before the Sanhedrin, Peter spoke of Christ, saying, "God exalted him at his right hand as Leader and Savior, to give *repentance* to Israel and forgiveness of sins" (Acts 5:31). And when Paul was preaching on the Areopagus in Athens to an assembly of Greek philosophers, he said, "The times of ignorance God overlooked, but now *he commands all men everywhere to repent*" (Acts 17:30). He also says in his epistles, "Do you not know that God's kindness is meant to lead you to repentance?" (Rom. 2:4), and he speaks of "a *repentance* that leads to salvation" (2 Cor. 7:10).

When we realize that genuine saving faith must be accompanied by genuine repentance for sin, it helps us to understand why some preaching of the gospel has such inadequate results today. If there is no mention of the need for repentance, sometimes the gospel message becomes only, "Believe in Jesus Christ and be saved" without any mention of repentance at all. But this watered-down version of the gospel does not ask for a wholehearted commitment to Christ—commitment *to* Christ, if genuine, must include a commitment to turn *from* sin. Preaching the need for faith without repentance is preaching only half of the gospel. It will result in many people being deceived, thinking that they have heard the Christian gospel and tried it, but nothing has happened. They might even say something like, "I accepted Christ as Savior over and over again and it never worked." Yet they never really did receive Christ as their Savior, for he comes to us in his majesty and invites us to receive him as he is—the one who deserves to be, and demands to be, absolute Lord of our lives as well.

Finally, what shall we say about the common practice of asking people to *pray* to receive Christ as their personal Savior and Lord? Since personal faith in Christ must involve an actual decision of the will, it is often very helpful to *express* that decision in spoken words, and this could very naturally take the form of a prayer to Christ in which we tell him of our sorrow for sin, our commitment to forsake it, and our decision actually to put our trust in him. Such a spoken prayer does not in itself save us, but the attitude of heart that it represents does constitute true conversion, and the decision to speak that prayer can often be the point at which a person truly comes to faith in Christ.

---

[3]See ch. 27, pp. 384–85, on the question of whether baptism is necessary for salvation.

C. Both Faith and Repentance Continue Throughout Life

Although we have been considering initial faith and repentance as the two aspects of conversion at the beginning of the Christian life, it is important to realize that faith and repentance are not confined to the beginning of the Christian life. They are rather attitudes of heart that continue throughout our lives as Christians. Jesus tells his disciples to pray daily, "*Forgive us our sins* as we also have forgiven those who sin against us" (Matt. 6:12, author's translation), a prayer that, if genuine, will certainly involve daily sorrow for sin and genuine repentance. And the risen Christ says to the church in Laodicea, "Those whom I love, I reprove and chasten; so be zealous *and repent*" (Rev. 3:19; cf. 2 Cor. 7:10).

With regard to faith, Paul tells us, "So *faith, hope, love abide*, these three; but the greatest of these is love" (1 Cor. 13:13). He certainly means that these three abide throughout the course of this life, but he probably also means that they abide for all eternity: If faith is trusting God to provide all our needs, then this attitude will never cease, not even in the age to come. But in any case, the point is clearly made that faith continues throughout this life. Paul also says, "The life I now live in the flesh *I live by faith in the Son of God,* who loved me and gave himself for me" (Gal. 2:20).

Therefore, although it is true that *initial* saving faith and *initial* repentance occur only once in our lives, and when they occur they constitute true conversion, nonetheless, the heart attitudes of repentance and faith only begin at conversion. These same attitudes should continue throughout the course of our Christian lives.[4] Each day there should be heartfelt repentance for sins that we have committed, and faith in Christ to provide for our needs and to empower us to live the Christian life.

II. REVIEW QUESTIONS

1. Describe the two components of conversion.
2. What three factors are necessary for there to be true, saving faith?
3. Define repentance. How does this differ from worldly grief or remorse (cf. 2 Cor. 7:9–10)?
4. Can a person have true saving faith without repentance? Explain.
5. Do faith and repentance occur only at the beginning of the Christian life? Why or why not?

III. QUESTIONS FOR PERSONAL APPLICATION

1. Have you come to trust in Christ personally, or are you still at the point of intellectual knowledge and emotional approval of the facts of salvation without having personally put your trust in Christ? If you have not put your trust in Christ yet, what do you think is making you hesitate?
2. If your knowledge about God has increased through reading this book, has your faith in God increased along with that knowledge? Why or why not? If not, what can you do to encourage your faith to grow more than it has?

---

[4]An excellent discussion of the way faith in God should pervade every moment of our Christian lives is found in John Piper, *Future Grace* (Sisters, Ore.: Multnomah, 1995).

3. In terms of human relationships, do you trust a person more when you do not know that person very well or after you have come to know him or her quite well? What does that fact tell you about how your trust in God might increase? What things might you do during the day to come to know God better and to come to know Jesus and the Holy Spirit better?

4. Have you ever truly repented of sin, or do you think you have been taught a watered-down gospel that did not include repentance? Do you think it is possible for someone genuinely to trust in Christ for forgiveness of sins without also sincerely repenting for sins?

5. Have faith and repentance remained a continuing part of your Christian life, or have those attitudes of heart grown somewhat weak in your life? What has been the result in your Christian life?

IV. SPECIAL TERMS

belief

conversion

faith

repentance

saving faith

trust

V. SCRIPTURE MEMORY PASSAGE

JOHN 3:16

For God so loved the world that he gave his only Son, that whoever believes in him should not perish but have eternal life.

CHAPTER TWENTY-TWO

Justification and Adoption

+ *How and when do we gain right legal standing before God?*

+ *What are the benefits of being a member of God's family?*

I. EXPLANATION AND SCRIPTURAL BASIS

In the previous chapters, we talked about the gospel call (in which God calls us to trust in Christ for salvation), regeneration (in which God imparts new spiritual life to us), and conversion (in which we respond to the gospel call in repentance for sin and faith in Christ for salvation). But *what about the guilt of our sin?* The gospel call invited us to trust in Christ for forgiveness of sins. Regeneration made it possible for us to respond to that invitation. In conversion we did respond, trusting in Christ for forgiveness of sins. Now the next step in the process of applying redemption to us is that God must respond to our faith and do what he promised, that is, actually declare our sins to be forgiven. This must be a *legal declaration* concerning our relationship to God's laws, stating that we are completely forgiven and no longer liable to punishment.

A right understanding of justification is absolutely crucial to the whole Christian faith. Once Martin Luther realized the truth of justification by faith alone, he became a Christian and overflowed with the newfound joy of the gospel. The primary issue in the Protestant Reformation was a dispute with the Roman Catholic Church over justification. If we are to safeguard the truth of the gospel for future generations, we must understand the truth of justification. Even today, a true view of justification is the dividing line between the biblical gospel of salvation by faith alone and all false gospels of salvation based on good works.

When Paul gives an overview of the process by which God applies salvation to us, he mentions justification explicitly: "Those whom he predestined he also called; and those whom he called he also *justified;* and those whom he justified he also glorified" (Rom. 8:30). As we explained in a previous chapter, the word "called" here refers to the effective calling of the gospel, which includes regeneration and brings forth the response of repentance and faith (or conversion) on our part. After effective calling and the response that it initiates on our part, the next step in the application of redemption is "justification." Here Paul mentions that this is something that God himself does: "Those whom he called *he also justified.*"

Moreover, Paul quite clearly teaches that this justification comes *after* our faith and *as God's response to* our faith. He says that God "*justifies him who has faith* in Jesus" (Rom. 3:26), and that "a man is *justified by faith* apart from works of law" (Rom. 3:28). He says, "Since we are *justified by faith,* we have peace with God through our Lord Jesus Christ" (Rom. 5:1). Moreover, "a man is not justified by works of the law but *through faith* in Jesus Christ" (Gal. 2:16).

Just what is justification? We may define it as follows: *Justification is an instantaneous legal act of God in which he (1) thinks of our sins as forgiven and Christ's righteousness as belonging to us, and (2) declares us to be righteous in his sight.*

In explaining the elements of this definition, we will look first at the second half of it, the aspect of justification in which God "declares us to be righteous in his sight." The reason for treating these items in reverse order is that the emphasis of the New Testament in the use of the word *justification* and related terms is on the second half of the definition, the legal declaration by God. But there are also passages that show that this declaration is based on the fact that God first thinks of righteousness as belonging to us. So both aspects must be treated, even though the New Testament terms for justification focus on the legal declaration by God.

A. Justification Includes a Legal Declaration by God

The use of the word *justify* in the Bible indicates that justification is a legal declaration by God. The verb *justify* in the New Testament (Gk. *Dikaioō*) has a range of meanings, but a very common sense is "to declare righteous." For example, we read, "When they heard this all the people and the tax collectors *justified* God, having been baptized with the baptism of John" (Luke 7:29). Of course the people and the tax collectors did not *make* God to be righteous—that would be impossible for anyone to do. Rather, they *declared* God to be righteous. This is also the sense of the term in passages where the New Testament talks about us being declared righteous by God (Rom. 3:20, 26, 28; 5:1; 8:30; 10:4, 10; Gal. 2:16; 3:24). This sense is particularly evident, for example, in Romans 4:5: "To one who does not work but trusts him who *justifies the ungodly,* his faith is reckoned as righteousness." Here Paul cannot mean that God "makes the ungodly to be righteous" (by changing them internally and making them morally perfect), for then they would have merit or works of their own on which to depend. Rather, he means that God declares the ungodly to be righteous in his sight, not on the basis of their good works, but in response to their faith.

The idea that justification is a legal declaration is quite evident also when justification is contrasted with condemnation. Paul says, "Who shall bring any charge against God's elect? It is God who *justifies;* who is to condemn?" (Rom. 8:33–34). To "condemn" someone is to declare that person guilty. The opposite of condemnation is justification, which, in this context, must mean "to declare someone not guilty." This is also evident from the fact that God's act of justifying is given as Paul's answer to the possibility of someone bringing an accusation or "charge" against God's people; such a declaration of guilt cannot stand in the face of God's declaration of righteousness.

In this sense of "*declare* to be righteous" or "*declare* to be not guilty," Paul frequently uses the word to speak of God's justification of us, his declaration that we, though guilty sinners, are nonetheless righteous in his sight. It is important to emphasize that this legal declaration in itself does not change our internal nature or character at all. In this sense of "justify," God issues a legal declaration about us. This is why theologians have also said that justification is *forensic,* where the word *forensic* means "having to do with legal proceedings."

John Murray makes an important distinction between regeneration and justification:

> Regeneration is an act of God in us; justification is a judgment of God with respect to us. The distinction is like that of the distinction between the act of a surgeon and the act of a judge. The surgeon, when he removes an inward cancer, does something in us. That is not what a judge does—he gives a verdict regarding our judicial status. If we are innocent he declares accordingly.
>
> The purity of the gospel is bound up with the recognition of this distinction. If justification is confused with regeneration or sanctification, then the door is opened for the perversion of the gospel at its center. Justification is still the article of the standing or falling of the Church.[1]

B. God Declares Us to Be Just in His Sight

In God's legal declaration of justification, he specifically declares that we are just *in his sight.* This declaration involves two aspects. First, it means that he declares that we have no penalty to pay for sin, including past, present, and future sins. After a long discussion of justification by faith alone (Rom. 4:1–5:21) and a parenthetical discussion on remaining sin in the Christian life, Paul returns to his main argument in the book of Romans and tells what is true of those who have been justified by faith: "There is therefore now *no condemnation* for those who are in Christ Jesus" (Rom. 8:1). In this sense, those who are justified have no penalty to pay for sin. This means that we are not subject to any charge of guilt or condemnation: "Who shall bring any charge against God's elect? It is God who *justifies;* who is to condemn?" (Rom. 8:33–34). In God's act of justification, he grants us full forgiveness of sins.

But if God merely declared us to be *forgiven from our sins,* that would not solve our problems entirely, for it would only make us morally neutral before God. We would be in the state that Adam was in before he had done anything right or wrong in God's sight—he was not guilty before God, but neither had he earned a record of righteousness before God. This first aspect of justification, in which God declares that our sins are forgiven, may be represented as in figure 22.1, in which the minus signs represent sins on our account that are completely forgiven in justification.

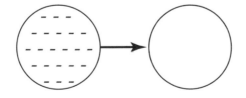

Forgiveness of Sins Is One Part of Justification

figure 22.1

---

[1]John Murray, *Redemption Accomplished and Applied* (Grand Rapids: Eerdmans, 1955), p. 121.

However, such a movement is not enough to earn us favor with God. We must rather move from a point of moral neutrality to a point of having positive righteousness before God, the righteousness of a life of perfect obedience to him. Our need may therefore be represented as in figure 22.2, in which the plus signs indicate a record of righteousness before God.

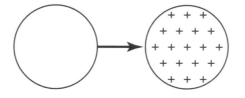

**Imputation of Christ's Righteousness to Us
Is the Other Part of Justification**

figure 22.2

Therefore, the second aspect of justification is that God must declare us not to be merely *neutral* in his sight, but actually to be *righteous* in his sight. In fact, he must declare us to have the merits of perfect righteousness before him. The Old Testament sometimes spoke of God as giving such righteousness to his people even though they had not earned it themselves. Isaiah says, "He has clothed me with the garments of salvation, *he has covered me with the robe of righteousness*" (Isa. 61:10). But Paul speaks more specifically about this in the New Testament. As a solution to our need for righteousness, Paul tells us that "the righteousness of God has been manifested apart from law, although the law and the prophets bear witness to it, *the righteousness of God through faith in Jesus Christ* for all who believe" (Rom. 3:21–22). He says, "Abraham believed God, and *it was reckoned to him as righteousness*" (Rom. 4:3; quoting Gen. 15:6). This came about through the obedience of Christ, for Paul says at the end of this extensive discussion of justification by faith that "by one man's obedience many will be *made righteous*" (Rom. 5:19). The second aspect of God's declaration in justification, then, is that we have the merits of perfect righteousness before him.

But questions arise: How can God declare that we have no penalty to pay for sin and that we have the merits of perfect righteousness if we are in fact guilty sinners? How can God declare us to be not guilty but righteous when in fact we are unrighteous? These questions lead to our next point.

C. God Can Declare Us to Be Just Because He Imputes Christ's Righteousness to Us

When we say that God *imputes* Christ's righteousness to us, it means that God thinks of Christ's righteousness as belonging to us, or regards it as belonging to us. He "reckons" it to our account. We read, "Abraham believed God, and *it was reckoned to him as righteousness*" (Rom. 4:3, quoting Gen. 15:6). Paul explains, "To one who does not work but trusts him who justifies the ungodly, his faith *is reckoned* as righteousness. So also David pronounces a blessing upon the man to whom *God reckons righteousness* apart from works" (Rom. 4:6). In this way, Christ's righteousness became ours. Paul says that we are those who received "the free gift of righteousness" (Rom. 5:17).

This is the third time in studying the doctrines of Scripture that we have encountered the idea of imputing guilt or righteousness to someone else. First, when Adam sinned, his guilt was imputed to us; God the Father viewed it as belonging to us, and therefore it did.[2] Second, when Christ suffered and died for our sins, our sin was imputed to Christ; God thought of it as belonging to him, and he paid the penalty for it.[3] Now in the doctrine of justification we see imputation for the third time. Christ's righteousness is imputed to us, and therefore God thinks of it as belonging to us. It is not our own righteousness, but Christ's righteousness, that is freely given to us. So Paul can say that God made Christ to be "our wisdom, *our righteousness* and sanctification and redemption" (1 Cor. 1:30). And Paul says that his goal is to be found in Christ, "not having a righteousness of my own, based on law, but that which is through faith in Christ, *the righteousness from God* that depends on faith" (Phil. 3:9). Paul knows that the righteousness he has before God is not anything of his own doing; it is the righteousness of God that comes through Jesus Christ (cf. Rom. 3:21–22).

It is essential to the heart of the gospel to insist that God declares us to be just or righteous not on the basis of our actual condition of righteousness or holiness, but rather on the basis of Christ's perfect righteousness, which God thinks of as belonging to us. This was the heart of the difference between Protestantism and Roman Catholicism at the Reformation. Protestantism since the time of Martin Luther has insisted that justification does not change us internally and it is not a declaration based in any way on any goodness that we have in ourselves.

If justification changed us internally and then declared us to be righteous based on how good we actually were, then (1) we could never be declared perfectly righteous in this life, because there is always sin that remains in our lives, and (2) there would be no provision for forgiveness of past sins (committed before we were changed internally), and therefore we could never have confidence that we are right before God. We would lose the confidence that Paul has when he says, "Therefore, *since we are justified by faith,* we have peace with God through our Lord Jesus Christ" (Rom. 5:1). If we thought of justification as based on something that we are internally we would never have the confidence to say with Paul, "There is therefore now *no condemnation* for those who are in Christ Jesus" (Rom. 8:1). We would have no assurance of forgiveness with God, no confidence to draw near to him "with a true heart in full assurance of faith" (Heb. 10:22). We would not be able to speak of "the *free gift* of righteousness" (Rom. 5:17), or say that "the *free gift* of God is eternal life in Christ Jesus our Lord" (Rom. 6:23).

The traditional Roman Catholic understanding of justification is very different from this. The Roman Catholic Church understands justification as something that changes us internally and makes us holier within. This view may be said to understand justification as based not on *imputed* righteousness but on *infused* righteousness—that is, righteousness that God actually *puts into us* and that changes us internally and in terms of our actual moral character.[4]

---

[2]See ch. 13, pp. 213–18, on the idea of Adam's sin being imputed to us.

[3]See ch. 15, pp. 250–58, on the fact that our guilt was imputed to Christ.

[4]It is noteworthy that on October 7, 1997, fifteen leading Roman Catholics joined eighteen evangelical leaders in signing a document called "The Gift of Salvation," in which they jointly declared:

> We agree that justification is not earned by any good works or merits of our own; it is entirely God's gift, conferred through the Father's sheer graciousness, out of the love that he bears us in his Son, who suffered on our behalf and rose from the dead for our justification. . . . In justification, God, on the basis of Christ's

The result of this traditional Roman Catholic view of justification is that people cannot be sure if they are in a "state of grace" where they experience God's complete acceptance and favor or not. Furthermore, under this view people experience varying degrees of justification according to the measure of righteousness that has been infused or placed within them. Ultimately, the logical consequence of this view of justification is that our eternal life with God is not based on God's grace alone but partially on our merit as well. As one Catholic theologian puts it, "For the justified eternal life is both a gift of grace promised by God and a reward for his own good works and merits. . . . Salutary works are, at the same time, gifts of God and meritorious acts of man."[5] To assign saving merit to man's internal righteousness and "good works" in this way ultimately destroys the heart of the gospel itself.

That is what Martin Luther so clearly saw and that is what gave such motivation to the Reformation. When the good news of the gospel truly became the good news of totally free salvation in Jesus Christ, it spread like wildfire throughout the civilized world. But this was simply a recovery of the original gospel, which declares, "The wages of sin is death, but the *free gift of God* is eternal life in Christ Jesus our Lord" (Rom. 6:23), and insists that "there is therefore now *no condemnation* for those who are in Christ Jesus" (Rom. 8:1).

D. Justification Comes to Us Entirely by God's Grace, Not on Account of Any Merit in Ourselves

After Paul explains in Romans 1:18–3:20 that no one will ever be able to make himself righteous before God ("For no human being will be justified in his sight by works of the law," Rom. 3:20), he goes on to explain that "since all have sinned and fall short of the glory of God, they are justified *by his grace as a gift,* through the redemption which is in Christ Jesus" (Rom. 3:23–24). God's "grace" means his "unmerited favor." Because we are completely unable to earn favor with God, the only way we could be declared righteous is if God freely provides salvation for us by grace, totally apart from our work. Paul explains, "For *by grace* you have been saved through faith; and this is not your own doing, it is the gift of God—not because of works, lest any man should boast" (Eph. 2:8–9; cf. Titus 3:7). Grace is clearly put in contrast to works or merit as the reason why God is willing to justify us. God did not have any obligation to impute our sin to Christ or to impute Christ's righteousness to us; it was only because of his unmerited favor that he did this.

---

righteousness alone, declares us to be no longer his rebellious enemies but his forgiven friends, and by virtue of his declaration it is so.

The New Testament makes it clear that the gift of justification is received through faith. . . . We understand that what we here affirm is in agreement with what the Reformation traditions have meant by justification by faith alone (*sola fide*). (*Christianity Today*, December 8, 1997, pp. 35–37)

On initial inspection, these words seem to be affirming an understanding of justification by imputed righteousness that is received by faith alone, and therefore this seems to be a declaration for which we can indeed be thankful. If it indeed signals complete agreement between influential evangelicals and Roman Catholics on the doctrine of justification, it would have historic significance. We may hope that a declaration of this sort may gain the assent of other leaders within the Roman Catholic Church and that it will indicate a departure from what I have termed in this section the traditional Roman Catholic position. However, not all evangelicals have assessed this document positively: See the "Appeal to Fellow Evangelicals," available from the Alliance of Confessing Evangelicals, 1716 Spruce Street, Philadelphia, PA 19103 (215 546-3696 or www.alliancenet.org).

[5]Ludwig Ott, *Fundamentals of Catholic Dogma*, ed. James Canon Bastible, trans. Patrick Lynch (St. Louis: Herder, 1955), p. 264.

For this reason, Luther and the other Reformers insisted that justification comes by grace *alone,* not by grace plus some merit on our part. This was in distinction from the Roman Catholic teaching that we are justified by God's grace plus some merit of our own that we attain as we make ourselves fit to receive the grace of justification and as we grow in this state of grace through our good works.

E. God Justifies Us Through Our Faith in Christ

1. Faith is an instrument to obtain justification, but it has no merit in itself. When we began this chapter, we noted that justification comes after saving faith. Paul makes this sequence clear when he says, "We *have believed in Christ Jesus, in order to be justified* by faith in Christ, and not by works of the law, because by works of the law shall no one be justified" (Gal. 2:16). Here Paul indicates that faith comes first and it is for the purpose of being justified. He also says that Christ is "to be received by faith" and that God "justifies him who has *faith* in Jesus" (Rom. 3:25, 26). The entire chapter of Romans 4 is a defense of the fact that we are justified by faith, not by works, just as Abraham and David themselves were. Paul says, "We are justified *by faith*" (Rom. 5:1).

Scripture never says that we are justified because of the inherent goodness of our faith, as if our faith has merit before God. It never allows us to think that our faith in itself earns favor with God. Rather, Scripture says that we are justified "by means of" our faith, understanding faith to be the instrument through which justification is given to us, but not at all an activity that earns us merit or favor with God. Rather, we are justified solely because of the merits of Christ's work (Rom. 5:17–19).

2. Why did God choose faith as the instrument for receiving justification? But we may ask *why* God chose *faith* to be the attitude of heart by which we would obtain justification. Why could God not have decided to give justification to all those who sincerely show love? Or who show joy? Or contentment? Or humility? Or wisdom? Why did God choose *faith* as the means by which we receive justification?

It is apparently because *faith* is the one attitude of heart that is the exact opposite of depending on ourselves. When we come to Christ in faith, we essentially say, "I give up! I will not depend on myself or my own good works any longer. I know that I can never make myself righteous before God. Therefore, Jesus, I trust you and depend on you completely to give me a righteous standing before God." In this way, faith is the opposite of trusting in ourselves, and therefore it is the attitude that perfectly fits salvation that depends not at all on our own merit but entirely on God's free gift of grace. Paul explains this when he says, "That is why it depends *on faith, in order that the promise may rest on grace* and be guaranteed to all his descendants" (Rom. 4:16). This is why the Reformers from Martin Luther on were so firm in their insistence that justification comes not through faith plus some merit or good work on our part but only *through faith alone.* "For by grace you have been saved *through faith;* and this is not your own doing, it is the gift of God—not because of works, lest any man should boast" (Eph. 2:8–9). Paul repeatedly says that "no human being will be justified in his sight by works of law" (Rom. 3:20); the same idea is repeated in Galatians 2:16; 3:11; 5:4.

3. What does James mean by saying we are justified by works? But is this consistent with the epistle of James? What can James mean when he says, "You see that a man is *justified by works* and not by faith alone" (James 2:24). Here we must realize that James is using the word *justified* in a different sense from the way Paul uses it. In the beginning of this chapter, we noted that the word *justify* has a range of meanings, and that one significant sense is "declare to be righteous," but we should also notice that the Greek word *dikaioō* can also mean "demonstrate or show to be righteous." For instance, Jesus said to the Pharisees, "You are those who *justify* yourselves before men, but God knows your hearts" (Luke 16:15). The point here was not that the Pharisees went around making legal declarations that they were "not guilty" before God, but rather that they were always attempting to show others that they were righteous by their outward deeds. Jesus knew that the truth was otherwise: "But God knows your hearts" (Luke 16:15). Similarly, the lawyer who put Jesus to a test by asking what he should do to inherit eternal life answered Jesus' first question well. But when Jesus told him, "Do this, and you will live," he was not satisfied. Luke tells us, "But he, *desiring to justify himself,* said to Jesus, 'And who is my neighbor?'" (Luke 10:28–29). Now he was not desiring to give a legal pronouncement about himself that he was not guilty in God's sight; rather, he was desiring to "show himself righteous" before others who were listening. Other examples of the word *justify* meaning "show to be righteous" can be found in Matthew 11:19; Luke 7:35; Romans 3:4.

Our interpretation of James 2 depends not only on the fact that "show to be righteous" is an acceptable sense for the word *justified,* but also on the consideration that this sense fits well with the primary purpose of James in this section. James is concerned to show that mere intellectual agreement with the gospel is a "faith" that is really no faith at all. He is concerned to argue against those who say they have faith but show no change in their lives. He says, "Show me your faith apart from your works, and I by my works will show you my faith" (James 2:18). "For as the body apart from the spirit is dead, so faith apart from works is dead" (James 2:26). James is simply saying here that "faith" that has no results or "works" is not real faith at all; it is "dead" faith. He is not denying Paul's clear teaching that justification (in the sense of a declaration of right legal standing before God) is by faith alone apart from works of the law; he is simply affirming a different truth—namely, that "justification" in the sense of an outward showing that one is righteous only occurs as we see evidence in a person's life. To paraphrase, James is saying that a person is "*shown to be righteous* by his works, and not by his faith alone." This is something with which Paul also would certainly agree (2 Cor. 13:5; Gal. 5:19–24).

4. Practical implications of justification by faith alone. The practical implications of the doctrine of justification by faith alone are very significant. First, this doctrine enables us to offer genuine *hope* to unbelievers who know they could never make themselves righteous before God. If salvation is a free gift to be received through faith *alone,* then anyone who hears the gospel may hope that eternal life is freely offered and may be obtained.

Second, this doctrine gives us confidence that God will never make us pay the penalty for sins that have been forgiven on Christ's merits. Of course, we may continue to suffer the ordinary *consequences* of sin (an alcoholic who quits drinking may still have physical weakness for the rest of his life, and a thief who is justified may still have to go to jail to pay the penalty for his crime). Moreover, God may *discipline* us if we continue to act in ways that are disobedient to him (see Heb. 12:5–11), doing this out of love and for our own good. But God never can or will *take vengeance* on us for past sins or *make us pay the penalty* that is due for them or *punish us out of wrath* and *for the purpose of doing us harm*. "There is therefore now no condemnation for those that are in Christ Jesus" (Rom 8:1). This fact should give us a great sense of joy and confidence before God that we are accepted by him and that we stand before him as "not guilty" but "righteous" forever.

F. Adoption

In addition to justification, there is another amazing privilege that God gives us at the time we become Christians, the privilege of *adoption*. We may define adoption as follows: *Adoption is an act of God whereby he makes us members of his family.*

Although adoption is a privilege that comes to us at the time we become Christians (John 1:12; Gal. 3:26; 1 John 3:1–2), it is, nevertheless, a privilege that is distinct from justification and distinct from regeneration. For example, God could have given us justification without the privileges of adoption into his family, for he could have forgiven our sins and given us right legal standing before him without making us his children. Similarly, he could have made us spiritually alive through regeneration and yet not members of his family with the special privileges of family members—angels, for example, apparently fall into that category. The biblical teaching on adoption focuses much more on the personal relationships that salvation gives us with God and with his people.

John mentions adoption at the beginning of his gospel, where he says, "But to all who received him, who believed in his name, he gave power *to become children of God*" (John 1:12). By contrast, those who do not believe in Christ are not children of God or adopted into his family but are "children of wrath" (Eph. 2:3) and "sons of disobedience" (Eph. 2:2; 5:6). Although those Jews who rejected Christ tried to claim that God was their father (John 8:41), Jesus told them, "If God were your Father, you would love me. . . . You are of your father the devil, and your will is to do your father's desires" (John 8:42–44).

The New Testament epistles bear repeated testimony to the fact that we are now God's children in a special sense, members of his family. Paul says: "For all who are led by the Spirit of God are *sons of God*. For you did not receive the spirit of slavery to fall back into fear, but you have received the *spirit of sonship*. When we cry, 'Abba! Father!' it is the Spirit himself bearing witness with our spirit that we are *children of God*, and if children, then heirs, heirs of God and fellow heirs with Christ, provided we suffer with him in order that we may also be glorified with him" (Rom. 8:14–17).

But if we are God's children, are we then related to one another as family members? Certainly so. In fact, this adoption into God's family makes us partakers together in *one family* even with the believing Jews of the Old Testament, for Paul says that we are Abraham's children as well: "Not all are children of Abraham because they are his descendants; but 'Through Isaac shall your descendants be named.' This means that it is not the children of the flesh who are the children of God, but the children of the promise are reckoned as descendants" (Rom. 9:7–8). He further explains in Galatians, "Now we, brethren, like Isaac, are children of promise. . . . we are not children of the slave but of the free woman" (Gal. 4:28, 31; cf. 1 Peter 3:6, where Peter sees believing women as daughters of Sarah in the new covenant).

Paul explains that this status of adoption as God's children was not fully realized in the old covenant. He says that "before faith came, we were confined under the law. . . . the law was our custodian until Christ came, that we might be justified by faith. But now that faith has come, we are no longer under a custodian; for *in Christ Jesus you are all sons of God, through faith*" (Gal. 3:23–26). This is not to say that the

Old Testament completely omitted talk of God as our Father, for God did call himself the Father of the children of Israel and called them his children in several places (Ps. 103:13; Isa. 43:6–7; Mal. 1:6; 2:10). But even though there was a consciousness of God as Father to the people of Israel, the full benefits and privileges of membership in God's family, and the full realization of that membership, did not come until Christ came and the Spirit of the Son of God was poured into our hearts, bearing witness with our spirit that we were God's children.

Although the New Testament says that we are *now* God's children (1 John 3:2), we should also note that there is another sense in which our adoption is still future because we will not receive the full benefits and privileges of adoption until Christ returns and we have new resurrection bodies. Paul speaks of this later, fuller sense of adoption when he says, "Not only the creation, but we ourselves, who have the first fruits of the Spirit, groan inwardly as we wait for adoption as sons, *the redemption of our bodies*" (Rom. 8:23). Here Paul sees the receiving of new resurrection bodies as the fulfillment of our privileges of adoption, so much so that he can refer to it as our "adoption as sons."

II. REVIEW QUESTIONS

1. Define the word *justify* as used in the New Testament in verses such as Romans 3:20, 26, 28; 4:5; and 8:33.

2. Does God's act of justification actually change our internal nature or character at all? Why or why not?

3. God's declaration of justification involves what two factors?

4. How can God declare us righteous when we are in fact guilty sinners? Is this righteousness based on our own actions or actual inner nature? If not, then on what is it based?

5. Briefly explain the difference between the Protestant view of justification and the traditional Roman Catholic understanding.

6. What is the relationship between faith and justification? Does faith earn us salvation? Explain.

7. Define the biblical doctrine of adoption. How is this privilege different from the blessing of justification?

III. QUESTIONS FOR PERSONAL APPLICATION

1. Are you confident that God has declared you "not guilty" forever in his sight? Do you know when that happened in your own life? Did you do or think anything that resulted in God's justifying of you? Did you do anything to deserve justification? If you are not sure that God has justified you fully and for all time, what would persuade you that God has certainly justified you?

2. If you think of yourself standing before God on the day of judgment, would you think that it is enough simply to have your sins all forgiven, or would you also feel a need to have the righteousness of Christ reckoned to your account?

3. Do you think the difference between the Roman Catholic and Protestant understanding of justification is an important one? Describe how you would feel about your relationship to God if you held the Roman Catholic view of justification.

4. Have you ever wondered if God is still continuing to punish you from time to time for sins you have done in the past, even long ago? How does the doctrine of justification help you deal with those feelings?

5. How many benefits can you think of that come to you because you are a member of God's family? Had you previously thought of these as automatically yours because you had been born again? Now how do you feel about the fact that God has adopted you into his family compared with the way you felt before reading this chapter?

IV. SPECIAL TERMS

adoption

forensic

impute

infused righteousness

justification

V. SCRIPTURE MEMORY PASSAGE

ROMANS 3:27–28

Then what becomes of our boasting? It is excluded. On what principle? On the principle of works? No, but on the principle of faith. For we hold that a man is justified by faith apart from works of law.

CHAPTER TWENTY-THREE

Sanctification (Growth in Likeness to Christ)

+ *How do we grow in Christian maturity?*
+ *What are the blessings of Christian growth?*

I. EXPLANATION AND SCRIPTURAL BASIS

The previous chapters have discussed several acts of God that occur at the beginning of our Christian lives: the gospel call (which God addresses to us), regeneration (by which God imparts new life to us), justification (by which God gives us right legal standing before him), and adoption (in which God makes us members of his family). We have also discussed conversion (in which we repent of sins and trust in Christ for salvation). These events all occur at the beginning of our Christian lives.

But now we come to a part of the application of redemption that is a *progressive* work that continues throughout our earthly lives. It is also a work in which *God and man cooperate,* each playing distinct roles. This part of the application of redemption is called sanctification: *Sanctification is a progressive work of God and man that makes us more and more free from sin and like Christ in our actual lives.*

A. Differences Between Justification and Sanctification

The following table specifies several differences between justification and sanctification:

Justification	Sanctification
Legal standing	Internal condition
Once for all time	Continuous throughout life
Entirely God's work	We cooperate
Perfect in this life	Not perfect in this life
The same in all Christians	Greater in some than in others

As this table indicates, sanctification is something that continues throughout our Christian life. The ordinary course of a Christian's life will involve continual growth in sanctification, and it is something that the New Testament encourages us to give effort and attention to.

B. Three Stages of Sanctification

1. Sanctification has a definite beginning at regeneration. A definite moral change occurs in our lives at the point of regeneration, for Paul talks about the "washing of regeneration and renewal in the Holy Spirit" (Titus 3:5). Once we have been born again, we cannot continue to sin as a habit or a pattern of life (1 John 3:9), because the power of new spiritual life within us keeps us from yielding to a life of sin.

This initial moral change is the first stage in sanctification. In this sense, there is some overlap between regeneration and sanctification, for this moral change is actually a part of regeneration. But when we view it from the standpoint of moral change within us, we can also see it as the first stage in sanctification. Paul looks back on a completed event when he says to the Corinthians, "You were washed, *you were sanctified,* you were justified in the name of the Lord Jesus Christ and in the Spirit of our God" (1 Cor. 6:11). Similarly, in Acts 20:32, Paul can refer to Christians as "all those who *are sanctified*" (using a perfect participle that expresses both a completed past action [they were sanctified] and a continuing result [they continue to experience the influence of that past action]).

This initial step in sanctification involves a definite break from the ruling power and love of sin, so that the believer is no longer ruled or dominated by sin and no longer loves to sin. Paul says, "So you also must *consider yourselves dead to sin* and alive to God in Christ Jesus. . . . For *sin will have no dominion over you*" (Rom. 6:11, 14). Paul says that Christians have been "set free from sin" (Rom. 6:18). In this context, to be dead to sin or to be set free from sin involves the power to overcome acts or patterns of sinful behavior in one's life. Paul tells the Romans not to let sin "reign in your mortal bodies," and he also says, "Do not yield your members to sin as instruments of wickedness, but yield yourselves to God" (Rom. 6:12–13). To be dead to the ruling power of sin means that we as Christians, by virtue of the power of the Holy Spirit and the resurrection life of Christ working within us, have power to overcome the temptations and enticements of sin. Sin will no longer be our master, as once it was before we became Christians.

In practical terms, this means that we must affirm two things to be true. On the one hand, we will never be able to say, "I am completely free from sin," because our sanctification will never be completed (see below). But on the other hand, a Christian should never say, for example, "This sin has defeated me. I give up. I have had a bad temper for thirty-seven years, and I will have one until the day I die, and people are just going to have to put up with me the way I am!" To say this is to say that sin has gained dominion. It is to allow sin to reign in our bodies. It is to admit defeat. It is to deny the truth of Scripture that tells us, "You also must consider yourselves dead to sin and alive to God in Christ Jesus" (Rom. 6:11). It is to deny the truth of Scripture that tells us that "sin will have no dominion over you" (Rom. 6:14).

This initial break with sin, then, involves a reorientation of our desires so that we no longer have a dominant love for sin in our lives. Paul knows that his readers were formerly slaves to sin (as all unbelievers are), but he says that they are enslaved no longer. "You who were once slaves of sin have become *obedient from the heart* to the standard of teaching to which you were committed, and, having been set free from sin, have become slaves of righteousness" (Rom. 6:17–18). This change of one's primary love and primary desires occurs at the beginning of sanctification.

2. Sanctification increases throughout life. Even though the New Testament speaks about a definite beginning to sanctification, it also sees it as a process that continues throughout our Christian lives. This is the primary sense in which sanctification is used in systematic theology and in Christian conversation generally today. Although Paul says that his readers have been set free from sin (Rom. 6:18) and that they are "dead to sin and alive to God" (Rom. 6:11), he nonetheless recognizes that sin remains in their lives so he tells them not to let it reign and not to yield to it (Rom. 6:12–13). Their task, therefore, as Christians is to grow more and more in sanctification, just as they previously grew more and more in sin: "Just as you once yielded your members to impurity and to greater and greater iniquity, so now yield your members to righteousness for sanctification" (Rom. 6:19).

Paul says that throughout the Christian life "we all . . . *are being changed* into his likeness from one degree of glory to another" (2 Cor. 3:18). We are progressively becoming more and more like Christ as we go on in the Christian life. Therefore, he says, "Forgetting what lies behind and straining forward to what lies ahead, *I press on* toward the goal for the prize of the upward call of God in Christ Jesus" (Phil. 3:13–14)—this is in the context of saying that he is not already perfect but he presses on to achieve all of the purposes for which Christ has saved him (vv. 9–12).

It is not necessary to list multiple additional quotations, because much of the New Testament is taken up with instructing believers in various churches on how they should grow in likeness to Christ. All of the moral exhortations and commands in the New Testament epistles apply here, because they all exhort believers to one aspect or another of greater sanctification in their lives. It is the expectation of all the New Testament authors that our sanctification will increase throughout our Christian lives.

3. Sanctification is completed at death (for our souls) and when the Lord returns (for our bodies). Because there is sin that still remains in our hearts even though we have become Christians (Rom. 6:12–13; 1 John 1:8), our sanctification will never be completed in this life (see below). But once we die and go to be with the Lord, then our sanctification is completed in one sense, for our souls are set free from indwelling sin and are made perfect. The author of Hebrews says that when we come into the presence of God to worship we come "to the spirits of just men *made perfect*" (Heb. 12:23). This is only appropriate because it is in anticipation of the fact that "nothing unclean shall enter" into the presence of God, the heavenly city (Rev. 21:27).

However, when we appreciate that sanctification involves the whole person, including our bodies (see 2 Cor. 7:1; 1 Thess. 5:23), then we realize that sanctification will not be entirely completed until the Lord returns and we receive new resurrection bodies. We await the coming of our Lord Jesus Christ from heaven, and he "will change our lowly body to be like his glorious body" (Phil. 3:21). It is "at his coming" (1 Cor. 15:23) that we will be made alive with a resurrection body and then we shall fully "bear the image of the Man of heaven" (1 Cor. 15:49).[1]

We may diagram the process of sanctification as in figure 23.1, showing that we are slaves to sin prior to conversion, (1) that there is a definite beginning to sanctification at the point of conversion, (2) that sanctification should increase throughout the Christian life, and (3) that sanctification is made perfect at death. (The completion of sanctification when we receive resurrection bodies is omitted from this chart for the sake of simplicity.)

---

[1]See ch. 25 on glorification—that is, receiving a resurrection body when Christ returns.

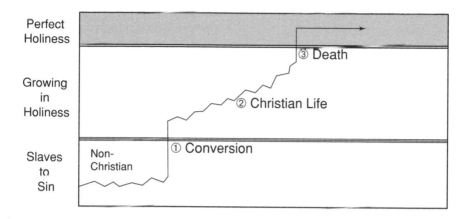

The Process of Sanctification

figure 23.1

I have shown the progress of sanctification as a jagged line on this chart, indicating that growth in sanctification is not always one-directional in this life, but that progress in sanctification occurs at some times, while at other times we realize that we are regressing somewhat. In the extreme case, a believer who makes very little use of the means of sanctification, but rather has bad teaching, lacks good Christian fellowship, and pays little attention to God's Word and prayer, may actually go for many years with very little progress in sanctification at all—but this is certainly not the normal or expected pattern of the Christian life. It is in fact highly abnormal.

4. Sanctification is never completed in this life. There have always been some in the history of the church who have taken commands such as Matthew 5:48 ("You, therefore, *must be perfect*, as your heavenly Father is perfect") or 2 Corinthians 7:1 ("Let us cleanse ourselves from every defilement of body and spirit, and *make holiness perfect* in the fear of God") and reasoned that since God gives us these commands, he must also give us the ability to obey them perfectly. Therefore, they have concluded, it is possible for us to attain a state of sinless perfection in this life. In fact, John even says, "No one who abides in him sins" (1 John 3:6)! Do these verses not point to the possibility of sinless perfection in the life of some Christians? In this discussion, I will use the term *perfectionism* to refer to this view that sinless perfection is possible in this life.

On closer inspection, these passages do not support the perfectionist position. First, it is simply not taught in Scripture that when God gives a command, he also gives the ability to obey it in every case. God commands all people everywhere to obey all of his moral laws and holds them accountable for failing to obey them, even though unredeemed people are sinners and, as such, dead in trespasses and sins, and thus unable to obey God's commands. When Jesus commands us to be perfect as our Father in heaven is perfect (Matt. 5:48), this simply shows that God's own absolute moral purity is the standard toward which we are to aim and the standard for which God holds us accountable. The fact that we are unable to attain that standard does not mean that it will be lowered; rather, it means that we need God's grace and forgiveness to overcome our remaining sin. Similarly, when Paul commands the

Corinthians to make holiness "perfect" in the fear of the Lord (2 Cor. 7:1), he is pointing to the goal that he desires them to reach. He does not imply that any reach it, but only that this is the high moral standard toward which God wants all believers to aspire.

John's statement that "no one who abides in him sins" (1 John 3:6) does not teach that some of us attain perfection, because the present-tense Greek verbs are better translated as indicating continual or habitual activity: "No one who lives in him *keeps on sinning*. No one who *continues to sin* has either seen him or known him" (1 John 3:6 NIV). This is similar to John's statement a few verses later, "No one who is born of God will *continue to sin*, because God's seed remains in him; he cannot go on sinning, because he has been born of God" (1 John 3:9 NIV). If these verses were taken to prove sinless perfection, they would have to prove it for all Christians, because they talk about what is true of everyone born of God, and everyone who has seen Christ and known him.

Therefore, there do not seem to be any convincing verses in Scripture that teach that it is possible for anyone to be completely free of sin in this life. On the other hand, there are passages throughout the Bible that clearly teach that we cannot be morally perfect in this life. The writer of Ecclesiastes explicitly says, *"Surely there is not a righteous man on earth who does good and never sins"* (7:20). Jesus commanded his disciples to pray, "Give us this day our daily bread; and *forgive us our sins,* as we also have forgiven those who sin against us" (Matt. 6:11–12, author's translation). Just as the prayer for daily bread provides a model for a prayer that should be repeated each day, so the prayer for the forgiveness of sins is included in the type of prayer that should be made each day in a believer's life.

As we noted above, when Paul talks about the new power over sin that is given to Christians, he does not say that there will be no sin in Christians' lives, but simply tells believers not to let sin "reign" in their bodies nor to "yield" their members to sin (Rom. 6:12–13). The very fact that he issues these directions shows his realization that sin will continue to be present in the lives of believers throughout their time on earth. Even James the brother of our Lord could say, *"We all make many mistakes"* (James 3:2), and if James himself can say this, then we certainly should be willing to say it as well. Finally, in the same letter in which John declares so frequently that a child of God will not continue in a pattern of sinful behavior, he also says clearly, *"If we say we have no sin, we deceive ourselves,* and the truth is not in us" (1 John 1:8). Here John explicitly excludes the possibility of being completely free from sin in our lives. In fact, he says that anyone who claims to be free from sin is simply deceiving himself, and the truth is not in him.

But once we have concluded that sanctification will never be completed in this life, we must exercise wisdom and caution in the way we use this truth. Some may take this fact and use it as an excuse not to strive for holiness or grow in sanctification— a procedure exactly contrary to dozens of New Testament commands. Others may think about the fact that we cannot be perfect in this life and lose hope of making any progress in the Christian life—an attitude that is also contrary to the clear teaching of Romans 6 and other passages about the resurrection power of Christ in our lives enabling us to overcome sin. Therefore, although sanctification will never be completed in this life, we must also emphasize that *sanctification should never stop increasing in this life.* Indeed, as Christians grow in maturity, it is certainly possible that they will at many times during the day be free from conscious or willful acts of disobedience to God in their words or their deeds. In fact, if Christian leaders are to "*set the believers an example* in speech and conduct, in love, in faith, in purity" (1 Tim. 4:12), then it will frequently be true that their lives will be free from words or deeds that others will count as blameworthy. But this is far removed from attaining total freedom from sin in our motives and in the thoughts and intents of our hearts.

C. God and Man Cooperate in Sanctification

Some object to saying that God and man "cooperate" in sanctification, because they want to insist that God's work is primary and our work in sanctification is only a secondary one (see Phil. 2:12–13). However, if we explain the nature of God's role and our role in sanctification clearly, it does not seem inappropriate to say that God and man cooperate in sanctification. We are not saying that we have equal roles in sanctification or that we both work in the same way, but simply that we cooperate with God in ways that are appropriate to our status as God's creatures. And the fact that Scripture emphasizes the role that we play in sanctification (with all the moral commands of the New Testament), makes it appropriate to teach that God calls us to cooperate with him in this activity.

1. God's role in sanctification. Since sanctification is primarily a work of God, it is appropriate that Paul prays, "*May the God of peace himself sanctify you wholly*" (1 Thess. 5:23). One specific role of God the Father in this sanctification is his process of disciplining us as his children (see Heb. 12:5–11). Paul tells the Philippians, "*God is at work in you*, both to will and to work for his good pleasure" (Phil. 2:13), thus indicating something of the way in which God sanctifies them—both by causing them to want his will and by giving them power to do it. The author of Hebrews speaks of the role of the Father and the role of the Son in a familiar benediction: "Now may the God of peace...equip you with everything good that you may do his will, working in you that which is pleasing in his sight, through Jesus Christ; to whom be glory for ever and ever" (Heb. 13:20–21).

While God the Son, Jesus Christ, certainly has a role in sanctification in that he *earned* our sanctification for us and serves as our example (see Heb. 12:2), it is specifically God the Holy Spirit who works within us to change us and sanctify us, giving us greater holiness of life. Peter speaks of the "sanctification of the Spirit" (1 Peter 1:2, author's translation), and Paul speaks of "sanctification by the Spirit" (2 Thess. 2:13). It is the Holy Spirit who produces in us the "fruit of the Spirit" (Gal. 5:22–23), those character traits that are part of greater and greater sanctification. If we grow in sanctification, we "walk by the Spirit" and are "led by the Spirit" (Gal. 5:16–18; cf. Rom. 8:14), that is, we are more and more responsive to the desires and promptings of the Holy Spirit in our life and character. The Holy Spirit is the spirit of holiness, and he produces holiness within us.

2. Our role in sanctification. The role that we play in sanctification is both a *passive* one in which we depend on God to sanctify us, and an *active* one in which we strive to obey God and take steps that will increase our sanctification. We can now consider both of these aspects of our role in sanctification.

First, what may be called the "passive" role that we play in sanctification is seen in texts that encourage us to trust God or to pray and ask that he sanctify us. Paul tells his readers, "*Yield yourselves to God* as men who have been brought from death to life" (Rom. 6:13; cf. v. 19), and he tells the Roman Christians, "Present your bodies as a living sacrifice, holy and acceptable to God" (Rom. 12:1). Paul realizes that we are dependent on the Holy Spirit's work to grow in sanctification, because he says, "If *by the Spirit* you put to death the deeds of the body you will live" (Rom. 8:13).

Unfortunately today, this "passive" role in sanctification, this idea of yielding to God and trusting him to work in us "to will and to work for his good pleasure" (Phil. 2:13), is sometimes so strongly emphasized that it is the only thing people are told about the path of sanctification. Sometimes the popular phrase "Let go and let God" is given as a summary of how to live the Christian life. But this is a tragic distortion of the doctrine of sanctification, for it only speaks of one half of the part we must play, and, by itself, will lead Christians to become lazy and to neglect the active role that Scripture commands them to play in their own sanctification.

That active role that we are to play is indicated by Romans 8:13, where Paul says, "If by the Spirit *you put to death the deeds of the body* you will live." Here Paul acknowledges that it is "by the Spirit" that we are able to do this. But he also says we must do it! It is not the Holy Spirit who is commanded to put to death the deeds of the flesh, but Christians! Similarly, Paul tells the Philippians, "Therefore, my beloved, as you have always obeyed, so now, not only as in my presence but much more in my absence, *work out your own salvation* with fear and trembling; for God is at work in you, both to will and to work for his good pleasure" (Phil. 2:12–13). Paul says that obedience is the way in which they "work out [their] own salvation," meaning that they will "work out" the further realization of the benefits of salvation in their Christian life. The Philippians are to work at this growth in sanctification, and to do it solemnly and with reverence ("with fear and trembling"), for they are doing it in the presence of God himself. But there is more: The reason why they are to work and to expect that their work will yield positive results is that "God is at work in you"—the prior and foundational work of God in sanctification means that their own work is empowered by God; therefore, it will be worthwhile and will bear positive results.

There are many aspects to this active role that we are to play in sanctification. We are to "*strive . . . for* the *holiness* without which no one will see the Lord" (Heb. 12:14); we are to "*abstain from immorality*" and so obey the will of God, which is our "sanctification" (1 Thess. 4:3). John says that those who hope to be like Christ when he appears will actively work at purification in this life: "Every one who thus hopes in him *purifies himself* as he is pure" (1 John 3:3). This kind of striving for obedience to God and for holiness may involve great effort on our part, for Peter tells his readers to "make every effort" to grow in character traits that accord with godliness (2 Peter 1:5). Many specific passages of the New Testament encourage detailed attention to various aspects of holiness and godliness in life (see Rom. 12:1–13:14; Eph. 4:17–6:20; Phil 4:4–9; Col. 3:5–4:6; 1 Peter 2:11–5:11; et al.). We are continually to build up patterns and habits of holiness, for one measure of maturity is that mature Christians "have their faculties trained by practice to distinguish good from evil" (Heb. 5:14).

The New Testament does not suggest any short-cuts by which we can grow in sanctification, but simply encourages us repeatedly to give ourselves to the old-fashioned, time-honored means of Bible reading and meditation (Ps. 1:2; Matt. 4:4; John 17:17), prayer (Eph. 6:18; Phil. 4:6), worship (Eph. 5:18–20), witnessing (Matt. 28:19–20), Christian fellowship (Heb. 10:24–25), and self-discipline or self-control (Gal. 5:23; Titus 1:8).

It is important that we continue to grow both in our passive trust in God to sanctify us and in our active striving for holiness and greater obedience in our lives. If we neglect active striving to obey God, we become passive, lazy Christians. If we neglect the passive role of trusting God and yielding to him, we become proud and overly confident in ourselves. In either case, our sanctification will be greatly deficient. We must maintain faith and diligence to obey at the same time. The old hymn wisely says, "*Trust and obey,* for there's no other way, to be happy in Jesus, but to trust and obey."

D. Sanctification Affects the Whole Person

We see that sanctification affects our *intellect* and our knowledge when Paul says that a life "worthy of the Lord, fully pleasing to him" is one that is continually "increasing in the *knowledge* of God" (Col. 1:10). Growth in sanctification will also affect our *emotions.* We will find it increasingly true that we do not "love the world or things in the world" (1 John 2:15), but that we, like our Savior, delight to do God's will. Sanctification will have an effect on our *will,* our decision-making faculty, because God is at work in us, "to *will* and to work for his good pleasure" (Phil. 2:13). Moreover, sanctification will also affect our *spirit,* the nonphysical part of our beings, and our *physical bodies,* as Paul encourages us to "cleanse ourselves from every defilement of *body* and *spirit,* and make holiness perfect in the fear of God" (2 Cor. 7:1; cf. 1 Cor. 7:34). He also says that a concern about the affairs of the Lord will mean taking thought for "how to be holy in body and *spirit*" (1 Cor. 7:34).[2] God's purpose for our lives is that we be increasingly "conformed to the image of his Son" (Rom. 8:29) in every dimension of our personhood.

E. Motives for Obedience to God in the Christian Life

Christians sometimes fail to recognize the wide range of motives for obedience to God that are found in the New Testament. (1) It is true that a desire to please God and express our love to him is a very important motive for obeying him—Jesus says, "If you love me, you will keep my commandments" (John 14:15), and, "He who has my commandments and keeps them, he it is who loves me" (John 14:21; cf. 1 John 5:3). But many other motives are also given to us: (2) the need to keep a clear conscience before God (Rom. 13:5; 1 Tim. 1:5, 19; 2 Tim. 1:3; 1 Peter 3:16); (3) the desire to be a "vessel for noble use" and have increased effectiveness in the work of the kingdom (2 Tim. 2:20–21); (4) the desire to see unbelievers come to Christ through observing our lives (1 Peter 3:1–2, 15–16); (5) the desire to receive present blessings from God on our lives and ministries (1 Peter 3:9–12); (6) the desire to avoid God's displeasure and discipline on our lives (sometimes called "the fear of God") (Acts 5:11; 9:31; 2 Cor. 5:11; 7:1; Eph. 4:30; Phil. 2:12; 1 Tim. 5:20; Heb. 12:3–11; 1 Peter 1:17; 2:17; cf. the state of unbelievers in Rom. 3:18); (7) the desire to seek greater heavenly reward (Matt. 6:19–21; Luke 19:17–19; 1 Cor. 3:12–15; 2 Cor. 5:9–10);[3] (8) the desire for a deeper walk with God (Matt. 5:8; John 14:21; 1 John 1:6; 3:21–22; and, in the Old Testament, Ps. 66:18; Isa. 59:2); (9) the desire that angels would glorify God for our obedience (1 Tim. 5:21; 1 Peter 1:12); (10) the desire for peace (Phil. 4:9) and joy (Heb. 12:1–2) in our lives; and (11) the desire to do what God commands simply because his commands are right and we delight in doing what is right (Phil. 4:8; cf. Ps. 40:8).

---

[2]See ch. 11, pp. 193–96, for a discussion of the fact that "soul" and "spirit" are used in a roughly synonymous way in the Bible.

[3]See ch. 33, pp. 456–57, for a discussion of degrees of reward in heaven.

F. The Beauty and Joy of Sanctification

It would not be right to end our discussion without noting that sanctification brings great joy to us. The more we grow in likeness to Christ, the more we will personally experience the "joy" and "peace" that are part of the fruit of the Holy Spirit (Gal. 5:22), and the more we will draw near to the kind of life that we will have in heaven. Paul says that as we become more and more obedient to God, "the *return* you get is sanctification and its end, eternal life" (Rom. 6:22). He realizes that this is the source of our true joy. "The kingdom of God is not food and drink but *righteousness* and *peace* and *joy* in the Holy Spirit" (Rom. 14:17). As we grow in holiness, we grow in conformity to the image of Christ, and more and more of the beauty of his character is seen in our own lives. This is the goal of perfect sanctification that we hope and long for and that will be ours when Christ returns. "Every one who thus hopes in him purifies himself as he is pure" (1 John 3:3).

II. REVIEW QUESTIONS

1. Describe at least three ways in which sanctification differs from justification.
2. What are the three stages of sanctification?
3. Will sanctification ever be completed in this life? Explain.
4. Differentiate between God's role and man's role in sanctification. Whose role is primary, and why is this so?
5. Is it wrong to say that we are to strive for holiness and greater obedience in our lives? Why or why not?
6. Name at least five motives for obedience to God given in Scripture.

III. QUESTIONS FOR PERSONAL APPLICATION

1. Can you remember in your own experience the definite beginning to sanctification that occurred when you became a Christian? Did you sense a clear break from the ruling power and love of sin in your life? Do you really believe that you are even now dead to the ruling power and love of sin in your life? How can this truth of the Christian life be of help to you in specific areas of your life where you still need to grow in sanctification?
2. As you look back over the last few years of your Christian life, can you see a pattern of definite growth in sanctification? What are some things that you used to delight in that no longer interest you? What are some things that you used to have no interest in that now hold great interest for you?
3. How does it affect your life to realize that the Holy Spirit is continually at work in you to increase your sanctification? Have you maintained a balance between your passive role and your active role in sanctification, or have you tended to emphasize one aspect over the other, and why? If there is imbalance in your life, what might you do to correct it?
4. Have you thought previously that sanctification affects your intellect and the way you think? What areas of your intellect still need growth in sanctification? With regard to your emotions, in what areas do you know that God

still needs to work to bring about greater sanctification? Are there areas or aspects of sanctification that need to be improved with respect to your physical body and its obedience to God's purposes?

5. Are there areas where your have struggled for years to grow in sanctification, but with no progress at all in your life? Has this chapter helped you regain hope for progress in those areas? (For Christians who have serious discouragement over lack of progress in sanctification, it is very important to talk personally to a pastor or other mature Christian about this situation, rather than letting it go on for a long period of time.)

IV. SPECIAL TERMS

perfectionism   sinless perfection

sanctification

V. SCRIPTURE MEMORY PASSAGE

ROMANS 6:11–14

So you also must consider yourselves dead to sin and alive to God in Christ Jesus. Let not sin therefore reign in your mortal bodies, to make you obey their passions. Do not yield your members to sin as instruments of wickedness, but yield yourselves to God as men who have been brought from death to life, and your members to God as instruments of righteousness. For sin will have no dominion over you, since you are not under law but under grace.

CHAPTER TWENTY-FOUR

The Perseverance of the Saints (Remaining a Christian)

+ *Can true Christians lose their salvation?*
+ *How can we know if we are truly born again?*

I. EXPLANATION AND SCRIPTURAL BASIS

Our previous discussion has dealt with many aspects of the full salvation that Christ has earned for us and that the Holy Spirit now applies to us. But how do we know that we shall continue to be Christians throughout our lives? Is there anything that will keep us from falling away from Christ, anything that will guarantee that we will remain Christians until we die and that we will in fact live with God in heaven forever? Or might it be that we will turn away from Christ and lose the blessings of our salvation? The topic of the perseverance of the saints speaks to these questions. *The perseverance of the saints means that all those who are truly born again will be kept by God's power and will persevere as Christians until the end of their lives, and that only those who persevere until the end have been truly born again.*

This definition has two parts to it. It indicates first that there is assurance to be given to those who are truly born again, for it reminds them that God's power will keep them as Christians until they die, and they will surely live with Christ in heaven forever. On the other hand, the second half of the definition makes it clear that continuing in the Christian life is one of the evidences that a person is truly born again. It is important to keep this aspect of the doctrine in mind as well, lest false assurance be given to people who were never really believers in the first place.

It should be noted that this question is one on which evangelical Christians have long had significant disagreement. Many within the Wesleyan/Arminian tradition have held that it is possible for someone who is truly born again to lose his or her salvation, while Reformed Christians have held that that is not possible.[1] Most Baptists have followed the Reformed tradition at this point; however, they have frequently used the term *eternal security* or the *eternal security of the believer* rather than the term *perseverance of the saints*.

A. All Who Are Truly Born Again Will Persevere to the End

Many passages teach that those who are truly born again, who are genuinely Christians, will continue in the Christian life until death and will then go to be with

---

[1]The doctrine of the perseverance of the saints is represented by P in the acronym TULIP, which is often used to summarize the "five points of Calvinism." (See full list at p. 288, n. 3.)

Christ in heaven. Jesus says: "I have come down from heaven, not to do my own will, but the will of him who sent me; and this is the will of him who sent me, that I should lose nothing of all that he has given me, but raise it up at the last day. For this is the will of my Father, that *every one who* sees the Son and *believes in* him should have eternal life; and *I will raise him up at the last day*" (John 6:38–40). Here Jesus says that everyone who believes in him will have eternal life. He says that he will raise that person up at the last day—which, in this context of believing in the Son and having eternal life, clearly means that Jesus will raise that person up to eternal life with him (not just raise him up to be judged and condemned). It seems hard to avoid the conclusion that everyone who truly believes in Christ will remain a Christian up to the day of final resurrection into the blessings of life in the presence of God. Moreover, this text emphasizes that Jesus does the will of the Father, which is that he should "*lose nothing* of all that he has given me" (John 6:39). Once again, those given to the Son by the Father will not be lost.

Another passage emphasizing this truth is John 10:27–29, in which Jesus says, "My sheep hear my voice, and I know them, and they follow me; and I give them eternal life, and *they shall never perish,* and no one shall snatch them out of my hand. My Father, who has given them to me, is greater than all, and no one is able to snatch them out of the Father's hand."

Here Jesus says that those who follow him, those who are his sheep, are given eternal life. He further says that "no one shall snatch them out of my hand" (v. 28). Now some have objected to this that even though no one else can take Christians out of Christ's hand, we might remove ourselves from Christ's hand. But that seems to be quibbling over words—does not "no one" also include the person who is in Christ's hand? Moreover, we know that our own hearts are far from trustworthy. Therefore, if the possibility remained that we could remove ourselves from Christ's hand, the passage would hardly give the assurance that Jesus intends by it.

But more importantly, the most forceful phrase in the passage is "*They shall never perish*" (v. 28). The Greek construction (*ou mē* plus aorist subjunctive) is especially emphatic and might be translated more explicitly, "and they shall *certainly not perish* forever." This emphasizes that those who are Jesus' "sheep" and who follow him, and to whom he has given eternal life, shall never lose their salvation or be separated from Christ—they shall "never perish."

There are several other passages that say those who believe have "eternal life." One example is John 3:36: "He who believes in the Son *has eternal life*" (cf. also John 5:24; 6:4–7; 10:28; 1 John 5:13). Now if this is truly *eternal* life that believers have, then it is life that lasts forever with God. It is often put in contrast to condemnation and eternal judgment (e.g., John 3:16–17, 36; 10:28), and the emphasis in this text with the adjective *eternal* further shows that this is life that goes on forever in God's presence.

Evidence in Paul's writings and the other New Testament epistles also indicates that those who are truly born again will persevere to the end. There remains "no condemnation for those who are in Christ Jesus" (Rom. 8:1); therefore, it would be unjust for God to give any kind of eternal punishment to those who are Christians—no condemnation remains for them, for the entire penalty for their sins has been paid.

Then in Romans 8:30, Paul emphasizes the clear connection between God's eternal purposes in predestination and his working out of those purposes in life, together with his final realization of those purposes in "glorifying" or giving final resurrection bodies to those whom he has brought into union with Christ: "Those whom he predestined he also called; and those whom he called he also justified; and those whom he justified he also glorified." Here Paul sees the future event of glorification as such a certainty in God's settled purpose that he can speak of it as if it were already accomplished ("he also glorified"). This is true of all those who are called and justified—that is, all those who truly become Christians.

Further evidence that God keeps those who are born again safe for eternity is the "seal" that God places upon us. This "seal" is the Holy Spirit within us, who also acts as God's "guarantee" that we will receive the inheritance promised to us: "In him you also, who have heard the word of truth, the gospel of your salvation, and have believed in him, were *sealed with the promised Holy Spirit,* which is the *guarantee* of our inheritance until we acquire possession of it, to the praise of his glory" (Eph. 1:13–14). The Greek word translated "guarantee" in this passage *(arrabōn)* is a legal and commercial term that means "first installment, deposit, down payment, pledge" and represents "a payment which obligates the contracting party to make further payments."[2] When God gave us the Holy Spirit within, he committed himself to give all the further blessings of eternal life and a great reward in heaven with him. This is why Paul can say that the Holy Spirit is the *"guarantee* of our inheritance until we acquire possession of it" (Eph. 1:14). All who have the Holy Spirit within them, all who are truly born again, have God's unchanging promise and guarantee that the inheritance of eternal life in heaven will certainly be theirs. God's own faithfulness is pledged to bring it about.

Peter tells his readers that they are those "who *by God's power are guarded* through faith for a salvation ready to be revealed in the last time" (1 Peter 1:5). The word "guarded" (Gk. *Phroureō*) can mean both "kept from escaping" and "protected from attack," and perhaps both kinds of guarding are intended here: God is preserving believers from escaping out of his kingdom, and he is protecting them from external attacks. "Salvation" is used here not of past justification or of present sanctification (speaking in theological categories), but of the future full possession of all the blessings of our redemption—of the final, complete fulfillment of our salvation (cf. Rom. 13:11; 1 Peter 2:2). Though already prepared or "ready," it will not be "revealed" by God to mankind generally until the "last time," the time of final judgment. If God's guarding has as its purpose the preservation of believers until they receive their full, heavenly salvation, then it is safe to conclude that God will accomplish that purpose and they will in fact attain that final salvation. Their attainment of final salvation ultimately depends on God's power.

B. Only Those Who Persevere to the End Have Been Truly Born Again

While Scripture repeatedly emphasizes that those who are truly born again will persevere to the end and will certainly have eternal life in heaven with God, there are other passages that speak of the necessity of continuing in faith throughout life. They make us realize that what Peter said in 1 Peter 1:5 ("who *by God's power* are guarded *through faith*") is true, namely, that God does not guard us *apart from* our faith, but only by working *through* our faith so that he enables us to continue to believe in him. In this way, those who continue to trust in Christ gain assurance that God is working in them and guarding them.

---

[2]BAGD, p. 109.

One example of this kind of passage is John 8:31–32: "Jesus then said to the Jews who had believed in him, '*If you continue in my word,* you are truly my disciples, and you will know the truth, and the truth will make you free.'" Jesus is here giving a warning that one evidence of genuine faith is continuing in his Word, that is, continuing to believe what he says and living a life of obedience to his commands. Similarly, Jesus says, "*He who endures to the end* will be saved" (Matt. 10:22), as a means of warning people not to fail away in times of persecution.

Paul says to the Colossian Christians that Christ has reconciled them to God "in order to present you holy and blameless and irreproachable before him, *provided that you continue in the faith,* stable and steadfast, not shifting from the hope of the gospel which you heard" (Col. 1:22–23). It is only natural that Paul and the other New Testament writers would speak this way, for they are addressing groups of people who profess to be Christians, without being able to know the actual state of every person's heart. There may have been people at Colossae who had joined in the fellowship of the church, and perhaps even professed that they had faith in Christ and had been baptized into membership of the church, but who never had true saving faith. How is Paul to distinguish such people from true believers? How can he avoid giving them false assurance, assurance that they will be saved eternally when in fact they will not, unless they come to true repentance and faith? Paul knows that those whose faith is not real will eventually fall away from participation in the fellowship of the church. Therefore, he tells his readers that they will ultimately be saved, "*provided that you continue in the faith*" (Col. 1:23). Those who continue show thereby that they are genuine believers. But those who do not continue in the faith show that there was no genuine faith in their hearts in the first place.

A similar emphasis is seen in Hebrews 3:14 (NASB): "For we have become partakers of Christ, *if we hold fast the beginning of our assurance firm to the end.*" This verse provides an excellent perspective on the doctrine of perseverance. How do we know if "we have become partakers of Christ"? How do we know if this being joined to Christ has happened to us at some time in the past? One way in which we know that we have come to genuine faith in Christ is *if we continue in faith* until the end of our lives.

We should remember that there are other evidences elsewhere in Scripture that give Christians assurance of salvation (see section D below), so *we should not think that assurance that we belong to Christ is impossible until we die.* However, continuing in faith is the one means of assurance that is named here by the author of Hebrews. Moreover, in this and in all of the other passages about the need to continue in faith, *the purpose is never to make those who are presently trusting in Christ worry that sometime in the future they might fall away.* We should never use these passages that way either, for that would be to give wrongful cause for worry in a way that Scripture does not intend. Rather, the purpose is always *to warn those who are thinking of falling away or have fallen away* that if they do this it is a strong indication that they were never saved in the first place. Thus, the necessity for continuing in faith should just be used as a warning against falling away, a warning that those who fall away give evidence that their faith was never real.

C. Those Who Finally Fall Away May Give Many External Signs of Conversion

Is it always clear which people in the church have genuine saving faith and which have only an intellectual persuasion of the truth of the gospel but no genuine faith in their hearts? It is not always easy to tell, and Scripture mentions in several places that unbelievers in fellowship with the visible church can give some external signs or indications that make them look or sound like genuine believers. For example, Judas, who betrayed Christ, must have acted almost exactly like the other disciples during the three years he was with Jesus. So convincing was his conformity to the behavior pattern of the other disciples, that at the end of three years of Jesus' ministry, when he said that one of his disciples would betray him, they did not all turn and suspect Judas, but they rather "began to say to him one after another, 'Is it I?'" (Matt. 26:22; cf. Mark 14:19; Luke 22:23; John 13:22). However, Jesus himself knew that there was no genuine faith in Judas's heart, because he said at one point, "Did I not choose you, the twelve, and one of you is a devil?" (John 6:70). John later wrote in his gospel that "Jesus knew from the first who those were that did not believe, and who it was that would betray him" (John 6:64). But the disciples themselves did not know.

Paul also speaks of "*false brethren* secretly brought in" (Gal. 2:4) and says that in his journeys he has been "in danger from *false brethren*" (2 Cor. 11:26). He also says that the servants of Satan "*disguise themselves* as servants of righteousness" (2 Cor. 11:15). This does not mean that all unbelievers in the church who nevertheless give some signs of true conversion are servants of Satan secretly undermining the work of the church, for some may be in process of considering the claims of the gospel and moving toward real faith, others may have heard only an inadequate explanation of the gospel message, and others may not have come under genuine conviction of the Holy Spirit yet. But Paul's statements do mean that some unbelievers in the church will be false brothers and sisters sent to disrupt the fellowship, while others will simply be unbelievers who will eventually come to genuine saving faith. In both cases, however, they give several external signs that make them look like genuine believers.

We can see this also in Jesus' statement about what will happen at the last judgment: "Not every one who says to me, 'Lord, Lord,' shall enter the kingdom of heaven, but he who does the will of my Father who is in heaven. On that day many will say to me, 'Lord, Lord, did we not prophesy in your name, and cast out demons in your name, and do many mighty works in your name?' And then will I declare to them, '*I never knew you;* depart from me, you evildoers'" (Matt. 7:21–23).

Although these people prophesied and cast out demons and did "many mighty works" in Jesus' name, the ability to do such works did not guarantee that they were Christians. Jesus says, "I never knew you." He does not say, "I knew you at one time but I no longer know you," or "I knew you at one time but you strayed away from me," but rather, "I *never* knew you." They never were genuine believers.

A similar teaching is found in the parable of the sower in Mark 4. Jesus says, "Other seed fell on rocky ground, where it had not much soil, and immediately it sprang up, since it had no depth of soil; and when the sun rose it was scorched, and since it had no root it withered away" (Mark 4:5–6). Jesus explains that the seed sown upon rocky ground represents people who "when they hear the word, immediately receive it with joy; and *they have no root in themselves,* but endure for a while; then, when tribulation or persecution arises on account of the word, immediately they fall away" (Mark 4:16–17). The fact that they "have no root in themselves" indicates that there is no source of life within these plants; similarly, the people represented by them have no genuine life of their own within. They have an appearance of conversion and they apparently have become Christians, because they receive the word "with joy," but when difficulty comes, they are nowhere to be found—their apparent conversion was not genuine and there was no real saving faith in their hearts.

The importance of continuing in faith is also affirmed in the parable of Jesus as the vine, in which Christians are portrayed as branches (John 15:1–7). Jesus says: "I am the true vine, and my Father is the vinedresser. Every branch of mine that bears no fruit, he takes away, and every branch that does bear fruit he prunes, that it may bear more fruit.... If a man does not abide in me, he is cast forth as a branch and withers; and the branches are gathered, thrown into the fire and burned" (John 15:1–2, 6).

Arminians have argued that the branches that do not bear fruit are still true branches on the vine—Jesus refers to "Every branch *of mine* that bears no fruit" (v. 2). Therefore, the branches that are gathered and thrown into the fire and burned must refer to true believers who were once part of the vine but fell away and became subject to eternal judgment. But that is not a necessary implication of Jesus' teaching at this point. The imagery of the vine used in this parable is limited in how much detail it can teach. In fact, if Jesus had wanted to teach that there were true and false believers associated with him, and if he wanted to use the analogy of a vine and branches, then the only way he could refer to people who do not have genuine life in themselves would be to speak of branches that bear no fruit (somewhat after the analogy of the seeds that fell on rocky ground and had "no root in themselves" in Mark 4:17). Here in John 15 the branches that do not bear fruit, though they are in some way connected to Jesus and give an outward appearance of being genuine branches, nonetheless give indication of their true state by the fact that they bear no fruit. This is similarly indicated by the fact that the person "does not abide" in Christ (John 15:6) and is cast off as a branch and withers. If we try to press the analogy any further, by saying, for example, that all branches on a vine really are alive or they would not be there in the first place, then we are simply trying to press the imagery beyond what it is able to teach—and in that case there would be nothing in the analogy that could represent false believers in any case. The point of the imagery is simply that those who bear fruit thereby give evidence that they are abiding in Christ; those who do not, are not abiding in him.

Finally, there are two passages in Hebrews that also affirm that those who finally fall away may give many external signs of conversion and may look in many ways like Christians. The first of these, Hebrews 6:4–6, has frequently been used by Arminians as proof that believers can lose their salvation. But on closer inspection such an interpretation is not convincing. The author writes, "For it is impossible to restore again to repentance those who have once been enlightened, who have tasted the heavenly gift, and have become partakers of the Holy Spirit, and have tasted the goodness of the word of God and the powers of the age to come, if they then commit apostasy, since they crucify the Son of God on their own account and hold him up to contempt" (Heb. 6:4–6).

At this point we may ask what kind of person is described by all of these terms. Does this text describe a person who has been genuinely born again?[3] These are no doubt people who have been *affiliated closely with the fellowship of the church.* They have had some sorrow for sin (repentance). They have clearly understood the gospel (they have been enlightened). They have come to appreciate the attractiveness of

---

[3]For a much lengthier discussion of this passage, see Wayne Grudem, "Perseverance of the Saints: A Case Study from Hebrews 6:4–6 and the Other Warning Passages in Hebrews," in *The Grace of God and the Bondage of the Will,* ed. Thomas Schreiner and Bruce Ware (Grand Rapids: Baker, 1995), 1:133–82.

the Christian life and the change that comes about in people's lives because of becoming a Christian, and they probably have had answers to prayer in their own lives and felt the power of the Holy Spirit at work, perhaps even using some spiritual gifts in the manner of the unbelievers in Matthew 7:22 (they have become "associated with" the work of the Holy Spirit or have become "partakers" of the Holy Spirit and have the heavenly gift and the powers of the age of come). They have been exposed to the true preaching of the Word and have appreciated much of its teachings (they have tasted the goodness of the Word of God).

But in spite of all this, if they "commit apostasy" and "crucify the Son of God on their own account and hold him up to contempt" (Heb. 6:6), then they are willfully rejecting all of these blessings and turning decidedly against them. The author tells us that if this occurs, it will be impossible to restore these people again to any kind of repentance or sorrow for sin. Their hearts will be hardened and their consciences calloused. Their repeated familiarity with the things of God and their experience of many influences of the Holy Spirit has simply served to harden them against conversion.

It is clear that there were some in the community to which this letter was written who were in danger of falling away in just this manner (see Heb. 2:3; 3:8, 12, 14–15; 4:1, 7, 11; 10:26, 29, 35–36, 38–39; 12:3, 15–17). The author wants to warn them that, though they have participated in the fellowship of the church and experienced a number of God's blessings in their lives, yet if they fall away after all that, there is no salvation for them. He wants to use the strongest language possible to say, "Here is how far a person can come in experiencing *temporary blessings* and still not really be saved." He is warning them to watch out, because depending on temporary blessings and experiences is not enough. This does not imply that he thinks that true Christians could fall away—Hebrews 3:14 implies quite the opposite. But he wants them to gain assurance of salvation through their continuing in faith and thereby implies that if they fall away, it would show that they never were Christ's people in the first place.

For this reason, he immediately passes from this description of those who commit apostasy to a further analogy that shows that these people who fell away never had any genuine fruit in their lives. Verses 7–8 speak of these same people in terms of "thorns and thistles," the kind of crop that is brought forth on land that has no worthwhile life in itself even though it receives repeated blessings from God (in terms of the analogy, even though rain frequently falls upon it). We should notice here that people who commit apostasy are *not compared to a field that once bore good fruit and now does not,* but that they are like *land that never bore good fruit,* but only thorns and thistles. The land may look good before the crops start to come up, but the fruit gives the genuine evidence, and it is bad.

Strong support for this interpretation of Hebrews 6:4–8 is found in the verse immediately following. Though the author has been speaking very harshly about the possibility of falling away, he then returns to speak to the situation of the great majority of the hearers whom he thinks to be genuine Christians. He says, "Though we speak thus, *yet in your case,* beloved, *we feel sure of better things that belong to salvation*" (Heb. 6:9). But the question is "better things" than what? The plural "better things" forms an appropriate contrast to the "good things" that have been mentioned in verses 4–6; the author is convinced that most of his readers have experienced *better things* than simply the partial and temporary influences of the Holy Spirit and the church talked about in verses 4–6.

In fact, the author talks about these things by saying (literally) that they are "better things, *also holding fast to salvation*" (Gk. *kai echomena sōterias*).[4] These are not only the temporary blessings talked about in verses 4–6, but these are *better things,* things having not only temporary influence, but *"also holding fast to salvation."* In this way, the Greek word *kai,* "also," shows that salvation is something that was not part of the things mentioned in verses 4–6 above. Therefore, this word *kai,* which is not explicitly translated in the RSV or NIV (but the NASB comes close),[5] provides a crucial key for understanding the passage. If the author had meant to say that the people mentioned in verses 4–6 were truly saved, then it is very difficult to understand why he would say in verse 9 that he is convinced of better things for them, *things that also (or "in addition") hold fast to salvation.* These things have "salvation" as an addition to those things mentioned above. He thus shows that he can use a brief phrase to say that people "have salvation" if he wishes to do so (he does not need to pile up many phrases), and he shows, moreover, that the people that he speaks of in verses 4–6 are not saved.

What exactly are these "better things"? In addition to salvation mentioned in verse 9, they are things that give real evidence of salvation—genuine fruit in their lives (v. 10), full assurance of hope (v. 11), and saving faith, of the type exhibited by those who inherit the promises (v. 12). In this way, he reassures those who are genuine believers—those who show fruit in their lives and show love for other Christians, who show hope and genuine faith that is continuing at the present time, and who are not about to fall away. He wants to reassure these readers (who are certainly the great majority of the ones to whom he writes) while still issuing a strong warning to those among them who may be in danger of falling away.

A similar teaching is found in Hebrews 10:26–31. There the author says, "If we deliberately keep on sinning after we have received the knowledge of the truth, no sacrifice for sins is left" (v. 26 NIV). A person who rejects Christ's salvation and "has treated as an unholy thing the blood of the covenant that sanctified him" (v. 29 NIV) deserves eternal punishment. This again is a strong warning against falling away, but it should not be taken as proof that someone who has truly been born again can lose his or her salvation. When the author talks about the blood of the covenant "that sanctified him," the word *sanctified* is used simply to refer to "external sanctification, like that of the ancient Israelites, by outward connection with God's people."[6] The passage does not talk about someone who is genuinely saved, but someone who has received some beneficial moral influence through contact with the church.

D. What Can Give a Believer Genuine Assurance?

If it is true, as explained in the previous section, that those who are unbelievers and who finally fall away may give many external signs of conversion, then what will serve as evidence of genuine conversion? What can give real assurance to a real believer? We can list three categories of questions that a person could ask of himself or herself.

---

[4]BAGD, p. 334, III, translates the middle participle of *echō* as "hold oneself fast, cling to," and lists Heb. 6:9 as the only New Testament example of this form used "of inner belonging and close association" (cf. LSJ, p. 750, C: "hold oneself fast, cling closely"). However, even if we translated the middle voice in the same way as the active, the phrase would mean, "things also *having* salvation," and my argument in this section would not be affected.

[5]The NASB translates, "and things that accompany salvation."

[6]Augustus H. Strong, *Systematic Theology* (Valley Forge, Pa.: Judson, 1907), p. 884. Outward ceremonial sanctification is also referred to in Heb. 9:13; cf. Matt. 23:17, 19.

1. Do I have a present trust in Christ for salvation? Paul tells the Colossians that they will be saved on the last day, "provided that you *continue in the faith*, stable and steadfast, not shifting from the hope of the gospel which you heard" (Col. 1:23). The author of Hebrews says, "We share in Christ, if only we hold our first confidence firm to the end" (Heb. 3:14) and encourages his readers to be imitators of those "who through faith and patience inherit the promises" (Heb. 6:12). In fact, the most famous verse in the entire Bible uses a present tense verb that may be translated, "whoever continues believing in him" may have eternal life (see John 3:16).

Therefore a person should ask himself or herself, "Do I today have trust in Christ to forgive my sins and take me without blame into heaven forever? Do I have confidence in my heart that he has saved me? If I were to die tonight and stand before God's judgment seat, and if he were to ask me why he should let me into heaven, would I begin to think of my good deeds and depend on them, or would I without hesitation say that I am depending on the merits of Christ and am confident that he is a sufficient Savior?"

This emphasis on *present* faith in Christ stands in contrast to the practice of some church "testimonies" where people repeatedly recite details of a conversion experience that may have happened twenty or thirty years ago. If a testimony of saving faith is genuine, it should be a testimony of faith that is active this very day.

2. Is there evidence of a regenerating work of the Holy Spirit in my heart? The evidence of the work of the Holy Spirit in our hearts comes in many different forms. Although we should not put confidence in the demonstration of miraculous works (Matt. 7:22), or long hours and years of work at some local church (which may simply be building with "wood, hay, straw" [in terms of 1 Cor. 3:12] to further one's own ego or power over others or to attempt to earn merit with God), there are many other evidences of a real work of the Holy Spirit in one's heart.

First, there is a subjective *testimony of the Holy Spirit within our hearts* bearing witness that we are God's children (Rom. 8:15–16; 1 John 4:13). This testimony will usually be accompanied by a sense of being led by the Holy Spirit in paths of obedience to God's will (Rom. 8:14).

In addition, if the Holy Spirit is genuinely at work in our lives, he will be producing the kind of character traits that Paul calls "the *fruit of the Spirit*" (Gal. 5:22). He lists several attitudes and character traits that are produced by the Holy Spirit: "love, joy, peace, patience, kindness, goodness, faithfulness, gentleness, self-control" (Gal. 5:22–23). Of course, the question is not, "Do I perfectly exemplify all of these characteristics in my life?" but rather, "Are these things a general characteristic of my life? Do I sense these attitudes in my heart? Do others (especially those closest to me) see these traits exhibited in my life? Have I been growing in them over a period of years?" There is no suggestion in the New Testament that any non-Christian, any unregenerate person, can convincingly fake these character traits, especially for those who know the person most closely.

Related to this kind of fruit, is another kind of fruit—the *results of one's life and ministry* as they have influence on others and on the church. There are some people who profess to be Christians but whose influence on others is to discourage them, to drag them down, to injure their faith, and to provoke controversy and divisiveness. The result of their life and ministry is not to build up others and to build up the church, but to tear it down. On the other hand, there are those who seem to edify others in every conversation, every prayer, and every work of ministry to which they put their hand. Jesus said, regarding false prophets, "You will know them by their fruits.... Every sound tree bears good fruit, but the bad tree bears evil fruit.... Thus you will know them by their fruits" (Matt. 7:16–20).

Another evidence of work of the Holy Spirit is *continuing to believe and accept the sound teaching of the church*. Those who begin to deny major doctrines of the faith give serious negative indications concerning their salvation: "No one who denies the Son has the Father.... If what you heard from the beginning abides in you, then you will abide in the Son and in the Father" (1 John 2:23–24). John also says, "Whoever knows God listens to us, and he who is not of God does not listen to us" (1 John 4:6). Since the New Testament writings are the current replacement for the apostles like John, we might also say that whoever knows God will continue to read and delight in God's Word, and will continue to believe it fully. Those who do not believe and delight in God's Word give evidence that they are not "of God."

Another evidence of genuine salvation is *a continuing present relationship with Jesus Christ*. Jesus says, "Abide in me, and I in you," and "If you abide in me, and my words abide in you, ask whatever you will, and it shall be done for you" (John 15:4, 7). This abiding in Christ will include not only day-by-day trust in him in various situations, but also certainly regular fellowship with him in prayer and worship. This abiding will also include *obedience* to God's commands. John says, "He who says 'I know him' but disobeys his commandments is a liar, and the truth is not in him; but whoever keeps his word, in him truly love for God is perfected. By this we may be sure that we are in him: he who says he abides in him ought to walk in the same way in which he walked" (1 John 2:4–6). A perfect life is not necessary, of course. John is rather saying that in general our lives ought to be ones of imitation of Christ and likeness to him in what we do and say. If we have genuine saving faith, there will be clear results in obedience in our lives (see also 1 John 3:9–10, 24; 5:18).

3. Do I see a long-term pattern of growth in my Christian life? The first two areas of assurance dealt with present faith and present evidence of the Holy Spirit at work in our lives. But Peter gives one more kind of test that we can use to ask whether we are genuinely believers. He tells us that there are some character traits which, if we keep on increasing in them, will guarantee that we will "never fall" (2 Peter 1:10). He tells his readers to add to their faith "virtue ... knowledge ... self-control ... steadfastness ... godliness ... brotherly affection ... love" (2 Peter 1:5–7). Then he says that these things are to belong to his readers and to continually "abound" in their lives (2 Peter 1:8). He adds that they are to "be the more zealous to confirm your call and election" and says then that "*if you do this* [lit. 'these things,' referring to the character traits mentioned in vv. 5–7] *you will never fall*" (2 Peter 1:10).

The way that we confirm our call and election, then, is to continue to grow in "these things." This implies that our assurance of salvation can be something that increases over time in our lives. Every year that we add to these character traits in our lives, we gain greater and greater assurance of our salvation. Thus, though young believers can have a quite strong confidence in their salvation, that assurance can increase to even deeper certainty over the years in which they grow toward Christian maturity. If they continue to add these things, they will confirm their call and election and will "never fall."

The result of these three questions that we can ask ourselves should be to give strong assurance to those who are genuinely believers. In this way, the doctrine of the perseverance of the saints will be a tremendously comforting doctrine. No one who has such assurance should wonder, "Will I be able to persevere to the end of my life and therefore be saved?" Everyone who gains assurance through such a self-examination should rather think, "I am truly born again; therefore, I will certainly persevere to the end, because I am being guarded 'by God's power' working through my faith (1 Peter 1:5) and therefore I will never be lost. Jesus will raise me up at the last day and I will enter into his kingdom forever" (John 6:40).

On the other hand, this doctrine of the perseverance of the saints, if rightly understood, should cause genuine worry, and even fear, in the hearts of any who are "backsliding" or straying away from Christ. Such persons must clearly be warned that only those who persevere to the end have been truly born again. If they fall away from their profession of faith in Christ and life of obedience to him, they may not really be saved—in fact, the evidence that they are then giving is that they are not saved, and they never really were saved. Once they stop trusting in Christ and obeying him, they have no genuine assurance of salvation, and they should consider themselves unsaved, and turn to Christ in repentance and ask him for forgiveness of their sins.

At this point, in terms of pastoral care with those who have strayed away from their Christian profession, we should realize that Calvinists and Arminians (those who believe in the perseverance of the saints and those who think that Christians can lose their salvation) will both counsel a "backslider" in the same way. According to the Arminian, this person was a Christian at one time but is no longer a Christian. According to the Calvinist, such a person never really was a Christian in the first place and is not one now. But in both cases the biblical counsel given would be the same: "You do not appear to be a Christian now—you must repent of your sins and trust in Christ for your salvation!" Though the Calvinist and Arminian would differ on their interpretation of the previous history, they would agree on what should be done in the present.

But here we see why the term *eternal security,* when used improperly, can be quite misleading. In some evangelical churches, instead of teaching the full and balanced presentation of the doctrine of the perseverance of the saints, pastors have sometimes taught a watered-down version, which in effect tells people that all who have once made a profession of faith and been baptized are "eternally secure." The result is that some people who are not genuinely converted at all may "come forward" at the end of an evangelistic sermon to profess faith in Christ and may be baptized shortly after that, but then they leave the fellowship of the church and live a life no different than the one they lived before they gained this "eternal security." In this way, people are given false assurance and are being cruelly deceived into thinking they are going to heaven when in fact they are not.

II. REVIEW QUESTIONS

1. Is it true that all who are truly born again will persevere in the Christian faith until the end of their lives? Support your answer from Scripture.

2. Given our earlier discussions on election, effective calling, and regeneration (chs. 18–20), is continuing in the Christian life a necessary evidence of genuine faith? Explain.

3. 　　　　　　　　　r a person to give external signs of conversion and later
　　　　　　　　.e Christian faith?

　　　　　　.1an perspective, can a believer ever really have any assurance
　　　.? Explain.

　　　.ree evidences of genuine faith that can give assurance to a true
　.iever.

III. QUESTIONS FOR PERSONAL APPLICATION

1. Do you have assurance that you are truly born again? What evidence do you
   see in your own life to give you that assurance? Do you think that God
   wants true believers to have this assurance? (See 1 John 5:13.) Have you
   seen a pattern of growth in your Christian life over time? Are you trusting in
   your own power to keep on believing in Christ, or in God's power to keep
   your faith active and alive?

2. If you have doubts about whether you are truly born again, what is it in
   your life that is giving reason for those doubts? What would Scripture
   encourage you to do to resolve those doubts (see 2 Peter 1:5–11; also Matt.
   11:28–30; John 6:37)?

3. Have you known people, perhaps in your church, whose "fruit" is always
   destructive or divisive or harmful to the ministry of the church and the faith
   of others? Do you think that an evaluation of the fruit of one's life and influence on others should be a qualification for church leadership? Is it possible
   that people would profess agreement with every true Christian doctrine and
   still not be born again? What are some more reliable evidences of genuine
   conversion other than intellectual adherence to sound doctrine?

IV. SPECIAL TERMS

assurance of salvation	perseverance of the saints
eternal security	temporary blessings

V. SCRIPTURE MEMORY PASSAGE

JOHN 10:27–28

*My sheep hear my voice, and I know them, and they follow me; and I
give them eternal life, and they shall never perish, and no one shall
snatch them out of my hand.*

CHAPTER TWENTY-FIVE

Death, the Intermediate State, and Glorification

+ *What is the purpose of death in the Christian life?*
+ *What happens to our bodies and souls when we die?*
+ *When will we receive resurrection bodies?*
+ *What will they be like?*

I. EXPLANATION AND SCRIPTURAL BASIS

A. Death: Why Do Christians Die?

Our treatment of the application of redemption must include a consideration of death and the question of how Christians should view their own death and the death of others. We also must ask what happens to us between the time we die and the time Christ returns to give us new resurrection bodies.

1. Death is not a punishment for Christians. Paul tells us clearly that there is "no condemnation for those who are in Christ Jesus" (Rom. 8:1). All the penalty for our sins has been paid. Therefore, even though we know that Christians die, we should not view the death of Christians as a punishment from God or in any way a result of a penalty due to us for our sins. It is true that the penalty for sin is death, but that penalty no longer applies to us—not in terms of physical death, and not in terms of spiritual death or separation from God. All of that has been paid for by Christ. Therefore, there must be another reason than punishment for our sins if we are to understand why Christians die.

2. Death is the final outcome of living in a fallen world. In his great wisdom, God decided that he would not apply to us the benefits of Christ's redemptive work all at once. Rather, he has chosen to apply the benefits of salvation to us gradually over time (as we have seen in chs. 19–25). Similarly, he has not chosen to remove all evil from the world immediately, but to wait until the final judgment and the establishment of the new heaven and new earth (see chs. 33 and 34). In short, we still live in a fallen world and our experience of salvation is still incomplete.

The last aspect of the fallen world to be removed will be death. Paul says: "Then comes the end, when he delivers the kingdom to God the Father after destroying every rule and every authority and power. For he must reign until he has put all his enemies under his feet. *The last enemy to be destroyed is death*" (1 Cor. 15:26).

When Christ returns,

> then shall come to pass the saying that is written:
> "Death is swallowed up in victory."
> "O death, where is your victory?
> O death, where is your sting?" (1 Cor. 15:54–55)

But until that time death remains a reality even in the lives of Christians. Although death does not come to us as a penalty for our individual sins (for that has been paid by Christ), it does come to us as a result of living in a fallen world, where the effects of sin have not all been removed. Related to the experience of death are other results of the fall that harm our physical bodies and signal the presence of death in the world—Christians as well as non-Christians experience aging, illnesses, injuries, and natural disasters (such as floods, violent storms, and earthquakes). Although God often answers prayers to deliver Christians (and also non-Christians) from some of these effects of the fall for a time (and thereby indicates the nature of his coming kingdom), nevertheless, Christians eventually experience all of these things to some measure, and, until Christ returns, all of us will grow old and die. The "last enemy" has not yet been destroyed. And God has chosen to allow us to experience death before we gain all the benefits of salvation that have been earned for us.

3. God uses the experience of death to complete our sanctification. Throughout our Christian lives we know that we never have to pay any penalty for sin, for that has all been taken by Christ (Rom. 8:1). Therefore, when we do experience pain and suffering in this life, we should never think it is because God is *punishing* us (for our harm). Sometimes suffering is simply a result of living in a sinful, fallen world, and sometimes it is because God is *disciplining* us (for our good), but in all cases we are assured by Romans 8:28 that "God causes *all things* to work together for good to those who love God, to those who are called according to His purpose" (NASB).

The positive purpose for God's discipline is clear in Hebrews 12, where we read, "The Lord disciplines him whom he loves.... He disciplines us for our good, that we may share his holiness. For the moment all discipline seems painful rather than pleasant; later it yields the peaceful fruit of righteousness to those who have been trained by it" (Heb. 12:6, 10–11). Not all discipline serves to correct us when we have committed sins; God may allow it to strengthen us so that we may gain greater ability to trust him and to resist sin in the challenging path of obedience. We see this clearly in the life of Jesus, who, though he was without sin, yet "learned obedience *through what he suffered*" (Heb. 5:8). He was made perfect *"through suffering"* (Heb. 2:10). Therefore, we should see all the hardship and suffering that comes to us in life as something that God brings to us *to do us good,* strengthening our trust in him and our obedience, and ultimately increasing our ability to glorify him.

The understanding that death is not in any way a punishment for sin, but simply something God brings us through in order to make us more like Christ, should be a great encouragement to us. It should take away from us the fear of death that haunts the minds of unbelievers (cf. Heb. 2:15). Nevertheless, although God will bring good to us through the process of death, we must still remember that death is not natural; it is not right; and in a world created by God, it is something that ought not to be. It is an enemy—something that Christ will finally destroy (1 Cor. 15:26).

4. Our obedience to God is more important than preserving our own lives. If God uses the experience of death to deepen our trust in him and to strengthen our obedience to him, then it is important that we remember that the world's goal of preserving one's own physical life at all costs is not the highest goal for a Christian: *Obedience to God and faithfulness to him in every circumstance is far more important.* This is why Paul could say, "I am ready not only to be imprisoned but even to die at Jerusalem for the name of the Lord Jesus" (Acts 21:13; cf. 25:11). He told the Ephesian elders, "I do not account my life of any value nor as precious to myself, if only I may accomplish my course and the ministry which I received from the Lord Jesus, to testify to the gospel of the grace of God" (Acts 20:24). When Paul was in prison, not knowing whether he would die there or come out alive, he could still say, "It is my eager expectation and hope that I shall not be at all ashamed, but that with full courage now as always *Christ will be honored* in my body, *whether by life or by death*" (Phil. 1:20).

The persuasion that we may honor the Lord even in our death and that faithfulness to him is far more important than preserving our lives, has given courage and motivation to martyrs throughout the history of the church. When faced with a choice of preserving their own lives and sinning, or giving up their own lives and being faithful, they chose to give up their own lives— *"they loved not their lives even unto death"* (Rev. 12:11). Even in times when there is little persecution and little likelihood of martyrdom, it would be good for us to fix this truth in our minds once for all, for if we are willing to give up even our lives for faithfulness to God, we shall find it much easier to give up everything else for the sake of Christ as well.

B. How Should We Think of Our Own Death and the Death of Others?

1. Our own death. The New Testament encourages us to view our own death, not with fear, but with joy at the prospect of going to be with Christ. Paul says, "We would rather be away from the body and at home with the Lord" (2 Cor. 5:8). When he is in prison, not knowing whether he will be executed or released, he can say: "For to me to live is Christ, and *to die is gain.* If it is to be life in the flesh, that means fruitful labor for me. Yet which I shall choose I cannot tell. I am hard pressed between the two. *My desire is to depart and be with Christ, for that is far better*" (Phil. 1:21–23).

We also read John's word in Revelation: "I heard a voice from heaven saying, 'Write this: *Blessed are the dead who die in the Lord henceforth.*' 'Blessed indeed,' says the Spirit, 'that they may rest from their labors, for their deeds follow them!'" (Rev. 14:13).

Believers need have no fear of death, therefore, for Scripture reassures us that not even "death" will "separate us from the love of God in Christ Jesus our Lord" (Rom. 8:38–39; cf. Ps. 23:4). In fact, Jesus died that he might "deliver all those who through fear of death were subject to lifelong bondage" (Heb. 2:15). This verse reminds us that a clear testimony to our lack of fear of death will provide a strong witness for Christians in an age that tries to avoid talking about death and has no answer for it.

2. The death of Christian friends and relatives. While we can look forward to our own death with a joyful expectation of being in Christ's presence, our attitude will be somewhat different when we experience the death of Christian friends and relatives. In these cases, we will experience genuine sorrow—but mixed with joy that they have gone to be with the Lord.

It is not wrong to express real sorrow at the loss of fellowship with loved ones who have died, and sorrow also for the suffering and hardship that they may have gone through prior to death. Sometimes Christians think it shows lack of faith if they mourn deeply for a brother or sister Christian who has died. But Scripture does not support that view, because when Stephen was stoned, we read that "Devout men buried Stephen, *and made great lamentation over him*" (Acts 8:2). Certainly there was no lack of faith on anyone's part that Stephen was in heaven experiencing great joy in the presence of the Lord. Yet the sorrow of his companions showed the genuine grief they felt at the loss of fellowship with someone whom they loved, and it was not wrong to express this sorrow—it was right. Even Jesus, at the tomb of Lazarus, "wept" (John 11:35), experiencing sorrow at the fact that Lazarus had died, that his sisters and others were experiencing such grief, and also, no doubt, at the fact that there was death in the world at all, for ultimately it is unnatural and ought not to be in a world created by God.

Nevertheless, the sorrow that we feel over the death of loved ones is clearly mingled with hope and joy. Paul does not tell the Thessalonians that they should not grieve *at all* concerning their loved ones who have died, but he writes, "that you may not grieve *as others do* who have no hope" (1 Thess. 4:13)—they should not grieve in the same way, with the same bitter despair, that unbelievers have. But certainly they should grieve. He assures them that Christ "died for us so that whether we wake or sleep we might live with him" (1 Thess. 5:10), and thereby encourages them that those who have died have gone to be with the Lord. That is why Scripture can say, "Blessed are the dead who die in the Lord henceforth . . . that they may rest from their labors" (Rev. 14:13). In fact, Scripture even tells us, "Precious in the sight of the LORD is the death of his saints" (Ps. 116:15).

Therefore, though we have genuine sorrow when Christian friends and relatives die, we also can say with Scripture, "O death, where is your victory? O death, where is your sting? . . . Thanks be to God, who gives us the victory through our Lord Jesus Christ" (1 Cor. 15:55–57). Though we mourn, our mourning should be mixed with worship of God and thanksgiving for the life of the loved one who has died.

3. The death of unbelievers. When unbelievers die, the sorrow we feel is not mingled with the joy of assurance that they have gone to be with the Lord forever. This sorrow, especially regarding those to whom we have been close, is very deep and real. Paul himself, when thinking about some of his Jewish brothers who had rejected Christ, said, "I am speaking the truth in Christ, I am not lying; my conscience bears me witness in the Holy Spirit, that *I have great sorrow and unceasing anguish in my heart.* For I could wish that I myself were accursed and cut off from Christ for the sake of my brethren, my kinsmen by race" (Rom. 9:1–3).

Yet it also must be said that we often do not have absolute certainty that a person has persisted in refusal to trust in Christ all the way to the point of death. The knowledge of one's impending death often will bring about genuine heart searching on the part of the dying person, and sometimes words of Scripture or words of Christian testimony that have been heard long ago will be recalled and the person may come to genuine repentance and faith. Certainly, we do not have any assurance that this has happened unless there is explicit evidence for it, but it is also good to realize that in many cases we have only probable but not absolute knowledge that those whom we have known as unbelievers have persisted in their unbelief until the point of death. In some cases we simply do not know.

Nevertheless, after a non-Christian has died, it would certainly be wrong to give any indication to others that we think that person has gone to heaven. This would simply be to give misleading information and false assurance and to diminish the urgency of the need for those who are still alive to trust in Christ. It is much better on such occasions, as God provides opportunity, to take time to reflect on our own lives and destiny and to share the gospel with others. In fact, the times when we are able to talk as a friend to the loved ones of an unbeliever who has died are often times when the Lord will open up opportunities to talk about the gospel with those who are still living.

C. What Happens When People Die?

1. The souls of believers go immediately into God's presence. Death is a temporary cessation of bodily life and a separation of the soul from the body. Once a believer has died, though his physical body remains on the earth and is buried, at the moment of death his soul (or spirit) goes immediately into the presence of God with rejoicing. When Paul thinks about death he says, "We would rather be *away from the body and at home with the Lord*" (2 Cor. 5:8). To be away from the body is to be at home with the Lord. He also says that his desire is "*to depart and be with Christ,* for that is far better" (Phil. 1:23). And Jesus said to the thief who was dying on the cross next to him, "*Today* you will be with me in Paradise" (Luke 23:43). The author of Hebrews says that when Christians come together to worship, they come not only into the presence of God in heaven, but also into the presence of "the spirits of just men made perfect" (Heb. 12:23). However, as we shall see in more detail below, God will not leave our dead bodies in the earth forever, for when Christ returns, the souls of believers will be reunited with their bodies, their bodies will be raised from the dead, and they will live with Christ eternally.

a. *The Bible does not teach the doctrine of purgatory.* The fact that the souls of believers go immediately into God's presence means that *there is no such thing as purgatory.* In Roman Catholic teaching, purgatory is the place where the souls of believers go to be further purified from sin until they are ready to be admitted into heaven. According to this view, the sufferings of purgatory are given to God in substitute for the punishment for sins that believers should have received in time, but did not.

But this doctrine is not taught in Scripture, and it is in fact contrary to the verses quoted immediately above. The Roman Catholic Church has found support for this doctrine, not in the pages of canonical Scripture as Protestants have accepted it since the Reformation, but in the writings of the Apocrypha. It should first be said that this literature is not equal to Scripture in authority and should not be taken as an authoritative source of doctrine.[1] Moreover, texts from which this doctrine is derived contradict clear affirmations of the New Testament and thereby oppose the teaching of Scripture. For example, the primary text used in this regard, 2 Maccabees 12:42–45, contradicts the clear scriptural affirmations about departing and being with Christ quoted above. The text reads:

> [Judas Maccabeus, the leader of the Jewish forces] also took a collection, man by man, to the amount of 2,000 drachmas of silver, and sent it to Jerusalem to provide for a sin offering. In doing this he acted very well and honorably, tak-

---

[1]See Wayne Grudem, *Systematic Theology* (Leicester: Inter-Varsity Press and Grand Rapids: Zondervan, 1994), ch. 3, pp. 57–59, on the Apocrypha.

ing into account the resurrection. For if he were not expecting that those who had fallen would rise again, it would have been superfluous and foolish *to pray for the dead*. But if he was looking to the splendid reward that is laid up for those who fall asleep in godliness, it was a holy and pious thought. Therefore he *made atonement for the dead, that they might be delivered from their sin*.

Here it is clear that prayer for the dead is approved and also making an offering to God to deliver the dead from their sin. But this contradicts the explicit teaching of the New Testament that Christ alone made atonement for us. This passage in 2 Maccabees is difficult to square even with Roman Catholic teaching, because it teaches that soldiers who had died in the mortal sin of idolatry (which cannot be forgiven according to Catholic teaching) should have prayers and sacrifices offered for them with the possibility that they will be delivered from their suffering.

Other passages sometimes used in support of the doctrine of purgatory include Matthew 12:32 and 1 Corinthians 3:15. In Matthew 12:32, Jesus says, "Whoever speaks against the Holy Spirit will not be forgiven, either in this age or in the age to come." Ludwig Ott says that this sentence "leaves open the possibility that sins are forgiven not only in this world but in the world to come."[2] However, this is simply an error in reasoning, for to say that something will not happen in the age to come does not imply that it might happen in the age to come! What is needed to prove the doctrine of purgatory is not a negative statement such as this but a positive statement that says that people suffer for the purpose of continuing purification after they die. But Scripture nowhere says this.

In 1 Corinthians 3:15 Paul says that on the day of judgment, the work that everyone has done will be judged and tested by fire, and then says, "*If any man's work is burned up,* he will suffer loss, though he himself will be saved, but only as through fire." But this does not speak of a *person* being burned or suffering punishment, but simply of *his work* as being tested by fire—that which is good will be like gold, silver, and precious stones that will last forever (v. 12). Moreover, Ott himself admits that this is something that occurs not during this age, but during the day of "the general judgment,"[3] and this further indicates that it can hardly be used as a convincing argument for purgatory.

An even more serious problem with this doctrine is that it teaches that we must add something to the redemptive work of Christ and that his redemptive work for us was not enough to pay the penalty for all our sins. But this is certainly contrary to the teaching of Scripture.[4] Moreover, in a pastoral sense, the doctrine of purgatory robs believers of the great comfort that should be theirs in knowing that those who have died have immediately gone into the presence of the Lord, and knowing that they also, when they die, will "depart and be with Christ, for that is far better" (Phil. 1:23).

b. *The Bible does not teach the doctrine of "soul sleep."* The fact that souls of believers go immediately into God's presence also means that *the doctrine of soul sleep is incorrect*. This doctrine teaches that when believers die they go into a state of unconscious existence, and the next thing that they are conscious of will be when Christ

[2]Ludwig Ott, *Fundamentals of Catholic Dogma*, ed. James Canon Bastible, trans. Patrick Lynch, 4th ed. (St. Louis: Herder, 1955), p. 483.
[3]Ibid., p. 483.
[4]See ch. 15, pp. 250–58, on the fact that Christ's death completely paid the penalty for all our sins.

returns and raises them to eternal life. This doctrine has never found wide acceptance in the church.

Support for this view has generally been found in the fact that Scripture several times speaks of the state of death as "sleep" or "falling asleep" (Matt. 9:24; 27:52; John 11:11; Acts 7:60; 13:36; 1 Cor. 15:6, 18, 20, 51; 1 Thess. 4:13; 5:10). Moreover, certain passages seem to teach that the dead do not have a conscious existence (see Ps. 6:5; 115:17 [but see v. 18!]; Eccl. 9:10; Isa. 38:19). But when Scripture represents death as "sleep," it is simply a metaphorical expression used to indicate that death is only temporary for Christians, just as sleep is temporary. This is clearly seen, for example, when Jesus tells his disciples about the death of Lazarus. He says, "Our friend Lazarus has fallen asleep, but I go to awake him out of sleep" (John 11:11). Then John explains, "Now Jesus had spoken of his death, but they thought that he meant taking rest in sleep. Then Jesus told them plainly, 'Lazarus is dead'" (John 11:12–13). The other passages that speak about people sleeping when they die are likewise to be interpreted as simply a metaphorical expression to teach that death is temporary.

As for the passages that indicate that the dead do not praise God, or that there is a ceasing of conscious activity when people die, these are all to be understood from the perspective of life in this world. From our perspective, it appears that once people die, they do not engage in these activities any longer. But Psalm 115 presents the full biblical perspective on this viewpoint. It says, "The dead do not praise the LORD, nor do any that go down into silence." But then it continues in the very next verse with a contrast indicating that those who believe in God *will* bless the Lord forever: "*But we will bless the LORD from this time forth and for evermore.* Praise the LORD!" (Ps. 115:17–18).

Finally, the passages quoted above demonstrating that the souls of believers go immediately into God's presence and enjoy fellowship with him there (2 Cor. 5:8; Phil. 1:23; Luke 23:43; Heb. 12:23) all indicate that there is conscious existence and fellowship with God immediately after death for the believer. Jesus did not say, "Today you will no longer have consciousness of anything that is going on," but, "Today *you will be with me in Paradise*" (Luke 23:43). Certainly the conception of paradise understood at that time was not one of unconscious existence but one of great blessing and joy in God's presence.[5] Paul did not say, "My desire is to depart and be unconscious for a long period of time," but rather, "My desire is to depart *and be with Christ*" (Phil. 1:23)—and he certainly knew that Christ was not an unconscious, sleeping Savior, but one who was living and reigning in heaven. To be with Christ was to enjoy the blessing of fellowship in his presence, and that is why to depart and be with him was "far better." (Phil. 1:23) Thus, he says, "We would rather be away from the body and at home with the Lord" (2 Cor. 5:8).

c. *Should we pray for the dead?* Finally, the fact that the souls of believers go immediately into God's presence means that *we should not pray for the dead.* Although praying for the dead is taught in 2 Maccabees 12:42–45 (see above), it is nowhere taught in the Bible itself. Moreover, there is no indication that this was the practice of any Christians at the time of the New Testament, nor should it have been.

---

[5]In both of the other New Testament uses, the word *Paradise* clearly means "heaven." In 2 Corinthians 12:4 it is the place to which Paul was caught up in his revelation of heaven, and in Revelation 2:7 it is the place where we find the tree of life.

Once *believers* die, they enter into God's presence and are in a state of perfect happiness with him. What good would it do to pray for them anymore? Final heavenly reward will be based on deeds done in this life, as Scripture repeatedly testifies (1 Cor. 3:12–15; 2 Cor. 5:10; et al.).[6] Further, the souls of *unbelievers* who die go to a place of punishment and eternal separation from God's presence. It would do no good to pray for them either, since their final destiny has been settled by their sin and their rebellion against God in this life. To pray for the dead, therefore, is simply to pray for something that God has told us has already been decided. Moreover, to teach that we should pray for the dead, or to encourage others to do so, would be to encourage false hope that the destinies of people might be changed after they die, something Scripture nowhere encourages us to think.

2. The souls of unbelievers go immediately to eternal punishment. Scripture never encourages us to think that people will have a second chance to trust in Christ after death. In fact, the situation is quite the contrary. Jesus' story about the rich man and Lazarus gives no hope that people can cross from hell to heaven after they have died. Though the rich man in hell called out, "Father Abraham, have mercy upon me, and send Lazarus to dip the end of his finger in water and cool my tongue; for I am in anguish in this flame," Abraham replied to him, "Between us and you a great chasm has been fixed, in order that those who would pass from here to you may not be able, and *none may cross from there to us*" (Luke 16:24–26).

The book of Hebrews connects death with the consequence of judgment in close sequence: "Just as it is appointed for men to die once, and after that comes judgment" (Heb. 9:27). Moreover, Scripture never represents the final judgment as depending on anything done after we die, but only on what has happened in this life (Matt. 25:31–46; Rom. 2:5–10; cf. 2 Cor. 5:10). Some have argued for a second chance to believe in the gospel on the basis of Christ's preaching to the spirits in prison in 1 Peter 3:18–20 and the preaching of the gospel "even to the dead" in 1 Peter 4:6, but those are inadequate interpretations of the verses in question, and, on closer inspection, do not support such a view.[7]

We should also realize that the idea that there will be a second chance to accept Christ after death is based on the assumption that everyone deserves a chance to accept Christ and that eternal punishment comes only to those who consciously decide to reject him. But certainly that idea is not supported by Scripture; we all are sinners by nature and choice, and no one actually deserves any of God's grace or deserves any opportunity to hear the gospel of Christ—those come only because of God's unmerited favor. Condemnation comes not only because of a willful rejection of Christ, but also because of the sins that we have committed and the rebellion against God that those sins represent (see John 3:18).[8]

Although unbelievers pass into a state of eternal punishment immediately upon death, their bodies will not be raised until the day of final judgment. On that day, their bodies will be raised and reunited with their souls, and they will stand before God's throne for final judgment to be pronounced upon them in the body (see Matt. 25:31–46; John 5:28–29; Acts 24:15; and Rev. 20:12, 15).[9] This leads us to a

---

[6]See ch. 33, pp. 456–57, on degrees of reward in heaven.

[7]See the discussion of these verses in ch. 15, pp. 257–58; see also Wayne Grudem, *The First Epistle of Peter* (Leicester: Inter-Varsity Press and Grand Rapids: Eerdmans, 1988), pp. 155–62, 170–72, 203–39.

[8]See ch. 33, pp. 453–62, for a discussion of the final judgment and the doctrine of hell.

[9]See below, ch. 33, pp. 454–55.

consideration of the resurrection of the body of the believer, which is the final step in the believer's redemption.

D. Glorification

As was mentioned earlier, God will not leave our dead bodies in the earth forever. When Christ redeemed us, he did not just redeem our spirits (or souls)—he redeemed us as whole persons, and this includes the redemption of our bodies. Therefore, the application of Christ's work of redemption to us will not be complete until our bodies are entirely set free from the effects of the fall and brought to that state of perfection for which God created them. In fact, the redemption of our bodies will only occur when Christ returns and raises our bodies from the dead. But at this present time, Paul says that we wait for *"the redemption of our bodies,"* and then adds, "for in this hope we were saved" (Rom. 8:23–24). The stage in the application of redemption when we receive resurrection bodies is called *glorification.* Referring to that future day, Paul says that we will be *"glorified* with him" (Rom. 8:17). Moreover, when Paul traces the steps in the application of redemption, the last one he names is glorification: "And those whom he predestined he also called; and those whom he called he also justified; and those whom he justified he also *glorified"* (Rom. 8:30).

We may define glorification as follows: *Glorification is the final step in the application of redemption. It will happen when Christ returns and raises from the dead the bodies of all believers for all time who have died, and reunites them with their souls, and changes the bodies of all believers who remain alive, thereby giving all believers at the same time perfect resurrection bodies like his own.*

1. Biblical evidence for glorification. The primary New Testament passage on glorification or the resurrection of the body is 1 Corinthians 15:12–58. Paul says, "So also in Christ shall all be made alive. But each in his own order: Christ the first fruits, then *at his coming* those who belong to Christ" (vv. 22–23). Paul discusses the nature of the resurrection body in some detail in verses 35–50 and then concludes the passage by saying that not all Christians will die, but some who remain alive when Christ returns will simply have their bodies instantaneously changed into a new, resurrection body that can never grow old or weak and can never die: "Lo! I tell you a mystery. We shall not all sleep, but *we shall all be changed,* in a moment, in the twinkling of an eye, at the last trumpet. For the trumpet will sound, and the dead will be raised imperishable, and we shall be changed" (1 Cor. 15:51–52).

Paul further explains in 1 Thessalonians that the souls of those who have died and gone to be with Christ will come back and be joined with their bodies on that day, for Christ will bring them with him: "For since we believe that Jesus died and rose again, even so, through Jesus, *God will bring with him those who have fallen asleep"* (1 Thess. 4:14). But here Paul affirms not only that God will bring with Christ those who have died; he also affirms that *"the dead in Christ will rise first"* (1 Thess. 4:16). So these believers who have died with Christ are also raised up to meet Christ (Paul says in v. 17, "We . . . shall be caught up together with them in the clouds to meet the Lord in the air"). This only makes sense if it is the *souls* of believers who have gone into Christ's presence who return with him, and if it is their *bodies* that are raised from the dead to be joined together with their souls, and then to ascend to be with Christ.

2. What will our resurrection bodies be like? If Christ will raise our bodies from the dead when he returns, and if our bodies will be like his resurrection body (1 Cor. 15:20, 23, 49; Phil. 3:21), then what will our resurrection bodies be like?

Using the example of sowing a seed in the ground and then watching it grow into something much more wonderful, Paul goes on to explain in more detail what our resurrection bodies will be like: "What is sown is perishable, what is raised is *imperishable*. It is sown in dishonor, it is raised *in glory*. It is sown in weakness, it is raised *in power*. It is sown a physical body, it is raised a *spiritual body*. . . . Just as we have borne the image of the man of dust, we shall also bear the image of the man of heaven" (1 Cor. 15:42 44, 49).

Paul first states that our resurrection bodies will be "imperishable." This means that they will not wear out or grow old or ever be subject to any kind of sickness or disease. They will be completely healthy and strong forever. Moreover, since the gradual process of aging is part of the process by which our bodies now are subject to "corruption," it is appropriate to think that our resurrection bodies will have no sign of aging, but will have the characteristics of youthful but mature manhood or womanhood forever. There will be no evidence of disease or injury, for all will be made perfect.[10] Our resurrection bodies will show the fulfillment of God's perfect wisdom in creating us as human beings who are the pinnacle of his creation and the appropriate bearers of his likeness and image. In these resurrection bodies, we will clearly see humanity as God intended it to be.

Paul also says our bodies will be raised "in glory." When this term is contrasted with "dishonor," as it is here, there is a suggestion of the beauty or the attractiveness of appearance our bodies will have. They will no longer be "dishonorable" or unattractive, but will look "glorious" in their beauty. They may even have a bright radiance about them (see Dan. 12:3; Matt. 13:43).

Our bodies will also be raised "in power" (1 Cor. 15:43). This is in contrast to the "weakness" we see in our bodies now. Our resurrection bodies will not only be free from disease and aging, they will also be given fullness of strength and power—not infinite power like God, of course, and probably not what we would think of as "superhuman" power in the sense possessed by the superheroes in modern fictional children's writing, for example, but nonetheless full and complete human power and strength, the strength that God intended human beings to have in their bodies when he created them. It will therefore be strength that is sufficient to do all that we desire to do in conformity with the will of God.

Finally, Paul says that the body is raised a "spiritual body" (1 Cor. 15:44). In the Pauline epistles, the word "spiritual" (Gk. *pneumatikos*) never means "nonphysical" but rather "consistent with the character and activity of the Holy Spirit" (see, for example, Rom. 1:11; 7:14; 1 Cor. 2:13, 15; 3:1; 14:37; Gal. 6:1 ["you who are spiritual"]; Eph. 5:19). The RSV translation, "It is sown a *physical* body, it is raised a *spiritual* body," is misleading, and a clearer paraphrase would be, "It is sown a *natural* body [that is, subject to the characteristics and desires of this age, and governed by its own sinful will], but it is raised a *spiritual* body [that is, completely subject to the will of the Holy Spirit and responsive to the Holy Spirit's guidance]." Such a body is not at all "nonphysical," but it is a physical body raised to the degree of perfection

---

[10]The fact that the scars of Jesus' nail prints remained on his hands is a special case to remind us of the price he paid for our redemption, and it should not be taken as an indication that any of our scars from physical injuries will remain. See ch. 16, p. 265.

for which God originally intended it. The repeated instances in which Jesus demonstrated to the disciples that he had a physical body that was able to be touched, that had flesh and bones (Luke 24:39), and that could eat food, show that Jesus' body, which is our pattern, was clearly a physical body that had been made perfect.

In conclusion, when Christ returns, he will give us new resurrection bodies to be like his resurrection body. "When he appears we shall be like him" (1 John 3:2; this statement is true not only in an ethical sense, but also in terms of our physical bodies; cf. 1 Cor. 15:49; also Rom. 8:29). Such assurance provides a clear affirmation of the goodness of God's physical creation. We will live in bodies that have all the excellent qualities God created us to have, and thereby we will forever be living proof of the wisdom of God in making a material creation that from the beginning was "very good" (Gen. 1:31). We will live as resurrected believers in those new bodies, and they will be suitable for inhabiting the "new heavens and a new earth in which righteousness dwells" (2 Peter 3:13).

II. REVIEW QUESTIONS

1. If the penalty for sin is death (Rom. 6:23), is death a punishment for Christians, since all Christians have sinned (cf. Rom. 3:23)? Why or why not? If not, then why do Christians die?

2. What is the purpose of death for the Christian?

3. Is death to be seen as a good thing for a Christian? Explain your answer.

4. What happens to a believer who dies? (Support your answer from Scripture.) Contrast this with the Roman Catholic teaching of purgatory.

5. What happens to an unbeliever who dies? Will nonbelievers receive a second chance to trust in Christ after death? Support your answer from Scripture.

III. QUESTIONS FOR PERSONAL APPLICATION

1. Have you thought very much about the possibility of your own death? Has there been an element of fear connected with those thoughts? What, if anything, do you fear about death, and where do these fears come from? How would the teachings of Scripture encourage you to deal with these fears?

2. Has this chapter changed your feelings about your own death in any way? Can you honestly contemplate it now as something that will bring you nearer to Christ and increase your own trust in God and faithfulness to him? How would you express your hopes regarding your own death?

3. Do you think you would have the courage to refuse to sin even if it meant being thrown to the lions in a Roman coliseum, or burned at the stake during the Reformation, or thrown in prison for years in some foreign country today? What happened to Christian martyrs in history to equip them for this suffering (read 1 Cor. 10:13)? Have you settled in your own mind that obedience to Christ is more important than preserving your own life? What would make you hesitant to believe this or act on this conviction?

4. If death itself is viewed as part of the process of sanctification, then how should we view the process of growing older and weaker in this world? Is that the way the world views aging?

5.   Paul says that the expectation of a future bodily resurrection is the "hope" in which we were saved (Rom. 8:24). Is the hope of a future resurrection of your body one of the major things you look forward to in the future? If not, why not?

IV. SPECIAL TERMS

death

glorification

purgatory

soul sleep

spiritual body

V. SCRIPTURE MEMORY PASSAGE

PHILIPPIANS 1:20–24

As it is my eager expectation and hope that I shall not be at all ashamed, but that with full courage now as always Christ will be honored in my body, whether by life or by death. For to me to live is Christ, and to die is gain. If it is to be life in the flesh, that means fruitful labor for me. Yet which I shall choose I cannot tell. I am hard pressed between the two. My desire is to depart and be with Christ, for that is far better. But to remain in the flesh is more necessary on your account.

PART VI

The Doctrine of the Church

CHAPTER TWENTY-SIX

The Nature of the Church

+ *How can we recognize a true church?*
+ *What are the purposes of the church?*
+ *What makes a church more or less pleasing to God?*

I. EXPLANATION AND SCRIPTURAL BASIS

A. The Nature of the Church

1. Definition: The church is the community of all true believers for all time.
This definition understands the church to be made of all those who are truly saved. Paul says, "Christ loved *the church* and gave himself up for her" (Eph. 5:25). Here "the church" is used to apply to all those whom Christ died to redeem, all those who are saved by the death of Christ. But that must include all true believers for all time, both in the New Testament age and in the Old Testament age as well.[1] So great is God's plan for the church that he has exalted Christ to a position of highest authority for the sake of the church: "He has put all things under his feet and has made him the head over all things *for the church*, which is his body, the fulness of him who fills all in all" (Eph. 1:22–23).

Jesus Christ himself builds the church by calling his people to himself. He promised, "I will build my church" (Matt. 16:18). But this process by which Christ builds the church is just a continuation of the pattern established by God in the Old Testament whereby he called people to himself to be a worshiping assembly before him. There are several indications in the Old Testament that God thought of his people as a "church," a people assembled for the purpose of worshiping God. When Moses tells the people that the Lord said to him, "*Gather the people to me,* that I may let them hear my words, so that they may learn to fear me all the days that they live upon the earth . . ." (Deut. 4:10), the Septuagint translates the word for "gather" (Heb. *Qāhal*) with the Greek term *ekklēsiazō*, "to summon an assembly," the verb that is cognate to the New Testament noun *ekklēsia*, "church."[2]

It is not surprising, then, that the New Testament authors can speak of the Old Testament people of Israel as a "church" *(ekklēsia)*. For example, Stephen speaks of

---

[1]See section 5 below for a discussion of the dispensational view that the church and Israel must be thought of as distinct groups. In this book, I have taken a nondispensational position on that question, though it should be pointed out that many evangelicals who agree with much of the rest of this book will differ with me on this particular question.

[2]In fact, the Greek word *ekklēsia*, the term translated "church" in the New Testament, is the word the Septuagint most frequently uses to translate the Old Testament term *qāhal*, the word used to speak of the "congregation" or the "assembly" of God's people. *Ekklēsia* translates *qāhal*, "assembly," 69 times in the Septuagint. The next most frequent translation is *synagōgē*, "synagogue" or "meeting, place of meeting" (37 times).

the people of Israel in the wilderness as "the church *[ekklēsia]* in the wilderness" (Acts 7:38, author's translation). And the author of Hebrews quotes Christ as saying that he would sing praise to God in the midst of the great assembly of God's people in heaven: "In the midst of the *church [ekklēsia]* I will sing praise to you" (Heb. 2:12, author's translation, quoting Ps. 22:22).

Therefore, the author of Hebrews understands the present-day Christians who constitute the church on earth to be surrounded by a great "cloud of witnesses" (Heb. 12:1) that reaches back into the earliest eras of the Old Testament and includes Abel, Enoch, Noah, Abraham, Sarah, Gideon, Barak, Samson, Jephthah, David, Samuel, and the prophets (Heb. 11:4–32). All these "witnesses" surround the present-day people of God, and it seems only appropriate that they, together with the New Testament people of God, should be thought of as God's great spiritual "assembly" or "church."[3]

Therefore, even though there are certainly new privileges and new blessings that are given to the people of God in the New Testament, both the usage of the term *church* in Scripture and the fact that throughout Scripture God has always called his people to assemble to worship himself, indicate that it is appropriate to think of the church as constituting all the people of God for all time, both Old Testament believers and New Testament believers.

2. The church is invisible yet visible. In its true spiritual reality as the fellowship of all genuine believers, the church is invisible. This is because we cannot see the spiritual condition of people's hearts. We can see those who outwardly attend the church, and we can see outward evidences of inward spiritual change, but we cannot actually see into people's hearts and view their spiritual state—only God can do that. This is why Paul says, *"The Lord knows those who are his"* (2 Tim. 2:19). Even in our own churches and our own neighborhoods, only God knows who are true believers with certainty and without error. In speaking of the church as invisible, the author of Hebrews speaks of the "assembly [lit. 'church'] of the first-born who are enrolled in heaven" (Heb. 12:23) and says that present-day Christians join with that assembly in worship.

We can give the following definition: *The invisible church is the church as God sees it.*

Both Martin Luther and John Calvin were eager to affirm this invisible aspect of the church over against the Roman Catholic teaching that the church was the one visible organization that had descended from the apostles in an unbroken line of succession (through the bishops of the church). The Roman Catholic Church had argued that only in the visible organization of the Roman Church could we find the one true church, the only true church. Even today such a view is held by the Roman Catholic Church.[4] Both Luther and Calvin disagreed with this idea, asserting that the Roman Catholic Church had the outward form, the organization, but it was just a shell. Calvin argued that just as Caiaphas (the high priest at the time of Christ) was descended from Aaron but was no true priest, so the Roman Catholic bishops had "descended" from the apostles in a line of succession but were not true bishops in Christ's church. Because they had departed from the true preaching of the gospel, their visible organization was not the true church.

---

[3]The Greek word *ekklēsia*, translated "church" in the New Testament, simply means "assembly."

[4]For a recent statement of this view, see the "Pastoral Statement for Catholics on Biblical Fundamentalism" in *Origins* 17, no. 21 (November 5, 1987): 376–77.

On the other hand, the true church of Christ certainly has a visible aspect as well. We may use the following definition: *The visible church is the church as Christians on earth see it.* In this sense, the visible church includes all who profess faith in Christ and give evidence of that faith in their lives.

In this definition, we do not say that the visible church is the church as any person in the world (such as an unbeliever or someone who held heretical teachings) might see it, but we mean to speak of the church as it is perceived by those who are genuine believers and have an understanding of the difference between believers and unbelievers.

The visible church throughout the world will always include some unbelievers, and individual congregations will usually include some unbelievers, because we cannot see hearts as God sees them. Paul speaks of "Hymenaeus and Philetus, who have swerved from the truth" and who "are upsetting the faith of some" (2 Tim. 2:17–18). But he is confident that "The Lord knows those who are his" (2 Tim. 2:19). Similarly, Paul warns the Ephesian elders that after his departure "fierce wolves will come in among you, not sparing the flock; and *from among your own selves* will arise men speaking perverse things, to draw away the disciples after them" (Acts 20:29–30). Jesus himself warned, "Beware of false prophets, who come to you in sheep's clothing but inwardly are ravenous wolves. You will know them by their fruits" (Matt. 7:15–16). Realizing this distinction between the church invisible and the church visible, Augustine said of the visible church, "Many sheep are without and many wolves are within."[5]

When we recognize that there are unbelievers in the visible church, there is a danger that we may become overly suspicious and begin to doubt the salvation of many true believers. Calvin warned against this danger by saying that we must make a "charitable judgment" whereby we recognize as members of the church all who "by confession of faith, by example of life, and by partaking of the sacraments, profess the same God and Christ with us."[6] We should not try to exclude people from the fellowship of the church until they by public sin bring discipline upon themselves. On the other hand, of course, the church should not tolerate in its membership "public unbelievers" who by profession or life clearly proclaim themselves to be outside the true church.

3. The church is local and universal. In the New Testament the word *church* may be applied to a group of believers at any level, ranging from a very small group meeting in a private home all the way to the group of all true believers in the universal church. A "*house* church" is called a "church" in Romans 16:5 ("greet also *the church in their house*") and 1 Corinthians 16:19 ("Aquila and Prisca, together with *the church in their house,* send you hearty greetings in the Lord"). The church in an entire *city* is also called "a church" (1 Cor. 1:2; 2 Cor. 1:1; 1 Thess. 1:1). The church in a *region* is referred to as a "church" in Acts 9:31: "So *the church throughout all Judea and Galilee and Samaria* had peace and was built up." Finally, the church throughout the entire *world* can be referred to as "the church." Paul says, "Christ loved *the church* and gave himself up for her" (Eph. 5:25), and "God has appointed *in the church* first apostles, second prophets, third teachers ..." (1 Cor.

---

[5]Quoted in John Calvin, *Institutes of the Christian Religion,* Library of Christian Classics, ed. John T. McNeill, trans. F. L. Battles, 2 vols. (Philadelphia: Westminster, 1960), 1:1022 (4.1.8).

[6]Ibid., 1:1022–23 (4.1.8).

12:28). In this latter verse, the mention of "apostles," who were not given to any individual church, guarantees that the reference is to the church universal.

We may conclude that the group of God's people considered at any level from local to universal may rightly be called "a church." We should not make the mistake of saying that only a church meeting in houses expresses the true nature of the church, or only a church considered at a city-wide level can rightly be called a church, or only the church universal can rightly be called by the name "church." Rather, the community of God's people considered at any level can be rightly called a church.

4. Metaphors for the church. To help us understand the nature of the church, Scripture uses a wide range of metaphors and images to describe to us what the church is like. There are several family images—for example, Paul views the church as a *family* when he tells Timothy to act as if all the church members were members of a larger family: "Do not rebuke an older man but exhort him as you would a father; treat younger men like brothers, older women like mothers, younger women like sisters, in all purity" (1 Tim. 5:1–2). God is our heavenly Father (Eph. 3:14), and we are his sons and daughters, for God says to us, "I will be a father to you, and you shall be my sons and daughters, says the Lord Almighty" (2 Cor. 6:18). We are therefore brothers and sisters with one another in God's family (Matt. 12:49–50; 1 John 3:14–18). A somewhat different family metaphor is seen when Paul refers to the church as the *bride of Christ*. He says that the relationship between a husband and wife "refers to Christ and the church" (Eph. 5:32), and he says that he brought about the engagement between Christ and the church at Corinth and that it resembles an engagement between a bride and her husband-to-be: "I betrothed you to one husband, that to Christ I might present you as a pure virgin" (2 Cor. 11:2 NASB)—here Paul is looking forward to the time of Christ's return as the time when the church will be presented to him as his bride.

In other metaphors, Scripture compares the church to *branches on a vine* (John 15:5), *an olive tree* (Rom. 11:17–24), *a field of crops* (1 Cor. 3:6–9), *a building* (1 Cor. 3:9), and *a harvest* (Matt. 13:1–30; John 4:35). The church is also viewed as *a new temple* not built with literal stones but built with Christian people who are "living stones" (1 Peter 2:5) built up on the "cornerstone" who is Christ Jesus (1 Peter 2:4–8). Yet the church is not only a new temple for worship of God; it is also *a new group of priests,* a "holy priesthood" that can offer "spiritual sacrifices acceptable to God" (1 Peter 2:5). We are also viewed as *God's house:* "We are his house" (Heb. 3:6), with Jesus Christ himself viewed as the "builder" of the house (Heb. 3:3). The church is also viewed as *"the pillar* and *bulwark of the truth"* (1 Tim. 3:15).

Finally, another familiar metaphor views the church as the *body of Christ* (1 Cor. 12:12–27). We should recognize that Paul in fact uses *two different metaphors* of the human body when he speaks of the church. Here in 1 Corinthians 12 *the whole body* is taken as a metaphor for the church, because Paul speaks of the "ear" and the "eye" and the "sense of smell" (1 Cor. 12:16–17). In this metaphor, Christ is not viewed as the head joined to the body, because the individual members are themselves the individual parts of the head. Christ is in this metaphor the Lord who is "outside" of that body that represents the church and is the one whom the church serves and worships.

But in Ephesians 1:22–23; 4:15–16, and in Colossians 2:19, Paul uses a different body metaphor to refer to the church. In these passages, Paul says that Christ is the head and the church is like *the rest of the body, as distinguished from the head:* "We are to grow up in every way into him who is the head, into Christ, from whom the whole body, joined and knit together by every joint with which it is supplied, when each part is working properly, makes bodily growth and upbuilds itself in love" (Eph. 4:15–16). We should not confuse these two metaphors in 1 Corinthians 12 and Ephesians 4, but keep them distinct.

The wide range of metaphors used for the church in the New Testament should remind us not to focus exclusively on any one. An undue emphasis on one metaphor to the exclusion of others will likely result in an unbalanced perspective on the church. Furthermore, each of the metaphors used for the church can help us to appreciate more of the richness of privilege that God has given us by incorporating us into the church. The fact that the church is like a family should increase our love and fellowship with one another. The thought that the church is like the bride of Christ should stimulate us to strive for greater purity and holiness and also greater love for Christ and submission to him. The image of the church as branches in a vine should cause us to rest in him more fully. These are but a few of the many applications that could be drawn from the rich diversity of metaphors for the church listed in Scripture.

5. *The church and Israel.* Among evangelical Protestants there has been a difference of viewpoint on the question of the relationship between Israel and the church. One viewpoint is called the *dispensational* view. On this view, God has two distinct plans for the two different groups of people he has redeemed: God's purposes and promises for Israel are for *earthly* blessings, and they will yet be fulfilled on this earth at some time in the future. On the other hand, God's purposes and promises for the church are for *heavenly* blessings, and those promises will be fulfilled in heaven. This distinction between the two different groups that God saves will especially be seen in the millennium, for at that time Israel will reign on earth as God's people and enjoy the fulfillment of Old Testament promises, but the church will already have been taken up into heaven at the time of Christ's secret return for his saints ("the rapture"). On this view, the church did not begin until Pentecost (Acts 2). And it is not right to think of Old Testament believers together with New Testament believers as constituting one church.[7]

A number of leaders among more recent dispensationalists have modified many of these points, referring to their theological framework as "progressive dispensationalism."[8] They *would not see the church as a parenthesis* in God's plan, but as the first step toward the establishment of the kingdom of God. There is thus a single purpose for Israel and the church—the establishment of the kingdom of God—in which Israel and the church will both share. Moreover, progressive dispensationalists would see *no distinction between Israel and the church in the future eternal state,* for all will be part of the one people of God.

However, there is still a difference between progressive dispensationalists and the rest of evangelicalism on one point: They would say that *the Old Testament*

---

[7]The most extensive systematic theology written from a dispensational perspective is Lewis Sperry Chafer's *Systematic Theology,* 7 vols. (Dallas: Dallas Seminary Press, 1947-48). For his treatment on Israel and the church, see esp. 4:45–53.

[8]See Robert L. Saucy, *The Case for Progressive Dispensationalism* (Grand Rapids: Zondervan, 1993), and Darrell L. Bock and Craig A. Blaising, eds., *Progressive Dispensationalism* (Wheaton, Ill.: Victor, 1993). See also John S. Feinberg, ed., *Continuity and Discontinuity: Perspectives on the Relationship Between the Old and New Testaments* (Wheaton, Ill.: Crossway, 1988).

prophecies concerning Israel will still be fulfilled in the millennium by ethnic Jewish people who will believe in Christ and live in the land of Israel as a "model nation" for all nations to see and learn from. Therefore, they would not say that the church is the "new Israel" or that all the Old Testament prophecies about Israel will be fulfilled in the church, for these prophecies will yet be fulfilled in ethnic Israel.

The position taken in this book differs quite a bit from traditional dispensational views on this issue and also differs somewhat with progressive dispensationalists. However, it must be said here that questions about the exact way in which biblical prophecies about the future will be fulfilled are, in the nature of the case, difficult to decide with certainty, and it is wise to have some tentativeness in our conclusions on these matters. With this in mind, the following may be said.

Both Protestant and Catholic theologians outside of the dispensational position have said that the church includes both Old Testament believers and New Testament believers in one church or one body of Christ. We should first notice the many New Testament verses that understand the church as the "new Israel" or new "people of God." The fact that "Christ loved *the church* and gave himself up for her" (Eph. 5:25) would suggest this. Moreover, this present church age, which has brought the salvation of many millions of Christians in the church, is not an interruption or a parenthesis in God's plan, but a continuation of his plan expressed throughout the Old Testament to call a people to himself. Paul says, "For he is not a real Jew who is one outwardly, nor is true circumcision something external and physical. *He is a Jew who is one inwardly,* and real circumcision is a matter of the heart, spiritual and not literal" (Rom. 2:28–29). Paul recognizes that though there is a literal or natural sense in which people who physically descended from Abraham are to be called Jews, there is also a deeper or spiritual sense in which a "true Jew" is one who is inwardly a believer and whose heart has been cleansed by God.

Paul says that Abraham is not only to be considered the father of the Jewish people in a physical sense. He is also in a deeper and more true sense "*the father of all who believe without being circumcised* . . . and likewise the father of the circumcised who are not merely circumcised but also follow the example of the faith which our father Abraham had" (Rom. 4:11–12; cf. vv. 16, 18). Therefore, Paul can say, "Not all who are descended from Israel belong to Israel, and not all are children of Abraham because they are his descendants. . . . it is not the children of the flesh who are the children of God, but the children of the promise are reckoned as descendants" (Rom. 9:6–8). Paul here implies that the true children of Abraham, those who are in the truest sense "Israel," are not the nation of Israel by physical descent from Abraham but those who have believed in Christ.

Far from thinking of the church as a separate group from the Jewish people, Paul writes to Gentile believers at Ephesus telling them that they were formerly "alienated from the commonwealth of Israel, and strangers to the covenants of promise" (Eph. 2:12), but that now they have been "brought near in the blood of Christ" (Eph. 2:13). And when the Gentiles were brought into the church, Jews and Gentiles were united into one new body. Paul says that God "has *made us both one,* and has broken down the dividing wall of hostility . . . that he might create in himself *one new man* in place of the two, so making peace, and might reconcile us both to God *in one body* through the cross" (Eph. 2:14–16). Therefore, Paul can say that Gentiles are "fellow citizens with the saints and members of the household of God, built upon the foundation of the apostles and prophets, Christ Jesus himself being the cornerstone" (Eph. 2:19–20). With his extensive awareness of the Old Testament background to the New Testament church, Paul can still say that "the Gentiles are fellow heirs, *members of the same body*" (Eph. 3:6). The entire passage speaks strongly of the unity of Jewish and Gentile believers in one body in Christ and gives no indication of any distinctive plan for Jewish people ever to be saved apart from inclusion in the one body of Christ, the church. The church incorporates into itself all the true people of God, and almost all of the titles used of God's people in the Old Testament are in one place or another applied to the church in the New Testament. These along with many other texts give us assurance that the church has now become the true Israel of God and will receive all the blessings promised to Israel in the Old Testament.

B. The "Marks" of the Church (Distinguishing Characteristics)

1. There are true churches and false churches. What makes a church a church? What is necessary to have a church? Might a group of people who claim to be Christians become so *unlike* what a church should be that they should no longer be called a church?

While in the early centuries of the Christian church there was little controversy about what was a true church, with the Reformation a crucial question emerged: *How can we recognize a true church*? Is the Roman Catholic Church a true church or not? To answer that question, people had to decide what were the "marks" of a true church, the distinguishing characteristics that lead us to recognize it as a true church.

Scripture certainly speaks of false churches. Paul says of the pagan temples in Corinth, "What pagans sacrifice they offer to demons and not to God" (1 Cor. 10:20). He tells the Corinthians that "when you were heathen, you were led astray to dumb idols" (1 Cor. 12:2). These pagan temples were certainly false churches or false religious assemblies. Moreover, Scripture can speak of a religious assembly that is really a "synagogue of Satan" (Rev. 2:9; 3:9). Here the risen Lord Jesus seems to be referring to Jewish assemblies where the people claimed to be Jews but were not true Jews who had saving faith. Their religious assemblies were not assemblies of Christ's people then but of those who still belonged to the kingdom of darkness, the kingdom of Satan. This also would certainly be a false church.

In large measure, there was agreement between Luther and Calvin on the question of what constituted a true church. The Lutheran statement of faith, which is called the Augsburg Confession (1530), defined the church as "the congregation of saints in which the gospel is rightly taught and the Sacraments rightly administered" (Article 7).[9] Similarly, John Calvin said, "Wherever we see the Word of God purely preached and heard, and the sacraments administered according to Christ's institution, there, it is not to be doubted, a church of God exists."[10] While slight differences appear in these confessions, their understanding of the distinguishing marks of a true church is quite similar. In contrast to the view of Luther and Calvin regarding the marks of a church, the Roman Catholic position has been that *the visible church* that descended from Peter and the apostles *is the true church.*

It seems appropriate that we take Luther and Calvin's view on the marks of a true church as correct still today. Their first mark was *right preaching of the Word.* Certainly

---

[9]Quoted from Philip Schaff, *The Creeds of Christendom*, 3 vols. (Grand Rapids: Baker, 1983, reprint of 1931 edition), pp. 11–12.

[10]Calvin, *Institutes,* p. 1023 (4.1.9).

if the Word of God is not being preached, but simply false doctrines or doctrines of men, then there is no true church. In some cases, we might have difficulty determining just how much wrong doctrine can be tolerated before a church can no longer be considered a true church, but there are many clear cases where we can say that a true church does not exist. For example, the Church of Jesus Christ of the Latter Day Saints (the Mormon Church) does not hold to any major Christian doctrines concerning salvation or the person of God or the person and work of Christ. It is clearly a false church. Similarly, the Jehovah's Witnesses teach salvation by works, not by trusting in Jesus Christ alone. This is a fundamental doctrinal deviation, because if people believe the teachings of the Jehovah's Witnesses, they simply will not be saved. So the Jehovah's Witnesses also must be considered a false church. When the preaching of a church conceals the gospel message of salvation by faith alone from its members so that the gospel message is not clearly proclaimed and has not been proclaimed for some time, the group meeting there is not really a church.

The second mark of the church, the *right administration of the sacraments* (baptism and the Lord's Supper) was probably stated in opposition to the Roman Catholic view that saving grace came through the sacraments and thereby the sacraments were made "works" by which we earned merit for salvation. In this way, the Roman Catholic Church was insisting on payment rather than teaching faith alone as the means of obtaining salvation, thus obscuring the true gospel. The need to protect the purity of the gospel is one reason for viewing right use of the sacraments (or "ordinances," as they are called by Baptists) as a mark or a true church.

But a second reason exists for including the sacraments (or ordinances) as a mark of the church. Once an organization begins to practice baptism and the Lord's Supper, it is a continuing organization and is attempting to function as a church. (In modern American society, an organization that begins to meet for worship and prayer and Bible teachings on Sunday mornings also would clearly be attempting to function as a church.)

A third reason for including right use of the sacraments (or ordinances) is that baptism and the Lord's Supper also serve as "membership controls" for the church. Baptism is the means for admitting people into the church, and the Lord's Supper is the means for allowing people to give a sign of continuing in the membership of the church—the church signifies that it considers those who receive baptism and the Lord's Supper to be saved. Therefore, these activities indicate what a church thinks about salvation, and they are appropriately listed as a mark of the church today as well. By contrast, groups who do not administer baptism and the Lord's Supper signify that they are not intending to function as a church. Someone may stand on a street corner with a small crowd and have true preaching and hearing of the Word, but the people there would not be a church. Even a neighborhood Bible study meeting in a home can have the true teaching and hearing of the Word without becoming a church. But if a local Bible study began baptizing its own new converts and regularly participating in the Lord's Supper, these things would signify an intention to function as a church, and it would be difficult to say why it should not be considered a church in itself.

2. True and false churches today. In view of the question posed during the Reformation, what about the Roman Catholic Church today? Is it a true church? Here it seems that we cannot simply make a decision regarding the Roman Catholic Church as a whole because it is far too diverse. Some Roman Catholic parishes certainly lack both marks—there is little or no true preaching of the Word, and the gospel message of salvation by faith in Christ alone is not known or received by people in the parish. Participation in the sacraments is seen as a "work" that can earn merit with God. Such a group of people is not a true Christian church. On the other hand, there are many Roman Catholic parishes in various parts of the world today where the local priest has a genuine saving knowledge of Christ and a vital personal relationship with Christ in prayer and Bible study. His own homilies and private teaching of the Bible place much emphasis on personal faith and the need for individual Bible reading and prayer. His teaching on the sacraments emphasizes their symbolic and commemorative aspects much more than it speaks of them as acts that merit some infusion of saving grace from God. In such a case, although we would have to say that we still have profound differences with Roman Catholic teaching on some doctrines, nonetheless, it would seem that such a church would have a close enough approximation to the two marks of the church that it would be hard to deny that it is in fact a true church. It would seem to be a genuine congregation of believers in which the gospel is taught (though not purely) and the sacraments are administered more rightly than wrongly.[11]

Are there false churches within Protestantism? Looking at the two distinguishing marks of the church, it seems to me that *many liberal Protestant churches are in fact false churches today.* Is the gospel of works-righteousness and unbelief in Scripture that these churches teach any more likely to save people than did Roman Catholic teaching at the time of the Reformation? And is not their administration of the sacraments without sound teaching to anyone who walks in the door likely to give as much false assurance to unregenerate sinners as did the Roman Catholic use of the sacraments at the time of the Reformation? When there is an assembly of people who take the name *Christian* but consistently teach that people cannot believe their Bibles—indeed, a church whose pastor and congregation seldom read their Bibles or pray in any meaningful way, and do not believe or perhaps even understand the gospel of salvation by faith in Christ alone, then how can we say that this is a true church?

C. The Purity and Unity of the Church

1. More pure and less pure churches. Beyond the question of whether a church is a true or a false church, a further distinction can be made between *more pure* and *less pure* churches. Such a distinction is evident from a brief comparison of Paul's epistles. For example, when we look at Philippians or 1 Thessalonians, we find evidence of Paul's great joy in these churches and the relative absence of major doctrinal or moral problems (see Phil. 1:3–11: 4:10–16; 1 Thess. 1:2–10; 3:6–10). On the other hand, there were all sorts of serious doctrinal and moral problems in the churches of Galatia (Gal. 1:6–9; 3:1–5) and Corinth (1 Cor. 3:1–4; 4:18–21; 5:1–2, 6; 6:1–8; 11:17–22; 14:20–23; 15:12; 2 Cor. 1:23–2:11; 11:3–5, 12–15).

We may define the purity of the church as follows: *The purity of the church is its degree of freedom from wrong doctrine and conduct, and its degree of conformity to God's revealed will for the church.* There are a number of factors that would indicate that a church is "more pure," including biblical doctrine, proper use of the sacraments (or ordinances), right use of church discipline, genuine worship, effective

---

[11]See ch. 22, n. 4, on "The Gift of Salvation," a public document in which several Roman Catholic leaders, in October 1997, endorsed the doctrine of justification by faith alone.

prayer, effective witness, personal holiness of life among members, care for the poor, and love for Christ. Of course, churches can be more pure in some areas and less pure in others—a church may have excellent doctrine and sound preaching, for example, yet be a dismal failure in witness to others or in meaningful worship. But the New Testament encourages us to work for the purity of the church in all of these areas. Christ's goal for the church is *"that he might sanctify her,* having cleansed her by the washing of water with the word, *that he might present the church to himself* in splendor, *without spot or wrinkle or any such thing,* that she might be holy and without blemish" (Eph. 5:26–27). Such an intention on the part of our Lord should encourage us to *work for the purity of the visible church* in all of its many facets.

2. The unity of the church. We must not neglect another New Testament emphasis, the need to work for the unity of the church. *The unity of the church is its degree of freedom from divisions among true Christians.* Jesus' goal is that "there shall be *one flock, one shepherd"* (John 10:16), and he prays for all future believers "that they may all be one" (John 17:21). This unity will be a witness to unbelievers, for Jesus prays "that they may become *perfectly one, so that the world may know that you have sent me* and have loved them even as you have loved me" (John 17:23). And Paul writes to Corinth, "I appeal to you, brethren, by the name of our Lord Jesus Christ, that *all of you agree* and that there be no dissensions among you, but *that you be united* in the same mind and the same judgment" (1 Cor. 1:10; cf. v. 13).

He also encourages the Philippians, "Complete my joy by being of the same mind, having the same love, *being in full accord and of one mind"* (Phil. 2:2). He tells the Ephesians that Christians are to be "eager to maintain the *unity* of the Spirit in the bond of peace" (Eph. 4:3), and that the Lord gives gifts to the church "for building up the body of Christ, *until we all attain to the unity of the faith and of the knowledge of the Son of God,* to mature manhood, to the measure of the stature of the fulness of Christ" (Eph. 4:12–13).

Consistent with this New Testament emphasis on the unity of believers is the fact that the direct commands to *separate* from other people are always commands to separate *from unbelievers,* not from Christians with whom one disagrees. When Paul says, "Therefore come out from them, and *be separate from them"* (2 Cor. 6:17), it is in support of his opening command of that section, "Do not be mismated *with unbelievers"* (2 Cor. 6:14). Of course, there is a kind of church discipline that requires separation from an individual who is causing trouble within the church (Matt. 18:17; 1 Cor. 5:11–13), and there may be other reasons for which Christians conclude that separation is required, but it is important to note here, in discussing the unity of the church, that there are no direct New Testament commands to separate from Christians with whom one has doctrinal differences (unless those differences involve such serious heresy that the Christian faith itself is denied, as in 2 John 10).

These passages on church unity tell us that, in addition to working for the purity of the visible church, *we are also to work for the unity of the visible church.* Yet we must realize that such unity does not require one worldwide church government over all Christians. In fact, the existence of different denominations, mission boards, Christian educational institutions, college ministries, and so forth is not necessarily a mark of disunity of the church, for there may be a great deal of cooperation and frequent demonstrations of unity among such diverse bodies as these. Another way of understanding the existence of many different denominations is that this is not just a mark of divisiveness but in many cases is rather the Lord's good provision to protect us from the alternative—one worldwide church government, which would have so much power it would inevitably become corrupt. Many Christians would argue that there should not be a worldwide government of the church, because the New Testament pattern of church government never shows elders having authority over any more than their own local congregations.[12] In fact, even in the New Testament, the apostles agreed that Paul should emphasize missionary work to the Gentiles while Peter would emphasize missionary work to the Jews (Gal. 2:7).

Unity among Christians is often demonstrated quite effectively through voluntary cooperation and affiliation among Christian groups. Moreover, different types of ministries and different emphases in ministry may result in different organizations, all under the universal headship of Christ as Lord of the church.

D. The Purposes of the Church

We can understand the purposes of the church in terms of ministry to God, ministry to believers, and ministry to the world.

1. Ministry to God: Worship. In relationship to God, the church's purpose is to worship him. Paul directs the church at Colossae to "sing psalms and hymns and spiritual songs with thankfulness in your hearts *to God*" (Col. 3:16). God has destined us and appointed us in Christ "to live for the praise of his glory" (Eph. 1:12). Worship in the church is not merely a preparation for something else; it is in itself fulfilling the major purpose of the church with reference to its Lord. That is why Paul can follow an exhortation that we are to be "making the most of the time" with a command to be filled with the Spirit and then to be "singing and making melody *to the Lord* with all your heart" (Eph. 5:16–19).

2. Ministry to believers: Nurture. According to Scripture, the church has an obligation to nurture those who are already believers and build them up to maturity in the faith. Paul said that his own goal was not simply to bring people to initial saving faith but to "present every man *mature* in Christ" (Col. 1:28). And he told the church at Ephesus that God gave the church gifted persons "to equip the saints for the work of ministry, for building up the body of Christ, until we all attain to the unity of the faith and of the knowledge of the Son of God, *to mature manhood,* to the measure of the stature of the fullness of Christ" (Eph. 4:12–13). It is clearly contrary to the New Testament pattern to think that our only goal with people is to bring them to initial saving faith. Our goal as a church must be to present to God every Christian "mature in Christ" (Col. 1:28).

3. Ministry to the world: Evangelism and mercy. Jesus told his disciples that they should "make disciples of all nations" (Matt. 28:19). This evangelistic work of declaring the gospel is the primary ministry that the church has toward the world. Yet accompanying the work of evangelism is also a ministry of mercy, a ministry that includes caring for the poor and needy in the name of the Lord. Although the emphasis of the New Testament is on giving material help to those who are part of the church (Acts 11:29; 2 Cor. 8:4; 1 John 3:17), there is still an affirmation that it is right to help unbelievers even if they do not respond with gratitude or acceptance

---

[12]The presence of the apostles at the Jerusalem Council in Acts 15 means that the elders present there do not set a pattern for authority of elders at more than the local level.

of the gospel message. Jesus tells us, "Love your enemies, and do good, and lend, expecting nothing in return; and your reward will be great, and you will be sons of the Most High; for *he is kind to the ungrateful and the selfish*. Be merciful, even as your Father is merciful" (Luke 6:35–36). The point of Jesus' explanation is that we are to imitate God in being kind to those who are being ungrateful and selfish as well.

Moreover, we have the example of Jesus who did not attempt to heal only those who accepted him as Messiah. Rather, when great crowds came to him, "he laid his hands *on every one of them* and healed them" (Luke 4:40). This should give us encouragement to carry out deeds of kindness and pray for healing and other needs in the lives of unbelievers as well as believers. Such ministries of mercy to the world may also include participation in civic activities or attempting to influence governmental policies to make them more consistent with biblical moral principles. In areas where there is systematic injustice manifested in the treatment of the poor and/or ethnic or religious minorities, the church should also pray and—as it has opportunity—speak against such injustice. All these are ways in which the church can supplement its evangelistic ministry to the world and indeed adorn the gospel it professes. But such ministries of mercy to the world should never become a substitute for genuine evangelism or for the other areas of ministry to God and to believers mentioned above.

4. Keeping these purposes in balance. Once we have listed these three purposes for the church, someone might ask, "Which is most important?" Or someone else might ask, "Might we neglect one of these three as less important than the others?"

To that we must respond that all three purposes of the church are commanded by the Lord in Scripture; therefore, all three are important and none can be neglected. In fact, a strong church will have effective ministries in all three of these areas. We should beware of any attempts to reduce the purpose of the church to only one of these three and say that it should be our primary focus. In fact, such attempts to make one of these purposes primary will always result in some neglect of the other two.

However, individuals are different from churches in placing a relative priority on one or another of these purposes of the church. Because we are like a body with diverse spiritual gifts and abilities, it is right for us to place most of our emphasis on the fulfillment of that purpose of the church that is most closely related to the gifts and interests God has given to us. Someone with the gift of evangelism should of course spend some time in worship and caring for other believers, but may end up spending the vast majority of his time in evangelistic work. Someone who is a gifted worship leader may end up devoting 90 percent of his or her time in the church toward preparation for and leading of worship. This is only an appropriate response to the diversity of gifts that God has given us.

II. REVIEW QUESTIONS

1. Does the definition of "church" in this chapter include only New Testament believers? Explain.
2. Define the terms "invisible church" and "visible church." Compare and contrast the two.

3. Does God have two distinct plans for Israel and the church, or should they be viewed as both constituting one people of God? Support your answer from Scripture.

4. What are the two primary marks of a true church? Why are these important?

5. Name and describe the three primary purposes of the church.

III. QUESTIONS FOR PERSONAL APPLICATION

1. When you think of the church as the invisible fellowship of all true believers throughout all time, how does it affect the way you think of yourself as an individual Christian? In the community in which you live, is there much visible unity among genuine believers (that is, is there much visible evidence of the true nature of the invisible church)? Does the New Testament say anything about the ideal size for an individual church?

2. Would you consider the church that you are now in to be a true church? Have you ever been a member of a church that you would think to be a false church? Viewed from the perspective of the final judgment, what good and what harm might come from our failure to state that we think unbelieving churches are false churches?

3. Did any of the metaphors for the church give you a new appreciation for the church that you currently attend?

4. To which purpose of the church do you think you can most effectively contribute? Which purpose has God placed in your heart a strong desire to fulfill?

IV. SPECIAL TERMS

body of Christ	marks of the church
church	purity of the church
ekklēsia	unity of the church
invisible church	visible church

V. SCRIPTURE MEMORY PASSAGE

EPHESIANS 4:11–13

And his gifts were that some should be apostles, some prophets, some evangelists, some pastors and teachers, to equip the saints for the work of ministry, for building up the body of Christ, until we all attain to the unity of the faith and of the knowledge of the Son of God, to mature manhood, to the measure of the stature of the fulness of Christ.

CHAPTER TWENTY-SEVEN

Baptism

+ *Who should be baptized?*
+ *How should it be done?*
+ *What does it mean?*

I. EXPLANATION AND SCRIPTURAL BASIS

In this chapter and the next we treat baptism and the Lord's Supper, two ceremonies Jesus commanded his church to perform. But before we begin consideration of either one of them, we must note that there is disagreement among Protestants even over the general term that should be applied to them. Because the Roman Catholic Church calls these two ceremonies "sacraments," and because the Catholic Church teaches that these sacraments *in themselves* actually *convey grace* to people (without requiring faith from the persons participating in them), some Protestants (especially Baptists) have refused to refer to baptism and the Lord's Supper as "sacraments." They have preferred the word *ordinances* instead. This is thought to be an appropriate term because baptism and the Lord's Supper were "ordained" by Christ. On the other hand, other Protestants such as those in the Anglican, Lutheran, and Reformed traditions have been willing to use the word *sacraments* to refer to baptism and the Lord's Supper, without thereby endorsing the Roman Catholic position.

It does not seem that any significant point is at issue here in the question of whether to call baptism and the Lord's Supper "ordinances" or "sacraments." Since Protestants who use both words explain clearly what they mean by them, the argument is not really over doctrine but over the meaning of an English word. If we are willing to explain clearly what we mean, it does not seem to make any difference whether we use the word *sacrament* or not. In this text, when referring to baptism and the Lord's Supper in Protestant teaching, I will use "ordinances" and "sacraments" interchangeably and regard them as synonymous in meaning.

Before beginning our discussion of baptism, we must recognize that there has been historically, and is today, a strong difference of viewpoint among evangelical Christians regarding this subject. The position advocated in this book is that baptism is not a "major" doctrine that should be the basis of division among genuine Christians,[1] but it is nonetheless a matter of importance for ordinary church life, and it is appropriate that we give it full consideration.

---

[1]See ch. 1, p. 21, for a discussion of major and minor doctrines. Not all Christians agree with my view that this is a minor doctrine. Many Christians in previous generations were persecuted and even put to death because they differed with the official state church and its practice of infant baptism. For them, the issue was not merely a ceremony; it was

The position advocated in this chapter is "Baptistic"—namely, that *baptism is appropriately administered only to those who give a believable profession of faith in Jesus Christ*. During the discussion, we shall interact particularly with the paedobaptist ("infant baptist") position as advocated by Louis Berkhof in his *Systematic Theology*, since this is a careful and responsible representation of the paedobaptist position, and it is in a widely used systematic theology text.

A. The Mode and Meaning of Baptism

The practice of baptism in the New Testament was carried out in one way: The person being baptized was *immersed*, or put completely under the water, and then brought back up again. Baptism *by immersion* is therefore the "mode" of baptism or the way in which baptism was carried out in the New Testament. This is evident for the following reasons:

First, the Greek word *baptizō* means "to plunge, dip, immerse" something in water. This is the commonly recognized and standard meaning of the term in ancient Greek literature both inside and outside of the Bible.[2]

Second, the sense "immerse" is appropriate and probably required for the word in several New Testament passages. In Mark 1:5 people were baptized by John "*in* the river Jordan" (the Greek text has *en*, "in," and not "beside" or "by" or "near" the river). Mark also tells us that when Jesus had been baptized "he came up *out of the water*" (Mark 1:10). The Greek text specifies that he came "out of" *(ek)* the water, not that he came away from it (this would be expressed by Gk. *apo*). The fact that John and Jesus went into the river and came up out of it strongly suggests immersion, since sprinkling or pouring of water could much more readily have been done standing beside the river, particularly because multitudes of people were coming for baptism. John's gospel tells us, further, that John the Baptist "was baptizing at Aenon near Salim, because there was much water there" (John 3:23). Again, it would not take "much water" to baptize people by sprinkling, but it would take much water to baptize by immersion. (See also Acts 8:36.)

Third, the symbolism of union with Christ in his death, burial, and resurrection seems to require baptism by immersion. Paul says, "Do you not know that all of us who have been baptized into Christ Jesus were baptized into his death? We were buried therefore with him by baptism into death, so that as Christ was raised from the dead by the glory of the Father, we too might walk in newness of life" (Rom. 6:3–4). Similarly, Paul tells the Colossians, "You were *buried with him in baptism*, in which you were also *raised with him* through faith in the working of God, who raised him from the dead" (Col. 2:12).

Now this truth is clearly symbolized in baptism by immersion. When the candidate for baptism goes down into the water, it is a picture of going down into the grave and being buried. Coming up out of the water is then a picture of being raised with Christ to walk in newness of life. Baptism thus very clearly pictures death to one's old way of life and rising to a new kind of life in Christ. But baptism by sprinkling or pouring simply misses this symbolism.

---

the right to have a believers' church, one that did not automatically include all the people born in a geographical region. Viewed in this light, the controversy over baptism involves a larger difference over the nature of the church: Does one become part of the church by birth into a believing family, or by voluntary profession of faith?

[2]So LSJ, p. 305: "plunge"; passive, "to be drowned." Similarly, BAGD, p. 131: "dip, immerse," and middle, "dip oneself, wash (in non-Christian literature also 'plunge, sink, drench, overwhelm')."

Sometimes it is objected that the essential thing symbolized in baptism is not death and resurrection with Christ but purification and cleansing from sins. Certainly it is true that water is an evident symbol of washing and cleansing, and the waters of baptism do symbolize washing and purification from sins as well as death and resurrection with Christ (cf. Titus 3:5; Acts 22:16).

But to say that washing away of sins is the only thing (or even the most essential thing) pictured in baptism does not faithfully represent New Testament teaching. Both washing and death and resurrection with Christ are symbolized in baptism, but Romans 6:1–11 and Colossians 2:11–12 place a clear emphasis on dying and rising with Christ. Even the washing is much more effectively symbolized by immersion than by sprinkling or pouring, and death and resurrection with Christ are symbolized only by immersion, not at all by sprinkling or pouring.

What then is the positive meaning of baptism? In all the discussion over the mode of baptism and the disputes over its meaning, it is easy for Christians to lose sight of the significance and beauty of baptism and to disregard the tremendous blessing that accompanies this ceremony. The amazing truths of dying and rising with Christ and of having our sins washed away are truths of momentous and eternal proportion and ought to be an occasion for giving great glory and praise to God. If churches would teach these truths more clearly, baptisms would be the occasion of much more blessing in the church.

B. The Subjects of Baptism

The pattern revealed at several places in the New Testament is that only those who give a believable profession of faith should be baptized. This view is often called "believers' baptism," since it holds that only those who themselves believed in Christ (or, more precisely, those who have given reasonable evidence of believing in Christ) should be baptized. This is because baptism, which is a *symbol of beginning the Christian life,* should only be given to those who have in fact begun the Christian life.

1. The argument from the New Testament narrative passages on baptism. The narrative examples of those who were baptized suggest that baptism was administered only to those who gave a believable profession of faith. After Peter's sermon at Pentecost, we read, "*Those who received his word* were baptized" (Acts 2:41). The text specifies that baptism was administered to those who "received his word" and therefore trusted in Christ for salvation. Similarly, when Philip preached the gospel in Samaria, we read, "*When they believed* Philip as he preached good news about the kingdom of God and the name of Jesus Christ, *they were baptized,* both men and women" (Acts 8:12). Likewise, when Peter preached to the Gentiles in Cornelius's household, he allowed baptism for those who had *heard* the Word and *received the Holy Spirit*—that is, for those who had given persuasive evidence of an internal work of regeneration. While Peter was preaching, "the Holy Spirit fell on all who heard the word," and Peter and his companions "heard them speaking in tongues and extolling God" (Acts 10:44–46). Peter's response was that baptism is appropriate for those who have received the regenerating work of the Holy Spirit: "Can any one forbid water for baptizing these people *who have received the Holy Spirit* just as we have?" Then Peter "commanded them to be baptized in the name of Jesus Christ" (Acts 10:47–48). The point of these three passages is that baptism is appropriately given to those who have received the gospel and trusted in Christ for salvation.

2. The argument from the meaning of baptism. A second consideration that argues for believers' baptism follows from the meaning of baptism: The outward symbol of *beginning* the Christian life should only be given to those who *show evidence* of having begun the Christian life. The New Testament authors wrote as though they clearly assumed that everyone who was baptized had also personally trusted in Christ and experienced salvation. For example, Paul says, *"As many of you as were baptized into Christ have put on Christ"* (Gal. 3:27). Paul here assumes that baptism is the outward sign of inward regeneration. This simply would not have been true of infants—Paul could not have said, "As many *infants* as have been baptized into Christ have put on Christ," for infants have not yet come to saving faith or given any evidence of regeneration.[3]

Paul speaks the same way in Romans 6:3–4: "Do you not know that *all of us who have been baptized into Christ Jesus* were baptized into his death? We were buried therefore with him by baptism into death." Could Paul have said this of infants? Could he have said that "all infants who have been baptized into Christ Jesus were baptized into his death" and "were buried therefore with him by baptism into death"? If Paul could not have said those things about infants, then those who advocate infant baptism must say that baptism means something *different* for infants than what Paul says it means for "all of us who have been baptized into Christ Jesus." Those who argue for infant baptism at this point resort to what seems to me to be vague language about infants being adopted "into the covenant" or "into the covenant community," but the New Testament does not speak that way about baptism. Rather, it says that all of those who have been baptized have been buried with Christ, have been raised with him, and have put on Christ (cf. also Col. 2:12).

3. Alternative #1: The Roman Catholic view. The Roman Catholic Church teaches that baptism should be administered to infants, an act often referred to as "christening." The reason for this is that the Catholic Church believes that baptism is necessary for salvation and that the act of baptism itself causes regeneration. Therefore, in this view, baptism is a means whereby the church bestows saving grace on people. And if it is this kind of a channel of saving grace, it should be given to all people.

Ludwig Ott, in his *Fundamentals of Catholic Dogma,* explains that through the sacrament of baptism a person is "spiritually reborn."[4] He further notes that baptism is necessary for salvation and is to be performed only by priests.[5] Moreover, even though infants cannot exercise saving faith themselves, the Roman Catholic Church teaches that the baptism of infants is valid because "the faith which infants lack is ... replaced by the faith of the Church."[6]

Essential to the Roman Catholic view of baptism is the belief that the sacraments work apart from the faith of the people participating in the sacrament. And if this is so, then it follows that baptism would confer grace even on infants who do not have the ability to exercise faith. The sacraments are believed to function *ex opere operato*[7]

---

[3]This is not to argue that *no* infants can be regenerated (see above, ch. 13, pp. 216–18), but simply that Paul could have no theological basis for saying that *all* infants who have been baptized have begun the Christian life. He is talking in Gal. 3:27 about "as many of you as were baptized into Christ."

[4]Ludwig Ott, *Fundamentals of Catholic Dogma,* ed. James Canon Bastible, trans. Patrick Lynch, 4th ed. (St. Louis: Herder, 1955), p. 350.

[5]Ibid., p. 356.

[6]Ibid., p. 359.

[7]Ibid., pp. 329–30.

("by work performed")—that is, the sacraments work in virtue of the actual activity done, and the power of the sacraments does not depend on any subjective attitude of faith in the people participating in them.

In giving a response to this Roman Catholic teaching, we should remember that the Reformation centered upon this issue. Martin Luther's great concern was to teach that salvation depends on faith alone, not on faith plus works. But if baptism and participating in the other sacraments are necessary for salvation because they are necessary for receiving saving grace, then salvation really is based on faith plus works. In contrast to this, the clear New Testament message is that justification is by faith alone. "By grace you have been saved *through faith;* and this is not your own doing, it is the gift of God—*not because of works,* lest any man should boast" (Eph. 2:8–9). Moreover, "the *free gift* of God is eternal life in Christ Jesus our Lord" (Rom. 6:23).

The Roman Catholic argument that baptism is necessary for salvation is very similar to the argument of Paul's opponents in Galatia who said that circumcision was necessary for salvation. Paul's response is that those who require circumcision are preaching "a different gospel" (Gal. 1:6). He says that "all who rely on works of the law are under a curse" (Gal. 3:10), and he speaks very severely to those who attempt to add any form of obedience as a requirement for justification: "You are severed from Christ, you who would be justified by the law; you have fallen away from grace" (Gal. 5:4). Therefore, we must conclude that no work is necessary for salvation. And therefore baptism is not necessary for salvation.

But what about 1 Peter 3:21, where Peter says, *"Baptism . . . now saves you"*? Does this not give clear support to the Roman Catholic view that baptism itself brings saving grace to the recipient?[8] No, for when Peter uses this phrase, he continues in the same sentence to explain exactly what he means by it. He says that baptism saves you *"not as a removal of dirt from the body"* (that is, not as an outward, physical act that washes dirt from the body—that is not the part that saves you), *"but as an appeal to God for a clear conscience"* (that is, as an inward, spiritual transaction between God and the individual, a transaction symbolized by the outward ceremony of baptism). We could paraphrase Peter's statement by saying, "Baptism now saves you—not the outward physical ceremony of baptism, but the inward spiritual reality that baptism represents." In this way, Peter guards against any view of baptism that would attribute automatic saving power to the physical ceremony itself.

In conclusion, the Roman Catholic teachings that baptism is necessary for salvation, that the act of baptism in itself confers saving grace, and that baptism is therefore appropriately administered to infants, are not persuasive in the light of New Testament teachings.

4. Alternative #2: The Protestant paedobaptist view. In contrast both to the Baptist position defended in the earlier part of this chapter and to the Roman Catholic view just discussed, another important view is that baptism is rightly administered to *all infant children of believing parents.* This is a common view in many Protestant groups (especially Presbyterian and Reformed churches). This view is sometimes known as the covenant argument for paedobaptism. It is called a "covenant" argument because it depends on seeing infants born to believers as part of the "covenant community" of God's people. The word *paedobaptism* means the practice of baptiz-

---

[8]This paragraph is adapted from Wayne Grudem, *The First Epistle of Peter* (Leicester: Inter-Varsity and Grand Rapids: Eerdmans, 1988), pp. 163–65, and is used by permission.

ing infants (the prefix *paedo-* means "child" and is derived from the Greek word *pais,* "child"). I will be interacting primarily with the arguments put forth by Louis Berkhof, who explains clearly and defends well the paedobaptist position.

The argument that infants of believers should be baptized depends primarily on the following three points:

a. *Infants were circumcised in the old covenant.* In the Old Testament, circumcision was the outward sign of entrance into the covenant community, or the community of God's people. Circumcision was administered to all Israelite males when they were eight days old.

b. *Baptism is parallel to circumcision.* In the New Testament, the outward sign of entrance into the covenant community is baptism. Therefore, baptism is the New Testament counterpart to circumcision. It follows that baptism should be administered to all infant children of believing parents. To deny them this benefit is to deprive them of a privilege and benefit that is rightfully theirs—the *sign* of belonging to the community of God's people, the "covenant community." The parallel between circumcision and baptism is seen quite clearly in Colossians 2: "In him also *you were circumcised* with a circumcision made without hands, by putting off the body of flesh in the circumcision of Christ; and *you were buried with him in baptism,* in which you were also raised with him through faith in the working of God, who raised him from the dead" (Col. 2:11–12). Here it is said that Paul makes an explicit connection between circumcision and baptism.

c. *Household baptisms.* Further support for the practice of baptizing infants is found in the "household baptisms" reported in Acts and the Epistles, particularly the baptism of the household of Lydia (Acts 16:15), the family of the Philippian jailer (Acts 16:33), and the household of Stephanas (1 Cor. 1:16). It is also claimed that Acts 2:39, which declares that the promised blessing of the gospel is "to you and to your children," supports this practice.

In response to these arguments for paedobaptism, the following points may be made:

1. It is certainly true that baptism and circumcision are in many ways similar, but we must not forget that what they symbolize is also different in some important ways. The old covenant had a *physical, external means of entrance* into the "covenant community." One became a Jew by being born of Jewish parents. Therefore, all Jewish males were circumcised. Circumcision was not restricted to people who had true inward spiritual life, but rather was given to *all who lived among the people of Israel.* God said: "Every male among you shall be circumcised. . . . He that is eight days old among you shall be circumcised; every male throughout your generations, whether born in your house, or bought with your money from any foreigner who is not of your offspring, *both he that is born in your house and he that is bought with your money,* shall be circumcised" (Gen. 17:10–13).

It was not only the physical descendants of the people of Israel who were circumcised, but also those servants who were purchased by them and lived among them (see Gen. 17:23; cf. Josh. 5:4). The presence or absence of inward spiritual life made no difference whatsoever in the question of whether one was circumcised.

We should realize that circumcision was given to every male living among the people of Israel even though true circumcision is something inward and spiritual:

"Real circumcision is a matter of the heart, spiritual and not literal" (Rom. 2:29). Moreover, Paul in the New Testament explicitly states that "not all who are descended from Israel belong to Israel" (Rom. 9:6). But even though there was in the time of the Old Testament (and more fully in the time of the New Testament) a realization of the inward spiritual reality that circumcision was intended to represent, there was no attempt to restrict circumcision only to those whose hearts were actually circumcised spiritually and who had genuine saving faith. Even among the adult males, circumcision was applied to everyone, not just those who gave evidence of inward faith.

2. But under the new covenant the situation is very different. The New Testament does not talk about a "covenant community" made up of believers *and* their unbelieving children and relatives and servants who happen to live among them. In the New Testament church, the only question that matters is whether one has saving faith and has been spiritually incorporated into the body of Christ, the true church. The only "covenant community" discussed is *the church,* the fellowship of the redeemed.

But how does one become a member of the church? The means of entrance into the church is *voluntary, spiritual, and internal.* One becomes a member of the true church by being born again and by having saving faith, not by physical birth. It comes about not by an external act, but by internal faith in one's heart. It is certainly true that baptism is the sign of entrance into the church, but this means that it should only be given to those who *give evidence* of membership in the church, only to those who profess faith in Christ.

This change in the way the covenant community was entered between the Old Testament (physical birth into the nation of Israel) and the New Testament (spiritual birth into the church) is paralleled by numerous changes between the old and new covenants. The old covenant had a physical temple to which Israel came for worship, but in the new covenant believers are built into a spiritual temple (1 Peter 2:5). Old covenant believers offered physical sacrifices of animals and crops upon an altar, but New Testament believers offer "spiritual sacrifices acceptable to God through Jesus Christ" (1 Peter 2:5; cf. Heb. 13:15–16).

In these and many other contrasts we see the truth of the distinction Paul emphasizes between the old covenant and the new covenant. The physical elements and activities of the old covenant were "only a shadow of what is to come," but the true reality, the "substance," is found in the new covenant relationship we have in Christ (Col. 2:17). Therefore, it is consistent with this change of systems that infant (male) children would automatically be circumcised in the old covenant, since their physical descent and physical presence in the community of Jewish people meant that they were members of that community in which faith was not an entrance requirement. But in the new covenant, it is appropriate that infants not be baptized and that baptism be given only to those who show evidence of genuine saving faith, because membership in the church is based on an internal spiritual reality, not on physical descent.

3. The examples of household baptisms in the New Testament are really not decisive for one position or another. When we look at the actual examples more closely, we see that in a number of them there are indications of saving faith on the part of all of those baptized. For example, it is true that the family of the Philippian jailer was baptized (Acts 16:33), but it is also true that Paul and Silas "spoke the

word of the Lord to him and *to all that were in his house*" (Acts 16:32). If the Word of the Lord was spoken to all in the house, there is an assumption that all were old enough to understand the word and believe it. Moreover, after the family had been baptized, we read that the Philippian jailer "*rejoiced with all his household* that he had believed in God" (Acts 16:34). So we have not only a household baptism but also a household reception of the Word of God and a household rejoicing in faith in God. These facts suggest quite strongly that the entire household had individually come to faith in Christ.

With regard to the fact that Paul baptized "the household of Stephanas" (1 Cor. 1:16), we must also note that Paul says at the end of 1 Corinthians that "the household of Stephanas were the first converts in Achaia, and they have devoted themselves to the service of the saints" (1 Cor. 16:15). So they were not only baptized; they were also converted and had worked at serving other believers. Once again, the example of *household baptism* gives indication of *household faith*.

Of all the examples of "household baptisms" in the New Testament, the only one that does not have some indication of household faith as well is Acts 16:14–15, speaking of Lydia: "The Lord opened her heart to give heed to what was said by Paul. And when she was baptized, with her household. . . ." The text simply does not contain any information about whether there were infants in her household or not. It is ambiguous and certainly not weighty evidence for infant baptism. It must be considered inconclusive in itself.

4. A further argument in objection to the paedobaptist position can be made when we ask the simple question, "What does baptism *do?*" In other words, we might ask, "What does it actually accomplish? What benefit does it bring?"

Roman Catholics have a clear answer to this question: Baptism *causes* regeneration. And Baptists have a clear answer: Baptism *symbolizes* the fact that inward regeneration has occurred. But paedobaptists cannot adopt either of these answers. They do not want to say that baptism causes regeneration, nor are they able to say (with respect to infants) that it symbolizes a regeneration that has already occurred.[9] The only alternative seems to be to say that it symbolizes a regeneration that will occur in the future, when the infant is old enough to come to saving faith. But even that is not quite accurate, because it is not certain that the infant will be regenerated in the future—some infants who are baptized never come to saving faith later. So it seems that the most accurate explanation of what baptism symbolizes for a paedobaptist is *probable future regeneration*. It does not cause regeneration, nor does it symbolize actual regeneration; therefore, it must be understood as symbolizing probable regeneration at some time in the future.

But at this point, it seems apparent that the paedobaptist understanding of baptism is quite different from that of the New Testament. The New Testament never views baptism as something that symbolizes a probable future regeneration. The New Testament authors do not say, "Can anyone forbid water for baptizing those who will probably someday be saved?" (cf. Acts 10:47), or, "As many of you as were baptized into Christ will probably someday put on Christ" (cf. Gal. 3:27), or "Do you not know that all of us who have been baptized into Christ Jesus will probably someday be baptized into his death?" (cf. Rom. 6:3). This is simply not the way the New Testament speaks of baptism. Baptism in the New Testament is a sign of being born

---

[9]However, some Protestant paedobaptists will *presume* that regeneration has occurred (and the evidence will be seen later). Others, including many Episcopalians and Lutherans, would say that regeneration occurs at the time of baptism.

again, being cleansed from sin, and beginning the Christian life. It seems fitting to reserve this sign for those who give evidence that that is actually true in their lives.

5. Finally, those who advocate believers' baptism often express concern about the practical consequences of paedobaptism. They argue that the practice of paedobaptism in actual church life frequently leads persons baptized in infancy to presume that they have been regenerated, and thereby they fail to feel the urgency of their need to come to personal faith in Christ. Over a period of years, this tendency is likely to result in more and more *unconverted* members of the "covenant community"—members who are not truly members of Christ's church. Of course, this would not make a paedobaptist church a false church, but it would make it a less pure church and one that will frequently be fighting tendencies toward liberal doctrine or other kinds of unbelief that are brought in by the unregenerate sector of the membership.

C. The Effect of Baptism

We have argued above that baptism symbolizes regeneration or spiritual rebirth. But does it only symbolize? Or is there some way in which it is also a "means of grace," that is, a means that the Holy Spirit uses to bring blessing to people? It seems proper to say that when baptism is properly carried out, of course it brings some spiritual benefit to believers as well. There is the blessing of God's favor that comes with all obedience, as well as the joy that comes through public profession of one's faith, and the reassurance of having a clear physical picture of dying and rising with Christ and of washing away sins. Certainly the Lord gave us baptism to strengthen and encourage our faith—and it should do so for everyone who is baptized and for every believer who witnesses a baptism.

D. The Necessity of Baptism

While we recognize that Jesus commanded baptism (Matt. 28:19), as did the apostles (Acts 2:38), we should not say that baptism is *necessary* for salvation.[10] This question was discussed to some extent above under the response to the Roman Catholic view of baptism. To say that baptism or any other action is *necessary* for salvation is to say that we are not justified by faith alone, but by faith plus a certain "work," the work of baptism. The apostle Paul would have opposed the idea that baptism is necessary for salvation just as strongly as he opposed the similar idea that circumcision was necessary for salvation (see Gal. 5:1–12).

Those who argue that baptism is necessary for salvation often point to Mark 16:16: "*He who believes and is baptized will be saved;* but he who does not believe will be condemned." But the very evident answer to this is simply to say that the verse says nothing about those who *believe* and *are not baptized*. The verse is simply talking about general cases without making a pedantic qualification for the unusual case of someone who believes and is not baptized. But certainly the verse should not be pressed into service and made to speak of something it is not talking about.[11]

More to the point is Jesus' statement to the dying thief on the cross, "Today you will be with me in Paradise" (Luke 23:43). The thief could not be baptized before

---

[10]At this point I am differing not only with Roman Catholic teaching, but also with the teaching of several Protestant denominations that teach that, in some sense, baptism is necessary for salvation. Although there are different nuances in their teaching, such a position is held by many Episcopalians, many Lutherans, and by the Churches of Christ.

[11]Moreover, it is doubtful whether this verse should be used in support of a theological position at all, since there are many ancient manuscripts that do not have this verse (or Mark 16:9–20), and it seems most likely that this verse was not in the gospel as Mark originally wrote it.

he died on the cross, but he was certainly saved that day. Moreover, the force of this point cannot be evaded by arguing that the thief was saved under the old covenant (under which baptism was not necessary to salvation), because the new covenant took effect at the death of Jesus (see Heb. 9:17), and Jesus died *before* either of the two thieves who were crucified with him (see John 19:32–33).

Another reason why baptism is not necessary for salvation is that our justification from sins takes place at the point of saving faith, not at the point of water baptism, which usually occurs later.[12] But if a person is already justified and has sins forgiven eternally at the point of saving faith, then baptism is not necessary for forgiveness of sins nor for the bestowal of new spiritual life.[13]

Baptism, then, is not necessary for salvation. But it is necessary if we are to be obedient to Christ, for he commanded baptism for all who believe in him.

E. The Age for Baptism

Those who are convinced by the arguments for believers' baptism must then begin to ask, "How old should children be before they are baptized?"

The most direct answer is that they should be old enough to give a *believable* profession of faith. It is impossible to set a precise age that will apply to every child, but when parents see convincing evidence of genuine spiritual life and also some degree of understanding regarding the meaning of trusting in Christ, then baptism is appropriate. Of course, this will require careful administration by the church, as well as a good explanation by parents in their homes. The exact age for baptism will vary from child to child, and church leaders may also give wise guidance regarding what they think to be appropriate for their church.

II. REVIEW QUESTIONS

1. How was baptism carried out in the New Testament? Support your answer with three pieces of evidence:
   - The meaning of the word translated *baptize* in the Bible
   - Scriptural references
   - The symbolism of baptism

2. Who should be baptized? Use both scriptural evidence and the meaning of baptism in your answer.

3. The Roman Catholic Church teaches that baptism is necessary for salvation and that the act of baptism by itself causes regeneration. How is this different from the view of baptism advocated in this chapter?

4. Unlike the Roman Catholic view, the Protestant paedobaptist view does not teach that baptism actually saves infants. What purpose does baptism serve in this view? What differences do you see between circumcision under the old covenant and baptism under the new covenant?

5. If baptism is not necessary for salvation, is it really important for believers to be baptized? Explain.

---

[12]See discussion of justification in ch. 22, pp. 316–23.
[13]See ch. 20, pp. 300–305, for a discussion of regeneration.

III. QUESTIONS FOR PERSONAL APPLICATION

1. Have you been baptized? When? If you were baptized as a believer, what was the effect of the baptism on your Christian life (if any)? If you were baptized as an infant, what effect did the knowledge of your baptism have in your own thinking when you eventually learned that you had been baptized as an infant?

2. What aspects of the meaning of baptism have you come to appreciate more as a result of reading this chapter (if any)? What aspects of the meaning of baptism would you like to see taught more clearly in your church?

3. When baptisms occur in your church, are they a time of rejoicing and praise to God? What do you think is happening to the person being baptized at that moment (if anything)? What do you think should be happening?

4. Have you modified your own view on the question of infant baptism versus believers' baptism as a result of reading this chapter? In what way?

5. How can baptism be an effective help to evangelism in your church? Have you seen it function in this way?

IV. SPECIAL TERMS

believable profession of faith	*ex opere operato*
believers' baptism	immersion
covenant community	paedobaptism

V. SCRIPTURE MEMORY PASSAGE

ROMANS 6:3–4

Do you not know that all of us who have been baptized into Christ Jesus were baptized into his death? We were buried therefore with him by baptism into death, so that as Christ was raised from the dead by the glory of the Father, we too might walk in newness of life.

Chapter Twenty-Eight

The Lord's Supper

+ *What is the meaning of the Lord's Supper?*
+ *How should it be observed?*

I. EXPLANATION AND SCRIPTURAL BASIS

The Lord Jesus instituted two ordinances (or sacraments) to be observed by the church. The previous chapter discussed *baptism,* an ordinance that is observed only once by each person as a sign of the beginning of his or her Christian life. This chapter discusses *the Lord's Supper,* an ordinance that is to be observed repeatedly throughout our Christian lives as a sign of continuing in fellowship with Christ.

A. Eating in God's Presence: A Special Blessing Throughout the Bible

Jesus instituted the Lord's Supper in the following way:

> Now as they were eating, Jesus took bread, and blessed, and broke it, and gave it to the disciples and said, "Take, eat; this is my body." And he took a cup, and when he had given thanks he gave it to them, saying, "Drink of it, all of you; for this is my blood of the covenant, which is poured out for many for the forgiveness of sins. I tell you I shall not drink again of this fruit of the vine until that day when I drink it new with you in my Father's kingdom." (Matt. 26:26–29)

Paul adds the following sentences from the tradition he received (1 Cor. 11:23): "This cup is the new covenant in my blood. Do this, as often as you drink it, in remembrance of me" (1 Cor. 11:25).

Is there a background to this ceremony in the Old Testament? It seems that there is, for there were instances of eating and drinking in the presence of God in the old covenant as well. For example, when the people of Israel were camped before Mount Sinai, just after God had given the Ten Commandments, God called the leaders of Israel up to the mountain to meet with him: "Then Moses and Aaron, Nadab, and Abihu, and seventy of the elders of Israel went up, and they saw the God of Israel. . . . *they beheld God, and ate and drank*" (Ex. 24:9–11).

Moreover, every year the people of Israel were to tithe (give one-tenth of) all their crops. Then the law of Moses specified, "*Before the LORD your God,* in the place which he will choose, to make his name dwell there, *you shall eat the tithe of your grain, of your wine, and of your oil, and the firstlings of your herd and flock;* that you may learn to fear the LORD your God always. . . . *You shall eat there before the LORD your God and rejoice,* you and your household" (Deut. 14:23, 26).

But even earlier than that, God had put Adam and Eve in the Garden of Eden and given them all of its abundance to eat (except the fruit of the tree of the knowledge of good and evil). Since there was no sin in that situation, and since God had created them for fellowship with himself and to glorify himself, every meal that Adam and Eve ate would have been a meal of feasting in the presence of the Lord.

When this fellowship in God's presence was later broken by sin, God still allowed some meals (such as the tithe of fruits mentioned above) that people would eat in his presence. These meals were a partial restoration of the fellowship with God that Adam and Eve enjoyed before the fall, even though it was marred by sin. But the fellowship of eating in the presence of the Lord that we find in the Lord's Supper is far better. The Old Testament sacrificial meals continually pointed to the fact that sins were not yet paid for, because the sacrifices in them were repeated year after year, and because they looked forward to the Messiah who was to come and take away sin (see Heb. 10:1–4). The Lord's Supper, however, reminds us that Jesus' payment for our sins has already been accomplished, so we now eat in the Lord's presence with great rejoicing.

Yet even the Lord's Supper looks forward to a more wonderful fellowship meal in God's presence in the future, when the fellowship of Eden will be restored and there will be even greater joy, because those who eat in God's presence will be forgiven sinners confirmed in righteousness, never able to sin again. That future time of eating in the presence of God is hinted at by Jesus when he says, "I tell you I shall not drink again of this fruit of the vine *until that day when I drink it new with you* in my Father's kingdom" (Matt. 26:29). We are told more explicitly in Revelation about the marriage supper of the Lamb: "The angel said to me, 'Write this: Blessed are those who are invited to the marriage supper of the Lamb'" (Rev. 19:9). This will be a time of great rejoicing in the presence of the Lord, as well as a time of reverence and awe before him.

From Genesis to Revelation, then, God's aim has been to bring his people into fellowship with himself, and one of the great joys of experiencing that fellowship is the fact that we can eat and drink in the presence of the Lord. It would be healthy for the church today to recapture a more vivid sense of God's presence at the table of the Lord.

B. The Meaning of the Lord's Supper

The meaning of the Lord's Supper is complex, rich, and full. Several things are symbolized and affirmed in the Lord's Supper.[1]

1. Christ's death. When we participate in the Lord's Supper, we symbolize the death of Christ because our actions give a picture of his death for us. When the bread is broken, it symbolizes the breaking of Christ's body; and when the cup is poured out, it symbolizes the pouring out of Christ's blood for us. This is why participating in the Lord's Supper is also a kind of proclamation: "For as often as you eat this bread and drink the cup, *you proclaim the Lord's death* until he comes" (1 Cor. 11:26).

2. Our participation in the benefits of Christ's death. Jesus commanded his disciples, "Take, eat; this is my body" (Matt. 26:26). As we individually reach out and take the cup for ourselves, each one of us is by that action proclaiming, "I am tak-

---

[1]The following seven points are adapted from Louis Berkhof, *Systematic Theology* (Grand Rapids: Eerdmans, 1932; reprint, Grand Rapids: Baker, 1979), pp. 650–51.

ing the benefits of Christ's death to myself." When we do this, we give a symbol of the fact that we participate or share in the benefits earned for us by Jesus' death.

3. Spiritual nourishment. Just as ordinary food nourishes our physical bodies, so the bread and wine of the Lord's Supper give nourishment to us. But they also picture the fact that there is spiritual nourishment and refreshment that Christ is giving to our souls—indeed, the ceremony that Jesus instituted is in its very nature designed to teach us this. Jesus said: "Unless you eat the flesh of the Son of man and drink his blood, you have no life in you; he who eats my flesh and drinks my blood has eternal life, and I will raise him up at the last day. For my flesh is food indeed, and my blood is drink indeed. He who eats my flesh and drinks my blood abides in me, and I in him. As the living Father sent me, and I live because of the Father, so he who eats me will live because of me" (John 6:53–57).

Certainly Jesus is not speaking of a literal eating of his flesh and blood. But if he is not speaking of a literal eating and drinking, then he must have in mind a spiritual participation in the benefits of the redemption he earns. This spiritual nourishment, so necessary for our souls, is both symbolized and experienced in our participation in the Lord's Supper.

4. The unity of believers. When Christians participate in the Lord's Supper together, they also give a clear sign of their unity with one another. In fact, Paul says, *"Because there is one bread, we who are many are one body,* for we all partake of the one bread" (1 Cor. 10:17).

When we put these four things together, we begin to realize some of the rich meaning of the Lord's Supper. When I participate I come into the presence of Christ; I remember that he died for me; I participate in the benefits of his death; I receive spiritual nourishment; and I am united with all other believers who participate in this Supper. What great cause for thanksgiving and joy is to be found in this Supper of the Lord!

But in addition to these truths visibly portrayed by the Lord's Supper, the fact that Christ has instituted this ceremony for us means that by it he is also promising or affirming certain things to us as well. When we participate in the Lord's Supper, we should be reminded again and again of two affirmations that Christ is making to us:

5. Christ affirms his love for me. The fact that I am able to participate in the Lord's Supper—indeed, that Jesus *invites me* to come—is a vivid reminder and visual reassurance that Jesus Christ loves *me,* individually and personally. When I come to partake of the Lord's Supper, I thereby find reassurance again and again of Christ's personal love for me.

6. Christ affirms that all the blessings of salvation are reserved for me. When I come at Christ's invitation to the Lord's Supper, the fact that he has invited me into his presence assures me that he has abundant blessings for me. In this Supper, I am actually eating and drinking at a foretaste of the great banquet table of the King. I come to his table as a member of his *eternal* family. When the Lord welcomes me to this table, he assures me that he will welcome me to all the other blessings of earth and heaven as well, and especially to the great marriage supper of the Lamb, at which a place has been reserved for me.

7. I affirm my faith in Christ. Finally, as I take the bread and cup for myself, by my actions I am proclaiming, "I need you and trust you, Lord Jesus, to forgive my sins and give life and health to my soul, for only by your broken body and shed blood can I be saved." In fact, as I partake in the breaking of the bread when I eat it and the pouring out of the cup when I drink from it, I proclaim again and again that my sins were part of the cause of Jesus' suffering and death. In this way sorrow, joy, thanksgiving, and deep love for Christ are richly intermingled in the beauty of the Lord's Supper.

C. How Is Christ Present in the Lord's Supper?

1. The Roman Catholic view: Transubstantiation. According to the teaching of the Roman Catholic Church, in the Eucharist the bread and wine *actually become* the body and blood of Christ.[2] This happens at the moment the priest says, "This is my body" during the celebration of the Mass. At the same time as the priest says this, the bread is raised up (elevated) and adored. This action of elevating the bread and pronouncing it to be Christ's body can only be performed by a priest.

When this happens, according to Roman Catholic teaching, grace is imparted to those present *ex opere operato,* that is, "by the work performed,"[3] but the amount of grace dispensed is in proportion to the subjective disposition of the recipient of grace.[4] Moreover, every time the Mass is celebrated, the sacrifice of Christ is repeated (in some sense), and the Catholic Church is careful to affirm that this is a real sacrifice, even though it is not the same as the sacrifice that Christ paid on the cross.

With respect to the actual sacrifice of Christ in the Mass, Ludwig Ott's *Fundamentals of Catholic Dogma* teaches as follows:

> The Holy Mass is a true and proper Sacrifice. (p. 402)

> The purpose of the Sacrifice is the same in the Sacrifice of the Mass as in the Sacrifice of the Cross; primarily the glorification of God, secondarily atonement, thanksgiving and appeal. (p. 408)

> *As a propitiatory sacrifice . . . the Sacrifice of the Mass effects the remission of sins and the punishment for sins;* as a sacrifice of appeal. . . . it brings about the conferring of supernatural and natural gifts. The Eucharistic Sacrifice of propitiation can, as the Council of Trent expressly asserted, be offered, not merely for the living, but also for the poor souls in Purgatory. (pp. 412–13)

In response to the Roman Catholic teaching on the Lord's Supper, it must be said that it first fails to recognize the symbolic character of Jesus' statements when he declared, "This is my body," or, "This is my blood." Jesus spoke in symbolic ways many times when speaking of himself. He said, for example, *"I am the true vine"* (John 15:1), or *"I am the door;* if any one enters by me, he will be saved" (John 10:9), or *"I am the bread* which came down from heaven" (John 6:41). In a similar way, when Jesus says, "This is my body," he means it in a symbolic way, not in an actual, literal, physical way. In fact, as he was sitting with his disciples holding the bread, the bread was in his hand but it was distinct from his body, and that was, of course, evident to the disciples. They naturally would have understood Jesus' state-

---

[2]The word *Eucharist* simply means the Lord's Supper. It is derived from the Greek word *eucharistia,* "giving of thanks." The term *Eucharist* is often used by Roman Catholics and frequently by Episcopalians as well. Among many Protestant churches the term *Communion* is commonly used to refer to the Lord's Supper.

[3]See discussion of the term *ex opere operato* in relationship to baptism in chapter 27 above, pp. 379–80.

[4]Ludwig Ott, *Fundamentals of Catholic Dogma,* ed. James Canon Bastible, trans. Patrick Lynch, 4th ed. (St. Louis: Herder, 1955), p. 399.

ment in a symbolic way. Similarly, when Jesus said, "*This cup* which is poured out for you *is the new covenant* in my blood" (Luke 22:20), he certainly did not mean that the cup was actually the new covenant, but that the cup *represented* the new covenant.

Moreover, the Roman Catholic view fails to recognize the clear New Testament teaching on the *finality* and *completeness* of Christ's sacrifice once for all time for our sins. The book of Hebrews emphasizes this many times, as when it says, "*Nor was it to offer himself repeatedly,* as the high priest enters the Holy Place yearly with blood not his own; for then he would have had to suffer repeatedly since the foundation of the world. But as it is, he has appeared *once* for all at the end of the age to put away sin by the sacrifice of himself . . . Christ, having been offered *once* to bear the sins of many" (Heb. 9:25–28). To say that Christ's sacrifice continues or is repeated in the Mass has been, since the Reformation, one of the most objectionable Roman Catholic doctrines from the standpoint of Protestants. When we realize that Christ's sacrifice for our sins is finished and completed (*"It is finished,"* John 19:30; cf. Heb. 1:3), it gives great assurance to us that our sins are *all* paid for, and there remains no sacrifice yet to be paid. But the idea of a continuation of Christ's sacrifice destroys that assurance that the payment has been made by Christ and accepted by God the Father and that there is "no condemnation" (Rom. 8:1) now remaining for us.

2. The Lutheran view: "In, with, and under." Martin Luther rejected the Roman Catholic view of the Lord's Supper, yet he insisted that the phrase "This is my body" had to be taken in some sense as a literal statement. His conclusion was not that the bread actually *becomes* the physical body of Christ, but that the physical body of Christ *is present* "in, with, and under" the bread of the Lord's Supper. The elements are not transformed into Christ's body and blood, but the latter are present with the elements. The example sometimes given is to say that Christ's body is present in the bread as water is present in a sponge—the water is not the sponge but is present "in, with, and under" a sponge, and is present wherever the sponge is present. Other examples given are that of magnetism in a magnet or a soul in the body. One passage that may be thought to give support to this position is 1 Corinthians 10:16, "The bread which we break, is it not a participation in the body of Christ?"

In response to the Lutheran view, it can be said that it too fails to realize that Jesus is speaking of a *spiritual* reality but using *physical* objects to teach us when he says, "This is my body." We should take this no more literally than we take the corresponding sentence, "*This cup* which is poured out for you *is the new covenant* in my blood" (Luke 22:20). In fact, Luther does not really do justice to Jesus' words in a literal sense at all. Berkhof rightly objects that Luther really makes the words of Jesus mean, "This accompanies my body."[5] In this matter it would help to read again John 6:27–59, where the context shows that Jesus is talking in literal, physical terms about bread, but he is continually explaining it in terms of spiritual reality.

3. The rest of Protestantism: A symbolic and spiritual presence of Christ. In distinction from Martin Luther, John Calvin and other Reformers argued that the bread and wine of the Lord's Supper did not change into the body and blood of Christ, nor did they somehow contain the body and blood of Christ. Rather, the bread and

---

[5]Berkhof, *Systematic Theology,* p. 653.

wine *symbolized* the body and blood of Christ, and they gave a visible sign of the fact that Christ himself was truly present.[6] Calvin said:

> By the showing of the symbol the thing itself is also shown. For unless a man means to call God a deceiver, he would never dare assert that an empty symbol is set forth by him. . . . And the godly ought by all means to keep this rule: whenever they see symbols appointed by the Lord, to think and be persuaded that the truth of the thing signified is surely present there. For why would the Lord put in your hand the symbol of his body, except to assure you of a true participation in it?[7]

Yet Calvin was careful to differ both with Roman Catholic teaching (which said that the bread became Christ's body) and with Lutheran teaching (which said that the bread contained Christ's body).

> But we must establish such a presence of Christ in the Supper as may neither fasten him to the element of bread, nor enclose him in bread, nor circumscribe him in any way (all which things, it is clear, detract from his heavenly glory).[8]

Today most Protestants would say, in addition to the fact that the bread and wine symbolize the body and blood of Christ, that Christ is also *spiritually present* in a special way as we partake of the bread and wine. Indeed, Jesus promised to be present whenever believers worship: "Where two or three are gathered in my name, there am I in the midst of them" (Matt. 18:20). And if he is especially present when Christians gather to worship, then we would expect that he will be present in a special way in the Lord's Supper. We meet him at *his* table, to which he comes to give himself to us. As we receive the elements of bread and wine in the presence of Christ, so we partake of him and all his benefits. We "feed upon him in our hearts" with thanksgiving. Indeed, even a child who knows Christ will understand this without being told and will expect to receive a special blessing from the Lord during this ceremony, because the meaning of it is so inherent in the very actions of eating and drinking. Yet we must not say that Christ is present apart from our personal faith, but only meets and blesses us there in accordance with our faith in him.

In what way is Christ present then? Certainly there is a symbolic presence of Christ, but it is also a genuine spiritual presence and there is genuine spiritual blessing in this ceremony.

D. Who Should Participate in the Lord's Supper?

Despite differences over some aspects of the Lord's Supper, most Protestants would agree, first, that *only those who believe in Christ* should participate in it, because it is a sign of being a Christian and continuing in the Christian life. Paul warns that those who eat and drink unworthily face serious consequences: "For any one who eats and drinks without discerning the body eats and drinks judgment upon himself. That is why many of you are weak and ill, and some have died" (1 Cor. 11:29–30).

---

[6]There was some difference between Calvin and another Swiss Reformer, Ulrich Zwingli (1484–1531) on the nature of the presence of Christ in the Lord's Supper, both agreeing that Christ was present in a symbolic way, but Zwingli being much more hesitant about affirming a real spiritual presence of Christ. However, the actual teaching of Zwingli in this regard is a matter of some difference among historians.

[7]John Calvin, *Institutes of the Christian Religion,* Library of Christian Classics, ed. John T. McNeill, trans. F. L. Battles, 2 vols. (Philadelphia: Westminster, 1960), 1:1371 (4.17.10).

[8]Ibid., 1:1381 (4.17.19).

A second qualification for participation is *self-examination:* "Whoever, therefore, eats the bread or drinks the cup of the Lord in an unworthy manner will be guilty of profaning the body and blood of the Lord. *Let a man examine himself, and so eat of the bread and drink of the cup.* For any one who eats and drinks without discerning the body eats and drinks judgment upon himself" (1 Cor. 11:27–29). In the context of 1 Corinthians 11, Paul is rebuking the Corinthians for their selfish and inconsiderate conduct when they come together as a church: "When you meet together, it is not the Lord's supper that you eat. For in eating, each one goes ahead with his own meal, and one is hungry and another is drunk" (1 Cor. 11:20–21). This helps us understand what Paul means when he talks about those who eat and drink "without discerning the body" (1 Cor. 11:29). The problem at Corinth was not a failure to understand that the bread and cup represented the body and blood of the Lord—they certainly knew that. The problem rather was their selfish, inconsiderate conduct toward each other while they were at the Lord's table. They were not understanding or "discerning" the true nature of the church *as one body.* This interpretation of "without discerning the body" is supported by Paul's mention of the church as the body of Christ just a bit earlier, in 1 Corinthians 10:17: "Because there is one bread, we who are many *are one body,* for we all partake of the one bread." So the phrase "not discerning the body" means "not understanding the unity and interdependence of people in the church, which is the body of Christ." It means not taking thought for our brothers and sisters when we come to the *Lord's* Supper, at which we ought to reflect his character.

What does it mean, then, to eat or drink "in an unworthy manner" (1 Cor. 11:27)? We might at first think the words apply rather narrowly and pertain only to the way we conduct ourselves when we actually eat and drink the bread and wine. But when Paul explains that unworthy participation involves "not discerning the body," he indicates that we are to take thought of all of our relationships within the body of Christ: Are we acting in ways that vividly portray, not the unity of the one bread and one body, but disunity? Are we conducting ourselves in ways that proclaim, not the self-giving sacrifice of our Lord, but enmity and selfishness? In a broad sense, then, "Let a man examine himself" means that we ought to ask whether our relationships in the body of Christ are in fact reflecting the character of the Lord whom we meet there and whom we represent.

In this connection, Jesus' teaching about coming to worship in general should also be mentioned: "So if you are offering your gift at the altar, and there remember that your brother has something against you, leave your gift there before the altar and go; first be reconciled to your brother, and then come and offer your gift" (Matt. 5:23–24). Jesus here tells us that whenever we come to worship we should be sure that our relationships with others are right, and if they are not, we should act quickly to make them right and then come to worship God. This admonition ought to be especially true when we come to the Lord's Supper.

E. Other Questions

Who should administer the Lord's Supper? Scripture gives no explicit teaching on this question, so we are left simply to decide what is wise and appropriate for the benefit of the believers in the church. To guard against abuse of the Lord's Supper, a responsible leader ought to be in charge of administering it, but it does not seem that Scripture requires that only ordained clergy or selected church officers could do this. In ordinary situations, of course, the pastor or other leader who ordinarily officiates at the worship services of the church would appropriately officiate at Communion as well. Similarly, some churches may feel that the leadership function of the church is so clearly tied up with the distribution of the elements that they would wish to continue with that restriction on their practice. But beyond this, there would seem to be no reason why only officers or only leaders, or only men, should distribute the elements. Would it not speak much more clearly of our unity and spiritual equality in Christ if both men and women, for example, assisted in distributing the elements of the Lord's Supper?

How often should the Lord's Supper be celebrated? Scripture does not tell us. Jesus simply said, "as often as you eat this bread and drink the cup . . ." (1 Cor. 11:26). Paul's directive here regarding worship services would also be appropriate to consider: "Let all things be done for edification" (1 Cor. 14:26). In actuality, it has been the practice of most of the church throughout its history to celebrate the Lord's Supper every week when believers gather. However, in many Protestant groups since the Reformation, there has been a less frequent celebration of the Lord's Supper—sometimes once a month or twice a month, or, in many Reformed churches, only four times a year. If the Lord's Supper is planned and explained and carried out in such a way that it is a time of self-examination, confession, thanksgiving, and praise, then it does not seem that celebrating it once a week would be too often, and it certainly could be observed that frequently "for edification."

II. REVIEW QUESTIONS

1. Why is baptism observed only once by each believer while the Lord's Supper is observed repeatedly throughout the believer's life?

2. Name at least four things symbolized by the Lord's Supper.

3. Respond to the following points of the Roman Catholic view of transubstantiation:
   - The bread and the wine of the Lord's Supper actually become the body and blood of Christ.
   - The Mass is in some sense a repetition of the death of Christ and a real sacrifice.

4. In the view held by most of Protestantism outside of Lutheranism, what relationship do the elements of the Lord's Supper have with the body and blood of Christ? In this view, in what way is Christ said to be present in the Lord's Supper?

5. Who should participate in the Lord's Supper? Why is self-examination for the participant in the Lord's Supper important?

III. QUESTIONS FOR PERSONAL APPLICATION

1. What things symbolized by the Lord's Supper have received new emphasis in your thinking as a result of reading this chapter? Do you feel more eager to participate in the Lord's Supper now than before you read the chapter? Why?

2. In what ways (if any) will you approach the Lord's Supper differently now? Which of the things symbolized in the Lord's Supper is most encouraging to your Christian life right now?

3. What view of the nature of Christ's presence in the Lord's Supper have you been taught in your church previously? What is your own view now?

4. Are there any broken personal relationships that you need to make right before you come to the Lord's Supper again?

5. Are there areas in which your church needs to do more teaching about the nature of the Lord's Supper? What are they?

IV. SPECIAL TERMS

Communion

Eucharist

"in, with, and under"

Lord's Supper

not discerning the body

spiritual presence

symbolic presence

transubstantiation

V. SCRIPTURE MEMORY PASSAGE

I Corinthians 11:23–26

For I received from the Lord what I also delivered to you, that the Lord Jesus on the night when he was betrayed took bread, and when he had given thanks, he broke it, and said, "This is my body which is for you. Do this in remembrance of me." In the same way also the cup, after supper, saying, "This cup is the new covenant in my blood. Do this, as often as you drink it, in remembrance of me." For as often as you eat this bread and drink the cup, you proclaim the Lord's death until he comes.

CHAPTER TWENTY-NINE

Gifts of the Holy Spirit (I): General Questions

+ *What are spiritual gifts?*
+ *How many are there?*
+ *Have some gifts ceased?*
+ *How do we seek and use spiritual gifts?*

I. EXPLANATION AND SCRIPTURAL BASIS

A. Questions Regarding Spiritual Gifts in General

In previous generations, systematic theology books did not have chapters on spiritual gifts, for there were few questions regarding the nature and use of spiritual gifts in the church. But the twentieth century has seen a remarkable increase in interest in spiritual gifts, primarily because of the influence of the Pentecostal and charismatic movements within the church.[1] In this chapter we will first look at some general questions regarding spiritual gifts, then examine the specific question of whether some (miraculous) gifts have ceased. In the next chapter we will analyze the New Testament teaching about particular gifts.

Before beginning the discussion, however, we may define spiritual gifts as follows: *A spiritual gift is any ability that is empowered by the Holy Spirit and used in any ministry of the church.* This broad definition includes both gifts that are related to natural abilities (such as teaching, showing mercy, or administration) and gifts that seem to be more "miraculous" and less related to natural abilities (such as prophecy, heal-

---

[1] I am using the terms *Pentecostal* and *charismatic* in the following way: *Pentecostal* refers to any denomination or group that traces its historical origin back to the Pentecostal revival that began in the United States in 1901, and that holds to the doctrinal positions (a) that baptism in the Holy Spirit is ordinarily an event subsequent to conversion, and (b) that baptism in the Holy Spirit is made evident by the sign of speaking in tongues, and (c) that all the spiritual gifts mentioned in the New Testament are to be sought and used today. Pentecostal groups usually have their own distinct denominational structures, the most prominent of which is the Assemblies of God.

Charismatic refers to any groups (or people) that trace their historical origin to the charismatic renewal movement of the 1960s and 1970s, seek to practice all the spiritual gifts mentioned in the New Testament (including prophecy, healing, miracles, tongues, interpretation, and distinguishing between spirits), and allow differing viewpoints on whether baptism in the Holy Spirit is subsequent to conversion and whether tongues is a sign of baptism in the Holy Spirit. Charismatics will very often refrain from forming their own denomination, but will view themselves as a force for renewal within existing Protestant and Roman Catholic churches.

The definitive reference work for these movements is now Stanley M. Burgess and Gary B. McGee, eds., *Dictionary of Pentecostal and Charismatic Movements* (Grand Rapids: Zondervan, 1988).

ing, or distinguishing between spirits). The reason for this is that when Paul lists spiritual gifts (in Rom. 12:6–8; 1 Cor. 7:7; 12:8–10, 28; and Eph. 4:11) he includes both kinds of gifts. Yet not every natural ability that people have is included here, because Paul is clear that all spiritual gifts must be empowered "by one and the same Spirit" (1 Cor. 12:11), that they are given "for the common good" (1 Cor. 12:7), and that they are all to be used for "edification" (1 Cor. 14:26), or for building up the church.

1. Spiritual gifts in the history of redemption. Certainly the Holy Spirit was at work in the Old Testament, bringing people to faith and working in remarkable ways in a few individuals such as Moses or Samuel, David or Elijah. But in general there was a less powerful activity of the Holy Spirit in the lives of most believers. There was little effective evangelism of the nations, there was no casting out of demons, miraculous healing was uncommon (though it did happen, especially in the ministries of Elijah and Elisha), prophecy was restricted to a few prophets or small bands of prophets, and there was very little experience of what New Testament believers would call "resurrection power" over sin, in the sense of Romans 6:1–14 and Philippians 3:10.

The pouring out of the Holy Spirit in new covenant fullness and power in the church occurred at Pentecost. With this a new era in redemptive history was inaugurated, and the new covenant empowering of the Holy Spirit that had been prophesied by the Old Testament prophets (cf. Joel 2:28–29) had come to God's people; the new covenant age had begun. And one characteristic of this new era was a widespread distribution of spiritual gifts to all people who were made partakers of this new covenant—sons and daughters, young men and old men, menservants and maidservants—all received a new covenant empowering of the Holy Spirit, and it would also be expected that all would receive gifts of the Holy Spirit then as well.

2. The purpose of spiritual gifts in the New Testament age. Spiritual gifts are given to equip the church to carry out its ministry until Christ returns. Paul tells the Corinthians, "You are not lacking in any spiritual gift, as you wait for the revealing of our Lord Jesus Christ" (1 Cor. 1:7). Here he connects the possession of spiritual gifts and their situation in the history of redemption (waiting for Christ's return), suggesting that gifts are given to the church for the period between Christ's ascension and his return. Similarly, Paul looks forward to the time of Christ's return and says, "When the perfect comes, the imperfect will pass away" (1 Cor. 13:10), indicating also that these "imperfect" gifts (mentioned in vv. 8–9) will be in operation until Christ returns, when they will be superseded by something far greater.[2] Indeed, the pouring out of the Holy Spirit in "power" at Pentecost (Acts 1:8) was to equip the church to preach the gospel (Acts 1:8)—something that will continue until Christ returns. And Paul reminds believers that in their use of spiritual gifts they are to "strive to excel in building up the church" (1 Cor. 14:12).

But spiritual gifts not only equip the church for the time until Christ returns, they also give a foretaste of the age to come. Paul reminds the Corinthians that they were "enriched" in all their speech and all their knowledge, and that the result of this enriching was that they were "not lacking in any spiritual gift" (1 Cor. 1:5, 7). Just as the Holy Spirit himself is in this age a "down payment" (2 Cor. 1:22 NASB mg; cf. 2 Cor. 5:5; Eph. 1:14) of the fuller work of the Holy Spirit within us in the age

---

[2]This interpretation of 1 Cor. 13:10 is defended at greater length in Section B below.

to come, so the gifts the Holy Spirit gives us are foretastes of the fuller working of the Holy Spirit that will be ours in the age to come.

In this way, gifts of insight and discernment prefigure the much greater discernment we will have when Christ returns. Gifts of knowledge and wisdom prefigure the much greater wisdom that will be ours when we "know as we are known" (cf. 1 Cor. 13:12). Gifts of healing give a foretaste of the perfect health which will be ours when Christ grants to us resurrection bodies. Similar parallels could be found with all the New Testament gifts. Even the diversity of gifts should lead to greater unity and interdependence in the church (see 1 Cor. 12:12–13, 24–25; Eph. 4:13), and this diversity in unity will itself be a foretaste of the unity which believers will have in heaven.

3. How many gifts are there? The New Testament epistles list specific spiritual gifts in six different passages.[3] Consider the following table:

1 Corinthians 12:28
1. apostle[5]
2. prophet
3. teacher
4. miracles
5. kinds of healing
6. helps
7. administration
8. tongues

1 Corinthians 12:8–10
9. word of wisdom
10. word of knowledge
11. faith
(5) gifts of healing
(4) miracles
(2) prophecy
12. distinguishing between spirits
(8) tongues
13. interpretation of tongues

Ephesians 4:11[4]
(1) apostle
(2) prophet
14. evangelist
15. pastor-teacher

Romans 12:6–8
(2) prophecy
16. serving
(3) teaching
17. encouraging
18. contributing
19. leadership
20. mercy

1 Corinthians 7:7
21. marriage
22. celebacy

1 Peter 4:11
whoever speaks
(covering several gifts)
whoever renders service
(covering several gifts)

What is obvious is that these lists are all quite different. No one list has all these gifts, and no gift is mentioned on all the lists. In fact, 1 Corinthians 7:7 mentions two gifts that are not on any other list: in the context of speaking of marriage and celibacy, Paul says, "Each has his own special gift[6] from God, one of one kind and one of another."

These facts indicate that Paul was not attempting to construct exhaustive lists of gifts when he specified the ones he did. Although there is sometimes an indication

---

[3]Some of the lists include both offices and gifts. Strictly speaking, for example, to be an apostle is an office, not a gift. In Eph. 4:11, the list gives four kinds of persons in terms of offices or functions, not, strictly speaking, four gifts. For three of the functions in Eph. 4:11, the corresponding gifts would be prophecy, evangelism, and teaching.

[4]This list gives four kinds of persons in terms of offices or functions, not, strictly speaking, four gifts. For three of the functions on the list, the corresponding gifts would be prophecy, evangelism, and teaching.

[5]Strictly speaking, to be an apostle is an office, not a gift.

[6]The Greek term for "gift" here is *charisma,* the same term Paul uses in 1 Cor. 12–14 to talk about spiritual gifts.

of some order (he puts apostles first, prophets second, and teachers third, but tongues last in 1 Cor. 12:28), it seems that in general Paul was almost randomly listing a series of different examples of gifts as they came to mind.

Moreover, there is some degree of overlap among the gifts listed at various places. No doubt the gift of administration (*kybernēsis*, 1 Cor. 12:28) is similar to the gift of leadership (*ho proistamenos*, Rom. 12:8), and both terms could probably be applied to many who have the office of pastor-teacher (Eph. 4:11). Moreover, in some cases Paul lists an activity and in other cases lists the related noun that describes the person (such as "prophecy" in Rom. 12:6 and 1 Cor. 12:10, but "prophet" in 1 Cor. 12:28 and Eph. 4:11).

How many different gifts are there then? It simply depends on how specific we wish to be. We can make a very short list of only two gifts as Peter does in 1 Peter 4:11: "whoever speaks" and "whoever renders service." In this list of only two items Peter includes all the gifts mentioned in any other list because all of them fit in one of these two categories. Other classifications of gifts include gifts of knowledge (such as distinguishing between spirits, word of wisdom, and word of knowledge), gifts of power (such as healing, miracles, and faith), and gifts of speech (tongues, interpretation, and prophecy).[7] Then again we could make a much longer list, such as the list of twenty-two gifts enumerated above.

The point of all of this is simply to say that God gives the church an amazing variety of spiritual gifts, and they are all tokens of his varied grace. In fact, Peter says as much: "As each has received a gift, employ it for one another, as good stewards of God's varied grace" (1 Peter 4:10; the word "varied" here is poikilos, which means "having many facets or aspects; having rich diversity").

The practical outcome of this discussion is that we should be willing to recognize and appreciate people who have gifts that differ from ours and whose gifts may differ from our expectations of what certain gifts should look like. Moreover, a healthy church will have a great diversity of gifts, and this diversity should not lead to fragmentation but to greater unity among believers in the church. Paul's whole point in the analogy of the body with many members (1 Cor. 12:12–26) is to say that God has put us in the body with these differences so that we might depend on each other. "The eye cannot say to the hand, 'I have no need of you,' nor again the head to the feet, 'I have no need of you.' On the contrary, the parts of the body which seem to be weaker are indispensable" (1 Cor. 12:21–22; cf. vv. 4–6).

4. Gifts may vary in strength. Paul says that if we have the gift of prophecy, we should use it "in proportion to our faith" (Rom. 12:6), indicating that the gift can be more or less strongly developed in different individuals, or in the same individual over a period of time. This is why Paul can remind Timothy, "Do not neglect the gift you have" (1 Tim. 4:14), and can say, "I remind you to rekindle the gift of God that is within you" (2 Tim. 1:6). It was possible for Timothy to allow his gift to weaken, apparently through infrequent use, and Paul reminds him to stir it up by using it and thereby strengthening it. This should not be surprising, for we realize that many gifts increase in strength and effectiveness as they are used, whether evangelism, teaching, encouraging, administration, or faith.

Texts such as these indicate that spiritual gifts may vary in strength. If we think of any gift, whether teaching or evangelism on the one hand, or prophecy or heal-

---

[7]This classification is adapted from Dennis and Rita Bennett, *The Holy Spirit and You* (Plainfield, NJ: Logos International, 1971), p. 83.

ing on the other, we should realize that within any congregation there will likely be people who are very effective in the use of that gift, perhaps through long use and experience, others who are moderately strong in that gift, and others who probably have the gift but are just beginning to use it. This variation in strength in spiritual gifts depends on a combination of divine and human influence. The divine influence is the sovereign working of the Holy Spirit as he "apportions to each one individually as he wills" (1 Cor. 12:11). The human influence comes from experience, training, wisdom, and natural ability in the use of that gift. It is usually not possible to know in what proportion the divine and human influences combine at any one time, nor is it really necessary to know, for even the abilities we think to be "natural" are from God (1 Cor. 4:7) and under his sovereign control.

But this leads to an interesting question: how strong does an ability have to be before it can be called a spiritual gift? How much teaching ability does someone need before he or she could be said to have a gift of teaching, for example? Or how effective in evangelism would someone need to be before we would recognize a gift of evangelism? Or how frequently would someone have to see prayers for healing answered before he or she could be said to have a gift of healing?

Scripture does not directly answer this question, but the fact that Paul speaks of these gifts as useful for the building up of the church (1 Cor. 14:12), and the fact that Peter likewise says that each person who has received a gift should remember to employ it "for one another" (1 Peter 4:10), suggest that both Paul and Peter thought of gifts as abilities that were strong enough to function for the benefit of the church, whether for the assembled congregation (as in prophecy or teaching), or for individuals at various times in the congregation (as helps or encouragement). Probably no definite line can be drawn in this matter, but Paul does remind us that not all have every gift or any one gift. He is quite clear in this in a set of questions that expect the answer "no" at each point: "Are all apostles? Are all prophets? Are all teachers? Do all work miracles? Do all possess gifts of healing? Do all speak with tongues? Do all interpret?" (1 Cor. 12:29–30).

The Greek text (with the particle *mē* before each question) clearly expects the answer "no" to every question. Therefore, not all are teachers, for example, nor do all possess gifts of healing, nor do all speak in tongues.

But even though not all have the gift of teaching, it is true that all people "teach" *in some sense* of the word *teach*. Even people who would never dream of teaching a Sunday school class will read Bible stories to their own children and explain the meaning to them—indeed, Moses commanded the Israelites to do this very thing with their children (Deut. 6:7), explaining God's words to them as they sat in their house or walked on the road. So we must say on the one hand that not everyone has the gift of teaching. But on the other hand we must say that there is some general ability related to the gift of teaching that all Christians have. Another way of saying this would be to say that there is no spiritual gift that all believers have, yet there is some general ability similar to every gift that all Christians have.

We can see this with a number of gifts. Not all Christians have a gift of evangelism, but all Christians have the ability to share the gospel with their neighbors. Not all Christians have gifts of healing, but nevertheless every Christian can and does pray for God to heal friends or relatives who are ill.

We can even say that other gifts, such as prophecy, not only vary in strength among those who have the gift, but also find a counterpart in some general abilities that are found in the life of every Christian. For example, if we understand prophecy (according to the definition given in ch. 30)[8] to be "reporting something that God brings to mind," then it is true that not everyone experiences this as a gift, for not everyone experiences God spontaneously bringing things to mind with such clarity and force that he or she feels free to speak about them among an assembled group of Christians. But probably every believer has at one time or another had a sense that God was bringing to mind the need to pray for a distant friend, or write or phone a word of encouragement to someone distant, and later found that that was exactly the thing that was needed at the moment. Few would deny that God sovereignly brought that need to mind in a spontaneous way, and, though this would not be called a gift of prophecy, it is a general ability to receive special direction or guidance from God that is similar to what happens in the gift of prophecy, but it is functioning at a weaker level.

The point of this whole discussion is simply to say that spiritual gifts are not as mysterious and "other worldly" as people sometimes make them out to be. Many of them are only intensifications or highly developed instances of phenomena that many Christians experience in their own lives. The other important point to be drawn from this discussion is that even though we have been given gifts by God, we are still responsible to use them effectively, and to seek to grow in their use that the church may receive more benefit from the gifts of which God has allowed us to be stewards.

5. Discovering and seeking spiritual gifts. Paul seems to assume that believers will know what their spiritual gifts are. He simply tells those in the church at Rome to use their gifts in various ways: "if prophecy, in proportion to our faith . . . he who contributes, in liberality; he who gives aid, with zeal; he who does acts of mercy, with cheerfulness" (Rom. 12:6–8). Similarly, Peter simply tells his readers how to use their gifts, but does not say anything about discovering what they are: "As each has received a gift, employ it for one another, as good stewards of God's varied grace" (1 Peter 4:10).

But what if many members in a church do not know what spiritual gift or gifts God has given to them? In such a case, the leaders of the church need to ask whether they are providing sufficient opportunities for varieties of gifts to be used. Though the lists of gifts given in the New Testament are not exhaustive, they certainly provide a good starting point for churches to ask whether at least there is opportunity for these gifts to be used. If God has placed people with certain gifts in a church when these gifts are not encouraged or perhaps not allowed to be used, they will feel frustrated and unfulfilled in their Christian ministries, and will perhaps move to another church where their gifts can function for the benefit of the church.

Beyond the question of discovering what gifts one has is the question of seeking additional spiritual gifts. Paul commands Christians, "Earnestly desire the higher gifts" (1 Cor. 12:31), and says later, "Make love your aim, and earnestly desire the spiritual gifts, especially that you may prophesy" (1 Cor. 14:1). In this context, Paul defines what he means by "higher gifts" or "greater gifts" because in 1 Corinthians 14:5 he repeats the word he used in 12:31 for "higher" (Gr. *meizōn*) when he says, "He who prophesies is greater than he who speaks in tongues, unless someone interprets, so that the church may be edified" (1 Cor. 14:5). Here the "greater" gifts are those that most edify the church. This is consistent with Paul's statement a few verses

---

[8]See ch. 30, pp. 408–15, for a definition of the gift of prophecy in the church.

later, when he says, "since you are eager for manifestations of the Spirit, strive to excel in building up the church" (1 Cor. 14:12). The higher gifts are those that build up the church more and bring more benefit to others.

But how do we seek more spiritual gifts? First, we should ask God for them. Paul says directly that "he who speaks in a tongue should pray for the power to interpret" (1 Cor. 14:13; cf. James. 1:5, where James tells people that they should ask God for wisdom). Next, people who seek additional spiritual gifts should have right motives. If spiritual gifts are sought only so that the person may be more prominent or have more influence or power, this certainly is wrong in God's eyes. This was the motivation of Simon the Sorcerer in Acts 8:19, when he said, "Give me also this power, that any one on whom I lay my hands may receive the Holy Spirit" (see Peter's rebuke in vv. 21–22). It is a fearful thing to want spiritual gifts or prominence in the church only for our own glory, not for the glory of God and for the help of others. Therefore those who seek spiritual gifts must first ask if they are seeking them out of love for others and a concern to be able to minister to their needs, because those who have great spiritual gifts but "have not love" are "nothing" in God's sight (cf. 1 Cor. 13:1–3).

After that, it is appropriate to seek opportunities to try the gift, just as in the case of a person trying to discover his or her gift, as explained above. Finally, those who are seeking additional spiritual gifts should continue to use the gifts they now have, and should be content if God chooses not to give them more. The master approved of the servant whose pound had "made ten pounds more," but condemned the one who hid his pound in a napkin and did nothing with it (Luke 19:16–17, 20–23)—certainly showing us that we have responsibility to use and attempt to increase whatever talents or abilities God has given to us as his stewards. We should balance this by remembering that spiritual gifts are apportioned to each person individually by the Holy Spirit "as he wills" (1 Cor. 12:11), and that "God arranged the organs in the body, each one of them, as he chose" (1 Cor. 12:18). In this way Paul reminds the Corinthians that ultimately the distribution of gifts is a matter of God's sovereign will, and it is for the good of the church and for our good that none of us have all of the gifts, and that we will need continually to depend on others who have gifts differing from ours. These considerations should make us content if God chooses not to give us the other gifts that we seek.

B. Have Some Gifts Ceased?

Within the evangelical world today there are differing positions over the question, "Are all the gifts mentioned in the New Testament valid for use in the church today?" Some would say yes. Others would say no, and would argue that some of the more miraculous gifts (such as prophecy, tongues plus interpretation, and perhaps healing and casting out of demons) were given only during the time of the apostles, as "signs" to authenticate the early preaching of the gospel. They first state that these gifts are no longer needed as signs today, and that they ceased at the end of the apostolic age, probably at the end of the first century or beginning of the second century A.D.[9]

---

[9]For an extensive discussion with representatives from four different views on this question, see Wayne Grudem, ed., *Are Miraculous Gifts for Today: Four Views* (Grand Rapids: Zondervan, 1996). The four contributors are Richard Gaffin (cessationist), Robert Saucy (open but cautious), Sam Storms (third wave), and Doug Oss (Pentecostal/charismatic). For further reading from a cessationist perspective, see John MacArthur Jr., *Charismatic Chaos* (Grand Rapids:

We should also realize that there is a large "middle" group with respect to this question, a group of "mainstream evangelicals" who are neither charismatics or Pentecostals on the one hand, nor "cessationists"[10] on the other hand, but are simply undecided and unsure whether this question can be decided from Scripture.[11]

Much of this debate centers on the meaning of 1 Corinthians 13:8–13, where Paul says:

> Love never ends; as for prophecies, they will pass away; as for tongues, they will cease; as for knowledge, it will pass away. For our knowledge is imperfect and our prophecy is imperfect; but when the perfect comes, the imperfect will pass away. When I was a child, I spoke like a child, I thought like a child, I reasoned like a child; when I became a man, I gave up childish ways. For now we see in a mirror dimly, but then face to face. Now I know in part; then I shall understand fully, even as I have been fully understood. So faith, hope, love abide, these three; but the greatest of these is love. (1 Cor. 13:8–13)

1. Does 1 Corinthians 13:8–13 tell us when miraculous gifts will cease? The purpose of this passage is to show that love is superior to gifts like prophecy because those gifts will pass away but love will not pass away. We should understand "the imperfect" in verse 10 to include not only prophecy but other gifts such as "tongues" and "knowledge" as well since these are also mentioned in verse 8 as things that will "pass away." The key issue is what time is meant by the word *when* in verse 10: "When the perfect is come, the imperfect will pass away."

Some who hold that these gifts have ceased believe that this phrase refers to a time earlier than the time of the Lord's return, such as "when the church is mature" or "when Scripture is complete." However, the meaning of verse 12 seems to require that this phrase is speaking about the time of the Lord's return. The phrase "see face to face" is several times used in the Old Testament to refer to seeing God personally[12]—not fully or exhaustively, for no finite creature can ever do that, but personally and truly nonetheless. So when Paul says, "but then face to face," he clearly means, "but then we shall see God face to face." Indeed, that will be the greatest blessing of heaven and our greatest joy for all eternity (Rev. 22:4: "They shall see his face"). This event can happen only when the Lord returns. Furthermore, the second half of verse 12 says, "Now I know in part; then I shall know even as I have been known." Paul does not expect to possess infinite knowledge, but rather when the Lord returns he expects to be freed from the misconceptions and inabilities to understand (especially to understand God and his work) that are part of this present life.

Zondervan, 1992), and Richard Gaffin, *Perspectives on Pentecost: Studies in New Testament Teaching on the Gifts of the Holy Spirit* (Phillipsburg, NJ: Presbyterian and Reformed, 1979). From a noncessationist perspective, see Jack Deere, *Surprised by the Power of the Spirit: A Former Dallas Seminary Professor Discovers that God Speaks and Heals Today* (Grand Rapids: Zondervan, 1993); Jack Deere, *Surprised by the Voice of God* (Grand Rapids: Zondervan, 1996); Jon Ruthven, *On the Cessation of the Charismata: The Protestant Polemic on Post-Biblical Miracles* (Sheffield: Sheffield University Academic Press, 1993); and Gary Greig and Kevin Springer, eds., *The Kingdom and the Power* (Ventura, Calif.: Regal, 1993). On the whole question, see also D. A. Carson, *Showing the Spirit: A Theological Exposition of 1 Corinthians 12–14* (Grand Rapids: Baker, 1987).

[10]The word *cessationist* means someone who thinks that certain miraculous spiritual gifts ceased long ago, when the apostles died and Scripture was complete.

[11]The discussion in the remainder of this section on the cessationist debate is adapted from Wayne Grudem, *The Gift of Prophecy in the New Testament and Today* (Eastbourne, UK: Kingsway, and Westchester, Ill.: Crossway, 1988), pp. 227–52, and is used by permission.

[12]See, for example, Gen. 32:30 and Judg. 6:22 (exactly the same Greek wording as 1 Cor. 13:12); Deut. 5:4; 34:10; Ezek. 20:35; Exod. 33:11.

His knowledge will resemble God's present knowledge of him because it will contain no false impressions and will not be limited to what is able to be perceived in this age. But such knowledge will occur only when the Lord returns.

This is the time to which verse 10 refers when it says "When the perfect comes, the imperfect will pass away." When Christ returns, "imperfect" or partial ways of acquiring knowledge about God will pass away because the kind of knowledge we will have in the final consummation of all things will render imperfect gifts obsolete. This would imply, however, that until Christ returns such gifts will continue to exist and be useful to the church, throughout the church age, including today, and right up to the day of Christ's second coming.

Moreover, this interpretation seems to fit best with the overall purpose of the passage. Paul is attempting to emphasize the greatness of love and to establish that "love never ends" (1 Cor. 13:8). To prove this point he argues that it will last beyond the time when the Lord returns, unlike present spiritual gifts. This makes a convincing argument: love is so fundamental to God's plans for the universe that it will last beyond the transition from this age to the age to come at Christ's return—it will continue for eternity.

Finally, a more general statement from Paul about the purpose of spiritual gifts in the New Testament age supports this interpretation. In 1 Corinthians 1:7 Paul ties the possession of spiritual gifts (Gr. *charismata*) to the activity of waiting for the Lord's return: "You are not lacking in any spiritual gift, as you wait for the revealing of our Lord Jesus Christ." This suggests that Paul saw the gifts as a temporary provision made to equip believers for ministry until the Lord returned. So this verse provides a close parallel to the thought of 1 Corinthians 13:8–13, where prophecy and knowledge (and no doubt tongues) are seen, similarly, as useful until Christ's return but unnecessary beyond that time.

First Corinthians 13:10, therefore, refers to the time of Christ's return and says that these spiritual gifts will last among believers until that time. This means that we have a clear biblical statement that Paul expected these gifts to continue through the entire church age and to function for the benefit of the church until the Lord returns.

2. Would the continuation of prophecy today challenge the sufficiency of Scripture? Some who take a "cessationist" view argue that to allow "words from God" from continuing prophetic utterances would be, in effect, either to add to Scripture or to compete with Scripture. In both cases, the sufficiency of Scripture itself would be challenged, and, in practice, its unique authority in our lives compromised. However, I have argued extensively elsewhere that ordinary congregational prophecy in New Testament churches did *not* have the authority of Scripture.[13] It was not spoken in words that were the very words of God, but rather in merely human words. And because it has this lesser authority, there is no reason to think that it will not continue in the church until Christ returns. It does not threaten or compete with Scripture in authority but is subject to Scripture, as well as to the mature judgment of the congregation.

Another objection is sometimes raised at this point. Some will argue that even if those who use the gift of prophecy today say that it does not equal Scripture in authority, in fact it functions in their lives to compete with or even replace Scripture

---

[13]For further discussion of the authority of the gift of prophecy, see ch. 30, pp. 408–15.

in giving guidance concerning God's will. Thus, prophecy today, it is said, challenges the doctrine of the sufficiency of Scripture for guidance in our lives.

Here it must be admitted that many mistakes have been made in the history of the church. But in this discussion the question must be, Are abuses *necessary* to the functioning of the gift of prophecy? If we are to argue that mistakes and abuses of a gift make the gift itself invalid, then we would have to reject Bible teaching (for many Bible teachers have taught error and started cults) and church administration as well (for many church leaders have led people astray) and so forth. The abuse of a gift does not mean that we must prohibit the proper use of the gift, unless it can be shown that there cannot be proper use—that all use has to be abuse.

3. Did miraculous gifts only accompany the giving of new Scripture? Another objection is to say that miraculous gifts accompanied the giving of Scripture, and since there is no new Scripture given today, we should expect no new miracles today.

But in response to that it must be said that this is not the only, nor even the major, purpose for miraculous gifts. Miracles have several other purposes in Scripture: (1) they authenticate the gospel message throughout the church age; (2) they give help to those in need, and thereby demonstrate God's mercy and love; (3) they equip people for ministry; and (4) they glorify God.

We should also note that not all miracles accompany the giving of additional Scripture. For example, the ministries of Elijah and Elisha were marked by several miracles in the Old Testament, but they wrote no books or sections of the Bible. In the New Testament, there were many occurrences of miracles that were not accompanied by the giving of Scripture. Both Stephen and Philip in the book of Acts worked miracles but wrote no Scripture. There were prophets who wrote no Scripture in Caesarea (Acts 21:4) and Tyre (Acts 21:9–11) and Rome (Rom. 12:6) and Thessalonica (1 Thess. 5:20–21) and Ephesus (Eph. 4:11) and the communities to which 1 John was written (1 John 4:1–6). There were apparently many miracles in the churches of Galatia (Gal. 3:5). And James expects that healing will occur at the hands of the elders in all the churches to which he writes (see James 5:14–16).

4. Is it dangerous for a church to allow for the possibility of miraculous gifts today? A final objection from the cessationist position is to say that a church that emphasizes the use of miraculous gifts is in danger of becoming imbalanced, and will likely neglect other important things such as evangelism, sound doctrine, and moral purity of life.

To say that the use of miraculous gifts is "dangerous" is not by itself an adequate criticism, because some things that are right are dangerous, at least in some sense. Missionary work is dangerous. Driving a car is dangerous. If we define *dangerous* to mean "something might go wrong," then we can criticize anything that anybody might do as "dangerous," and this just becomes an all-purpose criticism when there is no specific abuse to point to. A better approach with respect to spiritual gifts is to ask, "Are they being used in accordance with Scripture?" and "Are adequate steps being taken to guard against the dangers of abuse?"

Of course it is true that churches can become imbalanced, and some in fact have done so. But not all will, nor do they have to do so. Furthermore, since this argument is one based on actual results in the life of a church, it is also appropriate to ask, "Which churches in the world today have the most effective evangelism? Which have the most sacrificial giving among their members? Which, in fact, have the most emphasis on purity of life? Which have the deepest love for the Lord and for his Word?" While it is difficult to answer these questions clearly, I do not think that we can fairly say that those churches in the charismatic and Pentecostal movements by and large are weaker in these areas than other evangelical churches. In fact, in some cases they may be stronger in these areas. The point is simply that any argument that says that churches emphasizing miraculous gifts will become imbalanced is simply not proven in actual practice.

5. A final note: Cessationists and charismatics need each other. Finally, it can be argued that those in the charismatic and Pentecostal camps, and those in the cessationist camp (primarily Reformed and dispensational Christians) really need each other, and they would do well to appreciate each other more. The former tend to have more practical experience in the use of spiritual gifts and in vitality in worship that cessationists could benefit from, if they were willing to learn. On the other hand, Reformed and dispensational groups have traditionally been very strong in understanding of Christian doctrine and in deep and accurate understanding of the teachings of Scripture. Charismatic and Pentecostal groups could learn much from them if they would be willing to do so. But it certainly is not helpful to the church as a whole for both sides to think they can learn nothing from the other, or that they can gain no benefit from fellowship with one another.

II. REVIEW QUESTIONS

1. What is the purpose of spiritual gifts in the New Testament age? How do spiritual gifts relate to the age to come after Christ's return?

2. Refer to the lists of spiritual gifts on page 398:
    - What differences do you observe between the lists?
    - Which gifts are repeated on more than one list?
    - What inferences do you draw from these observations?

3. What evidence is there that spiritual gifts vary in strength from person to person?

4. Do we have scriptural warrant for desiring and seeking spiritual gifts? (Support your answer from Scripture.) List four recommendations as to how a person should go about this.

5. Did some spiritual gifts cease after the time of the apostles? Support your answer from Scripture.

6. Was the purpose of miracles only to accompany the giving of Scripture? What other purposes do miracles serve?

III. QUESTIONS FOR PERSONAL APPLICATION

1. Before reading this chapter, what spiritual gift or gifts did you think you had? Has your understanding of your own spiritual gift(s) changed after studying this chapter? In what way?

2. What can you do to stir up or strengthen the spiritual gifts in you that need strengthening? Are there some gifts that you have been given but have neglected? Why do you think you have neglected them?

3. As you think about your own church, which spiritual gifts do you think are most effectively functioning at present? Which are most needed in your church? Is there anything you can do to help meet those needs?

4. What do you think could be done to help churches avoid having controversies and divisions over the question of spiritual gifts? Are there tensions in your own church with regard to these questions today? If so, what can you do to help alleviate these tensions?

5. Do you think that some spiritual gifts mentioned in the New Testament ceased early in the history of the church and are no longer valid for today? Has your opinion on this question changed as a result of reading this chapter?

IV. SPECIAL TERMS

See the list at the end of the next chapter.

V. SCRIPTURE MEMORY PASSAGE

I PETER 4:10–11

As each has received a gift, employ it for one another, as good stewards of God's varied grace: whoever speaks, as one who utters oracles of God; whoever renders service, as one who renders it by the strength which God supplies; in order that in everything God may be glorified through Jesus Christ. To him belong glory and dominion for ever and ever. Amen.

CHAPTER THIRTY

Gifts of the Holy Spirit (II): Specific Gifts

+ *How should we understand and use specific spiritual gifts?*

I. EXPLANATION AND SCRIPTURAL BASIS

In this chapter we will build on the general discussion about spiritual gifts in the previous chapter and examine several specific gifts in more detail. We will not consider every gift mentioned in the New Testament but will focus on several gifts that are not well understood or whose use has aroused some controversy today. Therefore, we will not examine gifts whose meaning and use are self-evident from the term involved (such as serving, encouraging, contributing, showing leadership, or showing mercy), but will rather concentrate on the following gifts: (1) prophecy, (2) teaching, (3) healing, and (4) tongues and interpretation.

A. Prophecy

Although several definitions have been given for the gift of prophecy, a fresh examination of the New Testament teaching on this gift will show that it should be defined not as "predicting the future," nor as "proclaiming a word from the Lord," nor as "powerful preaching"—but rather as *"telling something that God has spontaneously brought to mind."* The first four points in the following material support this conclusion; the remaining points deal with other considerations regarding this gift.[1]

1. The New Testament counterparts to Old Testament prophets are New Testament apostles. Old Testament prophets had an amazing responsibility—they were able to speak and write words that had absolute divine authority. They could say, "Thus says the Lord," and the words that followed were the very words of God. The Old Testament prophets wrote their words as God's words in Scripture for all time (see Num. 22:38; Deut. 18:18–20; Jer. 1:9; Ezek. 2:7; et al.). Therefore, to disbelieve or disobey a prophet's words was to disbelieve or disobey God (see Deut. 18:19; 1 Sam. 8:7; 1 Kings 20:36; and many other passages).

---

[1]For a more extensive development of all of the following points about the gift of prophecy, see Wayne Grudem, *The Gift of Prophecy in 1 Corinthians* (Lanham, Md.: University Press of America, 1982), and Wayne Grudem, *The Gift of Prophecy in the New Testament and Today* (Eastbourne, U.K.: Kingsway, and Westchester, Ill.: Crossway, 1988). (The first book is more technical with more interaction with the scholarly literature.) Much of the following material on prophecy is adapted from my article "Why Christians Can Still Prophesy," in *Christianity Today* (September 16, 1988), pp. 29–35, and is used by permission.

In the New Testament there were also people who spoke and wrote God's very words and had them recorded in Scripture, but we may be surprised to find that Jesus no longer calls them "prophets" but uses a new term, "apostles." The apostles are the New Testament counterpart to the Old Testament prophets (see 1 Cor. 2:13; 2 Cor. 13:3; Gal. 1:8–9, 11–12; 1 Thess. 2:13; 4:8, 15; 2 Peter 3:2). It is the apostles, not the prophets, who have authority to write the words of New Testament Scripture.

When the apostles want to establish their unique authority, they never appeal to the title "prophet" but rather call themselves "apostles" (Rom. 1:1; 1 Cor. 1:1; 9:1–2; 2 Cor. 1:1; 11:12–13; 12:11–12; Gal. 1:1; Eph. 1:1; 1 Peter 1:1; 2 Peter 1:1; 3:2; et al.). This suggests that the words *prophet* and *prophesy* may not have been suitable to describe the authors of New Testament Scripture and that perhaps the words were frequently used in a broader sense at that time.

2. The meaning of the word prophet in the time of the New Testament. Why did Jesus choose the new term *apostle* to designate those who had the authority to write Scripture? It was probably because the Greek word *prophētēs* ("prophet") at the time of the New Testament had a very broad range of meanings. It generally did not have the sense "one who speaks God's very words" but rather "one who speaks on the basis of some external influence" (often a spiritual influence of some kind). Titus 1:12 uses the word in this sense, where Paul quotes the pagan Greek poet Epimenides: "One of themselves, a *prophet* of their own, said, 'Cretans are always liars, evil beasts, lazy gluttons.'" The soldiers who mock Jesus also seem to use the word *prophesy* in this way, when they blindfold Jesus and cruelly demand, "Prophesy! Who is it that struck you?" (Luke 22:64). They do not mean, "Speak words of absolute divine authority," but, "Tell us something that has been revealed to you" (cf. John 4:19).

Many writings outside the Bible use the word *prophet* (Gk. *Prophētēs*) in this way without signifying any divine authority in the words of one called a "prophet." In fact, by the time of the New Testament, the term *prophet* in everyday use often simply meant "one who has supernatural knowledge" or "one who predicts the future"—or even just "spokesman" (without any connotations of divine authority). Helmut Krämer surveys a number of examples of the use of this word near the time of the New Testament in his article in *Theological Dictionary of the New Testament,* concluding that the Greek word for "prophet" *(prophētēs)* "simply expresses the formal function of declaring, proclaiming, making known." Yet, because "every prophet declares something which is not his own," the Greek word for "herald" *(kēryx)* "is the closest synonym."[2]

Of course, the words *prophet* and *prophecy* were sometimes used of the apostles in contexts that emphasized the external spiritual influence (from the Holy Spirit) under which they spoke (so Eph. 2:20; 3:5; and Rev. 1:3; 22:7), but this was not the ordinary terminology used for the apostles, nor did the terms *prophet* and *prophecy* in themselves imply divine authority for their speech or writing. Much more commonly, the words *prophet* and *prophecy* were used of ordinary Christians who spoke not with absolute divine authority, but simply to report something that God had laid on their hearts or brought to their minds.

3. The gift of prophecy is given to all sorts of Christians in every congregation. With the giving of the Holy Spirit in new covenant fullness at Pentecost, one result

---

[2] *TDNT* 6, pp. 794–95.

was the widespread distribution of the gift of prophecy to thousands of God's people in thousands of Christian congregations throughout the early church. Peter said this would happen:

> . . . but this is what was spoken by the prophet Joel:
>
> "And in the last days it shall be, God declares,
> that I will pour out my Spirit upon all flesh,
> and *your sons and your daughters shall prophesy,*
> and your young men shall see visions,
> and your old men shall dream dreams;
> yea, and on my menservants and my maidservants in those days
> I will pour out my Spirit;
> and *they shall prophesy.*" (Acts 2:16–18)

Just as the Old Testament office of priest had been restricted to a very few people, but in the New Testament all of God's people become priests (or a "royal priesthood," 1 Peter 2:9), so there is a change in the office of prophet as well: The gift of prophecy is widely distributed to God's people, but the authority of prophecy is a lesser authority, no longer the authority of God's very words. We have specific evidence of prophets at least in Jerusalem (Acts 11:27), Antioch (Acts 13:1), Tyre (Acts 21:4), Caesarea (Acts 21:8–9), Rome (Rom. 12:6), Corinth (1 Cor. 14:29), Thessalonica (1 Thess. 5:20–21), and the churches to which John wrote (1 John 4:1–2). When we couple this evidence with the promise of the distribution of this gift in Acts 2:16–18 (above), it is likely that there were Christians with the gift of prophecy in every one of the thousands of Christian congregations in the ancient world. And Paul expected them to be prophesying at each church meeting (1 Cor. 14:1, 5, 26, 29–33).

Were all of these thousands of people with the gift of prophecy speaking the very words of God that were to be written down in Scripture, in God's "book of the covenant," to be preserved for all of God's people for all time? Certainly not. In fact, not one book of the New Testament was written by any one of these early Christian prophets. As we saw in chapter 2, the New Testament books were rather written by the apostles or people directly authorized by them. Then what kind of authority attached to the words of prophecies spoken in New Testament congregations? It must have been a lesser authority of some kind. In fact, this is what we find in several verses describing the gift of prophecy.

4. Indications that "prophets" did not speak with authority equal to the words of Scripture.

a. *Acts 21:4.* In Acts 21:4 we read of the disciples at Tyre: "Through the Spirit they told Paul not to go on to Jerusalem." This seems to be a reference to prophecy directed toward Paul, but Paul disobeyed it! He never would have done this if this prophecy contained God's very words and had authority equal to Scripture.

b. *Acts 21:10–11.* Then in Acts 21:10–11, Agabus prophesied that the Jews at Jerusalem would bind Paul and "deliver him into the hands of the Gentiles," a prediction that was nearly correct but not quite: The Romans, not the Jews, bound Paul (v. 33; also 22:29),[3] and the Jews, rather than delivering him voluntarily, tried to kill

---

[3] In both verses, Luke uses the same Greek verb (*deō*) that Agabus had used to predict that the Jews would bind Paul.

him and he had to be rescued by force (v. 32).[4] The prediction was not far off, but it had inaccuracies in detail that would have called into question the validity of any Old Testament prophet. On the other hand, this text could be perfectly well explained by supposing that Agabus had had a vision of Paul as a prisoner of the Romans in Jerusalem, surrounded by an angry mob of Jews. His own interpretation of such a "vision" or "revelation" from the Holy Spirit would be that the Jews had bound Paul and handed him over to the Romans, and that is what Agabus would (somewhat erroneously) prophesy. This is exactly the kind of fallible prophecy that would fit the definition of New Testament congregational prophecy proposed above—reporting in one's own words something that God has spontaneously brought to mind.[5]

c. *1 Thessalonians 5:19–21.* Paul tells the Thessalonians, "Do not despise prophesying, but *test everything;* hold fast what is good" (1 Thess. 5:20–21). If the Thessalonians had thought that prophecy equaled God's Word in authority, he never would have had to tell the Thessalonians not to despise it—they "received" and "accepted" God's Word "with joy from the Holy Spirit" (1 Thess. 1:6; 2:13; cf. 4:15). But when Paul tells them to "test everything," it must include at least the prophecies he mentioned in the previous phrase. He implies that prophecies contain some things that are good and some things that are not good when he encourages them to "hold fast *what is good.*" This is something that never could have been said of the words of an Old Testament prophet or of the authoritative teachings of a New Testament apostle.

d. *1 Corinthians 14:29–38.* More extensive evidence on New Testament prophecy is found in 1 Corinthians 14. When Paul says, "Let two or three prophets speak, and *let the others weigh what is said*" (1 Cor. 14:29), he suggests that they should listen carefully and sift the good from the bad, accepting some and rejecting the rest (for this is the implication of the Greek word *diakrinō,* here translated "weigh what is said"). We cannot imagine that an Old Testament prophet like Isaiah would have said, "Listen to what I say and weigh what is said—sort the good from the bad, what you accept from what you should not accept"! If prophecy had absolute divine authority, it would be sin to do this. But here Paul commands that it be done, suggesting that New Testament prophecy did not have the authority of God's very words.[6]

---

[4]The verb that Agabus used (*paradidōmi,* "to deliver, hand over") requires the sense of voluntarily, consciously, deliberately giving over or handing over something to someone else. That is the sense it has in all 119 other instances of the word in the New Testament. But that sense is not true with respect to the treatment of Paul by the Jews; they did not voluntarily hand Paul over to the Romans!

[5]It should not be objected that Acts 28:17 speaks of a fulfillment of Agabus's prophecy, because the whole narrative in Acts 28:17–19 refers to Paul's transfer out of Jerusalem to Caesarea (in Acts 23:12–35) and explains to the Jews in Rome why Paul is in Roman custody. In Acts 28:17, Paul refers to his transfer *out of (ex)* Jerusalem as a prisoner (Gk. *desmios*). (The NIV translation, "I was arrested in Jerusalem and handed over to the Romans," is an inaccurate paraphrase that completely misses the idea of being delivered *out of [ex]* Jerusalem and removes the idea that he was delivered as a prisoner, adding rather the idea that he was arrested in Jerusalem, an event that is not mentioned in the Greek text.) In the Greek text the language clearly refers to Paul's transfer *out of* the Jewish judicial system (the Jews were seeking to bring him again to be examined by the Sanhedrin in Acts 23:15, 20) *into* the Roman judicial system at Caesarea (Acts 23:23–35). Therefore, Paul correctly says in Acts 28:18 that the same Romans into whose hands he had been delivered as a prisoner (v. 17) were the ones who (*hoitines,* v. 18), "when they had examined me . . . wished to set me at liberty, because there was no reason for the death penalty in my case" (Acts 28:18).

[6]Paul's instructions are different from those in the early Christian document known as the *Didache,* which tells people, "Do not test or examine any prophet who is speaking in a spirit (or: in the Spirit)" (ch. 11). But the *Didache* says several things that are contrary to New Testament doctrine (see Wayne Grudem, *Systematic Theology* [Grand Rapids: Zondervan, 1994,], p. 67, n. 32), and we should not take it as a reliable guide to the nature of prophecy at the time of the New Testament. (For example, it says that apostles should not stay in a city more than two days [11:5]—but note that Paul stayed a year and a half in Corinth and three years in Ephesus!) The Bible is our authority, not the *Didache.*

In 1 Corinthians 14:30, Paul allows one prophet to interrupt another one: "If a revelation is made to another sitting by, let the first be silent. For you can all prophesy one by one." Again, if prophets had been speaking God's very words, equal in value to Scripture, it is hard to imagine that Paul would say they should be interrupted and not allowed to finish their message. But that is what Paul commands.

Paul indicates that no one at Corinth, a church that had much prophecy, was able to speak God's very words. He says in 1 Corinthians 14:36, "What! *Did the word of God come forth from you,* or are you the only ones it has reached?" (author's translation). Paul clearly implies that no "word of God" has come forth from all the prophets at Corinth.[7]

Then in verses 37 and 38, Paul claims authority far greater than any prophet at Corinth: "If any one thinks that he is a prophet, or spiritual, he should acknowledge that what I am writing to you is a command of the Lord. If any one does not recognize this, he is not recognized."

All these passages indicate that the common idea that prophets spoke "words of the Lord" when the apostles were not present in the early churches is simply incorrect.

5. How should we speak about the authority of prophecy today? Prophecies in the church today should be considered *merely human words, not God's words,* and not equal to God's words in authority.

Most Pentecostal and charismatic leaders would agree that contemporary prophecy is not equal to Scripture in authority. But it must be said that in actual practice much confusion results from the habit of prefacing prophecies with the common Old Testament phrase, "Thus says the Lord" (a phrase nowhere spoken in the New Testament by any prophets in New Testament churches). The use of this phrase is unfortunate because it gives the impression that the words that follow are God's very words, whereas the New Testament does not justify that position and, when pressed, most responsible charismatic spokesmen would not want to claim it for every part of their prophecies anyway. So there would be much gain and no loss if that introductory phrase were dropped.

Now it is true that Agabus uses a similar phrase ("Thus says the Holy Spirit") in Acts 21:11, but the same words (Gk. *tade legei*) are used by Christian writers just after the time of the New Testament to introduce very general paraphrases or greatly expanded interpretations of what is being reported (so Ignatius, *Epistle to the Philadelphians* 7:1–2 [about A.D. 108] and *Epistle of Barnabas* 6:8; 9:2, 5 [A.D. 70–100]). The phrase can apparently mean, "This is generally (or approximately) what the Holy Spirit is saying to us."

If someone really does think God is bringing something to mind that should be reported in the congregation, there is nothing wrong with saying, "*I think* the Lord is putting on my mind that . . ." or "*It seems to me that* the Lord is showing us . . ." or some similar expression. Of course that does not sound as "forceful" as "Thus says the Lord," but if the message is really from God, the Holy Spirit will cause it to speak with great power to the hearts of those who need to hear.

---

[7]Several recent translations of 1 Cor. 14:36 add the idea of the Word of God *first* or originally going forth from Corinth, but the Greek text clearly does not require that sense. Paul's statement is very simple and just says, "Did the word of God come forth [aorist of *exerchomai,* 'come out'] from you?" The KJV literally translates, "What? Came the word of God out from you?"

6. *A spontaneous "revelation" made prophecy different from other gifts.* If prophecy does not contain God's very words, then what is it? In what sense is it from God?

Paul indicates that God could bring something spontaneously to mind so that the person prophesying would report it in his or her own words. Paul calls this a "revelation": "If a revelation is made to another sitting by, let the first be silent. For you can all prophesy one by one, so that all may learn and all be encouraged" (1 Cor. 14:30–31). Here he uses the word *revelation* in a broader sense than the technical way theologians have used it to speak of the words of Scripture—but the New Testament elsewhere uses the terms *reveal* and *revelation* in this broader sense of communication from God that does not result in written Scripture or words equal to written Scripture in authority (see Matt. 11:27; Rom. 1:18; Eph. 1:17; Phil. 3:15).

Paul is simply referring to something that God may suddenly bring to mind, or something that God may impress on someone's consciousness in such a way that the person has a sense that it is from God. It may be that the thought brought to mind is surprisingly distinct from the person's own train of thought, or that it is accompanied by a sense of urgency or persistence, or in some other way gives the person a rather clear sense that it is from the Lord.

Figure 30.1 illustrates the idea of a revelation from God that is reported in the prophet's own (merely human) words.

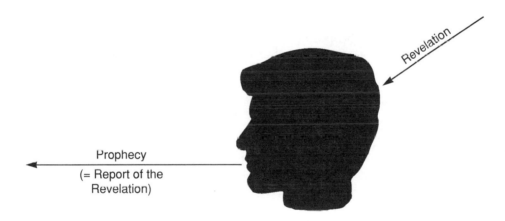

Prophecy Occurs When a Revelation from God Is Reported
in the Prophet's Own (Merely Human) Words
figure 30.1

Thus, if a stranger comes in and all prophesy, "the secrets of his heart are disclosed; and so, falling on his face, he will worship God and declare that God is really among you" (1 Cor. 14:25). I have heard a report of this happening in a clearly non-charismatic Baptist church in America. A missionary speaker paused in the middle of his message and said something like this: "I didn't plan to say this, but it seems the Lord is indicating that someone in this church has just walked out on his wife and family. If that is so, let me tell you that God wants you to return to them and learn to follow God's pattern for family life." The missionary did not know it, but in the unlit balcony sat a man who had entered the church moments before for the first time in his life. The description fit him exactly, and he made himself known, acknowledged his sin, and began to seek after God.

In this way, prophecy serves as a "sign" for believers (1 Cor. 14:22)—it is a clear demonstration that God is definitely at work in their midst, a "sign" of God's hand of blessing on the congregation. And since it will work for the conversion of unbelievers as well, Paul encourages this gift to be used when "unbelievers or outsiders enter" (1 Cor. 14:23).

Many Christians in all periods of the church have experienced or heard of similar events—for example, an unplanned but urgent request may have been given to pray for certain missionaries in Nigeria. Then much later those who prayed discovered that just at that time the missionaries had been in an auto accident or at a point of intense spiritual conflict and had needed those prayers. Paul would call the sense or intuition of those things a "revelation," and the report to the assembled church of that prompting from God would be called a "prophecy." It may have elements of the speaker's own understanding or interpretation in it and it certainly needs evaluation and testing, yet it has a valuable function in the church nonetheless.[8]

7. The difference between prophecy and teaching. While all New Testament "prophecy" was based on this kind of spontaneous prompting from the Holy Spirit (cf. Acts 11:28; 21:4, 10–11; and note the ideas of prophecy represented in Luke 7:39; 22:63–64; John 4:19; 11:51), no human speech act that is called a "teaching" or done by a "teacher," or described by the verb *teach,* is ever said to be based on a "revelation" in the New Testament. Rather, "teaching" is often simply an explanation or application of Scripture (Acts 15:35; 18:11, 24–28; Rom. 2:21; 15:4; Col. 3:16; Heb. 5:12) or a repetition and explanation of apostolic instructions (Rom. 16:17; 2 Tim. 2:2; 3:10; et al.). It is what we would call "Bible teaching" or "preaching" today.

So prophecy has less authority than "teaching," and prophecies in the church are always to be subject to the authoritative teaching of Scripture. Timothy was not told to *prophesy* Paul's instructions in the church; he was to *teach* them (1 Tim. 4:11; 6:2). The Thessalonians were not told to hold firm to the traditions that were "prophesied" to them but to the traditions that they were "taught" by Paul (2 Thess. 2:15). Contrary to some views, it was teachers, not prophets, who gave leadership and direction to the early churches.

Among the elders, therefore, were "those who labor in preaching and teaching" (1 Tim. 5:17), and an elder was to be "an apt teacher" (1 Tim. 3:2; cf. Titus 1:9)—but nothing is said about any elders whose work was prophesying, nor is it ever said that an elder has to be "an apt prophet" or that elders should be "holding firm to sound prophecies." In his leadership function, Timothy was to take heed to himself and to his "teaching" (1 Tim. 4:16), but he is never told to take heed to his prophesying. James warned that those who teach, not those who prophesy, will be judged with greater strictness (James 3:1).

The task of interpreting and applying Scripture, then, is called "teaching" in the New Testament. The distinction between this and prophecy is quite clear: If a mes-

---

[8]Some Christians today would consider reports of revelations from God to be "words of wisdom" or "words of knowledge." However, rather than these phrases, it seems that Paul's preferred term for this would be the broader category of "prophecy." Our conclusions concerning what Paul meant by "word of wisdom" and "word of knowledge" must be somewhat tentative, since the only place they are mentioned in the Bible (or any other early Christian literature) is 1 Cor. 12:8.

sage is the result of conscious reflection on the text of Scripture, containing interpretation of the text and application to life, then it is (in New Testament terms) a teaching. But if a message is the report of something God brings suddenly to mind, it is a prophecy. And even prepared teachings can be interrupted by unplanned additional material the Bible teacher suddenly feels God is bringing to his mind—in that case, it is a "teaching" with an element of prophecy mixed in.

B. Teaching

The gift of teaching in the New Testament is *the ability to explain Scripture and apply it to people's lives.* This is evident from a number of passages. In Acts 15:35, Paul and Barnabas and "many others" are in Antioch "*teaching* and preaching the word of the Lord." At Corinth, Paul stayed one and a half years "*teaching* the word of God among them" (Acts 18:11). And the readers of the epistle to the Hebrews, though they ought to have been teachers, needed rather to have someone to teach them again "the first principles of God's word" (Heb. 5:12). Paul tells the Romans that the words of the Old Testament Scriptures "were written for our instruction [or 'teaching,' Gk. *didaskalia*]" (Rom. 15:4), and writes to Timothy that "all scripture" is "profitable for teaching *[didaskalia]*" (2 Tim. 3:16).

Of course, if "teaching" in the early church was so often based on Old Testament Scripture, it is not surprising that it could also be based on something equal to Scripture in authority, namely, a received body of apostolic instructions. So Timothy was to take the teaching he had received from Paul and commit it to faithful men who would be able to "teach others also" (2 Tim. 2:2). And the Thessalonians were to "hold firm to the traditions" they were "taught" by Paul (2 Thess. 2:15). Far from being based on a spontaneous revelation that came during the worship service of the church (as prophecy was), this kind of "teaching" was the repetition and explanation of authentic apostolic teaching. To teach contrary to Paul's instructions was to teach different or heretical doctrine *(heterodidaskalō)* and to fail to give heed to "the sound words of our Lord Jesus Christ and the teaching which accords with godliness" (1 Tim. 6:3). In fact, Paul said that Timothy was to remind the Corinthians of Paul's ways "as I *teach* them everywhere in every church" (1 Cor. 4:17). Similarly, Timothy was to "command and teach" (1 Tim. 4:11) and to "teach and urge" (1 Tim. 6:2) Paul's instructions to the Ephesian church. Thus, it was not prophecy, but teaching, which in a primary sense (from the apostles) first provided the doctrinal and ethical norms by which the church was regulated. And as those who learned from the apostles also taught, their teaching guided and directed the local churches.

So teaching in terms of the New Testament epistles consisted of repeating and explaining the words of Scripture (or the equally authoritative teachings of Jesus and of the apostles) and applying them to the hearers. In the New Testament epistles, "teaching" is something very much like what is described by our phrase "Bible teaching" today.

C. Healing

1. Introduction: Sickness and health in the history of redemption. We must realize at the outset that physical sickness came as a result of the fall of Adam, and illness and disease are simply part of the outworking of the curse after the fall, and will eventually lead toward physical death. However, Christ redeemed us from that curse when he died on the cross: "Surely *he took up our infirmities* and carried our sorrows. . . . *by his wounds we are healed*" (Isa. 53:4–5 NIV). This passage refers to both physical and spiritual healing that Christ purchased for us, for Peter quotes it to refer to our salvation: "He himself *bore our sins* in his body on the tree, that we might die to sin and live to righteousness. *By his wounds you have been healed*" (1 Peter 2:24). But Matthew quotes the same passage from Isaiah with reference to the physical healings Jesus performed: "He cast out the spirits with a word, and healed all who were sick. This was to fulfil what was spoken by the prophet Isaiah, '*He took our infirmities* and bore our diseases'" (Matt. 8:16–17).

All Christians would probably agree that in the atonement Christ has purchased for us not only complete freedom from sin but also complete freedom from physical weakness and infirmity in his work of redemption (see ch. 25 on glorification). And all Christians would also probably agree that our full and complete possession of all the benefits that Christ earned for us will not come until Christ returns: it is only "at his coming" (1 Cor. 15:23) that we receive our perfect resurrection bodies. So it is with physical healing and redemption from the physical sickness that came as a result of the curse in Genesis 3. Our complete possession of redemption from physical illness will not be ours until Christ returns and we receive resurrection bodies.[9]

But the question that confronts us with respect to the gift of healing is whether God may from time to time grant us a foretaste or a down payment of the physical healing he will grant us fully in the future. The healing miracles of Jesus certainly demonstrate that at times God is willing to grant a partial foretaste of the perfect health that will be ours for eternity. And the ministry of healing seen in the lives of the apostles and among others in the early church also indicates that this was part of the ministry of the new covenant age. As such, it fits the larger pattern of blessings in the new covenant, many or all of which give partial foretastes of the blessings that will be ours when Christ returns. We "already" possess some of the blessings of the kingdom, but those blessings are "not yet" fully ours.

2. The purposes of healing. As with other spiritual gifts, healing has several purposes. Certainly it functions as a "sign" to authenticate the gospel message to show that the kingdom of God has come. Healing also brings comfort and health to those who are ill and thereby demonstrates God's attribute of mercy toward those in distress. Third, healing equips people for service as physical impediments to ministry are removed. Fourth, healing provides opportunity for God to be glorified as people see physical evidence of his goodness, love, power, wisdom, and presence.

3. What about the use of medicine? What is the relationship between prayer for healing and the use of medicine and the skill of a physician? Certainly we should use medicine if it is available, because God has also created substances in the earth that can be made into medicine with healing properties. Medicines thus should be considered part of the whole creation that God considered "very good" (Gen. 1:31). We should willingly use medicine with thankfulness to the Lord, for "The earth is the LORD's and the fulness thereof" (Ps. 24:1). In fact, when medicine is available and we refuse to use it (in cases where it would put ourselves or others in danger), then it seems that we are wrongly "forcing a test" on the Lord our God (cf. Luke 4:12): This is similar to the case of Satan tempting Jesus to jump from the temple rather than walking down the steps. Where ordinary means of getting down from the

---

[9]When people say that complete healing is "in the atonement," the statement is true in an ultimate sense, but it really does not tell us anything about when we will receive "complete healing" (or any part of it).

temple (the steps) are available, it is "forcing a test" on God to jump and thereby demand that he perform a miracle at that exact moment. To refuse to use effective medicine, insisting that God perform a miracle of healing instead of healing through the medicine, is very similar to this.

Of course, it is wrong to rely on doctors or medicine *instead of* relying on the Lord, a mistake tragically made by King Asa: "In the thirty-ninth year of his reign Asa was diseased in his feet, and his disease became severe; yet even in his disease he did not seek the LORD, but sought help from physicians. And Asa slept with his fathers, dying in the forty-first year of his reign" (2 Chron. 16:12–13). But if medicine is used in connection with prayer, then we should expect God to bless and often multiply the effectiveness of the medicine (cf. 1 Tim. 5:23). Even when Isaiah had received from the Lord a promise of healing for King Hezekiah, he told Hezekiah's servants to bring a cake of figs and apply it (as a medical remedy) to a boil that Hezekiah suffered from: "Isaiah said, 'Bring a cake of figs. And let them take and lay it on the boil, that he may recover'" (2 Kings 20:7).

However, sometimes there is no appropriate medicine available, or the medicine does not work. Certainly we must remember that God can heal where doctors and medicine cannot heal (and it may amaze us to realize how frequently doctors cannot heal, even in the most medically advanced countries). Moreover, there may be many times when an illness is not putting us or others in immediate danger, and we decide to ask God to heal our sickness without the use of medicine simply because we wish for another opportunity to exercise our faith and give him glory, and perhaps because we wish to avoid spending the time or money to use medical means, or wish to avoid the side-effects that some medicines have. In all of these cases, it is simply a matter of personal choice and would not seem to be "forcing a test" on God. (However, a decision not to use medicine in these cases should be a personal choice and not one that is forced on others.)

4. Does the New Testament show common methods used in healing? The methods used by Jesus and the disciples to bring healing varied from case to case, but most frequently they included laying on of hands. Jesus no doubt could have spoken a powerful word of command and healed everyone in the large crowd instantly, but instead, "*he laid his hands on every one of them* and healed them" (Luke 4:40). Laying on of hands seems to have been the primary means Jesus used to heal, because when people came and asked him for healing they did not simply ask for prayer but said, for example, "come and lay your hand on her, and she will live" (Matt. 9:18).

Another physical symbol of the Holy Spirit's power coming for healing was anointing with oil. Jesus' disciples "anointed with oil many that were sick and healed them" (Mark 6:13). And James tells the elders of the church to anoint the sick person with oil when they pray: "Is any among you sick? Let him call for the elders of the church, and let them pray over him, anointing him with oil in the name of the Lord; and the prayer of faith will save the sick man, and the Lord will raise him up; and if he has committed sins, he will be forgiven" (James 5:14–15).

The New Testament often emphasizes the role of faith in the healing process— sometimes the faith of the sick person (Luke 8:48; 17:19), but at other times the faith of others who bring the sick person for healing. In James 5:15 it is the elders who pray, and James says it is "the prayer of faith" that saves the sick person—this then must be the faith of the elders praying, not the faith of the one who is sick. When the four men let down a paralytic through a hole in the roof where Jesus was preaching, we read, "And when Jesus saw *their* faith . . ." (Mark 2:5). At other times Jesus mentions the faith of the Canaanite woman regarding the healing of her daughter (Matt. 15:28), or of the centurion for the healing of his servant (Matt. 8:10, 13).

5. How then should we pray for healing? How then should we pray regarding physical illness? Certainly it is right to ask God for healing, for Jesus tells us to pray, "Deliver us from evil" (Matt. 6:13), and the apostle John writes to Gaius, "I pray that all may go well with you and *that you may be in health*" (3 John 2). Moreover, Jesus frequently healed *all* who were brought to him, and he never sent people away telling them it would be good for them to remain ill for a longer time! Jesus reveals the character of God the Father to us, and his example of compassionate healing clearly displays God's will in sickness and healing. In addition to this, whenever we take any kind of medicine or seek any medical help for an illness, *by those actions we admit that we think it to be God's will that we seek to be well.* If we thought that God wanted us to continue in our illness, we would never seek medical means for healing! So when we pray it seems right that our first assumption, unless we have specific reason to think otherwise, should be that God would be pleased to heal the person we are praying for—as far as we can tell from Scripture, this is God's revealed will.[10]

How then should we pray? Certainly it is right to ask God for healing, and we should go to him with the simple request that he give physical healing in time of need. James warns us that simple unbelief can lead to prayerlessness and failure to receive answers from God: "You do not have, because you do not ask" (James 4:2). But when we pray for healing we should remember that we must pray for God to be glorified in the situation, whether he chooses to heal or not. And we also ought to pray out of the same compassion of heart that Jesus felt for those whom he healed. When we pray this way, God will sometimes—and perhaps often—grant answers to our prayers.

Someone may object at this point that, from a pastoral standpoint, much harm is done when people are encouraged to believe that a miracle of healing will occur and then nothing happens—disappointment with the church and anger at God may result. Those who pray for people to be healed today need to hear this objection and use wisdom in what they tell people who are ill.

But we also need to realize that there is more than one kind of mistake to make: (1) *Not praying for healing at all* is not a correct solution, for it involves disobedience to James 5. (2) Telling people that *God seldom heals today* and that they should expect nothing to happen is not a correct solution either, for it does not provide an atmosphere conducive to faith and is inconsistent with the pattern we see in the ministry of Jesus and the early church in the New Testament. (3) Telling people that *God always heals today* if we have enough faith is a cruel teaching not supported by Scripture (see section 6 below).

The pastorally wise solution, it seems, lies between (2) and (3) above. We can tell people that God frequently heals today (if we believe that is true), and that it is very possible that they will be healed, but that we are still living in an age when the kingdom of God is "already" here but "not yet" fully here. Therefore, Christians in this life will experience healing (and many other answers to prayer), but they will

---

[10]See discussion in ch. 5, pp. 95–98, on the secret and revealed will of God.

also experience continuing illness and eventual death. In each individual case it is God's sovereign wisdom that decides the outcome, and our role is simply to ask him and wait for him to answer (whether "yes" or "no" or "keep praying and wait").

Those with "gifts of healings" (a literal translation of the plurals in 1 Cor. 12:9, 28) will be those people who find that their prayers for healing are answered more frequently and more thoroughly than others. When that becomes evident, a church would be wise to encourage them in this ministry and give them more opportunities to pray for others who are ill. We should also realize that gifts of healing could include ministry not only in terms of physical healing, but also in terms of emotional healing. And it may at times include the ability to set people free from demonic attack, for this is also called "healing" sometimes in Scripture (see Luke 6:18; Acts 10:38). Perhaps the gifts of being able to pray effectively in different kinds of situations and for different kinds of needs are what Paul referred to when he used the plural expression "gifts of healing*s*."

6. But what if God does not heal? Nonetheless, we must realize that not all prayers for healing will be answered in this age. Sometimes God will not grant the special "faith" (James 5:15) that healing will occur, and at times God will choose not to heal because of his own sovereign purposes. In these cases we must remember that Romans 8:28 is still true: Though we experience the "sufferings of this present time," and though we "groan inwardly as we wait for . . . the redemption of our bodies" (Rom. 8:18, 23), nonetheless, "we know that in everything God works for good with those who love him, who are called according to his purpose" (Rom. 8:28). This includes working in our circumstances of suffering and illness as well. During such times we can be encouraged by the examples of Paul and others who, while often experiencing dramatic miracles, also endured circumstances of sickness and suffering (cf. 2 Cor. 4:16–18; 12:7–9; Phil. 2:25–27; 1 Tim. 5:23; 2 Tim. 4:20).

When God chooses not to heal, even though we ask him for it, then it is right that we "give thanks in all circumstances" (1 Thess. 5:18; cf. James 1:2–4) and realize that God can use sickness to draw us closer to himself and increase in us obedience to his will. So the psalmist can say, "It is good for me that I was afflicted, that I might learn your statutes" (Ps. 119:71), and "Before I was afflicted I went astray; but now I keep your word" (Ps. 119:67).

Therefore God can bring increased sanctification to us through illness and suffering—just as he can bring sanctification and growth in faith through miraculous healing. But the emphasis of the New Testament, both in Jesus' ministry and in the ministry of the disciples in Acts, seems to be one that encourages us in most cases eagerly and earnestly to seek God for healing, and then to continue to trust him to bring good out of the situation, whether he grants the physical healing or not. The point is that in everything God should receive glory and our joy and trust in him should increase.

D. Tongues and Interpretation

It should be said at the outset that the Greek word *glōssa,* translated "tongue," is used not only to mean the physical tongue in a person's mouth, but also to mean "language." In the New Testament passages where speaking in tongues is discussed, the meaning "languages" is certainly in view. It is unfortunate, therefore, that English translations have continued to use the phrase "speaking in tongues," which is an expression not otherwise used in ordinary English and which gives the impression of a strange experience, something completely foreign to ordinary human life. But if English translations were to use the expression "speaking in languages," it would not seem nearly as strange and would give the reader a sense much closer to what first-century Greek-speaking readers would have heard in the phrase when they read it in Acts or 1 Corinthians. However, because current usage of the phrase "speaking in tongues" is so widely established, we will continue to use it in this discussion.

1. Tongues in the history of redemption. The phenomenon of speaking in tongues is unique to the new covenant age. Before Adam and Eve fell into sin, there was no need to speak in other languages, because they spoke the *same language* and were *united in service of God* and in fellowship with him. After the fall, people spoke the *same language* but eventually became *united in opposition to God,* and "the wickedness of man was great in the earth" and "every imagination of the thoughts of his heart was only evil continually" (Gen. 6:5). This unified language used in rebellion against God culminated in the building of the tower of Babel at a time when "the whole earth had one language and few words" (Gen. 11:1). In order to stop this united rebellion against him, God at Babel "confused the language of all the earth" and scattered people abroad over the face of the earth (Gen. 11:9).

When God called Abraham to himself (Gen. 12:1), he promised to make of Abraham a "great nation" (Gen. 12:2), and the nation of Israel that resulted from this call had one language that God wanted them to use in service for him. Yet this language was not spoken by the rest of the nations of the world, and they remained outside the reach of God's plan of redemption. So the situation was improved somewhat, for *one language out of all the languages of the world was used in service of God,* whereas in Genesis 11 God was not praised with any language.

Now if we pass over the age of the New Testament church and look at eternity future, we see that once again unity of language will be restored, but this time everyone will once again speak *the same language in service of God,* and in praise to him (Rev. 7:9–12; cf. Zeph. 3:9; 1 Cor. 13:8; perhaps Isa. 19:18).

In the New Testament church, there is something of a foretaste of the unity of language that will exist in heaven, but it is given only at some times, and only in a partial way. At Pentecost, which was the point at which the gospel really began to go to all nations, it was appropriate that the disciples gathered in Jerusalem "*began to speak in other tongues,* as the Spirit gave them utterance" (Acts 2:4).[11] The result was that Jewish visitors to Jerusalem from various nations all heard in their own languages a proclamation of "the mighty works of God" (Acts 2:11). This was a remarkable symbol of the fact that the gospel message was about to go forth to all the nations of the world, inviting people in every place to turn to Christ and be saved.

Moreover, within the context of the worship service of the church, speaking in tongues plus interpretation gives further indication of a promise that one day the differences in languages that originated at Babel will be overcome. If this gift is operating in a church, no matter what language a word of prayer or praise is given in, once there is an interpretation, everyone can understand it. This is, of course, a two-step process that is "imperfect," as are all gifts in this age (1 Cor. 13:9), but it is still an improvement on the situation from Babel to Pentecost when there was no provision to enable people to understand a message in a language they did not know.

---

[11]This verse shows that the miracle was one of speaking, not of hearing. The disciples "began to *speak* in other tongues [or languages]."

Finally, prayer in tongues in a private setting is another form of prayer to God. Paul says, "If I pray in a tongue, *my spirit prays* but my mind is unfruitful" (1 Cor. 14:14). In the overall context of the history of redemption, this also may be seen as one more partial solution to the results of the fall, whereby we were cut off from fellowship with God. Of course, this does not mean that people's spirits can *only* have fellowship with God when they speak in tongues—for Paul affirms that he prays and sings both in tongues and in his own language (1 Cor. 14:15). However, Paul does see prayer in tongues as an additional means of fellowship directly with God in prayer and worship. Once again, this aspect of the gift of speaking in tongues was not operative, so far as we know, before the new covenant age.

2. What is speaking in tongues? We may define this gift as follows: *Speaking in tongues is prayer or praise spoken in syllables not understood by the speaker.*

a. *Words of prayer or praise spoken to God.* This definition indicates that speaking in tongues is primarily speech directed toward God (that is, prayer or praise). Therefore, it is unlike the gift of prophecy, which frequently consists of messages directed *from* God toward people in the church. Paul says, "One who speaks in a tongue speaks not to men but *to God*" (1 Cor. 14:2), and if there is no interpreter present at the church service, Paul says that someone who has a gift of speaking in tongues should "keep silence in church and speak to himself and *to God*" (1 Cor. 14:28).

What kind of speech is this that is directed toward God? Paul says, "If I *pray* in a tongue, *my spirit prays* but my mind is unfruitful" (1 Cor. 14:14; cf. vv. 14–17, where Paul categorizes speech in tongues as praying and giving thanks, and v. 28). Therefore, speaking in tongues apparently is prayer or praise directed to God, and it comes from the "spirit" of the person who is speaking. This is not inconsistent with the narrative in Acts 2, because the crowd said, "We hear them telling in our own tongues the mighty works of God" (Acts 2:11), a description that certainly could mean that the disciples were all glorifying God and proclaiming his mighty works in worship, and the crowd began to listen to this as it occurred in various languages. In fact, there is no indication that the disciples themselves were speaking to the crowd until Acts 2:14, when Peter then stands and addresses the crowd directly, presumably in Greek.

b. *Not understood by the speaker.* Paul says that "one who speaks in a tongue speaks not to men but to God; *for no one understands him,* but he utters mysteries in the Spirit" (1 Cor. 14:2). Similarly, he says that if there is speaking in tongues without interpretation, meaning will not be communicated: "I shall be a foreigner to the speaker and the speaker a foreigner to me" (1 Cor. 14:11). Moreover, the entire argument of 1 Corinthians 14:13–19 assumes that speech in tongues in the congregation, when it is not accompanied by interpretation, is not understood by those who hear.

At Pentecost speech in tongues was in known languages that were understood by those who heard: "Each one heard them speaking *in his own language*" (Acts 2:6). But once again the speech was not understood by the speakers, for what caused the amazement was that Galileans were speaking all these different languages (v. 7). It seems, therefore, that *at times* speaking in tongues may involve speech in actual human languages, sometimes even languages that are understood by some of those who hear. But at other times—and Paul assumes that this will ordinarily be the case—the speech will be in a language that "no one understands" (1 Cor. 14:2).

c. *Not ecstatic but self-controlled.* The *New English Bible* translates the phrase "speaking in tongues" as "ecstatic speech," thus giving further support to the idea that those who speak in tongues lose awareness of their surroundings or lose self-control or are forced to speak against their will. Moreover, some of the extreme elements in the Pentecostal movement have allowed frenzied and disorderly conduct at worship services, and this has, in the minds of some, perpetuated the notion that speaking in tongues is a kind of ecstatic speech.

But this is not the picture given in the New Testament. Even when the Holy Spirit came with overwhelming power at Pentecost, the disciples were able to stop speaking in tongues so that Peter could give his sermon to the assembled crowd. More explicitly, Paul says: "If any speak in a tongue, let there be only two or at most three, and each in turn; and let one interpret. But if there is no one to interpret, let each of them keep silence in church and speak to himself and to God" (1 Cor. 14:27–28). Here Paul requires that those who speak in tongues take turns, and he limits the number to three, indicating clearly that those who spoke in tongues were aware of what was going on around them and were able to control themselves so as to speak only when it was their turn and when no one else was speaking. If there was no one to interpret, they were easily able to keep silence and not speak. All of these factors indicate a high degree of self-control and give no support to the idea that Paul thought of tongues as ecstatic speech of some kind.

d. *Tongues without interpretation.* If no one known to have the gift of interpretation is present in the assembly, the passage just quoted indicates that speaking in tongues should be in private. No speech in tongues without interpretation should be given in the church service.

Paul speaks of praying in tongues and singing in tongues when he says, "I will pray with the spirit and I will pray with the mind also; I will *sing with the spirit* and I will sing with the mind also" (1 Cor. 14:15). This gives further confirmation to the definition given above in which we viewed tongues as something primarily directed toward God in prayer and praise. It also gives legitimacy to the practice of singing in tongues, whether publicly or privately. Yet the same rules apply for singing as for speaking: if there is no interpreter, it should only be done in private.

Nevertheless, however much Paul warns against using tongues without interpretation *in church,* he certainly views it positively and encourages it *in private.* He says, "He who speaks in a tongue *edifies himself,* but he who prophesies edifies the church" (1 Cor. 14:4). What is his conclusion? It is not (as some would argue) that Christians should decide not to use the gift or decide that it has no value when used privately. Rather he says, "What am I to do? I will pray with the spirit and I will pray with the mind also" (v. 15). And he says, "I thank God that I speak in tongues more than you all" (v. 18), and "Now *I want you all to speak in tongues,* but even more to prophesy" (v. 5), and "Earnestly desire to prophesy, and do not forbid speaking in tongues" (v. 39). If our previous understanding of tongues as prayer or praise to God is correct, we would certainly expect that edification would follow, even though the speaker's mind does not understand what is being said, for his or her own human spirit is communicating directly with God. Just as prayer and worship in general edify us as we engage in them, so this kind of prayer and worship edifies us too according to Paul.

e. *Tongues with interpretation: Edification for the church.* Paul says, "He who prophesies is greater than he who speaks in tongues, *unless someone interprets,* so that the church may be edified" (1 Cor. 14:5). Once a message in tongues is interpreted, all can understand. In that case, Paul says that the message in tongues is *as valuable to the church as prophecy.* We should note that *he does not say they have the same functions* (for other passages indicate that prophecy is communication from God toward human beings, while tongues is generally communication from human beings to God). But Paul clearly says they have equal value in edifying the church. We may define the gift of interpretation as *reporting to the church the general meaning of something spoken in tongues.*

f. *Not all speak in tongues.* Just as not all Christians are apostles, and not all are prophets or teachers, and not all possess gifts of healing, so not all speak with tongues. Paul clearly implies this when he asks a series of questions, all of which expect the answer "no," and includes the question "Do all speak with tongues?" (1 Cor. 12:30). The implied answer is no. Some have argued that Paul here only means that not all speak with tongues *publicly,* but that perhaps he would have admitted that all can speak in tongues privately. But this distinction seems foreign to the context and unconvincing. He does not specify that not all speak with tongues *publicly* or *in church,* but simply says that not all speak with tongues. His next question is, "Do all interpret?" (v. 30). His previous two questions were, "Do all work miracles? Do all possess gifts of healing?" (vv. 29–30). Would we wish to make the same arguments about these gifts—that not all interpret tongues *publicly,* but that all Christians are able to do it *privately?* Or that not all work miracles publicly, but that all are able to work miracles privately? Such a distinction seems unwarranted by the context in every case.

II. REVIEW QUESTIONS

1. Did prophets in the New Testament speak with the same authority as that of Scripture? Give scriptural support for your answer.

2. If prophecy is not equal to Scripture in authority, in what sense may we say that it is from God? Distinguish between a "revelation" (as defined in this chapter) and a prophecy.

3. How is the gift of teaching different from prophecy? Which is to carry greater authority in the church?

4. What is the relationship between the gift of healing in the church age and the resurrection bodies Christians will receive upon Christ's return?

5. Name at least four purposes for healing.

6. Define "speaking in tongues." To whom is speaking in tongues directed?

7. In a public church setting, what other spiritual gift is to accompany the gift of speaking in tongues? Can a person speak in tongues in private? Support your answer from Scripture.

III. QUESTIONS FOR PERSONAL APPLICATION

1. Have you ever experienced a gift of prophecy as defined in this chapter? What have you called it? Has this gift (or something like it) functioned in your church? If so, what have been the benefits—and dangers? If not, do you think this gift might be of help to your church? Why or why not?

2. Does the gift of teaching function effectively in your church? Who uses this gift in addition to the pastor or elders? Do you think your church adequately appreciates sound Bible teaching? In what areas (if any) do you think your church needs to grow in its knowledge and love of the teachings of Scripture?

3. Of the other gifts discussed in this chapter, have you ever used any of them yourself? Are there any that you think your church needs but does not have at this time? What do you think would be best for you to do in response to this need?

IV. SPECIAL TERMS

(This list applies to chapters 29 and 30.)

apostle	office
cessationist	prophecy
gifts of the Holy Spirit	speaking in tongues
healing	teaching
interpretation of tongues	

V. SCRIPTURE MEMORY PASSAGE

I Corinthians 12:7–11

To each is given the manifestation of the Spirit for the common good. To one is given through the Spirit the utterance of wisdom, and to another the utterance of knowledge according to the same Spirit, to another faith by the same Spirit, to another gifts of healing by the one Spirit, to another the working of miracles, to another prophecy, to another the ability to distinguish between spirits, to another various kinds of tongues, to another the interpretation of tongues. All these are inspired by one and the same Spirit, who apportions to each one individually as he wills.

PART VII

The Doctrine
of the Future

CHAPTER THIRTY-ONE

The Return of Christ: When and How?

+ *When and how will Christ return?*
+ *Could he come back at any hour?*

I. EXPLANATION AND SCRIPTURAL BASIS

As we begin the final unit of this book, we turn to consider events that will happen in the future. The study of future events is often called "eschatology," from the Greek word *eschatos,* which means "last." The study of eschatology, then, is the study of "the last things."

Unbelievers can make reasonable predictions about future events based on patterns of past occurrences, but in the nature of human experience it is clear that human beings of themselves cannot know the future. Therefore, unbelievers can have no certain knowledge of any future event. But Christians who believe the Bible are in a different situation. Although we cannot know everything about the future, God knows everything about the future and he has in Scripture told us about the major events yet to come in the history of the universe. About these events occurring we can have absolute confidence because God is never wrong and never lies.

Regarding our own personal future as individuals, we have already discussed the teaching of Scripture in chapter 25 (on death, the intermediate state, and glorification). The study of these future events that will happen to individuals is sometimes called "personal eschatology." But the Bible also talks about certain major events that will affect the entire universe. Specifically, it tells us about the second coming of Christ, the millennium, the final judgment, eternal punishment for unbelievers and eternal reward for believers, and life with God in the new heaven and new earth. The study of these events is sometimes called "general eschatology." In this chapter we will study the question of the return of Christ, or his "second coming." Subsequent chapters will deal with the remaining topics in a study of the last things.

There have been many debates—often heated ones—in the history of the church over questions regarding the future. In this chapter we will begin with aspects of Christ's second coming with which all evangelicals agree and then at the end move to one matter of disagreement: whether Christ could return at any time. In the following chapter, we will discuss the question of the millennium, a topic that has long been a source of disagreement among Christians.

A. There Will Be a Sudden, Personal, Visible, Bodily Return of Christ

Jesus often spoke about his return. "You also must be ready; for the Son of Man is coming at an hour you do not expect" (Matt. 24:44). He said, "*I will come again and will take you to myself, that where I am you may be also*" (John 14:3). Immediately after Jesus had ascended into heaven, two angels said to the disciples, "This Jesus, who was taken up from you into heaven, *will come* in the same way as you saw him go into heaven" (Acts 1:11). Paul taught, "*The Lord himself will descend from heaven* with a cry of command, with the archangel's call, and with the sound of the trumpet of God" (1 Thess. 4:16). The author of Hebrews wrote that Christ "*will appear a second time*, not to deal with sin but to save those who are eagerly waiting for him" (Heb. 9:28). James wrote, "the coming of the Lord is at hand" (James 5:8). Peter said, "The day of the Lord will come like a thief" (2 Peter 3:10). John wrote, "when he appears we shall be like him, for we shall see him as he is" (1 John 3:2). And the book of Revelation has frequent references to Christ's return, ending with Jesus' promise, "Surely *I am coming soon*," and John's response, "Amen. Come, Lord Jesus!" (Rev. 22:20).

This theme, then, is frequently mentioned throughout the New Testament. It is the dominant hope of the New Testament church. These verses predict a sudden return of Christ that will be dramatic and visible ("he is coming with the clouds, and every eye will see him," Rev. 1:7). The passages are far too explicit to allow the idea (once popular in liberal Protestant circles) that Christ himself will not return, but simply that the spirit of Christ, meaning an acceptance of his teaching and an imitation of his lifestyle of love, would increasingly return to the earth. It is not his teachings or his style of conduct, but "*the Lord himself*" who will descend from heaven (1 Thess. 4:16). It is Jesus himself "who was taken up from you into heaven" who "will come *in the same way* as you saw him go into heaven" (Acts 1:11). His appearing will not be a mere spiritual coming to dwell within people's hearts, but will be a *personal* and *bodily* return "in the same way as you saw him go into heaven."

B. We Should Eagerly Long for Christ's Return

John's response at the end of Revelation should characterize Christians' hearts in all ages: "Amen. Come, Lord Jesus!" (Rev. 22:20). True Christianity trains us "to live sober, upright, and godly lives in this world, *awaiting our blessed hope, the appearing of the glory of our great God and Savior Jesus Christ*" (Titus 2:12–13). Paul says, "Our commonwealth is in heaven, and from it we *await a Savior*, the Lord Jesus Christ" (Phil. 3:20). The term *Maranatha* in 1 Corinthians 16:22 (NASB) similarly means, "Our Lord, come!" (1 Cor. 16:22 RSV).

Do Christians in fact eagerly long for Christ's return? The more Christians are caught up in enjoying the good things of this life, and the more they neglect genuine Christian fellowship and their personal relationship with Christ, the less they will long for his return. On the other hand, many Christians who are experiencing suffering or persecution, or who are more elderly and infirm, and who have a vital and deep daily walk with Christ, will have a more intense longing for his return. To some extent, then, the degree to which we actually long for Christ's return is a measure of the spiritual condition of our own lives at the moment. It also gives some measure of the degree to which we see the world as it really is, as God sees it, in bondage to sin and rebellion against God, and in the power of the evil one (1 John 5:19).

But does this mean that we should not undertake long-term projects? If a scientist who is a Christian eagerly longs for Christ's return, then should he or she begin a ten-year research project? Or should a Christian begin a three-year course in a theological seminary or a Bible college? What if Christ were to return the day before graduation from that institution, before there was any chance to give a significant amount of one's time to actual ministry?

Certainly we should commit ourselves to long-term activities. It is precisely for this reason that Jesus does not allow us to know the actual time of his return (see below): He wants us to be engaged in obedience to him, no matter what our walk of life, up until the very moment of his return. To "be ready" for Christ's return (Matt. 24:44) is to be faithfully obeying him in the present, actively engaged in whatever work he has called us to. In the nature of the situation, since we do not know when he will return, on that day there will no doubt be some missionaries just departing for the mission field who will never reach their destination. There will be some men in their last year of theological education who will never use their training to pastor a church. There will be some researchers handing in their doctoral dissertations on that day, the fruit of years of research that will never be published and never have an influence on the world. But to all of those people who are Christians, Jesus will say, "Well done, good and faithful servant; you have been faithful over a little, I will set you over much; enter into the joy of your master" (Matt. 25:21).

C. We Do Not Know When Christ Will Return

Several passages indicate that we do not, and cannot, know the time when Christ will return. "The Son of man is coming *at an hour you do not expect*" (Matt. 24:44). "Watch therefore, for *you know neither the day nor the hour*" (Matt. 25:13). Moreover, Jesus said, "But of that day or that hour *no one knows*, not even the angels in heaven, nor the Son, but only the Father. Take heed, watch; for *you do not know* when the time will come" (Mark 13:32–33).

It is simply an evasion of the force of those passages to say that we cannot know the day or the hour but that we can know the month or the year. The fact remains that Jesus is coming "at an hour you do not expect" (Matt. 24:44) and "at an unexpected hour" (Luke 12:40). (In these verses the word "hour" *[hōra]* is best understood in a more general sense, to refer to the time when something will take place, not necessarily a sixty-minute period of time.)[1] The point of these passages is that Jesus is telling us that we *cannot* know when he is coming back. Since he will come at an unexpected time, we should be ready at all times for him to return.

The practical result of this is that anyone who claims to know specifically when Jesus is coming back is automatically to be considered wrong. The Jehovah's Witnesses have made many predictions of specific dates for Christ's return, and all of them have turned out to be wrong. But others in the history of the church have made such predictions as well, sometimes claiming new insight into biblical prophecies, and sometimes claiming to have received personal revelations from Jesus himself indicating the time of his return. It is unfortunate that many people have been deceived by these claims, because if people are convinced that Christ will return (for example) within a month, they will begin to withdraw from all long-term commitments. They will take their children out of school, sell their houses, quit their jobs,

---

[1]BAGD, p. 896, 3.

and give up work on any long-term projects whether in the church or elsewhere. They may initially have an increased zeal for evangelism and prayer, but the unreasonable nature of their behavior will offset any evangelistic impact they may have. Moreover, they are simply *disobeying* the teaching of Scripture that the date of Christ's return cannot be known, which means that even their prayer and fellowship with God will be hindered as well. Anyone who claims to know the date on which Christ will return—from whatever source—should be rejected as incorrect.

D. All Evangelicals Agree on the Final Results of Christ's Return

No matter what their differences on the details, all Christians who take the Bible as their final authority agree that the final and ultimate result of Christ's return will be the judgment of unbelievers and the final reward of believers, and that believers will live with Christ in new heavens and a new earth for all eternity. God the Father, Son, and Holy Spirit will reign and will be worshiped in a never-ending kingdom with no more sin, sorrow, or suffering. We will discuss these details more fully in the following chapters.

E. There Is Disagreement over the Details of Future Events

Nevertheless, Christians differ over specific details leading up to and immediately following Christ's return. Specifically, they differ over the nature of the millennium and the relationship of Christ's return to the millennium, the sequence of Christ's return and the great tribulation period that will come to the earth, and the question of the salvation of the Jewish people (and the relationship between Jews who are saved and the church).

Before we examine some of those questions in more detail, it is important to affirm the genuine evangelical standing of those who have differing positions on these questions. Evangelicals who hold to these various positions all agree that Scripture is inerrant, and they have a commitment to believe *whatever* is taught by Scripture. Their differences concern the interpretation of various passages relating to these events, but their differences on these matters should be seen as matters of secondary importance, not differences over primary doctrinal matters.

Nevertheless, it is worth our time to study these questions in more detail, both because we may gain further insight into the nature of the events that God has planned and promised for us, and because there is still hope that greater unity will come about in the church when we agree to examine these issues again in more detail and to engage in discussion about them.

F. Could Christ Come Back at Any Time?

One of the significant areas of disagreement is over the question of whether Christ could return at any time. On the one hand, many passages encourage us to be ready because Christ will return at an hour we do not expect. On the other hand, several passages speak of certain events that will happen before Christ returns. There have been different ways of resolving the apparent tension between these two sets of passages, with some Christians concluding that Christ could still return at any time, and others concluding that he could not return for at least a generation, since it would take that long to fulfill some of the predicted events that must occur before his return.

1. Verses predicting a sudden and unexpected coming of Christ. A number of verses in the Bible predict that Christ could come very soon. For example, Jesus told his disciples: "*Watch therefore,* for you do not know on what day your Lord is coming. But know this, that if the householder had known in what part of the night the thief was coming, he would have watched and would not have let his house be broken into. Therefore *you also must be ready;* for the Son of man is coming *at an hour you do not expect*" (Matt. 24:42–44; cf. vv. 36–39; 25:13; Mark 13:32–33; Luke 12:40; 1 Cor. 16:22; 1 Thess. 5:2; et al.).

What shall we say to the many passages such as this one? If there were no passages in the New Testament about signs that would precede Christ's return, we would probably conclude from the passage just quoted that Jesus could come at any moment. In this sense, we can say that Christ's return is *imminent.*[2] It would seem to blunt the force of the commands to *be ready* and to *watch* if there was a reason to think that Christ would not come soon.

Before we look at passages on signs that precede Christ's coming, another problem must be considered at this point. Were Jesus and the New Testament authors wrong in their expectation that he would return soon? Did they not *think* and even *teach* that the second coming of Christ would be in just a few years? In fact, a very prominent view among liberal New Testament scholars has been that Jesus mistakenly taught that he would return soon.

But none of the texts just cited require this interpretation. The texts that say to be ready do not say how long we will have to wait, nor do the texts that say that Jesus is coming at a time we do not expect. As for the texts that say Jesus is coming "soon," we must realize that biblical prophets often speak in terms of "prophetic foreshortening," which sees future events but does not see the intervening time before those events occur.

2. Signs that precede Christ's return. The other set of texts to be considered tells of several signs that Scripture says will precede the time of Christ's return. Here it will be helpful to list a few of those passages that most directly refer to signs that must occur before Christ's return.

a. *The preaching of the gospel to all nations.* "*The gospel must first be preached to all nations*" (Mark 13:10; cf. Matt. 24:14).

b. *The great tribulation.* "In those days *there will be such tribulation as has not been from the beginning of the creation which God created until now, and never will be. And if the Lord had not shortened the days, no human being would be saved;* but for the sake of the elect, whom he chose, he shortened the days" (Mark 13:19–20).

c. *False prophets working signs and wonders.* "*False Christs and false prophets will arise and show signs and wonders, to lead astray, if possible, the elect*" (Mark 13:22; cf. Matt. 24:23–24).

d. *Signs in the heavens.* "In those days, *after that tribulation, the sun will be darkened, and the moon will not give its light, and the stars will be falling from heaven, and the powers in the heavens will be shaken.* And then they will see the Son of man coming in clouds with great power and glory" (Mark 13:24–26; cf. Matt. 24:29–30; Luke 21:25–27).

---

[2]In this chapter, I am not using the term *imminent* to mean that Christ *certainly will* come soon (for then the verses teaching imminence would have been untrue when they were written). Rather, I am using the word *imminent* to mean that Christ *could* come and *might* come at any time, and that we are to be prepared for him to come at any day.

e. *The coming of the man of sin and the rebellion.* Paul writes to the Thessalonians that Christ will not come unless the man of sin is first revealed, and then the Lord Jesus will destroy him at his coming. This "man of sin" is sometimes identified with the beast in Revelation 13, and is sometimes called the antichrist, the final and worst of the series of "antichrists" mentioned in 1 John 2:18. Paul writes:

> Now concerning the coming of our Lord Jesus Christ . . . *that day will not come, unless the rebellion comes first, and the man of lawlessness is revealed,* the son of perdition, who opposes and exalts himself against every so-called god or object of worship, *so that he takes his seat in the temple of God, proclaiming himself to be God.* . . . And you know what is restraining him now so that he may be revealed in his time. For the mystery of lawlessness is already at work; only he who now restrains it will do so until he is out of the way. *And then the lawless one will be revealed, and the Lord Jesus will slay him with the breath of his mouth and destroy him by his appearing and his coming.* The coming of the lawless one by the activity of Satan will be with *all power and with pretended signs and wonders, and with all wicked deception for those who are to perish,* because they refused to love the truth and so be saved. (2 Thess. 2:1–10)

f. *The salvation of Israel.* Paul talks about the fact that many Jews have not trusted in Christ, but he says that sometime in the future a large number would be saved: "I do not want you, brethren, to be uninformed of this mystery, lest you be wise in your own estimation, that a partial hardening has happened to Israel until the fulness of the Gentiles has come in; *and thus all Israel will be saved*" (Rom. 11:25–26; cf. v. 12).

g. *Conclusions from these signs that precede Christ's return.* The impact of these passages seems so clear that, as was mentioned above, many Christians have felt that Christ simply cannot return at any moment. As we look over the list of signs given above, it would not seem to take much argument to demonstrate that most of these events, or perhaps all of them, have not yet occurred. Or at least that is what appears to be the case on a first reading of these passages.

3. Possible solutions. How can we reconcile the passages that seem to warn us to be ready because Christ could suddenly return with passages that indicate that several important and visible events must take place before Christ can return? Several solutions have been proposed.

One solution is to say that *Christ could not come at any time.* Just how long it would be before Christ would return depends on each person's estimate of how long it will take some of the signs to be fulfilled, such as the preaching of the gospel to all nations, the coming of the great tribulation, and the ingathering of the full number of the Jews who will be saved.

The difficulty with this view is twofold. First, it really seems to nullify the force of the warnings of Jesus that we should watch, be ready, and that he is returning at an hour we do not expect. What force is there in a warning to be ready for Christ to come at an unexpected time when we know that this coming cannot occur for many years? The sense of urgent expectancy of Christ's return is greatly diminished or denied altogether in this position, and that result seems quite contrary to Jesus' intention in giving these warnings.

Second, this position seems to use these signs in a way quite opposite from the way Jesus intended them to be used. The signs are given so that, when we see them, they will *intensify our expectation* of Christ's return. Jesus said, "Now *when these things begin to take place, look up and raise your heads, because your redemption is drawing near*" (Luke 21:28). And the warnings are also given to keep believers from going astray and following false messiahs: "Take heed that no one leads you astray. Many will come in my name, saying, 'I am he!' and they will lead many astray. . . . And then if any one says to you, 'Look, here is the Christ!' or 'Look, there he is!' do not believe it" (Mark 13:5–6, 21). So the signs are given to keep Christians from being surprised by these remarkable events, to assure them that God knows them all in advance, and to keep them from following after alleged messiahs who do not come in the dramatic, visible, world-conquering way in which Jesus himself will come. *But the signs are never given to make us think, "Jesus couldn't come for a few years."* There is no indication that Jesus gave these signs to provide Christians with a reason *not to be ready* for his return or to encourage them *not to expect* that he could come at any time!

The other major solution to this problem is to say that *Christ indeed could come at any time,* and to reconcile the two sets of passages in various ways. (1) One way to reconcile them is to say that *the New Testament talks about two distinct returns of Christ,* or two second comings of Christ, that is, a *secret* coming at which Christ takes Christians out of the world (a coming "for his saints"), and then, after seven years of tribulation have occurred on the earth, a visible, *public,* triumphant coming (a coming "with his saints") in which Christ comes to reign over the earth. During the seven-year interval, all the signs that have not yet been fulfilled (the great tribulation, the false prophets with signs and wonders, the antichrist, the salvation of Israel, and the signs in the heavens) will be fulfilled, so that there is no tension at all between waiting for a coming that could occur "at any moment" and realizing that a later coming will be preceded by many signs.[3]

The problem with this solution is that it is hard to derive two separate comings of Christ from the passages that predict his return. However, we will not discuss this matter here but will analyze it in the next chapter when considering the pretribulational premillennial view of Christ's return.[4] It should also be noted that this solution is historically quite recent, for it was unknown in the history of the church before it was proposed in the last century by John Nelson Darby (1800–1882). This should alert us to the fact that this solution is not the only possible one to the tension presented by the passages quoted above.

(2) Another solution is to say that *all the signs have been fulfilled, and therefore Christ in fact could return at any moment.* On this view, one could look for possible fulfillments of these signs in the events of the early church, even in the first century. In some sense, it might be said, the gospel was indeed preached to all nations, false prophets arose and opposed the gospel, there was great tribulation in the persecution the church suffered at the hands of some of the Roman emperors, the man of lawlessness was in fact the emperor Nero, and the full number of the Jewish people who are to be saved has gradually come about through the history of the church, since Paul even gives himself as one example of the beginning of this ingathering of the Jewish people (Rom. 11:1). We will discuss in more detail in the following section the view that the signs preceding Christ's return might have already been fulfilled, but here we can simply note that many people have not found convincing any

---

[3]This is the pretribulational view, often referred to as the pretribulational rapture view, which is discussed in ch. 32, pp. 445–46.

[4]See ch. 32, pp. 445–46, for an analysis of the pretribulational premillennial view of Christ's return.

view saying that they have happened, because these signs seem to them to point to much larger events than those that occurred in the first century.

(3) There is another possible way of resolving these two sets of passages. It is to say that it is *unlikely but possible that the signs have already been fulfilled,* and therefore we simply cannot know with certainty at any point in history whether all the signs have been fulfilled or not. This position is an attractive one because it takes seriously the primary purpose for the signs, the primary purpose for the warnings, and the fact that we are not to know when Christ will return. With regard to the signs, their primary purpose is to intensify our expectation of Christ's return. Therefore, whenever we see indications of things that resemble these signs, our expectation of Christ's return will be aroused and intensified. With regard to the warnings to be ready, advocates of this position would say that Christ *could* return at any time (since we cannot be certain that the signs have not been fulfilled), and so we must be ready, even though it is *unlikely* that Christ will return at once (because it seems that there are several signs yet to be fulfilled). Finally, this position agrees that we cannot know when Christ will return and that he is coming at an hour we do not expect.

But is it possible that these signs have been fulfilled? In each case, our conclusion that it is *unlikely, but possible, that the sign has been fulfilled already* seems very reasonable.

a. *The preaching of the gospel to all nations.* While it is unlikely that this sign has been fulfilled, Paul does speak in Colossians about the worldwide spread of the gospel. He speaks of "the gospel which has come to you, as indeed *in the whole world* it is bearing fruit and growing" (Col. 1:5–6). He also speaks of "the gospel which you heard, *which has been preached to every creature under heaven,* and of which I, Paul, became a minister" (Col. 1:23). In these verses, he certainly does not mean that every creature alive has heard the proclamation of the gospel, but that the proclamation has gone forth to the whole world and that, in a representative sense at least, the gospel has been preached to the whole world or to all nations. Therefore, it is unlikely but possible that this sign was initially fulfilled in the first century and has been fulfilled in a greater sense many times since then.

b. *Great tribulation.* Once again, it seems likely that the language of Scripture indicates a period of suffering coming to the earth that is far greater than anything that has yet been experienced. But it must be realized that many people have understood Jesus' warnings about great tribulation to refer to the Roman siege of Jerusalem in the Jewish War of A.D. 66–70. The suffering during that war was indeed terrible and could be what was described by Jesus in predicting this tribulation. In fact, since the first century, there have been many periods of violent and intense persecution of Christians that continue into our own century. Therefore, it seems appropriate to conclude that it is unlikely but possible that the prediction of a great tribulation has already been fulfilled.

c. *False christs and false prophets.* While demonic miracles and false signs have been done for centuries, it seems likely that Jesus' words predict a far greater manifestation of this kind of activity in the time just prior to his return. Again we must say, however, that it is difficult to be certain that this will be so. It is best to conclude that it is unlikely but still possible that this sign has been fulfilled already.

d. *Powerful signs in the heavens.* The occurrence of powerful signs in the heavens is the one sign that almost certainly has not yet occurred. Of course, there have been eclipses of the sun and moon, and comets have appeared, since the world began. But Jesus speaks of something far greater: *"The sun will be darkened, and the moon will not give its light, and the stars will fall from heaven, and the powers of the heavens will be shaken"* (Matt. 24:29). Although some attempt to explain this as symbolic language that refers to the destruction of Jerusalem and God's judgment on it,[5] it seems more likely that this verse, along with Isaiah 13:10 (from which Jesus' words in Matt. 24:29 seem to be drawn), speaks of a yet future literal falling of the stars and blackening of the sun and moon, something that would be a suitable prelude to the shaking of the earth and heaven and cosmic destruction that will come after the return of Christ (see Heb. 1:10–12; 12:27; 2 Peter 3:10–11). Nonetheless, they could occur very quickly—within the space of a few minutes or at most an hour or two—to be followed immediately by Christ's return. These particular signs are not the type that would lead us to deny that Christ could return at any time.

e. *The appearance of the man of lawlessness.* Many attempts have been made throughout history to identify the man of lawlessness (the "antichrist") with historical figures who had great authority and brought havoc and devastation among people on the earth. While such evil people might well be considered "antichrists" in the sense that they are precursors of the final antichrist (cf. 1 John 2:18), all past identifications of the antichrist have proved false, and it is likely that a yet worse "man of lawlessness" will arise on the world scene and bring unparalleled suffering and persecution, only to be destroyed by Jesus when he comes again. But the evil perpetrated by many of these other rulers has been so great that, at least while they were in power, it would have been difficult to be certain that the "man of lawlessness" mentioned in 2 Thessalonians 2 has not yet appeared. Once again, it is unlikely but possible that this sign has been fulfilled.

f. *The salvation of Israel.* With regard to the salvation of the fullness of Israel, again it must be said that Romans 9–11 seems to indicate that there will be a yet future massive ingathering of the Jewish people as they turn to accept Jesus as their Messiah. But it is not certain that Romans 9–11 predicts this, and many have argued that no further ingathering of the Jewish people will occur beyond the kind that we have already seen through the history of the church, since Paul gives himself as a primary example of this ingathering (Rom. 11:1–2). Once again, it is unlikely but possible that this sign has already been fulfilled.

g. *Conclusion.* Except for the spectacular signs in the heavens, it is unlikely but possible that these signs have already been fulfilled. Moreover, the only sign that seems certainly not to have occurred, the darkening of the sun and moon and the falling of the stars, could occur within the space of a few minutes, and therefore it seems appropriate to say that Christ could now return at any hour of the day or night. It is therefore unlikely but certainly possible that Christ could return at any time.

But does this position do justice to the warnings that we should be ready and that Christ is coming at a time we do not expect? Is it possible to *be ready* for something that we think *unlikely* to happen in the near future? Certainly it is. Everyone

---

[5]R. T. France, *The Gospel According to Matthew*, TNTC (Leicester: Inter-Varsity Press, and Grand Rapids: Eerdmans, 1985), pp. 343–44.

who wears a seatbelt when driving, or purchases auto insurance, gets ready for an event he or she thinks to be unlikely. In a similar way, it seems possible to take seriously the warnings that Jesus could come when we are not expecting him, and nonetheless to say that the signs preceding his coming will probably yet occur in the future.

This position has positive spiritual benefits as we seek to live the Christian life in the midst of a rapidly changing world. In the ebb and flow of world history, we see from time to time events that *could be* the final fulfillment of some of these signs. They happen, and then they fade away. With each successive wave of events, we do not know which one will be the last. And this is good, because God does not intend us to know. He simply wants us to continue to long for Christ's return and to expect that it could occur at any time. It is spiritually unhealthy for us to say that we know that these signs have not occurred, and it seems to stretch the bounds of credible interpretation to say that we know that these signs have occurred. But it seems to fit exactly in the middle of the New Testament approach toward Christ's return to say that we do not know with certainty if these events have occurred. Responsible exegesis, an expectation of Christ's sudden return, and a measure of humility in our understanding are all three preserved in this position.

Then if Christ does return suddenly, we will not be tempted to object, saying that one or another sign has not yet occurred. We will simply be ready to welcome him when he appears. And if there is great suffering yet to come, and if we begin to see intense opposition to the gospel, a large revival among the Jewish people, remarkable progress in the preaching of the gospel through the world, and even spectacular signs in the heavens, then we will not be dismayed or lose heart, because we will remember Jesus' words, "When these things begin to take place, look up and raise your heads, because your redemption is drawing near" (Luke 21:28).

II. REVIEW QUESTIONS

1. List Bible verses that support each of the following characteristics of the return of Christ:

   • Sudden

   • Personal

   • Visible

   • Bodily

2. What should be the Christian's attitude toward the return of Christ? How should the expectation of Christ's return affect the plans we make in life?

3. What should we think about predictions that are made about the timing of Christ's return? Support your answer from Scripture.

4. List five of the signs that according to Scripture will precede Christ's return. Which of these do you think have already occurred?

5. How does the author reconcile the Scriptures that teach that Christ could come at any time with those that refer to signs that will precede Christ's return?

III. QUESTIONS FOR PERSONAL APPLICATION

1. Before reading this chapter, did you think that Christ could return at any hour? How did that affect your Christian life? If your viewpoint has changed, what effect do you think it will have on your own life?

2. Why do you think Jesus decided to leave the world for a time and then return, rather than staying on earth after his resurrection and preaching the gospel throughout the world himself?

3. Do you now eagerly long for Christ's return? Have you had a greater longing for it in the past? If you do not have a very strong yearning for Christ's return, what factors in your life do you think contribute to that lack of longing?

4. Have you ever decided not to undertake a long-term project because you thought Christ's return was near? If so, do you think that hesitancy has any negative consequences on your life?

5. Are you ready for Christ to return today? If you knew he were going to return within twenty-four hours, what situations or relationships would you want to straighten out before he returned? Do you think that the command to "be ready" means that you should attempt to straighten out those things now, even if you think it unlikely that he would return today?

IV. SPECIAL TERMS

eschatology

general eschatology

imminent

Maranatha

personal eschatology

second coming of Christ

V. SCRIPTURE MEMORY PASSAGE

I THESSALONIANS 4:15–18

For this we declare to you by the word of the Lord, that we who are alive, who are left until the coming of the Lord, shall not precede those who have fallen asleep. For the Lord himself will descend from heaven with a cry of command, with the archangel's call, and with the sound of the trumpet of God. And the dead in Christ will rise first; then we who are alive, who are left, shall be caught up together with them in the clouds to meet the Lord in the air; and so we shall always be with the Lord. Therefore comfort one another with these words.

CHAPTER THIRTY-TWO

The Millennium

+ *What is the millennium?*
+ *When does it occur?*
+ *Will Christians go through the great tribulation?*

I. EXPLANATION AND SCRIPTURAL BASIS

The word *millennium* means "one thousand years" (from Lat. *millennium,* "thousand years"). The term comes from Revelation 20:4–5, where it says that certain people "came to life, and reigned with Christ *a thousand years.* The rest of the dead did not come to life until *the thousand years* were ended." Just prior to this statement, we read that an angel came down from heaven and seized the devil "and bound him for *a thousand years,* and threw him into the pit, and shut it and sealed it over him, that he should deceive the nations no more, till *the thousand years* were ended" (Rev. 20:2–3).

Throughout the history of the church there have been three major views on the time and nature of this "millennium."

A. Amillennialism

The first view to be explained here, amillennialism, is really the simplest. It can be pictured as in figure 32.1:

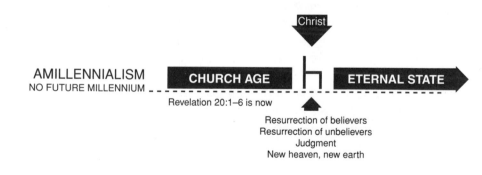

AMILLENNIALISM
NO FUTURE MILLENNIUM

Christ

CHURCH AGE ETERNAL STATE

Revelation 20:1–6 is now

Resurrection of believers
Resurrection of unbelievers
Judgment
New heaven, new earth

Amillennialism

figure 32.1

According to this position, Revelation 20:1–10 describes the present church age. This is an age in which Satan's influence over the nations has been greatly reduced so that the gospel can be preached to the whole world. Those who are said to be reigning with Christ for the thousand years are Christians who have died and are already reigning with Christ in heaven. Christ's reign in the millennium, according to this view, is not a bodily reign here on earth, but rather the heavenly reign he spoke of when he said, "All authority in heaven and on earth has been given to me" (Matt. 28:18).

This view is called "amillennial" because it maintains that there is no future millennium yet to come. Since amillennialists believe that Revelation 20 is now being fulfilled in the church age, they hold that the "millennium" described there is currently happening. The exact duration of the church age cannot be known, and the expression "thousand years" is simply a figure of speech for a long period of time in which God's perfect purposes will be accomplished.

From an amillennial viewpoint, the present church age will continue until the time of Christ's return (see figure 32.1). When Christ returns, there will be a resurrection of both believers and unbelievers. The bodies of believers will rise to be reunited with their spirits and enter into full enjoyment of heaven forever. Unbelievers will be raised to face the final judgment and eternal condemnation. Believers will also stand before the judgment seat of Christ (2 Cor. 5:10), but this judgment will only determine degrees of reward in heaven, for only unbelievers will be condemned eternally. At this time also, the new heavens and new earth will begin. Immediately after the final judgment, the eternal state will commence and continue forever.

This scheme is quite simple because all of the end-time events happen at once, immediately after Christ's return. Some amillennialists say that Christ could return at any time, while others (such as Berkhof) argue that certain signs have yet to be fulfilled.

In favor of the amillennial view, the following arguments are advanced:

1. When we look through the whole of the Bible, *only one passage* (Rev. 20:1–6) appears to teach a future earthly millennial rule of Christ, and that passage is itself obscure. It is unwise to base such a major doctrine on one passage of uncertain and widely disputed interpretation.

But how do amillennialists understand Revelation 20:1–6? The amillennial interpretation sees this passage as *referring to the present church age*. The passage reads as follows:

> Then I saw an angel coming down from heaven, holding in his hand the key of the bottomless pit and a great chain. And he seized the dragon, that ancient serpent, who is the Devil and Satan, and *bound him for a thousand years,* and threw him into the pit, and shut it and sealed it over him, that he should deceive the nations no more, till the thousand years were ended. After that he must be loosed for a little while.

> Then I saw thrones, and seated on them were those to whom judgment was committed. Also I saw the souls of those who had been beheaded for their testimony to Jesus and for the word of God, and who had not worshiped the beast or its image and had not received its mark on their foreheads or their hands. *They came to life, and reigned with Christ a thousand years.* The rest of the dead did not come to life until the thousand years were ended. This is the first resurrection. Blessed and holy is he who shares in the first resurrection! Over such the second death has no power, but they shall be priests of God and of Christ, and *they shall reign with him a thousand years.*

According to the amillennial interpretation,[1] the binding of Satan in verses 1–2 is the binding that occurred during Jesus' earthly ministry. He spoke of binding the strong man in order that he may plunder his house (Matt. 12:29) and said that the Spirit of God was at that time present in power to triumph over demonic forces: "If it is by the Spirit of God that I cast out demons, then the kingdom of God has come upon you" (Matt. 12:28). Similarly, with respect to the breaking of Satan's power, Jesus said during his ministry, "I saw Satan fall like lightning from heaven" (Luke 10:18).

The amillennialist argues that this binding of Satan in Revelation 20:1–3 is for a specific purpose: *"that he should deceive the nations no more"* (v. 3). This, then, is what happened when Jesus came and the gospel began to be proclaimed not simply to Jews but, after Pentecost, to all the nations of the world. In fact, the worldwide missionary activity of the church, and the presence of the church in most or all of the nations of the world, shows that the power that Satan had in the Old Testament, to "deceive the nations" and keep them in darkness, has been broken.

On the amillennial view, since John sees "souls" and not physical bodies in verse 4, it is argued that this scene must be occurring in heaven. When the text says that "they came to life," it does not mean that they received a bodily resurrection. It possibly means simply that "they lived," since the aorist verb *ezēsan* can readily be interpreted to be a statement of an event that occurred over a long period of time. On the other hand, some amillennial interpreters will take the verb *ezēsan* to mean "they came to life" in the sense of coming into heavenly existence in the presence of Christ and beginning to reign with him from heaven.

According to this view, the phrase "first resurrection" (v. 5) refers to going to heaven to be with the Lord. This is not a bodily resurrection but a coming into the presence of God in heaven. In a similar way, when verse 5 says, "The rest of the dead did not *come to life* until the thousand years were ended," this is understood to mean they did not come into God's presence for judgment until the end of the thousand years. So in both verses 4 and 5, the phrase "come to life" means "come into the presence of God." (Another amillennial view of "first resurrection" is that it refers to the resurrection of Christ, and to believers' participation in Christ's resurrection through union with Christ.)

2. A second argument often proposed in favor of amillennialism is the fact that Scripture teaches only *one resurrection,* when both believers and unbelievers will be raised, not two resurrections (a resurrection of believers before the millennium begins, and a resurrection of unbelievers to judgment after the end of the millennium). This is an important argument, because the premillennial view requires two separate resurrections separated by a thousand years.

Evidence in favor of only one resurrection is found in verses such as John 5:28–29, in which Jesus says, *"The hour is coming when all who are in the tombs will hear his voice and come forth,* those who have done good, to the resurrection of life, and those who have done evil, to the resurrection of judgment." Here Jesus speaks of a single "hour" when both believing and unbelieving dead will come forth from the tombs (cf. also Dan. 12:2; Acts 24:15).

3. The idea of glorified believers and sinners living on earth together is too difficult to accept. Berkhof says, "It is impossible to understand how a part of the old earth and of sinful humanity can exist alongside a part of the new earth and of a

---

[1]Here I am largely following the excellent discussion of Anthony A. Hoekema, "Amillennialism," in *The Meaning of the Millennium: Four Views,* ed. Robert G. Clouse (Downers Grove, Ill.: InterVarsity Press, 1977), pp. 155–87.

humanity that is glorified. How can perfect saints in glorified bodies have communion with sinners in the flesh? How can glorified sinners live in this sin-laden atmosphere and amid scenes of death and decay?"[2]

4. If Christ comes in glory to reign on the earth, then how could people still persist in sin? Once Jesus is actually present in his resurrection body and reigning as King over the earth, does it not seem highly unlikely that people would still reject him and that evil and rebellion would grow on the earth until eventually Satan could gather the nations for battle against Christ?

5. In conclusion, amillennialists say that Scripture seems to indicate that *all the major events yet to come* before the eternal state will occur at once. Christ will return, there will be one resurrection of believers and unbelievers, the final judgment will take place, and a new heaven and new earth will be established. Then we will enter immediately into the eternal state, with no future millennium.

B. Postmillennialism

The prefix *post-* means "after." According to this view, Christ will return *after* the millennium. The postmillennial view may be represented as in figure 32.2.

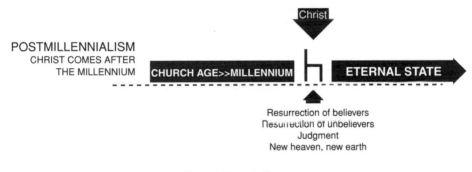

Postmillennialism

figure 32.2

According to this view, the progress of the gospel and the growth of the church will gradually increase so that a larger and larger proportion of the world's population will be Christians. As a result, there will be significant Christian influences on society, society will more and more function according to God's standards, and gradually a "millennial age" of peace and righteousness will occur on the earth. This "millennium" will last for a long period of time (not necessarily a literal one thousand years), and finally, *at the end of this period, Christ will return to earth,* believers and unbelievers will be raised, the final judgment will occur, and there will be a new heaven and new earth. We will then enter into the eternal state.

The primary characteristic of postmillennialism is that it is very optimistic about the power of the gospel to change lives and bring about much good in the world. Belief in postmillennialism tends to increase in times when the church is experiencing great revival, when there is an absence of war and international conflict, and when it appears that great progress is being made in overcoming the evil and suffering in

---

[2]Louis Berkhof, *Introduction to Systematic Theology* (Grand Rapids: Eerdmans, 1932; reprint, Grand Rapids: Baker, 1979), p. 715.

the world. But postmillennialism in its most responsible form is not based simply on the observation of events in the world around us, but on arguments from various Scripture passages.

The arguments in favor of postmillennialism are as follows:

1. The Great Commission leads us to expect that the gospel will go forth in power and eventually result in a largely Christian world. Jesus explicitly said, "*All authority in heaven and on earth* has been given to me. Go therefore and make disciples of all nations, baptizing them in the name of the Father and of the Son and of the Holy Spirit, teaching them to observe all that I have commanded you; and lo, I am with you always, to the close of the age" (Matt. 28:18–20). Since Christ has all authority in heaven and on earth, and since he promises to be with us in the fulfillment of this commission, we would expect that it would transpire without hindrance and eventually triumph in the whole world.

2. Parables of the gradual growth of the kingdom indicate that it eventually will fill the earth with its influence. Here postmillennialists point to the following: "Another parable he put before them, saying, 'The kingdom of heaven is like a grain of mustard seed which a man took and sowed in his field; it is the smallest of all seeds, but when it has grown it is the greatest of shrubs and becomes a tree, so that the birds of the air come and make nests in its branches'" (Matt. 13:31–32). According to postmillennialists, parables such as this one indicate that the kingdom will grow in influence until it permeates and in some measure transforms the entire world.

3. Postmillennialists will also argue that the world is becoming more Christian. The church is growing and spreading throughout the world, and even when it is persecuted and oppressed it grows remarkably by the power of God.

At this point, we must make a very significant distinction, however. The "millennium" which postmillennialists hold to is *very different* from the "millennium" which premillennialists talk about. In a sense, they are not even discussing the same topic. While *pre*millennialists talk about a renewed earth with Jesus Christ physically present and reigning as King, together with glorified believers in resurrection bodies, *post*millennialists are simply talking about an earth with many, many Christians influencing society. They do not envisage a millennium consisting of a renewed earth or glorified saints or Christ present in bodily form to reign (for they think that these things will only occur after Christ returns to inaugurate the eternal state). Therefore, the entire discussion of the millennium is more than simply a discussion of the sequence of events surrounding it. It also involves a significant difference over the nature of this period of time itself.

C. Premillennialism

1. Classic or historic premillennialism. The prefix *pre-* means "before," and the "premillennial" position says that Christ will come back *before* the millennium. This viewpoint has a long history from the earliest centuries onward. It may be represented as in figure 32.3

According to this viewpoint, the present church age will continue until, as it nears the end, a time of great tribulation and suffering comes on the earth (T in the figure above stands for tribulation).[3] After that time of tribulation *at the end of the church age, Christ will return to earth to establish a millennial kingdom.* When he

---

[3]An alternative type of premillennialism holds that Christ will come back *before* the period of great tribulation begins on earth. We shall examine that alternative form of premillennialism below.

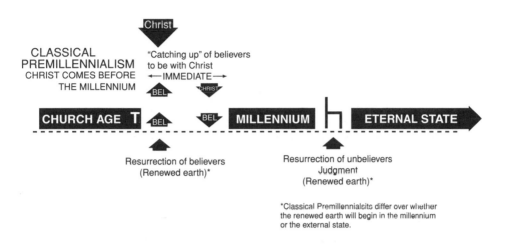

Classic or Historic Premillennialism

figure 32.3

comes back, believers who have died will be raised from the dead, their bodies will be reunited with their spirits, and *these believers will reign with Christ on earth for one thousand years.* (Some premillennialists take this to be a literal one thousand years, and others understand it to be a symbolic expression for a long period of time.) During this time, Christ will be physically present on the earth in his resurrected body and will reign as King over the entire earth. The believers who have been raised from the dead and those who were on earth when Christ returns will receive glorified resurrection bodies that will never die, and in these resurrection bodies they will live on the earth and reign with Christ. Of the unbelievers who remain on earth, many (but not all) will turn to Christ and be saved. Jesus will reign in perfect righteousness and there will be peace throughout the earth. During this time Satan will be bound and cast into the bottomless pit so that he will have no influence on the earth during the millennium (Rev. 20:1–3).

According to the premillennial viewpoint, at the end of the thousand years, Satan will be loosed from the bottomless pit and will join forces with many unbelievers who have submitted outwardly to Christ's reign but have inwardly been seething in rebellion against him. Satan will gather these rebellious people for battle against Christ, but they will be decisively defeated. Christ will then raise from the dead all the unbelievers who have died throughout history, and they will stand before him for final judgment. After the final judgment has occurred, believers will enter into the eternal state.

It seems that premillennialism has tended to increase in popularity as the church has experienced persecution and as suffering and evil have increased in the earth. But, as in the case of postmillennialism, the arguments for the premillennial position are not based on an observation of current events, but on specific passages of Scripture, especially (but not exclusively) Revelation 20:1–10.

The primary arguments for the premillennial position are listed below:

1. Several Old Testament passages seem to fit neither in the present age nor in the eternal state. These passages indicate some future stage in the history of redemption

that is far greater than the present church age but that still does not see the removal of all sin and rebellion and death from the earth.

Speaking of Jerusalem at some time in the future, Isaiah says:

> No more shall there be in it
> an infant that lives but a few days,
> or an old man who does not fill out his days,
> for the child shall die a hundred years old,
> and the sinner a hundred years old shall be accursed. (Isa. 65:20)

Here we read that there will be no more infants who die in infancy and no more old men who die prematurely, something far different from this present age. But death and sin will still be present, for the child who is a hundred years old shall die, and the sinner who is a hundred years old "shall be accursed." The larger context of this passage *may* mingle elements of the millennium and the eternal state (cf. vv. 17, 25), but it is in the nature of Old Testament prophecy not to distinguish among events in the future, just as these prophecies do not distinguish between the first and second comings of Christ. Therefore, in the larger context there may be mixed elements, but the point remains that this single element (the infants and old men who live long, the child dying a hundred years old, and the sinner being accursed) indicates a specific time in the future that is different from the present age. There are several other passages, especially in the Old Testament, that similarly speak of a future period that is far greater than the present age but that still fall short of the eternal state (see Ps. 72:8–14; Isa. 11:2–9; Zech. 14:6–21; 1 Cor. 15:24; Rev. 2:27; 12:5; 19:15).

2. There are also New Testament passages other than Revelation 20 that suggest a future millennium. When the risen Lord Jesus speaks to the church at Thyatira, he says, "*He who conquers and who keeps my works until the end, I will give him power over the nations,* and *he shall rule them with a rod of iron,* as when earthen pots are broken in pieces, even as I myself have received power from my Father" (Rev. 2:26–27). The imagery used (ruling with a rod of iron; shattering earthen pots) implies a rule of force over rebellious people. But when will believers who conquer over evil participate in this rule? The idea fits well into a future millennial kingdom when glorified saints rule with Christ on the earth but does not fit well at any time in the present age or in the eternal state. (The idea of ruling the nations "with a rod of iron" is also found in Rev. 12:5–6 and 19:15.)

When Paul talks about the resurrection, he says that each person will receive a resurrection body in his own order: "Christ the first fruits, *then* [Gk. *epeita*] at his coming those who belong to Christ. *Then* [Gk. *eita*] comes the end, when he delivers the kingdom to God the Father after destroying every rule and every authority and power. For he must reign until he has put all his enemies under his feet" (1 Cor. 15:23–25). The two words translated "then" in this passage (*epeita* and *eita*) both take the sense "after that," not the sense "at that same time." Therefore, the passage gives some support to the idea that, just as there is an interval of time between Christ's resurrection and his second coming when we receive a resurrection body (v. 23), so there is an interval of time between Christ's second coming and "the end" (v. 24), when Christ delivers the kingdom to God after having reigned for a time and put all his enemies under his feet.

3. With the background of a number of other passages that hint at or clearly suggest a future time far greater than the present age but short of the eternal state,

it is appropriate then to look at Revelation 20 once again. Several statements here are best understood as referring to a future earthly reign of Christ prior to the future judgment.

a. The binding and imprisonment of Satan in the bottomless pit (vv. 2–3) imply a far greater restriction of his activity than anything we know in this present age (see discussion above, under amillennialism).

b. The statement that those who were faithful "came to life" (v. 4) is best taken as referring to a bodily resurrection, for the next verse says, "This is the first resurrection." The verb *ezēsan*, "came to life," is the same verb and the same form of the verb used in Revelation 2:8, where Jesus identifies himself as the one "who died and *came to life*," here obviously referring to his resurrection.

c. On a premillennial interpretation, the reigning with Christ (in Rev. 20:4) is something that is still future, not something that is occurring now (as amillennialists claim). This is consistent with the rest of the New Testament, where we are frequently told that believers will reign with Christ and be given authority by him to reign over the earth (see Luke 19:17, 19; 1 Cor. 6:3; Rev. 2:26–27; 3:21). But nowhere does Scripture say that believers in the intermediate state (between their death and Christ's return) are reigning with Christ or sharing in rule with him.

Those who come to life and reign with Christ in Revelation 20 include people *"who had not worshiped the beast or its image and had not received its mark on their foreheads or their hands"* (Rev. 20:4). This is a reference to those who did not yield to the persecution by the beast spoken of in Revelation 13:1–18. But if the severity of persecution described in Revelation 13 leads us to conclude that the beast has not yet come on the world scene, but is yet future, then the persecution by this beast is still future as well. And if this persecution is still future, then the scene in Revelation 20 where those "who had not worshiped the beast . . . and had not received its mark on their foreheads or their hands" (Rev. 20:4) is still future as well. This means that Revelation 20:1–6 does not describe the present church age but is best understood to refer to a future millennial reign of Christ.

2. Pretribulational premillennialism (or dispensational premillennialism). Another variety of premillennialism has gained widespread popularity in the nineteenth and twentieth centuries, particularly in the United Kingdom and the United States. According to this position, Christ will return not only *before* the millennium (Christ's return is *pre*millennial), but also *before* the great tribulation (Christ's return is *pre*tribulational). This position is similar to the classical premillennial position mentioned above, but with one important difference: It will add another return of Christ before his return to reign on earth in the millennium. This return is thought to be a secret return of Christ to take believers out of the world.[4] The pretribulational premillennial view may be represented as in figure 32.4 on the following page.

According to this view, the church age will continue until, *suddenly, unexpectedly, and secretly, Christ will return part way to earth, and then will call believers to himself:* "The dead in Christ will rise first; then we who are alive, who are left, shall be caught up together with them in the clouds to meet the Lord in the air" (1 Thess. 4:16–17). *Christ will then return to heaven with the believers who have been removed from the earth. When that happens, there will be a great tribulation on the earth* for a period of seven years.

---

[4]Sometimes this secret coming of Christ for believers is called the "rapture," from the Latin word *rapio*, meaning "seize, snatch, carry away."

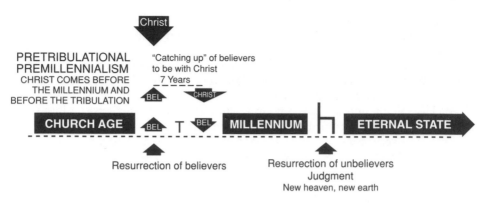

Pretribulational Premillennialism
figure 32.4

During this seven-year period of tribulation, many of the signs that were predicted to precede Christ's return will be fulfilled.[5] The great ingathering of the fullness of the Jewish people will occur as they trust Christ as their Messiah. In the midst of great suffering, there will also be much effective evangelism, especially carried out by the new Jewish Christians. *At the end of the tribulation, Christ will then come back with his saints to reign on the earth for one thousand years.* After this millennial period, there will be a rebellion resulting in the final defeat of Satan and his forces, and then will come the resurrection of unbelievers, the last judgment, and the beginning of the eternal state.

One further characteristic of pretribulational premillennialism should be mentioned: This view is found almost exclusively among dispensationalists who wish to maintain a clear distinction between the church and Israel. This pretribulational viewpoint allows the distinction to be maintained, since the church is taken out of the world before the widespread conversion of the Jewish people. These Jewish people therefore remain a distinct group from the church. Another characteristic of pretribulational premillennialism is its insistence on interpreting biblical prophecies "literally where possible." This especially applies to prophecies in the Old Testament concerning Israel. Those who hold this view argue that those prophecies of God's future blessing to Israel will yet be fulfilled among the Jewish people themselves; they are not to be "spiritualized" by finding their fulfillment in the church. Finally, one attractive feature about pretribulational premillennialism is that it allows people to insist that Christ's return could occur "at any moment" and therefore does justice to the full force of the passages that encourage us to be ready for Christ's return, while it still allows for a very literal fulfillment of the signs preceding Christ's return, since it says these will come to pass in the tribulation.

D. The Case in Favor of Classical Premillennialism

It is important to realize that the interpretation of the details of prophetic passages regarding future events is often a complex and difficult task involving many variable factors. Therefore, the degree of certainty that attaches to our conclusions

---

[5]See ch. 31, pp. 431–32, for discussion of the signs that will precede Christ's return.

in this area will be less than with many other doctrines. Even though it is important that Christians examine the scriptural data and attempt to reach convictions on what the Bible teaches about the millennium, I also think it is important for us to recognize that this area of study is complex and to extend a large measure of grace to others who hold different views regarding the millennium and the tribulation period.

In my view, the arguments in favor of classical premillennialism are the most persuasive. While the primary arguments for this position were listed above, some additional considerations relative to the other positions can now be made.

1. In response to the objection that only one passage teaches a future earthly millennium, it should be said that the Bible only needs to say something once in order for it to be true and something that we must believe. Moreover, it is not surprising that this doctrine should be clearly taught in the book of Revelation. Since Revelation is the New Testament book that most explicitly teaches about things yet future, it is appropriate that this more explicit revelation of the future millennium would be put at this point in the Bible.

2. The amillennial interpretation of Revelation 20:1–6 has significant difficulties. First, the binding of Satan described in Revelation 20 seems to be much more than a mere binding or restriction of activity as amillennialists hold. The imagery of throwing Satan into a pit and shutting it and sealing it over him gives a picture of total removal from influence on the earth, which seems much different than the present world situation during the church age in which Satan's activity is still very strong, in which he "prowls around like a roaring lion, seeking someone to devour" (1 Peter 5:8).

Moreover, amillennialist interpretations of the phrase "first resurrection" are unconvincing. The word *resurrection* (Gk. *anastasis*) never elsewhere means "going to heaven" or "going into the presence of God," but rather signifies a bodily resurrection. And it is hard to accept the contention that Scripture teaches only *one* resurrection when we realize that Revelation 20 explicitly speaks about "the *first* resurrection," thus implying that there will be a second resurrection as well. The passage distinguishes those who share in this first resurrection and are blessed from others who do not share in it. They are "the rest of the dead," and the implication is that "the second death" (that is, facing final judgment and being condemned to eternal punishment away from the presence of God) does have power over them, and they will experience it.

3. In response to the postmillennial position that the Great Commission leads us to expect that the power of the gospel will eventually result in a largely Christian world, we can agree that the Great Commission does indeed speak of the great authority that is given into Christ's hand. However, this does not necessarily imply that Christ will use that authority to bring about the conversion of the majority of the population of the world. The assumption that he will use it to bring about worldwide Christianization is not based on any specific evidence in the Great Commission or in other texts that talk about Christ's authority and power in this present age. In a similar way, the parable of the mustard seed and others like it do tell us that the kingdom of God will gradually grow from something very small to something very large, but they do not tell us the extent to which the kingdom will grow.

4. Several New Testament passages seem to give explicit denial to the postmillennial position. Jesus said, "Enter by the narrow gate; for the gate is wide and the way is easy, that leads to destruction, and those who enter by it are many. For

the gate is narrow and the way is hard, that leads to life, and *those who find it are few*" (Matt. 7:13–14). Rather than teaching that a majority of the world will become Christians, Jesus seems here to be saying that those who are saved will be few in contrast to the many who travel toward eternal destruction. Contrary to the view that the world will get better and better as the influence of the church grows, Paul writes to Timothy about the last days: "*In the last days* there will come times of stress. For men will be lovers of self, lovers of money, proud, arrogant, abusive, disobedient to their parents, ungrateful, unholy, inhuman, implacable, slanderers, profligates, fierce, haters of good, treacherous, reckless, swollen with conceit, lovers of pleasure rather than lovers of God, holding the form of religion but denying the power of it" (2 Tim. 3:1–5). He says further: "*All who desire to live a godly life in Christ Jesus will be persecuted, while evil men and impostors will go on from bad to worse, deceivers and deceived. . . .* the time is coming when people will not endure sound teaching, but having itching ears they will accumulate for themselves teachers to suit their own likings, and will turn away from listening to the truth and wander into myths" (2 Tim. 3:12–13; 4:3–4).

Finally, and perhaps most conclusively, Matthew 24:15–31 speaks of a great tribulation that will precede the time of Christ's return:

> For *then there will be great tribulation, such as has not been from the beginning of the world until now, no, and never will be. And if those days had not been short-ened, no human being would be saved;* but for the sake of the elect those days will be shortened. . . . *Immediately after the tribulation of those days the sun will be darkened, and the moon will not give its light, and the stars will fall from heaven, and the powers of the heavens will be shaken; then will appear the sign of the Son of man in heaven, and then all the tribes of the earth will mourn, and they will see the Son of man coming on the clouds of heaven with power and great glory.* (Matt. 24:21–30)

This passage pictures not a Christianized world but a world of great suffering and evil, a great tribulation that exceeds all previous periods of suffering on the earth. It does not say that the great majority of the world will welcome Christ when he comes, but rather that when the sign of the Son of man appears in heaven, "then all the tribes of the earth will mourn" (Matt. 24:30).

5. Finally, all of the passages indicating that Christ could return soon and that we must be ready for him to return at any time[6] must be considered a significant argument against postmillennialism as well. For if Christ could return at any time, and we are to be ready for his return, then the long period required for the establishment of the millennium on earth before Christ returns simply cannot be thought a persuasive theory.

These considerations combine to make a case in favor of premillennialism. Although we may not have much clarity on all the details of the nature of the millennium, we can be reasonably certain that there will be a future earthly reign of Christ that will be markedly different from this present age.

E. The Time of the Great Tribulation

For those who are persuaded by the arguments in favor of premillennialism, one further question must be decided: Will Christ return before or after the "great tribulation"?

---

[6]See ch. 31, pp. 430–36, on the passages teaching Christ's imminent return.

449

The expression "great tribulation" itself comes from Matthew 24:21 (and parallels), where Jesus says, "For then there will be *great tribulation,* such as has not been from the beginning of the world until now, no, and never will be." Historic premillennialism believes that Christ will return after that tribulation, for the passage continues, "Immediately after the tribulation of those days the sun will be darkened.... then will appear the sign of the Son of man in heaven, and then all the tribes of the earth will mourn, and they will see the Son of man coming on the clouds of heaven with power and great glory" (Matt. 24:29–30). But, as explained above, in the nineteenth and twentieth centuries, a variety of premillennialism that holds to a pretribulational coming of Christ became popular. This is often called a "pretribulation rapture" view because it holds that when Christ first returns, the church will be "raptured," or snatched up, into heaven to be with him.

The arguments for such a pretribulation rapture are as follows:[7]

1. The entire period of the tribulation will be a time of the outpouring of God's wrath on all the earth. Therefore, it would not be appropriate for Christians to be on the earth at that time.

2. Jesus promises in Revelation 3:10, "*I will keep you from the hour of trial which is coming on the whole world,* to try those who dwell upon the earth." This passage indicates that the church will be taken out of the world before that hour of trial comes.

3. If Christ returns *after* the tribulation and defeats all his enemies, then where will the unbelievers come from who are necessary to populate the millennial kingdom? The pretribulation position, however, envisages thousands of Jewish believers who have become Christians during the tribulation and who will go into the millennial kingdom in nonglorified bodies.

4. This view makes it possible to believe that Christ could come at any moment (his coming before the tribulation) and yet that many signs must be fulfilled before he comes (his coming after the tribulation when the signs will be fulfilled).

Although it is not specifically an argument in favor of a pretribulation position, it must also be noted that pretribulationists then view the teaching about the tribulation in Matthew 24 and the warnings and encouragements given to believers in that situation as applying to Jewish believers during the tribulation, and not to the church generally.

In response to these arguments, the following points may be made:

1. It is inconsistent with the New Testament descriptions of the tribulation to say that *all* the suffering that occurs during that time is specifically the result of the wrath of God. Much of the suffering is due to the fact that "wickedness is multiplied" (Matt. 24:12) and the fact that persecution of the church and opposition from Satan greatly increases during this period. Of course all Christians (whether Gentile or Jewish believers) will avoid the wrath of God at all times, but this does not mean they will avoid all suffering, even in times of intense hardship.

2. The fact that Jesus tells faithful believers in the church in Philadelphia (Rev. 3:10) that he will keep them from the hour of trial that is coming on the whole world is not strong enough evidence to say that the entire church will be taken out of the world before the tribulation. First, this statement is made to one specific church (Philadelphia) and should not be applied to the whole church at some future point in

history. Moreover, "the hour of trial which is coming on the whole world" need not refer to the time of the great tribulation, but more likely refers to a time of great suffering and persecution that would come upon the entire Roman Empire or the entire inhabited world. Finally, the promise that the church in Philadelphia will be *guarded* does not imply that they will be taken out of the world, but simply that they will be kept faithful and will be guarded from being harmed by that period of suffering and testing.

3. It is no argument for the pretribulation view to say that there must be some people in nonglorified bodies who will enter the millennium, because (on a posttribulational view) when Christ comes at the end of the tribulation, he will *defeat* all the forces arrayed against him, but that does not mean he will kill or annihilate all of them. Many will simply surrender without trusting Christ and will thus enter the millennium as unbelievers. And during the entire period of the millennium, no doubt many will be converted to Christ and become believers as well.

4. The pretribulational view is not the only one consistent with the ideas that Christ could come back at any time there are signs that precede his return. The position presented in the previous chapter—that it is unlikely but possible the signs have been fulfilled—is also consistent with these ideas.[8] But behind this argument of pretribulationists is probably a more fundamental concern: the desire to preserve a distinction between *the church* (which they think will be taken up into heaven to be with Christ) and *Israel* (which they think will constitute the people of God on earth during the tribulation and then during the millennial kingdom). But, as we noted in an earlier chapter,[9] the New Testament does not support a distinction of this kind between Israel and the church. Hence, it does not supply a need to see a distinction between these groups at the time of the tribulation and the millennium.

Finally, some objections to the *pre*tribulational rapture position can be stated in the form of arguments in favor of the *post*tribulational rapture view (the historic premillennial view that Christ will return after a period of tribulation on the earth):

1. The New Testament nowhere clearly says that the church will be taken out of the world before the tribulation. For example, it is very difficult to understand 1 Thessalonians 4:17, the only passage that explicitly speaks of the fact that the church will be "caught up" (or "raptured"), to speak of the idea of a secret coming of Christ to take believers out of the world prior to the tribulation. It says, "The Lord himself will descend from heaven *with a cry of command, with the archangel's call, and with the sound of the trumpet of God*" (1 Thess. 4:16). One noted commentator rightly says of these words, "It is difficult to see how he could more plainly describe something that is open and public."[10]

2. The tribulation is quite clearly linked with the Lord's return in some passages. First, the trumpet call to gather the elect in Matthew 24:31, the sound of the trumpet of God in 1 Thessalonians 4:16, and the last trumpet at which our bodies are changed in 1 Corinthians 15:51–52, all seem to be the same trumpet—the last trumpet that is blown just before the millennium. If it is indeed the "last trumpet" (1 Cor. 15:52), then it is hard to see how another loud trumpet call (Matt. 24:31) could follow it seven years later.

In addition, Matthew 24 is very difficult to understand as referring not to the church but to Jewish people who would be saved during the tribulation. Jesus is

---

[8]See ch. 31, pp. 434–36.

[9]See ch. 26, pp. 367–69, on the question of a distinction between Israel and the church.

[10]Leon Morris, *The First and Second Epistles to the Thessalonians*, New International Commentary on the New Testament (Grand Rapids: Eerdmans, 1959), p. 145.

addressing *his disciples* (Matt. 24:1–4) and warning them of persecution and suffering to come. It does not seem likely that Jesus, in saying all these things *to his disciples,* intended his words to apply not to the church but only to a future earthly kingdom of Jewish people who would be converted during the tribulation. Nor does it seem likely that the disciples are as representatives of a future Jewish kingdom and not as representatives of the church, with whose founding they were so integrally connected as to be its foundation (Eph. 2:20).

3. Finally, the New Testament does not seem to justify the idea of two separate returns of Christ (once *for* his church before the tribulation and then seven years later *with* his church to bring judgment on unbelievers). No such view is explicitly taught in any passage, but it is simply an inference drawn from differences between various passages that describe Christ's return from different perspectives. But it is not at all difficult to see these passages as referring to a single event occurring at one time.

It seems best to conclude, with the great majority of the church throughout history, that the church will go through the time of tribulation predicted by Jesus. We would probably not have chosen this path for ourselves, but the decision was not ours to make. And if God wills that any of us now alive remain on earth until the time of this great tribulation, then we should heed Peter's words, "If you are reproached for the name of Christ, you are blessed, because the spirit of glory and of God rests upon you" (1 Peter 4:14), and, "Christ also suffered for you, leaving you an example, that you should follow in his steps" (1 Peter 2:21). This idea that Christians should be prepared to endure suffering is also seen in Paul's words that we are fellow heirs with Christ, "provided we suffer with him in order that we may also be glorified with him" (Rom. 8:17). It is from the Savior who himself has suffered more than any of his children will ever suffer that we have the admonition, "Do not fear what you are about to suffer. . . . Be faithful unto death, and I will give you the crown of life" (Rev. 2:10).

II. REVIEW QUESTIONS

1. Summarize the sequence of events concerning Christ's return and the millennium for each of the following views:
   - Amillennialism
   - Postmillennialism
   - Classic premillennialism
   - Pretribulational premillennialism
2. How would a proponent of amillennialism answer the following questions concerning the interpretation of Revelation 20:1–6?
   - When did (or will) the binding of Satan in verses 1–2 occur?
   - Where does the scene described in verse 4 occur?
   - To what does the phrase "they came to life" in verse 4 refer?
   - Verse 4 says that the believers reigned with Christ for a thousand years. Where does this reigning take place? When?
   - To what does this "thousand years" refer?
3. Answer the previous questions from a classical premillennial perspective.
4. Describe the "millennium" that is envisioned by the postmillennial perspective.

5. What are the primary distinctions between the classical premillennial view and the dispensational premillennial view?

6. List four reasons in support of the view that Christ's return will come *after* a period of tribulation (the posttribulational rapture view).

III. QUESTIONS FOR PERSONAL APPLICATION

1. Before reading this chapter, did you have any conviction about whether Christ's return would be amillennial, postmillennial, or premillennial? Or whether it would be posttribulational or pretribulational? If so, how has your view now changed, if at all?

2. Explain how your present view of the millennium affects your Christian life today. Similarly, how your view of the tribulation affects your Christian life.

3. What do you think it will feel like to be living on earth with a glorified body, and with Jesus Christ as King over the whole world? Can you describe in any detail some of the attitudes and emotional responses you will have toward various situations in such a kingdom? (Your answers will differ somewhat depending on whether you expect a glorified body during the millennium or not until the eternal state.)

4. What might be both the positive and the negative results of a pretribulation rapture position in the everyday lives and attitudes of Christians? Similarly, what might be the positive and negative results of a posttribulation rapture position?

IV. SPECIAL TERMS

amillennialism	posttribulation rapture
dispensational premillennialism	posttribulational premillennialism
great tribulation	premillennialism
historic premillennialism	pretribulation rapture
millennium	pretribulational premillennialism
postmillennialism	rapture

V. SCRIPTURE MEMORY PASSAGE

REVELATION 20:4–6

Then I saw thrones, and seated on them were those to whom judgment was committed. Also I saw the souls of those who had been beheaded for their testimony to Jesus and for the word of God, and who had not worshiped the beast or its image and had not received its mark on their foreheads or their hands. They came to life, and reigned with Christ a thousand years. The rest of the dead did not come to life until the thousand years were ended. This is the first resurrection. Blessed and holy is he who shares in the first resurrection! Over such the second death has no power, but they shall be priests of God and of Christ, and they shall reign with him a thousand years.

CHAPTER THIRTY-THREE

The Final Judgment and Eternal Punishment

+ *Who will be judged?*
+ *What is hell?*

I. EXPLANATION AND SCRIPTURAL BASIS

A. The Fact of Final Judgment

Scripture frequently affirms the fact that there will be a great final judgment of believers and unbelievers. They will stand before the judgment seat of Christ in resurrected bodies and hear his proclamation of their eternal destiny.

The final judgment is vividly portrayed in John's vision in Revelation:

> *Then I saw a great white throne and him who sat upon it;* from his presence earth and sky fled away, and no place was found for them. *And I saw the dead, great and small, standing before the throne, and books were opened.* Also another book was opened, which is the book of life. *And the dead were judged by what was written in the books, by what they had done.* And the sea gave up the dead in it, Death and Hades gave up the dead in them, and all were judged by what they had done. Then Death and Hades were thrown into the lake of fire. This is the second death, the lake of fire; and if anyone's name was not found written in the book of life, he was thrown into the lake of fire. (Rev. 20:11–15)

Many other passages teach this final judgment. Paul tells the Greek philosophers in Athens that God "Now . . . commands all men everywhere to repent, because *he has fixed a day on which he will judge the world in righteousness* by a man whom he has appointed, and of this he has given assurance to all men by raising him from the dead" (Acts 17:30–31). Similarly, Paul talks about "the day of wrath when God's righteous judgment will be revealed" (Rom. 2:5). Other passages speak clearly of a coming day of judgment (see Matt. 10:15; 11:22, 24; 12:36; 25:31–46; 1 Cor. 4:5; Heb. 6:2; 2 Peter 2:4; Jude 6; et al.).

This final judgment is the culmination of many precursors in which God rewarded righteousness or punished unrighteousness throughout history. While he brought blessing and deliverance from danger to those who were faithful to him, including Abel, Noah, Abraham, Isaac, Jacob, Moses, David, and the faithful among the people of Israel, he also from time to time brought judgment on those who persisted in disobedience and unbelief: his judgments included the flood, the dispersion of the people from the tower of Babel, the judgments on Sodom and Gomorrah, and continuing judgments throughout history, both on individuals (Rom. 1:18–32) and on nations (Isa. 13–23; et al.) who persisted in sin. Moreover, in the unseen spiritual realm, he brought judgment on angels who sinned (2 Peter 2:4). Peter reminds us that God's judgments have been carried out periodically and with certainty, and this reminds us that a final judgment is yet coming, for "the Lord knows how to rescue the godly from trial, and to keep the unrighteous under punishment until the day of judgment, and especially those who indulge in the lust of defiling passion and despise authority" (2 Peter 2:9–10).

B. The Time of Final Judgment

The final judgment will occur after the millennium and the rebellion that occurs at the end of it. John pictures the millennial kingdom and the removal of Satan from influence on the earth in Revelation 20:1–6 (see discussion in ch. 32) and then says that "when the thousand years are ended, Satan will be loosed from his prison and will come out to deceive the nations . . . to gather them for battle" (Rev. 20:7–8). After God decisively defeats this final rebellion (Rev. 20:9–10), John tells us that judgment will follow: "Then I saw a great white throne and him who sat upon it" (v. 11).

C. The Nature of the Final Judgment

1. Jesus Christ will be the Judge. Paul speaks of "Jesus Christ who is to judge the living and the dead" (2 Tim. 4:1). Peter says that Jesus Christ "is the one ordained by God to be the judge of the living and the dead" (Acts 10:42; cf. 17:31; Matt. 25:31–33). This right to act as judge over the whole universe is something that the Father has given to the Son: "The Father . . . has given him authority to execute judgment, because he is the Son of Man" (John 5:26–27).

2. Unbelievers will be judged. It is clear that all unbelievers will stand before Christ for judgment, for this judgment includes "the dead, great and small" (Rev. 20:12), and Paul says that "on the day of wrath when God's righteous judgment will be revealed," "he will render to every man according to his works . . . for those who are factious and do not obey the truth, but obey wickedness, there will be wrath and fury" (Rom. 2:5–7).

This judgment of unbelievers will include *degrees of punishment,* for we read that the dead were judged "by what they had done" (Rev. 20:12, 13), and this judgment according to what people had done must therefore involve an evaluation of the works that people have done.[1] Similarly, Jesus says: "That servant who knew his master's will, but did not make ready or act according to his will, shall receive a severe beating. But he who did not know, and did what deserved a beating, shall receive a light beating" (Luke 12:47–48). When Jesus says to the cities of Chorazin and Bethsaida, "It shall be *more tolerable* on the day of judgment for Tyre and Sidon than for you" (Matt. 11:22; cf. v. 24), or when he says that the scribes "will receive the *greater condemnation*" (Luke 20:47), he implies that there will be degrees of punishment on the last day.

---

[1]The fact that there will be degrees of punishment for unbelievers according to their works does not mean that unbelievers can ever do enough good to merit God's approval or earn salvation, for salvation only comes as a free gift to those who trust in Christ: "He who believes in him is not condemned; he who does not believe is condemned already, because he has not believed in the name of the only Son of God" (John 3:18). For a discussion of the fact that there will be no "second chance" for people to accept Christ after they die, see ch. 25, pp. 355–56.

In fact, every wrong deed done will be remembered and taken account of in the punishment that is meted out on that day, because "on the day of judgment men will render account for every careless word they utter" (Matt. 12:36). Every word spoken, every deed done will be brought to light and receive judgment: "For God will bring every deed into judgment, with every secret thing, whether good or evil" (Eccl. 12:14).

As these verses indicate, on the day of judgment, the secrets of people's hearts will be revealed and made public. Paul speaks of the day when "God judges the secrets of men by Christ Jesus" (Rom. 2:16; cf. Luke 8:17). "Nothing is covered up that will not be revealed, or hidden that will not be known. Therefore whatever you have said in the dark shall be heard in the light, and what you have whispered in private rooms shall be proclaimed upon the housetops" (Luke 12:2–3).

3. Believers will be judged. In writing to Christians, Paul says, "*We shall all stand before the judgment seat of God....* Each of us shall give account of himself to God" (Rom. 14:10–12). He also tells the Corinthians, "For *we must all appear before the judgment seat of Christ, that each one may receive what is due him for the things done while in the body,* whether good or bad" (2 Cor. 5:10; cf. Rom. 2:6–11; Rev. 20:12, 15). In addition, the picture of the final judgment in Matthew 25:31–46 includes Christ separating the sheep from the goats, and rewarding those who receive his blessing.

It is important to realize that this judgment of believers will be a judgment to evaluate and bestow various degrees of reward (see below), but the fact that they will face such a judgment should never cause believers to fear that they will be eternally condemned. Jesus says, "He who hears my word and believes him who sent me, has eternal life; *he does not come into judgment,* but has passed from death to life" (John 5:24). Here judgment must be understood in the sense of eternal condemnation and death, since it is contrasted with passing from death into life. At the day of final judgment more than at any other time, it is of utmost importance that "there is therefore now *no condemnation for those who are in Christ Jesus*" (Rom. 8:1). Thus, the day of judgment can be portrayed as one in which believers are rewarded and unbelievers are punished: "The nations raged, but your wrath came, and the time for the dead to be judged, *for rewarding your servants,* the prophets and saints, and those who fear your name, both small and great, and for destroying the destroyers of the earth" (Rev. 11:18).

Will all the secret words and deeds of believers, and all their sins, also be revealed on that last day? We might at first think so, because in writing to *believers* about the day of judgment, Paul says that when the Lord comes he will "*bring to light the things now hidden in darkness* and will disclose the purposes of the heart. Then every man will receive his commendation from God" (1 Cor. 4:5; cf. Col. 3:25). On the other hand, this is a context that talks about "commendation" or praise (Gk. *epainos*) that comes from God, so it may not refer to sins. And other verses suggest that God will never again call our sins to remembrance: "You will cast all our sins into the depths of the sea" (Mic. 7:19); "As far as the east is from the west, so far does he remove our transgressions from us" (Ps. 103:12); "I, I am He who blots out your transgressions for my own sake, and *I will not remember your sins*" (Isa. 43:25); "For I will be merciful toward their iniquities, and *I will remember their sins no more*" (Heb. 8:12; cf. 10:17).[2]

---

[2]I had overlooked this scriptural emphasis on God's forgetting of our sins in my *Systematic Theology* (p. 1144), but it was called to my attention by my students at Trinity Evangelical Divinity School. This paragraph is therefore a revision of my earlier position.

In any case, the fact that we will appear before God for our lives to be evaluated should provide a motive for godly living, and Paul uses it that way in 2 Corinthians 5:9–10: "*We make it our aim to please him.* For we must all appear before the judgment seat of Christ." But this prospect should never cause terror or alarm on the part of believers, because even sins that are made public on that day will be made public as sins that have been *forgiven,* and thereby they will be the occasion for giving glory to God for the richness of his grace.

Scripture also teaches that there will be *degrees of reward for believers.* Paul encourages the Corinthians to be careful how they build the church on the foundation that has already been laid—Jesus Christ himself.

> Now if anyone builds on the foundation with gold, silver, precious stones, wood, hay, straw—each man's work will become manifest; for the Day will disclose it, because it will be revealed with fire, and the fire will test what sort of work each one has done. *If the work which any man has built on the foundation survives, he will receive a reward.* If any man's work is burned up, he will suffer loss, though he himself will be saved, but only as through fire. (1 Cor. 3:12–15)

Paul similarly says of Christians that "we must all appear before the judgment seat of Christ, that each one may receive *what is due him for the things done while in the body,* whether good or bad" (2 Cor. 5:10), again implying degrees of reward for what we have done in this life. Likewise, in the parable of the pounds, the one who made ten pounds more was told, "You shall have authority over ten cities," and the one whose pound had made five pounds more was told, "And you are to be over five cities" (Luke 19:17, 19). Many other passages likewise teach or imply degrees of reward for believers at the final judgment.[3]

But we must guard against misunderstanding here: Although there will be degrees of reward in heaven, the joy of each person will be full and complete for eternity. If we ask how this can be when there are different degrees of reward, it simply shows that our perception of happiness is based on the assumption that happiness depends on what we possess or the status or power that we have. In actuality, however, our true happiness consists in delighting in God and rejoicing in the status and recognition that he has given us. The foolishness of thinking that only those who have been highly rewarded and given great status will be fully happy in heaven is seen when we realize that no matter how great a reward we are given, there will always be those with greater rewards, or who have higher status and authority, including the apostles, the heavenly creatures, and Jesus Christ and God himself. Therefore, if highest status were essential for people to be fully happy, no one but God would be fully happy in heaven, which is certainly an incorrect idea. Moreover, those with greater reward and honor in heaven, those nearest the throne of God, delight not in their status but only in the privilege of falling down before God's throne to worship him (see Rev. 4:10–11).

It would be morally and spiritually beneficial for us to have a greater consciousness of this clear New Testament teaching on degrees of heavenly reward. Rather than making us competitive with one another, it would cause us to help and

---

[3]The Bible's teaching on degrees of reward in heaven is more extensive than Christians normally realize: see also Dan. 12:2; Matt. 6:20–21; 19:21; Luke 6:22–23; 12:18–21, 32, 42–48; 14:13–14; 1 Cor. 3:8; 9:18; 13:3; 15:19, 29–32, 58; Gal. 6:9–10; Eph. 6:7–8; Col. 3:23–24; 1 Tim. 6:18; Heb. 10:34, 35; 11:10, 14–16, 26, 35; 1 Peter 1:4; 2 John 8; Rev. 11:18; 22:12; cf. also Matt. 5:46; 6:2–6, 16–18, 24; Luke 6:35.

encourage one another that we all may increase our heavenly reward, for God has an infinite capacity to bring blessing to us all, and we are all members of one another (cf. 1 Cor. 12:26–27). We would more eagerly heed the admonition of the author of Hebrews, "*Let us consider how to stir up one another to love and good works,* not neglecting to meet together, as is the habit of some, but encouraging one another, and all the more as you see the Day drawing near" (Heb. 10:24–25). Moreover, in our own lives a heartfelt seeking of future heavenly reward would motivate us to work wholeheartedly for the Lord at whatever task he calls us to, whether great or small, paid or unpaid. It would also make us long for his approval rather than for wealth or success. It would motivate us to work at building up the church on the one foundation, Jesus Christ (1 Cor. 3:10–15).

4. Angels will be judged. Peter says that the rebellious angels have been committed to pits of nether gloom "to be kept until the judgment" (2 Peter 2:4), and Jude says that rebellious angels have been kept by God "until the judgment of the great day" (Jude 6). This means that at least the *rebellious* angels or demons will be subject to judgment on that last day as well.

Scripture does not clearly indicate whether righteous angels will undergo some kind of evaluation of their service as well, but it is possible that they are included in Paul's statement "Do you not know that *we are to judge angels?*" (1 Cor. 6:3). It is probable that this includes righteous angels, because there is no indication in the context that Paul is speaking of demons or fallen angels, and the word *angels* without further qualification in the New Testament would normally be understood to refer to righteous angels. But the text is not explicit enough to give us certainty.

D. Necessity of Final Judgment

Since believers pass immediately into the presence of God when they die, and unbelievers pass into a state of separation from God and the endurance of punishment when they die,[4] we may wonder why God has a time of final judgment established at all. Berkhof wisely points out that the final judgment is not for the purpose of letting God find out the condition of our hearts or the pattern of conduct of our lives, for he already knows that in every detail. Berkhof rather says of the final judgment:

> It will serve the purpose rather of displaying before all rational creatures the declarative glory of God in a formal, forensic act, which magnifies on the one hand His holiness and righteousness, and on the other hand, His grace and mercy. Moreover, it should be borne in mind that the judgment at the last day will differ from that of the death of each individual in more than one respect. It will not be secret, but public; it will not pertain to the soul only, but also to the body; it will not have reference to a single individual, but to all men.[5]

E. Justice of God in the Final Judgment

Scripture clearly affirms that God will be entirely just in his judgment and no one will be able to complain against him on that day. God is the one who "judges each one impartially according to his deeds" (1 Peter 1:17), and "God shows no partiality"

---

[4]See ch. 25, pp. 352–55, for evidence supporting the idea that believers go immediately into God's presence when they die and unbelievers go immediately to a place of punishment separated from God. (See also Luke 16:24–26; Heb. 9:27.)

[5]Louis Berkhof, *Introduction to Systematic Theology* (Grand Rapids: Eerdmans, 1932; reprint, Grand Rapids: Baker, 1979), p. 731.

(Rom. 2:11; cf. Col. 3:25). For this reason, on the last day, "every mouth" will be "stopped," and the whole world will be "held accountable to God" (Rom. 3:19), with no one being able to complain that God has treated him or her unfairly. In fact, one of the great blessings of the final judgment will be that saints and angels will see demonstrated the absolutely pure justice of God, and this will be a source of praise to him for all eternity. At the time of the judgment, there will be great praise in heaven, for John says, "I heard what seemed to be the loud voice of a great multitude in heaven, crying, '*Hallelujah!* Salvation and glory and power belong to our God, for *his judgments are true and just . . .*'" (Rev. 19:1–2).

F.   Moral Application of the Final Judgment

The doctrine of final judgment has several positive moral influences in our lives.

1. The doctrine of final judgment satisfies our inward sense of a need for justice in the world. The fact that there will be a final judgment assures us that ultimately God's universe is *fair,* for God is in control, and he keeps accurate records and renders just judgment. When Paul tells slaves to be submissive to their masters, he reassures them, "For the wrongdoer will be paid back for the wrong he has done, and there is no partiality" (Col. 3:25). When the picture of a final judgment mentions the fact that "books were opened" (Rev. 20:12; cf. Mal. 3:16), it reminds us (whether the books are literal or symbolic) that a permanent and accurate record of all our deeds has been kept by God, and ultimately all accounts will be settled and all will be made right.

2. The doctrine of final judgment enables us to forgive others freely. We realize that it is not up to us to take revenge on others who have wronged us, or even to want to do so, because God has reserved that right for himself. "Beloved, never avenge yourselves, but leave it to the wrath of God, for it is written, *'Vengeance is mine, I will repay, says the Lord'*" (Rom. 12:19). In this way, whenever we have been wronged, we can give into God's hands any desire to harm or pay back the person who has wronged us, knowing that every wrong in the universe will ultimately be paid for—either it will turn out to have been paid for by Christ when he died on the cross (if the wrongdoer becomes a Christian), or it will be paid for at the final judgment (for those who do not trust in Christ for salvation). But in either case, we can give the situation into God's hands and then pray that the wrongdoer will trust Christ for salvation and thereby receive forgiveness of his or her sins. This thought should keep us from harboring bitterness or resentment in our hearts for injustices we have suffered that have not been made right: God is just, and we can leave these situations in his hands, knowing that he will someday right all wrongs and give absolutely fair rewards and punishments. In this way, we are following in the example of Christ, who "when he was reviled, he did not revile in return; when he suffered, he did not threaten; but *he trusted to him who judges justly*" (1 Peter 2:22–23). He also prayed, "Father, forgive them, for they know not what they do" (Luke 23:34; cf. Acts 7:60, where Stephen followed Jesus' example in praying for those who put him to death).

3. The doctrine of the final judgment provides a motive for righteous living. For believers, the final judgment is an incentive to faithfulness and good works, not as a means of earning forgiveness of sins, but as a means of gaining greater eternal reward. This is a healthy and good motive for us—Jesus tells us, "Lay up for your-selves treasures in heaven" (Matt. 6:20)—though it runs counter to the popular views of our secular culture, a culture that does not really believe in heaven or eter-nal rewards at all.

For unbelievers the doctrine of final judgment still provides some moral restraint on their lives. If in a society there is widespread general acknowledgment that all will someday give account to the Creator of the universe for their lives, some "fear of God" will characterize many people's lives. By contrast, those who have no deep consciousness of final judgment give themselves up to greater and greater evil, demonstrating that "there is *no fear of God* before their eyes" (Rom. 3:18). Those who deny the final judgment, Peter says, will be "scoffers" who "will come in the last days with scoffing, *following their own passions* and saying, 'Where is the promise of his coming?'" (2 Peter 3:3–4). An awareness of final judgment is both a comfort to believers and a warning to unbelievers not to continue in their evil ways.

4. The doctrine of final judgment provides a great motive for evangelism. The decisions made by people in this life will affect their destiny for all eternity, and it is right that our hearts feel and our mouths echo the sentiment of the appeal of God through Ezekiel, *"Turn back, turn back from your evil ways; for why will you die, O house of Israel?"* (Ezek. 33:11). In fact, Peter indicates that the delay of the Lord's return is due to the fact that God "is forbearing toward you, not wishing that any should perish, but that all should reach repentance" (2 Peter 3:9).

G. Hell

It is appropriate to discuss the doctrine of hell in connection with the doctrine of final judgment. We may define hell as follows: *Hell is a place of eternal conscious punishment for the wicked.* Scripture teaches in several passages that there is such a place. At the end of the parable of the talents, the master says, "Cast the worthless servant into the outer darkness; there men will weep and gnash their teeth" (Matt. 25:30). This is one among several indications that there will be consciousness of punishment after the final judgment. Similarly, at the judgment the king will say to some, "Depart from me, you cursed, into *the eternal fire* prepared for the devil and his angels" (Matt. 25:41), and Jesus says that those thus condemned "will go away into *eternal punishment,* but the righteous into eternal life" (Matt. 25:46). In this text, the parallel between "eternal life" and "eternal punishment" indicates that both states will be without end.

Jesus refers to hell as "the unquenchable fire" (Mark 9:43) and says that hell is a place "where their worm does not die, and the fire is not quenched" (Mark 9:48). The story of the rich man and Lazarus also indicates a horrible consciousness of pun-ishment: "The rich man also died and was buried; and in Hades, being in torment, he lifted up his eyes, and saw Abraham far off and Lazarus in his bosom, and he called out, 'Father Abraham, have mercy upon me, and send Lazarus to dip the end of his finger in water and cool my tongue; for I am in anguish in this flame'" (Luke 16:22–24). He then begs Abraham to send Lazarus to his father's house, "for I have five brothers, so that he may warn them, lest they also come into *this place of tor-ment*" (Luke 16:28).

When we turn to Revelation, the descriptions of this eternal punishment are also very explicit:

If anyone worships the beast and its image, and receives a mark on his forehead or on his hand, he also shall drink the wine of God's wrath, poured unmixed into the cup of his anger, and he shall be tormented with fire and sulphur in the presence of the holy angels and in the presence of the Lamb. *And the smoke of their torment goes up forever and ever; and they have no rest, day or night, these worshipers of the beast and its image,* and whoever receives the mark of its name. (Rev. 14:9–11)

This passage very clearly affirms the idea of eternal conscious punishment of unbelievers.

With respect to the judgment on the wicked city of Babylon, a large multitude in heaven cries, "Hallelujah! *The smoke from her goes up for ever and ever*" (Rev. 19:3). After the final rebellion of Satan is crushed, we read, "The devil who had deceived them was thrown into the lake of fire and sulphur where the beast and the false prophet were, and *they will be tormented day and night for ever and ever*" (Rev. 20:10). This passage is also significant in connection with Matthew 25:41, in which unbelievers are sent "into the eternal fire prepared for the devil and his angels." These verses should make us realize the immensity of the evil that is found in sin and rebellion against God and the magnitude of the holiness and the justice of God that call forth this kind of punishment.

The idea that there will be *eternal* conscious punishment of unbelievers has been denied recently even by some evangelical theologians. It has previously been denied by the Seventh Day Adventist Church and by various individuals throughout church history. Those who deny eternal conscious punishment often advocate *"annihilationism,"* a teaching that, after the wicked have suffered the penalty of God's wrath for a time, God will "annihilate" them so that they no longer exist. Many who believe in annihilationism also hold to the reality of final judgment and punishment for sin, but they argue that after sinners have suffered for a certain period of time, bearing the wrath of God against their sin, they will finally cease to exist. The punishment will therefore be "conscious" but it will not be "eternal."

Arguments advanced in favor of annihilationism are: (1) the biblical references to the *destruction* of the wicked, which, some say, implies that they will no longer exist after they are destroyed (Phil. 3:19; 1 Thess. 5:3; 2 Thess. 1:9; 2 Peter 3:7; et al.); (2) the apparent inconsistency of eternal conscious punishment with the love of God; (3) the apparent injustice involved in the *disproportion* between sins committed in time and punishment that is eternal; and (4) the fact that the continuing presence of evil creatures in God's universe will eternally mar the perfection of a universe that God created to reflect his glory.

In response, (1) it must be said that the passages which speak of *destruction* (such as Phil. 3:19; 1 Thess. 5:3; 2 Thess. 1:9; 2 Peter 3:7) do not necessarily imply the cessation of existence, for in these passages the terms used for "destruction" do not necessarily imply a ceasing to exist or some kind of annihilation, but can simply be ways of referring to the harmful and destructive effects of final judgment on unbelievers.[6]

---

[6]In Phil. 3:19 and 2 Peter 3:7, the term for "destruction" is *apōleia,* which is the same word used by the disciples in Matt. 26:8 to speak of the "waste" (in their view) of the ointment that had just been poured on Jesus' head. Now the ointment did not cease to exist; it was very evident on Jesus' head. But it had been "destroyed" in the sense that it was no longer able to be used on someone else, or sold. In 1 Thess. 5:3 and 2 Thess. 1:9, another word, *olethros,* is used of the destruction of the wicked, but again this word does not imply that something will cease to exist, for it is used in 1 Cor. 5:5 of delivering a man to Satan (putting him out of the church) for the *destruction* of the flesh—but certainly his flesh did not cease to exist when he was put out of the church, even though he may have suffered in his body (this would be true whether we take "flesh" to mean his physical body or his sinful nature).

(2) With respect to the argument from the love of God, the same difficulty reconciling God's love with eternal punishment would seem to be present in reconciling God's love with the idea of divine punishment at all, and, conversely, if (as Scripture abundantly testifies) it is consistent for God to punish the wicked for a certain length of time after the last judgment, then there seems to be no necessary reason why it would be inconsistent of God to inflict the same punishment for an unending period of time.

This kind of reasoning may lead some people to adopt another kind of annihilationism, one in which there is no conscious suffering at all, not even for a brief time, and the only punishment is that unbelievers cease to exist after they die. But, in response, it may be wondered whether this kind of immediate annihilation can really be called a punishment, since there would be no consciousness of pain. In fact, the guarantee that there would be a cessation of existence would seem to many people, especially those who are suffering and in difficulty in this life, to be in some ways a desirable alternative. And if there was no punishment of unbelievers at all, even people like Hitler and Stalin would have nothing coming to them, and there would be no ultimate justice in the universe. Then people would have great incentive to be as wicked as possible in this life.

(3) The argument that *eternal* punishment is unfair (because there is a disproportion between temporary sin and eternal punishment) wrongly assumes that we know the extent of the evil done when sinners rebel against God. David Kingdon observes that "sin against the Creator is heinous to a degree utterly beyond our sin-warped imaginations' [ability] to conceive of.... Who would have the temerity to suggest to God what the punishment ... should be?"[7] He also responds to this objection by suggesting that unbelievers in hell may go on sinning and receiving punishment for their sin, but never repenting, and notes that Revelation 22:11 points in this direction: "Let the evildoer still do evil, and the filthy still be filthy."[8]

(4) Regarding the fourth argument, while evil *that remains unpunished* does detract from God's glory in the universe, we also must realize that when God *punishes* evil and *triumphs* over it, the glory of his justice, righteousness, and power to triumph over all opposition will be seen (see Rom. 9:17, 22–24). The depth of the riches of God's mercy will also then be revealed, for all redeemed sinners will recognize that they too deserve such punishment from God and have avoided it only by God's grace through Jesus Christ (cf. Rom. 9:23–24).

Yet after all this has been said, we have to admit that the ultimate resolution of the depths of this question lies far beyond our ability to understand, and remains hidden in the counsels of God. Were it not for the scriptural passages cited above that so clearly affirm eternal conscious punishment, annihilationism might seem to us to be an attractive option. Though annihilationism can be countered by theological arguments, it is ultimately the clarity and forcefulness of the passages themselves that convince us that annihilationism is incorrect and that Scripture does indeed teach the eternal conscious punishment of the wicked.

What are we to think of this doctrine? It is hard—and it should be hard—for us to think of this doctrine today. If our hearts are never moved with deep sorrow when we contemplate this doctrine, then there is a serious deficiency in our spiritual

---

[7]David Kingdon, "Annihilationism: Gain or Loss?" (March 1992; unpublished paper obtained from the author), p. 9.

[8]Ibid., pp. 9–10.

and emotional sensibilities. When Paul thinks of the lostness of his kinsmen the Jews, he says, "I have *great sorrow* and *unceasing anguish* in my heart" (Rom. 9:2). This is consistent with what God tells us of his own sorrow at the death of the wicked: "As I live, says the Lord God, *I have no pleasure in the death of the wicked,* but that the wicked turn from his way and live; turn back, turn back from your evil ways; for why will you die, O house of Israel?" (Ezek. 33:11). And Jesus' agony is evident as he cries out, "O Jerusalem, Jerusalem, killing the prophets and stoning those who are sent to you! How often would I have gathered your children together as a hen gathers her brood under her wings, and you would not! Behold, your house is forsaken and desolate" (Matt. 23:37–38; cf. Luke 19:41–42).

The reason it is hard for us to think of the doctrine of hell is because God has put in our hearts a portion of his own love for people created in his image, even his love for sinners who rebel against him. As long as we are in this life, and as long as we see and think about others who need to hear the gospel and trust in Christ for salvation, it should cause us great distress and agony of spirit to think about eternal punishment. Yet we must also realize that whatever God in his wisdom has ordained and taught in Scripture is *right.* Therefore, we must be careful that we not hate this doctrine or rebel against it, but rather we should seek, insofar as we are able, to come to the point where we acknowledge that eternal punishment is good and right, because in God there is no unrighteousness at all.

It may help us to realize that if God were not to execute eternal punishment, then, apparently, his justice would not be satisfied and his glory would not be furthered in the way he deems wise. And it will perhaps also help us to realize that from the perspective of the world to come there is a much greater recognition of the necessity and rightness of eternal punishment. Martyred believers in heaven are heard by John to cry out, "O sovereign Lord, holy and true, how long before you will judge and avenge our blood on those who dwell upon the earth?" (Rev. 6:10). Moreover, at the final destruction of Babylon, the loud voice of a great multitude in heaven cries out with praise to God for the rightness of his judgment as they finally see the heinous nature of evil for what it really is: "Hallelujah! Salvation and glory and power belong to our God, for his judgments are true and just; he has judged the great harlot who corrupted the earth with her fornication, and he has avenged on her the blood of his servants.... Hallelujah! The smoke from her goes up forever and ever" (Rev. 19:1–3). As soon as this happened, "the twenty-four elders and the four living creatures fell down and worshiped God who is seated on the throne, saying, 'Amen. Hallelujah!'" (Rev. 19:4). We cannot say that this great multitude of the redeemed and the living creatures in heaven have wrong moral judgment when they praise God for executing justice on evil, for they are all free from sin and their moral judgments are pleasing to God. They must see much more clearly than we do how terrible sin really is.

In this present age, however, we should only approach such a celebration of the punishment of evil when we meditate on the eternal punishment given to Satan and his demons. When we think of them, we do not instinctively love them, though they too were created by God. But now they are fully devoted to evil and beyond the potential of redemption. So we cannot long for their salvation as we long for the redemption of all humanity. We must believe that eternal punishment is true and just, yet we should also long that even those who most severely persecute the church should come to faith in Christ and thus escape eternal condemnation.

II. REVIEW QUESTIONS

1. Provide three scriptural evidences for the final judgment.

2. When will the final judgment occur?

3. How will the judgment of believers be different from that of unbelievers? Will the judgment of believers affect their legal standing before God? Explain.

4. Name four moral influences that the doctrine of final judgment should have on our lives.

5. Define *hell* and provide scriptural support for its existence.

6. What is "annihilationism"? Is this teaching scriptural? How would you respond to this teaching?

III. QUESTIONS FOR PERSONAL APPLICATION

1. Have you thought before that there will be a final judgment for believers? How do you think of it now? How does the awareness of the fact that we will all stand before the judgment seat of Christ affect your life today? What do you think it will feel like to have all your words and deeds made public on that last day? Is there an element of fear as you contemplate that day? If so, meditate on 1 John 4:16–18.

2. Have you previously thought very much about laying up treasures in heaven or about earning greater heavenly reward? If you really believe this doctrine, what kind of effect do you think it should have on your life?

3. Think of some of your Christian friends in your church. How do you think you will feel when you watch them stand before Christ at the final judgment? How will they feel about you at that time? Does the contemplation of this future judgment affect the way you think of your fellowship with each other as brothers and sisters in Christ today? Does the doctrine of final judgment help you to be more able to forgive people?

4. Are you glad that there will be a final judgment of both believers and unbelievers? Does it make you feel a sense of God's justice, or do you sense some unfairness and injustice in the whole idea?

5. Are you convinced that Scripture teaches that there will be eternal conscious punishment of the wicked? When you think of that idea in relationship to Satan and demons, do you feel that it is right?

IV. SPECIAL TERMS

annihilationism	final judgment
eternal conscious punishment	hell

V. SCRIPTURE MEMORY PASSAGE

REVELATION 20:11–13

Then I saw a great white throne and him who sat upon it; from his presence earth and sky fled away, and no place was found for them. And I saw the dead, great and small, standing before the throne, and books were opened. Also another book was opened, which is the book of life. And the dead were judged by what was written in the books, by what they had done. And the sea gave up the dead in it, Death and Hades gave up the dead in them, and all were judged by what they had done.

CHAPTER THIRTY-FOUR

The New Heavens and New Earth

+ *What is heaven?*
+ *Is it a place?*
+ *How will the earth be renewed?*
+ *What will it be like to live in the new heavens and new earth?*

I. EXPLANATION AND SCRIPTURAL BASIS

A. We Will Live Eternally with God in New Heavens and a New Earth

After the final judgment, believers will enter into the full enjoyment of life in the presence of God forever. Jesus will say to us, "Come, O blessed of my Father, inherit the kingdom prepared for you from the foundation of the world" (Matt. 25:34). We will enter a kingdom where "there shall no more be anything accursed, but the throne of God and of the Lamb shall be in it, and his servants shall worship him" (Rev. 22:3).

When referring to this place, Christians often talk about living with God "in heaven" forever. This is not wrong, but in fact the biblical teaching is richer than that: It tells us that there will be new heavens *and a new earth*—an entirely renewed creation—and we will live with God there.

The Lord promises through Isaiah, "For behold, I create *new heavens and a new earth;* and the former things shall not be remembered" (Isa. 65:17), and he speaks of "the new heavens and the new earth which I will make" (Isa. 66:22). Peter says, "According to his promise we wait for *new heavens and a new earth* in which righteousness dwells" (2 Peter 3:13). In John's vision of events to follow the final judgment, he says, "Then I saw a *new heaven and a new earth;* for the first heaven and the first earth had passed away" (Rev. 21:1). He goes on to tell us that there will also be a new kind of unification of heaven and earth, for he sees the holy city, the "new Jerusalem," coming "down out of heaven from God" (Rev. 21:2), and hears a voice proclaiming that "the dwelling of God is with men. He will dwell with them, and they shall be his people, and God himself will be with them" (v. 3). So there will be a joining of heaven and earth in this new creation, and there we will live in the presence of God.

1. What is heaven? During this present age, the place where God dwells is frequently called "heaven" in Scripture. The Lord says, "Heaven is my throne" (Isa.

66:1), and Jesus teaches us to pray, "Our Father who art in *heaven*" (Matt. 6:9). Jesus now "*has gone into heaven,* and is at the right hand of God" (1 Peter 3:22). In fact, heaven may be defined as follows: *Heaven is the place where God most fully makes known his presence to bless.*

We discussed earlier how God is present everywhere[1] but how he especially manifests his presence to bless in certain places. The greatest manifestation of God's presence to bless is seen in heaven, where he makes his glory known, and where angels, other heavenly creatures, and redeemed saints all worship him.

2. Heaven is a place, not just a state of mind. Someone may wonder how heaven can be joined together with earth. Clearly the earth is a *place* that exists at a certain location in our space-time universe, but can heaven also be thought of as a *place* that can be joined to the earth?

Outside of the evangelical world the idea of heaven as a place is often denied, chiefly on the ground that its existence can only be known from the testimony of Scripture. Recently, even some evangelical scholars have been hesitant to affirm that heaven is a place. Should the fact that we *only* know about heaven from the Bible and cannot give any empirical evidence for it be a reason not to believe that heaven is a real place?

The New Testament teaches the idea of a location for heaven in several different ways, and quite clearly. When Jesus ascended into heaven, the fact that he went to a *place* seems to be the entire point of the narrative, and this is the point that Jesus intended his disciples to understand by the way in which he gradually ascended even while speaking to them: "As they were looking on, he was lifted up, and a cloud took him out of their sight" (Acts 1:9; cf. Luke 24:51: "While he blessed them, he parted from them"). The angels exclaimed, "This Jesus, who was taken up from you *into heaven,* will come in the same way as you saw him go into heaven" (Acts 1:11). It is hard to imagine how the fact of Jesus' ascension to a *place* could be taught more clearly.

Admittedly, we cannot now see where Jesus is, but that is not because he passed into some ethereal "state of being" that has no location at all in the space-time universe, but rather because our eyes are unable to see the unseen spiritual world that exists all around us. There are angels around us, but we simply cannot see them because our eyes do not have that capacity: Elisha was surrounded by an army of angels and chariots of fire protecting him from the Syrians at Dothan, but Elisha's servant was not able to see those angels until God opened his eyes so that he could see things that existed in that spiritual dimension (2 Kings 6:17).

A similar conclusion can be drawn from the story of Stephen's death. Just before he was stoned, he, "full of the Holy Spirit, *gazed into heaven* and saw the glory of God, and Jesus standing at the right hand of God; and he said, 'Behold, I see the heavens opened, and the Son of Man standing at the right hand of God'" (Acts 7:55–56). He did not see mere symbols of a state of existence that is not in a place! It seems rather that his eyes were opened to see a spiritual dimension of reality that God has hidden from us in this present age, a dimension that nonetheless really does exist in our space-time universe and within which Jesus now lives in his physical resurrection body, waiting even now for the time when he will return to earth.[2] More-

---

[1]See ch. 4, pp. 78–81, on the omnipresence of God.

[2]See the discussion of Christ's resurrection body and his ascension in ch. 16, pp. 261–68.

over, the fact that we will have resurrection bodies like Christ's resurrection body indicates that heaven will be a place, for in such physical bodies (made perfect, never to become weak or die again),[3] we will inhabit a specific place at a specific time, just as Jesus now does in his resurrection body.

The idea of heaven as a place is also the easiest sense in which to understand Jesus' promise, "I go to prepare a *place* for you" (John 14:2). He speaks quite clearly of going from his existence in this world back to the Father, and then returning again: "When I go and prepare a *place* for you, I will come again and will take you to myself, that *where I am* you may be also" (John 14:3).

We cannot say exactly where heaven is. Scripture often pictures people as ascending up into heaven (as Jesus did, and Elijah) or coming down from heaven (as the angels in Jacob's dream, Gen. 28:12), so we are justified as thinking of heaven as somewhere "above" the earth. Admittedly the earth is round and it rotates, so where heaven is we are simply unable to say more precisely—Scripture does not tell us. But the repeated emphasis on the fact that Jesus went somewhere (as did Elijah, 2 Kings 2:11), and the fact that the New Jerusalem will come down from heaven from God (Rev. 21:2), all indicate that there is clearly a localization of heaven in the space-time universe. Those who do not believe in Scripture may scoff at such an idea and wonder how it can be so, just as the first Russian cosmonaut who came back from space and declared that he did not see God or heaven anywhere. But that simply points to the blindness of their eyes toward the unseen spiritual world; it does not indicate that heaven does not exist in a certain place.

These scriptural texts lead us to conclude that heaven is even now a place—though one whose location is now unknown to us and whose existence is now unable to be perceived by our natural senses. It is this place of God's dwelling that will be somehow made new at the time of the final judgment and will be joined to a renewed earth.

3. The physical creation will be renewed, and we will continue to exist and act in it. In addition to a renewed heaven, God will make a "new earth" (2 Peter 3:13; Rev. 21:1). Several passages indicate that the physical creation will be renewed in a significant way. "The creation waits with eager longing for the revealing of the sons of God; for the creation was subjected to futility, not of its own will but by the will of him who subjected it in hope; because *the creation itself will be set free from its bondage to decay and obtain the glorious liberty of the children of God*" (Rom. 8:19–21).

But will earth simply be renewed, or will it be completely destroyed and replaced by another earth, newly created by God? Some passages appear to speak of an entire new creation. For example, the author of Hebrews (quoting Ps. 102) tells us of the heavens and earth, "They will perish, but you remain; they will all grow old like a garment, like a mantle you will roll them up, and they will be changed" (Heb. 1:11–12). Later he tells us that God has promised, "Yet once more I will shake not only the earth but also the heaven," a shaking so severe as to involve "the removal of what is shaken . . . in order that what cannot be shaken may remain" (Heb. 12:26–27). Peter says, "The day of the Lord will come like a thief, and then *the heavens will pass away with a loud noise,* and the elements will be dissolved with fire, and *the earth and all the works that are upon it will be burned up*" (2 Peter 3:10). A similar picture is found in Revelation, where John says, "From his presence earth and sky fled away, and no place was found for them" (Rev. 20:11). Moreover, John says, "Then I saw

---

[3]See ch. 25, pp. 357–58, on the nature of our resurrection bodies.

a new heaven and a new earth; for the first heaven and the first earth had passed away, and the sea was no more" (Rev. 21:1).

Within the Protestant world, there has been disagreement as to whether the earth is to be destroyed completely and replaced or just changed and renewed. Berkhof says that Lutheran scholars have emphasized the fact that it will be an entirely new creation, while Reformed scholars have tended to emphasize those verses that say simply that this present creation will be renewed.[4] The Reformed position seems preferable here, for it is difficult to think that God would entirely annihilate his original creation, thereby seeming to give the devil the last word and scrapping the creation that was originally "very good" (Gen. 1:31). The passages above that speak of shaking and removing the earth and of the first earth passing away may simply refer to its existence in its present form, not its very existence itself, and even 2 Peter 3:10, which speaks of the elements dissolving and the earth and the works on it being burned up, may not be speaking of the earth as a planet but rather the surface things on the earth (that is, much of the ground and the things on the ground).

4. Our resurrection bodies will be part of the renewed creation. In the new heavens and new earth, there will be a place and activities for our resurrection bodies, which will never grow old or become weak or ill. A strong consideration in favor of this viewpoint is the fact that God made the original physical creation "very good" (Gen. 1:31). There is therefore nothing inherently sinful or evil or "unspiritual" about the physical world that God made or the creatures that he put in it, or about the physical bodies that he gave us at creation. Though all these things have been marred and distorted by sin, God will not completely destroy the physical world (which would be an acknowledgment that sin had frustrated and defeated God's purposes), but rather he will perfect the entire creation and bring it into harmony with the purposes for which he originally created it. Therefore, we can expect that in the new heavens and new earth there will be a fully perfect earth that is once again "very good." And we can expect that we will have physical bodies that will once again be "very good" in God's sight, and which will function to fulfill the purposes for which he originally placed man on the earth.

For that reason, it should not strike us as surprising to find that some of the descriptions of life in heaven include features that are very much part of the physical or material creation that God has made. We shall *eat and drink* at "the marriage supper of the Lamb" (Rev. 19:9). Jesus will once again *drink wine* with his disciples in the heavenly kingdom (Luke 22:18). The *"river* of the water of life" will flow "from the throne of God and of the Lamb through the middle of the *street of the city"* (Rev. 22:1). The *tree of life* will bear "twelve kinds of fruit, yielding its fruit each month" (Rev. 22:2). While there are, of course, symbolic descriptions in the book of Revelation, there is no strong reason to say these expressions are merely symbolic, without any literal reference. Are symbolic banquets and symbolic wine and symbolic rivers and trees somehow superior to real banquets and real wine and real rivers and trees in God's eternal plan? These things are just some of the excellent features of the perfection and final goodness of the physical creation that God has made.

Therefore, while we may have some uncertainty about the understanding of certain details, it does not seem inconsistent with this picture to say that we will eat and

---

[4]Louis Berkhof, *Introduction to Systematic Theology* (Grand Rapids: Eerdmans, 1932; reprint, Grand Rapids: Baker, 1979), p. 737.

drink in the new heavens and new earth, and carry on other physical activities as well. Music certainly is prominent in the descriptions of heaven in Revelation, and we might imagine that both musical and artistic activities would be done to the glory of God. It is not unlikely that people will continue to work at the whole range of investigation and development of the creation by technological, creative, and inventive means, thus exhibiting the full extent of their excellent creation in the image of God.

Moreover, since God is infinite and we can never exhaust his greatness (Ps. 145:3), and since we are finite creatures who will never equal God's knowledge or be omniscient, we may expect that for all eternity we will be able to go on learning more about God and about his relationship to his creation. In this way, we will continue the process of learning that was begun in this life, in which a life "fully pleasing to him" is one that includes continually "increasing in the knowledge of God" (Col. 1:10).

B. The Doctrine of the New Creation Provides a Great Motivation for Storing Up Treasures in Heaven Rather Than on Earth

When we consider that this present creation is a temporary one and that our life in the new creation will last for eternity, we have a strong motivation for godly living and for living in such a way as to store up treasures in heaven. In reflecting on the fact that heaven and earth will be destroyed, Peter says: "*Since all these things are thus to be dissolved, what sort of persons ought you to be in lives of holiness and godliness,* waiting for and hastening the coming of the day of God, because of which the heavens will be kindled and dissolved, and the elements will melt with fire! But according to his promise we wait for new heavens and a new earth in which righteousness dwells" (2 Peter 3:11–13). And Jesus very explicitly tells us: "Do not lay up for yourselves treasures on earth, where moth and rust consume and where thieves break in and steal, but *lay up for yourselves treasures in heaven,* where neither moth nor rust consumes and where thieves do not break in and steal. For where your treasure is, there will your heart be also" (Matt. 6:19–21).

C. The New Creation Will Be a Place of Great Beauty and Abundance and Joy in the Presence of God

Amid all the questions that we naturally have concerning the new heavens and new earth, we must not lose sight of the fact that Scripture consistently portrays this new creation as a place of great beauty and joy. In the description of heaven in Revelation 21 and 22, this theme is repeatedly affirmed. It is a "holy city" (21:2), a place "prepared as a bride adorned for her husband" (21:2). In that place "death shall be no more, neither shall there be mourning nor crying nor pain any more" (21:4). There we can drink "from the fountain of the water of life without payment" (21:6). It is a city "having the glory of God, its radiance like a most rare jewel, like a jasper, clear as crystal" (21:11). It is a city of immense size, whether the measurements be understood as literal or symbolic. Its length measures "12,000 stadia" (21:16), or about 1,400 miles, and "its length and breadth *and height* are equal" (21:6). Parts of the city are constructed of immense precious jewels of various colors (21:18–21). It will be free from all evil, for "nothing unclean shall enter it, nor anyone who practices abomination or falsehood, but only those who are written in the Lamb's book of life" (21:27). In that city we shall also have positions of rule over God's entire creation, for "they shall reign for ever and ever" (22:5).

But more important than all the physical beauty of the heavenly city, more important than the fellowship we will enjoy eternally with all God's people from all nations and all periods in history, more important than our freedom from pain and sorrow and physical suffering, and more important than reigning over God's kingdom—more important by far than any of these will be the fact that we will be in the presence of God and enjoying unhindered fellowship with him. "Behold, *the dwelling of God is with men.* He will dwell with them, and they shall be his people, and *God himself will be with them;* he will wipe away every tear from their eyes" (Rev. 21:3–4).

In the Old Testament, when the glory of God filled the temple, the priests were unable to stand and minister (2 Chron. 5:14). In the New Testament, when the glory of God surrounded the shepherds in the field outside Bethlehem, "they were filled with fear" (Luke 2:9). But here in the heavenly city, we will be able to endure the power and holiness of the presence of God's glory, for we will live continually in the atmosphere of the glory of God. "And the city has no need of sun or moon to shine upon it, *for the glory of God is its light, and its lamp is the Lamb*" (Rev. 21:23). This will be the fulfillment of God's purpose to call us "to his own glory and excellence" (2 Peter 1:3): Then we shall dwell continually in *"the presence of his glory with rejoicing"* (Jude 1:24; cf. Rom. 3:23; 8:18; 9:23; 1 Cor. 15:43; 2 Cor. 3:18; 4:17; Col. 3:4; 1 Thess. 2:12; Heb. 2:10; 1 Peter 5:1, 4, 10).

In that city we shall live in the presence of God, for "the throne of God and of the Lamb shall be in it, and his servants shall worship him" (Rev. 22:3). From time to time here on earth we experience the joy of genuine worship of God, and we realize that it is our highest joy to be giving him glory. But in that city, this joy will be multiplied many times over and we will know the fulfillment of that for which we were created. Our greatest joy will be in seeing the Lord himself and in being with him forever. When John speaks of the blessings of the heavenly city, the culmination of those blessings comes in the short statement, *"They shall see his face"* (22:4). When we look into the face of our Lord, we will see there the fulfillment of everything that we know to be good and right and desirable in the universe. In the face of God, we will see the fulfillment of all the longing we have ever had to know perfect love, peace, and joy, and to know truth and justice, holiness and wisdom, goodness and power, and glory and beauty. As we gaze into the face of our Lord, we will know more fully than ever before that *"in your presence there is fullness of joy, at your right hand are pleasures for evermore"* (Ps. 16:11). Then will be fulfilled the longing of our hearts with which we have cried out in the past,

> One thing have I asked of the LORD,
>   that will I seek after;
> that I may dwell in the house of the LORD
>   all the days of my life,
> *to behold the beauty of the LORD,*
>   and to inquire in his temple. (Ps. 27:4)

When we finally see the Lord face-to-face, our hearts will want nothing else. *"Whom have I in heaven but you?* And there is nothing upon earth that I desire besides you. . . . God is the strength of my heart and my portion forever" (Ps. 73:25–26). Then with joy our hearts and voices will join with the redeemed from all ages and with the mighty armies of heaven singing, "Holy, holy, holy, is the Lord God Almighty, who was and is and is to come!" (Rev. 4:8).

II. REVIEW QUESTIONS

1. Where will believers exist after the final judgment?
2. What is heaven? Is this an actual place?
3. Will the earth as we know it be destroyed? Support your answer from Scripture.
4. Will believers have a physical existence after the judgment? Explain.
5. What will be the most important characteristic of the new creation?

III. QUESTIONS FOR PERSONAL APPLICATION

1. Have you spent much time thinking about life in the new heavens and new earth? Do you think there is a very strong longing for this in your heart? If it has not been strong, why do you think this has been the case?
2. In what ways has this chapter made you more excited about entering the heavenly city? What positive effects on your Christian life do you think would come about because of a stronger longing for the life to come?
3. Are you convinced that the new creation is a place where we will exist with physical bodies that are made perfect? If so, are you encouraged or discouraged by this idea? Why? Why do you think it is necessary to insist that heaven is an actual place even today?
4. What are some ways in which you already have stored up treasure in heaven rather than on earth? Are there more ways you could do that in your own life now? Do you think you will?
5. Sometimes people have thought that they would be bored in the life to come. Do you feel that way yourself? What is a good answer to the objection that the eternal state will be boring?

IV. SPECIAL TERMS

heaven
new heavens and new earth

V. SCRIPTURE MEMORY PASSAGE

REVELATION 21:3–4

And I heard a loud voice from the throne saying, "Behold, the dwelling of God is with men. He will dwell with them, and they shall be his people, and God himself will be with them; he will wipe away every tear from their eyes, and death shall be no more, neither shall there be mourning nor crying nor pain any more, for the former things have passed away."

APPENDIX I

Historic Confessions of Faith

This appendix reprints three of the most significant confessions of faith from the ancient church: the Apostles' Creed (third–fourth centuries A.D.), the Nicene Creed (A.D. 325/381), and the Chalcedonian Creed (A.D. 451). I have also included the Chicago Statement on Biblical Inerrancy (1978) because it was the product of a conference representing a broad variety of evangelical traditions, and because it has gained widespread acceptance as a valuable doctrinal standard concerning an issue of recent and current controversy in the church.

THE APOSTLES' CREED
(third–fourth centuries A.D.)

I believe in God the Father Almighty; Maker of heaven and earth.

And in Jesus Christ his only Son our Lord; who was conceived by the Holy Spirit,[1] born of the virgin Mary; suffered under Pontius Pilate, was crucified, dead and buried;[2] the third day he rose from the dead; he ascended into heaven; and sitteth at the right hand of God the Father Almighty; from thence he shall come to judge the quick and the dead.

I believe in the Holy Spirit; the holy catholic Church; the communion of saints; the forgiveness of sins; the resurrection of the body; and the life everlasting. Amen.

THE NICENE CREED
(A.D. 325; revised at Constantinople A.D. 381)

I believe in one God the Father Almighty; Maker of heaven and earth, and of all things visible and invisible.

And in one Lord Jesus Christ, the only-begotten Son of God, begotten of the Father before all worlds, God of Gods, Light of Light, very God of very God, begotten, not made, being of one substance with the Father; by whom all things were made; who, for us men and for our salvation, came down from heaven, and was incarnate by the Holy Spirit of the Virgin Mary, and was made man; and was crucified also for us under Pontius Pilate; he suffered and was buried; and the third day he rose again, according to the Scriptures; and ascended into heaven, and sitteth on the right hand of the Father; and he shall come again, with glory, to judge both the quick and the dead; whose kingdom shall have no end.

---

[1]I have used the modern translation "Holy Spirit" instead of the archaic name "Holy Ghost" throughout the ancient creeds.

[2]I have not included the phrase "he descended into hell," because it is not attested in the earliest versions of the Apostles' Creed, and because of the doctrinal difficulties associated with it (see further discussion in ch. 15, pp. 257–58).

And in the Holy Spirit, the Lord and Giver of Life; who proceedeth from the Father and the Son;[3] who with the Father and the Son together is worshiped and glorified; who spake by the Prophets. And one Holy Catholic and Apostolic Church. I acknowledge one Baptism for the remission of sins; and I look for the resurrection of the dead, and the life of the world to come. Amen.

THE CHALCEDONIAN CREED
(A.D. 451)

We, then, following the holy Fathers, all with one consent, teach men to confess one and the same Son, our Lord Jesus Christ, the same perfect in Godhead and also perfect in manhood; truly God and truly man, of a reasonable soul and body; consubstantial with the Father according to the Godhead, and consubstantial with us according to the Manhood; in all things like unto us, without sin; begotten before all ages of the Father according to the Godhead, and in these latter days, for us and for our salvation, born of the Virgin Mary, the Mother of God, according to the Manhood; one and the same Christ, Son, Lord, Only-begotten, to be acknowledged in two natures, inconfusedly, unchangeably, indivisibly, inseparably; the distinction of natures being by no means taken away by the union, but rather the property of each nature being preserved, and concurring in one Person and one Subsistence, not parted or divided into two persons, but one and the same Son, and only begotten, God the Word, the Lord Jesus Christ, as the prophets from the beginning have declared concerning him, and the Lord Jesus Christ himself has taught us, and the Creed of the holy Fathers has handed down to us.

THE CHICAGO STATEMENT ON BIBLICAL INERRANCY
(1978)

Preface

The authority of Scripture is a key issue for the Christian Church in this and every age. Those who profess faith in Jesus Christ as Lord and Savior are called to show the reality of their discipleship by humbly and faithfully obeying God's written Word. To stray from Scripture in faith or conduct is disloyalty to our Master. Recognition of the total truth and trustworthiness of Holy Scripture is essential to a full grasp and adequate confession of its authority.

The following Statement affirms this inerrancy of Scripture afresh, making clear our understanding of it and warning against its denial. We are persuaded that to deny it is to set aside the witness of Jesus Christ and of Holy Spirit and to refuse that submission to the claims of God's own word which marks true Christian faith. We see it as our timely duty to make this affirmation in the face of current lapses from the truth of inerrancy among our fellow Christians and misunderstanding of this doctrine in the world at large.

This Statement consists of three parts: a Summary Statement, Articles of Affirmation and Denial, and an accompanying Exposition. It has been prepared in the course of a three-day consultation in Chicago. Those who have signed the Summary

---

[3]The phrase "and the Son" was added after the Council of Constantinople in 381 but is commonly included in the text of the Nicene Creed as used by Protestant and Roman Catholic churches today. The phrase is not included in the text used by Orthodox churches.

Statement and the Articles wish to affirm their own conviction as to the inerrancy of Scripture and to encourage and challenge one another and all Christians to growing appreciation and understanding of this doctrine. We acknowledge the limitations of a document prepared in a brief, intensive conference and do not propose that this Statement be given creedal weight. Yet we rejoice in the deepening of our own convictions through our discussions together, and we pray that the Statement we have signed may be used to the glory of our God toward a new reformation of the Church in its faith, life, and mission.

We offer this Statement in a spirit, not of contention, but of humility and love, which we purpose by God's grace to maintain in any future dialogue arising out of what we have said. We gladly acknowledge that many who deny the inerrancy of Scripture do not display the consequences of this denial in the rest of their belief and behavior, and we are conscious that we who confess this doctrine often deny it in life by failing to bring our thoughts and deeds, our traditions and habits, into true subjection to the divine Word.

We invite responses to this statement from any who see reason to amend its affirmations about Scripture by the light of Scripture itself, under whose infallible authority we stand as we speak. We claim no personal infallibility for the witness we bear, and for any help which enables us to strengthen this testimony to God's Word we shall be grateful.

A Short Statement

1. God, who is Himself Truth and speaks truth only, has inspired Holy Scripture in order thereby to reveal Himself to lost mankind through Jesus Christ as Creator and Lord, Redeemer and Judge. Holy Scripture is God's witness to Himself.

2. Holy Scripture, being God's own Word, written by men prepared and superintended by His Spirit, is of infallible divine authority in all matters upon which it touches: it is to be believed, as God's instruction, in all that it affirms; obeyed, as God's command, in all that it requires; embraced, as God's pledge, in all that it promises.

3. The Holy Spirit, Scripture's divine Author, both authenticates it to us by His inward witness and opens our minds to understand its meaning.

4. Being wholly and verbally God-given, Scripture is without error or fault in all its teaching, no less in what it states about God's acts in creation, about the events of world history, and about its own literary origins under God, than in its witness to God's saving grace in individual lives.

5. The authority of Scripture is inescapably impaired if this total divine inerrancy is in any way limited or disregarded, or made relative to a view of truth contrary to the Bible's own; and such lapses bring serious loss to both the individual and the Church.

Articles of Affirmation and Denial
Article I

We affirm that the Holy Scriptures are to be received as the authoritative Word of God.

We deny that the Scriptures receive their authority from the Church, tradition, or any other human source.

Article II

We affirm that the Scriptures are the supreme written norm by which God binds the conscience, and that the authority of the Church is subordinate to that of Scripture.

We deny that Church creeds, councils, or declarations have authority greater than or equal to the authority of the Bible.

Article III

We affirm that the written Word in its entirety is revelation given by God.

We deny that the Bible is merely a witness to revelation, or only becomes revelation in encounter, or depends on the responses of men for its validity.

Article IV

We affirm that God who made mankind in His image has used language as a means of revelation.

We deny that human language is so limited by our creatureliness that it is rendered inadequate as a vehicle for divine revelation. We further deny that the corruption of human culture and language through sin has thwarted God's work of inspiration.

Article V

We affirm that God's revelation in the Holy Scriptures was progressive.

We deny that later revelation, which may fulfill earlier revelation, ever corrects or contradicts it. We further deny that any normative revelation has been given since the completion of the New Testament writings.

Article VI

We affirm that the whole of Scripture and all its parts, down to the very words of original, were given by divine inspiration.

We deny that the inspiration of Scripture can rightly be affirmed of the whole without the parts, or of some parts but not the whole.

Article VII

We affirm that inspiration was the work in which God by His Spirit, through human writers, gave us His Word. The origin of Scripture is divine. The mode of divine inspiration remains largely a mystery to us.

We deny that inspiration can be reduced to human insight, or to heightened states of consciousness of any kind.

Article VIII

We affirm that God in His Work of inspiration utilized the distinctive personalities and literary styles of the writers whom He had chosen and prepared.

We deny that God, in causing these writers to use the very words that He chose, overrode their personalities.

Article IX

We affirm that inspiration, though not conferring omniscience, guaranteed true and trustworthy utterance on all matters of which the Bible authors were moved to speak and write.

We deny that the finitude or fallenness of these writers, by necessity or otherwise, introduced distortion or falsehood into God's Word.

Article X

We affirm that inspiration, strictly speaking, applies to the autographic text of Scripture, which in the providence of God can be ascertained from available manuscripts with great accuracy. We further affirm that copies and translations of Scripture are the Word of God to the extent that they faithfully represent the original.

We deny that any essential element of the Christian faith is affected by the absence of the autographs. We further deny that this absence renders the assertion of Biblical inerrancy invalid or irrelevant.

Article XI

We affirm that Scripture, having been given by divine inspiration, is infallible, so that, far from misleading us, it is true and reliable in all matters it addresses.

We deny that it is possible for the Bible to be at the same time infallible and errant in its assertions. Infallibility and inerrancy may be distinguished, but not separated.

Article XII

We affirm that Scripture in its entirety is inerrant, being free from all falsehood, fraud, or deceit.

We deny that Biblical infallibility and inerrancy are limited to spiritual, religious or redemptive themes, exclusive of assertions in the fields of history and science. We further deny that scientific hypotheses about earth history may properly be used to overturn the teaching of Scripture on creation and the flood.

Article XIII

We affirm the propriety of using inerrancy as a theological term with reference to the complete truthfulness of Scripture.

We deny that it is proper to evaluate Scripture according to standards of truth and error that are alien to its usage or purpose. We further deny that inerrancy is negated by Biblical phenomena such as a lack of modern technical precision, irregularities of grammar or spelling, observational descriptions of nature, the reporting of falsehoods, the use of hyperbole and round numbers, the topical arrangement of material, variant selections of material in parallel accounts, or the use of free citations.

Article XIV

We affirm the unity and internal consistency of Scripture.

We deny that alleged errors and discrepancies that have not yet been resolved vitiate the truth of claims of the Bible.

Article XV

We affirm that the doctrine of inerrancy is grounded in the teaching of the Bible about inspiration.

We deny that Jesus' teaching about Scripture may be dismissed by appeals to accommodation or to any natural limitation of His humanity.

Article XVI

We affirm that the doctrine of inerrancy has been integral to the Church's faith throughout its history.

We deny that inerrancy is a doctrine invented by Scholastic Protestantism, or is a reactionary position postulated in response to negative higher criticism.

Article XVII

We affirm that the Holy Spirit bears witness to the Scriptures, assuring believers of the truthfulness of God's written Word.

We deny that this witness of the Holy Spirit operates in isolation from or against Scripture.

Article XVIII

We affirm that the text of Scripture is to be interpreted by grammatico-historical exegesis, taking account of its literary forms and devices, and that Scripture is to interpret Scripture.

We deny the legitimacy of any treatment of the text or quest for sources lying behind it that leads to relativizing, dehistoricizing, or discounting its teaching, or rejecting its claims to authorship.

Article XIX

We affirm that a confession of the full authority, infallibility, and inerrancy of Scripture is vital to a sound understanding of the whole of the Christian faith. We further affirm that such confession should lead to increasing conformity to the image of Christ.

We deny that such confession is necessary for salvation. However, we further deny that inerrancy can be rejected without grave consequences, both to the individual and to the Church.

Appendix 2

Glossary

Numbers in parentheses refer to the chapter and section where the term is discussed.

absolute authority. The highest authority in one's life; an authority that cannot be disproved by appeal to any higher authority. (2A)

active obedience. Christ's perfect obedience to God during his entire earthly life, which earned the righteousness that God credits to those who place their faith in Christ. (15C.1)

adoption. An act of God whereby he makes us members of his family. (22F)

amillennialism. The view that there will be no literal thousand-year bodily reign of Christ on earth prior to the final judgment and the eternal state. In this view, scriptural references to the millennium in Revelation 20 are understood to describe the present church age. (32A.1)

angel. A created spiritual being with moral judgment and high intelligence but without a physical body. (10A)

annihilationism. The teaching that after death unbelievers suffer the penalty of God's wrath for a time and then are "annihilated," or destroyed, so that they no longer exist. Some forms of this teaching hold that annihilation occurs immediately upon death. (33G)

antichrist. The "man of lawlessness" who will appear prior to the second coming of Christ and will cause great suffering and persecution, only to be destroyed by Jesus. The term is also used to describe other figures who embody such an opposition to Christ and are precursors of the final antichrist. (31F.3.e)

Apollinarianism. The fourth-century heresy that held that Christ had a human body but not a human mind or spirit, and that the mind and spirit of Christ were from the divine nature of the Son of God. (14C.1.a)

apologetics. The discipline that seeks to provide a defense of the truthfulness of the Christian faith for the purpose of convincing unbelievers. (1A.1)

apostle. A recognized office of the early church. Apostles were the New Testament counterparts to the Old Testament prophets and as such had the authority to write words of Scripture. (30A.1)

archangel. An angel with authority over other angels. (10A.4)

Arianism. The erroneous doctrine that denies the full deity of Jesus Christ and the Holy Spirit. (6C.2)

Arminianism. A theological tradition that seeks to preserve the free choices of human beings and denies God's providential control over the details of all events. (8E)

ascension. The rising of Jesus from the earth into heaven forty days after his resurrection. (16B.1)

asceticism. An approach to living that renounces many comforts of the material world and practices rigid self-denial. (7D)

aseity. Another name for the attribute of God's independence or self-existence. (4D.1)

assurance of salvation. The confidence we may have based on certain evidences in our lives that we are truly born again and will persevere as Christians until the end of our lives. (24D)

atonement. The work Christ did in his life and death to earn our salvation. (15)

attributes of being. Aspects of God's character that describe his essential mode of existence. (5A)

attributes of purpose. Aspects of God's character that pertain to making and carrying out decisions. (5D)

authority of Scripture. The idea that all the words in Scripture are God's words in such a way that to disbelieve or disobey any word of Scripture is to disbelieve or disobey God. (2)

beauty. The attribute of God whereby he is the sum of all desirable qualities. (5E.16)

belief. In contemporary culture, this term usually refers to the acceptance of the truth of something, such as facts about Christ, with no necessary element of trust in Christ as a person. In the New Testament, this term often includes a sense of personal trust in or reliance on Christ (or, in other verses, trust in God the Father and reliance on him) (see John 3:16; see also "faith"). (21A.3)

believable profession of faith. A central component of the "Baptistic" view of baptism, which holds that only those who have given reasonable evidence of believing in Christ should be baptized. (27B)

believer's baptism. The view that baptism is appropriately administered only to those who give a believable profession of faith in Jesus Christ. (27B)

biblical theology. The study of the teaching of the individual authors and sections of the Bible and of the place of each teaching in the historical development of the Bible. (1A.1)

blameless. Morally perfect in God's sight, a characteristic of those who follow God's Word completely (Ps. 119:1). (3C)

blessedness. The attribute of God whereby he delights fully in himself and in all that reflects his character. (5E.15)

body of Christ. Scriptural metaphor for the church. This image is used for two different metaphors in the New Testament, one to stress the interdependence of the members of the body and one to stress Christ's headship of the church. (26A.4)

born again. Scriptural term (John 3:3–8) referring to God's work of regeneration by which he imparts new spiritual life to us. (20A)

born of the Spirit. Another term for regeneration that indicates the special role played by the Holy Spirit in imparting new spiritual life to us. (20C)

born of water. Phrase used by Jesus in John 3:5 that refers to the spiritual cleansing from sin that accompanies God's work of regeneration (cf. Ezek. 36:25–26). (20C)

Calvinism. A theological tradition named after the sixteenth-century French reformer John Calvin (1509–64) that emphasizes the sovereignty of God in all things and man's inability to do spiritual good before God. (8)

certain knowledge. Knowledge that is established beyond doubt or question. Because God alone knows all the facts of the universe and never lies, the only absolutely certain knowledge we can have in this age is found in God's words in Scripture. (3B.3)

cessationist. Someone who thinks that certain miraculous spiritual gifts (such as healing, prophecy, tongues, and interpretation of tongues) ceased when the apostles died and Scripture was complete. (29B)

Chalcedonian Definition. The statement produced by the Council of Chalcedon in A.D. 451, which has been regarded by most branches of Christianity as the orthodox definition of the biblical teaching on the person of Christ. (14.C.2; appendix)

charismatic. Term referring to any groups or people that trace their historical origin to the charismatic renewal movement of the 1960s and 1970s, seek to practice all the spiritual gifts mentioned in the New Testament, and allow differing viewpoints on whether baptism in the Holy Spirit is subsequent to conversion and whether tongues is a sign of baptism in the Holy Spirit. (29)

cherubim. A class of created spiritual beings who once guarded the entrance to the Garden of Eden and over whom God is enthroned. (10A.3.a)

Christian ethics. Any study that answers the question, "What does God require us to feel, think, and do today?" with regard to any given situation. (1A.1)

church. The community of all true believers for all time. (26A.1)

circular argument. An argument that seeks to prove its conclusion by appealing to a claim that depends on the truth of the conclusion. (2A.5)

clarity of Scripture. The idea that the Bible is written in such a way that its teachings are able to be understood by all who will read it seeking God's help and are willing to follow it. (3A.3)

common grace. The grace of God by which he gives people innumerable blessings that are not part of salvation. (17A)

communicable attributes. Aspects of God's character that he more fully shares or "communicates" with us. (4C)

Communion. Term commonly used to refer to the Lord's Supper. (28C.1)

compatibilism. Another term for the Reformed view of providence. The term indicates that absolute divine sovereignty is compatible with human significance and real human choices. (8A)

complementarian. The view that men and women are equal in value before God but have different roles in marriage and the church; specifically, that there is a unique leadership role for the husband in marriage and that some governing and teaching roles in the church are reserved for men. (12C.2.i)

concurrence. An aspect of God's providence whereby he cooperates with created things in every action, directing their distinctive properties to cause them to act as they do. (8B)

consequent absolute necessity. The view that the atonement was not absolutely necessary, but as a "consequence" of God's decision to save some human beings, the atonement was absolutely necessary, because there was no other way God could save any sinners except through the death and resurrection of his Son. (15B)

contradiction. A set of two statements, one of which denies the other. (1D.3)

conversion. Our willing response to the gospel call, in which we sincerely repent of sins and place our trust in Christ for salvation. (21)

covenant community. The community of God's people. Protestant proponents of infant baptism view baptism as a sign of entrance into the "covenant community" of God's people. (27B.4)

creation. The doctrine that God created the entire universe out of nothing; it was originally very good; and he created it to glorify himself. (7)

Darwinian evolution. The general theory of evolution (see also "macro-evolution") named after Charles Darwin, the British naturalist who expounded this theory in his *Origin of Species by Means of Natural Selection* in 1859. (7E.2.c.1)

death. The termination of our bodily life brought about by the entrance of sin into the world. (For the Christian, death brings us into the presence of God because of Christ's payment of the penalty for our sins.) (25A)

decrees of God. The eternal plans of God whereby, before the creation of the world, he determined to bring about everything that happens. (5D.12.b; 6D.1)

deism. The view that God created the universe but is not now directly involved in it. (7B)

demon possession. A misleading phrase found in some English translations of the Bible that seems to suggest that a person's will is completely dominated by a demon. The Greek term *daimonizomai* is better translated "under demonic influence," which could range from mild to strong influence or attack. (10F.3)

demonized. To be under demonic influence (Gk. *daimonizomai*); in the New Testament, the term often suggests more extreme cases of demonic influence. (10F.3)

demons. Evil angels who sinned against God and who now continually work evil in the world. (10D)

depravity. Another term for "inherited corruption." (13C.2)

determinism. The idea that acts, events, and decisions are the inevitable results of some condition or decision prior to them that is independent of the human will. (18C.2.d)

dichotomy. The view that man is made up of two parts—body and soul/spirit. (11D.1)

dictation. The idea that God expressly spoke every word of Scripture to the human authors. (2A.6)

difference in role. The idea that men and women have been given by God different primary functions in the family and the church. (12C)

discerning of spirits. Another term for distinguishing between spirits. (29A.3)

dispensational premillennialism. Another term for "pretribulational premillennialism." The term *dispensational* is used because most proponents of this view wish to maintain a clear distinction between the church and Israel, with whom God deals under different arrangements, or "dispensations." (32C.2)

dispensationalism. A theological system that began in the nineteenth century with the writings of J. N. Darby (1800–1882). Among the general doctrines of this system are the distinction between Israel and the church as two groups in God's overall plan, the pretribulational rapture of the church, a future literal fulfillment of Old Testament prophecies concerning Israel, and the dividing of biblical history into seven periods or "dispensations" of God's ways of relating to his people. (32C.2)

distinguishing between spirits. A special ability to recognize the influence of the Holy Spirit or of demonic spirits in a person. (29A.3)

distortion of roles. The idea that in the punishments God gave to Adam and Eve after their sin, he did not introduce new roles or functions, but simply introduced pain and distortion into the functions they previously had. (12C.2.g)

docetism. The heretical teaching that Jesus was not really a man, but only seemed to be one (from the Greek verb *dokeō*, "to seem, to appear to be"). (14A.5)

doctrine. What the whole Bible teaches us today about some particular topic. (1A.4)

dualism. The idea that both God and the material universe (or some evil force) have eternally existed side by side as two ultimate forces in the universe. (7B; also 13B)

economic subordination. The teaching that certain members of the Trinity have roles or functions that are subject to the authority of other members; specifically, that the Son is eternally subject to the Father, and the Holy Spirit is eternally subject to the Father and Son. (To be distinguished from ontological subordination or subordinationism, an erroneous teaching that has been rejected by the church.) (6D.2)

effective calling. An act of God the Father, speaking through the human proclamation of the gospel, in which he summons people to himself in such a way that they respond in saving faith. (19A)

egalitarian. The view that all functions and roles in the family and the church are open to men and women alike (except those based on physical differences, such as bearing children). Specifically, egalitarianism holds that there is no unique leadership role for the husband in marriage and that no governing or teaching roles in the church are reserved for men. (12C.2.i)

ekklēsia. Greek term translated "church" in the New Testament. The word literally means "assembly" and in the Bible indicates the assembly or congregation of the people of God. (26A.1)

election. An act of God before creation in which he chose some people to be saved, not on account of any foreseen merit in them, but only because of his sovereign good pleasure. (18)

equality in personhood. The idea that men and women are both created in God's image and therefore are equally important to God and equally valuable to him. (12B)

eschatology. The study of "the last things," or future events (from Gk. *eschatos*, "last"). (31)

eternal conscious punishment. Description of the nature of punishment in hell, which will be unending and of which the wicked will be aware. (33G)

eternal security. Another term for "perseverance of the saints." However, this term can be misunderstood to mean that all who have once made a profession of faith are "eternally secure" in their salvation when they may not have been genuinely converted at all. (24D.3)

eternity. When used of God, the doctrine that God has no beginning, end, or succession of moments in his own being, and that he sees all time equally vividly yet sees events in time and acts in time. (4D.3)

ethics. See "Christian ethics."

Eucharist. Another term for the Lord's Supper (from Gk. *eucharistia*, "giving of thanks"). (28C.1)

Eutychianism. Another term for monophysitism, named after the fifth-century monk Eutyches. (14C.1.c)

evangelism. The proclamation of the gospel to unbelievers (from Gk. *Euangelizō,* "to announce good news"). (19)

ex nihilo. Latin phrase meaning "out of nothing." Refers to God's creation of the universe "out of nothing," or without the use of any previously existing materials. (7A.1)

ex opere operato. Latin phrase meaning "by the work performed." In Roman Catholic teaching the phrase is used to indicate that the sacraments (such as baptism or the Eucharist) are effective because of the actual activity done, and this effectiveness does not depend on a subjective attitude of faith in the participants. (28C.1)

example theory. The view that in the atonement Christ did not bear the just penalty of God for our sins but that he simply provided us with an example of how we should trust and obey God perfectly, even if this leads to death. (15C.2.d.[3])

exegesis. The process of interpreting a text of Scripture. (3A.4)

external calling. The general gospel invitation offered to all people that comes through human proclamation of the gospel. Also referred to as "general calling" or "the gospel call," this call can be rejected by people. (19A)

faith. Trust or dependence on God based on the fact that we take him at his word and believe what he has said (see also "saving faith"). (9C.2; 21A.3)

faith and practice. Some people who deny the inerrancy of the Bible claim that the Bible's purpose is only to tell us about these two subjects. (2D.2.a)

faithfulness. The attribute of God whereby he will always do what he has said and will fulfill what he has promised. (5B.5)

fatalism. A system in which human choices and human decisions make no real difference because things will turn out as they have been previously ordained. This is in contrast to the biblical doctrines of providence and election, in which people make real choices that have real consequences and for which they will be held accountable. (18C.1)

final judgment. The last and ultimate proclamation by Jesus Christ of the eternal destinies of all people, which will take place after the millennium and the rebellion that occurs at the end of it. (33A)

first fruits. The first portion of a ripening harvest (Gk. *Aparchē*). In describing Christ in his resurrection as the "first fruits" (1 Cor. 15:20), the Bible indicates that our resurrection bodies will be like his when God raises us from the dead. (16A.4.c)

foreknowledge. Relative to the doctrine of election, the personal, relational knowledge by which God thought of certain people in a saving relationship to himself before creation. This is to be distinguished from the mere knowledge of facts about a person. (18C.2.a)

forensic. Having to do with legal proceedings; used to describe justification as being a legal declaration by God that in itself does not change our internal nature or character. (22A)

free choices. Choices made according to our free will (see "free will").

free will. The ability to make willing choices that have real effects (however, other people define this in other ways, including the ability to make choices that are not determined by God). (8B.9)

freedom. The attribute of God whereby he does whatever he pleases. (5D.12.b)

general eschatology. The study of future events that will affect the entire universe, such as the second coming of Christ, the millennium, and the final judgment. (31)

general revelation. The knowledge of God's existence, character, and moral law, which comes through creation to all humanity. (3B.4)

gifts of the Holy Spirit. All abilities that are empowered by the Holy Spirit and used in any ministry of the church. (29A)

glorification. The final step in the application of redemption. It will happen when Christ returns and raises from the dead the bodies of all believers for all time who have died, and reunites them with their souls, and changes the bodies of all believers who remain alive, thereby giving all believers at the same time perfect resurrection bodies like his own. (25D)

God. In the New Testament, a translation of the Greek word *theos,* which is usually, but not always, used to refer to God the Father. (14B.1.a)

God-breathed. Translation of the Greek word *theopneustos* (sometimes translated "inspired by God"), which the Bible (2 Tim. 3:16) uses metaphorically to describe the words of Scripture as being spoken by God. (2A.1)

goodness. The attribute of God whereby he is the final standard of good and all that he is and does is worthy of approval. (5C.6)

gospel call. The general gospel invitation to all people that comes through human proclamation of the gospel. Also referred to as "external calling." (19A)

government. An aspect of God's providence that indicates that God has a purpose in all he does in the world and that he providentially governs or directs all things so they accomplish his purposes. (8C)

governmental theory. The theory that Christ's death was not a payment for our sins but God's demonstration of the fact that, since he is the moral governor of the universe, some kind of penalty must be paid whenever his laws are broken. (15C.2.d.[4])

grace. God's goodness toward those who deserve only punishment. (5C.6)

Great Commission. The final commands of Jesus to the disciples recorded in Matthew 28:18–20. (1C.1)

great tribulation. Expression from Matthew 24:21 referring to a period of great hardship and suffering prior to the return of Christ. (32E)

healing. A gift of the Holy Spirit that functions to bring a restoration to health as a foretaste of the complete freedom from physical weakness and infirmity that Christ purchased for us by his death and resurrection. (30C)

heaven. The place where God most fully makes known his presence to bless. It is in heaven where God most fully reveals his glory and where angels, other heavenly creatures, and redeemed saints all worship him. (34A.1)

hell. A place of eternal conscious punishment for the wicked. (33G)

hermeneutics. The study of correct methods of interpreting texts. (3A.4)

historic premillennialism. The view that Christ will return to the earth after a period of great tribulation and establish a millennial kingdom. At this time, believers who have died will be raised from the dead and believers who are alive will receive glorified resurrection bodies, and both will reign with Christ on earth for a thousand years. (32C.1; 32E)

historical theology. The historical study of how Christians in different periods since the time of the New Testament have understood various theological topics. (1A.1)

holiness. The attribute of God whereby he is separated from sin and devoted to seeking his own honor. (5C.8)

Holy Spirit. One of the three persons of the Trinity, whose work is to manifest the active presence of God in the world, and especially in the church. (17)

homoiousios. Greek word meaning "of a similar nature," which was used by Arius in the fourth century to affirm that Christ was a supernatural heavenly being but not of the *same* nature as God the Father. (6C.2)

homoousios. A Greek word meaning "of the same nature," which was included in the Nicene Creed to teach that Christ was of the exact same nature as God the Father and therefore was fully divine as well as fully human. (6C.2)

image of God. The nature of man such that he is like God and represents God. (11C)

immanent. Existing or remaining in; used in theology to speak of God's involvement in creation. (7B)

immersion. The mode of baptism in the New Testament in which the person was put completely underwater and then brought back up again. (27A)

imminent. Refers to the fact that Christ could return and might return at any time, and that we are to be prepared for him to come at any day. (31F.1)

immutability. Another term for God's unchangeableness. (4D.2)

impassibility. The doctrine, often based on a misunderstanding of Acts 14:15, that God does not have passions or emotions. Scripture instead teaches that God does have emotions, but he does not have sinful passions or emotions. (4D.2.c)

impeccability. The doctrine that Christ was not able to sin. (14A.4)

impute. To think of as belonging to someone and therefore to cause it to belong to that person. God "thinks of" Adam's sin as belonging to us, and it therefore belongs to us. In justification, God thinks of Christ's righteousness as belonging to us, and on that basis he declares that it belongs to us, and therefore it does (13C.1; 22C)

"in Jesus' name." Refers to prayer made on Jesus' authorization and consistent with his character. (9B.3)

"in, with, and under." Phrase descriptive of the Lutheran view of the Lord's Supper, which holds, not that the bread actually becomes the physical body of Christ, but that the physical body of Christ is present "in, with, and under" the bread of the Lord's Supper. (28C.2)

incarnation. The act of God the Son whereby he took to himself a human nature. (14B)

incommunicable attributes. Aspects of God's character that he less fully shares with us. (4C)

incomprehensible. Not able to be fully understood. As this applies to God, it means that nothing about God can be understood fully or exhaustively, although we can know true things about God. (4B.1)

incorruptible. The nature of our future resurrection bodies, which will be like Christ's resurrection body and therefore will not wear out, grow old, or be subject to any kind of sickness or disease. (16A.4.c)

independence. The attribute of God whereby he does not need us or the rest of creation for anything, yet we and the rest of creation can glorify him and bring him joy. (4D.1)

inerrancy. The idea that Scripture in the original manuscripts does not affirm anything that is contrary to fact. (2D.1)

infallibility. The idea that Scripture is not able to lead us astray in matters of faith and practice. (2D.2.a)

infant baptism. See "paedobaptism."

infinite. When used of God, refers to the fact that he is not subject to any of the limitations of humanity or of creation in general. (4D.2.d)

infinity with respect to space. Another term for God's omnipresence. (4D.4)

infinity with respect to time. Another term for God's eternity. (4D.3)

infused righteousness. Righteousness that God actually puts into us and that changes us internally. The Roman Catholic Church understands justification to be based on such an infusion, which differs from Protestantism's view that justification is a legal declaration by God based on imputed righteousness. (22C)

inherited corruption. The sinful nature, or the tendency to sin, which all people inherit because of Adam's sin (often referred to as "original pollution"). This idea entails that (1) in our nature we totally lack spiritual good before God, and (2) in our actions we are totally unable to do spiritual good before God. (13C.2)

inherited guilt. The idea that God counts all people guilty because of Adam's sin (often referred to as "original guilt"). (13C.1)

inherited sin. The guilt and the tendency to sin that all people inherit because of Adam's sin (often referred to as "original sin"). Inherited sin includes both inherited guilt and inherited corruption. (13C)

inner sense of God. An instinctive awareness of God's existence possessed by every human being. (4A)

inspiration. Refers to the fact that the words of Scripture are spoken by God. Because of the weak sense of this word in ordinary usage, this text prefers the term "God-breathed" to indicate that the words of Scripture are spoken by God. (2A.1)

intelligent design. The view that God directly created the world and its many life forms, which stands against the view that new species came about through an evolutionary process of random mutation. (7E.2.b)

intermediate state. The state of a person between his or her death and the time that Christ returns to give believers new resurrection bodies. In the intermediate state, believers exist as spirits without physical bodies. (25)

internal calling. Another term for "effective calling." (19A)

interpretation of tongues. The gift of the Holy Spirit by which the general meaning of something spoken in tongues is reported to the church. (30D.2.e)

invisible church. The church as God sees it. (26A.2)

invisibility. The attribute of God whereby his total essence, all of his spiritual being, will never be able to be seen by us, yet God still shows himself to us through visible, created things. (5A.2)

irresistible grace. The action of God whereby he effectively calls people and also gives them regeneration, both of which guarantee that we will respond in saving faith. This term is subject to misunderstanding since it *seems* to imply that people do not make a voluntary, willing choice in responding to the gospel. (20A)

jealousy. The doctrine that God continually seeks to protect his own honor. (5C.10)

judgment. See "final judgment."

justice. Another term for God's righteousness. (5C.9)

justification. An instantaneous legal act of God in which he (1) thinks of our sins as forgiven and Christ's righteousness as belonging to us, and (2) declares us to be righteous in his sight. (22)

kenosis theory. The erroneous theory that Christ gave up some of his divine attributes while he was on earth as a man (from the Greek verb *kenoō*, which means "to empty"). (14B.3)

knowable. Refers to the fact that we can know true things about God, and we can know God himself and not simply facts about him. (4B)

knowledge. The attribute of God whereby he fully knows himself and all things actual and possible in one simple and eternal act. (5B.3)

likeness. Refers to something that is similar but not identical to the thing it represents (Heb. *demût* in Gen. 1:26: Man was made after God's "likeness"). (11C.1)

living creatures. A class of created spiritual beings with appearances like a lion, an ox, a man, and an eagle, who are said to worship around the throne of God. (10A.3.c)

Lord. In the New Testament, a translation of the Greek word *kyrios,* which is usually, but not always, used to refer to Christ. In the Greek translation of the Old Testament, this word is used to translate the Hebrew *yhwh,* the personal name of the omnipotent God. (14B.1.b)

Lord's Supper. One of the two ordinances that Jesus commanded his church to observe. This is an ordinance to be observed repeatedly throughout our Christian lives, as a sign of continuing in fellowship with Christ. (28)

love. When used of God, the doctrine that God eternally gives of himself to others. (5C.7)

macro-evolution. The "general theory of evolution," or the view that nonliving substance gave rise to the first living material, which then reproduced and diversified to produce all living things that now exist or ever existed in the past. (7E.2.c.[1])

major doctrine. A doctrine that has a significant impact on our thinking about other doctrines or that has a significant impact on how we live the Christian life. (1A.5)

Maranatha. Aramaic term used in 1 Corinthians 16:22 meaning "Our Lord, come," expressing eager longing for Christ's return. (31B)

marks of the church. The distinguishing characteristics of a true church. In Protestant tradition, these have usually been recognized as the right preaching of the Word of God and the right administration of the sacraments (baptism and the Lord's Supper). (26B.1)

materialism. The view that the material universe is all that exists. (7B)

mediator. The role that Jesus plays in coming between God and us, enabling us to come into the presence of God. (9B.2)

mental attributes. The aspects of God's character that describe the nature of his knowing and reasoning. (5B)

mercy. God's goodness toward those in misery and distress. (5C.6)

Michael. An archangel who appears as a leader in the angelic army. (10A.4)

micro-evolution. The view that small developments occur within individual species without creating any new species. (7E.2.c.[1])

millennium. The period of one thousand years (mentioned in Rev. 20:4–5) when Christ will be physically present and reign in perfect peace and justice over the earth (from Lat. *millennium*, "thousand years"). (32)

minor doctrine. A doctrine that has very little impact on how we think about other doctrines and that has very little impact on how we live the Christian life. (1A.5)

modalism. The heretical teaching that holds that God is not really three distinct persons, but only one person who appears to people in different "modes" at different times. Also called Sabellianism. (6C.1)

monism. The view that man is made of only one element, the physical body, and that his body is the person. (11D.1)

monophysitism. The fifth-century heresy that held that Christ had only one nature, which was a mixture of divine and human natures (from Gk. *monos*, "one," and *physis*, "nature"). (14C.1.c)

moral attributes. Aspects of God's character that describe his moral or ethical nature. (5C)

moral influence theory. The theory that Christ's death was not a payment for sins but simply a demonstration of how much God loved human beings, because it showed how God identified with their sufferings, even to the point of death. The atonement becomes, then, an example designed to draw from us a grateful response. (15C.2.d.[2])

natural selection. The idea, assumed in evolutionary theory, that living organisms that are most fitted to their environment survive and multiply while others perish (also called "survival of the fittest"). (7E.2.c.[1])

necessity of Scripture. The idea that the Bible is necessary for knowing the gospel, for maintaining spiritual life, and for knowing God's will, but is not necessary for knowing that God exists or for knowing something about his character and moral laws. (3B)

neoorthodoxy. Twentieth-century theological movement represented by the teachings of Karl Barth. Instead of the orthodox position that all the words of Scripture were spoken by God, Barth taught that the words of Scripture become God's words to us as we encounter them. (2A.2)

Nestorianism. The fifth-century heresy that taught that there were two separate persons in Christ, a human person and a divine person. (14C.1.b)

new heavens and new earth. A description of the entirely renewed creation in which believers will dwell after the final judgment. (34A)

New Testament theology. The study of the teaching of the individual authors and sections of the New Testament and of the place of each teaching in the historical development of the New Testament. (1A.1)

"not discerning the body." Phrase used in 1 Corinthians 11:29 of the Corinthians' abuse of the Lord's Supper. In their selfish, inconsiderate conduct toward each other during the Lord's Supper, they were not understanding the unity and interdependence of people in the church, which is the body of Christ. (28D)

office. A publicly recognized position of a person who has the right and responsibility to perform certain functions for the benefit of the whole church. (29A.3)

old earth theory. A theory of creation that views the earth as very old, perhaps as old as 4.5 billion years. (7E.3)

Old Testament theology. The study of the teaching of the individual authors and sections of the Old Testament and of the place of each teaching in the historical development of the Old Testament. (1A.1)

omnipotence. The attribute of God whereby he is able to do all his holy will (from Lat. *omni,* "all," and *potens,* "powerful"). (5D.13)

omnipresence. The attribute of God whereby he does not have size or spatial dimensions and is present at every point of space with his whole being, yet God acts differently in different places. (4D.4)

omniscience. The attribute of God whereby he fully knows himself and all things actual and possible in one simple and eternal act. (5B.3)

only begotten. A mistranslation of the Greek word *monogenēs* (John 3:16; et al.), which actually means "unique" or "one-of-a-kind." The Arians used this word to deny Christ's deity, but the rest of the church understood it to mean that the Son eternally related as a son to the Father. (6C.2)

ontological equality. Phrase that describes the members of the Trinity as eternally equal in being or existence. (6D.2)

order of salvation. A list of the events in which God applies salvation to us, arranged in the specific order in which they occur in our lives. (18)

original guilt. Another term for "inherited guilt." (13C.1)

original pollution. Another term for our inherited sinful nature (see "inherited corruption"). (13C.2)

original sin. The traditional term for the doctrine referred to in this text as "inherited sin." Original sin includes both original guilt and original pollution. (13C)

paedobaptism. The practice of baptizing infants (the prefix *paido-* is derived from Gk. *pais,* "child"). (27B.4)

pantheism. The idea that the whole universe is God or part of God. (7B)

paradox. A seemingly contradictory statement that may nonetheless be true; an apparent but not real contradiction. (1D.3)

passive obedience. Refers to Christ's sufferings for us in which he took the penalty due for our sins and as a result died for our sins. (15C.2)

Pelagius. A fifth-century monk who taught that every person has the ability to obey God's commands and can take the first and most important steps toward salvation on his or her own. (13D.2)

penal substitution. The view of the atonement that holds that Christ in his death bore the just penalty of God for our sins, and did so as a substitute for us. (15C.2.b.[4])

Pentecostal. Any denomination or group that traces its historical origin back to the Pentecostal revival that began in the United States in 1901 and that holds to the doctrinal positions (1) that baptism in the Holy Spirit is ordinarily an event subsequent to conversion, (2) that baptism in the Holy Spirit is made evident by the sign of speaking in tongues, and (3) that all the spiritual gifts mentioned in the New Testament are to be sought and used today. (29)

perfection. The attribute of God whereby he completely possesses all excellent qualities and lacks no part of any qualities that would be desirable for him. (5E.14)

perfectionism. The view that sinless perfection, or freedom from conscious sin, is possible in this life for the Christian. (23B.4)

perseverance of the saints. The doctrine that all those who are truly born again will be kept by God's power and will persevere as Christians until the end of their lives and that only those who persevere until the end have been truly born again. (24)

personal eschatology. The study of future events that will happen to individuals, such as death, the intermediate state, and glorification. (31)

philosophical theology. The study of theological topics that primarily employs the tools and methods of philosophical reasoning and uses information that can be known about God from observing the universe, but not information that comes from Scripture. (1A.1)

postmillennialism. The view that Christ will return to the earth after the millennium. In this view, the millennium is an age of peace and righteousness on the earth that is brought about by the progress of the gospel and the growth of the church but not by Christ's physical presence on earth. (32B)

posttribulational premillennialism. Another term for historic premillennialism (or "classic premillennialism"). This position is distinguished from other premillennial views by the idea that Christ will return after the great tribulation. (32)

posttribulational rapture. The taking up of believers after the great tribulation to meet with Christ in the air just a few moments prior to his coming to earth with them to reign during the millennial kingdom (or, on the amillennial view, during the eternal state). (32E)

power. Another term for God's omnipotence. (5D.13)

prayer. Personal communication from us to God. (9)

predestination. Sometimes used as another term for "election." However, in Reformed theology generally, predestination is a broader term that includes not only election (for believers) but also reprobation (for nonbelievers). (18)

premillennialism. Includes a variety of views that have in common the belief that Christ will return to the earth before the millennium. (32C)

pretribulation rapture. The taking up of believers into heaven when (according to this view) Christ returns secretly, prior to the great tribulation. (32E)

pretribulational premillennialism. The view that Christ will return secretly before the great tribulation to call believers to himself, and then again after the tribulation to reign on earth for a thousand years. (32C.2)

preservation. An aspect of God's providence whereby he keeps all created things existing and maintaining the properties with which he created them. (8A)

presupposition. An assumption that forms the beginning point of any study. (1B)

primary cause. The divine, invisible, directing cause of everything that happens. (8B.4)

primogeniture. The Old Testament practice in which the firstborn in any generation in a human family has leadership in the family for that generation. (12C.2.a)

principalities and powers. Other names for demonic powers (and perhaps angelic powers) in some verses of the Bible. (10G.2)

prophecy. In the New Testament, a gift of the Holy Spirit that involves telling something that God has spontaneously brought to mind. (30A)

propitiation. A sacrifice that bears God's wrath to the end and in so doing changes God's wrath toward us into favor. (15C.2.b.[4])

providence. The doctrine that God is continually involved with all created things in such a way that he (1) keeps them existing and maintaining the properties with which he created them; (2) cooperates with created things in every action, directing their distinctive properties to cause them to act as they do; and (3) directs them to fulfill his purposes. (8)

purgatory. In Roman Catholic doctrine, the place where the souls of believers go to be further purified from sin until they are ready to be admitted into heaven. (25C.1.a)

purity of the church. The church's degree of freedom from wrong doctrine and conduct, and its degree of conformity to God's revealed will for the church. (26C.1)

raised in glory. Phrase describing our future resurrection bodies, which will exhibit a beauty and radiance appropriate to the position of exaltation and rule over creation that God will give us, bearing some similarity to Christ's glorified body. (16A.4.c; 25D.2)

raised in power. Phrase describing our future resurrection bodies, which will exhibit the fullness of strength and power that God intended human beings to have in their bodies when he created them. (16A.2; 25D.2)

random mutation. According to evolutionary theory, the entirely random mechanism by which differences occurred when cells reproduced themselves, with the result that all life forms developed from the simplest form without any intelligent direction or design. (7E.2.b)

ransom to Satan theory. The erroneous view that in the atonement Christ paid a ransom to Satan to redeem us out of his kingdom. (15C.2.d.[1])

rapture. The taking up or snatching up (from Lat. *rapio,* "seize, snatch, carry away") of believers to be with Christ when he returns to the earth. (32E)

reconciliation. The removal of enmity and the restoration of fellowship between two parties; in the atonement, we were reconciled to God. (15C.2.c.[3])

redemption. The act of buying back sinners out of their bondage to sin and to Satan through the payment of a ransom. (15C.2.c.[4])

Reformed. Another term for the theological tradition known as Calvinism. (8)

regeneration. A secret act of God in which he imparts new spiritual life to us; sometimes called "being born again." (20)

repentance. A heartfelt sorrow for sin, a renouncing of it, and a sincere commitment to forsake it and walk in obedience to Christ. (21B)

reprobation. The sovereign decision of God before creation to pass over some persons, in sorrow deciding not to save them, and to punish them for their sins, and thereby to manifest his justice. (18E)

resurrection. A rising from the dead into a new kind of life not subject to sickness, aging, deterioration, or death. (16A.2)

revealed will. God's declared will concerning what pleases him or what he commands us to do. God's revealed will is found in Scripture. (5D.12.b)

righteousness. The attribute of God whereby he always acts in accordance with what is right and is himself the final standard of what is right. (5C.9)

sacrifice. Christ's death on the cross viewed from the standpoint that he paid the penalty that we deserved. (15C.2.c.[1])

sanctification. A progressive work of God and man that makes us more and more free from sin and like Christ in our actual lives. (23)

Satan. The personal name of the head of the demons. (10E)

saving faith. Trust in Jesus Christ as a living person for forgiveness of sins and for eternal life with God. (21A.3)

saving grace. The grace of God that brings people to salvation; also known as "special grace." (17A)

Scripture. The writings (Gr. *graphē*) of the Old and New Testaments, which have historically been recognized as God's words in written form. Another term for the Bible. (2A)

second coming of Christ. The sudden, personal, visible, bodily return of Christ from heaven to earth. (32)

secondary cause. The properties and actions of created things that bring about events in the world. (8B.4)

secret will. God's hidden decrees by which he governs the universe and determines everything that will happen. (5D.12.b)

self-attesting. The self-authenticating nature of the Bible by which it convinces us that its words are God's words. (2A.4)

self-existence. Another term for God's independence. (4D.1)

seraphim. A class of created spiritual beings who are said to continually worship God. (10A.3.b)

session. The "sitting down" of Christ at God's right hand after his ascension, indicating that his work of redemption was complete and that he had received authority over the universe. (16B.3)

sin. Any failure to conform to the moral law of God in act, attitude, or nature. (13A)

sinless perfection. The state of being totally free from sin. Some erroneously hold that such a state is possible in this life (see also "perfectionism"). (23B.4)

Son of God. A title often used of Jesus to designate him as the heavenly, eternal Son who is equal in nature to God himself. (14B.1.c)

Son of Man. The term by which Jesus referred to himself most often, which had an Old Testament background, especially in the heavenly figure who was given eternal rule over the world in the vision in Daniel 7:13. (14B.1.c)

soul. The immaterial part of man; used interchangeably with "spirit." (11D.1)

soul sleep. The erroneous doctrine that believers go into a state of unconscious existence when they die and that they return to consciousness when Christ returns and raises them to eternal life. (25C.1.b)

sovereignty. God's exercise of power over his creation. (5D.13)

speaking in tongues. Prayer or praise spoken in syllables not understood by the speaker. (30D.2)

special revelation. God's words addressed to specific people, including the words of the Bible. To be distinguished from general revelation, which is given to all people generally. (3B.4)

Spirit. The immaterial part of man; used interchangeably with "soul." (11D.1)

spiritual body. The type of body we will receive at our future resurrection, which will not be "immaterial" but rather suited to and responsive to the guidance of the Holy Spirit. (16A.2)

spiritual presence. Phrase descriptive of the Reformed perspective of the Lord's Supper, which views Christ as spiritually present in a special way as we partake of the bread and wine. (28C.3)

spirituality. The doctrine that God exists as a being who is not made of any matter, has no parts or dimensions, is unable to be perceived by our bodily senses, and is more excellent than any other kind of existence. (5A.1)

subordinationism. The heretical teaching that the Son was inferior or "subordinate" in being to God the Father. Also called "ontological subordination," but different from economic subordination, which has been the historic view of the church. (6C.2)

sufficiency of Scripture. The idea that Scripture contained all the words of God he intended his people to have at each stage of redemptive history and that it now contains all the words of God we need for salvation, for trusting him perfectly, and for obeying him perfectly. (3C)

summary attributes. Qualities of God's character that emphasize the excellence of his entire being, such as perfection (he lacks no desirable quality), blessedness (he delights in all his qualities), and beauty (he is the sum of everything desirable). (5E)

symbolic presence. The common Protestant view that the bread and wine of the Lord's Supper symbolize the body and blood of Christ, rather than change into or somehow contain the body and blood of Christ. (28C.3)

systematic theology. Any study that answers the question, "What does the whole Bible teach us today?" about any given topic. (1A)

teaching. In the New Testament, the ability to explain Scripture and apply it to people's lives. (30B)

temporary blessings. Influences of the Holy Spirit and the church that make unbelievers look or sound like genuine believers when in fact they are not. (24C)

textual variants. Occurrences of different words in different ancient copies of the same verse of Scripture. (2D.2.c)

theistic evolution. The theory that God used the process of evolution to bring about all of the life forms on earth. (7E.2.b)

theophany. An "appearance of God" in which he takes on a visible form to show himself to people. (5A.2)

total depravity. The traditional term for the doctrine referred to in this text as "total inability." (13C.2.a)

total inability. Man's total lack of spiritual good and inability to do good before God (often referred to as "total depravity"). (13C.2.a)

transcendent. The term used to describe God as being greater than the creation and independent of it. (7B)

transitional types. In evolutionary theory, fossils showing some characteristics of one animal and some of the next developmental type, which, if found, would provide evidence for evolutionary theory by filling in the gaps between distinct kinds of animals. (7E.2.c.[1])

transubstantiation. The Roman Catholic teaching that the bread and wine of the Lord's Supper (often referred to as the Eucharist) actually become the body and blood of Christ. (28C.1)

trichotomy. The view that man is made up of three parts: body, soul, and spirit. (11D.1)

Trinity. The doctrine that God eternally exists as three persons, Father, Son, and Holy Spirit, and each person is fully God, and there is one God. (6)

tritheism. The belief that there are three gods. (6C.3)

trust. An aspect of biblical faith or belief in which we not only know and agree with facts about Jesus, but we also place personal trust in him as a living person. (21A.3)

truthfulness. The doctrine that God is the true God, and that all his knowledge and words are both true and the final standard of truth. (5B.5)

unchangeableness. The doctrine that God is unchanging in his being, perfections, purposes, and promises, yet God does act and feel emotions, and he acts and feels differently in response to different situations. (4D.2)

unity. The doctrine that God is not divided into parts, yet we see different attributes of God emphasized at different times. (4D.5)

unity of the church. The church's degree of freedom from divisions among true Christians. (26C.2)

unpardonable sin. The unusually malicious, willful rejection and slander against the Holy Spirit's work attesting to Christ, and attributing that work to Satan. (13D.5)

veracity. Another term for God's truthfulness. (5B.5; 5B.4)

vicarious atonement. The work Christ did in his life and death to earn our salvation by standing in our place as our "vicar," or representative (15C.2.b.[4])

virgin birth. The biblical teaching that Jesus was conceived in the womb of his mother Mary by a miraculous work of the Holy Spirit and without a human father. (14A.1)

visible church. The church as Christians on earth see it. Because only God sees our hearts, the visible church will always include some unbelievers. (26A.2)

watchers. Another name for angels (Dan. 4:13, 17, 23). (10A.2)

will. The attribute of God whereby he approves and determines to bring about every action necessary for the existence and activity of himself and all creation. (5D.12)

willing choices. Choices that are made in accord with our desires and with no awareness of restraints on our will. (8B.9).

wisdom. The attribute of God whereby he always chooses the best goals and the best means to those goals. (5B.4)

wrath. The attribute of God whereby he intensely hates all sin. (5C.11)

young earth theory. A theory of creation that views the earth as relatively young, perhaps as young as ten thousand to twenty thousand years old. (7E.3)

Appendix 3

Annotated Bibliography of Evangelical Systematic Theologies

This bibliography lists most of the major evangelical systematic theologies available in English and a few shorter guides to Christian doctrine. With the exception of the two Roman Catholic theologies (the traditional theology text by Ott, and the 1994 *Catechism*), which are included to give some access to Roman Catholicism, all of the authors on this list fall generally within a "conservative evangelical" theological position, although some are at the far left of the evangelical spectrum, especially with regard to the inerrancy of the Bible (see notes after each author).[1]

Arminius, James. *The Writings of James Arminius*. 3 vols. Vols. 1 and 2 translated by James Nichols. Vol. 3 translated by W. R. Bagnell. Grand Rapids: Baker, 1956.

Arminius (1560–1609) was a Reformed pastor in Amsterdam and later professor of theology at the University of Leyden. His disagreement with some of the central tenets of Calvinism led to great controversy in the Netherlands that continued long after his death. His ideas became the foundation of a system of thought now known as Arminianism, which continues today in conservative Wesleyan and Methodist churches and in many other Protestant groups. This collection of writings, assembled after his death, is not strictly organized as a systematic theology but does contain discussions of most important theological topics.

Bavinck, Herman. *The Doctrine of God*. Translated by William Hendriksen. Grand Rapids: Eerdmans, 1951. Reprint edition: Carlisle, Pa.: Banner of Truth, 1977.

_____. *Our Reasonable Faith*. Translated by Henry Zylstra. Grand Rapids: Eerdmans, 1956. Reprint edition: Grand Rapids: Baker, 1977.

_____. *The Philosophy of Revelation*. Translated by Geerhardus Vos, Nikolas Steffens, and Henry Dosker. Reprint edition: Grand Rapids: Baker, 1979. First published in 1909 by Longmans, Green, and Co.

Bavinck (1854–1921) was a Dutch theologian and one of this century's most brilliant spokesmen for a Reformed theological position. His great four-volume systematic theology, *Gereformeerde Dogmatiek*, still awaits translation into English (only vol. 2, *The Doctrine of God*, has been translated).

---

[1]A very helpful and more broadly-based annotated bibliography, including notes on works from several prominent liberal scholars, may be found in John Jefferson Davis, *Theology Primer* (Grand Rapids: Baker, 1981), pp. 74–79; see also his "Brief Guide to Modern Theologians" on pp. 39–55. In addition, valuable brief notes on dozens of important theologians from all theological traditions may be found in Millard Erickson, *Concise Dictionary of Christian Theology* (Grand Rapids: Baker, 1986). See also Stanley J. Grenz and Roger E. Olson, *Twentieth-Century Theology* (Downers Grove, Ill.: InterVarsity Press, 1992).

Berkhof, Louis. *Introduction to Systematic Theology*. Reprint edition: Grand Rapids: Baker, 1979. First published in 1932 by Eerdmans.

_____. *Systematic Theology*. Fourth edition, Grand Rapids: Eerdmans, 1939. In 1996 this book was reissued with Berkhof's *Introduction to Systematic Theology* bound together with it in one volume.

This is the standard Reformed textbook for systematic theology by a former president of Calvin Seminary in Grand Rapids, Michigan. This book is a great treasurehouse of information and analysis and is probably the most useful one-volume systematic theology available from any theological perspective. Berkhof lived from 1873 to 1957.

Berkouwer, G. C. *Studies in Dogmatics*. 14 vols. (1952–76).

_____. *The Church*. Translated by James E. Davidson. Grand Rapids: Eerdmans, 1976.

_____. *Divine Election*. Translated by Hugo Bekker. Grand Rapids: Eerdmans, 1960.

_____. *Faith and Justification*. Translated by Lewis B. Smedes. Grand Rapids: Eerdmans, 1954.

_____. *Faith and Perseverance*. Translated by Robert D. Knudsen. Grand Rapids: Eerdmans, 1958.

_____. *Faith and Sanctification*. Translated by John Vriend. Grand Rapids: Eerdmans, 1952.

_____. *General Revelation*. (No translator named.) Grand Rapids: Eerdmans, 1955.

_____. *Holy Scripture*. Translated and edited by Jack B. Rogers. Grand Rapids: Eerdmans, 1975.

_____. *Man: The Image of God*. Translated by Dirk W. Jellema. Grand Rapids: Eerdmans, 1962.

_____. *The Person of Christ*. Translated by John Vriend. Grand Rapids: Eerdmans, 1954.

_____. *The Providence of God*. Translated by Lewis B. Smedes. Grand Rapids: Eerdmans, 1952.

_____. *The Return of Christ*. Translated by James Van Oosterom. Edited by Marlin J. Van Elderen. Grand Rapids: Eerdmans, 1972.

_____. *The Sacraments*. Translated by Hugo Bekker. Grand Rapids: Eerdmans, 1969.

_____. *Sin*. Translated by Philip C. Holtrop. Grand Rapids: Eerdmans, 1971.

_____. *The Work of Christ*. Translated by Cornelius Lambregtse. Grand Rapids: Eerdmans, 1965.

These are major contemporary studies by a Reformed theologian who was professor of systematic theology at the Free University of Amsterdam.

Bloesch, Donald G. *Christian Foundations*. Downers Grove, Ill.: InterVarsity Press, 1997.

_____. *Essentials of Evangelical Theology*. 2 vols., New York: Harper and Row, 1978–79.

Bloesch is a contemporary theologian who is more or less in the Reformed tradition but is much less clear on the doctrines of election and the authority of Scripture, for example, than other writers whom I have classified as "Reformed" in this bibliography.

Boice, James Montgomery. *Foundations of the Christian Faith*. Revised one-volume edition. Downers Grove, Ill.: InterVarsity Press, 1986.

This is a recent Reformed guide to systematic theology written by the theologian-pastor of Tenth Presbyterian Church, Philadelphia. This work is written in a popular, readable style, with helpful application of doctrines to life. It was previously published in four separate volumes: *The Sovereign God* (1978), *God the Redeemer* (1978), *Awakening to God* (1979), and *God and History* (1981).

Boyce, James Pettigru. *Abstract of Systematic Theology*. Reprint edition: Christian Gospel Foundation, n.d. First published 1887.

This Baptist systematic theology by a former president and professor of systematic theology in the Southern Baptist Seminary, Louisville, Kentucky, is also Reformed in doctrinal orientation. Boyce lived from 1827 to 1888.

Buswell, James Oliver, Jr. *A Systematic Theology of the Christian Religion*. 2 vols. Grand Rapids: Zondervan, 1962–63.

This Reformed systematic theology is by the former dean of the graduate faculty at Covenant College and Seminary in St. Louis, Missouri.

Calvin, John. *Institutes of the Christian Religion*. 2 vols. Edited by John T. McNeill. Translated and indexed by Ford Lewis Battles. The Library of Christian Classics, vols. 20–21. Philadelphia: Westminster, 1960. Translated from the 1559 text and collated with earlier versions.

This is the best available English translation of Calvin's systematic exposition of the Christian faith. Calvin (1509–64) was a French reformer who became the greatest theologian of the Reformation and, according to many estimates, the greatest theologian in the history of the church. Reformed in doctrinal perspective.

Carter, Charles W., editor. *A Contemporary Wesleyan Theology: Biblical, Systematic, and Practical*. 2 vols. Grand Rapids: Zondervan, Francis Asbury Press, 1983.

This is a collection of twenty-four essays on major doctrinal themes by several scholars representing a wide range of conservative Wesleyan denominations and institutions. The set also includes some essays on practical theology and ethics. Charles Carter, who contributed four of the chapters, was professor of religion and missions at Marion College, Marion, Indiana. The advisory committee for the volumes included representatives of the United Methodist and Free Methodist denominations, Church of the Nazarene, Missionary Church, Salvation Army, Wesleyan Church, and others.

Catechism of the Catholic Church. English translation. San Francisco: Ignatius Press, 1994.

This is the best current statement of the doctrinal positions of the Roman Catholic Church. It was prepared by a commission of cardinals and bishops under the direction of Cardinal Joseph Ratzinger. In its publication, Pope John Paul II wrote that it "is a statement of the Church's faith and of catholic doctrine.... I declare it to be a sure norm for teaching the faith.... This catechism is given ... that it may be a sure and authentic reference text for teaching catholic doctrine ..." (p. 5).

Chafer, Lewis Sperry. *Systematic Theology*. 7 vols. plus index. Dallas: Dallas Seminary Press, 1947–48.

_____. *Systematic Theology: Abridged edition*. 2 vols. Edited by John F. Walvoord, Donald K. Campbell, and Roy B. Zuck. Wheaton, Ill.: Victor, 1988.

Chafer (1871–1952) was the first president of Dallas Theological Seminary. The seven-volume edition is the most extensive dispensational systematic theology ever written. The two-volume edition is a condensation of the earlier work.

Cottrell, Jack. *What the Bible Says About God the Creator*. Joplin, Mo.: College Press, 1983.

_____. *What the Bible Says About God the Ruler*. Joplin, Mo.: College Press, 1984.

_____. *What the Bible Says About God the Redeemer*. Joplin, Mo.: College Press, 1987.

Cottrell is an articulate and thoughtful Arminian theologian who teaches at Cincinnati Bible Seminary (Christian Church/Churches of Christ).

Dabney, Robert L. *Discussions: Evangelical and Theological.* London: Banner of Truth, 1967. Reprint of 1890 edition.

_____. *Systematic Theology.* Edinburgh: Banner of Truth, 1985. Reprint of 1878 edition.

A Southern Presbyterian who represented a strongly Reformed position, Dabney (1820–98) was professor of theology at Union Seminary in Virginia. He was also chaplain and later chief of staff for General Stonewall Jackson during the American Civil War.

Edwards, Jonathan. *The Works of Jonathan Edwards.* 2 vols. Revised and corrected by Edward Hickman. Edinburgh: Banner of Truth, 1974. Reprint of 1834 edition.

Edwards (1703–58) was a pastor in Northampton, Massachusetts, and, for one month before his death from a smallpox injection, president of Princeton. Some consider him the greatest American philosopher-theologian. He did not write an entire systematic theology, but his works contain writings on most theological topics. He is strongly Reformed in outlook and combines profound thought with warm-hearted devotion to Christ. (A new edition of Edwards' works is in process of publication from Yale University Press.)

Erickson, Millard. *Christian Theology.* Grand Rapids: Baker, 1985.

This is a clear and very thorough recent textbook in systematic theology from a Baptist perspective. Erickson, who was academic dean at Bethel Theological Seminary in St. Paul, Minnesota, now teaches at Southwestern Baptist Seminary in Ft. Worth, Texas. This book includes interaction with all the major trends in contemporary nonevangelical theology, as well as helpful material for personal application. Erickson has also published a condensed version of this book, *Introducing Christian Doctrine,* edited by L. Arnold Hustad (Grand Rapids: Baker, 1992).

Finney, Charles G. *Finney's Lectures on Systematic Theology.* Edited by J. H. Fairchild. Grand Rapids: Eerdmans, 1953. Reprint of 1878 edition.

Finney (1792–1875) was a revivalist and president of Oberlin College 1851–66. This work is not representative of any one theological position, but articulates some strong Arminian arguments. Emphasis is placed on personal holiness and perfectionism. This is not really a complete systematic theology, because many topics are not covered.

Garrett, James Leo. *Systematic Theology: Biblical, Historical, Evangelical.* 2 vols. Grand Rapids: Eerdmans, 1990, 1995.

Garrett is a Southern Baptist who is Distinguished Professor of Theology at Southwestern Baptist Theological Seminary in Fort Worth, Texas. He interacts extensively and with scrupulous fairness with both evangelical and nonevangelical authors, though he himself is firmly within the evangelical camp. He is Baptistic in his convictions yet gives much more space to representing different positions clearly than to arguing for his own position. With 1,530 total pages, these volumes are an amazingly rich resource for historical, bibliographical, and biblical data on each doctrine treated.

Gill, John. *Complete Body of Doctrinal and Practical Divinity.* 2 vols. Grand Rapids: Baker, 1978. First published as *A Body of Doctrinal Divinity* (1767) and *A Body of Practical Divinity* (1770).

Gill (1697–1771) was a highly influential Baptist pastor, prolific writer, and respected theologian in eighteenth-century England. He was also Reformed (or Calvinistic) in his view of God's sovereignty. His book *The Cause of God and Truth*

(1735–38; reprinted Grand Rapids: Baker, 1981) is one of the most thorough defenses of Calvinistic theology ever written.

Grenz, Stanley J. *Theology for the Community of God.* Nashville: Broadman and Holman, 1994.

Grenz is a Baptist who teaches at Carey Theological College and also at Regent College in Vancouver. He organizes his treatment of theology around the "integrative motif" of the establishment of "community," which he sees as God's central program for creation. Grenz is a representative of the new "evangelical left," theologians who are reluctant to affirm a conservative view of biblical inerrancy, and who place less emphasis on deriving theology from the propositions of Scripture and more on the narrative patterns they see in Scripture, as well as on church history and contemporary thought.

Grudem, Wayne. *Systematic Theology: An Introduction to Biblical Doctrine.* Leicester: Inter-Varsity Press and Grand Rapids: Zondervan, 1994.

A much larger and more detailed version of this book.

Henry, Carl F. H. *God, Revelation, and Authority.* 6 vols. Waco, Tex.: Word, 1976–83.

This major work contains detailed interaction with hundreds of other scholarly positions. Henry is a leading evangelical theologian with great strengths especially in the areas of apologetics and philosophical theology.

Heppe, Heinrich. *Reformed Dogmatics: Set Out and Illustrated from the Sources.* Revised and edited by Ernst Bizer. Translated by G. T. Thompson. Reprint edition: Grand Rapids: Baker, 1978. First published 1861. English translation first published 1950.

Heppe (1820–79) was a German scholar who collected and quoted extensively from many earlier Reformed theologians. Because the quotations are arranged according to the topics of systematic theology, this book is a valuable sourcebook.

Hodge, Charles. *Systematic Theology.* 3 vols. Reprint edition: Grand Rapids: Eerdmans, 1970. First published 1871–73.

This major Reformed systematic theology is still widely used today. Hodge (1797–1878) was professor of systematic theology at Princeton Theological Seminary.

Lewis, Gordon R., and Bruce Demarest. *Integrative Theology.* 3 vols. Grand Rapids: Zondervan, 1987, 1990, 1994. Published as one volume in 1996.

Lewis and Demarest are both professors of systematic theology at Denver Seminary in Colorado (a Conservative Baptist seminary). This is an excellent contemporary work that integrates historical, biblical, apologetic, and practical material with systematic theology.

Litton, Edward Arthur. *Introduction to Dogmatic Theology.* New edition, edited by Philip E. Hughes. London: James Clarke, 1960. First published 1882–92.

This is a standard Anglican (or Episcopalian) systematic theology by an evangelical British theologian of the nineteenth century. Litton lived from 1813 to 1897.

McGrath, Alister E. *Christian Theology: An Introduction.* Second edition. Oxford: Blackwell, 1997.

McGrath is principal of Wycliffe Hall, Oxford; research lecturer in theology at Oxford University, and research professor of theology at Regent College, Vancouver. The first part of this useful book (pp. 3–137) provides a clear overview of the history of doctrine. The second part (pp. 141–235) discusses sources and methods in theology. The last part (pp. 239–563) treats in topical order the subjects ordinarliy covered in systematic theology, primarily with a wide-ranging survey of ancient and modern viewpoints on each subject. McGrath does not advocate a particular theological tradition within this book, for he explains that it "does not seek to tell its readers what to believe, but rather aims to explain to them what has been believed, and to equip them to make up their minds for themselves, by describing the options available to them and their historical origins" (p. xvi).

Miley, John. *Systematic Theology.* 2 vols. Library of Biblical and Theological Literature, vols. 5–6. New York: Eaton and Mains, 1892–94. Reprint: Peabody, Mass.: Hendriksen, 1989.

This is probably the most scholarly and extensive Arminian systematic theology ever written. Miley was a professor at Drew Theological Seminary, Madison, New Jersey.

Milne, Bruce. *Know the Truth.* Leicester: Inter-Varsity Press, 1982.

This thoughtful, clearly written evangelical guide to Christian doctrine has found wide use among students. Milne lectures in biblical and historical theology at Spurgeon's College, London.

Mueller, John Theodore. *Christian Dogmatics.* St. Louis: Concordia, 1934.

This is a condensation and translation of Francis Pieper's *Christliche Dogmatik* (Christian Dogmatics) by a professor of systematic theology at Concordia Seminary in St. Louis, a Missouri Synod Lutheran seminary. An excellent statement of conservative Lutheran theology.

Mullins, Edgar Young. *The Christian Religion in Its Doctrinal Expression.* Philadelphia: Judson, 1917.

This evangelical systematic theology is by a former president of the Southern Baptist Seminary in Louisville, Kentucky. Mullins lived from 1860 to 1928. This book is weak in its doctrine of the authority and inerrancy of Scripture. This weakness may have contributed to a drift toward liberalism in Southern Baptist seminaries in the mid-twentieth century, a trend that has only been reversed in the 1990s.

Murray, John. *Collected Writings of John Murray.* 4 vols. Carlisle, Pa.: Banner of Truth, 1976–82.

_____. *The Imputation of Adam's Sin.* Reprint edition: Nutley, N.J.: Presbyterian and Reformed, 1977. First published Grand Rapids: Eerdmans, 1959.

_____. *Principles of Conduct.* Grand Rapids: Eerdmans, 1957.

_____. *Redemption Accomplished and Applied.* Grand Rapids: Eerdmans, 1955.

Murray (1898–1975) was professor of systematic theology at Westminster Seminary in Philadelphia and one of the most articulate modern defenders of Reformed theology.

Oden, Thomas. *Systematic Theology.*
Vol. 1: *The Living God.* San Francisco: Harper and Row, 1987.
Vol. 2: *The Word of Life.* San Francisco: Harper and Row, 1989.
Vol. 3: *Life in the Spirit.* San Francisco: Harper and Row, 1992.

Oden is a Methodist theologian who has moved from his previous liberal theological convictions to a conservative evangelical position. He is professor of theology and ethics at Drew University. His method is "to make no new contribution to theology" but to ascertain and document the "consental teaching" on which all the major figures and movements in the history of the church have agreed. This is a monumental work of great value, with thousands of quotations (especially from early Christian writers) on every aspect of systematic theology.

Olson, Arnold T. *This We Believe: The Background and Exposition of the Doctrinal Statement of The Evangelical Free Church of America.* Minneapolis, Minn.: Free Church Publications, 1961.

This guide to Christian doctrine is based on the widely used statement of faith of the Evangelical Free Church of America. Olson was the first president of the Evangelical Free Church.

Ott, Ludwig. *Fundamentals of Catholic Dogma.* Edited by James Canon Bastible. Translated by Patrick Lynch. St. Louis: Herder, 1955. First published in German in 1952.

This is a standard textbook of traditional Roman Catholic theology.

Packer, J. I. *Concise Theology: A Guide to Historic Christian Beliefs.* Wheaton, Ill.: Tyndale, 1993.

This readable volume lives up to its name, because Packer, an Anglican with strong Reformed convictions, is a master of saying much in a few words. He is a professor of theology at Regent College in Vancouver, British Columbia, and one of the most widely respected evangelical theologians today.

Pieper, Francis. *Christian Dogmatics.* 3 vols. Translated by Theodore Engelder, et al. St. Louis: Concordia, 1950–57. First published in German, 1917–24.

This is a standard systematic theology of conservative Lutheranism. Pieper (1852–1931) was a Missouri Synod theologian and professor and president of Concordia Seminary in St. Louis.

Pope, William Burt. *A Compendium of Christian Theology.* Second edition. 3 vols. New York: Phillips and Hunt, n.d.

This work, first published in 1875–76, is one of the greatest systematic theologies written from a Wesleyan or Arminian perspective.

Purkiser, W. T., editor. *Exploring Our Christian Faith.* Kansas City, Mo.: Beacon Hill Press, 1960.

This is a more popular Arminian systematic theology with contributions from several authors.

Ryrie, Charles. *Basic Theology.* Wheaton, Ill.: Victor, 1986.

This is a very clearly written introduction to systematic theology from a dispensationalist perspective by a former professor of systematic theology at Dallas Theological Seminary.

Shedd, William G. T. *Dogmatic Theology.* 3 vols. in 4. Reprint edition: Minneapolis: Klock and Klock, 1979. Originally published by Charles Scribner's Sons, 1889.

This is a useful Reformed systematic theology by a former professor at Union Theological Seminary in New York. (Note that the entire range of systematic theology is treated in vols. 1 and 2, and that vol. 3 contains supplementary material for every part of vols. 1 and 2. Vol. 3 is not well indexed.) Shedd lived from 1820 to 1894.

Strong, Augustus H. *Systematic Theology.* Valley Forge, Pa.: Judson, 1907.

Strong (1836–1921) was president and professor of theology at Rochester Theological Seminary, and, from 1905 to 1910, was the first president of the Northern Baptist Convention. This text was widely used in Baptist circles for most of the twentieth century until it was largely replaced by Millard Erickson's *Christian Theology* (1983–85).

Thiessen, Henry Clarence. *Introductory Lectures in Systematic Theology.* Revised by Vernon D. Doerksen. Grand Rapids: Eerdmans, 1977. First published 1949.

This is an evangelical systematic theology textbook by a former chairman of the faculty of the graduate school at Wheaton College. Thiessen is Baptistic and Dispensational in theological perspective.

Thomas, W. H. Griffith. *The Principles of Theology: An Introduction to the Thirty-nine Articles.* Fifth edition, revised. London: Church Book Room Press, 1956. First published 1930.

Although this book is structured around the Anglican Thirty-nine Articles, it functions well as a thoughtful introductory text in Christian doctrine even for those outside the Anglican tradition. It has been widely used in British evangelical circles for many years. Thomas (1861–1924) was principal of Wycliffe Hall, Oxford, and then professor of Old Testament at Wycliffe College, Toronto. He also played a role in founding Dallas Seminary just before his death.

Thornwell, James Henley. *The Collected Writings of James Henley Thornwell.* 4 vols. Edited by John B. Adger. New York: Robert Carter and Brothers, 1871–73. Reprint: Edinburgh and Carlisle, Pa.: Banner of Truth, 1974.

Thornwell (1812–62) was a Reformed theologian who was professor of theology in the Presbyterian Theological Seminary at Columbia, South Carolina.

Turretin, Francis. *Institutes of Elenctic Theology.* 3 vols. Translated by George Musgrave Giger. Edited by James T. Dennison, Jr. Phillipsburg, N.J.: Presbyterian and Reformed, 1992, 1994, 1997.

Turretin (1623–87) taught theology for more than thirty years at the Academy in Geneva. His work, written in Latin, is said to be one of the fullest expressions of Calvinistic theology ever published. It was reprinted (in Latin) in 1847 and widely used as a theological textbook for American Presbyterians, most notably by Charles Hodge at Princeton. George Giger translated Turretin's *Institutes* in the mid-nineteenth century, but the translation lay unpublished for over a century. James Dennison of Westminster Seminary has done extensive editorial work to make this great theology text finally available to English readers.

Van Til, Cornelius. *In Defense of the Faith,* vol. 5: *An Introduction to Systematic Theology.* Philadephia: Presbyterian and Reformed, 1976.

This volume contains Van Til's discussions of the nature of systematic theology, of revelation, and of the doctrine of God. Van Til was a Reformed theologian and philosopher who taught at Westminster Theological Seminary in Philadelphia and is best known for his "presuppositional" system of apologetics.

Warfield, Benjamin B. *Biblical and Theological Studies.* Philadelphia: Presbyterian and Reformed, 1976.

_____. *Christology and Criticism.* London and New York: Oxford University Press, 1929.

_____. *The Inspiration and Authority of the Bible.* Edited by Samuel G. Craig. Introduction by Cornelius Van Til. Philadelphia: Presbyterian and Reformed, 1967.

_____. *The Lord of Glory.* New York: American Tract Society, 1907.

_____. *Perfectionism.* Philadelphia: Presbyterian and Reformed, 1958.

This is a condensation of Warfield's earlier two-volume work on perfectionism published by Oxford University Press, omitting extensive interaction with particular German theologians.

_____. *The Person and Work of Christ.* Philadelphia: Presbyterian and Reformed, 1950.

This contains reprints of two articles from *Studies in Theology,* five from *Bible Doctrine,* six from *Christology and Criticism,* and one other article.

_____. *The Plan of Salvation*. Revised edition: Grand Rapids: Eerdmans, 1942.

_____. *Selected Shorter Writings of Benjamin B. Warfield*. 2 vols. Nutley, N.J.: Presbyterian and Reformed, 1970–73.

_____. *Studies in Theology*. New York: Oxford University Press, 1932.

_____. *Works*. 10 vols. Grand Rapids: Baker, 1991.

Warfield (1851–1921) was a Reformed theologian who taught New Testament and then systematic theology at Princeton Theological Seminary from 1887 to 1921. In the estimate of many people, he was one of the greatest American theologians.

Watson, Richard. *Theological Institutes*. 2 vols. New York: G. Lane and P. Sandford, 1843. First published 1823.

This is the earliest systematic theology by a Methodist. Watson (1781–1833) was Arminian in theological perspective.

Wiley, H. Orton. *Christian Theology*. 3 vols. Kansas City, Mo.: Nazarene Publishing House, 1940–43.

This recent work by a respected theologian in the Church of the Nazarene is probably the best Arminian systematic theology published in the twentieth century, but it does not match Miley in scholarly depth.

Williams, J. Rodman. *Renewal Theology: Systematic Theology from a Charismatic Perspective*. 3 vols. Grand Rapids: Zondervan, 1988–92. Published in one volume in 1996.

Williams is a charismatic scholar who teaches at Regent University (formerly CBN University). This clearly written theology interacts extensively with the biblical text and with other literature. It is the first published work from an explicitly charismatic perspective.

AUTHOR INDEX

SUBJECT INDEX

Bold type indicates more extensive treatment of a subject or the location of a chapter or section dealing with that subject.

INDEX OF SCRIPTURE PASSAGES DISCUSSED

Scripture passages cited in the text without comment are not included in this index.